Vulkan Cookboo

Work through recipes to unlock the full potential of the next generation graphics API—Vulkan

Pawel Lapinski

BIRMINGHAM - MUMBAI

Vulkan Cookbook

Copyright © 2017 Packt Publishing

All rights reserved. No part of this book may be reproduced, stored in a retrieval system, or transmitted in any form or by any means, without the prior written permission of the publisher, except in the case of brief quotations embedded in critical articles or reviews.

Every effort has been made in the preparation of this book to ensure the accuracy of the information presented. However, the information contained in this book is sold without warranty, either express or implied. Neither the author, nor Packt Publishing, and its dealers and distributors will be held liable for any damages caused or alleged to be caused directly or indirectly by this book.

Packt Publishing has endeavored to provide trademark information about all of the companies and products mentioned in this book by the appropriate use of capitals. However, Packt Publishing cannot guarantee the accuracy of this information.

First published: April 2017

Production reference: 1260417

Published by Packt Publishing Ltd.
Livery Place
35 Livery Street
Birmingham
B3 2PB, UK.
ISBN 978-1-78646-815-4

www.packtpub.com

Credits

Author

Pawel Lapinski

Reviewer

Chris Forbes

Commissioning Editor

Ashwin Nair

Acquisition Editor

Nitin Dasan

Content Development Editor

Aditi Gour

Technical Editor

Murtaza Tinwala

Copy Editor

Safis Editing

Project Coordinator

Ritika Manoj

Proofreader

Safis Editing

Indexer

Tejal Daruwale Soni

Production Coordinator

Arvindkumar Gupta

Graphics

Jason Monteiro

About the Author

Pawel Lapinski is a graphics software engineer at Intel Corporation. His professional career started 10 years ago when he and his friends were hired to develop a 3D training/simulation application using C++, OpenGL, and Cg, which was later improved with added head-mounted display support and stereoscopic image generation.

Since his studies, Pawel has been interested in 3D graphics and especially in the open multiplatform OpenGL library. He wrote a diploma about the "Effective usage of vertex and fragment shaders." Since then, he has continued to pursue opportunities to work with 3D graphics and expand his knowledge in the field. He had the opportunity to join a team that was developing one of the biggest CAVE-like installations at the Polish Gdansk University of Technology. His responsibility was to prepare 3D visualizations using Unity3D engine and add stereoscopic image generation and support for motion tracking.

Pawel's whole career has involved working with computer graphics, the OpenGL library, and shaders. However, some time ago, already as a programmer at Intel, he had the opportunity to start working with the Vulkan API when he prepared validation tests for the Vulkan graphics driver. He also prepared a series of tutorials teaching people how to use Vulkan and now he wants to share more of his knowledge in the form of a Vulkan Cookbook.

Acknowledgments

This is my first published book and it is a very important moment of my life. That's why I'd like to include quite many people in this "special thanks" list.

First and foremost, I want to thank my wife, Agata, my children, and the whole family for all their love, patience, and continuous support.

I wouldn't have written this book if Mr. Jacek Kuffel hadn't been my language teacher in my primary school. He taught me how important our language is and he also taught me how to express myself with written words. I learned all my love of writing from him.

My affection for 3D graphics programming started during my studies. It started growing thanks to my thesis supervisor Mariusz Szwoch, Ph.D., and my 3D graphics teacher Jacek Lebiedz, Ph.D. I'd like to thank them for their support and help. Without them I would not have started learning OpenGL and, as the next step, the Vulkan API.

Kind regards and a huge thank you to my team here at Intel Poland. I couldn't have joined a better team or started working with better people. They are not only specialists at what they do, but they are all kind, sincere and warmhearted friends. I'd like to thank them for patiently answering my many questions, for sharing their knowledge. And for the great atmosphere that they create every day. Special thanks are required to Slawek, Boguslaw, Adam, Jacek, and to my manager Jan.

And last but not least – the Packt team. I've always dreamt about writing a book and they not only allowed me to do it, but they helped me realize my dreams, showing their support at every step from the very beginning. Aditi, Murtaza, Nitin, Sachin – You are great. It was much easier to write this book with you on my side.

About the Reviewer

Chris Forbes works as a software developer for Google, working on Vulkan validation support and other ecosystem components. Previously he has been involved in implementing OpenGL 3 and 4 support in open source graphics drivers for Linux [www.mesa3d.org], as well as rebuilding classic strategy games to run on modern systems [www.openra.net]. He also served as a technical reviewer on Packt's previous Vulkan title, *Learning Vulkan*.

www.PacktPub.com

For support files and downloads related to your book, please visit `www.PacktPub.com`.

Did you know that Packt offers eBook versions of every book published, with PDF and ePub files available? You can upgrade to the eBook version at `www.PacktPub.com` and as a print book customer, you are entitled to a discount on the eBook copy. Get in touch with us at `service@packtpub.com` for more details.

At `www.PacktPub.com`, you can also read a collection of free technical articles, sign up for a range of free newsletters and receive exclusive discounts and offers on Packt books and eBooks.

`https://www.packtpub.com/mapt`

Get the most in-demand software skills with Mapt. Mapt gives you full access to all Packt books and video courses, as well as industry-leading tools to help you plan your personal development and advance your career.

Why subscribe?

- Fully searchable across every book published by Packt
- Copy and paste, print, and bookmark content
- On demand and accessible via a web browser

Customer Feedback

Thanks for purchasing this Packt book. At Packt, quality is at the heart of our editorial process. To help us improve, please leave us an honest review on this book's Amazon page at `https://www.amazon.com/Vulkan-Cookbook-Pawel-Lapinski/dp/1786468158`.

If you'd like to join our team of regular reviewers, you can e-mail us at `customerreviews@packtpub.com`. We award our regular reviewers with free eBooks and videos in exchange for their valuable feedback. Help us be relentless in improving our products!

Table of Contents

Preface   1

Chapter 1: Instance and Devices   9
- **Introduction**   10
- **Downloading Vulkan's SDK**   10
  - Getting ready   10
  - How to do it...   10
  - How it works...   12
  - See also   12
- **Enabling validation layers**   13
  - How to do it...   14
  - How it works...   15
  - See also   16
- **Connecting with a Vulkan Loader library**   16
  - How to do it...   17
  - How it works...   17
  - See also   18
- **Preparing for loading Vulkan API functions**   18
  - How to do it...   19
  - How it works...   21
  - See also   21
- **Loading functions exported from a Vulkan Loader library**   22
  - How to do it...   22
  - How it works...   23
  - See also   24
- **Loading global-level functions**   24
  - How to do it...   25
  - How it works...   25
  - See also   26
- **Checking available Instance extensions**   27
  - How to do it...   27
  - How it works...   28
  - See also   29
- **Creating a Vulkan Instance**   29
  - How to do it...   29

      How it works... 30
      See also 33
Loading instance-level functions 33
      How to do it... 33
      How it works... 34
      See also 37
Enumerating available physical devices 37
      How to do it... 37
      How it works... 38
      See also 39
Checking available device extensions 40
      How to do it... 40
      How it works... 41
      See also 42
Getting features and properties of a physical device 42
      How to do it... 42
      How it works... 43
      See also 44
Checking available queue families and their properties 44
      How to do it... 45
      How it works... 46
      See also 47
Selecting the index of a queue family with the desired capabilities 47
      How to do it... 48
      How it works... 49
      See also 50
Creating a logical device 50
      Getting ready 51
      How to do it... 51
      How it works... 53
      See also 56
Loading device-level functions 56
      How to do it... 57
      How it works... 57
      See also 61
Getting a device queue 61
      How to do it... 61
      How it works... 62
      See also 63

Creating a logical device with geometry shaders, graphics, and compute queues — 63
- How to do it... — 63
- How it works... — 65
- See also — 67

Destroying a logical device — 67
- How to do it... — 67
- How it works... — 68
- See also — 68

Destroying a Vulkan Instance — 68
- How to do it... — 68
- How it works... — 69
- See also — 69

Releasing a Vulkan Loader library — 69
- How to do it... — 69
- How it works... — 70
- See also — 70

Chapter 2: Image Presentation — 71

Introduction — 72

Creating a Vulkan Instance with WSI extensions enabled — 72
- How to do it... — 73
- How it works... — 74
- See also — 76

Creating a presentation surface — 76
- Getting ready — 76
- How to do it... — 77
- How it works... — 80
- See also — 81

Selecting a queue family that supports presentation to a given surface — 81
- How to do it... — 82
- How it works... — 00
- See also — 83

Creating a logical device with WSI extensions enabled — 84
- How to do it... — 84
- How it works... — 85
- See also — 86

Selecting a desired presentation mode — 86
- How to do it... — 86
- How it works... — 87

[iii]

See also	92
Getting the capabilities of a presentation surface	92
How to do it...	92
How it works...	93
See also	93
Selecting a number of swapchain images	94
How to do it...	94
How it works...	94
See also	95
Choosing a size of swapchain images	96
How to do it...	96
How it works...	97
See also	97
Selecting desired usage scenarios of swapchain images	98
How to do it...	98
How it works...	99
See also	99
Selecting a transformation of swapchain images	100
How to do it...	100
How it works...	100
See also	101
Selecting a format of swapchain images	101
Getting ready	101
How to do it...	102
How it works...	103
See also	105
Creating a swapchain	105
How to do it...	105
How it works...	107
See also	108
Getting handles of swapchain images	109
How to do it...	109
How it works...	110
See also	111
Creating a swapchain with R8G8B8A8 format and a mailbox present mode	111
How to do it...	112
How it works...	113
See also	115

Acquiring a swapchain image — 115
  Getting ready — 116
  How to do it... — 116
  How it works... — 117
  See also — 118
Presenting an image — 119
  Getting ready — 119
  How to do it... — 119
  How it works... — 120
  See also — 121
Destroying a swapchain — 122
  How to do it... — 122
  How it works... — 122
  See also — 122
Destroying a presentation surface — 122
  How to do it... — 123
  How it works... — 123
  See also — 123

Chapter 3: Command Buffers and Synchronization — 125
Introduction — 125
Creating a command pool — 126
  How to do it... — 126
  How it works... — 127
  See also — 128
Allocating command buffers — 129
  How to do it... — 129
  How it works... — 130
  See also — 131
Beginning a command buffer recording operation — 131
  How to do it... — 131
  How it works... — 133
  See also — 134
Ending a command buffer recording operation — 135
  How to do it... — 135
  How it works... — 135
  See also — 136
Resetting a command buffer — 136
  How to do it... — 136
  How it works... — 137

See also	137
Resetting a command pool	137
How to do it...	138
How it works...	138
See also	139
Creating a semaphore	139
How to do it...	139
How it works...	140
See also	141
Creating a fence	141
How to do it...	142
How it works...	142
See also	143
Waiting for fences	143
How to do it...	144
How it works...	144
See also	145
Resetting fences	145
How to do it...	145
How it works...	146
See also	146
Submitting command buffers to a queue	147
Getting ready	147
How to do it...	147
How it works...	149
See also	150
Synchronizing two command buffers	151
Getting ready	151
How to do it...	151
How it works...	152
See also	153
Checking if processing of a submitted command buffer has finished	153
How to do it...	153
How it works...	154
See also	155
Waiting until all commands submitted to a queue are finished	155
How to do it...	155
How it works...	155
See also	156

Waiting for all submitted commands to be finished	156
How to do it...	156
How it works...	157
See also	157
Destroying a fence	157
How to do it...	158
How it works...	158
See also	158
Destroying a semaphore	158
How to do it...	159
How it works...	159
See also	160
Freeing command buffers	160
How to do it...	160
How it works...	161
See also	161
Destroying a command pool	161
How to do it...	162
How it works...	162
See also	162
Chapter 4: Resources and Memory	**163**
Introduction	164
Creating a buffer	164
How to do it...	165
How it works...	165
See also	167
Allocating and binding a memory object for a buffer	168
How to do it...	168
How it works...	170
There's more...	171
See also	172
Setting a buffer memory barrier	172
Getting ready	172
How to do it...	173
How it works...	174
There's more...	177
See also	178
Creating a buffer view	178
How to do it...	178

How it works...	179
See also	180
Creating an image	**180**
How to do it...	180
How it works...	182
See also	184
Allocating and binding a memory object to an image	**185**
How to do it...	185
How it works...	187
There's more...	188
See also	189
Setting an image memory barrier	**189**
Getting ready	189
How to do it...	190
How it works...	192
See also	196
Creating an image view	**196**
How to do it...	196
How it works...	197
See also	199
Creating a 2D image and view	**199**
How to do it...	199
How it works...	200
See also	201
Creating a layered 2D image with a CUBEMAP view	**202**
How to do it...	202
How it works...	203
See also	204
Mapping, updating and unmapping host-visible memory	**204**
How to do it...	204
How it works...	206
See also	207
Copying data between buffers	**207**
How to do it...	207
How it works...	208
See also	209
Copying data from a buffer to an image	**209**
How to do it...	209
How it works...	211

  See also   213
Copying data from an image to a buffer   213
  How to do it...   213
  How it works...   214
  See also   216
Using a staging buffer to update a buffer with a device-local memory bound   216
  How to do it...   216
  How it works...   219
  See also   221
Using a staging buffer to update an image with a device-local memory bound   222
  How to do it...   222
  How it works...   224
  See also   226
Destroying an image view   227
  How to do it...   227
  How it works...   227
  See also   227
Destroying an image   228
  How to do it...   228
  How it works...   228
  See also   228
Destroying a buffer view   228
  How to do it...   229
  How it works...   229
  See also   229
Freeing a memory object   229
  How to do it...   230
  How it works...   230
  See also   230
Destroying a buffer   231
  How to do it...   231
  How it works...   231
  See also   231

Chapter 5: Descriptor Sets   233
Introduction   234
Creating a sampler   234
  How to do it...   234

How it works...	236
See also	237
Creating a sampled image	**237**
How to do it...	237
How it works...	238
See also	241
Creating a combined image sampler	**241**
How to do it...	241
How it works...	242
See also	243
Creating a storage image	**243**
How to do it...	243
How it works...	244
See also	246
Creating a uniform texel buffer	**247**
How to do it...	247
How it works...	248
See also	250
Creating a storage texel buffer	**250**
How to do it...	251
How it works...	252
See also	254
Creating a uniform buffer	**254**
How to do it...	254
How it works...	255
See also	257
Creating a storage buffer	**257**
How to do it...	257
How it works...	257
See also	259
Creating an input attachment	**259**
How to do it...	259
How it works...	260
See also	263
Creating a descriptor set layout	**264**
How to do it...	264
How it works...	265
See also	266
Creating a descriptor pool	**266**

How to do it...	266
How it works...	267
See also	268
Allocating descriptor sets	268
How to do it...	269
How it works...	270
See also	271
Updating descriptor sets	272
Getting ready	272
How to do it...	273
How it works...	275
See also	277
Binding descriptor sets	277
How to do it...	278
How it works...	279
See also	279
Creating descriptors with a texture and a uniform buffer	279
How to do it...	280
How it works...	282
See also	284
Freeing descriptor sets	285
How to do it...	285
How it works...	285
See also	286
Resetting a descriptor pool	286
How to do it...	286
How it works...	287
See also	287
Destroying a descriptor pool	288
How to do it...	288
How it works...	288
See also	288
Destroying a descriptor set layout	289
How to do it...	289
How it works...	289
See also	289
Destroying a sampler	290
How to do it...	290
How it works...	290

See also — 290

Chapter 6: Render Passes and Framebuffers — 291
Introduction — 291
Specifying attachments descriptions — 292
- How to do it... — 292
- How it works... — 293
- See also — 295
Specifying subpass descriptions — 295
- Getting ready — 295
- How to do it... — 296
- How it works... — 298
- See also — 299
Specifying dependencies between subpasses — 300
- How to do it... — 300
- How it works... — 301
- See also — 303
Creating a render pass — 303
- Getting ready — 303
- How to do it... — 303
- How it works... — 305
- See also — 306
Creating a framebuffer — 307
- How to do it... — 307
- How it works... — 308
- See also — 310
Preparing a render pass for geometry rendering and postprocess subpasses — 310
- Getting ready — 310
- How to do it... — 310
- How it works... — 313
- See also — 316
Preparing a render pass and a framebuffer with color and depth attachments — 317
- Getting ready — 317
- How to do it... — 317
- How it works... — 320
- See also — 322
Beginning a render pass — 322
- How to do it... — 322

How it works...	323
See also	325
Progressing to the next subpass	325
How to do it...	325
How it works...	326
See also	326
Ending a render pass	326
How to do it...	327
How it works...	327
See also	327
Destroying a framebuffer	328
How to do it...	328
How it works...	328
See also	328
Destroying a render pass	329
How to do it...	329
How it works...	329
See also	329
Chapter 7: Shaders	**331**
Introduction	331
Converting GLSL shaders to SPIR-V assemblies	332
How to do it...	332
How it works...	333
See also	334
Writing vertex shaders	334
How to do it...	334
How it works...	335
See also	337
Writing tessellation control shaders	337
How to do it...	338
How it works...	339
See also	341
Writing tessellation evaluation shaders	341
How to do it...	341
How it works...	343
See also	344
Writing geometry shaders	344
How to do it...	344
How it works...	346

See also	348
Writing fragment shaders	348
How to do it...	348
How it works...	349
See also	351
Writing compute shaders	351
How to do it...	351
How it works...	352
See also	353
Writing a vertex shader that multiplies vertex position by a projection matrix	354
How to do it...	354
How it works...	355
See also	356
Using push constants in shaders	356
How to do it...	356
How it works...	357
See also	358
Writing texturing vertex and fragment shaders	358
How to do it...	359
How it works...	359
See also	361
Displaying polygon normals with a geometry shader	362
How to do it...	362
How it works...	365
See also	368
Chapter 8: Graphics and Compute Pipelines	369
Introduction	370
Creating a shader module	371
How to do it...	371
How it works...	372
See also	373
Specifying pipeline shader stages	373
Getting ready	373
How to do it...	374
How it works...	375
See also	376
Specifying a pipeline vertex binding description, attribute description, and input state	377

[xiv]

How to do it...	377
How it works...	378
See also	381
Specifying a pipeline input assembly state	**381**
How to do it...	381
How it works...	382
See also	383
Specifying a pipeline tessellation state	**383**
How to do it...	383
How it works...	384
See also	385
Specifying a pipeline viewport and scissor test state	**385**
Getting ready	385
How to do it...	385
How it works...	387
See also	389
Specifying a pipeline rasterization state	**389**
How to do it...	390
How it works...	391
See also	392
Specifying a pipeline multisample state	**392**
How to do it...	392
How it works...	393
See also	394
Specifying a pipeline depth and stencil state	**394**
How to do it...	395
How it works...	396
See also	397
Specifying a pipeline blend state	**398**
How to do it...	398
How it works...	399
See also	403
Specifying pipeline dynamic states	**403**
How to do it...	404
How it works...	405
See also	406
Creating a pipeline layout	**407**
How to do it...	407
How it works...	409

See also	411
Specifying graphics pipeline creation parameters	411
How to do it...	412
How it works...	415
See also	416
Creating a pipeline cache object	417
How to do it...	417
How it works...	418
See also	419
Retrieving data from a pipeline cache	419
How to do it...	419
How it works...	420
See also	421
Merging multiple pipeline cache objects	421
How to do it...	422
How it works...	422
See also	423
Creating a graphics pipeline	423
How to do it...	424
How it works...	425
See also	426
Creating a compute pipeline	427
How to do it...	427
How it works...	428
See also	429
Binding a pipeline object	429
How to do it...	430
How it works...	430
See also	430
Creating a pipeline layout with a combined image sampler, a buffer, and push constant ranges	431
How to do it...	431
How it works...	432
See also	433
Creating a graphics pipeline with vertex and fragment shaders, depth test enabled, and with dynamic viewport and scissor tests	433
How to do it...	434
How it works...	436
See also	439

Creating multiple graphics pipelines on multiple threads	440
Getting ready	440
How to do it...	440
How it works...	441
See also	443
Destroying a pipeline	443
How to do it...	444
How it works...	444
See also	444
Destroying a pipeline cache	445
How to do it...	445
How it works...	445
See also	446
Destroying a pipeline layout	446
How to do it...	446
How it works...	447
See also	447
Destroying a shader module	447
How to do it...	448
How it works...	448
See also	448

Chapter 9: Command Recording and Drawing   449

Introduction	450
Clearing a color image	450
How to do it...	450
How it works...	451
See also	452
Clearing a depth-stencil image	452
How to do it...	453
How it works...	454
See also	454
Clearing render pass attachments	454
How to do it...	454
How it works...	455
See also	455
Binding vertex buffers	456
Getting ready	456
How to do it...	456
How it works...	457

See also	458
Binding an index buffer	**458**
How to do it...	459
How it works...	459
See also	460
Providing data to shaders through push constants	**460**
How to do it...	460
How it works...	461
See also	462
Setting viewport states dynamically	**462**
How to do it...	462
How it works...	463
See also	464
Setting scissor states dynamically	**464**
How to do it...	464
How it works...	465
See also	465
Setting line width states dynamically	**466**
How to do it...	466
How it works...	466
See also	467
Setting depth bias states dynamically	**467**
How to do it...	467
How it works...	467
See also	468
Setting blend constants states dynamically	**468**
How to do it...	468
How it works...	469
See also	469
Drawing a geometry	**469**
How to do it...	470
How it works...	471
See also	472
Drawing an indexed geometry	**473**
How to do it...	473
How it works...	474
See also	474
Dispatching compute work	**475**
How to do it...	475

How it works...	476
See also	477
Executing a secondary command buffer inside a primary command buffer	**477**
How to do it...	477
How it works...	478
See also	478
Recording a command buffer that draws a geometry with dynamic viewport and scissor states	**478**
Getting ready	479
How to do it...	479
How it works...	483
See also	487
Recording command buffers on multiple threads	**487**
Getting ready	488
How to do it...	488
How it works...	489
See also	492
Preparing a single frame of animation	**492**
How to do it...	492
How it works...	494
See also	497
Increasing the performance through increasing the number of separately rendered frames	**498**
Getting ready	498
How to do it...	499
How it works...	501
See also	504
Chapter 10: Helper Recipes	**505**
Introduction	**505**
Preparing a translation matrix	**506**
How to do it...	506
How it works...	506
See also	508
Preparing a rotation matrix	**509**
How to do it...	509
How it works...	510
See also	512
Preparing a scaling matrix	**512**

How to do it...	513
How it works...	513
See also	515
Preparing a perspective projection matrix	**515**
How to do it...	516
How it works...	517
See also	519
Preparing an orthographic projection matrix	**519**
How to do it...	520
How it works...	521
See also	522
Loading texture data from a file	**522**
Getting ready	522
How to do it...	523
How it works...	524
See also	525
Loading a 3D model from an OBJ file	**525**
Getting ready	526
How to do it...	527
How it works...	528
See also	531

Chapter 11: Lighting — 533

Introduction	**533**
Rendering a geometry with a vertex diffuse lighting	**534**
Getting ready	535
How to do it...	536
How it works...	543
See also	551
Rendering a geometry with a fragment specular lighting	**551**
Getting ready	552
How to do it...	554
How it works...	556
See also	557
Rendering a normal mapped geometry	**558**
Getting ready	559
How to do it...	560
How it works...	564
See also	569
Drawing a reflective and refractive geometry using cubemaps	**570**

Getting ready	570
How to do it...	572
How it works...	575
See also	580
Adding shadows to the scene	581
Getting ready	581
How to do it...	582
How it works...	588
See also	595

Chapter 12: Advanced Rendering Techniques — 597

Introduction	597
Drawing a skybox	598
Getting ready	598
How to do it...	599
How it works...	602
See also	606
Drawing billboards using geometry shaders	607
How to do it...	608
How it works...	610
See also	614
Drawing particles using compute and graphics pipelines	615
How to do it...	616
How it works...	618
See also	627
Rendering a tessellated terrain	627
Getting ready	629
How to do it...	630
How it works...	634
See also	643
Rendering a full-screen quad for post-processing	643
How to do it...	644
How it works...	646
See also	651
Using input attachments for a color correction post-process effect	652
How to do it...	653
How it works...	655
See also	661

Index — 663

Preface

Computer graphics have a very long and interesting history. Many APIs or custom approaches to the generation of 2D or 3D images have come and gone. A landmark in this history was the invention of OpenGL, one of the first graphics libraries, which allowed us to create real-time, high-performance 3D graphics, and which was available for everyone on multiple operating systems. It is still developed and widely used even today. And this year we can celebrate its 25th birthday!

But many things have changed since OpenGL was created. The graphics hardware industry is evolving very quickly. And recently, to accommodate these changes, a new approach to 3D graphics rendering was presented. It took the form of a low-level access to the graphics hardware. OpenGL was designed as a high-level API, which allows users to easily render images on screen. But this high-level approach, convenient for users, is difficult for graphics drivers to handle. This is one of the main reasons for restricting the hardware to show its full potential. The new approach tries to overcome these struggles–it gives users much more control over the hardware, but also many more responsibilities. This way application developers can release the full potential of the graphics hardware, because the drivers no longer block them. Low-level access allows drivers to be much smaller, much thinner. But these benefits come at the expense of much more work that needs to done by the developers.

The first evangelist of the new approach to graphics rendering was a Mantle API designed by AMD. When it proved that low-level access can give considerable performance benefits, other companies started working on their own graphics libraries. One of the most notable representatives of the new trend were Metal API, designed by Apple, and DirectX 12, developed by Microsoft.

But all of the above libraries were developed with specific operating systems and/or hardware in mind. There was no open and multiplatform standard such as OpenGL. Until last year. Year 2016 saw the release of the Vulkan API, developed by Khronos consortium, which maintains the OpenGL library. Vulkan also represents the new approach, a low-level access to the graphics hardware, but unlike the other libraries it is available for everyone on multiple operating systems and hardware platforms–from high-performance desktop computers with Windows or Linux operating systems, to mobile devices with Android OS. And as it is still being very new, there are few resources teaching developers how to use it. This book tries to fill this gap.

What this book covers

Chapter 1, *Instance and Devices*, shows how to get started with the Vulkan API. This chapter explains where to download the Vulkan SDK from, how to connect with the Vulkan Loader library, how to select the physical device on which operations will be performed, and how to prepare and create a logical device.

Chapter 2, *Image Presentation*, describes how to display Vulkan-generated images on screen. It explains what a swapchain is and what parameters are required to create it, so we can use it for rendering and see the results of our work.

Chapter 3, *Command Buffers and Synchronization*, is about recording various operations into command buffers and submitting them to queues, where they are processed by the hardware. Also, various synchronization mechanisms are presented in this chapter.

Chapter 4, *Resources and Memory*, presents two basic and most important resource types, images and buffers, which allow us to store data. We explain how to create them, how to prepare memory for these resources, and, also, how to upload data to them from our application (CPU).

Chapter 5, *Descriptor Sets*, explains how to provide created resource to shaders. We explain how to prepare resources so they can be used inside shaders and how to set up descriptor sets, which form the interface between the application and the shaders.

Chapter 6, *Render Passes and Framebuffers*, shows how to organize drawing operations into sets of separate steps called subpasses, which are organized into render passes. In this chapter we also show how to prepare descriptions of attachments (render targets) used during drawing and how to create framebuffers, which bind specific resources according to these descriptions.

Chapter 7, *Shaders*, describes the specifics of programming all available graphics and compute shader stages. This chapter presents how to implement shader programs using GLSL programming language and how to convert them into SPIR-V assemblies – the only form core Vulkan API accepts.

Chapter 8, *Graphics and Compute Pipelines*, presents the process of creating two available pipeline types. They are used to set up all the parameters graphics hardware needs to properly process drawing commands or computational work.

Chapter 9, *Command Recording and Drawing*, is about recording all the operations needed to successfully draw 3D models or dispatch computational work. Also, various optimization techniques are presented in this chapter, which can help increase the performance of the application.

Chapter 10, *Helper Recipes*, shows convenient set of tools no 3D rendering application can do without. It is shown how to load textures and 3D models from files and how to manipulate the geometry inside shaders.

Chapter 11, *Lighting*, presents commonly used lighting techniques from simple diffuse and specular lighting calculations to normal mapping and shadow mapping techniques.

Chapter 12, *Advanced Rendering Techniques*, explains how to implement impressive graphics techniques, which can be found in many popular 3D applications such as games and benchmarks.

What you need for this book

This book explains various aspects of the Vulkan graphics API, which is open and multiplatform. It is available on Microsoft Windows (version 7 and newer) or Linux (preferably Ubuntu 16.04 or newer) systems. (Vulkan is also supported on Android devices with the 7.0+ / Nougat version of the operating system, but the code samples available with this book weren't designed to be executed on the Android OS.)

To execute sample programs or to develop our own applications, apart from Windows 7+ or Linux operating systems, graphics hardware and drivers that support Vulkan API are also required. Refer to 3D graphics vendors' sites and/or support to check which hardware is capable of running Vulkan-enabled software.

When using the Windows operating system, code samples can be compiled using the Visual Studio Community 2015 IDE (or newer), which is free and available for everyone. To generate a solution for the Visual Studio IDE the CMAKE 3.0 or newer is required.

On Linux systems, compilation is performed using a combination of the CMAKE 3.0 and the make tool. But the samples can also be compiled using other tools such as QtCreator.

Who this book is for

This book is ideal for developers who know C/C++ languages, have some basic familiarity with graphics programming, and now want to take advantage of the new Vulkan API in the process of building next generation computer graphics. Some basic familiarity with Vulkan would be useful to follow the recipes. OpenGL developers who want to take advantage of the Vulkan API will also find this book useful.

Preface

Sections

In this book, you will find several headings that appear frequently (Getting ready, How to do it, How it works, There's more, and See also).

To give clear instructions on how to complete a recipe, we use these sections as follows:

Getting ready

This section tells you what to expect in the recipe, and describes how to set up any software or any preliminary settings required for the recipe.

How to do it…

This section contains the steps required to follow the recipe.

How it works…

This section usually consists of a detailed explanation of what happened in the previous section.

There's more…

This section consists of additional information about the recipe in order to make the reader more knowledgeable about the recipe.

See also

This section provides helpful links to other useful information for the recipe.

Conventions

In this book, you will find a number of text styles that distinguish between different kinds of information. Here are some examples of these styles and an explanation of their meaning.

Code words in text, database table names, folder names, filenames, file extensions, pathnames, dummy URLs, user input, and Twitter handles are shown as follows: "Just assign the names of the layers you want to activate to the `VK_INSTANCE_LAYERS` environment variable"

A block of code is set as follows:

```
{
  if( (result != VK_SUCCESS) ||
      (extensions_count == 0) ) {
    std::cout << "Could not enumerate device extensions." << std::endl;
    return false;
  }
}
```

Any command-line input or output is written as follows:

```
setx VK_INSTANCE_LAYERS
VK_LAYER_LUNARG_api_dump;VK_LAYER_LUNARG_core_validation
```

New terms and **important words** are shown in bold. Words that you see on the screen, for example, in menus or dialog boxes, appear in the text like this: "Select **System info** from the **Administration** panel."

Warnings or important notes appear in a box like this.

Tips and tricks appear like this.

Reader feedback

Feedback from our readers is always welcome. Let us know what you think about this book-what you liked or disliked. Reader feedback is important for us as it helps us develop titles that you will really get the most out of.

To send us general feedback, simply e-mail feedback@packtpub.com, and mention the book's title in the subject of your message.

If there is a topic that you have expertise in and you are interested in either writing or contributing to a book, see our author guide at www.packtpub.com/authors.

Customer support

Now that you are the proud owner of a Packt book, we have a number of things to help you to get the most from your purchase.

Downloading the example code

You can download the example code files for this book from your account at http://www.packtpub.com. If you purchased this book elsewhere, you can visit http://www.packtpub.com/support and register to have the files e-mailed directly to you.

You can download the code files by following these steps:

1. Log in or register to our website using your e-mail address and password.
2. Hover the mouse pointer on the **SUPPORT** tab at the top.
3. Click on **Code Downloads & Errata**.
4. Enter the name of the book in the **Search** box.
5. Select the book for which you're looking to download the code files.
6. Choose from the drop-down menu where you purchased this book from.
7. Click on **Code Download**.

You can also download the code files by clicking on the **Code Files** button on the book's webpage at the Packt Publishing website. This page can be accessed by entering the book's name in the **Search** box. Please note that you need to be logged in to your Packt account.

Once the file is downloaded, please make sure that you unzip or extract the folder using the latest version of:

- WinRAR / 7-Zip for Windows
- Zipeg / iZip / UnRarX for Mac
- 7-Zip / PeaZip for Linux

The code bundle for the book is also hosted on GitHub at https://github.com/PacktPublishing/Vulkan-Cookbook. We also have other code bundles from our rich catalog of books and videos available at https://github.com/PacktPublishing/. Check them out!

Downloading the color images of this book

We also provide you with a PDF file that has color images of the screenshots/diagrams used in this book. The color images will help you better understand the changes in the output. You can download this file from https://www.packtpub.com/sites/default/files/downloads/VulkanCookbook_ColorImages.pdf.

Errata

Although we have taken every care to ensure the accuracy of our content, mistakes do happen. If you find a mistake in one of our books-maybe a mistake in the text or the code-we would be grateful if you could report this to us. By doing so, you can save other readers from frustration and help us improve subsequent versions of this book. If you find any errata, please report them by visiting http://www.packtpub.com/submit-errata, selecting your book, clicking on the **Errata Submission Form** link, and entering the details of your errata. Once your errata are verified, your submission will be accepted and the errata will be uploaded to our website or added to any list of existing errata under the Errata section of that title.

To view the previously submitted errata, go to https://www.packtpub.com/books/content/support and enter the name of the book in the search field. The required information will appear under the **Errata** section.

Piracy

Piracy of copyrighted material on the Internet is an ongoing problem across all media. At Packt, we take the protection of our copyright and licenses very seriously. If you come across any illegal copies of our works in any form on the Internet, please provide us with the location address or website name immediately so that we can pursue a remedy.

Please contact us at copyright@packtpub.com with a link to the suspected pirated material.

We appreciate your help in protecting our authors and our ability to bring you valuable content.

Questions

If you have a problem with any aspect of this book, you can contact us at questions@packtpub.com, and we will do our best to address the problem.

1
Instance and Devices

In this chapter, we will cover the following recipes:

- Downloading Vulkan SDK
- Enabling validation layers
- Connecting with a Vulkan Loader library
- Preparing for loading Vulkan API functions
- Loading function exported from a Vulkan Loader library
- Loading global-level functions
- Checking available Instance extensions
- Creating a Vulkan Instance
- Loading instance-level functions
- Enumerating available physical devices
- Checking available device extensions
- Getting features and properties of a physical device
- Checking available queue families and their properties
- Selecting the index of a queue family with the desired capabilities
- Creating a logical device
- Loading device-level functions
- Getting a device queue
- Creating a logical device with geometry shaders and graphics and compute queues
- Destroying a logical device
- Destroying a Vulkan Instance
- Releasing a Vulkan Loader library

Instance and Devices

Introduction

Vulkan is a new graphics API developed by the Khronos Consortium. It is perceived as a successor to the OpenGL: it is open source and cross-platform. However, as it is possible to use Vulkan on different types of devices and operating systems, there are some differences in the basic setup code we need to create in order to use Vulkan in our application.

In this chapter, we will cover topics that are specific to using Vulkan on Microsoft Windows and Ubuntu Linux operating systems. We will learn Vulkan basics such as downloading the **Software Development Kit (SDK)** and setting **validation layers,** which enable us to debug the applications that use the Vulkan API. We will start using the **Vulkan Loader** library, load all the Vulkan API functions, create a Vulkan Instance, and select the device our work will be executed on.

Downloading Vulkan's SDK

To start developing applications using the Vulkan API, we need to download a SDK and use some of its resources in our application.

Vulkan's SDK can be found at `https://vulkan.lunarg.com`.

Getting ready

Before we can execute any application that uses the Vulkan API, we also need to install a graphics drivers that supports the Vulkan API. These can be found on a graphics hardware vendor's site.

How to do it...

On the Windows operating system family:

1. Go to `https://vulkan.lunarg.com`.
2. Scroll to the bottom of the page and choose **WINDOWS** operating system.
3. Download and save the SDK installer file.

4. Run the installer and select the destination at which you want to install the SDK. By default, it is installed to a `C:\VulkanSDK\<version>\` folder.
5. When the installation is finished, open the folder in which the Vulkan SDK was installed and then open the `RunTimeInstaller` sub-folder. Execute `VulkanRT-<version>-Installer` file. This will install the latest version of the Vulkan Loader.
6. Once again, go to the folder in which the SDK was installed and open the `Include\vulkan` sub-folder. Copy the `vk_platform.h` and `vulkan.h` header files to the project folder of the application you want to develop. We will call these two files *Vulkan header files*.

On the Linux operating system family:

1. Update system packages by running the following commands:

   ```
   sudo apt-get update
   sudo apt-get dist-upgrade
   ```

2. To be able to build and execute Vulkan samples from the SDK, install additional development packages by running the following command:

   ```
   sudo apt-get install libglm-dev graphviz libxcb-dri3-0
   libxcb-present0 libpciaccess0 cmake libpng-dev libxcb-dri3-
   dev libx11-dev
   ```

3. Go to `https://vulkan.lunarg.com`.
4. Scroll to the bottom of the page and choose **LINUX** operating system.
5. Download the Linux package for the SDK and save it in the desired folder.
6. Open Terminal and change the current directory to the folder to which the SDK package was downloaded.
7. Change the access permissions to the downloaded file by executing the following command:

   ```
   chmod ugo+x vulkansdk-linux-x86_64-<version>.run
   ```

8. Run the downloaded SDK package installer file with the following command:

   ```
   ./vulkansdk-linux-x86_64-<version>.run
   ```

9. Change the current directory to the `VulkanSDK/<version>` folder that was created by the SDK package installer.

10. Set up environment variables by executing the following command:

```
sudo su
VULKAN_SDK=$PWD/x86_64
echo export PATH=$PATH:$VULKAN_SDK/bin >> /etc/environment
echo export VK_LAYER_PATH=$VULKAN_SDK/etc/explicit_layer.d >> /etc/environment
echo $VULKAN_SDK/lib >> /etc/ld.so.conf.d/vulkan.conf
ldconfig
```

11. Change the current directory to the `x86_64/include/vulkan` folder.
12. Copy `vk_platform.h` and `vulkan.h` header files to the project folder of the application you want to develop. We will call these two files *Vulkan header files*.
13. Restart the computer for the changes to take effect.

How it works...

The SDK contains resources needed to create applications using the Vulkan API. Vulkan header files (the `vk_platform.h` and `vulkan.h` files) need to be included in the source code of our application so we can use the Vulkan API functions, structures, enumerations, and so on, inside the code.

The Vulkan Loader (`vulkan-1.dll` file on Windows, `libvulkan.so.1` file on Linux systems) is a dynamic library responsible for exposing Vulkan API functions and forwarding them to the graphics driver. We connect with it in our application and load Vulkan API functions from it.

See also

The following recipes in this chapter:

- *Enabling validation layers*
- *Connecting with a Vulkan Loader library*
- *Releasing a Vulkan Loader library*

Enabling validation layers

The Vulkan API was designed with performance in mind. One way to increase its performance is to lower state and error checking performed by the driver. This is one of the reasons Vulkan is called a "thin API" or "thin driver," it is a minimal abstraction of the hardware, which is required for the API to be portable across multiple hardware vendors and device types (high-performance desktop computers, mobile phones, and integrated and low-power embedded systems).

However, this approach makes creating applications with the Vulkan API much more difficult, compared to the traditional high-level APIs such as OpenGL. It's because very little feedback is given to developers by the driver, as it expects that programmers will correctly use the API and abide by rules defined in the Vulkan specification.

To mitigate this problem, Vulkan was also designed to be a layered API. The lowest layer, the core, is the **Vulkan API** itself, which communicates with the **Driver**, allowing us to program the **Hardware** (as seen in the preceding diagram). On top of it (between the **Application** and the **Vulkan API**), developers can enable additional layers, to ease the debugging process.

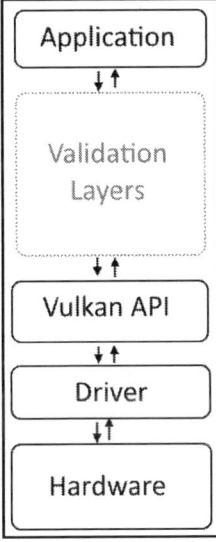

How to do it...

On the Windows operating system family:

1. Go to the folder in which the SDK was installed and then open the `Config` sub-directory.
2. Copy the `vk_layer_settings.txt` file into the directory of the executable you want to debug (into a folder of an application you want to execute).
3. Create an environment variable named `VK_INSTANCE_LAYERS`:
    1. Open the command-line console (Command Prompt/`cmd.exe`).
    2. Type the following:

        ```
        setx VK_INSTANCE_LAYERS
        VK_LAYER_LUNARG_standard_validation
        ```

    3. Close the console.
4. Re-open the command prompt once again.
5. Change the current directory to the folder of the application you want to execute.
6. Run the application; potential warnings or errors will be displayed in the standard output of the command prompt.

On the Linux operating system family:

1. Go to the folder in which the SDK was installed and then open the `Config` sub-directory.
2. Copy the `vk_layer_settings.txt` file into the directory of the executable you want to debug (into a folder of an application you want to execute).
3. Create an environment variable named `VK_INSTANCE_LAYERS`:
    1. Open the Terminal window.
    2. Type the following:

        ```
        export
        VK_INSTANCE_LAYERS=VK_LAYER_LUNARG_standard_validation
        ```

4. Run the application; potential warnings or errors will be displayed in the standard output of the Terminal window.

How it works...

Vulkan validation layers contain a set of libraries which help find potential problems in created applications. Their debugging capabilities include, but are not limited to, validating parameters passed to Vulkan functions, validating texture and render target formats, tracking Vulkan objects and their lifetime and usage, and checking for potential memory leaks or dumping (displaying/printing) Vulkan API function calls. These functionalities are enabled by different validation layers, but most of them are gathered into a single layer called `VK_LAYER_LUNARG_standard_validation` which is enabled in this recipe. Examples of names of other layers include `VK_LAYER_LUNARG_swapchain`, `VK_LAYER_LUNARG_object_tracker`, `VK_LAYER_GOOGLE_threading`, or `VK_LAYER_LUNARG_api_dump`, among others. Multiple layers can be enabled at the same time, in a similar way as presented here in the recipe. Just assign the names of the layers you want to activate to the `VK_INSTANCE_LAYERS` environment variable. If you are a Windows OS user, remember to separate them with a semicolon, as in the example:

```
setx VK_INSTANCE_LAYERS
VK_LAYER_LUNARG_api_dump;VK_LAYER_LUNARG_core_validation
```

If you are a Linux OS user, separate them with a colon. Here is an example:

```
export VK_INSTANCE_LAYERS=VK_LAYER_LUNARG_api_dump:VK_LAYER_LUNARG
_core_validation
```

The environment variable named `VK_INSTANCE_LAYERS` can be also set with other OS specific ways such as, advanced operating system settings on Windows or `/etc/environment` on Linux.

The preceding examples enable validation layers globally, for all applications, but they can also be enabled only for our own application, in its source code during Instance creation. However, this approach requires us to recompile the whole program every time we want to enable or disable different layers. So, it is easier to enable them using the preceding recipe. This way, we also won't forget to disable them when we want to ship the final version of our application. To disable validation layers, we just have to delete `VK_INSTANCE_LAYERS` environment variable.

> Validation layers should not be enabled in the released (shipped) version of the applications as they may drastically decrease performance.

Instance and Devices

For a full list of available validation layers, please refer to the documentation, which can be found in the `Documentation` sub-folder of the directory in which the Vulkan SDK was installed.

See also

The following recipes in this chapter:

- *Downloading Vulkan's SDK*
- *Connecting with a Vulkan Loader library*
- *Releasing a Vulkan Loader library*

Connecting with a Vulkan Loader library

Support for the Vulkan API is implemented by the graphics-hardware vendor and provided through graphics drivers. Each vendor can implement it in any dynamic library they choose, and can even change it with the driver update.

That's why, along with the drivers, Vulkan Loader is also installed. We can also install it from the folder in which the SDK was installed. It allows developers to access Vulkan API entry points, through a `vulkan-1.dll` library on Windows OS or `libvulkan.so.1` library on Linux OS, no matter what driver, from what vendor, is installed.

Vulkan Loader is responsible for transmitting Vulkan API calls to an appropriate graphics driver. On a given computer, there may be more hardware components that support Vulkan, but with Vulkan Loader, we don't need to wonder which driver we should use, or which library we should connect with to be able to use Vulkan. Developers just need to know the name of a Vulkan library: `vulkan-1.dll` on Windows or `libvulkan.so.1` on Linux. When we want to use Vulkan in our application, we just need to connect with it in our code (load it).

> On Windows OS, Vulkan Loader library is called `vulkan-1.dll`.
> On Linux OS, Vulkan Loader library is called `libvulkan.so.1`.

How to do it...

On the Windows operating system family:

1. Prepare a variable of type `HMODULE` named `vulkan_library`.
2. Call `LoadLibrary( "vulkan-1.dll" )` and store the result of this operation in a `vulkan_library` variable.
3. Confirm that this operation has been successful by checking if a value of a `vulkan_library` variable is different than `nullptr`.

On the Linux operating system family:

1. Prepare a variable of type `void*` named `vulkan_library`.
2. Call `dlopen( "libvulkan.so.1", RTLD_NOW )` and store the result of this operation in a `vulkan_library` variable.
3. Confirm that this operation has been successful by checking if a value of a `vulkan_library` variable is different than `nullptr`.

How it works...

`LoadLibrary()` is a function available on Windows operating systems. `dlopen()` is a function available on Linux operating systems. They both load (open) a specified dynamic-link library into a memory space of our application. This way we can load (acquire pointers of) functions implemented and exported from a given library and use them in our application.

In the case of a function exported from a Vulkan API, in which we are, of course, most interested, we load a `vulkan-1.dll` library on Windows or `libvulkan.so.1` library on Linux as follows:

```
#if defined _WIN32
vulkan_library = LoadLibrary( "vulkan-1.dll" );
#elif defined __linux
vulkan_library = dlopen( "libvulkan.so.1", RTLD_NOW );
#endif

if( vulkan_library == nullptr ) {
  std::cout << "Could not connect with a Vulkan Runtime library." << std::endl;
  return false;
}
return true;
```

Instance and Devices

After a successful call, we can load a Vulkan-specific function for acquiring the addresses of all other Vulkan API procedures.

See also

The following recipes in this chapter:

- *Downloading Vulkan SDK*
- *Enabling validation layers*
- *Releasing a Vulkan Loader library*

Preparing for loading Vulkan API functions

When we want to use Vulkan API in our application, we need to acquire procedures specified in the Vulkan documentation. In order to do that, we can add a dependency to the Vulkan Loader library, statically link with it in our project, and use function prototypes defined in the `vulkan.h` header file. The second approach is to disable the function prototypes defined in the `vulkan.h` header file and load function pointers dynamically in our application.

The first approach is little bit easier, but it uses functions defined directly in the Vulkan Loader library. When we perform operations on a given device, Vulkan Loader needs to redirect function calls to the proper implementation based on the handle of the device we provide as an argument. This redirection takes some time, and thus impacts performance.

The second option requires more work on the application side, but allows us to skip the preceding redirection (jump) and save some performance. It is performed by loading functions directly from the device we want to use. This way, we can also choose only the subset of Vulkan functions if we don't need them all.

In this book, the second approach is presented, as this gives developers more control over the things that are going in their applications. To dynamically load functions from a Vulkan Loader library, it is convenient to wrap the names of all Vulkan API functions into a set of simple macros and divide declarations, definitions and function loading into multiple files.

How to do it...

1. Define the `VK_NO_PROTOTYPES` preprocessor definition in the project: do this in the project properties (when using development environments such as Microsoft Visual Studio or Qt Creator), or by using the `#define VK_NO_PROTOTYPES` preprocessor directive just before the `vulkan.h` file is included in the source code of our application.
2. Create a new file, named `ListOfVulkanFunctions.inl`.
3. Type the following contents into the file:

```
#ifndef EXPORTED_VULKAN_FUNCTION
#define EXPORTED_VULKAN_FUNCTION( function )
#endif

#undef EXPORTED_VULKAN_FUNCTION
//
#ifndef GLOBAL_LEVEL_VULKAN_FUNCTION
#define GLOBAL_LEVEL_VULKAN_FUNCTION( function )
#endif

#undef GLOBAL_LEVEL_VULKAN_FUNCTION
//
#ifndef INSTANCE_LEVEL_VULKAN_FUNCTION
#define INSTANCE_LEVEL_VULKAN_FUNCTION( function )
#endif

#undef INSTANCE_LEVEL_VULKAN_FUNCTION
//
#ifndef INSTANCE_LEVEL_VULKAN_FUNCTION_FROM_EXTENSION
#define INSTANCE_LEVEL_VULKAN_FUNCTION_FROM_EXTENSION( function, extension )
#endif

#undef INSTANCE_LEVEL_VULKAN_FUNCTION_FROM_EXTENSION
//
#ifndef DEVICE_LEVEL_VULKAN_FUNCTION
#define DEVICE_LEVEL_VULKAN_FUNCTION( function )
#endif

#undef DEVICE_LEVEL_VULKAN_FUNCTION
//
#ifndef DEVICE_LEVEL_VULKAN_FUNCTION_FROM_EXTENSION
#define DEVICE_LEVEL_VULKAN_FUNCTION_FROM_EXTENSION( function, extension )
#endif
```

Instance and Devices

```
#undef DEVICE_LEVEL_VULKAN_FUNCTION_FROM_EXTENSION
```

4. Create a new header file, named `VulkanFunctions.h`.
5. Insert the following contents into the file:

```
#include "vulkan.h"

namespace VulkanCookbook {

#define EXPORTED_VULKAN_FUNCTION( name ) extern PFN_##name name;
#define GLOBAL_LEVEL_VULKAN_FUNCTION( name ) extern PFN_##name name;
#define INSTANCE_LEVEL_VULKAN_FUNCTION( name ) extern PFN_##name name;
#define INSTANCE_LEVEL_VULKAN_FUNCTION_FROM_EXTENSION( name, extension ) extern PFN_##name name;
#define DEVICE_LEVEL_VULKAN_FUNCTION( name ) extern PFN_##name name;
#define DEVICE_LEVEL_VULKAN_FUNCTION_FROM_EXTENSION( name, extension ) extern PFN_##name name;

#include "ListOfVulkanFunctions.inl"

} // namespace VulkanCookbook
```

6. Create a new file with a source code named `VulkanFunctions.cpp`.
7. Insert the following contents into the file:

```
#include "VulkanFunctions.h"

namespace VulkanCookbook {

#define EXPORTED_VULKAN_FUNCTION( name ) PFN_##name name;
#define GLOBAL_LEVEL_VULKAN_FUNCTION( name ) PFN_##name name;
#define INSTANCE_LEVEL_VULKAN_FUNCTION( name ) PFN_##name name;
#define INSTANCE_LEVEL_VULKAN_FUNCTION_FROM_EXTENSION( name, extension ) PFN_##name name;
#define DEVICE_LEVEL_VULKAN_FUNCTION( name ) PFN_##name name;
#define DEVICE_LEVEL_VULKAN_FUNCTION_FROM_EXTENSION( name, extension ) PFN_##name name;

#include "ListOfVulkanFunctions.inl"

} // namespace VulkanCookbook
```

How it works...

The preceding set of files may seem unnecessary, or even overwhelming, at first. `VulkanFunctions.h` and `VulkanFunctions.cpp` files are used to declare and define variables in which we will store pointers to Vulkan API functions. Declarations and definitions are done through a convenient macro definition and an inclusion of a `ListOfVulkanFunctions.inl` file. We will update this file and add the names of many Vulkan functions, from various levels. This way, we don't need to repeat the names of functions multiple times, in multiple places, which helps us avoid making mistakes and typos. We can just write the required names of Vulkan functions only once, in the `ListOfVulkanFunctions.inl` file, and include it when it's needed.

How do we know the types of variables for storing pointers to Vulkan API functions? It's quite simple. The type of each function's prototype is derived directly from the function's name. When a function is named `<name>`, its type is `PFN_<name>`. For example, a function that creates an image is called `vkCreateImage()`, so the type of this function is `PFN_vkCreateImage`. That's why macros defined in the presented set of files have just one parameter for function name, from which the type can be easily derived.

Last, but not least, remember that declarations and definitions of variables, in which we will store addresses of the Vulkan functions, should be placed inside a namespace, a class, or a structure. This is because, if they are made global, this could lead to problems on some operating systems. It's better to remember about namespaces and increase the portability of our code.

 Place declarations and definitions of variables containing Vulkan API function pointers inside a structure, class, or namespace.

Now that we are prepared, we can start loading Vulkan functions.

See also

The following recipes in this chapter:

- *Loading function exported from a Vulkan Loader library*
- *Loading global-level functions*
- *Loading instance-level functions*
- *Loading device-level functions*

Loading functions exported from a Vulkan Loader library

When we load (connect with) a Vulkan Loader library, we need to load its functions to be able to use the Vulkan API in our application. Unfortunately, different operating systems have different ways of acquiring the addresses of functions exported from dynamic libraries (.dll files on Windows or .so files on Linux). However, the Vulkan API strives to be portable across many operating systems. So, to allow developers to load all functions available in the API, no matter what operating system they are targeting, Vulkan introduced a function which can be used to load all other Vulkan API functions. However, this one single function can only be loaded in an OS specific way.

How to do it...

On the Windows operating system family:

1. Create a variable of type PFN_vkGetInstanceProcAddr named vkGetInstanceProcAddr.
2. Call GetProcAddress(vulkan_library, "vkGetInstanceProcAddr"), cast the result of this operation onto a PFN_vkGetInstanceProcAddr type, and store it in the vkGetInstanceProcAddr variable.
3. Confirm that this operation succeeded by checking if a value of the vkGetInstanceProcAddr variable does not equal to nullptr.

On the Linux operating system family:

1. Create a variable of type PFN_vkGetInstanceProcAddr named vkGetInstanceProcAddr.
2. Call dlsym(vulkan_library, "vkGetInstanceProcAddr"), cast the result of this operation onto a PFN_vkGetInstanceProcAddr type, and store it in the vkGetInstanceProcAddr variable.
3. Confirm that this operation succeeded by checking if a value of the vkGetInstanceProcAddr variable does not equal to nullptr.

How it works...

`GetProcAddress()` is a function available on Windows operating systems. `dlsym()` is a function available on Linux operating systems. They both acquire an address of a specified function from an already loaded dynamic-link library. The only function that must be publicly exported from all Vulkan implementations is called `vkGetInstanceProcAddr()`. It allows us to load any other Vulkan function in a way that is independent of the operating system we are working on.

To ease and automate the process of loading multiple Vulkan functions, and to lower the probability of making mistakes, we should wrap the processes of declaring, defining, and loading functions into a set of convenient macro definitions, as described in the *Preparing for loading Vulkan API functions* recipe. This way, we can keep all Vulkan API functions in just one file which contains a list of macro-wrapped names of all Vulkan functions. We can then include this single file in multiple places and get use of the C/C++ preprocessor. By redefining macros, we can declare and define the variables in which we will store function pointers, and we can also load all of them.

Here is the updated fragment of the `ListOfVulkanFunctions.inl` file:

```
#ifndef EXPORTED_VULKAN_FUNCTION
#define EXPORTED_VULKAN_FUNCTION( function )
#endif

EXPORTED_VULKAN_FUNCTION( vkGetInstanceProcAddr )

#undef EXPORTED_VULKAN_FUNCTION
```

The rest of the files (`VulkanFunctions.h` and `VulkanFunctions.h`) remain unchanged. Declarations and definitions are automatically performed with preprocessor macros. However, we still need to load functions exported from the Vulkan Loader library. The implementation of the preceding recipe may look as follows:

```
#if defined _WIN32
#define LoadFunction GetProcAddress
#elif defined __linux
#define LoadFunction dlsym
#endif

#define EXPORTED_VULKAN_FUNCTION( name )                             \
name = (PFN_##name)LoadFunction( vulkan_library, #name );            \
if( name == nullptr ) {                                              \
  std::cout << "Could not load exported Vulkan function named: "     \
    #name << std::endl;                                              \
  return false;                                                      \
```

Instance and Devices

```
    }

    #include "ListOfVulkanFunctions.inl"

    return true;
```

First we define a macro that is responsible for acquiring an address of a `vkGetInstanceProcAddr()` function. It gets it from the library represented by the `vulkan_library` variable, casts the result of this operation onto a `PFN_kGetInstanceProcAddr` type, and stores it in a variable named `vkGetInstanceProcAddr`. After that, the macro checks whether the operation succeeded, and displays the proper message on screen in the case of a failure.

All the preprocessor "magic" is done when the `ListOfVulkanFunctions.inl` file is included and the preceding operations are performed for each function defined in this file. In this case, it is performed for only the `vkGetInstanceProcAddr()` function, but the same behavior is achieved for functions from other levels.

Now, when we have a function loading function, we can acquire pointers to other Vulkan procedures in an OS-independent way.

See also

The following recipes in this chapter:

- *Connecting with a Vulkan Loader library*
- *Preparing for loading Vulkan API functions*
- *Loading global-level functions*
- *Loading instance-level functions*
- *Loading device-level functions*

Loading global-level functions

We have acquired a `vkGetInstanceProcAddr()` function, through which we can load all other Vulkan API entry points in an OS-independent way.

Vulkan functions can be divided into three levels, which are **global**, **instance**, and **device**. Device-level functions are used to perform typical operations such as drawing, shader-modules creation, image creation, or data copying. Instance-level functions allow us to create **logical devices**. To do all this, and to load device and instance-level functions, we need to create an Instance. This operation is performed with global-level functions, which we need to load first.

How to do it...

1. Create a variable of type `PFN_vkEnumerateInstanceExtensionProperties` named `vkEnumerateInstanceExtensionProperties`.
2. Create a variable of type `PFN_vkEnumerateInstanceLayerProperties` named `vkEnumerateInstanceLayerProperties`.
3. Create a variable of type `PFN_vkCreateInstance` named `vkCreateInstance`.
4. Call `vkGetInstanceProcAddr( nullptr, "vkEnumerateInstanceExtensionProperties" )`, cast the result of this operation onto the `PFN_vkEnumerateInstanceExtensionProperties` type, and store it in a `vkEnumerateInstanceExtensionProperties` variable.
5. Call `vkGetInstanceProcAddr( nullptr, "vkEnumerateInstanceLayerProperties" )`, cast the result of this operation onto the `PFN_vkEnumerateInstanceLayerProperties` type, and store it in a `vkEnumerateInstanceLayerProperties` variable.
6. Call `vkGetInstanceProcAddr( nullptr, "vkCreateInstance" )`, cast the result of this operation onto a `PFN_vkCreateInstance` type, and store it in the `vkCreateInstance` variable.
7. Confirm that the operation succeeded by checking whether, values of all the preceding variables are not equal to `nullptr`.

How it works...

In Vulkan, there are only three global-level functions: `vkEnumerateInstanceExtensionProperties()`, `vkEnumerateInstanceLayerProperties()`, and `vkCreateInstance()`. They are used during Instance creation to check, what instance-level extensions and layers are available and to create the Instance itself.

Instance and Devices

The process of acquiring global-level functions is similar to the loading function exported from the Vulkan Loader. That's why the most convenient way is to add the names of global-level functions to the `ListOfVulkanFunctions.inl` file as follows:

```
#ifndef GLOBAL_LEVEL_VULKAN_FUNCTION
#define GLOBAL_LEVEL_VULKAN_FUNCTION( function )
#endif

GLOBAL_LEVEL_VULKAN_FUNCTION( vkEnumerateInstanceExtensionProperties )
GLOBAL_LEVEL_VULKAN_FUNCTION( vkEnumerateInstanceLayerProperties )
GLOBAL_LEVEL_VULKAN_FUNCTION( vkCreateInstance )

#undef GLOBAL_LEVEL_VULKAN_FUNCTION
```

We don't need to change the `VulkanFunctions.h` and `VulkanFunctions.h` files, but we still need to implement the preceding recipe and load global-level functions as follows:

```
#define GLOBAL_LEVEL_VULKAN_FUNCTION( name )                       \
name = (PFN_##name)vkGetInstanceProcAddr( nullptr, #name );        \
if( name == nullptr ) {                                            \
  std::cout << "Could not load global-level function named: "      \
    #name << std::endl;                                            \
  return false;                                                    \
}

#include "ListOfVulkanFunctions.inl"

return true;
```

A custom `GLOBAL_LEVEL_VULKAN_FUNCTION` macro takes the function name and provides it to a `vkGetInstanceProcAddr()` function. It tries to load the given function and, in the case of a failure, returns `nullptr`. Any result returned by the `vkGetInstanceProcAddr()` function is cast onto a `PFN_<name>` type and stored in a proper variable.

In the case of a failure, a message is displayed so the user knows which function couldn't be loaded.

See also

The following recipes in this chapter:

- *Preparing for loading Vulkan API functions*
- *Loading function exported from a Vulkan Loader library*

- *Loading instance-level functions*
- *Loading device-level functions*

Checking available Instance extensions

Vulkan Instance gathers per application state and allows us to create a logical device on which almost all operations are performed. Before we can create an Instance object, we should think about the instance-level extensions we want to enable. An example of one of the most important instance-level extensions are swapchain related extensions, which are used to display images on screen.

Extensions in Vulkan, as opposed to OpenGL, are enabled explicitly. We can't create a Vulkan Instance and request extensions that are not supported, because the Instance creation operation will fail. That's why we need to check which extensions are supported on a given hardware platform.

How to do it...

1. Prepare a variable of type `uint32_t` named `extensions_count`.
2. Call `vkEnumerateInstanceExtensionProperties( nullptr, &extensions_count, nullptr )`. All parameters should be set to `nullptr`, except for the second parameter, which should point to the `extensions_count` variable.
3. If a function call is successful, the total number of available instance-level extensions will be stored in the `extensions_count` variable.
4. Prepare a storage for the list of extension properties. It must contain elements of type `VkExtensionProperties`. The best solution is to use a `std::vector` container. Call it `available_extensions`.
5. Resize the vector to be able to hold at least the `extensions_count` elements.
6. Call `vkEnumerateInstanceExtensionProperties( nullptr, &extensions_count, &available_extensions[0] )`. The first parameter is once again set to `nullptr`; the second parameter should point to the `extensions_count` variable; the third parameter must point to an array of at least `extensions_count` elements of type `VkExtensionProperties`. Here, in the third parameter, provide an address of the first element of the `available_extensions` vector.

7. If the function returns successfully, the `available_extensions` vector variable will contain a list of all extensions supported on a given hardware platform.

How it works...

Code that acquires instance-level extensions can be divided into two stages. First we get the total number of available extensions as follows:

```
uint32_t extensions_count = 0;
VkResult result = VK_SUCCESS;

result = vkEnumerateInstanceExtensionProperties( nullptr,
&extensions_count, nullptr );
if( (result != VK_SUCCESS) ||
    (extensions_count == 0) ) {
  std::cout << "Could not get the number of Instance extensions." << std::endl;
  return false;
}
```

When called with the last parameter set to `nullptr`, the `vkEnumerateInstanceExtensionProperties()` function stores the number of available extensions in the variable pointed to in the second parameter. This way, we know how many extensions are on a given platform and how much space we need to be able to store parameters for all of them.

When we are ready to acquire extensions' properties, we can call the same function once again. This time the last parameter should point to the prepared space (an array of `VkExtensionProperties` elements, or a vector, in our case) in which these properties will be stored:

```
available_extensions.resize( extensions_count );
result = vkEnumerateInstanceExtensionProperties( nullptr,
&extensions_count, &available_extensions[0] );
if( (result != VK_SUCCESS) ||
    (extensions_count == 0) ) {
  std::cout << "Could not enumerate Instance extensions." << std::endl;
  return false;
}

return true;
```

 The pattern of calling the same function twice is common in Vulkan. There are multiple functions, which store the number of elements returned in the query when their last argument is set to `nullptr`. When their last element points to an appropriate variable, they return the data itself.

Now that we have the list, we can look through it and check whether the extensions we would like to enable are available on a given platform.

See also

- The following recipes in this chapter:
    - *Checking available device extensions*
- The following recipe in `Chapter 2`, *Image Presentation*:
    - *Creating a Vulkan Instance with WSI extensions enabled*

Creating a Vulkan Instance

A Vulkan Instance is an object that gathers the state of an application. It encloses information such as an application name, name and version of an engine used to create an application, or enabled instance-level extensions and layers.

Through the Instance, we can also enumerate available physical devices and create logical devices on which typical operations such as image creation or drawing are performed. So, before we proceed with using the Vulkan API, we need to create a new Instance object.

How to do it...

1. Prepare a variable of type `std::vector<char const *>` named `desired_extensions`. Store the names of all extensions you want to enable in the `desired_extensions` variable.
2. Create a variable of type `std::vector<VkExtensionProperties>` named `available_extensions`. Acquire the list of all available extensions and store it in the `available_extensions` variable (refer to the *Checking available Instance extensions* recipe).

3. Make sure that the name of each extension from the `desired_extensions` variable is also present in the `available_extensions` variable.
4. Prepare a variable of type `VkApplicationInfo` named `application_info`. Assign the following values for members of the `application_info` variable:
    1. `VK_STRUCTURE_TYPE_APPLICATION_INFO` value for `sType`.
    2. `nullptr` value for `pNext`.
    3. Name of your application for `pApplicationName`.
    4. Version of your application for the `applicationVersion` structure member; do that by using `VK_MAKE_VERSION` macro and specifying major, minor, and patch values in it.
    5. Name of the engine used to create an application for `pEngineName`.
    6. Version of the engine used to create an application for `engineVersion`; do that by using `VK_MAKE_VERSION` macro.
    7. `VK_MAKE_VERSION( 1, 0, 0 )` for `apiVersion`.
5. Create a variable of type `VkInstanceCreateInfo` named `instance_create_info`. Assign the following values for members of the `instance_create_info` variable:
    1. `VK_STRUCTURE_TYPE_INSTANCE_CREATE_INFO` value for `sType`.
    2. `nullptr` value for `pNext`.
    3. `0` value for `flags`.
    4. Pointer to the `application_info` variable in `pApplicationInfo`.
    5. `0` value for `enabledLayerCount`.
    6. `nullptr` value for `ppEnabledLayerNames`.
    7. Number of elements of the `desired_extensions` vector for `enabledExtensionCount`.
    8. Pointer to the first element of the `desired_extensions` vector (or `nullptr` if is empty) for `ppEnabledExtensionNames`.
6. Create a variable of type `VkInstance` named `instance`.
7. Call the `vkCreateInstance( &instance_create_info, nullptr, &instance )` function. Provide a pointer to the `instance_create_info` variable in the first parameter, a `nullptr` value in the second, and a pointer to the `instance` variable in the third parameter.
8. Make sure the operation was successful by checking whether the value returned by the `vkCreateInstance()` function call is equal to `VK_SUCCESS`.

How it works...

To create an Instance, we need to prepare some information. First, we need to create an array of names of instance-level extensions that we would like to enable. Next, we need to check if they are supported on a given hardware. This is done by acquiring the list of all available instance-level extensions and checking if it contains the names of all the extensions we want to enable:

```
std::vector<VkExtensionProperties> available_extensions;
if( !CheckAvailableInstanceExtensions( available_extensions ) ) {
  return false;
}

for( auto & extension : desired_extensions ) {
  if( !IsExtensionSupported( available_extensions, extension ) ) {
    std::cout << "Extension named '" << extension << "' is not supported." << std::endl;
    return false;
  }
}
```

Next, we need to create a variable in which we will provide information about our application, such as its name and version, the name and version of an engine used to create an application, and the version of a Vulkan API we want to use (right now only the first version is supported by the API):

```
VkApplicationInfo application_info = {
  VK_STRUCTURE_TYPE_APPLICATION_INFO,
  nullptr,
  application_name,
  VK_MAKE_VERSION( 1, 0, 0 ),
  "Vulkan Cookbook",
  VK_MAKE_VERSION( 1, 0, 0 ),
  VK_MAKE_VERSION( 1, 0, 0 )
};
```

Instance and Devices

The pointer to the `application_info` variable in the preceding code sample is provided in a second variable with the actual parameters used to create an Instance. In it, apart from the previously mentioned pointer, we provide information about the number and names of extensions we want to enable, and also the number and names of layers we want to enable. Neither extensions nor layers are required to create a valid Instance object and we can skip them. However, there are very important extensions, without which it will be hard to create a fully functional application, so it is recommended to use them. Layers may be safely omitted. Following is the sample code preparing a variable used to define Instance parameters:

```
VkInstanceCreateInfo instance_create_info = {
  VK_STRUCTURE_TYPE_INSTANCE_CREATE_INFO,
  nullptr,
  0,
  &application_info,
  0,
  nullptr,
  static_cast<uint32_t>(desired_extensions.size()),
  desired_extensions.size() > 0 ? &desired_extensions[0] : nullptr
};
```

Finally, when we have prepared the preceding data, we can create an Instance object. This is done with the `vkCreateInstance()` function. Its first parameter must point to the variable of type `VkInstanceCreateInfo`. The third parameter must point to a variable of type `VkInstance`. The created Instance handle will be stored in it. The second parameter is very rarely used: It may point to a variable of type `VkAllocationCallbacks`, in which allocator callback functions are defined. These functions control the way host memory is allocated and are mainly used for debugging purposes. Most of the time, the second parameter defining allocation callbacks can be set to `nullptr`:

```
VkResult result = vkCreateInstance( &instance_create_info, nullptr,
  &instance );
if( (result != VK_SUCCESS) ||
    (instance == VK_NULL_HANDLE) ) {
  std::cout << "Could not create Vulkan Instance." << std::endl;
  return false;
}

return true;
```

See also

- The following recipes in this chapter:
    - *Checking available Instance extensions*
    - *Destroying a Vulkan Instance*
- The following recipe in `Chapter 2`, *Image Presentation*:
    - *Creating a Vulkan Instance with WSI extensions enabled*

Loading instance-level functions

We have created a Vulkan Instance object. The next step is to enumerate physical devices, choose one of them, and create a logical device from it. These operations are performed with instance-level functions, of which we need to acquire the addresses.

How to do it...

1. Take the handle of a created Vulkan Instance. Provide it in a variable of type `VkInstance` named `instance`.
2. Choose the name (denoted as `<function name>`) of an instance-level function you want to load.
3. Create a variable of type `PFN_<function name>` named `<function name>`.
4. Call `vkGetInstanceProcAddr( instance, "<function name>" )`. Provide a handle for the created Instance in the first parameter and a function name in the second. Cast the result of this operation onto a `PFN_<function name>` type and store it in a `<function name>` variable.
5. Confirm that this operation succeeded by checking if a value of a `<function name>` variable is not equal to `nullptr`.

How it works...

Instance-level functions are used mainly for operations on physical devices. There are multiple instance-level functions, with `vkEnumeratePhysicalDevices()`, `vkGetPhysicalDeviceProperties()`, `vkGetPhysicalDeviceFeatures()`, `vkGetPhysicalDeviceQueueFamilyProperties()`, `vkCreateDevice()`, `vkGetDeviceProcAddr()`, `vkDestroyInstance()` or `vkEnumerateDeviceExtensionProperties()` among them. However, this list doesn't include all instance-level functions.

How can we tell if a function is instance- or device-level? All device-level functions have their first parameter of type `VkDevice`, `VkQueue`, or `VkCommandBuffer`. So, if a function doesn't have such a parameter and is not from the global level, it is from an instance level. As mentioned previously, instance-level functions are used for manipulating with physical devices, checking their properties, abilities and, creating logical devices.

Remember that extensions can also introduce new functions. You need to add their functions to the function loading code in order to be able to use the extension in the application. However, you shouldn't load functions introduced by a given extension without enabling the extension first during Instance creation. If these functions are not supported on a given platform, loading them will fail (it will return a null pointer).

So, in order to load instance-level functions, we should update the `ListOfVulkanFunctions.inl` file as follows:

```
#ifndef INSTANCE_LEVEL_VULKAN_FUNCTION
#define INSTANCE_LEVEL_VULKAN_FUNCTION( function )
#endif

INSTANCE_LEVEL_VULKAN_FUNCTION( vkEnumeratePhysicalDevices )
INSTANCE_LEVEL_VULKAN_FUNCTION( vkGetPhysicalDeviceProperties )
INSTANCE_LEVEL_VULKAN_FUNCTION( vkGetPhysicalDeviceFeatures )
INSTANCE_LEVEL_VULKAN_FUNCTION( vkCreateDevice )
INSTANCE_LEVEL_VULKAN_FUNCTION( vkGetDeviceProcAddr )
//...

#undef INSTANCE_LEVEL_VULKAN_FUNCTION

//

#ifndef INSTANCE_LEVEL_VULKAN_FUNCTION_FROM_EXTENSION
#define INSTANCE_LEVEL_VULKAN_FUNCTION_FROM_EXTENSION( function, extension )
#endif
```

```
INSTANCE_LEVEL_VULKAN_FUNCTION_FROM_EXTENSION(
vkGetPhysicalDeviceSurfaceSupportKHR, VK_KHR_SURFACE_EXTENSION_NAME )
INSTANCE_LEVEL_VULKAN_FUNCTION_FROM_EXTENSION(
vkGetPhysicalDeviceSurfaceCapabilitiesKHR, VK_KHR_SURFACE_EXTENSION_NAME )
INSTANCE_LEVEL_VULKAN_FUNCTION_FROM_EXTENSION(
vkGetPhysicalDeviceSurfaceFormatsKHR, VK_KHR_SURFACE_EXTENSION_NAME )

#ifdef VK_USE_PLATFORM_WIN32_KHR
INSTANCE_LEVEL_VULKAN_FUNCTION_FROM_EXTENSION( vkCreateWin32SurfaceKHR,
VK_KHR_WIN32_SURFACE_EXTENSION_NAME )
#elif defined VK_USE_PLATFORM_XCB_KHR
INSTANCE_LEVEL_VULKAN_FUNCTION_FROM_EXTENSION( vkCreateXcbSurfaceKHR,
VK_KHR_XLIB_SURFACE_EXTENSION_NAME )
#elif defined VK_USE_PLATFORM_XLIB_KHR
INSTANCE_LEVEL_VULKAN_FUNCTION_FROM_EXTENSION( vkCreateXlibSurfaceKHR,
VK_KHR_XCB_SURFACE_EXTENSION_NAME )
#endif

#undef INSTANCE_LEVEL_VULKAN_FUNCTION_FROM_EXTENSION
```

In the preceding code, we added the names of several (but not all) instance-level functions. Each of them is wrapped into an INSTANCE_LEVEL_VULKAN_FUNCTION or an INSTANCE_LEVEL_VULKAN_FUNCTION_FROM_EXTENSION macro, and is placed between #ifndef and the #undef preprocessor definitions.

To implement the instance-level functions loading recipe using the preceding macros, we should write the following code:

```
#define INSTANCE_LEVEL_VULKAN_FUNCTION( name )                          \
name = (PFN_##name)vkGetInstanceProcAddr( instance, #name );            \
if( name == nullptr ) {                                                 \
  std::cout << "Could not load instance-level Vulkan function named: "\
    #name << std::endl;                                                 \
  return false;                                                         \
}

#include "ListOfVulkanFunctions.inl"

return true;
```

The preceding macro calls a vkGetInstanceProcAddr() function. It's the same function used to load global-level functions, but this time, the handle of a Vulkan Instance is provided in the first parameter. This way, we can load functions that can work properly only when an Instance object is created.

Instance and Devices

This function returns a pointer to the function whose name is provided in the second parameter. The returned value is of type `void*`, which is why it is then cast onto a type appropriate for a function we acquire the address of.

 The type of a given function's prototype is defined based on its name, with a `PFN_` before it. So, in the example, the type of the `vkEnumeratePhysicalDevices()` function's prototype will be defined as `PFN_vkEnumeratePhysicalDevices`.

If the `vkGetInstanceProcAddr()` function cannot find an address of the requested procedure, it returns `nullptr`. That's why we should perform a check and log the appropriate message in case of any problems.

The next step is to load functions that are introduced by extensions. Our function loading code acquires pointers of all functions that are specified with a proper macro in the `ListOfVulkanFunctions.inl` file, but we can't provide extension-specific functions in the same way, because they can be loaded only when appropriate extensions are enabled. When we don't enable any extension, only the core Vulkan API functions can be loaded. That's why we need to distinguish core API functions from extension-specific functions. We also need to know which extensions are enabled and which function comes from which extension. That's why a separate macro is used for functions introduced by extensions. Such a macro specifies a function name, but also the name of an extension in which a given function is specified. To load such functions, we can use the following code:

```
#define INSTANCE_LEVEL_VULKAN_FUNCTION_FROM_EXTENSION( name, extension ) \
for( auto & enabled_extension : enabled_extensions ) {                  \
  if( std::string( enabled_extension ) == std::string( extension ) )    \
{                                                                       \
    name = (PFN_##name)vkGetInstanceProcAddr( instance, #name );        \
    if( name == nullptr ) {                                             \
      std::cout << "Could not load instance-level Vulkan function named: " \
      #name << std::endl;                                               \
      return false;                                                     \
    }                                                                   \
  }                                                                     \
}

#include "ListOfVulkanFunctions.inl"

return true;
```

`enabled_extensions` is a variable of type `std::vector<char const *>`, which contains the names of all enabled instance-level extensions. We iterate over all its elements and check whether the name of a given extension matches the name of an extension that introduces the provided function. If it does, we load the function in the same way as a normal core API function. Otherwise, we skip the pointer-loading code. If we don't enable the given extension, we can't load functions introduced by it.

See also

The following recipes in this chapter:

- *Preparing for loading Vulkan API functions*
- *Loading function exported from a Vulkan Loader library*
- *Loading global-level functions*
- *Loading device-level functions*

Enumerating available physical devices

Almost all the work in Vulkan is performed on logical devices: we create resources on them, manage their memory, record command buffers created from them, and submit commands for processing to their queues. In our application, logical devices represent physical devices for which a set of features and extensions were enabled. To create a logical device, we need to select one of the physical devices available on a given hardware platform. How do we know how many and what physical devices are available on a given computer? We need to enumerate them.

How to do it...

1. Take the handle of a created Vulkan Instance. Provide it through a variable of type `VkInstance` named `instance`.
2. Prepare a variable of type `uint32_t` named `devices_count`.
3. Call `vkEnumeratePhysicalDevices( instance, &devices_count, nullptr )`. In the first parameter, provide a handle of the Vulkan Instance; in second, provide a pointer to the `devices_count` variable, and leave the third parameter set to `nullptr` right now.

Instance and Devices

4. If a function call is successful, the `devices_count` variable will contain the total number of available physical devices.
5. Prepare storage for the list of physical devices. The best solution is to use a variable of type `std::vector` with elements of type `VkPhysicalDevice`. Call it `available_devices`.
6. Resize the vector to be able to hold at least the `devices_count` elements.
7. Call `vkEnumeratePhysicalDevices( instance, &devices_count, &available_devices[0] )`. Again, the first parameter should be set to the handle of a Vulkan Instance object, the second parameter should still point to the `extensions_count` variable, and the third parameter must point to an array of at least `devices_count` elements of type `VkPhysicalDevice`. Here, in the third parameter, provide an address of the first element of an `available_devices` vector.
8. If the function returns successfully, the `available_devices` vector will contain a list of all physical devices installed on a given hardware platform that supports a Vulkan API.

How it works...

Enumerating the available physical devices operation is divided into two stages: First, we check how many physical devices are available on any given hardware. This is done by calling the `vkEnumeratePhysicalDevices()` function with the last parameter set to `nullptr`, as follows:

```
uint32_t devices_count = 0;
VkResult result = VK_SUCCESS;

result = vkEnumeratePhysicalDevices( instance, &devices_count, nullptr );
if( (result != VK_SUCCESS) ||
    (devices_count == 0) ) {
  std::cout << "Could not get the number of available physical devices." << std::endl;
  return false;
}
```

This way, we know how many devices are supporting Vulkan and how much storage we need to prepare for their handles. When we are ready and have prepared enough space, we can go to the second stage and get the actual handles of physical devices. This is done with the call of the same `vkEnumeratePhysicalDevices()` function, but this time, the last parameter must point to an array of `VkPhysicalDevice` elements:

```
available_devices.resize( devices_count );
result = vkEnumeratePhysicalDevices( instance, &devices_count,
&available_devices[0] );
if( (result != VK_SUCCESS) ||
    (devices_count == 0) ) {
  std::cout << "Could not enumerate physical devices." << std::endl;
  return false;
}

return true;
```

When the call is successful, the prepared storage is filled with the handles of physical devices installed on any computer on which our application is executed.

Now that we have the list of devices, we can look through it and check the properties of each device, check operations we can perform on it, and see what extensions are supported by it.

See also

The following recipes in this chapter:

- *Loading instance-level functions*
- *Checking available device extensions*
- *Checking available queue families and their properties*
- *Creating a logical device*

Checking available device extensions

Some Vulkan features we would like to use, require us to explicitly enable certain extensions (contrary to OpenGL, in which extensions were automatically/implicitly enabled). There are two kinds, or two levels, of extensions: Instance-level and device-level. Like Instance extensions, device extensions are enabled during logical device creation. We can't ask for a device extension if it is not supported by a given physical device or we won't be able to create a logical device for it. So, before we start creating a logical device, we need to make sure that all requested extensions are supported by a given physical device, or we need to search for another device that supports them all.

How to do it...

1. Take one of the physical device handles returned by the `vkEnumeratePhysicalDevices()` function and store it in a variable of type `VkPhysicalDevice` called `physical_device`.
2. Prepare a variable of type `uint32_t` named `extensions_count`.
3. Call `vkEnumerateDeviceExtensionProperties( physical_device, nullptr, &extensions_count, nullptr )`. In the first parameter, provide the handle of a physical device available on a given hardware platform: the `physical_device` variable; the second and last parameters should be set to `nullptr`, and the third parameter should point to the `extensions_count` variable.
4. If a function call is successful, the `extensions_count` variable will contain the total number of available device-level extensions.
5. Prepare the storage for the list of extension properties. The best solution is to use a variable of type `std::vector` with elements of type `VkExtensionProperties`. Call it `available_extensions`.
6. Resize the vector to be able to hold at least the `extensions_count` elements.
7. Call `vkEnumerateDeviceExtensionProperties( physical_device, nullptr, &extensions_count, &available_extensions[0] )`. However, this time, replace the last parameter with a pointer to the first element of an array with elements of type `VkExtensionProperties`. This array must have enough space to contain at least `extensions_count` elements. Here, provide a pointer to the first element of the `available_extensions` variable.
8. If the function returns successfully, the `available_extensions` vector will contain a list of all extensions supported by a given physical device.

How it works...

The process of acquiring the list of supported device-level extensions can be divided into two stages: Firstly, we check how many extensions are supported by a given physical device. This is done by calling a function named `vkEnumerateDeviceExtensionProperties()` and setting its last parameter to `nullptr` as follows:

```
uint32_t extensions_count = 0;
VkResult result = VK_SUCCESS;

result = vkEnumerateDeviceExtensionProperties( physical_device, nullptr,
&extensions_count, nullptr );
if( (result != VK_SUCCESS) ||
    (extensions_count == 0) ) {
  std::cout << "Could not get the number of device extensions." << std::endl;
  return false;
}
```

Secondly, we need to prepare an array that will be able to store enough elements of type `VkExtensionProperties`. In the example, we create a vector variable and resize it so it has the `extensions_count` number of elements. In the second `vkEnumerateDeviceExtensionProperties()` function call, we provide an address of the first element of the `available_extensions` variable. When the call is successful, the variable will be filled with properties (names and versions) of all extensions supported by a given physical device.

```
available_extensions.resize( extensions_count );
result = vkEnumerateDeviceExtensionProperties( physical_device, nullptr,
&extensions_count, &available_extensions[0] );
if( (result != VK_SUCCESS) ||
    (extensions_count == 0) ) {
  std::cout << "Could not enumerate device extensions." << std::endl;
  return false;
}

return true;
```

Once again, we can see the pattern of calling the same function twice: The first call (with the last parameter set to `nullptr`) informs us of the number of elements returned by the second call. The second call (with the last parameter pointing to an array of `VkExtensionProperties` elements) returns the requested data, in this case device extensions, which we can iterate over and check whether the extensions we are interested in are available on a given physical device.

Instance and Devices

See also

- The following recipes in this chapter:
    - *Checking available Instance extensions*
    - *Enumerating available physical devices*
- The following recipe in `Chapter 2`, *Image Presentation:*
    - *Creating a logical device with WSI extensions enabled*

Getting features and properties of a physical device

When we create a Vulkan-enabled application, it can be executed on many different devices. It may be a desktop computer, a notebook, or a mobile phone. Each such device may have a different configuration, and may contain different graphics hardware that provide different performance, or, more importantly, different capabilities. A given computer may have more than one graphics card installed. So, in order to find a device that suits our needs, and is able to perform operations we want to implement in our code, we should check not only how many devices there are, but also, to be able to properly choose one of them, we need to check what the capabilities of each device are.

How to do it...

1. Prepare the handle of the physical device returned by the `vkEnumeratePhysicalDevices()` function. Store it in a variable of type `VkPhysicalDevice` named `physical_device`.
2. Create a variable of type `VkPhysicalDeviceFeatures` named `device_features`.
3. Create a second variable of type `VkPhysicalDeviceProperties` named `device_properties`.
4. To get the list of features supported by a given device ,call `vkGetPhysicalDeviceFeatures( physical_device, &device_features )`. Set the handle of the physical device returned by the `vkEnumeratePhysicalDevices()` function for the first parameter. The second parameter must point to the `device_features` variable.

5. To acquire the properties of a given physical device call the `vkGetPhysicalDeviceProperties( physical_device, &device_properties )` function. Provide the handle of the physical device in the first argument. This handle must have been returned by the `vkEnumeratePhysicalDevices()` function. The second parameter must be a pointer to a `device_properties` variable.

How it works...

Here you can find an implementation of the preceding recipe:

```
vkGetPhysicalDeviceFeatures( physical_device, &device_features );

vkGetPhysicalDeviceProperties( physical_device, &device_properties );
```

This code, while short and simple, gives us much information about the graphics hardware on which we can perform operations using the Vulkan API.

The `VkPhysicalDeviceProperties` structure contains general information about a given physical device. Through it, we can check the name of the device, the version of a driver, and a supported version of a Vulkan API. We can also check the type of a device: Whether it is an **integrated** device (built into a main processor) or a **discrete** (dedicated) graphics card, or maybe even a CPU itself. We can also read the limitations (limits) of a given hardware, for example, how big images (textures) can be created on it, how many buffers can be used in shaders, or we can check the upper limit of vertex attributes used during drawing operations.

The `VkPhysicalDeviceFeatures` structure lists additional features that may be supported by the given hardware, but are not required by the core Vulkan specification. Features include items such as **geometry** and **tessellation** shaders, **depth clamp** and **bias**, **multiple viewports**, or **wide lines**. You may wonder why geometry and tessellation shaders are on the list. Graphics hardware has supported these features for many years now. However, don't forget that the Vulkan API is portable and can be supported on many different hardware platforms, not only high-end PCs, but also mobile phones or even dedicated, portable devices, which should be as power efficient as possible. That's why these performance-hungry features are not in the core specification. This allows for some driver flexibility and, more importantly, power efficiency and lower memory consumption.

Instance and Devices

There is one additional thing you should know about the physical device features. Like extensions, they are not enabled by default and can't be used just like that. They must be implicitly enabled during the logical device creation. We can't request all features during this operation, because if there is any feature that is not supported, the logical device creation process will fail. If we are interested in a specific feature, we need to check if it is available and specify it during the creation of a logical device. If the feature is not supported, we can't use such a feature on this device and we need to look for another device that supports it.

If we want to enable all features supported by a given physical device, we just need to query for the available features and provide the acquired data during logical device creation.

See also

The following recipes in this chapter:

- *Creating a logical device*
- *Creating a logical device with geometry shaders, graphics, and compute queues*

Checking available queue families and their properties

In Vulkan, when we want to perform operations on hardware, we submit them to queues. The operations within a single queue are processed one after another, in the same order they were submitted--that's why it's called a **queue**. However, operations submitted to different queues are processed independently (if we need, we can synchronize them):

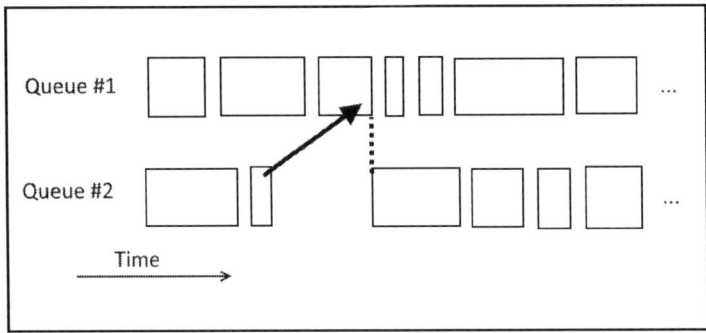

[44]

Different queues may represent different parts of the hardware, and thus may support different kinds of operations. Not all operations may be performed on all queues.

Queues with the same capabilities are grouped into families. A device may expose any number of queue families, and each family may contain one or more queues. To check what operations can be performed on the given hardware, we need to query the properties of all queue families.

How to do it...

1. Take one of the physical device handles returned by the `vkEnumeratePhysicalDevices()` function and store it in a variable of type `VkPhysicalDevice` called `physical_device`.
2. Prepare a variable of type `uint32_t` named `queue_families_count`.
3. Call `vkGetPhysicalDeviceQueueFamilyProperties( physical_device, &queue_families_count, nullptr )`. Provide the handle of a physical device in the first parameter; the second parameter should point to the `queue_families_count` variable, and the final parameter should be set to `nullptr`.
4. After the successful call, the `queue_families_count` variable will contain the number of all queue families exposed by a given physical device.
5. Prepare a storage for the list of queue families and their properties. A very convenient solution is to use a variable of type `std::vector`. Its elements must be of type `VkQueueFamilyProperties`. Call the variable `queue_families`.
6. Resize the vector to be able to hold at least the `queue_families_count` elements.
7. Call `vkGetPhysicalDeviceQueueFamilyProperties( physical_device, &queue_families_count, &queue_families[0] )`. The first and second argument should be the same as in the previous call; the last parameter should point to the first element of the `queue_families` vector.
8. To be sure that everything went okay, check that the `queue_families_count` variable is greater than zero. If successful, the properties of all queue families will be stored in the `queue_families` vector.

How it works...

The implementation of the preceding recipe, similarly to other queries, can be divided into two stages: Firstly, we acquire information about the total number of queue families available on a given physical device. This is done by calling a `vkGetPhysicalDeviceQueueFamilyProperties()` function, with the last argument set to `nullptr`:

```
uint32_t queue_families_count = 0;

vkGetPhysicalDeviceQueueFamilyProperties( physical_device,
&queue_families_count, nullptr );
if( queue_families_count == 0 ) {
  std::cout << "Could not get the number of queue families." << std::endl;
  return false;
}
```

Secondly, when we know how many queue families there are, we can prepare sufficient memory to be able to store the properties of all of them. In the presented example, we create a variable of type `std::vector` with `VkQueueFamilyProperties` elements and resize it to the value returned by the first query. After that, we perform a second `vkGetPhysicalDeviceQueueFamilyProperties()` function call, with the last parameter pointing to the first element of the created vector. In this vector, the parameters of all available queue families will be stored.

```
queue_families.resize( queue_families_count );
vkGetPhysicalDeviceQueueFamilyProperties( physical_device,
&queue_families_count, &queue_families[0] );
if( queue_families_count == 0 ) {
  std::cout << "Could not acquire properties of queue families." << std::endl;
  return false;
}

return true;
```

The most important information we can get from properties is the types of operations that can be performed by the queues in a given family. Types of operations supported by queues are divided into:

- **Graphics**: For creating graphics pipelines and drawing
- **Compute**: For creating compute pipelines and dispatching compute shaders
- **Transfer**: Used for very fast memory-copying operations
- **Sparse**: Allows for additional memory management features

Queues from the given family may support more than one type of operation. There may also be a situation where different queue families support exactly the same types of operation.

Family properties also inform us about the number of queues that are available in the given family, about the timestamp support (for time measurements), and the granularity of image transfer operations (how small parts of image can be specified during copy/blit operations).

With the knowledge of the number of queue families, their properties, and the available number of queues in each family, we can prepare for logical device creation. All this information is needed, because we don't create queues by ourselves. We just request them during logical device creation, for which we must specify how many queues are needed and from which families. When a device is created, queues are created automatically along with it. We just need to acquire the handles of all requested queues.

See also

- The following recipes in this chapter:
    - *Selecting index of a queue family with desired capabilities*
    - *Creating a logical device*
    - *Getting a device queue*
    - *Creating a logical device with geometry shaders, graphics, and compute queues*
- The following recipe in `Chapter 2`, *Image Presentation*:
    - *Selecting a queue family that supports presentation to a given surface*

Selecting the index of a queue family with the desired capabilities

Before we can create a logical device, we need to think about what operations we want to perform on it, because this will affect our choice of a queue family (or families) from which we want to request queues.

For simple use cases, a single queue from a family that supports graphics operations should be enough. More advanced scenarios will require graphics and compute operations to be supported, or even an additional transfer queue for very fast memory copying.

In this recipe, we will look at how to search for a queue family that supports the desired type of operations.

How to do it...

1. Take one of the physical device handles returned by the `vkEnumeratePhysicalDevices()` function and store it in a variable of type `VkPhysicalDevice` called `physical_device`.
2. Prepare a variable of type `uint32_t` named `queue_family_index`. In it, we will store an index of a queue family that supports selected types of operations.
3. Create a bit field variable of type `VkQueueFlags` named `desired_capabilities`. Store the desired types of operations in the `desired_capabilities` variables--it can be a logical OR operation of any of the `VK_QUEUE_GRAPHICS_BIT`, `VK_QUEUE_COMPUTE_BIT`, `VK_QUEUE_TRANSFER_BIT` or `VK_QUEUE_SPARSE_BINDING_BIT` values.
4. Create a variable of type `std::vector` with `VkQueueFamilyProperties` elements named `queue_families`.
5. Check the number of available queue families and acquire their properties as described in the *Checking available queue families and their properties* recipe. Store the results of this operation in the `queue_families` variable.
6. Loop over all elements of the `queue_families` vector using a variable of type `uint32_t` named `index`.
7. For each element of the `queue_families` variable:
    1. Check if the number of queues (indicated by the `queueCount` member) in the current element is greater than zero.
    2. Check if the logical AND operation of the `desired_capabilities` variable and the `queueFlags` member of the currently iterated element is not equal to zero.
    3. If both checks are positive, store the value of an `index` variable (current loop iteration) in the `queue_family_index` variable, and finish iterating.
8. Repeat steps from **7.1** to **7.3** until all elements of the `queue_families` vector are viewed.

How it works...

First, we acquire the properties of queue families available on a given physical device. This is the operation described in the *Checking available queue families and their properties* recipe. We store the results of the query in the `queue_families` variable, which is of `std::vector` type with `VkQueueFamilyProperties` elements:

```
std::vector<VkQueueFamilyProperties> queue_families;
if( !CheckAvailableQueueFamiliesAndTheirProperties( physical_device,
queue_families ) ) {
  return false;
}
```

Next, we start inspecting all elements of a `queue_families` vector:

```
for( uint32_t index = 0; index <
static_cast<uint32_t>(queue_families.size()); ++index ) {
  if( (queue_families[index].queueCount > 0) &&
      (queue_families[index].queueFlags & desired_capabilities ) ) {
    queue_family_index = index;
    return true;
  }
}
return false;
```

Each element of the `queue_families` vector represents a separate queue family. Its `queueCount` member contains the number of queues available in a given family. The `queueFlags` member is a bit field, in which each bit represents a different type of operation. If a given bit is set, it means that the corresponding type of operation is supported by the given queue family. We can check for any combination of supported operations, but we may need to search for separate queues for every type of operation. This solely depends on the hardware support and the Vulkan API driver.

To be sure that the data we have acquired is correct, we also check if each family exposes at least one queue.

More advanced real-life scenarios would require us to store the total number of queues exposed in each family. This is because we may want to request more than one queue, but we can't request more queues than are available in a given family. In simple use cases, one queue from a given family is enough.

Instance and Devices

See also

- The following recipes in this chapter:
    - *Checking available queue families and their properties*
    - *Creating a logical device*
    - *Getting a device queue*
    - *Creating a logical device with geometry shader, graphics, and compute queues*
- The following recipe in `Chapter 2`, *Image Presentation*:
    - *Selecting a queue family that supports the presentation to a given surface*

Creating a logical device

The logical device is one the most important objects created in our application. It represents real hardware, along with all the extensions and features enabled for it and all the queues requested from it:

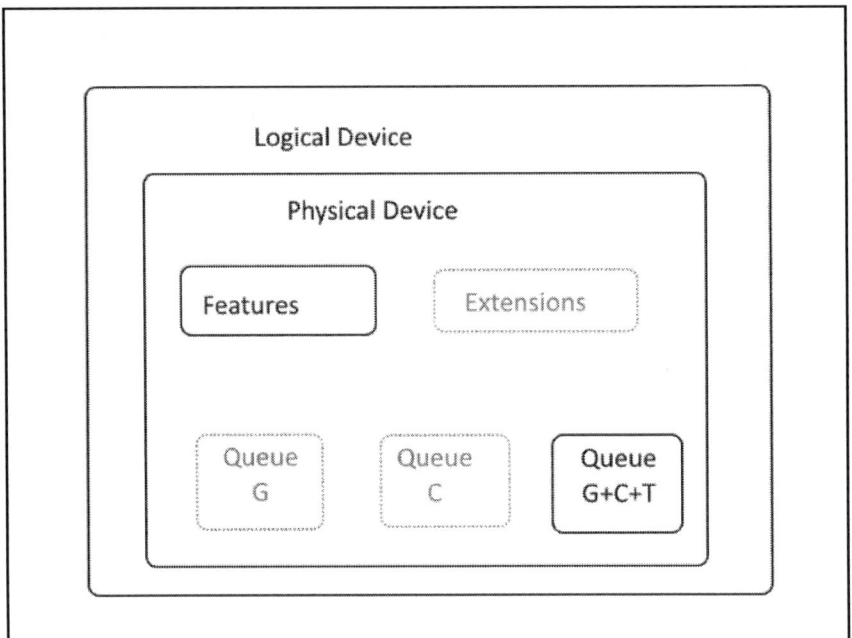

The logical device allows us to perform almost all the work typically done in rendering applications, such as creating images and buffers, setting the pipeline state, or loading shaders. The most important ability it gives us is recording commands (such as issuing draw calls or dispatching computational work) and submitting them to queues, where they are executed and processed by the given hardware. After such execution, we acquire the results of the submitted operations. These can be a set of values calculated by compute shaders, or other data (not necessarily an image) generated by draw calls. All this is performed on a logical device, so now we will look at how to create one.

Getting ready

In this recipe, we will use a variable of a custom structure type. The type is called `QueueInfo` and is defined as follows:

```
struct QueueInfo {
  uint32_t           FamilyIndex;
  std::vector<float> Priorities;
};
```

In a variable of this type, we will store information about the queues we want to request for a given logical device. The data contains an index of a family from which we want the queues to be created, the total number of queues requested from this family, and the list of priorities assigned to each queue. As the number of priorities must be equal to the number of queues requested from a given family, the total number of queues we request from a given family is equal to the number of elements in the `Priorities` vector.

How to do it...

1. Based on the features, limits, available extensions and supported types of operations, choose one of the physical devices acquired using the `vkEnumeratePhysicalDevices()` function call (refer to *Enumerating available physical devices* recipe). Take its handle and store it in a variable of type `VkPhysicalDevice` called `physical_device`.
2. Prepare a list of device extensions you want to enable. Store the names of the desired extensions in a variable of type `std::vector<char const *>` named `desired_extensions`.

Instance and Devices

3. Create a variable of type `std::vector<VkExtensionProperties>` named `available_extensions`. Acquire the list of all available extensions and store it in the `available_extensions` variable (refer to *Checking available device extensions* recipe).
4. Make sure that the name of each extension from the `desired_extensions` variable is also present in the `available_extensions` variable.
5. Create a variable of type `VkPhysicalDeviceFeatures` named `desired_features`.
6. Acquire a set of features supported by a physical device represented by the `physical_device` handle and store it in the `desired_features` variable (refer to *Getting features and properties of a physical device* recipe).
7. Make sure that all the required features are supported by a given physical device represented by the `physical_device` variable. Do that by checking if the corresponding members of the acquired `desired_features` structure are set to one. Clear the rest of the `desired_features` structure members (set them to zero).
8. Based on the properties (supported types of operations), prepare a list of queue families, from which queues should be requested. Prepare a number of queues that should be requested from each selected queue family. Assign a priority for each queue in a given family: A floating point value from `0.0f` to `1.0f` (multiple queues may have the same priority value). Create a `std::vector` variable named `queue_infos` with elements of a custom type `QueueInfo`. Store the indices of queue families and a list of priorities in the `queue_infos` vector, the size of `Priorities` vector should be equal to the number of queues from each family.
9. Create a variable of type `std::vector<VkDeviceQueueCreateInfo>` named `queue_create_infos`. For each queue family stored in the `queue_infos` variable, add a new element to the `queue_create_infos` vector. Assign the following values for members of a new element:
    1. `VK_STRUCTURE_TYPE_DEVICE_QUEUE_CREATE_INFO` value for `sType`.
    2. `nullptr` value for `pNext`.
    3. `0` value for `flags`.
    4. Index of a queue family for `queueFamilyIndex`.
    5. Number of queues requested from a given family for `queueCount`.
    6. Pointer to the first element of a list of priorities of queues from a given family for `pQueuePriorities`.

Chapter 1

10. Create a variable of type `VkDeviceCreateInfo` named `device_create_info`. Assign the following values for members of a `device_create_info` variable:
    1. `VK_STRUCTURE_TYPE_DEVICE_CREATE_INFO` value for `sType`.
    2. `nullptr` value for `pNext`.
    3. 0 value for `flags`.
    4. Number of elements of the `queue_create_infos` vector variable for `queueCreateInfoCount`.
    5. Pointer to the first element of the `queue_create_infos` vector variable in `pQueueCreateInfos`.
    6. 0 value for `enabledLayerCount`.
    7. `nullptr` value for `ppEnabledLayerNames`.
    8. Number of elements of the `desired_extensions` vector variable in `enabledExtensionCount`.
    9. Pointer to the first element of the `desired_extensions` vector variable (or `nullptr` if it is empty) in `ppEnabledExtensionNames`.
    10. Pointer to the `desired_features` variable in `pEnabledFeatures`.
11. Create a variable of type `VkDevice` named `logical_device`.
12. Call `vkCreateDevice( physical_device, &device_create_info, nullptr, &logical_device )`. Provide a handle of the physical device in the first argument, a pointer to the `device_create_info` variable in the second argument, a `nullptr` value in the third argument, and a pointer to the `logical_device` variable in the final argument.
13. Make sure the operation succeeded by checking that the value returned by the `vkCreateDevice()` function call is equal to `VK_SUCCESS`.

How it works...

To create a logical device, we need to prepare a considerable amount of data. First we need to acquire the list of extensions that are supported by a given physical device, and then we need check that all the extensions we want to enable can be found in the list of supported extensions. Similar to Instance creation, we can't create a logical device with extensions that are not supported. Such an operation will fail:

```
std::vector<VkExtensionProperties> available_extensions;
if( !CheckAvailableDeviceExtensions( physical_device, available_extensions
) ) {
  return false;
}
```

[53]

Instance and Devices

```
for( auto & extension : desired_extensions ) {
  if( !IsExtensionSupported( available_extensions, extension ) ) {
    std::cout << "Extension named '" << extension << "' is not supported by a physical device." << std::endl;
    return false;
  }
}
```

Next we prepare a vector variable named `queue_create_infos` that will contain information about queues and queue families we want to request for a logical device. Each element of this vector is of type `VkDeviceQueueCreateInfo`. The most important information it contains is an index of the queue family and the number of queues requested for that family. We can't have two elements in the vector that refer to the same queue family.

In the `queue_create_infos` vector variable, we also provide information about queue priorities. Each queue in a given family may have a different priority: A floating-point value between `0.0f` and `1.0f`, with higher values indicating higher priority. This means that hardware will try to schedule operations performed on multiple queues based on this priority, and may assign more processing time to queues with higher priorities. However, this is only a hint and it is not guaranteed. It also doesn't influence queues from other devices:

```
std::vector<VkDeviceQueueCreateInfo> queue_create_infos;

for( auto & info : queue_infos ) {
  queue_create_infos.push_back( {
    VK_STRUCTURE_TYPE_DEVICE_QUEUE_CREATE_INFO,
    nullptr,
    0,
    info.FamilyIndex,
    static_cast<uint32_t>(info.Priorities.size()),
    info.Priorities.size() > 0 ? &info.Priorities[0] : nullptr
  } );
};
```

The `queue_create_infos` vector variable is provided to another variable of type `VkDeviceCreateInfo`. In this variable, we store information about the number of different queue families from which we request queues for a logical device, number and names of enabled layers, and extensions we want to enable for a device, and also features we want to use.

Layers and extensions are not required for the device to work properly, but there are quite useful extensions, which must be enabled if we want to display Vulkan-generated images on screen.

Features are also not necessary, as the core Vulkan API gives us plenty of features to be able to generate beautiful images or perform complicated calculations. If we don't want to enable any feature, we can provide a `nullptr` value for the `pEnabledFeatures` member, or provide a variable filled with zeros. However, if we want to use more advanced features, such as **geometry** or **tessellation** shaders, we need to enable them by providing a pointer to a proper variable, previously acquiring the list of supported features, and making sure the ones we need are available. Unnecessary features can (and even should) be disabled, because there are some features that may impact performance. This situation is very rare, but it's good to bear this in mind. In Vulkan, we should do and use only those things that need to be done and used:

```
VkDeviceCreateInfo device_create_info = {
  VK_STRUCTURE_TYPE_DEVICE_CREATE_INFO,
  nullptr,
  0,
  static_cast<uint32_t>(queue_create_infos.size()),
  queue_create_infos.size() > 0 ? &queue_create_infos[0] : nullptr,
  0,
  nullptr,
  static_cast<uint32_t>(desired_extensions.size()),
  desired_extensions.size() > 0 ? &desired_extensions[0] : nullptr,
  desired_features
};
```

The `device_create_info` variable is provided to the `vkCreateDevice()` function, which creates a logical device. To be sure that the operation succeeded, we need to check that the value returned by the `vkCreateDevice()` function call is equal to `VK_SUCCESS`. If it is, the handle of a created logical device is stored in the variable pointed to by the final argument of the function call:

```
VkResult result = vkCreateDevice( physical_device, &device_create_info,
nullptr, &logical_device );
if( (result != VK_SUCCESS) ||
    (logical_device == VK_NULL_HANDLE) ) {
  std::cout << "Could not create logical device." << std::endl;
  return false;
}

return true;
```

See also

The following recipes in this chapter:

- *Enumerating available physical devices*
- *Checking available device extensions*
- *Getting features and properties of a physical device*
- *Checking available queue families and their properties*
- *Selecting the index of a queue family with the desired capabilities*
- *Destroying a logical device*

Loading device-level functions

We have created a logical device on which we can perform any desired operations, such as rendering a 3D scene, calculating collisions of objects in a game, or processing video frames. These operations are performed with device-level functions, but they are not available until we acquire them.

How to do it...

1. Take the handle of a created logical device object. Store it in a variable of type `VkDevice` named `logical_device`.
2. Choose the name (denoted as `<function name>`) of a device-level function you want to load.
3. For each device-level function that will be loaded, create a variable of type `PFN_<function name>` named `<function name>`.
4. Call `vkGetDeviceProcAddr( device, "<function name>" )`, in which you provide the handle of created logical device in the first argument and the name of the function in the second argument. Cast the result of this operation onto a `PFN_<function name>` type and store it in a `<function name>` variable.
5. Confirm that the operation succeeded by checking that the value of a `<function name>` variable is not equal to `nullptr`.

How it works...

Almost all the typical work done in 3D rendering applications is performed using device-level functions. They are used to create buffers, images, samplers, or shaders. We use device-level functions to create pipeline objects, synchronization primitives, framebuffers, and many other resources. And, most importantly, they are used to record operations that are later submitted (using device-level functions too) to queues, where these operations are processed by the hardware. This all is done with device-level functions.

Device-level functions, like all other Vulkan functions, can be loaded using the `vkGetInstanceProcAddr()` function, but this approach is not optimal. Vulkan is designed to be a flexible API. It gives the option to perform operations on multiple devices in a single application, but when we call the `vkGetInstanceProcAddr()` function, we can't provide any parameter connected with the logical device. So, the function pointer returned by this function can't be connected with the device on which we want to perform the given operation. This device may not even exist at the time the `vkGetInstanceProcAddr()` function is called. That's why the `vkGetInstanceProcAddr()` function returns a dispatch function which, based on its arguments, calls the implementation of a function, that is proper for a given logical device. However, this jump has a performance cost: It's very small, but it nevertheless takes some processor time to call the right function.

If we want to avoid this unnecessary jump and acquire function pointers corresponding directly to a given device, we should do that by using a `vkGetDeviceProcAddr()`. This way, we can avoid the intermediate function call and improve the performance of our application. Such an approach also has some drawbacks: We need to acquire function pointers for each device created in an application. If we want to perform operations on many different devices, we need a separate list of function pointers for each logical device. We can't use functions acquired from one device to perform operations on a different device. But using C++ language's preprocessor, it is quite easy to acquire function pointers specific to a given device:

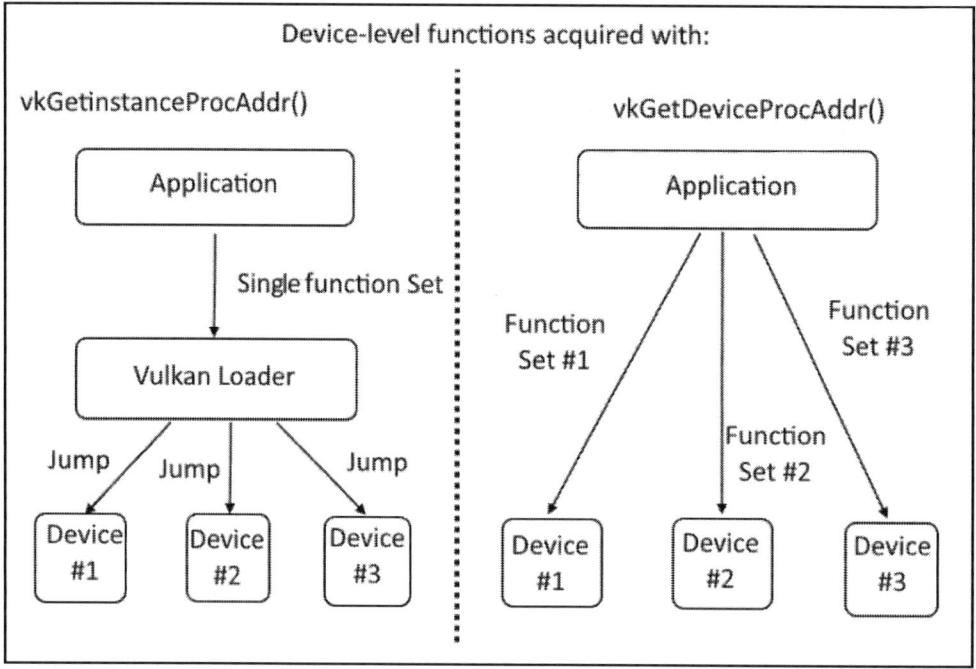

How do we know if a function is from the device-level and not from the global or instance-level? The first argument of device-level functions is of type `VkDevice`, `VkQueue`, or `VkCommandBuffer`. Most of the functions that will be introduced from now on are from the device level.

To load device-level functions, we should update the `ListOfVulkanFunctions.inl` file as follows:

```
#ifndef DEVICE_LEVEL_VULKAN_FUNCTION
#define DEVICE_LEVEL_VULKAN_FUNCTION( function )
#endif

DEVICE_LEVEL_VULKAN_FUNCTION( vkGetDeviceQueue )
DEVICE_LEVEL_VULKAN_FUNCTION( vkDeviceWaitIdle )
DEVICE_LEVEL_VULKAN_FUNCTION( vkDestroyDevice )

DEVICE_LEVEL_VULKAN_FUNCTION( vkCreateBuffer )
DEVICE_LEVEL_VULKAN_FUNCTION( vkGetBufferMemoryRequirements )
// ...

#undef DEVICE_LEVEL_VULKAN_FUNCTION

//

#ifndef DEVICE_LEVEL_VULKAN_FUNCTION_FROM_EXTENSION
#define DEVICE_LEVEL_VULKAN_FUNCTION_FROM_EXTENSION( function, extension )
#endif

DEVICE_LEVEL_VULKAN_FUNCTION_FROM_EXTENSION( vkCreateSwapchainKHR,
VK_KHR_SWAPCHAIN_EXTENSION_NAME )
DEVICE_LEVEL_VULKAN_FUNCTION_FROM_EXTENSION( vkGetSwapchainImagesKHR,
VK_KHR_SWAPCHAIN_EXTENSION_NAME )
DEVICE_LEVEL_VULKAN_FUNCTION_FROM_EXTENSION( vkAcquireNextImageKHR,
VK_KHR_SWAPCHAIN_EXTENSION_NAME )
DEVICE_LEVEL_VULKAN_FUNCTION_FROM_EXTENSION( vkQueuePresentKHR,
VK_KHR_SWAPCHAIN_EXTENSION_NAME )
DEVICE_LEVEL_VULKAN_FUNCTION_FROM_EXTENSION( vkDestroySwapchainKHR,
VK_KHR_SWAPCHAIN_EXTENSION_NAME )

#undef DEVICE_LEVEL_VULKAN_FUNCTION_FROM_EXTENSION
```

In the preceding code, we added, names of multiple device-level functions. Each of them is wrapped into a `DEVICE_LEVEL_VULKAN_FUNCTION` macro (if it is defined in the core API) or a `DEVICE_LEVEL_VULKAN_FUNCTION_FROM_EXTENSION` macro (if it is introduced by an extension), and is placed between proper `#ifndef` and `#undef` preprocessor directives. The list is, of course, incomplete, as there are too many functions to present them all here.

Instance and Devices

Remember that we shouldn't load functions introduced by a given extension without first enabling the extension during the logical device creation. If an extension is not supported, its functions are not available and the operation of loading them will fail. That's why, similarly to loading instance-level functions, we need to divide function-loading code into two blocks.

First, to implement the device-level core API functions loading using the preceding macros, we should write the following code:

```
#define DEVICE_LEVEL_VULKAN_FUNCTION( name )                                    \
name = (PFN_##name)vkGetDeviceProcAddr( device, #name );                        \
if( name == nullptr ) {                                                         \
  std::cout << "Could not load device-level Vulkan function named: " #name      \
<< std::endl;                                                                   \
  return false;                                                                 \
}

#include "ListOfVulkanFunctions.inl"

return true;
```

In this code sample, we create a macro that, for each occurrence of a DEVICE_LEVEL_VULKAN_FUNCTION() definition found in the ListOfVulkanFunctions.inl file, calls a vkGetDeviceProcAddr() function and provides the name of a procedure we want to load. The result of this operation is cast onto an appropriate type and stored in a variable with exactly the same name as the name of the acquired function. Upon failure, any additional information is displayed on screen.

Next, we need to load functions introduced by extensions. These extensions must have been enabled during logical device creation:

```
#define DEVICE_LEVEL_VULKAN_FUNCTION_FROM_EXTENSION( name,
extension )                                                                     \
for( auto & enabled_extension : enabled_extensions ) {                          \
  if( std::string( enabled_extension ) == std::string( extension )
) {                                                                             \
    name = (PFN_##name)vkGetDeviceProcAddr( logical_device, #name );\
    if( name == nullptr ) {                                                     \
      std::cout << "Could not load device-level Vulkan function named: "        \
      #name << std::endl;                                                       \
      return false;                                                             \
    }                                                                           \
  }                                                                             \
}
```

[60]

```
#include "ListOfVulkanFunctions.inl"

return true;
```

In the preceding code, we define the macro which iterates over all enabled extensions. They are defined in a variable of type `std::vector<char const *>` named `enabled_extensions`. In each loop iteration, the name of the enabled extension from the vector is compared with the name of an extension specified for a given function. If they match, the function pointer is loaded; if not, the given function is skipped as we can't load functions from un-enabled extensions.

See also

The following recipes in this chapter:

- *Preparing for loading Vulkan API functions*
- *Loading function exported from a Vulkan Loader library*
- *Loading global-level functions*
- *Loading instance-level functions*

Getting a device queue

In Vulkan, in order to harness the processing power of a given device, we need to submit operations to the device's queues. Queues are not created explicitly by an application. They are requested during device creation: We check what families are available and how many queues each family contains. We can ask only for the subset of available queues from existing queue families, and we can't request more queues than the given family exposes.

Requested queues are created automatically along with the logical device. We don't manage them and create them explicitly. We can't destroy them either; they are also destroyed with a logical device. To use them and to be able to submit any work to the device's queues, we just need to acquire their handles.

How to do it...

1. Take the handle of a created logical device object. Store it in a variable of type `VkDevice` named `logical_device`.

Instance and Devices

2. Take the index of one of the queue families that was provided during the logical device creation in a `queueFamilyIndex` member of a structure of type `VkDeviceQueueCreateInfo`. Store it in a variable of type `uint32_t` named `queue_family_index`.
3. Take the index of one of the queues requested for a given queue family: The index must be smaller than the total number of queues requested for a given family in a `queueCount` member of the `VkDeviceQueueCreateInfo` structure. Store the index in a variable of type `uint32_t` named `queue_index`.
4. Prepare a variable of type `VkQueue` named `queue`.
5. Call `vkGetDeviceQueue( logical_device, queue_family_index, queue_index, &queue )`. Provide a handle to the created logical device in the first argument; the second argument must be equal to the selected queue family index; the third argument must contain a number of one of the queues requested for a given family; then, in the final parameter, provide a pointer to the `queue` variable. A handle to the device queue will be stored in this variable.
6. Repeat steps 2 to 5 for all queues requested from all queue families.

How it works...

Code that acquires the handle of a given queue is very simple:

```
vkGetDeviceQueue( logical_device, queue_family_index, queue_index, &queue );
```

We provide a handle to the created logical device, an index of the queue family, and an index of the queue requested for a given family. We must provide one of the family indices that were provided during logical device creation. This means that we can't acquire the handle of a queue from a family that wasn't specified during the logical device creation. Similarly, we can only provide an index of a queue that is smaller than the total number of queues requested from a given family.

Let's imagine the following situation: A given physical device supports five queues in the queue family No. 3. During logical device creation, we request only two queues from this queue family No. 3. So here, when we call the `vkGetDeviceQueue()` function, we must provide the value 3 as the queue family index. For the queue index, we can provide only values 0 and 1.

The handle of the requested queue is stored in a variable to which we provide a pointer in the final argument of the `vkGetDeviceQueue()` function call. We can ask for a handle of the same queue multiple times. This call doesn't create queues--they are created implicitly during logical device creation. Here, we just ask for the handle of an existing queue, so we can do it multiple times (although it may not make much sense to do so).

See also

The following recipes in this chapter:

- *Checking available queue families and their properties*
- *Selecting the index of a queue family with the desired capabilities*
- *Creating a logical device*
- *Creating a logical device with geometry shaders, graphics, and compute queues*

Creating a logical device with geometry shaders, graphics, and compute queues

In Vulkan, when we create various objects, we need to prepare many different structures that describe the creation process itself, but they may also require other objects to be created.

A logical device is no different: We need to enumerate physical devices, check their properties and supported queue families, and prepare a `VkDeviceCreateInfo` structure that requires much more information.

To organize these operations, we will present a sample recipe that creates a logical device from one of the available physical devices that support geometry shaders, and both graphics and compute queues.

How to do it...

1. Prepare a variable of type `VkDevice` named `logical_device`.
2. Create two variables of type `VkQueue`, one named `graphics_queue` and one named `compute_queue`.

Instance and Devices

3. Create a variable of type `std::vector<VkPhysicalDevice>` named `physical_devices`.
4. Get the list of all physical devices available on a given platform and store it in the `physical_devices` vector (refer to the *Enumerating available physical devices* recipe).
5. For each physical device from the `physical_devices` vector:
    1. Create a variable of type `VkPhysicalDeviceFeatures` named `device_features`.
    2. Acquire the list of features supported by a given physical device and store it in the `device_features` variable.
    3. Check whether the `geometryShader` member of the `device_features` variable is equal to `VK_TRUE` (is not 0). If it is, reset all the other members of the `device_features` variable (set their values to zero); if it is not, start again with another physical device.
    4. Create two variables of type `uint32_t` named `graphics_queue_family_index` and `compute_queue_family_index`.
    5. Acquire indices of queue families that support graphics and compute operations, and store them in the `graphics_queue_family_index` and `compute_queue_family_index` variables, respectively (refer to the *Selecting index of a queue family with desired capabilities* recipe). If any of these operations is not supported, search for another physical device.
    6. Create a variable of type `std::vector` with elements of type `QueueInfo` (refer to *Creating a logical device* recipe). Name this variable `requested_queues`.
    7. Store the `graphics_queue_family_index` variable and one-element vector of `floats` with a `1.0f` value in the `requested_queues` variable. If a value of the `compute_queue_family_index` variable is different than the value of the `graphics_queue_family_index` variable, add another element to the `requested_queues` vector, with the `compute_queue_family_index` variable and a one-element vector of `floats` with `1.0f` value.
    8. Create a logical device using the `physical_device`, `requested_queues`, `device_features` and `logical_device` variables (refer to the *Creating a logical device* recipe). If this operation failed, repeat the preceding operations with another physical device.

9. If the logical device was successfully created, load the device-level functions (refer to the *Loading device-level functions* recipe). Get the handle of the queue from the `graphics_queue_family_index` family and store it in the `graphics_queue` variable. Get the queue from the `compute_queue_family_index` family and store it in the `compute_queue` variable.

How it works...

To start the process of creating a logical device, we need to acquire the handles of all physical devices available on a given computer:

```
std::vector<VkPhysicalDevice> physical_devices;
EnumerateAvailablePhysicalDevices( instance, physical_devices );
```

Next we need to loop through all available physical devices. For each such device, we need to acquire its features. This will give us the information about whether a given physical device supports geometry shaders:

```
for( auto & physical_device : physical_devices ) {
  VkPhysicalDeviceFeatures device_features;
  VkPhysicalDeviceProperties device_properties;
  GetTheFeaturesAndPropertiesOfAPhysicalDevice( physical_device,
device_features, device_properties );

  if( !device_features.geometryShader ) {
    continue;
  } else {
    device_features = {};
    device_features.geometryShader = VK_TRUE;
  }
}
```

If geometry shaders are supported, we can reset all the other members of a returned list of features. We will provide this list during the logical device creation, but we don't want to enable any other feature. In this example, geometry shaders are the only additional feature we want to use.

Next we need to check if a given physical device exposes queue families that support graphics and compute operations. This may be just one single family or two separate families. We acquire the indices of such queue families:

```
uint32_t graphics_queue_family_index;
  if( !SelectIndexOfQueueFamilyWithDesiredCapabilities( physical_device,
VK_QUEUE_GRAPHICS_BIT, graphics_queue_family_index ) ) {
```

Instance and Devices

```
      continue;
    }

    uint32_t compute_queue_family_index;
    if( !SelectIndexOfQueueFamilyWithDesiredCapabilities( physical_device,
  VK_QUEUE_COMPUTE_BIT, compute_queue_family_index ) ) {
      continue;
    }
```

Next, we need to prepare a list of queue families, from which we want to request queues. We also need to assign priorities to each queue from each family:

```
    std::vector<QueueInfo> requested_queues = { {
  graphics_queue_family_index, { 1.0f } } };
    if( graphics_queue_family_index != compute_queue_family_index ) {
      requested_queues.push_back( { compute_queue_family_index, { 1.0f } } );
    }
```

If graphics and compute queue families have the same index, we request only one queue from one queue family. If they are different, we need to request two queues: One from the graphics family and one from the compute family.

We are ready to create a logical device for which we provide the prepared data. Upon success, we can the load device-level functions and acquire the handles of the requested queues:

```
    if( !CreateLogicalDevice( physical_device, requested_queues, {},
  &device_features, logical_device ) ) {
      continue;
    } else {
      if( !LoadDeviceLevelFunctions( logical_device, {} ) ) {
        return false;
      }
      GetDeviceQueue( logical_device, graphics_queue_family_index, 0,
  graphics_queue );
      GetDeviceQueue( logical_device, compute_queue_family_index, 0,
  compute_queue );
      return true;
    }
  }
  return false;
```

[66]

See also

The following recipes in this chapter:

- *Enumerating available physical devices*
- *Getting features and properties of a physical device*
- *Selecting the index of a queue family with the desired capabilities*
- *Creating a logical device*
- *Loading device-level functions*
- *Getting a device queue*
- *Destroying a logical device*

Destroying a logical device

After we have finished and we want to quit the application, we should clean up after ourselves. Despite the fact that all the resources should be destroyed automatically by the driver when the Vulkan Instance is destroyed, we should also do this explicitly in the application to follow good programming guidelines. The order of destroying resources should be opposite to the order in which they were created.

> Resources should be released in the reverse order to the order of their creation.

In this chapter, the logical device was the last created object, so it will be destroyed first.

How to do it...

1. Take the handle of the logical device that was created and stored in a variable of type `VkDevice` named `logical_device`.
2. Call `vkDestroyDevice( logical_device, nullptr );` provide the `logical_device` variable in the first argument, and a `nullptr` value in the second.
3. For safety reasons, assign the `VK_NULL_HANDLE` value to the `logical_device` variable.

How it works...

The implementation of the logical device-destroying recipe is very straightforward:

```
if( logical_device ) {
  vkDestroyDevice( logical_device, nullptr );
  logical_device = VK_NULL_HANDLE;
}
```

First, we need to check if the logical device handle is valid, because, we shouldn't destroy objects that weren't created. Then, we destroy the device with the `vkDestroyDevice()` function call and we assign the `VK_NULL_HANDLE` value to the variable in which the logical device handle was stored. We do this just in case--if there is a mistake in our code, we won't destroy the same object twice.

Remember that, when we destroy a logical device, we can't use device-level functions acquired from it.

See also

- The recipe *Creating a logical device* in this chapter

Destroying a Vulkan Instance

After all the other resources are destroyed, we can destroy the Vulkan Instance.

How to do it...

1. Take the handle of the created Vulkan Instance object stored in a variable of type `VkInstance` named `instance`.
2. Call `vkDestroyInstance( instance, nullptr )`, provide the `instance` variable as the first argument and a `nullptr` value as the second argument.
3. For safety reasons, assign the `VK_NULL_HANDLE` value to the `instance` variable.

How it works...

Before we close the application, we should make sure that all the created resources are released. The Vulkan Instance is destroyed with the following code:

```
if( instance ) {
  vkDestroyInstance( instance, nullptr );
  instance = VK_NULL_HANDLE;
}
```

See also

- The recipe *Creating a Vulkan Instance* in this chapter

Releasing a Vulkan Loader library

Libraries that are loaded dynamically must be explicitly closed (released). To be able to use Vulkan in our application, we opened the Vulkan Loader (a `vulkan-1.dll` library on Windows, or `libvulkan.so.1` library on Linux). So, before we can close the application, we should free it.

How to do it...

On the Windows operating system family:

1. Take the variable of type `HMODULE` named `vulkan_library`, in which the handle of a loaded Vulkan Loader was stored (refer to the *Connecting with a Vulkan Loader library* recipe).
2. Call `FreeLibrary( vulkan_library )` and provide the `vulkan_library` variable in the only argument.
3. For safety reasons, assign the `nullptr` value to the `vulkan_library` variable.

Instance and Devices

On the Linux operating system family:

1. Take the variable of type `void*` named `vulkan_library` in which the handle of a loaded Vulkan Loader was stored (refer to *Connecting with a Vulkan Loader library* recipe).
2. Call `dlclose( vulkan_library )`, provide the `vulkan_library` variable in the only argument.
3. For safety reasons, assign the `nullptr` value to the `vulkan_library` variable.

How it works...

On the Windows operating system family, dynamic libraries are opened using the `LoadLibrary()` function. Such libraries must be closed (released) by calling the `FreeLibrary()` function to which the handle of a previously opened library must be provided.

On the Linux operating system family, dynamic libraries are opened using the `dlopen()` function. Such libraries must be closed (released) by calling the `dlclose()` function, to which the handle of a previously opened library must be provided:

```
#if defined _WIN32
FreeLibrary( vulkan_library );
#elif defined __linux
dlclose( vulkan_library );
#endif
vulkan_library = nullptr;
```

See also

- The recipe *Connecting with a Vulkan Loader library* in this chapter

2
Image Presentation

In this chapter, we will cover the following recipes:

- Creating a Vulkan Instance with WSI extensions enabled
- Creating a presentation surface
- Selecting a queue family that supports presentation to a given surface
- Creating a logical device with WSI extensions enabled
- Selecting a desired presentation mode
- Getting capabilities of a presentation surface
- Selecting a number of swapchain images
- Choosing a size of swapchain images
- Selecting desired usage scenarios of swapchain images
- Selecting a transformation of swapchain images
- Selecting a format of swapchain images
- Creating a swapchain
- Getting handles of swapchain images
- Creating a swapchain with R8G8B8A8 format and a mailbox present mode
- Acquiring a swapchain image
- Presenting an image
- Destroying a swapchain
- Destroying a presentation surface

Introduction

APIs such as Vulkan can be used for many different purposes, such as mathematical and physical computations, image or video stream processing, and data visualizations. But the main purpose Vulkan was designed for and its most common usage is efficiently rendering 2D and 3D graphics. And when our application generates an image, we usually would like to display it on screen.

At first, it may seem surprising that the core of the Vulkan API doesn't allow for displaying generated images in the application's window. This is because Vulkan is a portable, cross-platform API but, unfortunately, there is no universal standard for presenting images on screen in different operating systems because they have drastically different architectures and standards.

That's why a set of extensions was introduced for the Vulkan API which allow us to present generated images in an application's window. These extensions are commonly referred to as Windowing System Integration (WSI). Each operating system on which Vulkan is available has its own set of extensions that integrate Vulkan with the windowing system specific for a given OS.

The most important extension is the one which allows us to create a swapchain. A swapchain is an array of images that can be presented (displayed) to the user. In this chapter, we will be preparing for drawing images on screen--setting up image parameters such as format, size, and so on. We will also take a look at the various available **presentation** modes that determine the way images are displayed, that is, define whether vertical sync is enabled or disabled. And, finally, we will see how to present the images--display them in the application's window.

Creating a Vulkan Instance with WSI extensions enabled

To be able to properly display images on screen, we need to enable a set of WSI extensions. They are divided into instance- and device-levels, depending on the functionality they introduce. The first step is to create a Vulkan Instance with a set of enabled extensions that allow us to create a presentation surface--a Vulkan representation of an application's window.

How to do it...

On the Windows operating systems family, perform the following steps:

1. Prepare a variable of type `VkInstance` named `instance`.
2. Prepare a variable of type `std::vector<char const *>` named `desired_extensions`. Store the names of all extensions you want to enable in the `desired_extensions` variable.
3. Add another element to the `desired_extensions` vector with the `VK_KHR_SURFACE_EXTENSION_NAME` value.
4. Add yet another element to the `desired_extensions` vector with the `VK_KHR_WIN32_SURFACE_EXTENSION_NAME` value.
5. Create a Vulkan Instance object for which enable all of the extensions specified in the `desired_extensions` variable (refer to the *Creating a Vulkan Instance* recipe from Chapter 1, *Instance and Devices*).

On the Linux operating systems family with an **X11** windowing system through an **XLIB** interface, perform the following steps:

1. Prepare a variable of type `VkInstance` named `instance`.
2. Prepare a variable of type `std::vector<char const *>` named `desired_extensions`. Store the names of all extensions you want to enable in the `desired_extensions` variable.
3. Add another element to the `desired_extensions` vector with the `VK_KHR_SURFACE_EXTENSION_NAME` value.
4. Add yet another element to the `desired_extensions` vector with the `VK_KHR_XLIB_SURFACE_EXTENSION_NAME` value.
5. Create a Vulkan Instance object for which enable all of the extensions specified in the `desired_extensions` variable (refer to the *Creating a Vulkan Instance* recipe from Chapter 1, *Instance and Devices*).

On the Linux operating systems family with an X11 windowing system through an **XCB** interface, perform the following steps:

1. Prepare a variable of type `VkInstance` named `instance`.
2. Prepare a variable of type `std::vector<char const *>` named `desired_extensions`. Store the names of all extensions you want to enable in the `desired_extensions` variable.

3. Add another element to the `desired_extensions` vector with the `VK_KHR_SURFACE_EXTENSION_NAME` value.
4. Add yet another element to the `desired_extensions` vector with the `VK_KHR_XCB_SURFACE_EXTENSION_NAME` value.
5. Create a Vulkan Instance object for which enable all of the extensions specified in the `desired_extensions` variable (refer to the *Creating a Vulkan Instance* recipe from `Chapter 1`, *Instance and Devices*).

How it works...

Instance-level extensions are responsible for managing, creating, and destroying a presentation surface. It is a (cross-platform) representation of an application's window. Through it, we can check whether we are able to draw to the window (displaying an image, a presentation, is an additional property of a queue family), what its parameters are, or what presentation modes are supported (if we want the vertical sync to be enabled or disabled).

The presentation surface is directly connected to our application's window, so it can be created only in a way that is specific for a given operating system. That's why this functionality is introduced through extensions and each operating system has its own extension for creating a presentation surface. On the Windows operating systems family, this extension is called `VK_KHR_win32_surface`. On the Linux operating systems family with an X11 windowing system, this extension is called `VK_KHR_xlib_surface`. On the Linux operating systems family with an XCB windowing system, this extension is called `VK_KHR_xcb_surface`.

The functionality of destroying a presentation surface is enabled via an additional extension called `VK_KHR_surface`. It is available on all operating systems. So in order to properly manage a presentation surface, check its parameters, and verify the ability to present to it, we need to enable two extensions during Vulkan Instance creation.

Chapter 2

VK_KHR_win32_surface and VK_KHR_surface extensions introduce the ability to create and destroy a presentation surface on the Windows OS family.

VK_KHR_xlib_surface and VK_KHR_surface extensions introduce the ability to create and destroy a presentation surface on the Linux OS family with an X11 windowing system and an XLIB interface.

VK_KHR_xcb_surface and VK_KHR_surface extensions introduce the ability to create and destroy a presentation surface on the Linux OS family with an X11 windowing system and an XCB interface.

In order to create a Vulkan Instance that supports the process of creating and destroying a presentation surface, we need to prepare the following code:

```
desired_extensions.emplace_back( VK_KHR_SURFACE_EXTENSION_NAME );
desired_extensions.emplace_back(
#ifdef VK_USE_PLATFORM_WIN32_KHR
  VK_KHR_WIN32_SURFACE_EXTENSION_NAME

#elif defined VK_USE_PLATFORM_XCB_KHR
  VK_KHR_XCB_SURFACE_EXTENSION_NAME

#elif defined VK_USE_PLATFORM_XLIB_KHR
  VK_KHR_XLIB_SURFACE_EXTENSION_NAME
#endif
);

return CreateVulkanInstance( desired_extensions, application_name, instance
);
```

In the preceding code, we begin with a vector variable in which the names of all extensions we want to enable are stored. We then add the required WSI extensions to the vector. The names of these extensions are provided through convenient preprocessor definitions. They are defined in the vulkan.h file. With them, we don't need to remember the exact names of extensions and if we make a mistake, compiler will tell us about it.

After we are done preparing the list of required extensions, we can create a Vulkan Instance object in the same way as described in the *Creating a Vulkan Instance* recipe from Chapter 1, *Instance and Devices*.

[75]

See also

- In Chapter 1, *Instance and Devices* see the following recipes:
    - *Checking available Instance extensions*
    - *Creating a Vulkan Instance*
- The following recipe in this chapter:
    - *Creating a logical device with WSI extensions enabled*

Creating a presentation surface

A presentation surface represents an application's window. It allows us to acquire the window's parameters, such as dimensions, supported color formats, required number of images, or presentation modes. It also allows us to check whether a given physical device is able to display an image in a given window.

That's why, in situations where we want to show an image on screen, we need to create a presentation surface first, as it will help us choose a physical device that suits our needs.

Getting ready

To create a presentation surface, we need to provide the parameters of an application's window. In order to do that, the window must have been already created. In this recipe, we will provide its parameters through a structure of type `WindowParameters`. Its definition looks like this:

```
struct WindowParameters {
#ifdef VK_USE_PLATFORM_WIN32_KHR
  HINSTANCE          HInstance;
  HWND               HWnd;
#elif defined VK_USE_PLATFORM_XLIB_KHR
  Display          * Dpy;
  Window             Window;
#elif defined VK_USE_PLATFORM_XCB_KHR
  xcb_connection_t * Connection;
  xcb_window_t       Window;
#endif
};
```

On Windows, the structure contains the following parameters:

- A variable of type `HINSTANCE` named `HInstance` in which we store the value acquired using the `GetModuleHandle()` function
- A variable of type `HWND` named `HWnd` in which we store a value returned by the `CreateWindow()` function

On Linux with an X11 windowing system and an XLIB interface, the structure contains the following members:

- A variable of type `Display*` named `Dpy` in which the value of the `XOpenDisplay()` function call is stored
- A variable of type `Window` named `Window` to which we assign a value returned by `XCreateWindow()` or `XCreateSimpleWindow()` functions

On Linux with an X11 windowing system and an XCB interface, the `WindowParameters` structure contains the following members:

- A variable of type `xcb_connection_t*` named `Connection` in which we store a value returned by the `xcb_connect()` function
- A variable of type `xcb_window_t` named `Window` in which a value returned by the `xcb_generate_id()` function is stored

How to do it...

On the Windows operating systems family, perform the following steps:

1. Take the variable of type `VkInstance` named `instance` in which a handle of a created Vulkan Instance is stored.
2. Create a variable of type `WindowParameters` named `window_parameters`. Assign the following values for its members:
    - A value returned by the `CreateWindow()` function for `HWnd`
    - A value returned by the `GetModuleHandle(nullptr)` function for `HInstance`
3. Create a variable of type `VkWin32SurfaceCreateInfoKHR` named `surface_create_info` and initialize its members with the following values:
    - VK_STRUCTURE_TYPE_WIN32_SURFACE_CREATE_INFO_KHR value for `sType`

[77]

Image Presentation

- `nullptr` value for `pNext`
- `0` value for `flags`
- `window_parameters.HInstance` member for `hinstance`
- `window_parameters.HWnd` member for `hwnd`

4. Create a variable of type `VkSurfaceKHR` named `presentation_surface` and assign a `VK_NULL_HANDLE` value to it.
5. Call `vkCreateWin32SurfaceKHR(instance, &surface_create_info, nullptr, &presentation_surface)`. Provide a handle of a created Instance in the first parameter, a pointer to the `surface_create_info` variable in the second parameter, a `nullptr` value in the third parameter, and a pointer to the `presentation_surface` variable in the last parameter.
6. Make sure the `vkCreateWin32SurfaceKHR()` function call was successful by checking whether the value returned by it is equal to `VK_SUCCESS` and the value of the `presentation_surface` variable is not equal to a `VK_NULL_HANDLE`.

On the Linux operating systems family with an X11 windowing system and an XLIB interface, perform the following steps:

1. Take the variable of type `VkInstance` named `instance` in which a handle of a created Vulkan Instance is stored.
2. Create a variable of type `WindowParameters` named `window_parameters`. Assign the following values for its members:
   - A value returned by the `XOpenDisplay()` function for `Dpy`
   - A value returned by the `XCreateSimpleWindow()` or `XCreateWindow()` functions for `Window`
3. Create a variable of type `VkXlibSurfaceCreateInfoKHR` named `surface_create_info` and initialize its members with the following values:
   - `VK_STRUCTURE_TYPE_XLIB_SURFACE_CREATE_INFO_KHR` value for `sType`
   - `nullptr` value for `pNext`
   - `0` value for `flags`
   - `window_parameters.Dpy` member for `dpy`
   - `window_parameters.Window` member for `window`
4. Create a variable of type `VkSurfaceKHR` named `presentation_surface` and assign a `VK_NULL_HANDLE` value to it.

5. Call `vkCreateXlibSurfaceKHR(instance, &surface_create_info, nullptr, &presentation_surface)`. Provide a handle of a created Instance in the first parameter, pointer to the `surface_create_info` variable in the second parameter, a `nullptr` value in the third parameter, and a pointer to the `presentation_surface` variable in the last parameter.
6. Make sure the `vkCreateXlibSurfaceKHR()` function call was successful by checking whether the value returned by it is equal to `VK_SUCCESS` and the value of the `presentation_surface` variable is not equal to `VK_NULL_HANDLE`.

On the Linux operating systems family with an X11 windowing system and an XCB interface, perform the following steps:

1. Take the variable of type `VkInstance` named `instance` in which a handle of a created Vulkan Instance is stored.
2. Create a variable of type `WindowParameters` named `window_parameters`. Assign the following values for its members:
    - A value returned by the `xcb_connect()` function for `Connection`
    - A value returned by the `xcb_generate_id()` functions for `Window`
3. Create a variable of type `VkXcbSurfaceCreateInfoKHR` named `surface_create_info` and initialize it's members with the following values:
    - `VK_STRUCTURE_TYPE_XCB_SURFACE_CREATE_INFO_KHR` value for `sType`
    - `nullptr` value for `pNext`
    - `0` value for `flags`
    - `window_parameters.Connection` member for `connection`
    - `window_parameters.Window` member for `window`
4. Create a variable of type `VkSurfaceKHR` named `presentation_surface` and assign a `VK_NULL_HANDLE` value to it.
5. Call `vkCreateXcbSurfaceKHR( instance, &surface_create_info, nullptr, &presentation_surface )`. Provide a handle of a created Instance in the first parameter, a pointer to the `surface_create_info` variable in the second parameter, a `nullptr` value in the third parameter, and a pointer to the `presentation_surface` variable in the last parameter.
6. Make sure the `vkCreateXcbSurfaceKHR()` function call was successful by checking whether the value returned by it is equal to `VK_SUCCESS` and the value of the `presentation_surface` variable is not equal to `VK_NULL_HANDLE`.

How it works...

Presentation surface creation depends heavily on parameters that are specific for a given operating system. On each OS, we need to create a variable of a different type and call a different function. Here is a code that creates a presentation surface on Windows:

```
#ifdef VK_USE_PLATFORM_WIN32_KHR

VkWin32SurfaceCreateInfoKHR surface_create_info = {
  VK_STRUCTURE_TYPE_WIN32_SURFACE_CREATE_INFO_KHR,
  nullptr,
  0,
  window_parameters.HInstance,
  window_parameters.HWnd
};

VkResult result = vkCreateWin32SurfaceKHR( instance, &surface_create_info, nullptr, &presentation_surface );
```

Here is a part of the code that does the same on the Linux operating system, when we are using the X11 windowing system:

```
#elif defined VK_USE_PLATFORM_XLIB_KHR

VkXlibSurfaceCreateInfoKHR surface_create_info = {
  VK_STRUCTURE_TYPE_XLIB_SURFACE_CREATE_INFO_KHR,
  nullptr,
  0,
  window_parameters.Dpy,
  window_parameters.Window
};

VkResult result = vkCreateXlibSurfaceKHR( instance, &surface_create_info, nullptr, &presentation_surface );
```

And finally, here is the part for the XCB windowing system, also on Linux:

```
#elif defined VK_USE_PLATFORM_XCB_KHR

VkXcbSurfaceCreateInfoKHR surface_create_info = {
  VK_STRUCTURE_TYPE_XCB_SURFACE_CREATE_INFO_KHR,
  nullptr,
  0,
  window_parameters.Connection,
  window_parameters.Window
};

VkResult result = vkCreateXcbSurfaceKHR( instance, &surface_create_info,
```

```
    nullptr, &presentation_surface );

#endif
```

The preceding code samples are very similar. In each, we create a variable of a structure type whose members we initialize with parameters of a created window. Next we call a `vkCreate???SurfaceKHR()` function which creates a presentation surface and stores its handle in the `presentation_surface` variable. After that, we should check whether everything worked as expected:

```
if( (VK_SUCCESS != result) ||
    (VK_NULL_HANDLE == presentation_surface) ) {
  std::cout << "Could not create presentation surface." << std::endl;
  return false;
}
return true;
```

See also

The following recipes in this chapter:

- *Getting capabilities of a presentation surface*
- *Creating a swapchain*
- *Destroying a presentation surface*

Selecting a queue family that supports presentation to a given surface

Displaying an image on screen is performed by submitting a special command to the device's queue. We can't display images using any queues we want or, in other words, we can't submit this operation to any queue. This is because it may not be supported. Image presentation, along with the graphics, compute, transfer, and sparse operations, is another property of a queue family. And similar to all types of operations, not all queues may support it and, more importantly, not even all devices may support it. That's why we need to check what queue family from which physical device allows us to present an image on screen.

Image Presentation

How to do it...

1. Take the handle of a physical device returned by the `vkEnumeratePhysicalDevices()` function. Store it in a variable of type `VkPhysicalDevice` named `physical_device`.
2. Take the created presentation surface and store its handle in a variable of type `VkSurfaceKHR` named `presentation_surface`.
3. Create a `std::vector` with elements of type `VkQueueFamilyProperties` and call it `queue_families`.
4. Enumerate all queue families that are available on a physical device represented by the `physical_device` variable (refer to the *Checking available queue families and their properties* recipe from Chapter 1, *Instance and Devices*). Store the results of this operation in the `queue_families` variable.
5. Create a variable of type `uint32_t` named `queue_family_index`.
6. Create a variable of type `uint32_t` named `index`. Use it to loop over all elements of the `queue_families` vector. For each element of the `queue_families` variable, perform the following steps:
   1. Create a variable of type `VkBool32` named `presentation_supported`. Assign a value of `VK_FALSE` to this variable.
   2. Call `vkGetPhysicalDeviceSurfaceSupportKHR(physical_device, index, presentation_surface, &presentation_supported)`. Provide a handle of the physical device in the first argument, the number of the current loop iteration in the second argument, and a handle of the presentation surface in the third argument. Also, provide a pointer to the `presentation_supported` variable in the last argument.
   3. Check whether the value returned by the `vkGetPhysicalDeviceSurfaceSupportKHR()` function is equal to `VK_SUCCESS` and whether the value of the `presentation_supported` variable is equal to `VK_TRUE`. If it is, store the value of a current loop iteration (`index` variable) in the `queue_family_index` variable and finish the loop.

How it works...

First we need to check what queue families are exposed by a given physical device. This operation is performed the same way as described in the *Checking available queue families and their properties* recipe from Chapter 1, *Instance and Devices*:

```
std::vector<VkQueueFamilyProperties> queue_families;
if( !CheckAvailableQueueFamiliesAndTheirProperties( physical_device,
queue_families ) ) {
  return false;
}
```

Next we can iterate over all available queue families and check whether a given family supports image presentation. This is performed by calling a vkGetPhysicalDeviceSurfaceSupportKHR() function which stores the information in a specified variable. If the image presentation is supported, we can remember an index of a given family. All queues from this family will support image presentation:

```
for( uint32_t index = 0; index <
static_cast<uint32_t>(queue_families.size()); ++index ) {
  VkBool32 presentation_supported = VK_FALSE;
  VkResult result = vkGetPhysicalDeviceSurfaceSupportKHR( physical_device,
index, presentation_surface, &presentation_supported );
  if( (VK_SUCCESS == result) &&
      (VK_TRUE == presentation_supported) ) {
    queue_family_index = index;
    return true;
  }
}
return false;
```

When there is no queue family exported by a given physical device that supports image presentation, we must check whether this operation is available on another physical device.

See also

In Chapter 1, *Instance and Devices* see the following recipes:

- *Checking available queue families and their properties*
- *Selecting index of a queue family with desired capabilities*
- *Creating a logical device*

Creating a logical device with WSI extensions enabled

When we have created an Instance with WSI extensions enabled and have found a queue family that supports image presentation, it is time to create a logical device with another extension enabled. A device-level WSI extension allows us to create a swapchain. This is a collection of images which are managed by the presentation engine. In order to use any of these images and to render into them, we need to acquire them. After we are done, we give it back to the presentation engine. This operation is called a presentation and it informs the driver that we want to show an image to the user (present or display it on screen). The presentation engine displays it according to the parameters defined during swapchain creation. And we can create it only on logical devices with an enabled swapchain extension.

How to do it...

1. Take the handle of a physical device, for which there is a queue family that supports image presentation, and store it in a variable of type `VkPhysicalDevice` named `physical_device`.
2. Prepare a list of queue families and a number of queues from each family. Assign a priority (a floating-point value between `0.0f` and `1.0f`) for each queue from each family. Store these parameters in a `std::vector` variable named `queue_infos` with elements of a custom type `QueueInfo` (refer to the *Creating a logical device* recipe from Chapter 1, *Instance and Devices*). Remember to include at least one queue from a family that supports image presentation.
3. Prepare a list of extensions that should be enabled. Store it in a variable of type `std::vector<char const *>` named `desired_extensions`.
4. Add another element to the `desired_extensions` variable with value equal to `VK_KHR_SWAPCHAIN_EXTENSION_NAME`.
5. Create a logical device using the parameters prepared in the `physical_device` and `queue_infos` variable and with all extensions enabled from the `desired_extensions` vector (refer to the *Creating a logical device* recipe from Chapter 1, *Instance and Devices*).

How it works...

When we want to display images on screen, there is only one device-level extension that needs to be enabled during logical device creation. This is called VK_KHR_swapchain and allows us to create a swapchain.

A swapchain defines parameters that are very similar to the parameters of a default drawing buffer in the OpenGL API. It specifies, among others, the format of an image we want to render to, the number of images (which can be thought of as double or triple buffering), or a presentation mode (v-sync enabled or disabled). Images created along the swapchain are owned and managed by the presentation engine. We are not allowed to create or destroy them by ourselves. We can't even use them until we ask to do this. When we want to display an image on screen, we need to ask for one of the swapchain images (acquire it), render into it, and then give the image back to the presentation engine (present it).

> The ability to specify a set of presentable images, to acquire them, and to display them on screen is defined in a VK_KHR_swapchain extension.

The functionality described is defined in the VK_KHR_swapchain extension. To enable it during logical device creation, we need to prepare the following code:

```
desired_extensions.emplace_back( VK_KHR_SWAPCHAIN_EXTENSION_NAME );

return CreateLogicalDevice( physical_device, queue_infos,
  desired_extensions, desired_features, logical_device );
```

The logical device creation code is identical to the operation described in the *Creating a logical device* recipe from Chapter 1, *Instance and Devices*. Here, we just need to remember that we must check whether a given physical device supports a VK_KHR_swapchain extension, and after that, we need to include it in a list of extensions that should be enabled.

The name of the extension is specified through a VK_KHR_SWAPCHAIN_EXTENSION_NAME preprocessor definition. It is defined in the vulkan.h header file and it helps us avoid making typos in the name of the extension.

See also

- The following recipes in Chapter 1, *Instance and Devices*:
    - *Checking available device extensions*
    - *Creating a logical device*
- The recipe *Creating a Vulkan Instance with WSI extensions* enabled in this chapter

Selecting a desired presentation mode

The ability to display images on screen is one of the most important features of a Vulkan's swapchain--and, in fact, it's what a swapchain was designed for. In OpenGL, when we finished rendering to a back buffer, we just switched it with a front buffer and the rendered image was displayed on screen. We could only determine whether we wanted to display an image along with blanking intervals (if we wanted a v-sync to be enabled) or not.

In Vulkan, we are not limited to only one image (back buffer) to which we can render. And, instead of two (v-sync enabled or disabled), we can select one of more ways in which images are displayed on screen. This is called a presentation mode and we need to specify it during swapchain creation.

How to do it...

1. Take the handle of a physical device enumerated with the `vkEnumeratePhysicalDevices()` function. Store it in a variable of type `VkPhysicalDevice` named `physical_device`.
2. Take the created presentation surface and store its handle in a variable of type `VkSurfaceKHR` named `presentation_surface`.
3. Create a variable of type `VkPresentModeKHR` named `desired_present_mode`. Store a desired presentation mode in this variable.

4. Prepare a variable of type `uint32_t` named `present_modes_count`.
5. Call `vkGetPhysicalDeviceSurfacePresentModesKHR(physical_device, presentation_surface, &present_modes_count, nullptr)`. Provide a handle of a physical device and a handle of a presentation surface as the first two arguments. In the third parameter, provide a pointer to the `present_modes_count` variable.
6. If a function call is successful, the `present_modes_count` variable will contain the number of supported presentation modes.
7. Create a variable of type `std::vector<VkPresentModeKHR>` named `present_modes`. Resize the vector to be large enough to contain at least `present_modes_count` elements.
8. Once again, call `vkGetPhysicalDeviceSurfacePresentModesKHR( physical_device, presentation_surface, &present_modes_count, &present_modes[0])`, but this time, in the last parameter, provide a pointer to the first element of the `present_modes` vector.
9. If the function returns a `VK_SUCCESS` value, the `present_modes` variable will contain the present modes supported on a given platform.
10. Iterate over all elements of the `present_modes` vector. Check whether one of the elements is equal to the desired present mode stored in the `desired_present_mode` variable.
11. If the desired present mode is not supported (none of the elements of the `present_modes` vector is equal to the `desired_present_mode` variable), select a FIFO present mode--a value of `VK_PRESENT_MODE_FIFO_KHR`--which always should be supported.

How it works...

The presentation mode defines the way in which images are displayed on screen. Currently, there are four modes defined in a Vulkan API.

Image Presentation

The simplest is an **IMMEDIATE** mode. Here, when an image is presented, it immediately replaces the image that is being displayed. There is no waiting involved, no queue, and no other parameters that should be considered from the application perspective. And because of that, screen tearing may (and probably will) be observed:

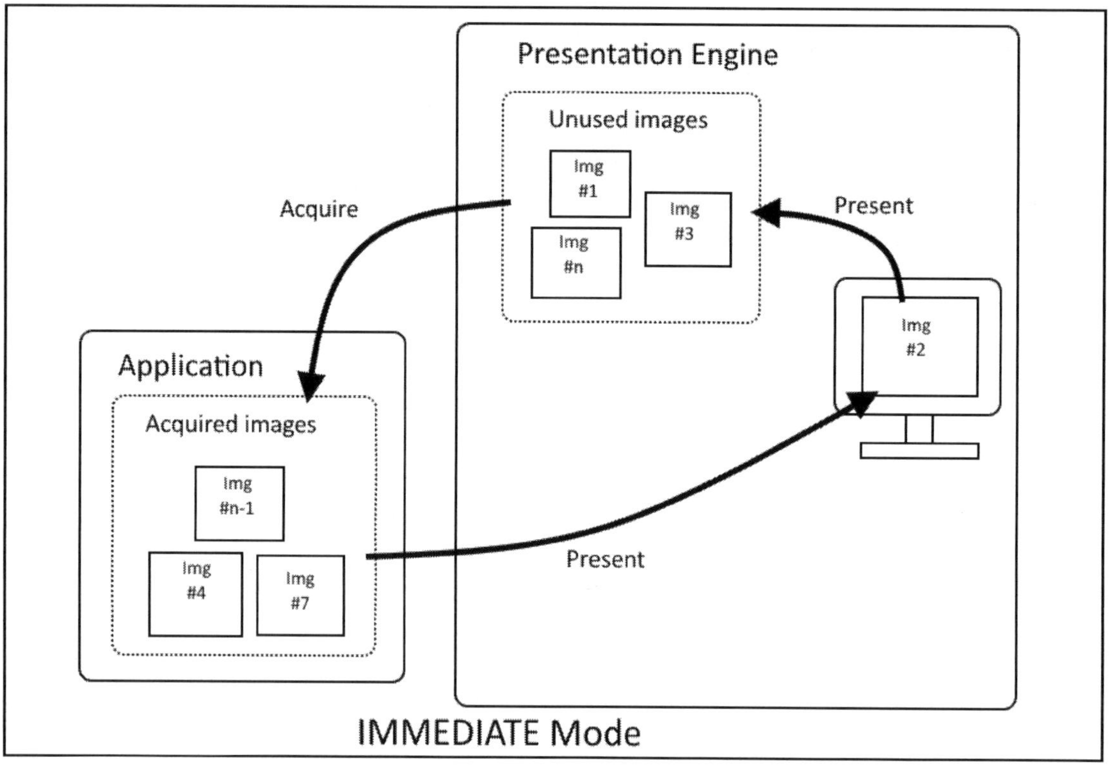

IMMEDIATE Mode

The presentation mode that is mandatory, that every Vulkan API implementation must support, is a **FIFO mode**. Here, when an image is presented, it is added to the First In First Out queue (the length of this queue is equal to the number of images in a swapchain minus one, $n - 1$). From this queue, images are displayed on screen in sync with blanking periods (v-sync), always in the same order they were added to the queue. There is no tearing in this mode, as v-sync is enabled. This mode is similar to OpenGL's buffer swapping with swap interval set to one.

 The FIFO presentation mode must always be supported.

[88]

There is also a slight modification of a FIFO mode called **FIFO RELAXED**. The difference between these two is that in **RELAXED** mode, images are displayed on screen in sync with blanking periods only when they are presented quick enough, faster than the refresh rate. If an image is presented by the application and the time that has elapsed from the last presentation is greater than the refresh time between two blanking periods (the FIFO queue is empty), the image is presented immediately. So if we are quick enough, there is no screen tearing, but if we are drawing slower than the monitor's refresh rate, screen tearing will be visible. This behavior is similar to that specified in OpenGL's `EXT_swap_control_tear` extension:

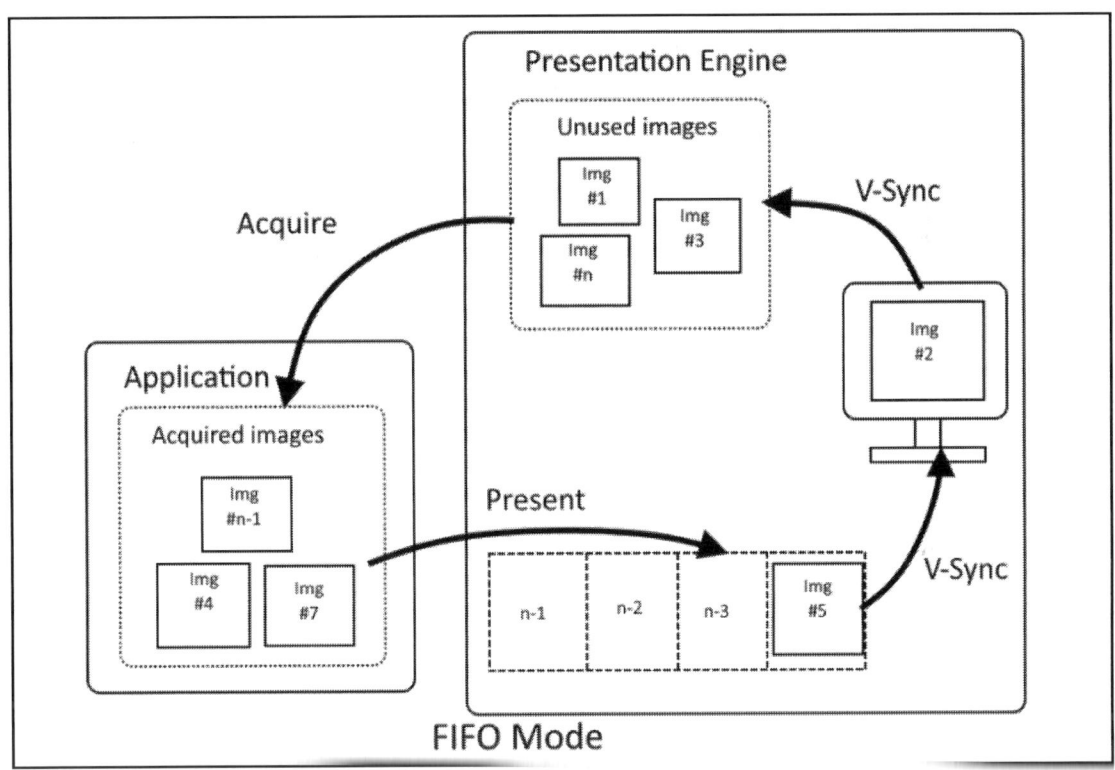

Image Presentation

The last presentation mode is called **mailbox** mode. It can be perceived as a triple buffering. Here also, there is a queue involved, but it contains just one element. An image that is waiting in this queue is displayed in sync with the blanking periods (v-sync is enabled). But when the application presents an image, the new image replaces the one waiting in the queue. So the presentation engine always displays the latest, the most recent, image available. And there is no screen tearing:

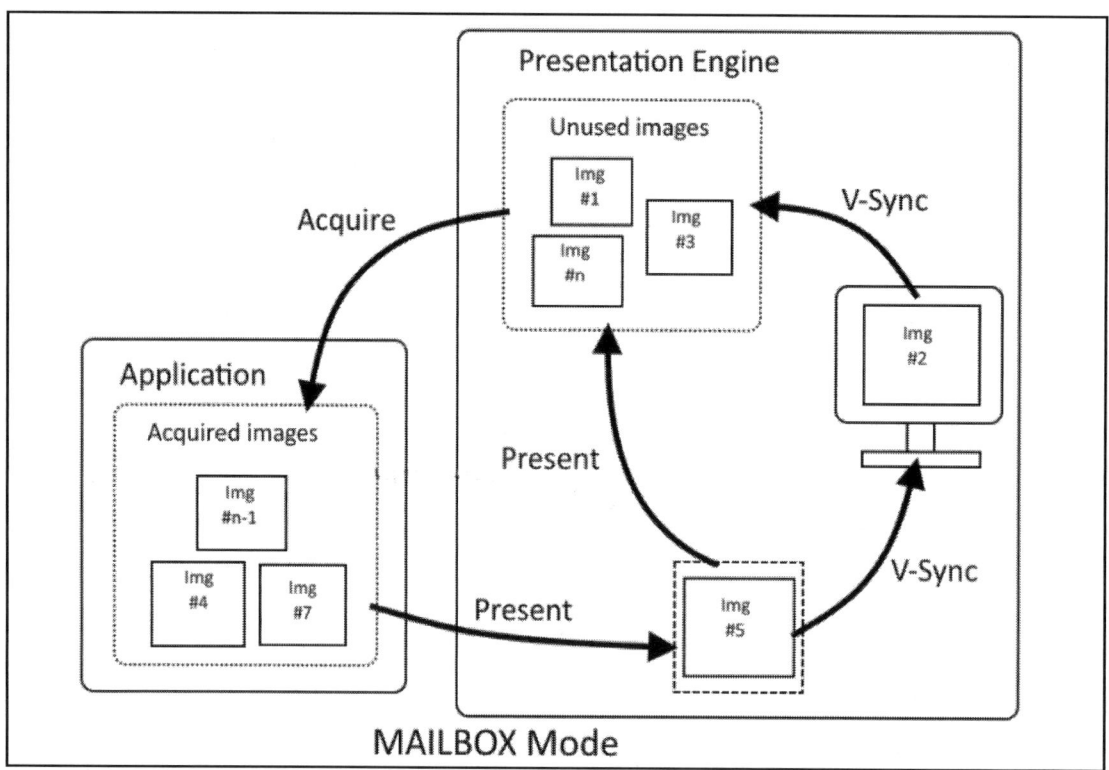

To select the desired presentation mode, we need to check what modes are available on the current platform. First, we need to acquire the number of all supported presentation modes. This is done by calling a vkGetPhysicalDeviceSurfacePresentModesKHR() function with the last parameter set to nullptr:

```
uint32_t present_modes_count = 0;
VkResult result = VK_SUCCESS;

result = vkGetPhysicalDeviceSurfacePresentModesKHR( physical_device,
  presentation_surface, &present_modes_count, nullptr );
if( (VK_SUCCESS != result) ||
    (0 == present_modes_count) ) {
```

```
    std::cout << "Could not get the number of supported present modes." <<
std::endl;
    return false;
}
```

Next we can prepare storage for all supported modes and once again call the same function, but this time with the last parameter pointing to the allocated storage:

```
std::vector<VkPresentModeKHR> present_modes( present_modes_count );
result = vkGetPhysicalDeviceSurfacePresentModesKHR( physical_device,
presentation_surface, &present_modes_count, &present_modes[0] );
if( (VK_SUCCESS != result) ||
   (0 == present_modes_count) ) {
    std::cout << "Could not enumerate present modes." << std::endl;
    return false;
}
```

Now that we know what presentation modes are available, we can check whether the selected mode is available. If it is not, we can choose another presentation mode from the acquired list or we just fall back to the default FIFO mode that is mandatory and should always be available:

```
for( auto & current_present_mode : present_modes ) {
  if( current_present_mode == desired_present_mode ) {
    present_mode = desired_present_mode;
    return true;
  }
}

std::cout << "Desired present mode is not supported. Selecting default FIFO mode." << std::endl;
for( auto & current_present_mode : present_modes ) {
  if( current_present_mode == VK_PRESENT_MODE_FIFO_KHR ) {
    present_mode = VK_PRESENT_MODE_FIFO_KHR;
    return true;
  }
}
```

See also

The following recipes in this chapter:

- *Selecting a number of swapchain images*
- *Creating a swapchain*
- *Creating a swapchain with R8G8B8A8 format and a mailbox present mode*
- *Acquiring a swapchain image*
- *Presenting an image*

Getting the capabilities of a presentation surface

When we create a swapchain, we need to specify creation parameters. But we can't choose whatever values we want. We must provide values that fit into supported limits, which can be obtained from a presentation surface. So in order to properly create a swapchain, we need to acquire the surface's capabilities.

How to do it...

1. Take the handle of a selected physical device enumerated using the `vkEnumeratePhysicalDevices()` function and store it in a variable of type `VkPhysicalDevice` named `physical_device`.
2. Take the handle of a created presentation surface. Store it in a variable of type `VkSurfaceKHR` named `presentation_surface`.
3. Create a variable of type `VkSurfaceCapabilitiesKHR` named `surface_capabilities`.
4. Call `vkGetPhysicalDeviceSurfaceCapabilitiesKHR( physical_device, presentation_surface, &surface_capabilities )` for which provide the handles of the physical device and a presentation surface, and a pointer to the `surface_capabilities` variable.
5. If the function call is successful, the `surface_capabilities` variable will contain the presentation surface's parameters, limits, and capabilities that can be used to create a swapchain.

How it works...

Acquiring the supported capabilities and ranges of parameters that can be used during swapchain creation is very straightforward:

```
VkResult result = vkGetPhysicalDeviceSurfaceCapabilitiesKHR(
physical_device, presentation_surface, &surface_capabilities );

if( VK_SUCCESS != result ) {
  std::cout << "Could not get the capabilities of a presentation surface."
<< std::endl;
  return false;
}
return true;
```

We just call a `vkGetPhysicalDeviceSurfaceCapabilitiesKHR()` function, which stores the parameters in a variable of type `VkSurfaceCapabilitiesKHR`. It is a structure which contains members defining the following parameters:

- Minimal and maximal allowed number of swapchain images
- Minimal, maximal, and current extent of a presentation surface
- Supported image transformations (which can be applied before presentation) and the transformation currently in use
- Maximal number of supported image layers
- Supported usages
- A list of the supported compositions of a surface's alpha value (how an image's alpha component should affect the application's window desktop composition)

See also

The following recipes in this chapter:

- *Creating a presentation surface*
- *Selecting a number of swapchain images*
- *Choosing a size of swapchain images*
- *Selecting desired usage scenarios of swapchain images*
- *Selecting a transformation of swapchain images*
- *Selecting a format of swapchain images*
- *Creating a swapchain*

Selecting a number of swapchain images

When an application wants to render into a swapchain image, it must acquire it from the presentation engine. An application can acquire more images; we are not limited to just one image at a time. But the number of images that are available (unused by the presentation engine at a given time) depends on the specified presentation mode, the application's current situation (rendering/presenting history), and the number of images--when we create a swapchain, we must specify the (minimal) number of images that should be created.

How to do it...

1. Acquire the capabilities of a presentation surface (refer to the *Getting capabilities of a presentation surface* recipe). Store them in a variable of type `VkSurfaceCapabilitiesKHR` named `surface_capabilities`.
2. Create a variable of type `uint32_t` named `number_of_images`.
3. Assign a value of `surface_capabilities.minImageCount + 1` to the `number_of_images` variable.
4. Check whether the value of the `maxImageCount` member of the `surface_capabilities` variable is greater than zero. If it is, this means there is a limit to the maximal allowed number of created images. In this case, check whether the value of the `number_of_images` variable is greater than the value of `surface_capabilities.maxImageCount`. If it is, clamp the value of the `number_of_images` variable to the limit defined in the `maxImageCount` member of the `surface_capabilities` variable.

How it works...

Images created (automatically) along with a swapchain are mainly used for presentation purposes. But they also allow the presentation engine to work properly. One image is (always) displayed on screen. The application can't use it until it is replaced by another image. Images that are presented replace the displayed image immediately, or wait in a queue for the proper moment (v-sync) to replace it, depending on the selected mode. An image that was displayed and is now being replaced becomes unused and can be acquired by the application.

An application can acquire only images that are currently in an unused state (refer to the *Selecting a desired presentation mode* recipe). We can acquire all of them. But as soon as all unused images are acquired, we need to present at least one of them in order to be able to acquire another one. If we don't do this, the acquiring operation may block indefinitely.

The number of unused images depends mainly on the presentation mode and the total number of images created with a swapchain. So the number of images that we want to create should be chosen based on the rendering scenarios we want to implement (how many images an application wants to possess at the same time) and the selected present mode.

Choosing the minimal number of images may look like this:

```
number_of_images = surface_capabilities.minImageCount + 1;
if( (surface_capabilities.maxImageCount > 0) &&
    (number_of_images > surface_capabilities.maxImageCount) ) {
  number_of_images = surface_capabilities.maxImageCount;
}
return true;
```

Usually, in the most typical rendering scenarios, we will be rendering into a single image at a given time. So the minimal supported number of images may be enough. Creating more images allows us to acquire more of them at the same time, but, more importantly, it may also increase the performance of our application if a proper rendering algorithm is implemented. But we can't forget that images consume a considerable amount of memory. So the number of images we choose for the swapchain should be a compromise between our needs, memory usage, and the performance of our application.

In the preceding example, such a compromise is presented in which the application chooses one image more than the minimal value that allows the presentation engine to work properly. After that, we also need to check whether there is an upper limit and whether we exceed it. If we do, we need to clamp the selected value to the supported range.

See also

The following recipes in this chapter:

- *Selecting a desired presentation mode*
- *Getting the capabilities of a presentation surface*
- *Creating a swapchain*
- *Acquiring a swapchain image*
- *Presenting an image*

Choosing a size of swapchain images

Usually, images created for a swapchain should fit into an application's window. The supported dimensions are available in the presentation surface's capabilities. But on some operating systems, the size of the images defines the final size of the window. We also should keep that in mind and check what dimensions are proper for the swapchain images.

How to do it...

1. Acquire the capabilities of a presentation surface (refer to the *Getting capabilities of a presentation surface* recipe). Store them in a variable of type `VkSurfaceCapabilitiesKHR` named `surface_capabilities`.
2. Create a variable of type `VkExtent2D` named `size_of_images` in which we will store the desired size of swapchain images.
3. Check whether the `currentExtent.width` member of the `surface_capabilities` variable is equal to `0xFFFFFFFF` (-1 converted to an unsigned value of `uint32_t` type). If it is, it means that the size of images determines the size of the window. In this situation:
    - Assign the desired values for `width` and `height` members of the `size_of_images` variable
    - Clamp the value of the `width` member of a `size_of_images` variable to the range defined
      by `surface_capabilities.minImageExtent.width` and `surface_capabilities.maxImageExtent.width`
    - Clamp the value of the `height` member of the `size_of_images` variable to the range defined
      by `surface_capabilities.minImageExtent.height` and `surface_capabilities.maxImageExtent.height`
4. If the value of the `currentExtent.width` member of the `surface_capabilities` variable is not equal to `0xFFFFFFFF`, in the `size_of_images` variable, store the value of `surface_capabilities.currentExtent`.

How it works...

The size of swapchain images must fit into supported limits. These are defined by the surface capabilities. In most typical scenarios, we want to render into an image that has the same dimensions as the application window's client area. This value is specified in the `currentExtent` member of surface's capabilities.

But there are operating systems on which the window's size is determined by the size of swapchain images. This situation is signaled by the `0xFFFFFFFF` value of the `currentExtent.width` or `currentExtent.height` member of the surface's capabilities. In this case, we can define the size of images, but it still must fall within a specified range:

```
if( 0xFFFFFFFF == surface_capabilities.currentExtent.width ) {
  size_of_images = { 640, 480 };

  if( size_of_images.width < surface_capabilities.minImageExtent.width ) {
    size_of_images.width = surface_capabilities.minImageExtent.width;
  } else if( size_of_images.width > surface_capabilities.maxImageExtent.width ) {
    size_of_images.width = surface_capabilities.maxImageExtent.width;
  }

  if( size_of_images.height < surface_capabilities.minImageExtent.height ) {
    size_of_images.height = surface_capabilities.minImageExtent.height;
  } else if( size_of_images.height > surface_capabilities.maxImageExtent.height ) {
    size_of_images.height = surface_capabilities.maxImageExtent.height;
  }
} else {
  size_of_images = surface_capabilities.currentExtent;
}
return true;
```

See also

The following recipes in this chapter:

- *Getting capabilities of a presentation surface*
- *Creating a swapchain*

Selecting desired usage scenarios of swapchain images

Images created with a swapchain are usually used as color attachments. This means that we want to render into them (use them as render targets). But we are not limited only to this scenario. We can use swapchain images for other purposes--we can sample from them, use them as a source of data in copy operations, or copy data into them. These are all different image usages and we can specify them during swapchain creation. But, again, we need to check whether these usages are supported.

How to do it...

1. Acquire the capabilities of a presentation surface (refer to the *Getting capabilities of a presentation surface* recipe). Store them in a variable of type `VkSurfaceCapabilitiesKHR` named `surface_capabilities`.
2. Choose the desired image usages and store them in a variable of a bit field type `VkImageUsageFlags` named `desired_usages`.
3. Create a variable of type `VkImageUsageFlags` named `image_usage` in which a list of requested usages that are supported on a given platform will be stored. Assign a value of 0 to the `image_usage` variable.
4. Iterate over all bits of the `desired_usages` bit field variable. For each bit in the variable:
    - Check whether the bit is set (is equal to one)
    - Check whether the corresponding bit of the `supportedUsageFlags` member of the `surface_capabilities` variable is set
    - If the preceding checks are true, set the same bit in the `image_usage` variable
5. Make sure that all of the requested usages are supported on a given platform by checking if the values of the `desired_usages` and `image_usage` variables are equal.

How it works...

The list of usages that can be selected for swapchain images is available in a `supportedUsageFlags` member of a presentation surface's capabilities. This member is a bit field in which each bit corresponds to a specific usage. If a given bit is set, it means that a given usage is supported.

> Color attachment usage (`VK_IMAGE_USAGE_COLOR_ATTACHMENT_BIT`) must always be supported.

`VK_IMAGE_USAGE_COLOR_ATTACHMENT_BIT` usage is mandatory and all Vulkan implementations must support it. Other usages are optional. That's why we shouldn't rely on their availability. Also, we shouldn't request usages that we don't need as this may impact the performance of our application.

Selecting a desired usage may look like this:

```
image_usage = desired_usages & surface_capabilities.supportedUsageFlags;

return desired_usages == image_usage;
```

We take only the common part of desired usages and the supported usages. We then check whether all requested usages are supported. We do this by comparing the values of the requested and the "final" usages. If their values differ, we know that not all of the desired usages are supported.

See also

The following recipes in this chapter:

- *Getting capabilities of a presentation surface*
- *Creating a swapchain*

Selecting a transformation of swapchain images

On some (especially mobile) devices, images can be viewed from different orientations. Sometimes we would like to be able to specify how an image should be oriented when it is displayed on screen. In Vulkan, we have such a possibility. When creating a swapchain, we need to specify the transformation which should be applied to an image before it is presented.

How to do it...

1. Acquire the capabilities of a presentation surface (refer to the *Getting capabilities of a presentation surface* recipe). Store them in a variable of type `VkSurfaceCapabilitiesKHR` named `surface_capabilities`.
2. Store the desired transformations in a bit field variable of type `VkSurfaceTransformFlagBitsKHR` named `desired_transform`.
3. Create a variable of type `VkSurfaceTransformFlagBitsKHR` named `surface_transform` in which we will store the supported transformation.
4. Check whether all bits set in the `desired_transform` variable are also set in the `supportedTransforms` member of the presentation surface's capabilities. If they are, assign the value of the `desired_transform` variable to the `surface_transform` variable.
5. If not all desired transformations are supported, fall back to the current transformation by assigning a value of `surface_capabilities.currentTransform` to the `surface_transform` variable.

How it works...

The `supportedTransforms` member of a presentation surface's capabilities defines a list of all image transformations that are available on a given platform. Transformations define how an image should be rotated or mirrored before it is displayed on screen. During swapchain creation, we can specify the desired transformation and a presentation engine applies it to the image as part of the displaying process.

We can choose any of the supported values. Here is a code sample that selects a desired transformation if it is available or otherwise just takes the currently used transformation:

```
if( surface_capabilities.supportedTransforms & desired_transform ) {
  surface_transform = desired_transform;
} else {
  surface_transform = surface_capabilities.currentTransform;
}
```

See also

The following recipes in this chapter:

- *Getting capabilities of a presentation surface*
- *Creating a swapchain*

Selecting a format of swapchain images

The format defines the number of color components, the number of bits for each component, and the used data type. During swapchain creation, we must specify whether we want to use red, green, and blue channels with or without an alpha component, whether the color values should be encoded using unsigned integer or floating-point data types, and what their precision is. We must also choose whether we are encoding color values using linear or nonlinear color space. But as with other swapchain parameters, we can use only values that are supported by the presentation surface.

Getting ready

In this recipe, we use several terms that may seem identical, but in fact they specify different parameters:

- Image format is used to describe the number of components, precision, and data type of an image's pixels. It corresponds to variables of type `VkFormat`.
- Color space determines the way the values of color components are interpreted by the hardware, whether they are encoded or decoded using a linear or nonlinear function. Color space corresponds to variables of type `VkColorSpaceKHR`.
- Surface format is a pair of image format and color space and is represented by variables of type `VkSurfaceFormatKHR`.

Image Presentation

How to do it...

1. Take the handle of a physical device returned by the `vkEnumeratePhysicalDevices()` function. Store it in a variable of type `VkPhysicalDevice` named `physical_device`.
2. Take the created presentation surface and store its handle in a variable of type `VkSurfaceKHR` named `presentation_surface`.
3. Select the desired image format and color space and assign them to the members of a variable of type `VkSurfaceFormatKHR` named `desired_surface_format`.
4. Create a variable of type `uint32_t` named `formats_count`.
5. Call `vkGetPhysicalDeviceSurfaceFormatsKHR( physical_device, presentation_surface, &formats_count, nullptr )`, provide a handle of the physical device in the first parameter, a handle of the presentation surface in the second parameter, and a pointer to the `formats_count` variable in the third variable. Leave the value of the last parameter set to `nullptr`.
6. If a function call is successful, the `formats_count` variable will contain the number of all supported format-color space pairs.
7. Create a variable of type `std::vector<VkSurfaceFormatKHR>` named `surface_formats`. Resize the vector so it is able to hold at least `formats_count` elements.
8. Make the following call, `vkGetPhysicalDeviceSurfaceFormatsKHR( physical_device, presentation_surface, &formats_count, &surface_formats[0] )`. Provide the same arguments for the first three parameters. In the last parameter, provide a pointer to the first element of the `surface_formats` vector.
9. If the call is successful, all available image format-color space pairs will be stored in the `surface_formats` variable.
10. Create a variable of type `VkFormat` named `image_format` and a second variable of type `VkColorSpaceKHR` named `image_color_space` in which we will store selected values of format and color space used later during swapchain creation.
11. Check the number of elements in the `surface_formats` vector. If it holds only one element with a value of `VK_FORMAT_UNDEFINED`, it means that we can choose whatever surface format we want. Assign the members of the `desired_surface_format` variable to the `image_format` and `image_color_space` variables.

12. If the `surface_formats` vector contains more elements, iterate over each element of the vector and compare the `format` and `colorSpace` members with the same members of the `desired_surface_format` variable. If we find an element in which both members are identical, it means that the desired surface format is supported and we can use it for swapchain creation. Assign the members of the `desired_surface_format` variable to the `image_format` and `image_color_space` variables.
13. If we haven't found a match, iterate over all elements of the `surface_formats` vector. Check whether the `format` member of any of its elements is identical to the value of a chosen `surface_format.format`. If there is such an element, assign the `desired_surface_format.format` value to the `image_format` variable, but take the corresponding color space from the currently viewed element of the `surface_formats` vector and assign it to the `image_color_space` variable.
14. If the `surface_formats` variable doesn't contain any element with the selected image format, take the first element of the vector and assign its `format` and `colorSpace` members to the `image_format` and `image_color_space` variables.

How it works...

To obtain a list of all supported surface formats, we need to make a double call of a `vkGetPhysicalDeviceSurfaceFormatsKHR()` function. First we acquire the number of all supported format-color space pairs:

```
uint32_t formats_count = 0;
VkResult result = VK_SUCCESS;

result = vkGetPhysicalDeviceSurfaceFormatsKHR( physical_device,
presentation_surface, &formats_count, nullptr );
if( (VK_SUCCESS != result) ||
    (0 == formats_count) ) {
  std::cout << "Could not get the number of supported surface formats." << std::endl;
  return false;
}
```

Image Presentation

Next we can prepare storage for the actual values and make the second call to acquire them:

```
std::vector<VkSurfaceFormatKHR> surface_formats( formats_count );
result = vkGetPhysicalDeviceSurfaceFormatsKHR( physical_device,
presentation_surface, &formats_count, &surface_formats[0] );
if( (VK_SUCCESS != result) ||
    (0 == formats_count) ) {
  std::cout << "Could not enumerate supported surface formats." <<
std::endl;
  return false;
}
```

After that, we can choose one of the supported surface formats that is the best match for our needs. If only one surface format was returned and it has a value of VK_FORMAT_UNDEFINED, it means that there are no restrictions on the supported format-color space pairs. In such a situation, we can choose any surface format we want and use it during swapchain creation:

```
if( (1 == surface_formats.size()) &&
    (VK_FORMAT_UNDEFINED == surface_formats[0].format) ) {
  image_format = desired_surface_format.format;
  image_color_space = desired_surface_format.colorSpace;
  return true;
}
```

If there are more elements returned by the vkGetPhysicalDeviceSurfaceFormatsKHR() function, we need to take one of them. First we check whether the chosen surface format is supported "entirely"--both selected image format and color space are available:

```
for( auto & surface_format : surface_formats ) {
  if( (desired_surface_format.format == surface_format.format) &&
      (desired_surface_format.colorSpace == surface_format.colorSpace) ) {
    image_format = desired_surface_format.format;
    image_color_space = desired_surface_format.colorSpace;
    return true;
  }
}
```

If we can't find a match, we look for a member that has an identical image format, but other color space. We can't take any of the supported formats and any of the supported color spaces--we must take the same color space that corresponds to a given format:

```
for( auto & surface_format : surface_formats ) {
  if( (desired_surface_format.format == surface_format.format) ) {
    image_format = desired_surface_format.format;
    image_color_space = surface_format.colorSpace;
    std::cout << "Desired combination of format and colorspace is not
```

```
supported. Selecting other colorspace." << std::endl;
      return true;
    }
  }
}
```

Finally, if the format we wanted to use is not supported, we just take the first available image format-color space pair:

```
image_format = surface_formats[0].format;
image_color_space = surface_formats[0].colorSpace;
std::cout << "Desired format is not supported. Selecting available format -
colorspace combination." << std::endl;
return true;
```

See also

The following recipes in this chapter:

- *Creating a swapchain*
- *Creating a swapchain with R8G8B8A8 format and a mailbox present mode*

Creating a swapchain

A swapchain is used to display images on screen. It is an array of images which can be acquired by the application and then presented in our application's window. Each image has the same defined set of properties. When we have prepared all of these parameters, meaning that we chose a number, a size, a format, and usage scenarios for swapchain images, and also acquired and selected one of the available presentation modes, we are ready to create a swapchain.

How to do it...

1. Take the handle of a created logical device object. Store it in a variable of type `VkDevice` named `logical_device`.
2. Assign the handle of a created presentation surface to a variable of type `VkSurfaceKHR` named `presentation_surface`.
3. Take the desired number of swapchain images assigned to a variable of type `uint32_t` named `image_count`.

Image Presentation

4. Store the values of the selected image format and color space in a variable of type `VkSurfaceFormatKHR` named `surface_format`.
5. Prepare the required image size and assign it to a variable of type `VkExtent2D` named `image_size`.
6. Choose the desired usage scenarios for swapchain images. Store them in a bit field variable of type `VkImageUsageFlags` named `image_usage`.
7. Take the selected surface transformations stored in a variable of type `VkSurfaceTransformFlagBitsKHR` named `surface_transform`.
8. Prepare a variable of type `VkPresentModeKHR` named `present_mode` and assign a desired presentation mode to it.
9. Create a variable of type `VkSwapchainKHR` named `old_swapchain`. If there was a swapchain created previously, store a handle of that swapchain in this variable. Otherwise, assign a `VK_NULL_HANDLE` value to this variable.
10. Create a variable of type `VkSwapchainCreateInfoKHR` named `swapchain_create_info`. Assign the following values to the members of this variable:
    - `VK_STRUCTURE_TYPE_SWAPCHAIN_CREATE_INFO_KHR` value for `sType`
    - `nullptr` value for `pNext`
    - `0` value for `flags`
    - `presentation_surface` variable for `surface`
    - `image_count` variable for `minImageCount`
    - `surface_format.format` member for `imageFormat`
    - `surface_format.colorSpace` member for `imageColorSpace`
    - `image_size` variable for `imageExtent`
    - `1` value for `imageArrayLayers` (or more if we want to perform layered/stereoscopic rendering)
    - `image_usage` variable for `imageUsage`
    - `VK_SHARING_MODE_EXCLUSIVE` value for `imageSharingMode`
    - `0` value for `queueFamilyIndexCount`
    - `nullptr` value for `pQueueFamilyIndices`
    - `surface_transform` variable for `preTransform`
    - `VK_COMPOSITE_ALPHA_OPAQUE_BIT_KHR` value for `compositeAlpha`
    - `present_mode` variable for `presentMode`
    - `VK_TRUE` for `clipped`
    - `old_swapchain` variable for `oldSwapchain`

11. Create a variable of type `VkSwapchainKHR` named `swapchain`.
12. Call `vkCreateSwapchainKHR( logical_device, &swapchain_create_info, nullptr, &swapchain )`. Use the handle of a created logical device, a pointer to the `swapchain_create_info` variable, a `nullptr` value, and a pointer to the `swapchain` variable as the function's arguments.
13. Make sure the call was successful by comparing the returned value with a `VK_SUCCESS` value.
14. Call `vkDestroySwapchainKHR( logical_device, old_swapchain, nullptr )` to destroy the old swapchain. Provide a handle to the created logical device, a handle of an old swapchain, and a `nullptr` value for the function call.

How it works...

As was mentioned earlier, a swapchain is a collection of images. They are created automatically along with a swapchain. They are also destroyed when the swapchain is destroyed. Though an application can obtain handles of these images, it is not allowed to create or destroy them.

The process of swapchain creation isn't too complicated, but there is a considerable amount of data we need to prepare before we are able to create it:

```
VkSwapchainCreateInfoKHR swapchain_create_info = {
  VK_STRUCTURE_TYPE_SWAPCHAIN_CREATE_INFO_KHR,
  nullptr,
  0,
  presentation_surface,
  image_count,
  surface_format.format,
  surface_format.colorSpace,
  image_size,
  1,
  image_usage,
  VK_SHARING_MODE_EXCLUSIVE,
  0,
  nullptr,
  surface_transform,
  VK_COMPOSITE_ALPHA_OPAQUE_BIT_KHR,
  present_mode,
  VK_TRUE,
  old_swapchain
};
```

Image Presentation

```
VkResult result = vkCreateSwapchainKHR( logical_device,
&swapchain_create_info, nullptr, &swapchain );
if( (VK_SUCCESS != result) ||
    (VK_NULL_HANDLE == swapchain) ) {
  std::cout << "Could not create a swapchain." << std::endl;
  return false;
}
```

Only one swapchain can be associated with a given application's window. When we create a new swapchain, we need to destroy any swapchain that was previously created for the same window:

```
if( VK_NULL_HANDLE != old_swapchain ) {
  vkDestroySwapchainKHR( logical_device, old_swapchain, nullptr );
  old_swapchain = VK_NULL_HANDLE;
}
```

When the swapchain is ready, we can acquire its images and perform tasks that fit into specified usage scenarios. We are not limited to acquiring just a single image, like we were used to in an OpenGL API (single back buffer). The number of images depends on the minimal specified number of images that should be created along with a swapchain, the chosen presentation mode, and current rendering history (number of images currently acquired and recently presented).

After we have acquired an image, we can use it in our application. The most common usage is rendering into the image (using it as a color attachment), but we are not limited to just this usage and we can perform other tasks with swapchain images. But we must make sure respective usages are available on a given platform and that they were specified during swapchain creation. Not all platforms may support all usages. Only color attachment usage is mandatory.

When we are done rendering into an image (or images) or performing other tasks, we can display an image by presenting it. This operation returns the image to the presentation engine which replaces the currently displayed image with the new one according to the specified presentation mode.

See also

The following recipes in this chapter:

- *Creating a presentation surface*
- *Selecting a queue family that supports presentation to a given surface*
- *Creating a logical device with WSI extensions enabled*

Chapter 2

- *Selecting a desired presentation mode*
- *Getting capabilities of a presentation surface*
- *Selecting a number of swapchain images*
- *Choosing a size of swapchain images*
- *Selecting desired usage scenarios of swapchain images*
- *Selecting a transformation of swapchain images*
- *Selecting a format of swapchain images*

Getting handles of swapchain images

When the swapchain object is created, it may be very useful to acquire the number and handles of all images that were created along with the swapchain.

How to do it...

1. Take the handle of a created logical device object. Store it in a variable of type `VkDevice` named `logical_device`.
2. Assign the handle of a created swapchain to a variable of type `VkSwapchainKHR` named `swapchain`.
3. Create a variable of type `uint32_t` named `images_count`.
4. Call `vkGetSwapchainImagesKHR( logical_device, swapchain, &images_count, nullptr )` for which provide the handle to the created logical device in the first parameter, the handle of the swapchain in the second, and a pointer to the `images_count` variable in the third parameter. Provide a `nullptr` value in the last parameter.
5. If the call is successful, meaning that the returned value is equal to `VK_SUCCESS`, the `images_count` variable will contain the total number of images created for a given swapchain object.
6. Create a `std::vector` with elements of type `VkImage`. Name the vector `swapchain_images` and resize it so it is able to hold at least `images_count` number of elements.

[109]

Image Presentation

7. Call `vkGetSwapchainImagesKHR(logical_device, swapchain, &images_count, &swapchain_images[0])` and provide the same arguments for the first three parameters as previously. In the last parameter, provide a pointer to the first element of the `swapchain_images` vector.
8. On success, the vector will contain the handles of all swapchain images.

How it works...

Drivers may create more images than were requested in the swapchain's creation parameters. There, we just defined the minimum required number but Vulkan implementations are allowed to create more.

We need to know the total number of created images to be able to acquire their handles. In Vulkan, when we want to render into an image, we need to know its handle. It is required to create an image view that wraps the image and is used during framebuffer creation. A framebuffer, as in OpenGL, specifies a set of images that are used during the rendering process (mostly that we render into them).

But this is not the only case in which we need to know what images were created along with a swapchain. It's been said that when an application wants to use a presentable image, it must acquire it from the presentation engine. The process of image acquisition returns a number, not the handle itself. The provided number represents an index of an image in the array of images acquired with the `vkGetSwapchainImagesKHR()` function (a `swapchain_images` variable). So the knowledge of the total number of images, their order, and their handles is necessary to properly use a swapchain and its images.

To acquire the total number of images, we need to use the following code:

```
uint32_t images_count = 0;
VkResult result = VK_SUCCESS;

result = vkGetSwapchainImagesKHR( logical_device, swapchain, &images_count,
nullptr );
if( (VK_SUCCESS != result) ||
    (0 == images_count) ) {
  std::cout << "Could not get the number of swapchain images." <<
std::endl;
  return false;
}
```

Next, we can prepare storage for all images and acquire their handles:

```
swapchain_images.resize( images_count );
result = vkGetSwapchainImagesKHR( logical_device, swapchain, &images_count,
&swapchain_images[0] );
if( (VK_SUCCESS != result) ||
  (0 == images_count) ) {
  std::cout << "Could not enumerate swapchain images." << std::endl;
  return false;
}

return true;
```

See also

The following recipes in this chapter:

- *Selecting a number of swapchain images*
- *Creating a swapchain*
- *Acquiring a swapchain image*
- *Presenting an image*

Creating a swapchain with R8G8B8A8 format and a mailbox present mode

To create a swapchain, we need to acquire a lot of additional information and prepare a considerable number of parameters. To present the order of all the steps required for the preparation phases and how to use the acquired information, we will create a swapchain with arbitrarily chosen parameters. For it, we will set a mailbox presentation mode, the most commonly used R8G8B8A8 color format with unsigned normalized values (similar to OpenGL's RGBA8 format), no transformations, and a standard color attachment image usage.

Image Presentation

How to do it...

1. Prepare a physical device handle. Store it in a variable of type `VkPhysicalDevice` named `physical_device`.
2. Take the handle of a created presentation surface and assign it to a variable of type `VkSurfaceKHR` named `presentation_surface`.
3. Take the logical device created from the handle represented by the `physical_device` variable. Store the handle of the logical device in a variable of type `VkDevice` named `logical_device`.
4. Create a variable of type `VkSwapchainKHR` named `old_swapchain`. If a swapchain was previously created, assign its handle to the `old_swapchain` variable. Otherwise, assign a `VK_NULL_HANDLE` to it.
5. Create a variable of type `VkPresentModeKHR` named `desired_present_mode`.
6. Check whether the `VK_PRESENT_MODE_MAILBOX_KHR` presentation mode is supported and assign it to the `desired_present_mode` variable. If this mode is not supported, use a `VK_PRESENT_MODE_FIFO_KHR` mode (refer to *Selecting a desired presentation mode* recipe).
7. Create a variable of type `VkSurfaceCapabilitiesKHR` named `surface_capabilities`.
8. Get the capabilities of a presentation surface and store them in the `surface_capabilities` variable.
9. Create a variable of type `uint32_t` named `number_of_images`. Based on the acquired surface capabilities, assign a minimal required number of images to the `number_of_images` variable (refer to the *Selecting a number of swapchain images* recipe).
10. Create a variable of type `VkExtent2D` named `image_size`. Based on the acquired surface capabilities, assign a size of swapchain images to the `image_size` variable (refer to the *Choosing a size of swapchain images* recipe).
11. Make sure the `width` and `height` members of the `image_size` variable are greater than zero. If they are not, do not attempt to create a swapchain, but don't close the application--such a situation may occur when a window is minimized.
12. Create a variable of type `VkImageUsageFlags` named `image_usage`. Assign a `VK_IMAGE_USAGE_COLOR_ATTACHMENT_BIT` image usage to it (refer to the *Selecting desired usage scenarios of swapchain images* recipe).

13. Create a variable of type `VkSurfaceTransformFlagBitsKHR` named `surface_transform`. Store an identity transform (a value of `VK_SURFACE_TRANSFORM_IDENTITY_BIT_KHR`) in the variable. Based on the acquired surface capabilities, check whether it is supported. If it is not, assign the `currentTransform` member of the acquired capabilities to the `surface_transform` variable (refer to the *Selecting a transformation of swapchain images* recipe).
14. Create a variable of type `VkFormat` named `image_format` and a variable of type `VkColorSpaceKHR` named `image_color_space`.
15. Using the acquired capabilities, try to use the `VK_FORMAT_R8G8B8A8_UNORM` image format with a `VK_COLOR_SPACE_SRGB_NONLINEAR_KHR` color space. If format or color space, or both, are not supported, select other values from the surface capabilities (refer to the *Selecting a format of swapchain images* recipe).
16. Create a variable of type `VkSwapchainKHR` named `swapchain`.
17. Using the `logical_device`, `presentation_surface`, `number_of_images`, `image_format`, `image_color_space`, `size_of_images`, `image_usage`, `surface_transform`, `desired_present_mode`, and `old_swapchain` variables, create a swapchain and store its handle in the `swapchain` variable. Remember to check if the swapchain creation was successful. (refer to the *Creating a swapchain* recipe).
18. Create a variable of type `std::vector<VkImage>` named `swapchain_images` and store the handles of the created swapchain images in it (refer to the *Getting handles of swapchain images* recipe).

How it works...

When we want to create a swapchain, we first need to think what presentation mode we would like to use. As the mailbox mode allows us to present the most recent image without screen tearing (it is similar to a triple buffering), it looks like a good choice:

```
VkPresentModeKHR desired_present_mode;
if( !SelectDesiredPresentationMode( physical_device, presentation_surface,
VK_PRESENT_MODE_MAILBOX_KHR, desired_present_mode ) ) {
  return false;
}
```

Image Presentation

Next we need to acquire the presentation surface capabilities and use them to set up the required number of images, their size (dimensions), usage scenarios, transformations applied during presentation, and their format and color space:

```
VkSurfaceCapabilitiesKHR surface_capabilities;
if( !GetCapabilitiesOfPresentationSurface( physical_device,
presentation_surface, surface_capabilities ) ) {
  return false;
}

uint32_t number_of_images;
if( !SelectNumberOfSwapchainImages( surface_capabilities, number_of_images
) ) {
  return false;
}

VkExtent2D image_size;
if( !ChooseSizeOfSwapchainImages( surface_capabilities, image_size ) ) {
  return false;
}
if( (0 == image_size.width) ||
    (0 == image_size.height) ) {
  return true;
}

VkImageUsageFlags image_usage;
if( !SelectDesiredUsageScenariosOfSwapchainImages( surface_capabilities,
VK_IMAGE_USAGE_COLOR_ATTACHMENT_BIT, image_usage ) ) {
  return false;
}

VkSurfaceTransformFlagBitsKHR surface_transform;
SelectTransformationOfSwapchainImages( surface_capabilities,
VK_SURFACE_TRANSFORM_IDENTITY_BIT_KHR, surface_transform );

VkFormat image_format;
VkColorSpaceKHR image_color_space;
if( !SelectFormatOfSwapchainImages( physical_device, presentation_surface,
{ VK_FORMAT_R8G8B8A8_UNORM, VK_COLOR_SPACE_SRGB_NONLINEAR_KHR },
image_format, image_color_space ) ) {
  return false;
}
```

Finally, with all these preparations, we can create a swapchain, destroy an old one (if we want to replace a previously created swapchain with the new one), and acquire the handles of images created along with it:

```
if( !CreateSwapchain( logical_device, presentation_surface,
  number_of_images, { image_format, image_color_space }, image_size,
  image_usage, surface_transform, desired_present_mode, old_swapchain,
  swapchain ) ) {
  return false;
}

if( !GetHandlesOfSwapchainImages( logical_device, swapchain,
  swapchain_images ) ) {
  return false;
}
return true;
```

See also

The following recipes in this chapter:

- *Creating a presentation surface*
- *Creating a logical device with WSI extensions enabled*
- *Selecting a desired presentation mode*
- *Getting capabilities of a presentation surface*
- *Selecting a number of swapchain images*
- *Choosing a size of swapchain images*
- *Selecting desired usage scenarios of swapchain images*
- *Selecting a transformation of swapchain images*
- *Selecting a format of swapchain images*
- *Creating a swapchain*
- *Getting handles of swapchain images*

Acquiring a swapchain image

Before we can use a swapchain image, we need to ask a presentation engine for it. This process is called **image acquisition**. It returns an image's index into the array of images returned by the vkGetSwapchainImagesKHR() function as described in the *Getting handles of swapchain images* recipe.

Getting ready

To acquire an image in Vulkan, we need to specify one of two types of objects that haven't been described yet. These are semaphores and fences.

Semaphores are used to synchronize device's queues. It means that when we submit commands for processing, these commands may require another job to be finished. In such a situation, we can specify that these commands should wait for the other commands before they are executed. And this is what semaphores are for. They are for internal queue synchronization, but we can't use them to synchronize an application with the submitted commands (refer to the *Creating a semaphore* recipe from Chapter 3, *Command Buffers and Synchronization*).

To do so, we need to use fences. They are used to inform an application about some work being finished. An application can acquire the state of a fence and, based on the acquired information, check whether some commands are still being processed or whether they have finished the assigned tasks (refer to the *Creating a fence* recipe from Chapter 3, *Command Buffers and Synchronization*).

How to do it...

1. Take the handle of a created logical device and store it in a variable of type `VkDevice` named `logical_device`.
2. Prepare the handle of a swapchain object and assign it to a `VkSwapchainKHR` variable named `swapchain`.
3. Prepare a semaphore in the form of a variable of type `VkSemaphore` named `semaphore` or prepare a fence and assign its handle to the variable of type `VkFence` named `fence`. You can prepare both synchronization objects but at least one of them is required (no matter which one).
4. Create a variable of type `uint32_t` named `image_index`.
5. Call `vkAcquireNextImageKHR( logical_device, swapchain, <timeout>, semaphore, fence, &image_index )`. Provide a handle of the logical device in the first parameter and a handle of a swapchain object in the second. For the third parameter, named `<timeout>`, provide a value of time after which the function will return a timeout error. You also need to provide one or both synchronization primitives--a swapchain and/or a fence. For the last parameter, provide a pointer to the `image_index` variable.

6. Check the value returned by the `vkAcquireNextImageKHR()` function. If the returned value was equal to `VK_SUCCESS` or `VK_SUBOPTIMAL_KHR`, the call was successful and an `image_index` variable will hold an index of swapchain images which points to the element of an array returned by the `vkGetSwapchainImagesKHR()` function (refer to the *Getting handles of swapchain images* recipe). But if the `VK_ERROR_OUT_OF_DATE_KHR` value was returned, you can't use any images from the swapchain. You must destroy the given swapchain and recreate it once again in order to acquire images.

How it works...

The `vkAcquireNextImageKHR()` function returns an index into the array of swapchain images returned by the `vkGetSwapchainImagesKHR()` function. It does not return the handle of that image. The following code illustrates the recipe:

```
VkResult result;

result = vkAcquireNextImageKHR( logical_device, swapchain, 2000000000,
semaphore, fence, &image_index );
switch( result ) {
  case VK_SUCCESS:
  case VK_SUBOPTIMAL_KHR:
    return true;
default:
  return false;
}
```

In the code sample, we call the `vkAcquireNextImageKHR()` function. Sometimes images may not be available immediately due to the internal mechanism of a presentation engine. It is even possible that we may wait indefinitely! It occurs in situations when we want to acquire more images than the presentation engine can provide. That's why in the third parameter of the preceding function, we provide a timeout value in nanoseconds. It tells the hardware how long we can wait for the image. After this time, the function will inform us that it took too long to acquire an image. In the preceding sample, we inform the driver that we don't want to wait more than 2 seconds for the image to be acquired.

Image Presentation

The other interesting parameters are a semaphore and a fence. When we acquire an image, we still may not use it immediately for our purposes. We need to wait for all previously submitted operations that referenced this image to finish. For this purpose, a fence can be used, using which an application can check when it is safe to modify an image. But we can also tell the driver that it should wait before it starts processing new commands that use a given image. For this purpose, a semaphore is used, which, in general, is a better option.

> Waiting on the application side hurts the performance much more than waiting solely on the GPU.

Return values are also very important during swapchain image acquisition. When the function returns a `VK_SUBOPTIMAL_KHR` value, it means we can still use an image but it may no longer be best suited for the presentation engine. We should recreate the swapchain from which an image was acquired. But we don't need to do it immediately. When the function returns a `VK_ERROR_OUT_OF_DATE_KHR` value, we can't use images from a given swapchain anymore and we need to recreate it as soon as possible.

And the last thing to note about swapchain image acquisition is that before we can use an image, we need to change (transition) its layout. The layout is the image's internal memory organization, which may be different depending on the current purpose for which image is used. And if we want to use the image in a different way, we need to change its layout.

For example, images used by the presentation engine must have a `VK_IMAGE_LAYOUT_PRESENT_SRC_KHR` layout. But if we want to render into an image, it must have a `VK_IMAGE_LAYOUT_COLOR_ATTACHMENT_OPTIMAL` layout. The operation of changing the layout is called a transition (refer to the *Setting an image memory barrier* recipe from `Chapter 4`, *Resources and Memory*).

See also

- The following recipes in this chapter:
    - *Selecting a desired presentation mode*
    - *Creating a swapchain*
    - *Getting handles of swapchain images*
    - *Presenting an image*
- In `Chapter 4`, *Resources and Memory* see the following recipe:
    - *Setting an image memory barrier*

- In `Chapter 3`, *Command Buffers and Synchronization* see the following recipe:
    - *Creating a semaphore*
    - *Creating a fence*

Presenting an image

After we are done rendering into a swapchain image or using it for any other purposes, we need to give the image back to the presentation engine. This operation is called a presentation and it displays an image on screen.

Getting ready

In this recipe, we will be using a custom structure defined as follows:

```
struct PresentInfo {
  VkSwapchainKHR  Swapchain;
  uint32_t        ImageIndex;
};
```

It is used to define a swapchain from which we want to present an image, and an image (its index) that we want to display. For each swapchain, we can present only one image at a time.

How to do it...

1. Prepare a handle of a queue that supports presenting. Store it in a variable of type `VkQueue` named `queue`.
2. Prepare a variable of type `std::vector<VkSemaphore>` named `rendering_semaphores`. Into this vector, insert semaphores associated with rendering commands that reference images which we want to present.
3. Create a variable of type `std::vector<VkSwapchainKHR>` named `swapchains` in which store the handles of all swapchains from which we want to present images.
4. Create a variable of type `std::vector<uint32_t>` named `image_indices`. Resize the vector to be the same size as the `swapchains` vector. For each element of the `image_indices` variable, assign an index of an image from the corresponding swapchain (at the same position in the `swapchains` vector).

Image Presentation

5. Create a variable of type `VkPresentInfoKHR` named `present_info`. Assign the following values for its members:
   - `VK_STRUCTURE_TYPE_PRESENT_INFO_KHR` value for `sType`
   - `nullptr` value for `pNext`
   - A number of elements of the `rendering_semaphores` vector for `waitSemaphoreCount`
   - A pointer to the first element of the `rendering_semaphores` vector for `pWaitSemaphores`
   - The number of elements in the `swapchains` vector for `swapchainCount`
   - A pointer to the first element of the `swapchains` vector for `pSwapchains`
   - A pointer to the first element of the `image_indices` vector for `pImageIndices`
   - `nullptr` value for `pResults`
6. Call `vkQueuePresentKHR( queue, &present_info )` and provide the handle of the queue to which we want to submit this operation, and a pointer to the `present_info` variable.
7. Make sure the call was successful by comparing the returned value with a `VK_SUCCESS`.

How it works...

A presentation operation gives an image back to the presentation engine, which displays an image according to the presentation mode. We can present multiple images at the same time, but only one image from a given swapchain. To present an image, we provide its index into the array returned by the `vkGetSwapchainImagesKHR()` function (refer to the *Getting handles of swapchain images* recipe):

```
VkPresentInfoKHR present_info = {
  VK_STRUCTURE_TYPE_PRESENT_INFO_KHR,
  nullptr,
  static_cast<uint32_t>(rendering_semaphores.size()),
  rendering_semaphores.size() > 0 ? &rendering_semaphores[0] : nullptr,
  static_cast<uint32_t>(swapchains.size()),
  swapchains.size() > 0 ? &swapchains[0] : nullptr,
  swapchains.size() > 0 ? &image_indices[0] : nullptr,
  nullptr
};
```

```
result = vkQueuePresentKHR( queue, &present_info );
switch( result ) {
case VK_SUCCESS:
  return true;
default:
  return false;
}
```

In the preceding sample, the handles of swapchains from which we want to present images and the indices of images are placed in the `swapchains` and `image_indices` vectors.

Before we can submit an image, we need to change its layout to a `VK_IMAGE_LAYOUT_PRESENT_SRC_KHR` or the presentation engine may be not able to correctly display such an image.

Semaphores are used to inform the hardware when it can safely display an image. When we submit a rendering command, we can associate a semaphore with such a submission. This semaphore will then change its state to signaled when the commands are finished. We should create and associate a semaphore with commands that reference a presentable image. This way, when we present an image and provide such a semaphore, the hardware will know when an image is no longer in use and displaying it will not interrupt any previously issued operations.

See also

- The following recipes in this chapter:
    - *Selecting a desired presentation mode*
    - *Creating a swapchain*
    - *Getting handles of swapchain images*
    - *Acquiring a swapchain image*
- In `Chapter 3`, *Command Buffers and Synchronization* see the following recipe:
    - *Creating a semaphore*
    - *Creating a fence*
- In `Chapter 4`, *Resources and Memory* see the following recipe:
    - *Setting an image memory barrier*

Destroying a swapchain

When we are done using a swapchain, because we don't want to present images any more, or because we are just closing our application, we should destroy it. We need to destroy it before we destroy a presentation surface which was used during a given swapchain creation.

How to do it...

1. Take the handle of a logical device and store it in a variable of type `VkDevice` named `logical_device`.
2. Take the handle of a swapchain object that needs to be destroyed. Store it in a variable of type `VkSwapchainKHR` named `swapchain`.
3. Call `vkDestroySwapchainKHR( logical_device, swapchain, nullptr )` and provide the `logical_device` variable as the first argument and the swapchain handle as the second argument. Set the last parameter to `nullptr`.
4. For safety reasons, assign a `VK_NULL_HANDLE` value to the `swapchain` variable.

How it works...

To destroy a swapchain, we can prepare code that is similar to the following example:

```
if( swapchain ) {
  vkDestroySwapchainKHR( logical_device, swapchain, nullptr );
  swapchain = VK_NULL_HANDLE;
}
```

First we check whether a swapchain was really created (if its handle is not empty). Next we call the `vkDestroySwapchainKHR()` function and then we assign a `VK_NULL_HANDLE` value to the `swapchain` variable to be sure that we won't try to delete the same object twice.

See also

- *Creating a swapchain* recipe in this chapter

Destroying a presentation surface

The presentation surface represents the window of our application. It is used, among other purposes, during swapchain creation. That's why we should destroy the presentation surface after the destruction of a swapchain that is based on a given surface is finished.

How to do it...

1. Prepare the handle of a Vulkan Instance and store it in a variable of type `VkInstance` named `instance`.
2. Take the handle of a presentation surface and assign it to the variable of type `VkSurfaceKHR` named `presentation_surface`.
3. Call `vkDestroySurfaceKHR( instance, presentation_surface, nullptr )` and provide the `instance` and `presentation_surface` variables in the first two parameters and a `nullptr` value in the last parameter.
4. For safety reasons, assign a `VK_NULL_HANDLE` value to the `presentation_surface` variable.

How it works...

The presentation surface's destruction is very similar to the destruction of other Vulkan resources presented so far. We make sure we don't provide a `VK_NULL_HANDLE` value and we call a `vkDestroySurfaceKHR()` function. After that, we assign a `VK_NULL_HANDLE` value to the `presentation_surface` variable:

```
if( presentation_surface ) {
  vkDestroySurfaceKHR( instance, presentation_surface, nullptr );
  presentation_surface = VK_NULL_HANDLE;
}
```

See also

- *Creating a presentation surface* recipe in this chapter

3
Command Buffers and Synchronization

In this chapter, we will cover the following recipes:

- Creating a command pool
- Allocating command buffers
- Beginning a command buffer recording operation
- Ending a command buffer recording operation
- Resetting a command buffer
- Resetting a command pool
- Creating a semaphore
- Creating a fence
- Waiting for fences
- Resetting fences
- Submitting command buffers to a queue
- Synchronizing two command buffers
- Checking if processing of a submitted command buffer has finished
- Waiting until all commands submitted to a queue are finished
- Waiting for all submitted commands to be finished
- Destroying a fence
- Destroying a semaphore
- Freeing command buffers
- Destroying a command pool

Introduction

Low level APIs like Vulkan give us much more control over the hardware than higher level APIs similar to OpenGL. This control is achieved not only through resources we can create, manage, and operate on, but especially through communication and interaction with the hardware. The control Vulkan gives us is fine grained, because we explicitly specify which commands are sent to hardware, how and when. For this purpose **command buffers** have been introduced; these are one of the most important objects Vulkan API exposes to developers. They allow us to record operations and submit them to hardware, where they are processed or executed. And what's more important, we can record them in multiple threads, unlike in high level APIs like OpenGL, where not only are commands recorded in a single thread, but they are recorded implicitly by the driver and sent to hardware without any control from the developers. Vulkan also allows us to reuse existing command buffers, saving additional processing time. This all gives us much more flexibility, but also many more responsibilities.

Because of this, we need to control not only what operations we submit, but also when. Especially when some operations depend on the results of other operations, we need to take extra care and properly synchronize submitted commands. For this purpose, semaphores and fences have been introduced.

In this chapter we will learn how to allocate, record and submit command buffers, how to create synchronization primitives and use them to control the execution of submitted operations, how to synchronize command buffers internally, directly on the GPU, and also how to synchronize applications with the work processed by the hardware.

Creating a command pool

Command pools are objects from which command buffers acquire their memory. Memory itself is allocated implicitly and dynamically, but without it command buffers wouldn't have any storage space to hold the recorded commands. That's why, before we can allocate command buffers, we first need to create a memory pool for them.

How to do it...

1. Create a variable of type `VkDevice` named `logical_device` and initialize it with a handle of a created logical device.

2. Take the index of one of the queue families requested for the logical device. Store this index in a variable of type `uint32_t` named `queue_family`.
3. Create a variable of type `VkCommandPoolCreateInfo` named `command_pool_create_info`. Use the following values for the members of this variable:
   - `VK_STRUCTURE_TYPE_COMMAND_POOL_CREATE_INFO` value for `sType`
   - `nullptr` value for `pNext`
   - Bit field indicating selected parameters of type `VkCommandPoolCreateFlags` for `flags`
   - `queue_family` variable for `queueFamilyIndex`
4. Create a variable of type `VkCommandPool` named `command_pool` in which command pool's handle will be stored.
5. Call `vkCreateCommandPool( logical_device, &command_pool_create_info, nullptr, &command_pool )` using the `logical_device` variable, a pointer to the `command_pool_create_info` variable, a `nullptr` value and a pointer to the `command_pool` variable.
6. Make sure the call returned a `VK_SUCCESS` value.

How it works...

Command pools are used mainly as a source of memory for the command buffers, but this is not the only reason for which they are created. They inform the driver about the intended usage of command buffers allocated from them, and whether we must reset or free them in bulk, or if we can do it separately per each command buffer. These parameters are specified through a `flags` member (represented as follows by a `parameters` variable) of the variables of type `VkCommandPoolCreateInfo`, like this:

```
VkCommandPoolCreateInfo command_pool_create_info = {
  VK_STRUCTURE_TYPE_COMMAND_POOL_CREATE_INFO,
  nullptr,
  parameters,
  queue_family
};
```

Command Buffers and Synchronization

When we specify `VK_COMMAND_POOL_CREATE_TRANSIENT_BIT` bit, it means that the command buffers allocated from a given pool will live for a very short amount of time, they will be submitted very few times, and will be immediately reset or freed. When we use `VK_COMMAND_POOL_CREATE_RESET_COMMAND_BUFFER_BIT`, we can reset command buffers individually. Without this flag, we can do this only in groups - on all command buffers allocated from a given pool. Recording a command buffer implicitly resets it so, without this flag, we can record a command buffer only once. If we want to record it again, we need to reset the whole pool from which it was allocated.

Command pools also control the queues to which command buffers can be submitted. This is achieved through a queue family index, which we must provide during pool creation (only families requested during logical device creation can be provided). Command buffers that are allocated from a given pool can be submitted *only* to queues from the specified family.

To create a pool, we need to prepare the following code:

```
VkResult result = vkCreateCommandPool( logical_device,
&command_pool_create_info, nullptr, &command_pool );
if( VK_SUCCESS != result ) {
  std::cout << "Could not create command pool." << std::endl;
  return false;
}
return true;
```

Command pools cannot be accessed at the same time from multiple threads (command buffers from the same pool cannot be recorded on multiple threads at the same time). That's why each application thread on which a command buffer will be recorded should use separate command pools.

Now, we are ready to allocate command buffers.

See also

The following recipes in this chapter:

- *Allocating command buffers*
- *Resetting a command buffer*
- *Resetting a command pool*
- *Destroying a command pool*

Allocating command buffers

Command buffers are used to store (record) commands that are later submitted to queues, where they are executed and processed by the hardware to give us results. When we have created a command pool, we can use it to allocate command buffers.

How to do it...

1. Take the handle of a created logical device and store it in a variable of type `VkDevice` named `logical_device`.
2. Take the handle of a command pool and use it to initialize a variable of type `VkCommandPool` named `command_pool`.
3. Create a variable of type `VkCommandBufferAllocateInfo` named `command_buffer_allocate_info` and use the following values for its members:
   - `VK_STRUCTURE_TYPE_COMMAND_BUFFER_ALLOCATE_INFO` value for `sType`
   - `nullptr` value for `pNext`
   - `command_pool` variable for `commandPool`
   - `VK_COMMAND_BUFFER_LEVEL_PRIMARY` value or a `VK_COMMAND_BUFFER_LEVEL_SECONDARY` value for `level`
   - The number of command buffers we want to allocate for `commandBufferCount`
4. Create a vector of type `std::vector<VkCommandBuffer>` named `command_buffers`. Resize the vector to be able to hold the number of command buffers we want to create.
5. Call `vkAllocateCommandBuffers( logical_device, &command_buffer_allocate_info, &command_buffers[0] )` for which provide a handle of the logical device, a pointer to the `command_buffer_allocate_info` variable and a pointer to the first element of the `command_buffers` vector.
6. Upon success, indicated by the `VK_SUCCESS` value returned by the call, handles of all created command buffers will be stored in the `command_buffers` vector.

How it works...

Command buffers are allocated from command pools. This allows us to control some of their properties in whole groups. First, we can submit command buffers only to queues from a family selected during command pool creation. Second, as command pools cannot be used concurrently, we should create separate command pools for each thread of our application in which we want to record commands, to minimize synchronization and improve performance.

But, command buffers also have their individual properties. Some of them are specified when we start recording operations, but we need to choose a very important parameter during command buffer allocation - whether we want to allocate **primary** or **secondary** command buffers:

- Primary command buffers can be directly submitted to queues. They can also execute (call) secondary command buffers.
- Secondary command buffers can only be executed from primary command buffers, and we are not allowed to submit them.

These parameters are specified through variables of type `VkCommandBufferAllocateInfo`, like this:

```
VkCommandBufferAllocateInfo command_buffer_allocate_info = {
  VK_STRUCTURE_TYPE_COMMAND_BUFFER_ALLOCATE_INFO,
  nullptr,
  command_pool,
  level,
  count
};
```

Next, to allocate command buffers, we need the following code:

```
command_buffers.resize( count );

VkResult result = vkAllocateCommandBuffers( logical_device,
&command_buffer_allocate_info, &command_buffers[0] );
if( VK_SUCCESS != result ) {
  std::cout << "Could not allocate command buffers." << std::endl;
  return false;
}
return true;
```

Now that we have allocated command buffers, we can use them in our application. To do this, we need to record operations in one or multiple command buffers and then submit them to a queue.

See also

The following recipes in this chapter:

- *Creating a command pool*
- *Beginning a command buffer recording operation*
- *Ending a command buffer recording operation*
- *Submitting command buffers to a queue*
- *Freeing command buffers*

Beginning a command buffer recording operation

When we want to perform operations using hardware, we need to record them and submit them to a queue. Commands are recorded into command buffers. So when we want to record them, we need to begin a recording operation of a selected command buffer, effectively setting it in the recording state.

How to do it...

1. Take the handle of a command buffer, in which commands should be recorded, and store it in a variable of type VkCommandBuffer named command_buffer. Make sure the command buffer is allocated from a pool with a VK_COMMAND_POOL_CREATE_RESET_COMMAND_BUFFER_BIT flag set, or that it is in the initial state (it was reset).
2. Create a variable of a bit field type VkCommandBufferUsageFlags named usage and set the following bits depending on which conditions are met:
    1. If the command buffer will be submitted only once and then reset or re-recorded, set the VK_COMMAND_BUFFER_USAGE_ONE_TIME_SUBMIT_BIT bit.

Command Buffers and Synchronization

2. If it is the secondary command buffer and is considered to be entirely inside a render pass, set the `VK_COMMAND_BUFFER_USAGE_RENDER_PASS_CONTINUE_BIT` bit.
3. If the command buffer needs to be resubmitted to a queue while it is still being executed on a device (before the previous submission of this command buffer has ended), set the `VK_COMMAND_BUFFER_USAGE_SIMULTANEOUS_USE_BIT` bit.

3. Create a variable of type `VkCommandBufferInheritanceInfo *` named `secondary_command_buffer_info`. If it is a primary command buffer, initialize the variable with a `nullptr` value. If it is a secondary command buffer, initialize the variable with an address of a variable of type `VkCommandBufferInheritanceInfo` whose members are initialized with the following values:
   - `VK_STRUCTURE_TYPE_COMMAND_BUFFER_INHERITANCE_INFO` value for `sType`.
   - `nullptr` value for `pNext`.
   - For `renderPass` use a handle of a compatible render pass, in which the command buffer will be executed; if the command buffer won't be executed inside a render pass, this value is ignored (refer to *Creating a render pass* recipe from `Chapter 6`, *Render Passes and Framebuffers*).
   - An index of a subpass within a render pass, in which the command buffer will be executed, for `subpass` (if the command buffer won't be executed inside a render pass, this value is ignored).
   - For `framebuffer`, use an optional handle of a framebuffer into which the command buffer will render, or a `VK_NULL_HANDLE` value if a framebuffer is not known or the command buffer won't be executed from within a render pass.
   - For `occlusionQueryEnable` member use a `VK_TRUE` value, if the command buffer can be executed while an occlusion query is active in the primary command buffer that executes this secondary command buffer. Otherwise, use a `VK_FALSE` value to indicate that the command buffer cannot be executed along with an enabled occlusion query.
   - A set of flags that can be used by an active occlusion query for `queryFlags`.
   - A set of statistics that can be counted by an active query for `pipelineStatistics`.

4. Create a variable of type `VkCommandBufferBeginInfo` named `command_buffer_begin_info`. Use the following values to initialize its members:
    - `VK_STRUCTURE_TYPE_COMMAND_BUFFER_BEGIN_INFO` value for `sType`
    - `nullptr` value for `pNext`
    - `usage` variable for `flags`
    - `secondary_command_buffer_info` variable for `pInheritanceInfo`
5. Call `vkBeginCommandBuffer( command_buffer, &command_buffer_begin_info )` and provide the handle of the command buffer in the first parameter, and a pointer to the `command_buffer_begin_info` variable in the second parameter.
6. Make sure the call was successful by checking if the value returned by the call was equal to `VK_SUCCESS`.

How it works...

Recording command buffers is the most important operation we can do in Vulkan. This is the only way to tell the hardware what it should do and how. When we start recording command buffers, their state is undefined. In general, command buffers don't inherit any state (as opposed to an OpenGL, in which the current state is maintained). So when we record operations, we also need to remember to set the state that is relevant to these operations. An example of such a state is a drawing command, which uses vertex attributes and indices. Before we record a drawing operation, we need to bind appropriate buffers with vertex data and a buffer with vertex indices.

Primary command buffers can call (execute) commands recorded in the secondary command buffers. Executed secondary command buffers don't inherit the state from the primary command buffers that executed them. What's more, the state of the primary command buffer is also undefined after the execution of the secondary command buffer is recorded (when we record a primary command buffer, and execute a secondary command buffer in it, and we want to continue recording the primary command buffer, we need to set its state once again). There is only one exception to the state inheritance rule - when the primary command buffer is inside a render pass and we execute a secondary command buffer from it, the primary command buffer's render pass and subpass states are preserved.

Before we can begin a recording operation, we need to prepare a variable of type `VkCommandBufferBeginInfo`, through which we provide recording parameters:

```
VkCommandBufferBeginInfo command_buffer_begin_info = {
  VK_STRUCTURE_TYPE_COMMAND_BUFFER_BEGIN_INFO,
  nullptr,
  usage,
  secondary_command_buffer_info
};
```

 For performance reasons, we should avoid recording command buffers with a `VK_COMMAND_BUFFER_USAGE_SIMULTANEOUS_USE_BIT` flag.

Next, we can begin a recording operation:

```
VkResult result = vkBeginCommandBuffer( command_buffer,
&command_buffer_begin_info );
if( VK_SUCCESS != result ) {
  std::cout << "Could not begin command buffer recording operation." << std::endl;
  return false;
}
return true;
```

From now on, we can record selected operations into the command buffer. But how do we know which commands can be recorded into command buffers? The names of all such functions begin with a `vkCmd` prefix and their first parameter is always a command buffer (a variable of type `VkCommandBuffer`). But, we need to remember that not all commands can be recorded into both primary and secondary command buffers.

See also

The following recipes in this chapter:

- *Allocating command buffers*
- *Ending a command buffer recording operation*
- *Resetting a command buffer*
- *Resetting a command pool*
- *Submitting command buffers to a queue*

Ending a command buffer recording operation

When we don't want to record any more commands in a command buffer, we need to stop recording it.

How to do it...

1. Take the handle of a command buffer that is in a recording state (for which a recording operation was started). Store the handle in a variable of type `VkCommandBuffer` named `command_buffer`.
2. Call `vkEndCommandBuffer( command_buffer )` and provide the `command_buffer` variable.
3. Make sure the recording operation was successful by checking whether the call returned a `VK_SUCCESS` value.

How it works...

Commands are recorded into the command buffer between the `vkBeginCommandBuffer()` and `vkEndCommandBuffer()` function calls. We can't submit a command buffer until we stop recording it. In other words, when we finish recording a command buffer, it is said to be in the executable state and can be submitted.

For the recording operation to be as fast as possible and to have as small impact on the performance as possible, recorded commands don't report any errors. If any problems occur, they are reported by the `vkEndCommandBuffer()` function.

So when we stop recording a command buffer, we should make sure that the recording was successful. We can do that like this:

```
VkResult result = vkEndCommandBuffer( command_buffer );
if( VK_SUCCESS != result ) {
  std::cout << "Error occurred during command buffer recording." << std::endl;
  return false;
}
return true;
```

If there were errors during the recording operation (the value returned by the `vkEndCommandBuffer()` function is not equal to `VK_SUCCESS`), we can't submit such a command buffer and we need to reset it.

See also

The following recipes in this chapter:

- *Beginning a command buffer recording operation*
- *Submitting command buffers to a queue*
- *Resetting a command buffer*

Resetting a command buffer

When a command buffer was previously recorded, or if there were errors during the recording operation, the command buffer must be reset before it can be rerecorded once again. We can do this implicitly, by beginning another record operation. But, we can also do it explicitly.

How to do it...

1. Take the handle of a command buffer allocated from a pool that was created with a `VK_COMMAND_POOL_CREATE_RESET_COMMAND_BUFFER_BIT` flag. Store the handle in a variable of type `VkCommandBuffer` named `command_buffer`.
2. Create a variable of type `VkCommandBufferResetFlags` named `release_resources`. In the variable, store a value of `VK_COMMAND_BUFFER_RESET_RELEASE_RESOURCES_BIT` if you want to release memory allocated by the buffer and give it back to the pool. Otherwise, store a `0` value in the variable.
3. Call `vkResetCommandBuffer( command_buffer, release_resources )` and provide the handle of the command buffer in the first parameter, and the `release_resources` variable in the second parameter.
4. Make sure the call was successful by checking if the returned value is equal to `VK_SUCCESS`.

How it works...

Command buffers can be reset in bulk, by resetting a whole command pool, or individually. Separate resets can be performed only if a pool, from which the command buffers were allocated, was created with a `VK_COMMAND_POOL_CREATE_RESET_COMMAND_BUFFER_BIT` flag.

Resetting a command buffer is performed implicitly, when we start recording it, or explicitly by calling a `vkResetCommandBuffer()` function. Explicit reset gives us control over the memory allocated by the command buffer from its pool. During explicit reset, we can decide whether we want to return the memory to a pool, or if the command buffer should keep it and reuse it during the next command recording.

Individual command buffers are reset explicitly like this:

```
VkResult result = vkResetCommandBuffer( command_buffer, release_resources ?
VK_COMMAND_BUFFER_RESET_RELEASE_RESOURCES_BIT : 0 );
if( VK_SUCCESS != result ) {
  std::cout << "Error occurred during command buffer reset." << std::endl;
  return false;
}
return true;
```

See also

The following recipes in this chapter:

- *Creating a command pool*
- *Beginning a command buffer recording operation*
- *Resetting a command pool*

Resetting a command pool

When we don't want to reset command buffers individually, or if we created a pool without a `VK_COMMAND_POOL_CREATE_RESET_COMMAND_BUFFER_BIT` flag, we can reset all command buffers allocated from a given pool at once.

How to do it...

1. Take the handle of a logical device and store it in a variable of type `VkDevice` named `logical_device`.
2. Take the handle of a created command pool. Use it to initialize a variable of type `VkCommandPool` named `command_pool`.
3. Create a variable of type `VkCommandPoolResetFlags` named `release_resources` and initialize it with a value of `VK_COMMAND_POOL_RESET_RELEASE_RESOURCES_BIT`, if memory reserved by all command buffers allocated from the command pool should be released and returned to the pool, or with a `0` value otherwise.
4. Call `vkResetCommandPool( logical_device, command_pool, release_resources )` and provide the `logical_device`, `command_pool` and `release_resources` variables.
5. Make sure the call returned a `VK_SUCCESS` value, which indicates it was successful.

How it works...

Resetting a command pool causes all command buffers allocated from it to return to their initial state, as if they were never recorded. This is similar to resetting all command buffers separately, but is faster and we don't have to create a command pool with a `VK_COMMAND_POOL_CREATE_RESET_COMMAND_BUFFER_BIT` flag specified.

When command buffers are recorded, they take their memory from the pool. This is done automatically, without our control. When we reset the command pool, we can choose if command buffers should keep their memory for later use, or if it should be returned to the pool.

To reset all command buffers allocated from the specified pool at once, we need the following code:

```
VkResult result = vkResetCommandPool( logical_device, command_pool,
release_resources ? VK_COMMAND_POOL_RESET_RELEASE_RESOURCES_BIT : 0 );
if( VK_SUCCESS != result ) {
  std::cout << "Error occurred during command pool reset." << std::endl;
  return false;
}
return true;
```

See also

The following recipes in this chapter:

- *Creating a command pool*
- *Allocating command buffers*
- *Resetting a command buffer*

Creating a semaphore

Before we can submit commands and utilize the device's processing power, we need to know how to synchronize operations. Semaphores are one of the primitives used for synchronization. They allow us to coordinate operations submitted to queues, not only within one queue, but also between different queues in one logical device.

Semaphores are used when we submit commands to queues. So before we can use them during the submission of command buffers, we need to create them.

How to do it...

1. Take the handle of a created logical device. Store the handle in a variable of type `VkDevice` named `logical_device`.
2. Create a variable of type `VkSemaphoreCreateInfo` named `semaphore_create_info`. Use the following values to initialize its members:
   - VK_STRUCTURE_TYPE_SEMAPHORE_CREATE_INFO value for `sType`
   - `nullptr` value for `pNext`
   - 0 value for `flags`
3. Create a variable of type `VkSemaphore` named `semaphore`. In this variable, a handle of a created semaphore will be stored.
4. Make the following function call: `vkCreateSemaphore( logical_device, &semaphore_create_info, nullptr, &semaphore )`. For this call use the `logical_device` variable, a pointer to the `semaphore_create_info` variable, a `nullptr` value and a pointer to the `semaphore` variable.
5. Make sure the semaphore creation was successful by checking if the returned value was equal to `VK_SUCCESS`.

How it works...

Semaphores, as synchronization primitives, have only two different states: signaled or un-signaled. Semaphores are used during command buffer submissions. When we provide them to a list of semaphores to be signaled, they change their state to signaled as soon as all work submitted within a given batch is finished. In a similar way, when we submit commands to queues, we can specify that submitted commands should wait until all semaphores from a specified list become signaled. This way, we can coordinate work submitted to queues and postpone processing of commands that depend on the results of other commands.

 When semaphores are signaled and all commands waiting for them are resumed, semaphores are automatically reset (they change their state to un-signaled) and can be reused.

Semaphores are also used when we acquire images from a swapchain. In this case, such semaphores must be used when we submit commands that reference acquired images. These commands should wait until swapchain images are no longer used by the presentation engine, which is indicated by the semaphore signal operation. This is shown in the following screenshot:

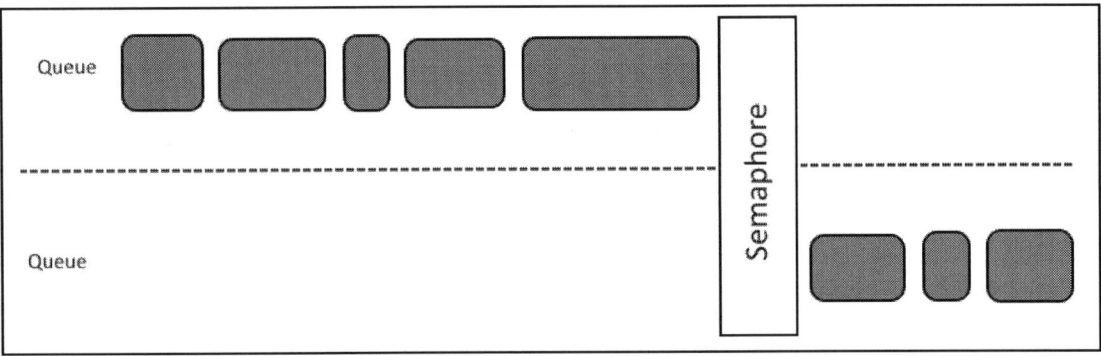

Semaphores are created with a `vkCreateSemaphore()` function call. Parameters needed during the creation process are provided through a variable of type `VkSemaphoreCreateInfo`, like this:

```
VkSemaphoreCreateInfo semaphore_create_info = {
  VK_STRUCTURE_TYPE_SEMAPHORE_CREATE_INFO,
  nullptr,
  0
};
```

To create a semaphore, we need to prepare a code similar to this one:

```
VkResult result = vkCreateSemaphore( logical_device,
&semaphore_create_info, nullptr, &semaphore );
if( VK_SUCCESS != result ) {
  std::cout << "Could not create a semaphore." << std::endl;
  return false;
}
return true;
```

Semaphores can be used only to synchronize work submitted to queues, as they coordinate graphics hardware internally. The application doesn't have access to the state of the semaphores. If the application should be synchronized with the submitted commands, fences need to be used.

See also

In Chapter 2, *Image Presentation*, see the following recipes:

- *Acquiring a swapchain image*
- *Presenting an image*

The following recipes in this chapter:

- *Creating a fence*
- *Submitting command buffers to a queue*
- *Synchronizing two command buffers*
- *Destroying a semaphore*

Creating a fence

Fences, opposite to semaphores, are used to synchronize an application with commands submitted to the graphics hardware. They inform the application when the processing of a submitted work has been finished. But before we can use fences, we need to create them.

Command Buffers and Synchronization

How to do it...

1. Take the created logical device and use its handle to initialize a variable of type `VkDevice` named `logical_device`.
2. Create a variable of type `VkFenceCreateInfo` named `fence_create_info`. Use the following values to initialize its members:
    - `VK_STRUCTURE_TYPE_FENCE_CREATE_INFO` value for `sType`
    - `nullptr` value for `pNext`
    - For `flags` use a `0` value if a created fence should be un-signaled, or a `VK_FENCE_CREATE_SIGNALED_BIT` value if a created fence should be signaled
3. Create a variable of type `VkFence` named `fence` that will hold the handle of a created fence.
4. Call `vkCreateFence( logical_device, &fence_create_info, nullptr, &fence )` and provide the `logical_device` variable, a pointer to the `fence_create_info` variable, a `nullptr` value and a pointer to the `fence` variable.
5. Make sure the call was successful by comparing the returned value with a `VK_SUCCESS` enum.

How it works...

Fences, similarly to other synchronization primitives, have only two states: signaled and un-signaled. They can be created in either of these two states, but they are reset by the application--this changes their state from signaled to un-signaled.

To signal a fence, we need to provide it during command buffer submission. Such a fence, similarly to semaphores, will become signaled as soon as all work submitted along with the fence is finished. But, fences can't be used to synchronize command buffers. Their state can be queried by the application and the application can wait on fences until they become signaled.

 Semaphores are used to synchronize submitted command buffers with each other. Fences are used to synchronize an application with submitted commands.

[142]

Chapter 3

To create a fence, we need to prepare a variable of type `VkFenceCreateInfo`, in which we must choose whether we want the created fence to be already in a signaled state or if it should be un-signaled:

```
VkFenceCreateInfo fence_create_info = {
  VK_STRUCTURE_TYPE_FENCE_CREATE_INFO,
  nullptr,
  signaled ? VK_FENCE_CREATE_SIGNALED_BIT : 0
};
```

Next, this structure is provided to the `vkCreateFence()` function, which creates a fence using specified parameters:

```
VkResult result = vkCreateFence( logical_device, &fence_create_info,
nullptr, &fence );
if( VK_SUCCESS != result ) {
  std::cout << "Could not create a fence." << std::endl;
  return false;
}
return true;
```

See also

The following recipes in this chapter:

- *Creating a semaphore*
- *Waiting on fences*
- *Resetting fences*
- *Submitting command buffers to a queue*
- *Checking if processing of a submitted command buffer has finished*
- *Destroying a fence*

Waiting for fences

When we want to know when the processing of submitted commands is finished, we need to use a fence and provide it during command buffer submission. Then, the application can check the fence's state and wait until it becomes signaled.

How to do it...

1. Take the created logical device and use its handle to initialize a variable of type `VkDevice` named `logical_device`.
2. Create a list of fences on which the application should wait. Store the handles of all fences in a variable of type `std::vector<VkFence>` named `fences`.
3. Create a variable of type `VkBool32` named `wait_for_all`. Initialize it with a value of `VK_TRUE`, if the application should wait until all specified fences become signaled. If the application should wait until any of the fences becomes signaled (at least one of them), then initialize the variable with a `VK_FALSE` value.
4. Create a variable of type `uint64_t` named `timeout`. Initialize the variable with a value indicating how much time (in nanoseconds) the application should spend waiting.
5. Call `vkWaitForFences( logical_device, static_cast<uint32_t>(fences.size()), &fences[0], wait_for_all, timeout )`. Provide a handle of the logical device, a number of elements in the `fences` vector, a pointer to the first element of the `fences` variable, the `wait_for_all` and the `timeout` variables.
6. Check the value returned by the call. If it was equal to `VK_SUCCESS` it means that the condition was satisfied--one or all fences (depending on the value of the `wait_for_all` variable) became signaled within the specified time. If the condition is not met, `VK_TIMEOUT` will be returned.

How it works...

The `vkWaitForFences()` function blocks the application for a specified period of time or until the provided fences becomes signaled. This way, we can synchronize our application with work submitted to the device's queues. This is also the way for us to know when the processing of submitted commands is finished.

During the call we can provide multiple fences, not just one. We can also wait until all fences become signaled, or just any one of them. If the condition is not met within the specified period of time, the function returns a `VK_TIMEOUT` value. Otherwise, it returns `VK_SUCCESS`.

We can also check a fence's state by simply providing its handle to the function and specifying a timeout value of 0. This way, the vkWaitForFences() function won't block and will immediately return the value indicating the current state of the provided fence - a VK_TIMEOUT value if the fence was un-signaled (though no real wait was performed) or a VK_SUCCESS value if the fence was already signaled.

The code that causes the application to wait may look like this:

```
if( fences.size() > 0 ) {
   VkResult result = vkWaitForFences( logical_device,
   static_cast<uint32_t>(fences.size()), &fences[0], wait_for_all, timeout );
   if( VK_SUCCESS != result ) {
      std::cout << "Waiting on fence failed." << std::endl;
      return false;
   }
   return true;
}
return false;
```

See also

The following recipes in this chapter:

- *Creating a fence*
- *Resetting fences*
- *Submitting command buffers to a queue*
- *Checking if processing of a submitted command buffer has finished*

Resetting fences

Semaphores are automatically reset. But when a fence becomes signaled, it is the application's responsibility to reset the fence back to the un-signaled state.

How to do it...

1. Store the handle of a created logical device in a variable of type VkDevice named logical_device.

Command Buffers and Synchronization

2. Create a vector variable named `fences`. It should contain elements of type `VkFence`. In the variable, store the handles of all fences that should be reset.
3. Call `vkResetFences( logical_device, static_cast<uint32_t>(fences.size()), &fences[0] )` and provide the `logical_device` variable, the number of elements in the `fences` vector and a pointer to the first element of the `fences` vector.
4. Make sure the function succeeded by checking if the value returned by the call was equal to `VK_SUCCESS`.

How it works...

When we want to know when submitted commands are finished, we use a fence. But we can't provide a fence that was already signaled. We must first reset it, which means that we change its state from signaled to un-signaled. Fences are reset explicitly by the application, not automatically like semaphores. Resetting fences is done like this:

```
if( fences.size() > 0 ) {
  VkResult result = vkResetFences( logical_device,
static_cast<uint32_t>(fences.size()), &fences[0] );
  if( VK_SUCCESS != result ) {
    std::cout << "Error occurred when tried to reset fences." << std::endl;
    return false;
  }
  return VK_SUCCESS == result;
}
return false;
```

See also

The following recipes in this chapter:

- *Creating a fence*
- *Waiting on fences*
- *Submitting command buffers to a queue*
- *Checking if processing of a submitted command buffer has finished*

Submitting command buffers to a queue

We have recorded command buffers and we want to harness the graphics hardware's power to process the prepared operations. What to do next? We need to submit prepared work to a selected queue.

Getting ready

In this recipe we will use variables of a custom `WaitSemaphoreInfo` type. It is defined as follows:

```
struct WaitSemaphoreInfo {
   VkSemaphore          Semaphore;
   VkPipelineStageFlags WaitingStage;
};
```

Through it, we provide a handle of a semaphore on which hardware should wait before processing the given `command buffer`, and we also specify in which pipeline stages the wait should occur.

How to do it...

1. Take the handle of a queue to which work should be submitted. Use the handle to initialize a variable of type `VkQueue` named `queue`.
2. Create a variable of type `std::vector<VkSemaphore>` named `wait_semaphore_handles`. If submitted commands should wait for other commands to end, in the variable store the handles of all semaphores for which a given queue should wait before processing the submitted command buffers.
3. Create a variable of type `std::vector<VkPipelineStageFlags>` named `wait_semaphore_stages`. If submitted commands should wait for other commands to end, initialize the vector with pipeline stages at which the queue should wait for a corresponding semaphore from the `wait_semaphore_handles` variable to become signaled.
4. Prepare a variable of type `std::vector<VkCommandBuffer>` named `command_buffers`. Store the handles of all recorded command buffers that should be submitted to the selected queue. Make sure that none of these command buffers is currently processed by the device, or were recorded with a `VK_COMMAND_BUFFER_USAGE_SIMULTANEOUS_USE_BIT` flag.

Command Buffers and Synchronization

5. Create a variable of type `std::vector<VkSemaphore>` named `signal_semaphores`. In this vector, store the handles of all semaphores that should be signaled when the processing of all command buffers, submitted in the `command_buffers` variable, is finished.
6. Create a variable of type `VkFence` named `fence`. If a fence should be signaled when the processing of all command buffers submitted in the `command_buffers` variable is finished, store the handle of this fence in the `fence` variable. Otherwise, initialize this variable with a `VK_NULL_HANDLE` value.
7. Create a variable of type `VkSubmitInfo` named `submit_info`. Use the following values to initialize its members:
    - `VK_STRUCTURE_TYPE_SUBMIT_INFO` value for `sType`
    - `nullptr` value for `pNext`
    - Number of elements in the `wait_semaphore_handles` vector for `waitSemaphoreCount`
    - Pointer to the first element of the `wait_semaphore_handles` vector or a `nullptr` value, if the vector is empty, for `pWaitSemaphores`
    - Pointer to the first element of the `wait_semaphore_stages` vector or a `nullptr` value, if the vector is empty, for `pWaitDstStageMask`
    - Number of submitted command buffers (number of elements in the `command_buffers` vector) for `commandBufferCount`
    - Pointer to the first element of the `command_buffers` vector or a `nullptr` value, if the vector is empty, for `pCommandBuffers`
    - Number of elements in the `signal_semaphores` vector for `signalSemaphoreCount`
    - Pointer to the first element of the `signal_semaphores` vector or a `nullptr` value, if the vector is empty, for `pSignalSemaphores`
8. Call `vkQueueSubmit( queue, 1, &submit_info, fence )` and provide the handle of the queue to which work should be submitted, a 1 value, a pointer to the `submit_info` variable, and the `fence` variable.
9. Make sure the call was successful by checking whether it returned a `VK_SUCCESS` value.

How it works...

When we submit command buffers to the device's queue, they will be executed as soon as the processing of earlier commands submitted to the same queue is finished. From the application's perspective, we don't know when the commands are going to be executed. It may start immediately or after a while.

When we want to postpone the processing of submitted commands, we need to synchronize them by providing a list of semaphores on which a given queue should wait before the submitted command buffers are executed.

When we submit command buffers and provide a list of semaphores, each semaphore is associated with a pipeline stage. Commands are executed until they reach a specified pipeline stage, where they are paused and wait for the semaphore to become signaled.

During the submission, semaphores and pipeline stages are in separate arrays. So, we need to split the vector with elements of a custom type `WaitSemaphoreInfo` into two separate vectors:

```
std::vector<VkSemaphore>         wait_semaphore_handles;
std::vector<VkPipelineStageFlags> wait_semaphore_stages;

for( auto & wait_semaphore_info : wait_semaphore_infos ) {
  wait_semaphore_handles.emplace_back( wait_semaphore_info.Semaphore );
  wait_semaphore_stages.emplace_back( wait_semaphore_info.WaitingStage );
}
```

Now, we are ready for the usual submission. For the submission, semaphores on which command buffers should wait, pipeline stages at which the wait should be performed, command buffers and another list of semaphores that should be signaled, are all specified through a variable of type `VkSubmitInfo`:

```
VkSubmitInfo submit_info = {
  VK_STRUCTURE_TYPE_SUBMIT_INFO,
  nullptr,
  static_cast<uint32_t>(wait_semaphore_infos.size()),
  wait_semaphore_handles.size() > 0 ? &wait_semaphore_handles[0] : nullptr,
  wait_semaphore_stages.size() > 0 ? &wait_semaphore_stages[0] : nullptr,
  static_cast<uint32_t>(command_buffers.size()),
  command_buffers.size() > 0 ? &command_buffers[0] : nullptr,
  static_cast<uint32_t>(signal_semaphores.size()),
  signal_semaphores.size() > 0 ? &signal_semaphores[0] : nullptr
};
```

This batch of data is then submitted like this:

```
VkResult result = vkQueueSubmit( queue, 1, &submit_info, fence );
if( VK_SUCCESS != result ) {
  std::cout << "Error occurred during command buffer submission." << std::endl;
  return false;
}
return true;
```

When we submit command buffers, the device will execute the recorded commands and produce the desired results, as an example it will draw a 3D scene on screen.

Here we submit just one batch of command buffers, but it is possible to submit multiple batches.

For performance reasons, we should submit as many batches as possible in as few function calls as possible.

We shouldn't submit command buffers if they were already submitted and their execution hasn't ended yet. We can do this only when command buffers were recorded with a `VK_COMMAND_BUFFER_USAGE_SIMULTANEOUS_USE_BIT` flag, but we should avoid using this flag for performance reasons.

See also

The following recipes in this chapter:

- *Beginning a command buffer recording operation*
- *Ending a command buffer recording operation*
- *Creating a semaphore*
- *Creating a fence*

Synchronizing two command buffers

We know how to prepare work and submit it to queues. We also know how to create semaphores. In this sample recipe, we will see how to use semaphores to synchronize two command buffers. More specifically, we will learn how to postpone the processing of a command buffer until the processing of another command buffer is finished.

Getting ready

In this recipe we will use the `WaitSemaphoreInfo` structure introduced in the *Submitting command buffers to a queue* recipe. For reference, here is its definition:

```
struct WaitSemaphoreInfo {
  VkSemaphore          Semaphore;
  VkPipelineStageFlags WaitingStage;
};
```

How to do it...

1. Take the handle of a queue to which the first batch of command buffers will be submitted. Store this handle in a variable of type `VkQueue` named `first_queue`.
2. Create semaphores that should be signaled when the processing of the first batch of command buffers is finished (refer to *Creating a semaphore* recipe). Store the semaphores in a variable of type `std::vector<WaitSemaphoreInfo>` named `synchronizing_semaphores`. Prepare a list of stages at which command buffers from the second batch should wait for each semaphore. Include these stages in the `synchronizing_semaphores` vector.
3. Prepare the first batch of command buffers and submit them to the queue represented by the `first_queue` variable. Include semaphores from the `synchronizing_semaphores` vector on a list of semaphores to signal (see *Submitting command buffers to a queue* recipe).
4. Take the handle of a queue, to which the second batch of command buffers will be submitted. Store this handle in a variable of type `VkQueue` named `second_queue`.
5. Prepare the second batch of command buffers and submit them to the queue, represented by the `second_queue` variable. Include semaphores and stages from the `synchronizing_semaphores` vector on a list of semaphores and stages to wait for (see *Submitting command buffers to a queue* recipe).

How it works...

In this recipe we submit two batches of command buffers. When the first batch is processed by the hardware and finished, it signals all the semaphores included in the list of semaphores to be signaled. We take only the handles of semaphores, because pipeline stages are not required during the process of signaling the semaphores:

```
std::vector<VkSemaphore> first_signal_semaphores;
for( auto & semaphore_info : synchronizing_semaphores ) {
  first_signal_semaphores.emplace_back( semaphore_info.Semaphore );
}
if( !SubmitCommandBuffersToQueue( first_queue, first_wait_semaphore_infos,
first_command_buffers, first_signal_semaphores, VK_NULL_HANDLE ) ) {
  return false;
}
```

Next, we take these same semaphores and use them when we submit the second batch of command buffers. This time, we use both handles and pipeline stages. The second batch will wait for all the provided semaphores at the specified pipeline stages. This means that some parts of the submitted command buffers may start being processed, but when they reach the provided stages processing is paused, as seen in the following diagram:

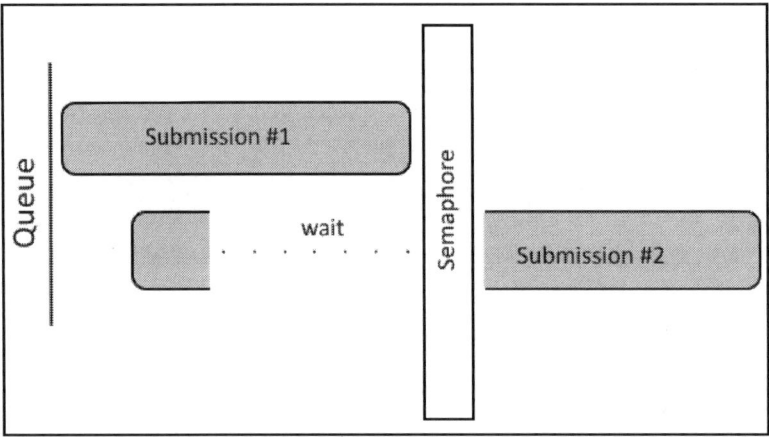

```
if( !SubmitCommandBuffersToQueue( second_queue, synchronizing_semaphores,
second_command_buffers, second_signal_semaphores, second_fence ) ) {
  return false;
}
return true;
```

This shows how to synchronize the work of multiple command buffers submitted to different queues from the same logical device. The processing of the command buffers from the second submission will be postponed until all commands from the first batch are finished.

See also

The following recipes in this chapter:

- *Creating a semaphore*
- *Submitting command buffers to a queue*

Checking if processing of a submitted command buffer has finished

When we use semaphores, the application is not involved in the process of synchronizing the command buffers. It doesn't know when the processing of submitted commands has finished and when other commands start being processed. It all takes place "behind the stage", and is transparent to the application.

But, when we want to know when the processing of a given command buffer has ended, we need to use fences. This way, we can check when a submitted command buffer is fully processed by the device.

How to do it...

1. Create an un-signaled fence and store it in a variable of type `VkFence` named `fence`.
2. Prepare a batch of command buffers, semaphores to wait on submission and semaphores to signal after the submission is fully processed. Use the prepared data when submitting command buffers to the selected queue. Use the `fence` variable during the submission (refer to *Submitting command buffers to a queue* recipe).

3. Wait on the created fence object by providing a handle of a logical device, from which all the utilized resources were created, the `fence` variable, `VK_FALSE` value for the parameter defining whether to wait on all provided fences, and a selected value for timeout (refer to the *Waiting for fences* recipe).
4. When the wait is finished and the `VK_SUCCESS` value was returned, it means that the processing of all command buffers submitted to the queue within the batch in which the `fence` variable was used, has been successfully finished.

How it works...

Synchronizing the application with submitted command buffers is done in two steps. First we create a fence, prepare the command buffers and submit them to a queue. We need to remember to provide the created fence within the same submission:

```
if( !SubmitCommandBuffersToQueue( queue, wait_semaphore_infos,
command_buffers, signal_semaphores, fence ) ) {
  return false;
}
```

Next, we just need to wait in our application, until the fence becomes signaled.

```
return WaitForFences( logical_device, { fence }, VK_FALSE, timeout );
```

This way, we are sure that the submitted command buffer has been successfully processed by the device.

But typical rendering scenarios should not cause our application to be fully paused, as this is just a waste of time. We should check if a fence becomes signaled. If it does not, we should spend the remaining time on other tasks, for example on improving the artificial intelligence or calculating physics more accurately, and check periodically the state of the fence. When the fence becomes signaled, we then perform the tasks that depended on the submitted commands.

Fences can also be used when we want to reuse command buffers. Before we can re-record them, we must be sure they are no longer executed by the device. We should have a number of command buffers recorded and submitted one after another. Only then, when we use all of them, do we start waiting on fences (each submitted batch should have an associated fence). The more separate batches of command buffers we have, the less time we spend on waiting for fences (refer to *Increasing the performance through increasing the number of separately rendered frames* recipe from `Chapter 9`, *Command Recording and Drawing*).

See also

The following recipes in this chapter:

- *Creating a fence*
- *Waiting for fences*
- *Resetting fences*
- *Submitting command buffers to a queue*

Waiting until all commands submitted to a queue are finished

When we want to synchronize the application with work submitted to a selected queue, we don't always have to use fences. It is possible for the application to wait until all tasks submitted to a selected queue are finished.

How to do it...

1. Take the handle of the queue into which tasks were submitted. Store it in a variable of type `VkQueue` named `queue`.
2. Call `vkQueueWaitIdle( queue )` and provide the `queue` variable.
3. We can make sure that no errors occurred by checking if the value returned by the call is equal to a `VK_SUCCESS`.

How it works...

The `vkQueueWaitIdle()` function pauses the application until all work (processing of all command buffers) submitted to the given queue is finished. This way, we don't need to create fences.

But such synchronization should be performed only on very rare occasions. Graphics hardware (GPU) is usually much faster than the general processor (CPU), and may require work to be constantly submitted for the application to fully utilize its performance.

Command Buffers and Synchronization

 Performing a wait on the application side may introduce stalls in the graphics hardware's pipeline, which causes the device to be inefficiently utilized.

To wait for the queue until it finishes all submitted work, we need to prepare the following code:

```
VkResult result = vkQueueWaitIdle( queue );
if( VK_SUCCESS != result ) {
  std::cout << "Waiting for all operations submitted to queue failed." << std::endl;
  return false;
}
return true;
```

See also

The following recipes in this chapter:

- *Waiting on fences*
- *Submitting command buffers to a queue*
- *Waiting for all commands to be finished*

Waiting for all submitted commands to be finished

Sometimes we would like to wait until all the work submitted to all the logical devices' queues is finished. This type of wait is typically done before we close our application and we want to destroy all created or allocated resources.

How to do it...

1. Take the handle of a created logical device and store it in a variable of type `VkDevice` named `logical_device`.

2. Make the following call: `vkDeviceWaitIdle( logical_device )`, for which provide the handle of the logical device.
3. You can check if there were no errors by comparing the returned value with a `VK_SUCCESS`.

How it works...

The `vkDeviceWaitIdle()` function causes our application to wait until a logical device is no longer busy. This is similar to waiting on all queues requested for a given device--until commands, which were submitted to all queues, are finished.

The above function is usually called just before the exit from our application. When we want to destroy resources, we must make sure they are no longer used by the logical device. This function guarantees we can safely perform such destruction.

Waiting for all commands submitted to the device is performed like this:

```
VkResult result = vkDeviceWaitIdle( logical_device );
if( VK_SUCCESS != result ) {
  std::cout << "Waiting on a device failed." << std::endl;
  return false;
}
return true;
```

See also

The following recipes in this chapter:

- *Waiting on fences*
- *Waiting until all commands submitted to a queue are finished*

Destroying a fence

Fences can be reused multiple times. But when we don't need them anymore, typically just before we close our application, we should destroy them.

How to do it...

1. Take the handle of a logical device and store it in a variable of type `VkDevice` named `logical_device`.
2. Take the handle of a fence that should be destroyed. Use the handle to initialize a variable of type `VkFence` named `fence`.
3. Call `vkDestroyFence( logical_device, fence, nullptr )` and provide the logical device's handle, the `fence` variable and a `nullptr` value.
4. For safety reasons, assign the `VK_NULL_HANDLE` value to the `fence` variable.

How it works...

Fences are destroyed using the `vkDestroyFence()` function, like this:

```
if( VK_NULL_HANDLE != fence ) {
  vkDestroyFence( logical_device, fence, nullptr );
  fence = VK_NULL_HANDLE;
}
```

We don't need to check if a value of the `fence` variable is not equal to the `VK_NULL_HANDLE` value because destruction of a null handle will be ignored by the driver. But, we do this to skip an unnecessary function call.

But, we can't destroy an invalid object - an object that wasn't created on a given logical device or that has already been destroyed. That's why we assign a `VK_NULL_HANDLE` value to the variable with the fence's handle.

See also

- In this chapter, the recipe: *Creating a fence*.

Destroying a semaphore

Semaphores can be reused multiple times, so usually we don't need to delete them when the application is executing. But when we don't need a semaphore any more, and if we are sure it is not being used by the device (there are both no pending waits, and no pending signal operations), we can destroy it.

How to do it...

1. Take the handle of a logical device. Store this handle in a variable of type `VkDevice` named `logical_device`.
2. Initialize a variable of type `VkSemaphore` named `semaphore` with a handle of the semaphore that should be destroyed. Make sure it is not referenced by any submissions.
3. Make the following call: `vkDestroySemaphore( logical_device, semaphore, nullptr )`, for which provide the logical device's handle, the handle of the semaphore and a `nullptr` value.
4. For safety reasons, assign a `VK_NULL_HANDLE` value to the `semaphore` variable.

How it works...

Deleting a semaphore is quite easy:

```
if( VK_NULL_HANDLE != semaphore ) {
  vkDestroySemaphore( logical_device, semaphore, nullptr );
  semaphore = VK_NULL_HANDLE;
}
```

Before we can destroy a semaphore, we must make sure it is not referenced any more by any of the performed queue submissions.

If we performed a submission and provided a semaphore in the list of semaphores to be signaled, or in the list of the semaphores for which a given submission should wait, we must make sure the submitted commands have finished. For this purpose we need to use a fence on which the application should wait, or one of the functions waiting for all the operations to be submitted to a given queue or the whole device to be finished (refer to the *Waiting for fences*, *Waiting until all commands submitted to a queue are finished* and *Waiting for all submitted commands to be finished* recipes).

See also

The following recipes in this chapter:

- *Creating a semaphore*
- *Waiting for fences*
- *Waiting until all commands submitted to a queue are finished*
- *Waiting for all submitted commands to be finished*

Freeing command buffers

When command buffers are no longer necessary and when they are not pending for execution on a device, they can be freed.

How to do it...

1. Take the handle of a logical device and use it to initialize a variable of type `VkDevice` named `logical_device`.
2. Take the handle of a command pool created from the logical device. Store this handle in a variable of type `VkCommandPool` named `command_pool`.
3. Create a vector variable with elements of type `VkCommandBuffer`, name the variable `command_buffers`. Resize the vector to be able to hold all command buffers that should be freed. Initialize the vector's elements with the handles of all the command buffers that should be freed.
4. Call `vkFreeCommandBuffers( logical_device, command_pool, static_cast<uint32_t>(command_buffers.size()), &command_buffers[0] )`. During the call, provide the handles of the logical device and the command pool, provide the number of elements in the `command_buffers` vector (the number of command buffers to be freed) and a pointer to the first element of the `command_buffers` vector.
5. For safety reasons, clear the `command_buffers` vector.

How it works...

Command buffers can be freed in groups, but during a single `vkFreeCommandBuffers()` function call we can only free command buffers from the same command pool. We can free any number of command buffers at once:

```
if( command_buffers.size() > 0 ) {
  vkFreeCommandBuffers( logical_device, command_pool,
static_cast<uint32_t>(command_buffers.size()), &command_buffers[0] );
  command_buffers.clear();
}
```

> Before we can free command buffers, we must make sure they are not referenced by the logical device, and that all submissions in which command buffers were provided have already finished.

Command buffers allocated from a given pool are implicitly freed when we destroy a command pool. So when we want to destroy a pool, we don't need to separately free all command buffers allocated from it.

See also

The following recipes in this chapter:

- *Creating a command pool*
- *Allocating command buffers*
- *Waiting for fences*
- *Waiting for all commands to be finished*
- *Destroying a command pool*

Destroying a command pool

When all command buffers allocated from a given pool are not used any more, and we also don't need the pool, we can safely destroy it.

How to do it...

1. Take the handle of a logical device and store it in a variable of type `VkDevice` named `logical_device`.
2. Use a handle of the pool that should be destroyed to initialize a variable of type `VkCommandPool` named `command_pool`.
3. Call `vkDestroyCommandPool( logical_device, command_pool, nullptr )`, for which provide the handles of the logical device and the command pool, and a `nullptr` value.
4. For safety reasons, assign the `VK_NULL_HANDLE` value to the `command_pool` variable.

How it works...

The command pool is destroyed with the following code:

```
if( VK_NULL_HANDLE != command_pool ) {
  vkDestroyCommandPool( logical_device, command_pool, nullptr );
  command_pool = VK_NULL_HANDLE;
}
```

But, we can't destroy the pool until all command buffers allocated from it are not pending for execution on a device. To do that, we can wait on fences or use one of the functions that causes the application to wait until the selected queue stops processing commands, or while the whole device is busy (the work submitted to all queues from a given device is still being processed). Only then can we safely destroy the command pool.

See also

The following recipes in this chapter:

- *Creating a command pool*
- *Waiting for all submitted commands to be finished*

4
Resources and Memory

In this chapter, we will cover the following recipes:

- Creating a buffer
- Allocating and binding a memory object for a buffer
- Setting a buffer memory barrier
- Creating a buffer view
- Creating an image
- Allocating and binding a memory object to an image
- Setting an image memory barrier
- Creating an image view
- Creating a 2D image and view
- Creating a layered 2D image with a CUBEMAP view
- Mapping, updating, and unmapping host-visible memory
- Copying data between buffers
- Copying data from a buffer to an image
- Copying data from an image to a buffer
- Using a staging buffer to update a buffer with a device-local memory bound
- Using a staging buffer to update an image with a device-local memory bound
- Destroying an image view
- Destroying an image
- Destroying a buffer view
- Freeing a memory object
- Destroying a buffer

Introduction

In Vulkan, there are two very important types of resources in which data can be stored--buffers and images. Buffers represent linear arrays of data. Images, similarly to OpenGL's textures, represent one-, two-, or three-dimensional data organized in a way that is (generally) specific for a given hardware (so we don't know the internal memory structure). Buffers and images can be used for various purposes: in shaders, we can read or sample data from them, or store data in them. Images can be used as color or depth/stencil attachments (render targets), which means that we can render into them. Buffers can also store vertex attributes, indices, or parameters used during indirect drawing.

What is very important is that each of the mentioned usages must be specified during resource creation (we can provide many of them at once). We also need to inform the driver when we change the way in which a given resource is used in our application.

As opposed to high-level APIs such as OpenGL, buffers and images in Vulkan don't have their own storage. They require us to specifically create and bind appropriate memory objects.

In this chapter, we will learn how to use these resources and how to allocate memory for them and bind it to them. We will also learn how to upload data from the CPU to the GPU, and how to copy data between resources.

Creating a buffer

Buffers are the simplest resources because they represent data which can be laid out in memory only linearly, just like in typical C/C++ arrays:

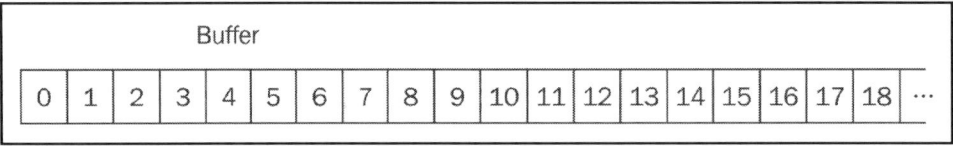

Buffers can be used for various purposes. They can be used in pipelines via descriptor sets to back data stores for uniform buffers, storage buffers, or texel buffers, among others. They can be a source of data for vertex indices or attributes, or can be used as **staging resources**--intermediate resources for data transfer from the CPU to the GPU. For all these purposes, we just need to create a buffer and specify its usage.

How to do it...

1. Take the handle of a created logical device stored in a variable of type `VkDevice` named `logical_device`.
2. Create a variable of type `VkDeviceSize` named `size`, in which store a value that will represent the size of data (in bytes) which a buffer will be able to store.
3. Think of desired scenarios a buffer will be used for. Create a variable of a bitfield type `VkBufferUsageFlags` named `usage`. Assign a value that is a logical sum (OR) of all desired buffer usages.
4. Create a variable of type `VkBufferCreateInfo` named `buffer_create_info`. Assign the following values to its members:
   - `VK_STRUCTURE_TYPE_BUFFER_CREATE_INFO` value for `sType`
   - `nullptr` value for `pNext`
   - `0` value for `flags`
   - `size` variable for `size`
   - `usage` variable for `usage`
   - `VK_SHARING_MODE_EXCLUSIVE` value for `sharingMode`
   - `0` value for `queueFamilyIndexCount`
   - `nullptr` value for `pQueueFamilyIndices`
5. Create a variable of type `VkBuffer` named `buffer`, in which a handle of a created buffer will be stored.
6. Call `vkCreateBuffer( logical_device, &buffer_create_info, nullptr, &buffer )`, and provide a handle of the logical device in the first parameter, a pointer to the `buffer_create_info` variable in the second parameter, a `nullptr` value in the third parameter, and a pointer to the `buffer` variable in the last parameter.
7. Make sure the function call was successful by checking whether the returned valued is equal to `VK_SUCCESS`.

How it works...

Before we can create a buffer, we need to know how big the buffer should be and how we want to use it. A buffer's size is determined by the amount of data we would like to store in it. All the ways in which buffer will be used in our application are specified by the buffer's usage. We can't use a buffer in a way that wasn't defined during buffer creation.

 Buffers can only be used for purposes (usages) specified during their creation.

Here is a list of supported ways in which buffers can be used:

- VK_BUFFER_USAGE_TRANSFER_SRC_BIT specifies that the buffer can be a source of data for copy operations
- VK_BUFFER_USAGE_TRANSFER_DST_BIT specifies that we can copy data to the buffer
- VK_BUFFER_USAGE_UNIFORM_TEXEL_BUFFER_BIT indicates that the buffer can be used in shaders as a uniform texel buffer
- VK_BUFFER_USAGE_STORAGE_TEXEL_BUFFER_BIT specifies that the buffer can be used in shaders as a storage texel buffer
- VK_BUFFER_USAGE_UNIFORM_BUFFER_BIT indicates that the buffer can be used in shaders as a source of values for uniform variables
- VK_BUFFER_USAGE_STORAGE_BUFFER_BIT indicates that we can store data in the buffer from within shaders
- VK_BUFFER_USAGE_INDEX_BUFFER_BIT specifies that the buffer can be used as a source of vertex indices during drawing
- VK_BUFFER_USAGE_VERTEX_BUFFER_BIT indicates that the buffer can be a source of data for vertex attributes specified during drawing
- VK_BUFFER_USAGE_INDIRECT_BUFFER_BIT indicates that the buffer can contain data that will be used during indirect drawing

To create a buffer, we need to prepare a variable of type VkBufferCreateInfo in which we provide the following data:

```
VkBufferCreateInfo buffer_create_info = {
  VK_STRUCTURE_TYPE_BUFFER_CREATE_INFO,
  nullptr,
  0,
  size,
  usage,
  VK_SHARING_MODE_EXCLUSIVE,
  0,
  nullptr
};
```

The `size` and `usage` variables define the amount of data the buffer can hold and the ways in which we can use the buffer in our application, respectively.

The preceding `VK_SHARING_MODE_EXCLUSIVE` value provided for the `sharingMode` member is another very important parameter. Through it, we specify whether queues from multiple families can access the buffer at the same time. **Exclusive sharing mode** tells the driver that the buffer can be referenced only by queues from one family at a single time. If we want to use the buffer in commands submitted to queues from another family, we must explicitly tell the driver when the ownership has changed (when we transferred ownership from one family to another). This option gives us a better performance, but with a cost of more work.

We can also specify a `VK_SHARING_MODE_CONCURRENT` sharing mode. With it, multiple queues from multiple families can access a buffer at the same time and we don't need to perform an ownership transfer. But, the trade-off is that a **concurrent access** may have lower performance.

After we have prepared the creation data, we can create a buffer like this:

```
VkResult result = vkCreateBuffer( logical_device, &buffer_create_info, nullptr, &buffer );
if( VK_SUCCESS != result ) {
  std::cout << "Could not create a buffer." << std::endl;
  return false;
}
return true;
```

See also

The following recipes in this chapter:

- *Allocating and binding a memory object for a buffer*
- *Setting a buffer memory barrier*
- *Creating a buffer view*
- *Using a staging buffer to update a buffer with a device-local memory bound*
- *Destroying a buffer*

Resources and Memory

Allocating and binding a memory object for a buffer

In Vulkan, buffers don't have their own memory. To be able to use buffers in our application and to store any data inside them, we need to allocate a memory object and bind it to a buffer.

How to do it...

1. Take the handle of a physical device from which the logical device was created. Store it in a variable of type `VkPhysicalDevice` named `physical_device`.
2. Create a variable of type `VkPhysicalDeviceMemoryProperties` named `physical_device_memory_properties`.
3. Call `vkGetPhysicalDeviceMemoryProperties( physical_device, &physical_device_memory_properties )`, for which provide the handle of a physical device and a pointer to the `physical_device_memory_properties` variable. This call will store memory parameters (number of heaps, their size, and types) of the physical device used for processing.
4. Take the handle of a logical device created from the physical device, represented by the `physical_device` variable. Store the handle in a variable of type `VkDevice` named `logical_device`.
5. Take the handle of a created buffer represented by a variable of type `VkBuffer` named `buffer`.
6. Create a variable of type `VkMemoryRequirements` named `memory_requirements`.
7. Acquire parameters of a memory that needs to be used for the buffer. Do this by calling `vkGetBufferMemoryRequirements( logical_device, buffer, &memory_requirements )`, and providing the handle of the logical device in the first parameter, the handle of the created buffer in the second parameter, and a pointer to the `memory_requirements` variable in the third parameter.
8. Create a variable of type `VkDeviceMemory` named `memory_object` that will represent the created buffer's memory object, and assign a `VK_NULL_HANDLE` value to it.
9. Create a variable of type `VkMemoryPropertyFlagBits` named `memory_properties`. Store additional (chosen) memory properties in the variable.

10. Iterate over the available physical device's memory types represented by the `memoryTypeCount` member of a `physical_device_memory_properties` variable. Do this by using the variable of type `uint32_t` named `type`. For each loop iteration, perform the following steps:
    1. Make sure that the bit of the `memoryTypeBits` member of the `memory_requirements` variable on the position represented by the `type` variable is set.
    2. Make sure that the `memory_properties` variable has the same bits set as a `propertyFlags` member of the memory type, at index `type` of the `memoryTypes` array in the `physical_device_memory_properties` variable.
    3. If points 1 and 2 are not true, continue iterating the loop.
    4. Create a variable of type `VkMemoryAllocateInfo` named `buffer_memory_allocate_info`, and assign the following values for its members:
        - `VK_STRUCTURE_TYPE_MEMORY_ALLOCATE_INFO` value for `sType`
        - `nullptr` value for `pNext`
        - `memory_requirements.size` variable for `allocationSize`
        - `type` variable for `memoryTypeIndex`
    5. Call `vkAllocateMemory( logical_device, &buffer_memory_allocate_info, nullptr, &memory_object )`, for which provide the handle of the logical device, a pointer to the `buffer_memory_allocate_info` variable, a `nullptr` value, and a pointer to the `memory_object` variable.
    6. Make sure the call was successful by checking if the value returned by the call was equal to `VK_SUCCESS`, and stop iterating the loop.
11. Make sure that memory object allocation inside the loop was successful by checking whether the `memory_object` variable is not equal to `VK_NULL_HANDLE`.
12. Bind the memory object to the buffer by calling `vkBindBufferMemory( logical_device, buffer, memory_object, 0 )`, for which provide the `logical_device`, `buffer`, and `memory_object` variables and a 0 value.
13. Make sure the call was successful and the returned value was equal to `VK_SUCCESS`.

How it works...

To allocate a memory object for a buffer (or memory object in general), we need to know what memory types are available on a given physical device, and how many of them there are. This is done by calling the `vkGetPhysicalDeviceMemoryProperties()` function, like this:

```
VkPhysicalDeviceMemoryProperties physical_device_memory_properties;
vkGetPhysicalDeviceMemoryProperties( physical_device,
&physical_device_memory_properties );
```

Next, we need to know how much storage a given buffer requires (the buffer's memory may need to be bigger than the buffer's size) and what memory type is compatible with it. All this is stored in a variable of type `VkMemoryRequirements`:

```
VkMemoryRequirements memory_requirements;
vkGetBufferMemoryRequirements( logical_device, buffer, &memory_requirements
);
```

Next, we need to check which memory type corresponds to the buffer's memory requirements:

```
memory_object = VK_NULL_HANDLE;
for( uint32_t type = 0; type <
physical_device_memory_properties.memoryTypeCount; ++type ) {
   if( (memory_requirements.memoryTypeBits & (1 << type)) &&
       ((physical_device_memory_properties.memoryTypes[type].propertyFlags &
memory_properties) == memory_properties) ) {

    VkMemoryAllocateInfo buffer_memory_allocate_info = {
      VK_STRUCTURE_TYPE_MEMORY_ALLOCATE_INFO,
      nullptr,
      memory_requirements.size,
      type
    };

    VkResult result = vkAllocateMemory( logical_device,
&buffer_memory_allocate_info, nullptr, &memory_object );
    if( VK_SUCCESS == result ) {
      break;
    }
  }
}
```

Here, we iterate over all available memory types and check whether a given type can be used for our buffer. We can also request some additional memory properties that need to be fulfilled. For example, if we want to upload data directly from our application (from the CPU), memory mapping must be supported. In this case, we need to use a memory type that is **host-visible**.

When we have found a proper memory type, we can use it to allocate a memory object and we can stop the loop. After that, we make sure that the memory was allocated properly (if we didn't leave the loop without allocating the object) and next, we bind it to our buffer:

```
if( VK_NULL_HANDLE == memory_object ) {
  std::cout << "Could not allocate memory for a buffer." << std::endl;
  return false;
}

VkResult result = vkBindBufferMemory( logical_device, buffer,
memory_object, 0 );
if( VK_SUCCESS != result ) {
  std::cout << "Could not bind memory object to a buffer." << std::endl;
  return false;
}
return true;
```

During binding, we specify a memory offset, among other parameters. This allows us to bind a part of the memory that's not at the beginning of the memory object. We can (and should) use the `offset` parameter to bind multiple, separate parts of a memory object to multiple buffers.

From now on, the buffer can be used in our application.

There's more...

This recipe shows how to allocate and bind a memory object to a buffer. But in general, we shouldn't use a separate memory object for each buffer. We should allocate bigger memory objects and use parts of them for multiple buffers.

In this recipe, we also acquired the parameters of a physical device's available memory types by calling a `vkGetPhysicalDeviceMemoryProperties()` function. But in general, to improve the performance of our application, we don't need to call it every time we want to allocate a memory object. We can call this function only once, after we choose a physical device that will be used for a logical device (refer to the *Creating a logical device* recipe from `Chapter 1`, *Instance and Devices*) and use the variable in which the parameters were stored.

Resources and Memory

See also

The following recipes in this chapter:

- *Creating a buffer*
- *Setting a buffer memory barrier*
- *Mapping, updating, and unmapping host-visible memory*
- *Using a staging buffer to update a buffer with a device-local memory bound*
- *Freeing a memory object*
- *Destroying a buffer*

Setting a buffer memory barrier

Buffers can be used for various purposes. For each buffer, we can upload data to it or copy data from it; we can bind a buffer to a pipeline via descriptor sets and use it inside shaders as a source of data, or we can store data in the buffer from within the shaders.

We must inform a driver about each such usage, not only during buffer creation, but also before the intended usage. When we have been using a buffer for one purpose and from now on we want to use it differently, we must tell the driver about a change in the buffer's usage. This is done through buffer memory barriers. They are set as part of the pipeline barriers during command buffer recording (refer to the *Beginning a command buffer recording operation* recipe from `Chapter 3`, *Command Buffers and Synchronization*).

Getting ready

For the purpose of this recipe, we will use a custom structure type named `BufferTransition` with the following definition:

```
struct BufferTransition {
    VkBuffer          Buffer;
    VkAccessFlags     CurrentAccess;
    VkAccessFlags     NewAccess;
    uint32_t          CurrentQueueFamily;
    uint32_t          NewQueueFamily;
};
```

Through this structure, we will define the parameters we want to use for the buffer memory barrier. In `CurrentAccess` and `NewAccess`, we store information about how the buffer has been used so far and how it will be used from now on, respectively (in this case, usage is defined as types of memory operations that will involve a given buffer). The `CurrentQueueFamily` and `NewQueueFamily` members are used when we want to transfer ownership from queues from one family to another. We need to do this when we have specified **exclusive sharing mode** during buffer creation.

How to do it...

1. Prepare parameters for each buffer you want to set up a barrier for. Store them in a vector of type `std::vector<BufferTransition>` named `buffer_transitions`. For each buffer, store the following parameters:
    1. Buffer's handle in the `Buffer` member
    2. Type of memory operations that have involved the buffer so far in the `CurrentAccess` member
    3. Type of memory operations that will be performed on the buffer from now on (after the barrier) in the `NewAccess` member
    4. Index of a queue family that has been referencing the buffer so far (or a `VK_QUEUE_FAMILY_IGNORED` value if we don't want to transfer queue ownership) in the `CurrentQueueFamily` member
    5. Index of a queue family that will be referencing the buffer from now on (or a `VK_QUEUE_FAMILY_IGNORED` value if we don't want to transfer queue ownership) in the `NewQueueFamily` member
2. Create a vector variable of type `std::vector<VkBufferMemoryBarrier>` named `buffer_memory_barriers`.
3. For each element of the `buffer_transitions` variable, add a new element to the `buffer_memory_barriers` vector. Use the following values for members of the new element:
    - `VK_STRUCTURE_TYPE_BUFFER_MEMORY_BARRIER` value for `sType` member
    - `nullptr` value for `pNext`
    - `CurrentAccess` value of the current element for `srcAccessMask`
    - `NewAccess` value of the current element for `dstAccessMask`
    - `CurrentQueueFamily` value of the current element for `srcQueueFamilyIndex`

- `NewQueueFamily` value of the current element for `dstQueueFamilyIndex`
    - Buffer's handle for `buffer`
    - 0 value for `offset`
    - `VK_WHOLE_SIZE` value for `size`
4. Take the handle of the command buffer and store it in a variable of type `VkCommandBuffer` named `command_buffer`.
5. Make sure the command buffer represented by the `command_buffer` handle is in the recording state (that the recording operation was started for the command buffer).
6. Create a variable of a bit field type `VkPipelineStageFlags` named `generating_stages`. In this variable, store values representing pipeline stages that have been using the buffer so far.
7. Create a variable of a bit field type `VkPipelineStageFlags` named `consuming_stages`. In this variable, store values representing pipeline stages in which the buffer will be used after the barrier.
8. Call `vkCmdPipelineBarrier( command_buffer, generating_stages, consuming_stages, 0, 0, nullptr, static_cast<uint32_t>(buffer_memory_barriers.size()), &buffer_memory_barriers[0], 0, nullptr )`, and provide the handle of the command buffer in the first parameter, and `generating_stages` and `consuming_stages` variables in the second and third parameters respectively. The number of elements of the `buffer_memory_barriers` vector should be provided in the seventh parameter, and the eighth parameter should point to the first element of the `buffer_memory_barriers` vector.

How it works...

In Vulkan, operations that are submitted to queues are executed in order, but they are independent. Sometimes, it is possible for some operations to start before the previous operations have finished. This parallel execution is one of the most important performance factors of current graphics hardware. But sometimes, it is crucial that some operations should wait for the results of earlier operations: this is when memory barriers come in handy.

 Memory barriers are used to define moments in command buffers' executions, in which later commands should wait for the earlier commands to finish their job. They also cause the results of these operations to become visible for other operations.

In the case of buffers, through memory barriers, we specify how the buffer was used and which pipeline stages were using it up to the moment in which we placed a barrier. Next we need to define which pipeline stages will be using it and how, after the barrier. With this information, the driver can pause operations that need to wait for the results of earlier operations to become available, but execute operations that won't reference the buffer at all.

Buffers can be used only for purposes defined during creation. Each such usage corresponds with the type of memory operation through which the buffer's contents can be accessed. Here is a list of supported memory access types:

- VK_ACCESS_INDIRECT_COMMAND_READ_BIT is used when the buffer's contents are a source of data for indirect drawing
- VK_ACCESS_INDEX_READ_BIT indicates the buffer's contents are used for indices during drawing operations
- VK_ACCESS_VERTEX_ATTRIBUTE_READ_BIT specifies that the buffer is a source of vertex attributes that are read during drawing
- VK_ACCESS_UNIFORM_READ_BIT is used when the buffer will be accessed through shaders as an uniform buffer
- VK_ACCESS_SHADER_READ_BIT indicates that the buffer can be read inside shaders (but not as a uniform buffer)
- VK_ACCESS_SHADER_WRITE_BIT specifies that shaders will write data to the buffer
- VK_ACCESS_TRANSFER_READ_BIT is used when we want to copy data from the buffer
- VK_ACCESS_TRANSFER_WRITE_BIT is used when we want to copy data to the buffer
- VK_ACCESS_HOST_READ_BIT specifies that the application will read the buffer's contents (via memory mapping)
- VK_ACCESS_HOST_WRITE_BIT is used when the application will write data to the buffer (via memory mapping)
- VK_ACCESS_MEMORY_READ_BIT is used when the buffer's memory will be read in any other way not specified above
- VK_ACCESS_MEMORY_WRITE_BIT is used when the buffer's memory will be written through any other way not described above

Resources and Memory

Barriers are needed for memory operations to become visible for later commands. Without them, commands that read the buffer's contents may start reading them before the contents were even properly written by the previous operations. But, such a break in the command buffer's execution causes stalls in the graphics hardware's processing pipeline. And this, unfortunately, may impact the performance of our application:

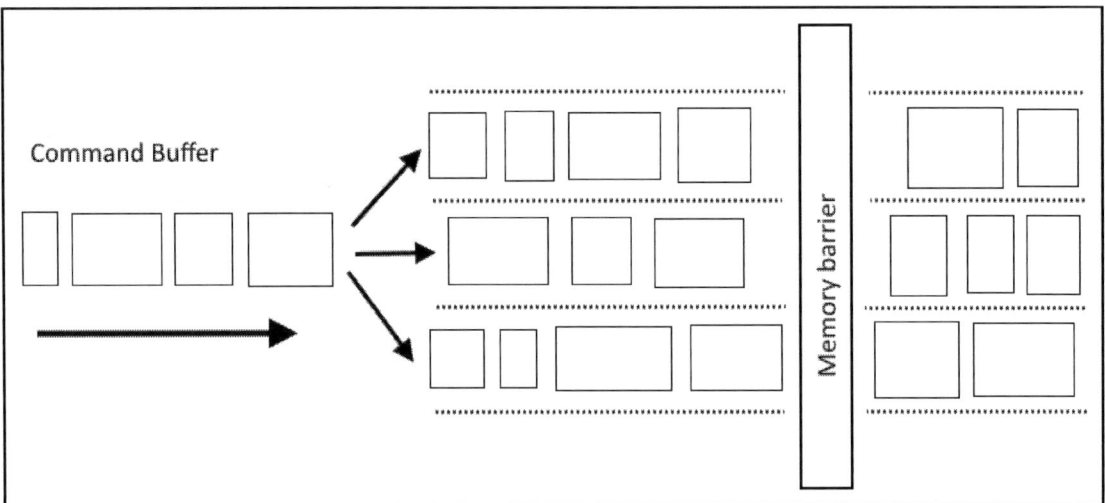

 We should aggregate usage and ownership transitions for as many buffers as possible in as few barriers as possible.

To set up a memory barrier for a buffer, we need to prepare a variable of type `VkBufferMemoryBarrier`. If possible, we should aggregate data for multiple buffers in one memory barrier. That's why a vector with elements of type `VkBufferMemoryBarrier` seems very useful for this reason, and can be filled like this:

```
std::vector<VkBufferMemoryBarrier> buffer_memory_barriers;

for( auto & buffer_transition : buffer_transitions ) {
  buffer_memory_barriers.push_back( {
    VK_STRUCTURE_TYPE_BUFFER_MEMORY_BARRIER,
    nullptr,
    buffer_transition.CurrentAccess,
    buffer_transition.NewAccess,
    buffer_transition.CurrentQueueFamily,
    buffer_transition.NewQueueFamily,
    buffer_transition.Buffer,
```

```
    0,
    VK_WHOLE_SIZE
  } );
}
```

Next, we set up a memory barrier in the command buffer. This is done during the command buffer's recording operation:

```
if( buffer_memory_barriers.size() > 0 ) {
  vkCmdPipelineBarrier( command_buffer, generating_stages,
consuming_stages, 0, 0, nullptr,
static_cast<uint32_t>(buffer_memory_barriers.size()),
&buffer_memory_barriers[0], 0, nullptr );
}
```

In the barrier we specify which pipeline stages of the commands, executed after the barrier, should wait for the results of which pipeline stages of commands executed before the barrier.

Remember that we need to set a barrier only when the usage is changed. We don't need to do it if the buffer is used for the same purpose multiple times. Imagine a situation in which we want to copy data to a buffer two times, from two different resources. First, we need to set one barrier that will inform the driver that we will perform operations involving memory access of a VK_ACCESS_TRANSFER_WRITE_BIT type. After that, we can copy data to the buffer as many times as we want. Next, if we want to use a buffer, for example, as a vertex buffer (source of vertex attributes during rendering), we need to set another barrier indicating that we will read vertex attribute data from the buffer--these operations are represented by a VK_ACCESS_VERTEX_ATTRIBUTE_READ_BIT memory access. When we are done drawing and a buffer will be used for yet another purpose, even if once again we want to copy data to the buffer, we yet again need to set a memory barrier with proper parameters.

There's more...

We don't need to set up a barrier for the whole buffer. We can do it only for part of the buffer's memory. To do this, we just need to specify proper values for the offset and size members of a variable of type VkBufferMemoryBarrier, defined for a given buffer. Through these members, we define where the contents of the memory start, and what the size of the memory is for which we want to define a barrier. These values are specified in machine units (bytes).

Resources and Memory

See also

The following recipes in this chapter:

- *Beginning a command buffer recording operation*
- *Creating a buffer*
- *Allocating and binding a memory object to a buffer*
- *Setting an image memory barrier*
- *Using a staging buffer to update a buffer with a device-local memory bound*
- *Using a staging buffer to update an image with a device-local memory bound*

Creating a buffer view

When we want to use a given buffer as a uniform texel buffer or as a storage texel buffer, we need to create a buffer view for it.

How to do it...

1. Take the handle of a logical device from which a given buffer was created. Store it in a variable of type `VkDevice` named `logical_device`.
2. Take the handle of a created buffer and store it in a variable of type `VkBuffer` named `buffer`.
3. Choose a format for a buffer view (how the buffer's contents should be interpreted) and use it to initialize a variable of type `VkFormat` named `format`.
4. Select the part of a buffer's memory for which a view should be created. Set the starting point of this memory (offset from the beginning of the buffer's memory) in a variable of type `VkDeviceSize` named `memory_offset`. Define the size of this memory through a variable of type `VkDeviceSize` named `memory_range`.
5. Create a variable of type `VkBufferViewCreateInfo` named `buffer_view_create_info`. Use the following values to initialize its members:
    - `VK_STRUCTURE_TYPE_BUFFER_VIEW_CREATE_INFO` value for `sType`
    - `nullptr` value for `pNext`
    - `0` value for `flags`
    - `buffer` variable for `buffer`

- `format` variable for `format`
- `memory_offset` variable for `offset`
- `memory_range` variable for `range`

6. Create a variable of type `VkBufferView` named `buffer_view`. It will be used to store the handle of a created buffer view.
7. Call `vkCreateBufferView( logical_device, &buffer_view_create_info, nullptr, &buffer_view )`, for which provide the handle of the logical device in the first parameter, a pointer to the `buffer_view_create_info` variable in the second parameter, a `nullptr` value as the third parameter, and a pointer to the `buffer_view` variable in the last parameter.
8. Make sure the call was successful by checking whether the value returned by the call was equal to `VK_SUCCESS`.

How it works...

To create a buffer view, the most important things we need to think about are the view's format and the memory parts for which the view will be created. This way, inside shaders, a buffer's contents can be interpreted similarly to images (textures). We define these parameters as follows:

```
VkBufferViewCreateInfo buffer_view_create_info = {
  VK_STRUCTURE_TYPE_BUFFER_VIEW_CREATE_INFO,
  nullptr,
  0,
  buffer,
  format,
  memory_offset,
  memory_range
};
```

Next, we create the buffer itself using the specified parameters:

```
VkResult result = vkCreateBufferView( logical_device,
  &buffer_view_create_info, nullptr, &buffer_view );
if( VK_SUCCESS != result ) {
  std::cout << "Could not creat buffer view." << std::endl;
  return false;
}
return true;
```

See also

The following recipes in this chapter:

- *Creating a buffer*
- *Allocating and binding a memory object to a buffer*
- *Destroying an image view*

In Chapter 5, *Descriptor Sets*, see the following recipes:

- *Creating a descriptor set layout*
- *Updating descriptor sets*

Creating an image

Images represent data that can have one, two, or three dimensions, and can have additional mipmap levels and layers. Each element of an image's data (a texel) can also have one or more samples.

Images can be used for many different purposes. We can use them as a source of data for copy operations. We can bind images to pipelines via descriptor sets and use them as textures (similarly to OpenGL). We can render into images, in which case we use images as color or depth attachments (render targets).

We specify image parameters such as size, format, and its intended usages during image creation.

How to do it...

1. Take the handle of a logical device on which we want to create an image. Store it in a variable of type `VkDevice` named `logical_device`.
2. Choose an image type (if an image should have one, two, or three dimensions) and use a proper value to initialize a variable of type `VkImageType` named `type`.
3. Select the image's format--the number of components and number of bits each image's element should contain. Store the format in a variable of type `VkFormat` named `format`.
4. Select the image's size (dimensions) and use it to initialize a variable of type `VkExtent3D` named `size`.

5. Choose the number of mipmap levels that should be defined for the image. Store the number of mipmap levels in a variable of type `uint32_t` named `num_mipmaps`.
6. Choose the number of layers that should be defined for the image and store it in a variable of type `uint32_t` named `num_layers`. If an image will be used as a cubemap, the number of layers must be a multiple of six.
7. Create a variable of type `VkSampleCountFlagBits` named `samples`, and initialize it with a value representing the number of samples.
8. Select the intended image usages. Define them in a variable of type `VkImageUsageFlags` named `usage_scenarios`.
9. Create a variable of type `VkImageCreateInfo` named `image_create_info`. Use the following values for its members:
    - `VK_STRUCTURE_TYPE_IMAGE_CREATE_INFO` value for `sType`
    - `nullptr` value for `pNext`
    - For `flags`, use the `VK_IMAGE_CREATE_CUBE_COMPATIBLE_BIT` value if the image should be used as a cubemap, otherwise use a 0 value
    - `type` variable for `imageType`
    - `format` variable for `format`
    - `size` variable for `extent`
    - `num_mipmaps` variable for `mipLevels`
    - `num_layers` variable for `arrayLayers`
    - `samples` variable for `samples`
    - `VK_IMAGE_TILING_OPTIMAL` value for `tiling`
    - `usage_scenarios` variable for `usage`
    - `VK_SHARING_MODE_EXCLUSIVE` value for `sharingMode`
    - 0 value for `queueFamilyIndexCount`
    - `nullptr` value for `pQueueFamilyIndices`
    - `VK_IMAGE_LAYOUT_UNDEFINED` value for `initialLayout`
10. Create a variable of type `VkImage` named `image`. In it, a handle of a created image will be stored.
11. Call `vkCreateImage( logical_device, &image_create_info, nullptr, &image )`, for which provide the handle of the logical device, a pointer to the `image_create_info` variable, a `nullptr` value, and a pointer to the `image` variable.
12. Make sure the value return by the `vkCreateImage()` call was equal to `VK_SUCCESS`.

Resources and Memory

How it works...

When we want to create an image, we need to prepare multiple parameters: the image's type, dimensions (size), number of components, and the number of bits for each component (format). We also need to know whether the image will contain mipmaps or whether it will have multiple layers (a normal image must contain at least one, and a cubemap image must contain at least six). We should also think about the intended usage scenarios, which are also defined during image creation. We can't use an image in a way that wasn't defined during its creation.

 Images can only be used for purposes (usages) specified during their creation.

Here is a list of purposes for which images can be used:

- `VK_IMAGE_USAGE_TRANSFER_SRC_BIT` specifies that the image can be used as a source of data for copy operations
- `VK_IMAGE_USAGE_TRANSFER_DST_BIT` specifies that we can copy data to the image
- `VK_IMAGE_USAGE_SAMPLED_BIT` indicates that we can sample data from the image inside shaders
- `VK_IMAGE_USAGE_STORAGE_BIT` specifies that the image can be used as a storage image inside shaders
- `VK_IMAGE_USAGE_COLOR_ATTACHMENT_BIT` specifies that we can render into an image (use it as a color render target/attachment in a framebuffer)
- `VK_IMAGE_USAGE_DEPTH_STENCIL_ATTACHMENT_BIT` indicates that the image can be used as a depth and/or stencil buffer (as a depth render target/attachment in a framebuffer)
- `VK_IMAGE_USAGE_TRANSIENT_ATTACHMENT_BIT` indicates that the memory bound to the image will be allocated lazily (on demand)
- `VK_IMAGE_USAGE_INPUT_ATTACHMENT_BIT` specifies that the image can be used as an input attachment inside shaders

Different usage scenarios require different image layouts to be used. These are changed (transitioned) using image memory barriers. But during creation, we can specify only VK_IMAGE_LAYOUT_UNDEFINED (if we don't care about the initial contents) or VK_IMAGE_LAYOUT_PREINITIALIZED (if we want to upload data by mapping the **host-visible** memory), and we always need to transition to another layout before the actual use.

All the image parameters are specified through a variable of type VkImageCreateInfo, like this:

```
VkImageCreateInfo image_create_info = {
  VK_STRUCTURE_TYPE_IMAGE_CREATE_INFO,
  nullptr,
  cubemap ? VK_IMAGE_CREATE_CUBE_COMPATIBLE_BIT : 0u,
  type,
  format,
  size,
  num_mipmaps,
  cubemap ? 6 * num_layers : num_layers,
  samples,
  VK_IMAGE_TILING_OPTIMAL,
  usage_scenarios,
  VK_SHARING_MODE_EXCLUSIVE,
  0,
  nullptr,
  VK_IMAGE_LAYOUT_UNDEFINED
};
```

When we create an image, we also need to specify the tiling. It defines the image's memory structure. There are two available types of image tiling: linear and optimal.

When using **linear tiling**, as the name suggests, an image's data is laid out in memory linearly, similarly to buffers or C/C++ arrays. This allows us to map an image's memory and read it or initialize it directly from our application, because we know how the memory is organized. Unfortunately, it restricts us from using an image for many purposes; for example, we can't use an image as a depth texture or as a cubemap (some drivers may support it, but it is not required by the specification and, in general, we shouldn't rely on it). Linear tiling can also lower the performance of our application.

For the best performance, it is recommended to create images with optimal tiling.

Resources and Memory

Images with **optimal tiling** can be used for all purposes; they also have much better performance. But this comes with a trade-off--we don't know how the image's memory is organized. In the following diagram we can see an example of image's data and it's internal structure:

Each type of graphics hardware can store image data in a different way that is optimal for it. Because of that, we can't map an image's memory and initialize or read it directly from our application. In this situation, we are required to use **staging resources**.
When we are ready, we can create an image with the following code:

```
VkResult result = vkCreateImage( logical_device, &image_create_info,
nullptr, &image );
if( VK_SUCCESS != result ) {
  std::cout << "Could not create an image." << std::endl;
  return false;
}
return true;
```

See also

The following recipes in this chapter:

- *Allocating and binding a memory object to an image*
- *Setting an image memory barrier*
- *Creating an image view*
- *Creating a 2D image and view*
- *Using a staging buffer to update an image with a device-local memory bound*
- *Destroying an image*

Allocating and binding a memory object to an image

Images, similarly to buffers, are not created with a bound memory storage. We need to implicitly create a memory object and bind it to the image. We can also use an existing memory object for this purpose.

How to do it...

1. Take the handle of a physical device from which a logical device was created. Store it in a variable of type `VkPhysicalDevice` named `physical_device`.
2. Create a variable of type `VkPhysicalDeviceMemoryProperties` named `physical_device_memory_properties`.
3. Call `vkGetPhysicalDeviceMemoryProperties( physical_device, &physical_device_memory_properties )`, for which provide the handle of the physical device and a pointer to the `physical_device_memory_properties` variable. This call will store memory parameters (number of heaps, their size, and types) of the physical device used for processing submitted operations.
4. Take the handle of a logical device created from the physical device, represented by the `physical_device` variable. Store the handle in a variable of type `VkDevice` named `logical_device`.
5. Take the handle of a created image represented by a variable of type `VkImage` named `image`.
6. Create a variable of type `VkMemoryRequirements` named `memory_requirements`.
7. Acquire the parameters of the memory that needs to be used for the image. Do this by calling `vkGetImageMemoryRequirements( logical_device, image, &memory_requirements )` and providing the handle of the logical device in the first parameter, the handle of the created image in the second parameter, and a pointer to the `memory_requirements` variable in the third parameter.
8. Create a variable of type `VkDeviceMemory` named `memory_object`, that will represent the memory object created for the image and assign a `VK_NULL_HANDLE` value to it.

Resources and Memory

9. Create a variable of type `VkMemoryPropertyFlagBits` named `memory_properties`. Store additional (chosen) memory properties in the variable, or a 0 value if no additional properties are required.

10. Iterate over the available physical device's memory types, represented by the `memoryTypeCount` member of a `physical_device_memory_properties` variable. Do this by using a variable of type `uint32_t` named `type`. For each loop iteration:
    1. Make sure that the bit on the position, represented by the `type` variable in the `memoryTypeBits` member of the `memory_requirements` variable, is set.
    2. Make sure that the `memory_properties` variable has the same bits set as a `propertyFlags` member of the memory type `memoryTypes`, at index `type` in the `physical_device_memory_properties` variable.
    3. If points 1 and 2 are not true, continue iterating the loop.
    4. Create a variable of type `VkMemoryAllocateInfo` named `image_memory_allocate_info` and assign the following values for its members:
        - `VK_STRUCTURE_TYPE_MEMORY_ALLOCATE_INFO` value for `sType`
        - `nullptr` value for `pNext`
        - `memory_requirements.size` variable for `allocationSize`
        - `type` variable for `memoryTypeIndex`
    5. Call `vkAllocateMemory( logical_device, &image_memory_allocate_info, nullptr, &memory_object )`, for which provide the handle of the logical device, a pointer to the `image_memory_allocate_info` variable, a `nullptr` value, and a pointer to the `memory_object` variable.
    6. Make sure the call was successful by checking whether the value returned by the call was equal to `VK_SUCCESS`, and stop iterating the loop.

11. Make sure that memory object allocation inside the loop was successful by checking whether the `memory_object` variable is not equal to `VK_NULL_HANDLE`.

Chapter 4

12. Bind the memory object to the image by calling `vkBindImageMemory( logical_device, image, memory_object, 0 )`, for which provide the `logical_device`, `image` and `memory_object` variables and a 0 value.
13. Make sure the call was successful and the returned value was equal to `VK_SUCCESS`.

How it works...

Similarly to the memory object created for a buffer, we start by checking what memory types are available on a given physical device and what their properties are. We can, of course, omit these steps and gather this information once at the initialization stage of our application:

```
VkPhysicalDeviceMemoryProperties physical_device_memory_properties;
vkGetPhysicalDeviceMemoryProperties( physical_device,
&physical_device_memory_properties );
```

Next, we acquire the specific memory requirements of a given image. These can (and probably will) be different for each image, as they depend on the format, size, number of mipmaps and layers, and other properties of the image:

```
VkMemoryRequirements memory_requirements;
vkGetImageMemoryRequirements( logical_device, image, &memory_requirements );
```

The next step is to find a memory type that has proper parameters and is compatible with the image's memory requirements:

```
memory_object = VK_NULL_HANDLE;
for( uint32_t type = 0; type < physical_device_memory_properties.memoryTypeCount; ++type ) {
    if( (memory_requirements.memoryTypeBits & (1 << type)) &&
        ((physical_device_memory_properties.memoryTypes[type].propertyFlags &
        memory_properties) == memory_properties) ) {

        VkMemoryAllocateInfo image_memory_allocate_info = {

            VK_STRUCTURE_TYPE_MEMORY_ALLOCATE_INFO,
            nullptr,
            memory_requirements.size,
            type
        };

        VkResult result = vkAllocateMemory( logical_device,
```

Resources and Memory

```
      &image_memory_allocate_info, nullptr, &memory_object );
    if( VK_SUCCESS == result ) {
      break;
    }
  }
}
```

Here, we iterate over all available memory types. If a given bit of the `memoryTypeBits` member of an image's memory properties is set, this means that a memory type with the same number is compatible with the image and we can use it for the memory object. We can also check for other properties of the memory type and find the one that is suitable for our needs. For example, we may want to use a memory that can be mapped on the CPU (a **host-visible** memory).

Next, we check whether the memory object allocation inside the loop was successful. And if yes, we bind the created memory object with our image:

```
if( VK_NULL_HANDLE == memory_object ) {
  std::cout << "Could not allocate memory for an image." << std::endl;
  return false;
}

VkResult result = vkBindImageMemory( logical_device, image, memory_object, 0 );
if( VK_SUCCESS != result ) {
  std::cout << "Could not bind memory object to an image." << std::endl;
  return false;
}
return true;
```

From now on, we can use the image for all purposes defined during its creation.

There's more...

Similarly to binding memory objects to buffers, we should allocate bigger memory objects and bind parts of them to multiple images. This way, we perform fewer memory allocations and the driver has to track a smaller number of memory objects. This may improve the performance of our application. It may also allow us to save some memory, as each allocation may require more memory than requested during allocation (in other words, its size may always be rounded up to a multiple of the memory page size). Allocating bigger memory objects and reusing parts of them for multiple images spares us the wasted area.

See also

The following recipes in this chapter:

- *Creating an image*
- *Setting an image memory barrier*
- *Mapping, updating, and unmapping host-visible memory*
- *Using a staging buffer to update an image with a device-local memory bound*
- *Destroying an image*
- *Freeing a memory object*

Setting an image memory barrier

Images are created for various purposes--they are used as textures, by binding them to a pipeline via descriptor sets, as render targets, or as presentable images in swapchains. We can copy data to or from images--these are also separate usages defined during image creation.

Before we start using an image for any purpose, and every time we want to change the current usage of a given image, we need to inform a driver about this operation. We do this by using image memory barriers which are set during command buffer recording.

Getting ready

For the purpose of this recipe, a custom structure type `ImageTransition` is introduced. It has the following definition:

```
struct ImageTransition {
  VkImage              Image;
  VkAccessFlags        CurrentAccess;
  VkAccessFlags        NewAccess;
  VkImageLayout        CurrentLayout;
  VkImageLayout        NewLayout;
  uint32_t             CurrentQueueFamily;
  uint32_t             NewQueueFamily;
  VkImageAspectFlags   Aspect;
};
```

Resources and Memory

The `CurrentAccess` and `NewAccess` members define types of memory operations that were taking place in regard to a given image before the barrier, and that will occur after the barrier.

In Vulkan, images used for different purposes may have different internal memory organization. In other words, the memory of a given image may have a different layout for different image usages. When we want to start using an image in a different way, we also need to change this memory layout. This is done through the `CurrentLayout` and `NewLayout` members.

Memory barriers also allow us to transfer queue family ownership if an image was created with an exclusive sharing mode. In the `CurrentQueueFamily` member, we define the index of a family from which queues have been using an image so far. In `NewQueueFamily`, we need to define a family index for queues that will be using an image after the barrier. We can also use a `VK_QUEUE_FAMILY_IGNORED` special value for both when we don't want to transfer an ownership.

The `Aspect` member defines the image's usage "context". We can choose from color, depth, or stencil aspects.

How to do it...

1. Prepare parameters for each image you want to set up a barrier for. Store them in a vector of type `std::vector<ImageTransition>` named `image_transitions`. For each image, use the following values:
    - Image's handle in an `Image` member
    - Type of memory operations that involved the image so far in the `CurrentAccess` member
    - Type of memory operations that will be performed on the image from now on, after the barrier, in the `NewAccess` member
    - Current image's internal memory layout in `CurrentLayout` member
    - Layout image's memory should change into after the barrier in `NewLayout` member
    - Index of a queue family that has been referencing the image so far (or a `VK_QUEUE_FAMILY_IGNORED` value if we don't want to transfer queue ownership) in the `CurrentQueueFamily` member

- Index of a queue family that will be referencing the image from now on (or a `VK_QUEUE_FAMILY_IGNORED` value if we don't want to transfer queue ownership) in the `NewQueueFamily` member
- Image's aspect (color, depth, or stencil) in the `Aspect` member

2. Create a vector variable of type `std::vector<VkImageMemoryBarrier>` named `image_memory_barriers`.

3. For each element of the `image_transitions` variable, add a new element to the `image_memory_barriers` vector. Use the following values for members of the new element:
    - `VK_STRUCTURE_TYPE_IMAGE_MEMORY_BARRIER` value for `sType` member.
    - `nullptr` value for `pNext`.
    - `CurrentAccess` value of the current element for `srcAccessMask`.
    - `NewAccess` value of the current element for `dstAccessMask`.
    - `CurrentLayout` member of the current element for `oldLayout`.
    - `NewLayout` value of the current element for `newLayout`.
    - `CurrentQueueFamily` value of the current element for `srcQueueFamilyIndex`.
    - `NewQueueFamily` value of the current element for `dstQueueFamilyIndex`.
    - Image's handle for `image`.
    - The following values for the `subresourceRange` member of the new element:
        - `Aspect` member of the current element for `aspectMask`
        - 0 value for `baseMipLevel`
        - `VK_REMAINING_MIP_LEVELS` value for `levelCount`
        - 0 value for `baseArrayLayer`
        - `VK_REMAINING_ARRAY_LAYERS` value for `layerCount`

4. Take the handle of the command buffer and store it in a variable of type `VkCommandBuffer` named `command_buffer`.

5. Make sure the command buffer represented by the `command_buffer` handle is in the recording state (that the recording operation was started for the command buffer).

6. Create a variable of a bitfield type `VkPipelineStageFlags` named `generating_stages`. In this variable, store values representing pipeline stages that have been using the image so far.
7. Create a variable of a bitfield type `VkPipelineStageFlags` named `consuming_stages`. In this variable, store values representing pipeline stages in which the image will be referenced after the barrier.
8. Call `vkCmdPipelineBarrier( command_buffer, generating_stages, consuming_stages, 0, 0, nullptr, 0, nullptr, static_cast<uint32_t>(image_memory_barriers.size()), &image_memory_barriers[0] )` and provide the handle of the command buffer in the first parameter, and the `generating_stages` and `consuming_stages` variables in the second and third parameters respectively. The number of elements of the `image_memory_barriers` vector should be provided in the second to last parameter, and the last parameter should point to the first element of the `image_memory_barriers` vector.

How it works...

In Vulkan, operations are processed in a pipeline. Even though the processing of operations needs to be started in the order in which they were submitted, parts of the pipeline may still be executed concurrently. But sometimes, we may need to synchronize these operations and tell the driver that we want some of them to wait for results of other operations.

Memory barriers are used to define moments in command buffers' execution, in which later commands should wait for the earlier commands to finish their job. They also cause the results of these operations to become visible for other operations.

Barriers are needed for memory operations to become visible for later commands. In cases where the operations write data to images and further operations will read from them, we need to use image memory barriers. The opposite situation also requires memory barriers to be used--operations that overwrite images' data should wait for earlier operations to stop reading data from them. Failing to do so, in both cases, will make the contents of an image invalid. But such situations should be as rare as possible or our application may suffer from performance loss. This is because such a pause in the command buffer's execution causes stalls in the graphics hardware's processing pipeline and, as a result, time being wasted:

Chapter 4

TIP — To avoid a negative impact on the performance of our application, we should set up parameters for as many images as possible in as few barriers as possible.

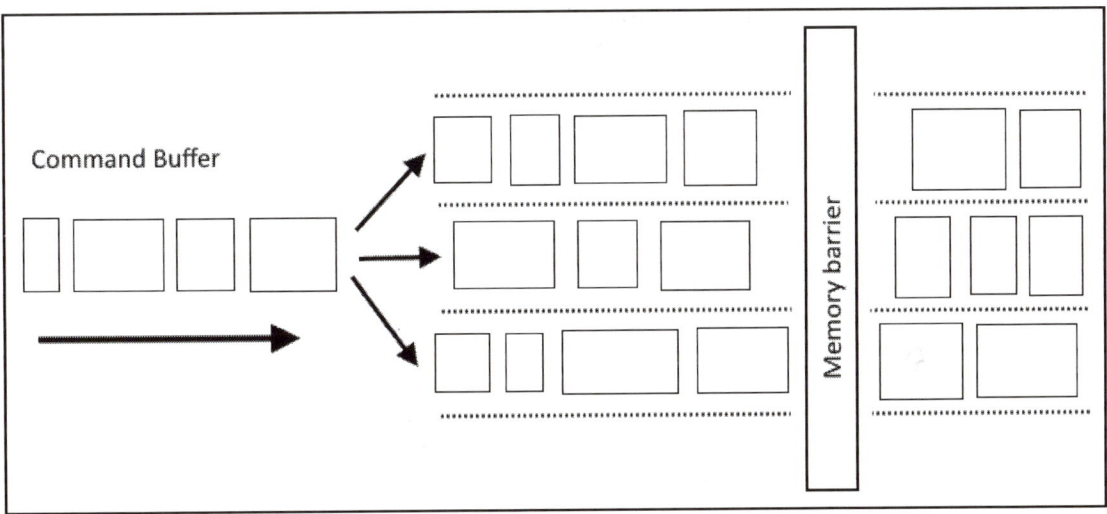

Image memory barriers are also used to define a change in how images are used. Such a usage change typically also requires us to synchronize submitted operations; that's why this is also done through memory barriers. For the purpose of changing an image's usage, we need to define types of memory operations that were performed on an image before and after the barrier (memory access). We also specify what the memory layout was before the barrier, and how memory should be laid out after the barrier. This is because images may have different memory organization when they are used for different purposes. For example, sampling data from images inside shaders may need them to be cached in such a way that neighbor texels are also neighbors in memory. But, writing data to images may be performed faster when a memory is laid out linearly. That's why image layouts were introduced in Vulkan. Each image usage has its own, designated layout. There is one, general layout, which can be used for all purposes. But, using the general layout is not recommended because it may impact the performance on some hardware platforms.

TIP — For the best performance, it is recommended to use designated image memory layouts for specific usages, though care must be taken if layout transitions are performed too frequently.

[193]

Resources and Memory

Parameters that define usage change are specified through the variables of a `VkImageMemoryBarrier` type, like this:

```
std::vector<VkImageMemoryBarrier> image_memory_barriers;

for( auto & image_transition : image_transitions ) {
  image_memory_barriers.push_back( {
    VK_STRUCTURE_TYPE_IMAGE_MEMORY_BARRIER,
    nullptr,
    image_transition.CurrentAccess,
    image_transition.NewAccess,
    image_transition.CurrentLayout,
    image_transition.NewLayout,
    image_transition.CurrentQueueFamily,
    image_transition.NewQueueFamily,
    image_transition.Image,
    {
      image_transition.Aspect,
      0,
      VK_REMAINING_MIP_LEVELS,
      0,
      VK_REMAINING_ARRAY_LAYERS
    }
  } );
}
```

But for the barrier to work properly, we also need to define pipeline stages in which images have been used so far, and in which images will be used from now on:

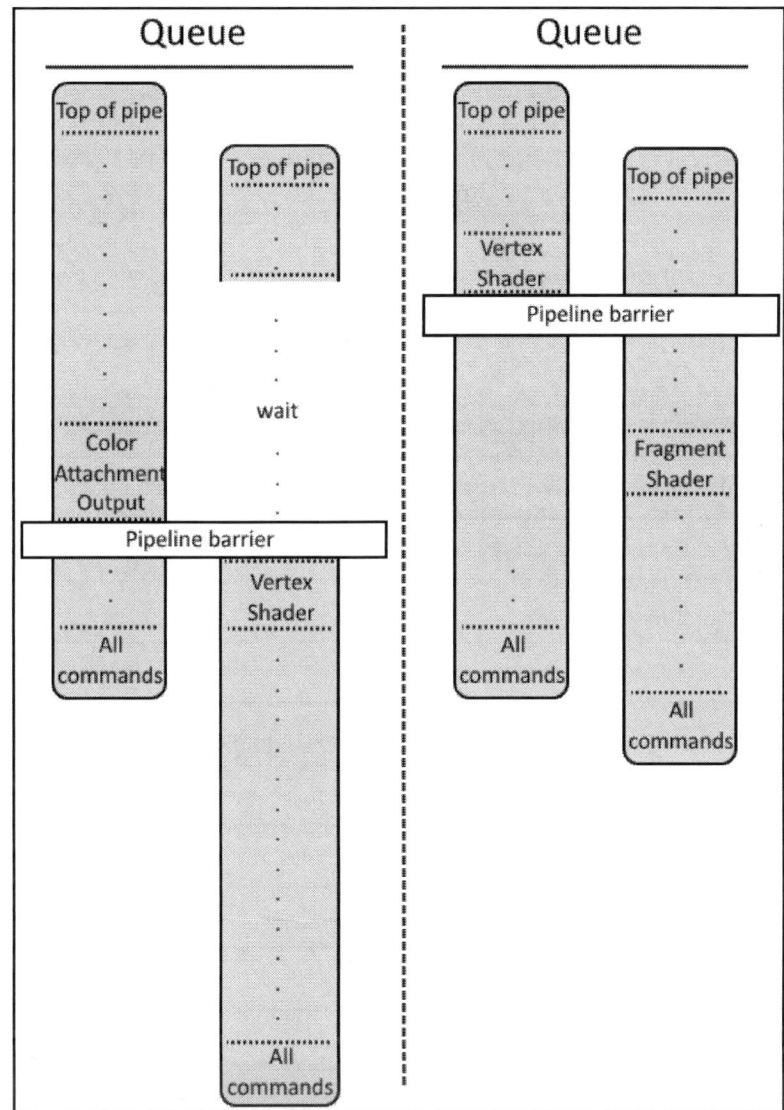

In the preceding diagram, we can see two examples of pipeline barriers. On the left, color is generated by the fragment shader and, after all the fragment tests (depth test, blending), color data is written into the image. This image is then used in the vertex shader of the successive commands. There is a high chance that such a setup will generate stalls in the pipeline.

The example on the right shows another dependency in graphics commands. Here, data is written into a resource in the vertex shader. Such data is then used by the fragment shader of the next command. This time, there is a high probability that all instances of the vertex shader will finish their jobs before the fragment shader of the next command begins executing. That's why it is important to lower the number of pipeline barriers and, if required, to properly set up drawing commands and choose pipeline stages for the barrier. The parameters of the barrier (generating and consuming stages) are aggregated for all images specified in the barrier using the following call:

```
if( image_memory_barriers.size() > 0 ) {
  vkCmdPipelineBarrier( command_buffer, generating_stages,
consuming_stages, 0, 0, nullptr, 0, nullptr,
static_cast<uint32_t>(image_memory_barriers.size()),
&image_memory_barriers[0] );
}
```

If the image is used in the same way multiple times and is not used for other purposes in between, we don't need to set a barrier before the image is actually used. We set it to signal the usage change, not the usage itself.

See also

In `Chapter 3`, *Command Buffers and Synchronization*, see the following recipe:

- *Beginning a command buffer recording operation*

See the following recipes in this chapter:

- *Creating an image*
- *Allocating and binding a memory object to an image*
- *Using a staging buffer to update an image with a device-local memory bound*

Creating an image view

Images are rarely used directly in Vulkan commands. Framebuffers and shaders (via descriptor sets) access images through image views. Image views define a selected part of an image's memory and specify additional information needed to properly read an image's data. That's why we need to know how to create an image view.

How to do it...

1. Take the handle of a logical device and use it to initialize a variable of type `VkDevice` named `logical_device`.
2. Use the handle of a created image to initialize a variable of type `VkImage` named `image`.
3. Create a variable of type `VkImageViewCreateInfo` named `image_view_create_info`. Use the following values for its members:
   - `VK_STRUCTURE_TYPE_IMAGE_VIEW_CREATE_INFO` value for `sType`
   - `nullptr` value for `pNext`
   - 0 value for `flags`
   - `image` variable for `image`
   - Type of image view for `viewType`
   - Format of an image or other compatible format (if you want to reinterpret it inside the view) for `format`
   - `VK_COMPONENT_SWIZZLE_IDENTITY` value for all members of a `components` member
   - Use the following values for members of a `subresourceRange` member:
     - Image's aspect (color, depth, or stencil) for `aspectMask`
     - 0 value for `baseMipLevel`
     - `VK_REMAINING_MIP_LEVELS` value for `levelCount`
     - 0 for `baseArrayLayer`
     - `VK_REMAINING_ARRAY_LAYERS` for `layerCount`
4. Create a variable of type `VkImageView` named `image_view`. We will store a handle of a created image view in it.
5. Call `vkCreateImageView( logical_device, &image_view_create_info, nullptr, &image_view )`, for which provide the handle of the logical device, a pointer to the `image_view_create_info` variable, a `nullptr` value, and a pointer to the `image_view` variable.
6. Make sure the call was successful by comparing the returned value with the `VK_SUCCESS` value.

How it works...

Image view defines additional metadata used for accessing the image. Through it, we can specify the parts of an image that should be accessed by the commands. Though this recipe shows how to create an image view for the whole image data, it is possible to specify a smaller range of the resource which should be accessed. For example, when we render into an image inside a render pass, we can specify that only one mipmap level should be updated.

Image view also defines how an image's memory should be interpreted. A good example is an image with multiple layers. For it, we can define an image view that interprets the image directly, as a layered image, or we can use image view to create a cubemap from it.

These parameters are specified like this:

```
VkImageViewCreateInfo image_view_create_info = {
  VK_STRUCTURE_TYPE_IMAGE_VIEW_CREATE_INFO,
  nullptr,
  0,
  image,
  view_type,
  format,
  {
    VK_COMPONENT_SWIZZLE_IDENTITY,
    VK_COMPONENT_SWIZZLE_IDENTITY,
    VK_COMPONENT_SWIZZLE_IDENTITY,
    VK_COMPONENT_SWIZZLE_IDENTITY
  },
  {
    aspect,
    0,
    VK_REMAINING_MIP_LEVELS,
    0,
    VK_REMAINING_ARRAY_LAYERS
  }
};
```

The image view creation is performed through a single call of the `vkCreateImageView()` function. An example of such a call is shown here:

```
VkResult result = vkCreateImageView( logical_device,
&image_view_create_info, nullptr, &image_view );
if( VK_SUCCESS != result ) {
  std::cout << "Could not create an image view." << std::endl;
  return false;
}
return true;
```

See also

The following recipes in this chapter:

- *Creating an image*
- *Creating a 2D image and view*
- *Destroying an image view*

Creating a 2D image and view

The most common image type that is used in many popular applications or games is typical 2D textures with four RGBA components and 32 bits per texel. To create such a resource in Vulkan, we need to create a 2D image and a proper image view.

How to do it...

1. Take a handle of a logical device and use it to initialize a variable of type `VkDevice` named `logical_device`.
2. Select the data format used in the image and initialize a variable of type `VkFormat` named `format` with the selected value.
3. Choose the size of the image. Store it in a variable of type `VkExtent2D` named `size`.
4. Choose the number of mipmap levels that should compose the image. Initialize a variable of type `uint32_t` named `num_mipmaps` with the selected number of mipmaps.
5. Specify the number of image layers using a variable of type `uint32_t` named `num_layers`.
6. Select the number of per texel samples and store it in a variable of type `VkSampleCountFlagBits` named `samples`.
7. Think of all the purposes for which the image will be used in the application. Store the value that is a logical sum (**OR**) of all these usages in a variable of type `VkImageUsageFlags` named `usage`.
8. Create an image of `VK_IMAGE_TYPE_2D` type using the `logical_device`, `format`, `size`, `num_mipmaps`, `num_layers`, `samples`, and `usage` variables. Store the handle of the created image in a variable of type `VkImage` named `image` (refer to the *Creating an image* recipe).

Resources and Memory

9. Take the handle of a physical device from which the `logical_device` handle was acquired. Store the physical device's handle in a variable of type `VkPhysicalDevice` named `physical_device`.
10. Acquire the memory properties of the `physical_device` and use them to allocate a memory object that will be bound to an image represented by the `image` variable. Make sure a memory type with a `VK_MEMORY_PROPERTY_DEVICE_LOCAL_BIT` property is used. Store the allocated memory object in a variable of type `VkDeviceMemory` named `memory_object` (refer to the *Allocating and binding memory object to an image* recipe).
11. Select the image's aspect used for the image view creation (color or depth and/or stencil) and store it in a variable of type `VkImageAspectFlags` named `aspect`.
12. Create an image view of a `VK_IMAGE_VIEW_TYPE_2D` type. Use the `logical_device`, image, format, and `aspect` variables during image view creation. Store the created handle in a variable of type `VkImageView` named `image_view` (refer to the *Creating an image view* recipe).

How it works...

Image creation requires us to perform three general steps:

1. Create an image.
2. Create a memory object (or use an existing one) and bind it to the image.
3. Create an image view.

For an image typically used as a texture, we need to create an image of the type `VK_IMAGE_TYPE_2D` and the format `VK_FORMAT_R8G8B8A8_UNORM`, but we can set these parameters as we want. The rest of the image's properties depend on the size of the image (in other words, we are creating a texture from an existing image file and we need to match its dimensions), the type of filtering that should applied to an image (if we want to use mipmapping), the number of samples (if it should be multisampled), and the desired usage scenarios.

Image creation defined in the *Creating an image* recipe can be simplified to the following code:

```
if( !CreateImage( logical_device, VK_IMAGE_TYPE_2D, format, { size.width,
size.height, 1 }, num_mipmaps, num_layers, samples, usage, false, image ) )
{
  return false;
}
```

Next, we need to allocate and bind a memory object to the image as described in the *Allocating and binding a memory object to an image* recipe. For the best performance, the memory object should be allocated on a fast, **device-local** memory like this:

```
if( !AllocateAndBindMemoryObjectToImage( physical_device, logical_device,
image, VK_MEMORY_PROPERTY_DEVICE_LOCAL_BIT, memory_object ) ) {
  return false;
}
```

We can of course use an existing memory object if it fulfills the image's memory requirements and has enough storage.

After that, we must create an image view. With it, we can tell the hardware how the image data should be interpreted. We can also use a different (but still compatible) format for an image view. But for many (if not most) purposes, it is not necessary and we will specify the same format that was used for the image. For standard 2D textures, we also use a color aspect for view creation, but for images with depth data (in other words, for images used as depth attachments), depth aspect must be specified. For more details on image view creation, follow the *Creating an image view* recipe:

```
if( !CreateImageView( logical_device, image, VK_IMAGE_VIEW_TYPE_2D, format,
aspect, image_view ) ) {
  return false;
}
```

Now, the image is ready to be used in our application. We can upload data from a file to the image and use it as a texture inside shaders (in this case, we also need a sampler and descriptor sets). We can also bind the image's view to a framebuffer and use it as a color attachment (render target).

See also

The following recipes in this chapter:

- *Creating an image*
- *Allocating and binding a memory object to an image*
- *Creating an image view*
- *Destroying an image view*
- *Destroying an image*
- *Freeing a memory object*

Resources and Memory

Creating a layered 2D image with a CUBEMAP view

A quite common example of images used in 3D applications or games are CUBEMAPs, used for simulating an object reflecting its environment. For this purpose, we don't create a CUBEMAP image. We need to create a layered image and through image view, we tell the hardware that it should interpret its layers as six CUBEMAP faces.

How to do it...

1. Take a handle of a logical device. Store it in a variable of type `VkDevice` named `logical_device`.
2. Choose the size of an image and remember it must be square. Save the image's dimensions in a variable of type `uint32_t` named `size`.
3. Select the number of the image's mipmap levels. Initialize a variable of type `uint32_t` named `num_mipmaps` with the chosen number.
4. Think about all different scenarios in which the image will be used. Store the logical sum (OR) of all these usages in a variable of type `VkImageUsageFlags` named `usage`.
5. Create an image of a `VK_IMAGE_TYPE_2D` type, a `VK_FORMAT_R8G8B8A8_UNORM` format, six layers, and one sample per texel. Use the `logical_device`, `size`, `num_mipmaps`, and `usage` variables for the rest of the image parameters. Store the handle of the created image in a variable of type `VkImage` named `image` (refer to the *Creating an image* recipe).
6. Take the handle of the physical device from which the `logical_device` handle was acquired. Store it in a variable of type `VkPhysicalDevice` named `physical_device`.
7. Acquire the memory properties of a `physical_device`. Use them to allocate a memory object using a memory type with a `VK_MEMORY_PROPERTY_DEVICE_LOCAL_BIT` property. Store the handle of the allocated memory object in a variable of type `VkDeviceMemory` named `memory_object`, and bind it to the image (refer to the *Allocating and binding a memory object to an image* recipe).

8. Select the color aspect and store it in a variable of a `VkImageAspectFlags` type named `aspect`.
9. Create an image view of a `VK_IMAGE_VIEW_TYPE_CUBE` type and a `VK_FORMAT_R8G8B8A8_UNORM` format. Use the `logical_device`, `image`, and `aspect` variables during image view creation. Store the created handle in a variable of type `VkImageView` named `image_view` (refer to the *Creating an image view* recipe).

How it works...

The process of creating a CUBEMAP is very similar to creating any other type of images. First, we create the image itself. We just need to remember that the image should have at least six layers that will be interpreted as six CUBEMAP faces. For CUBEMAPs, we also cannot use more than one sample per texel:

```
if( !CreateImage( logical_device, VK_IMAGE_TYPE_2D,
VK_FORMAT_R8G8B8A8_UNORM, { size, size, 1 }, num_mipmaps, 6,
VK_SAMPLE_COUNT_1_BIT, usage, true, image ) ) {
  return false;
}
```

Next, we allocate and bind a memory object in the same way as for other resources:

```
if( !AllocateAndBindMemoryObjectToImage( physical_device, logical_device,
image, VK_MEMORY_PROPERTY_DEVICE_LOCAL_BIT, memory_object ) ) {
  return false;
}
```

Finally, we need to create an image view. Through it, we specify a CUBEMAP view type:

```
if( !CreateImageView( logical_device, image, VK_IMAGE_VIEW_TYPE_CUBE,
VK_FORMAT_R8G8B8A8_UNORM, aspect, image_view ) ) {
  return false;
}
```

> When using a CUBEMAP image view, image layers correspond to faces in the order +X, -X, +Y, -Y, +Z, and -Z.

See also

The following recipes in this chapter:

- *Creating an image*
- *Allocating and binding a memory object to an image*
- *Creating an image view*
- *Destroying an image view*
- *Destroying an image*
- *Freeing a memory object*

Mapping, updating and unmapping host-visible memory

For images and buffers that are used during rendering, it is recommended to bind a memory that is located on the graphics hardware (**device-local** memory). This gives us the best performance. But we can't access such memory directly, and we need to use intermediate (staging) resources which mediate the data transfer between a GPU (device) and a CPU (host).

Staging resources, on the other hand, need to use memory that is **host-visible**. To upload data to such memory, or to read data from it, we need to map it.

How to do it...

1. Take the handle of a created logical device and store it in a variable of type `VkDevice` named `logical_device`.
2. Select a memory object that was allocated on a memory type with a `VK_MEMORY_PROPERTY_HOST_VISIBLE_BIT` property. Store the memory object's handle in a variable of type `VkDeviceMemory` named `memory_object`.
3. Choose a memory region that should be mapped and updated. Store the offset (in bytes) from the beginning of a memory object's memory in a variable of type `VkDeviceSize` named `offset`.

4. Select the size of data to be copied to the selected region of the memory object. Represent the data size with a variable of type `VkDeviceSize` named `data_size`.
5. Prepare data that should be copied to the memory object. Set up a pointer to the beginning of the data and use it to initialize a variable of type `void*` named `data`.
6. Create a variable of type `void*` named `pointer`. It will contain a pointer to the mapped memory range.
7. Map the memory with a `vkMapMemory( logical_device, memory_object, offset, data_size, 0, &local_pointer )` call. Provide handles of the logical device and the memory object, offset from the start of the memory and the size (in bytes) of the region we want to map, a 0 value, and a pointer to the `pointer` variable.
8. Make sure the call was successful by checking whether the returned value was equal to `VK_SUCCESS`.
9. Copy the prepared data to the memory pointed to by the `pointer` variable. It can be done with the following call: `std::memcpy( local_pointer, data, data_size )`.
10. Create a variable of type `std::vector<VkMappedMemoryRange>` named `memory_ranges`. For each modified range, add an element to the vector and use the following values to initialize its members:
    - `VK_STRUCTURE_TYPE_MAPPED_MEMORY_RANGE` value for `sType`
    - `nullptr` value for `pNext`
    - `memory_object` variable for `memory`
    - Offset of each range for `offset`
    - Size of each range for `size`

5. Inform the driver which parts of the memory have changed. Do this by making the `vkFlushMappedMemoryRanges( logical_device, static_cast<uint32_t>(memory_ranges.size()), &memory_ranges[0] )` call, for which provide the `logical_device` variable, the number of modified ranges (elements in the `memory_ranges` vector), and a pointer to the first element of the `memory_ranges` vector.
6. Make sure the flushing was successful and the call returned a `VK_SUCCESS` value.
7. To unmap the memory, call `vkUnmapMemory( logical_device, memory_object )`.

How it works...

Mapping the memory is the simplest way to upload data to the Vulkan resources. During the mapping, we specify which part of the memory should be mapped (offset from the beginning of the memory object and a size of the mapped range):

```
VkResult result;
void * local_pointer;
result = vkMapMemory( logical_device, memory_object, offset, data_size, 0,
&local_pointer );
if( VK_SUCCESS != result ) {
  std::cout << "Could not map memory object." << std::endl;
  return false;
}
```

Mapping gives us a pointer to the requested memory part. We can use this pointer like we use other pointers in typical C++ applications. There are no restrictions on whether we write or read data from such memory. In this recipe, we copy data from the application to the memory object:

```
std::memcpy( local_pointer, data, data_size );
```

When we update the mapped memory range, we need to inform the driver that memory contents were modified or the uploaded data may not immediately become visible for other operations submitted to queues. Informing about the memory data modifications performed by the CPU (host) is called flushing. For this, we prepare a list of updated memory ranges which don't need to cover the whole mapped memory:

```
std::vector<VkMappedMemoryRange> memory_ranges = {
  {
  VK_STRUCTURE_TYPE_MAPPED_MEMORY_RANGE,
  nullptr,
  memory_object,
  offset,
  data_size
  }
};

vkFlushMappedMemoryRanges( logical_device,
static_cast<uint32_t>(memory_ranges.size()), &memory_ranges[0] );
if( VK_SUCCESS != result ) {
  std::cout << "Could not flush mapped memory." << std::endl;
  return false;
}
```

After we are done dealing with a mapped memory, we can unmap it. Memory mapping shouldn't influence the performance of our application and we can keep the acquired pointer for the whole lifetime of our application. But, we should release it (unmap) before we close the application and destroy all resources:

```
if( unmap ) {
  vkUnmapMemory( logical_device, memory_object );
} else if( nullptr != pointer ) {
  *pointer = local_pointer;
}

return true;
```

See also

The following recipes in this chapter:

- *Allocating and binding a memory object to a buffer*
- *Allocating and binding a memory object to an image*
- *Using a staging buffer to update a buffer with a device-local memory bound*
- *Using a staging buffer to update an image with a device-local memory bound*
- *Freeing a memory object*

Copying data between buffers

In Vulkan, to upload data to a buffer, we are not limited only to the memory mapping technique. It is possible to copy data between buffers, even if the memory objects bound to them were allocated from different memory types.

How to do it...

1. Take the handle of a command buffer. Store it in a variable of type `VkCommandBuffer` named `command_buffer`. Make sure the command buffer is in the recording state (refer to the *Beginning a command buffer recording operation* recipe from `Chapter 3`, *Command Buffers and Synchronization*).

2. Take the buffer from which data will be copied. Represent this buffer with a variable of type `VkBuffer` named `source_buffer`.
3. Take the buffer to which data will be uploaded. Represent this buffer using a variable of type `VkBuffer` named `destination_buffer`.
4. Create a variable of type `std::vector<VkBufferCopy>` named `regions`. For each memory region from which data should be copied, add an element to the `regions` vector. In each element, specify the memory offset in the source buffer from which data should be copied, a memory offset in the target buffer to which data should be copied, and the size of data to be copied from a given region.
5. Call `vkCmdCopyBuffer( command_buffer, source_buffer, destination_buffer, static_cast<uint32_t>(regions.size()), &regions[0] )`, for which use the `command_buffer`, `source_buffer` and `destination_buffer` variables, the number of elements in the `regions` vector, and a pointer to the first element of that vector.

How it works...

Copying data between buffers is another way of updating the memory contents of a given resource. This operation needs to be recorded to the command buffer, like this:

```
if( regions.size() > 0 ) {
  vkCmdCopyBuffer( command_buffer, source_buffer, destination_buffer,
static_cast<uint32_t>(regions.size()), &regions[0] );
}
```

For the best performance, resources that are used during rendering should have a device-local memory bound. But, we can't map such memory. Using the `vkCmdCopyBuffer()` function, we can copy data to such a buffer from another buffer that has a host-visible memory bound to it. Such memory can be mapped and updated directly from our application.

> Buffers from which data can be copied must be created with a `VK_BUFFER_USAGE_TRANSFER_SRC_BIT` usage.
>
> Buffers into which we transfer data must be created with a `VK_BUFFER_USAGE_TRANSFER_DST_BIT` usage.

When we want to use a buffer as a target for transfer operations (we want to copy data to the buffer), we should set a memory barrier that will inform the driver that from now on, operations performed on the buffer are represented by a `VK_ACCESS_TRANSFER_WRITE_BIT` memory access scheme. After we are done copying data to the destination buffer and we want to use it for the desired purpose, we should set another memory barrier. This time, we should specify that previously we were transferring data to the buffer (so the operations were represented by the `VK_ACCESS_TRANSFER_WRITE_BIT` memory access type), but after the barrier the buffer will be used differently, with another memory access type representing operations performed on it (refer to the *Setting a buffer memory barrier* recipe).

See also

The following recipes in this chapter:

- *Creating a buffer*
- *Setting a buffer memory barrier*
- *Mapping, updating, and unmapping host-visible memory*
- *Using a staging buffer to update a buffer with a device-local memory bound*

Copying data from a buffer to an image

For images, we can bind memory objects that are allocated from different memory types. Only host-visible memory can be mapped and updated directly from our application. When we want to update the memory of an image that uses a device-local memory, we need to copy data from a buffer.

How to do it...

1. Take the handle of a command buffer and store it in a variable of type `VkCommandBuffer` named `command_buffer`. Make sure the command buffer is already in a recording state (refer to the *Beginning a command buffer recording operation* recipe from `Chapter 3`, *Command Buffers and Synchronization*).
2. Take a buffer from which data will be copied. Store its handle in a variable of type `VkBuffer` named `source_buffer`.

3. Take the image to which data will be copied. Represent this image with a variable of type `VkImage` named `destination_image`.
4. Create a variable of type `VkImageLayout` named `image_layout`, in which the image's current layout will be stored.
5. Create a variable of type `std::vector<VkBufferImageCopy>` named `regions`. For each memory region from which data should be copied, add an element to the `regions` vector. Specify the following values for members of each element:
   - Offset from the beginning of a buffer's memory from which data should be copied for `bufferOffset`.
   - The length of data that represents a single row in the buffer or a 0 value if the data is tightly packed (according to the size of the destination image) for `bufferRowLength`.
   - The height of the imaginary image stored in the buffer or a 0 value if the buffer's data is tightly packed (according to the size of the destination image) for `bufferImageHeight`.
   - Initialize the `imageSubresource` member with the following values:
     - Image's aspect (color, depth or stencil) for `aspectMask`
     - Number (index) of mipmap level to be updated for `mipLevel`
     - Number of the first array layer to be updated for `baseArrayLayer`
     - Number of array layers that will be updated for `layerCount`
   - Initial offset (in texels) of image's sub region that should be updated for `imageOffset`
   - The size (dimensions) of an image for `imageExtent`
6. Call `vkCmdCopyBufferToImage( command_buffer, source_buffer, destination_image, image_layout, static_cast<uint32_t>(regions.size()), &regions[0] )`, for which use the `command_buffer`, `source_buffer`, `destination_image` and `image_layout` variables, the number of elements in the `regions` vector, and a pointer to the first element of that vector.

How it works...

Copying data between a buffer and an image is done through a command buffer, in which we record the following operation:

```
if( regions.size() > 0 ) {
  vkCmdCopyBufferToImage( command_buffer, source_buffer, destination_image,
  image_layout, static_cast<uint32_t>(regions.size()), &regions[0] );
}
```

We need to know how the image data is laid out inside the buffer, so the image's memory is properly uploaded. We need to provide a memory offset (from the beginning of the buffer's memory), the length of the data row, and the height of the data in a buffer. This allows the driver to properly address the memory and copy the buffer's contents into the image. We can also provide zeros for row length and a height, which means that the buffer contains data that is tightly packed and it corresponds to the destination image's dimensions.

We also need to provide information about the destination of a data transfer operation. This involves defining an offset from the image's origin (from the upper-left corner in texels) for x, y, and z dimensions, the mipmap level into which data will be copied and a base array layer, and the number of layers that will be updated. We also need to specify the destination image's dimensions.

All the preceding parameters are specified through an array of `VkBufferImageCopy` elements. We can provide many regions at once and copy memory ranges that are not continuous.

On hardware architectures with several different memory types exposed by a physical device, it is recommended to use a device-local-only memory for resources that are used during rendering (performance-critical paths of our application). Such memory is usually faster than the memory that is also host-visible. Host-visible memory should be used only for staging resources which are used to upload data from, or download data to, the CPU (our application).

On architectures with only one memory type that is both device local and host-visible, we don't need to bother with intermediate staging resources for data upload. But, the presented approach is still valid and may unify the application's behavior across different execution environments. This may make maintenance of our application easier.

Resources and Memory

In both cases, we can easily map the staging resource's memory and access it in our application. Next we can use it to transfer data to and from a device-local memory, which (generally) cannot be mapped. This is achieved with the copy operation described in this recipe.

> Buffers from which data can be copied must be created with a VK_BUFFER_USAGE_TRANSFER_SRC_BIT usage.
>
> Images into which we transfer data must be created with a VK_BUFFER_USAGE_TRANSFER_DST_BIT usage. Before the transfer operation, we also need to transition the image layout to a VK_IMAGE_LAYOUT_TRANSFER_DST_OPTIMAL.

Before we can transfer data to an image, we must change its memory layout. We can only copy data to an image whose current memory layout is set to VK_IMAGE_LAYOUT_TRANSFER_DST_OPTIMAL. We can also use a VK_IMAGE_LAYOUT_GENERAL layout, but it is not recommended due to lower performance.

So before we can copy data to an image, we should set a memory barrier that will change the image's memory access type from the one that occurred so far to a VK_ACCESS_TRANSFER_WRITE_BIT. The barrier should also perform a layout transition from the current layout to the VK_IMAGE_LAYOUT_TRANSFER_DST_OPTIMAL layout. After we are done copying data to the image and we want to use it for other purposes, we should set another memory barrier. This time, we should change the memory access type from VK_ACCESS_TRANSFER_WRITE_BIT to the access that corresponds to the purpose for which the image will be used. And we should also transition the image's layout from VK_IMAGE_LAYOUT_TRANSFER_DST_OPTIMAL to the one that is compatible with the image's next usage (refer to the *Setting an image memory barrier* recipe). Without these barriers, not only might the data transfer operation be invalid, but the data might not become visible for other operations performed on the image.

If the buffer that is a source of data is used for other purposes, we should also set a memory barrier for it and perform similar memory access changes before and after the transfer operation. But as the buffer is a source of data, we set a VK_ACCESS_TRANSFER_READ_BIT access type in the first barrier. It can be done with the same pipeline barriers which changed the parameters of the image. Refer to the *Setting a buffer memory barrier* recipe for more details.

See also

The following recipes in this chapter:

- *Creating a buffer*
- *Allocating and binding a memory object to a buffer*
- *Setting a buffer memory barrier*
- *Creating an image*
- *Allocating and binding a memory object to an image*
- *Setting an image memory barrier*
- *Mapping, updating, and unmapping host-visible memory*
- *Copying data from an image to a buffer*

Copying data from an image to a buffer

In Vulkan, we can not only transfer data from a buffer to an image, but also the other way-- we can copy data from an image to the buffer. It doesn't matter what the properties of memory objects bound to them are. But, the data copy operation is the only way to update a device-local memory which cannot be mapped.

How to do it...

1. Take the handle of a command buffer and store it in a variable of type `VkCommandBuffer` named `command_buffer`. Make sure the command buffer is already in a recording state (refer to the *Beginning a command buffer recording operation* recipe from Chapter 3, *Command Buffers and Synchronization*).
2. Take an image from which data will be copied. Store its handle in a variable of type `VkImage` named `source_image`.
3. Take the source image's current memory layout and use it to initialize a variable of type `VkImageLayout` named `image_layout`.
4. Take the buffer to which data will be copied. Prepare its handle in a variable of type `VkBuffer` named `destination_buffer`.

5. Create a variable of type `std::vector<VkBufferImageCopy>` named `regions`. For each region in the memory from which data should be copied, add an element to the `regions` vector. Specify the following values for members of each element:
    - Offset from the beginning of a buffer's memory to which data should be copied for `bufferOffset`.
    - The length of data that will compose a single row in the buffer or a 0 value if the data is tightly packed (according to the size of the source image) for `bufferRowLength`.
    - The height of the image in the buffer (number of rows) or a 0 value if the buffer's data is tightly packed (according to the size of the source image) for `bufferImageHeight`.
    - Initialize `imageSubresource` member with the following values:
        - Image's aspect (color, depth or stencil) for `aspectMask`
        - Number (index) of a mipmap level from which data will be copied for `mipLevel`
        - Index of the first array layer from which contents will be copied for `baseArrayLayer`
        - Number of array layers to copy for `layerCount`
    - Initial offset (in texels) of image's subregion from which data will be read and copied to buffer for `imageOffset`.
    - The size of an image for `imageExtent`.
6. Call `vkCmdCopyImageToBuffer( command_buffer, source_image, image_layout, destination_buffer, static_cast<uint32_t>(regions.size()), &regions[0] )`, for which use the `command_buffer`, `source_image`, `image_layout`, and `destination_buffer` variables, the number of elements in the `regions` vector, and a pointer to the first element of that vector.

How it works...

Data copy from an image to a buffer is an operation that is recorded to the command buffer like this:

```
if( regions.size() > 0 ) {
  vkCmdCopyImageToBuffer( command_buffer, source_image, image_layout,
destination_buffer, static_cast<uint32_t>(regions.size()), &regions[0] );
}
```

The command buffer must be already in a recording state.

For the data to be copied properly, we need to provide multiple parameters that define the source of the data and the destination to which the data will be copied. These parameters consist of an offset from the image's origin (from the upper-left corner in texels) for x, y, and z dimensions, the mipmap level and a base array layer from which data will be copied, and the number of layers that will be the source of the data. Image dimensions are also required.

For the destination buffer, we specify a memory offset (from the beginning of the buffer's memory), the length of the data row and the height of the data in a buffer. We can also provide zeros for row length and height, which means that the data copied to the buffer will be tightly packed and will correspond to the source image's dimensions.

The preceding parameters are specified using an array of VkBufferImageCopy elements, similar to copying data from a buffer to an image as described in the *Copying data from a buffer to an image* recipe. We can provide many regions and copy memory ranges that are not continuous all as part of one copy operation.

> Images from which we copy data must be created with a VK_BUFFER_USAGE_TRANSFER_SRC_BIT usage. Before the transfer operation, we also need to transition the image's layout to a VK_IMAGE_LAYOUT_TRANSFER_SRC_OPTIMAL.
>
> Buffers to which data can be copied must be created with a VK_BUFFER_USAGE_TRANSFER_DST_BIT usage.

Before we can copy data from an image, we should set a memory barrier and change the image's layout from the one currently used to the VK_IMAGE_LAYOUT_TRANSFER_SRC_OPTIMAL layout. We also should change the type of memory access from the one that occurred so far to VK_ACCESS_TRANSFER_READ_BIT. A barrier should also be set after we are done copying data from the image, if it will be used for other purposes from now on. This time, we should change the memory access type from VK_ACCESS_TRANSFER_READ_BIT to the access that corresponds to the purpose for which the image will be used. At the same time, we should transition the layout from VK_IMAGE_LAYOUT_TRANSFER_SRC_OPTIMAL to the one that is compatible with the image's next usage (refer to the *Setting an image memory barrier* recipe). Without these barriers, not only might the data transfer operation be performed in the wrong way, but later commands may overwrite the image's contents before the transfer operation has finished.

Resources and Memory

Similar barriers should be set for the buffer (but they can be a part of the same pipeline barrier). If previously the buffer was used for other purposes, we should change the memory access to `VK_ACCESS_TRANSFER_WRITE_BIT` before the transfer operation, as described in the *Setting a buffer memory barrier* recipe.

See also

The following recipes in this chapter:

- *Creating a buffer*
- *Allocating and binding a memory object to a buffer*
- *Setting a buffer memory barrier*
- *Creating an image*
- *Allocating and binding a memory object to an image*
- *Setting an image memory barrier*
- *Mapping, updating, and unmapping host-visible memory*
- *Copying data from a buffer to an image*

Using a staging buffer to update a buffer with a device-local memory bound

Staging resources are used to update the contents of a memory that is not host-visible. Such memory cannot be mapped, so we need an intermediate buffer whose contents can be easily mapped and updated, and from which data can be transferred.

How to do it...

1. Take the handle of a logical device stored in a variable of type `VkDevice` named `logical_device`.
2. Prepare the data that should be uploaded to the target buffer. Set up a pointer to the beginning of a data source and store it in a variable of type `void*` named `data`. The size of the data (in bytes) should be represented with a variable of type `VkDeviceSize` named `data_size`.

3. Create a variable of type `VkBuffer` named `staging_buffer`. In it, the handle of a staging buffer will be stored.
4. Create a buffer that is big enough to hold the `data_size` number of bytes. Specify `VK_BUFFER_USAGE_TRANSFER_SRC_BIT` usage during buffer creation. Use the `logical_device` variable during the creation process and store the created handle in the `staging_buffer` variable (refer to the *Creating a buffer* recipe).
5. Take the handle of the physical device from which the `logical_device` handle was created. Use the physical device's handle to initialize a variable of type `VkPhysicalDevice` named `physical_device`.
6. Create a variable of type `VkDeviceMemory` named `memory_object` that will be used to create a memory object for the staging buffer.
7. Allocate a memory object using the `physical_device`, `logical_device`, and `staging_buffer` variables. Allocate a memory object from a memory type that has a `VK_MEMORY_PROPERTY_HOST_VISIBLE_BIT` property. Store the created handle in the `memory_object` variable and bind it to the staging buffer (refer to the *Allocating and binding a memory object to a buffer* recipe).
8. Map the memory of the `memory_object` using the `logical_device` variable, a 0 value for offset, and the `data_size` variable for the size of the mapped memory. Copy the data from the `data` pointer to the memory pointed to by the acquired pointer. Un-map the memory (refer to the *Mapping, updating, and unmapping host-visible memory* recipe).
9. Take the handle of an allocated primary command buffer and use it to initialize a variable of type `VkCommandBuffer` named `command_buffer`.
10. Begin recording of the `command_buffer`. Provide a `VK_COMMAND_BUFFER_USAGE_ONE_TIME_SUBMIT_BIT` flag (refer to the *Beginning a command buffer recording operation* recipe from `Chapter 3`, *Command Buffers and Synchronization*).
11. Take the handle of a buffer to which data will be transferred. Make sure it was created with a `VK_BUFFER_USAGE_TRANSFER_DST_BIT` usage. Store its handle in a variable of type `VkBuffer` named `destination_buffer`.

12. Record a memory barrier for a `destination_buffer` in the `command_buffer` variable. Provide pipeline stages which have been referencing the `destination_buffer` so far for the generating stages, and use a `VK_PIPELINE_STAGE_TRANSFER_BIT` stage for the consuming stages. Provide the type of memory access operations that have been referencing the buffer so far and use a `VK_ACCESS_TRANSFER_WRITE_BIT` value for the new memory access type. Ignore queue family indices--provide `VK_QUEUE_FAMILY_IGNORED` for both indices (refer to the *Setting a buffer memory barrier* recipe).
13. Create a variable of type `VkDeviceSize` named `destination_offset`, and initialize it with an offset value to which data should be transferred to in the target buffer's memory.
14. Copy data from the `staging_buffer` to the `destination_buffer` using the `command_buffer` variable. Provide a 0 value for the source offset, the `destination_offset` variable for the destination offset, and the `data_size` variable for the size of the data to be transferred (refer to the *Copying data between buffers* recipe).
15. Record another memory barrier for the `destination_buffer` in the `command_buffer` variable. Provide a `VK_PIPELINE_STAGE_TRANSFER_BIT` value for the generating stages and a set of pipeline stages in which `destination_buffer` will be used from now on. Use the `VK_ACCESS_TRANSFER_WRITE_BIT` value for the current memory access type and a value that is proper for the way in which the buffer will be used after the memory transfer. Use a `VK_QUEUE_FAMILY_IGNORED` value for queue family indices (refer to the *Setting a buffer memory barrier* recipe).
16. End recording of the `command_buffer` (refer to the *Ending a command buffer recording operation* recipe in Chapter 3, *Command Buffers and Synchronization*).
17. Take the handle of the queue on which the transfer operation will be performed and store it in a variable of type `VkQueue` named `queue`.
18. Create a list of semaphores that should be signaled when the transfer operation is completed. Store their handles in a variable of type `std::vector<VkSemaphore>` named `signal_semaphores`.
19. Create a variable of type `VkFence` named `fence`.
20. Create an unsignaled fence using the `logical_device` variable. Store the created handle in the `fence` variable (refer to the *Creating a fence* recipe from Chapter 3, *Command Buffers and Synchronization*).

Chapter 4

21. Submit `command_buffer` to the `queue`. Provide a list of semaphores from the `signal_semaphores` vector as a list of semaphores to be signaled, and the `fence` variable for the fence to be signaled (refer to the *Submitting command buffers to the queue* recipe in `Chapter 3`, *Command Buffers and Synchronization*).
22. Wait for the fence object to be signaled using the `logical_device` and `fence` variables. Provide a desired timeout value (refer to the *Waiting for fences* recipe in `Chapter 3`, *Command Buffers and Synchronization*).
23. Destroy the buffer represented by the `staging_buffer` variable (refer to the *Destroying a buffer* recipe).
24. Free the memory object represented by the `memory_object` variable (refer to the *Freeing a memory object* recipe).

How it works...

To use a staging resource for a transfer operation, we need a buffer with a memory that can be mapped. We can use an existing buffer or create a new one like this:

```
VkBuffer staging_buffer;
if( !CreateBuffer( logical_device, data_size,
VK_BUFFER_USAGE_TRANSFER_SRC_BIT, staging_buffer ) ) {
  return false;
}

VkDeviceMemory memory_object;
if( !AllocateAndBindMemoryObjectToBuffer( physical_device, logical_device,
staging_buffer, VK_MEMORY_PROPERTY_HOST_VISIBLE_BIT, memory_object ) ) {
  return false;
}
```

Next, we need to map the buffer's memory and update its contents:

```
if( !MapUpdateAndUnmapHostVisibleMemory( logical_device, memory_object, 0,
data_size, data, true, nullptr ) ) {
  return false;
}
```

[219]

Resources and Memory

With a staging buffer ready, we can begin a transfer operation that will copy the data to the desired, target buffer. First, we start by beginning the command buffer recording operation and setting a memory barrier for the destination buffer to change its usage to the target for data copy operation. We don't need the memory barrier for the staging buffer. When we map and update the buffer's memory, its contents become visible for other commands, because an implicit barrier is set for the host writer when we start a command buffer recording:

```
if( !BeginCommandBufferRecordingOperation( command_buffer,
VK_COMMAND_BUFFER_USAGE_ONE_TIME_SUBMIT_BIT, nullptr ) ) {
  return false;
}

SetBufferMemoryBarrier( command_buffer,
destination_buffer_generating_stages, VK_PIPELINE_STAGE_TRANSFER_BIT, { {
destination_buffer, destination_buffer_current_access,
VK_ACCESS_TRANSFER_WRITE_BIT, VK_QUEUE_FAMILY_IGNORED,
VK_QUEUE_FAMILY_IGNORED } } );
```

Next, we can record data copying from the **staging resource** to the destination buffer:

```
CopyDataBetweenBuffers( command_buffer, staging_buffer, destination_buffer,
{ { 0, destination_offset, data_size } } );
```

After this, we need a second memory barrier for the target buffer. This time, we change its usage from being a target of copy operations to the one the buffer will be used for after the data transfer. We can also end command buffer recording:

```
SetBufferMemoryBarrier( command_buffer, VK_PIPELINE_STAGE_TRANSFER_BIT,
destination_buffer_consuming_stages, { { destination_buffer,
VK_ACCESS_TRANSFER_WRITE_BIT, destination_buffer_new_access,
VK_QUEUE_FAMILY_IGNORED, VK_QUEUE_FAMILY_IGNORED } } );

if( !EndCommandBufferRecordingOperation( command_buffer ) ) {
  return false;
}
```

Next, we create a fence and submit the command buffer to the queue, where it will be processed and the data transfer will be actually performed:

```
VkFence fence;
if( !CreateFence( logical_device, false, fence ) ) {
  return false;
}
if( !SubmitCommandBuffersToQueue( queue, {}, { command_buffer },
signal_semaphores, fence ) ) {
  return false;
}
```

If we don't want to use a staging buffer any more, we can destroy it. But, we can't do this until the staging buffer won't be used any more by the commands submitted to the queue: that's why we need a fence. We wait on it until the driver signals when the processing of a submitted command buffer has finished. Then, we can safely destroy a staging buffer and free the memory object bound to it:

```
if( !WaitForFences( logical_device, { fence }, VK_FALSE, 500000000 ) ) {
  return false;
}

DestroyBuffer( logical_device, staging_buffer );
FreeMemoryObject( logical_device, memory_object );
return true;
```

In real-life scenarios, we should use an existing buffer and reuse it as a staging buffer as many times as possible to avoid unnecessary buffer creation and destruction operations. This way, we also avoid waiting on a fence.

See also

In Chapter 3, *Command Buffers and Synchronization*, see the following recipes:

- *Beginning a command buffer recording operation*
- *Ending a command buffer recording operation*
- *Creating a fence*
- *Waiting for fences*
- *Submitting command buffers to the queue*

Resources and Memory

See the following recipes in this chapter:

- *Creating a buffer*
- *Allocating and binding a memory object to a buffer*
- *Setting an image memory barrier*
- *Mapping, updating, and unmapping host-visible memory*
- *Copying data from a buffer to an image*
- *Using a staging buffer to update an image with a device-local memory bound*
- *Freeing a memory object*
- *Destroying a buffer*

Using a staging buffer to update an image with a device-local memory bound

Staging buffers can be used not only to transfer data between buffers, but also to and from an image. Here, we will show how to map a buffer's memory and copy its contents to a desired image.

How to do it...

1. Create a staging buffer big enough to hold the entire data to be transferred. Specify a `VK_BUFFER_USAGE_TRANSFER_SRC_BIT` usage for the buffer and store its handle in a variable of type `VkBuffer` named `staging_buffer`. Allocate a memory object that supports the `VK_MEMORY_PROPERTY_HOST_VISIBLE_BIT` property and bind it to the staging buffer. Store the memory object's handle in a variable of type `VkDeviceMemory` named `memory_object`. Map the memory and update its contents with the data to be transferred to the image. Unmap the memory. Perform these steps as described in more detail in the *Using a staging buffer to update a buffer with a device-local memory bound* recipe.
2. Take the handle of a primary command buffer and use it to initialize a variable of type `VkCommandBuffer` named `command_buffer`.
3. Begin recording of the `command_buffer`. Provide a `VK_COMMAND_BUFFER_USAGE_ONE_TIME_SUBMIT_BIT` flag (refer to the *Beginning a command buffer recording operation* recipe from `Chapter 3`, *Command Buffers and Synchronization*).

4. Take the handle of the image to which data will be transferred and make sure it was created with a `VK_IMAGE_USAGE_TRANSFER_DST_BIT` specified. Use the handle to initialize a variable of type `VkImage` named `destination_image`.
5. Record an image memory barrier in the `command_buffer`. Specify the stages in which the image was used so far and use a `VK_PIPELINE_STAGE_TRANSFER_BIT` stage for the consuming stages. Use the `destination_image` variable, provide the image's current access, and use a `VK_ACCESS_TRANSFER_WRITE_BIT` value for the new access. Specify the image's current layout and use a `VK_IMAGE_LAYOUT_TRANSFER_DST_OPTIMAL` value for the new layout. Provide the image's aspect, but ignore queue family indices--use `VK_QUEUE_FAMILY_IGNORED` values for both (refer to the *Setting an image memory barrier* recipe).
6. In the `command_buffer`, record the data transfer operation from `staging_buffer` to `destination_image`. Provide a `VK_IMAGE_LAYOUT_TRANSFER_DST_OPTIMAL` value as an image layout, a 0 value for the buffer's offset, a 0 value for the buffer's row lengths, and a 0 value for the buffer's image height. Specify the image's memory region into which data should be copied by providing the desired mipmap level, base array layer index, and the number of layers to be updated. Provide the image's aspect too. Specify the offset into the image's x, y, and z coordinates (in texels) and the image's size (refer to the *Copying data from a buffer to an image* recipe).
7. Record another image memory barrier into the `command_buffer`. This time, specify a `VK_PIPELINE_STAGE_TRANSFER_BIT` value for generating stages and set proper stages in which the target image will be used after the data transfer. In the barrier, change the image's layout from `VK_IMAGE_LAYOUT_TRANSFER_DST_OPTIMAL` into the value proper for the new usage. Set a `VK_QUEUE_FAMILY_IGNORED` value for both queue families and also provide the image's aspect (refer to the *Setting an image memory barrier* recipe).
8. End the command buffer recording operation, create an unsignaled fence and use it, along with semaphores that should be signaled, during submitting the command buffer to the queue. Wait for the created fence to be signaled, destroy the staging buffer, and free its memory object as described in the *Using a staging buffer to update a buffer with a device-local memory bound* recipe.

Resources and Memory

How it works...

This recipe is very similar to the *Using a staging buffer to update a buffer with a device-local memory bound* recipe; that's why only the differences are described in more detail.

First we create a staging buffer, allocate a memory object for it, bind it to the buffer, and map it to upload data from our application to the GPU:

```
VkBuffer staging_buffer;
if( !CreateBuffer( logical_device, data_size,
VK_BUFFER_USAGE_TRANSFER_SRC_BIT, staging_buffer ) ) {
  return false;
}

VkDeviceMemory memory_object;
if( !AllocateAndBindMemoryObjectToBuffer( physical_device, logical_device,
staging_buffer, VK_MEMORY_PROPERTY_HOST_VISIBLE_BIT, memory_object ) ) {
  return false;
}

if( !MapUpdateAndUnmapHostVisibleMemory( logical_device, memory_object, 0,
data_size, data, true, nullptr ) ) {
  return false;
}
```

Next we begin command buffer recording, and set one barrier for the destination image so it can be used as a target for data transfer. We also record the data transfer operation:

```
if( !BeginCommandBufferRecordingOperation( command_buffer,
VK_COMMAND_BUFFER_USAGE_ONE_TIME_SUBMIT_BIT, nullptr ) ) {
  return false;
}

SetImageMemoryBarrier( command_buffer, destination_image_generating_stages,
VK_PIPELINE_STAGE_TRANSFER_BIT,
{
  {
    destination_image,
    destination_image_current_access,
    VK_ACCESS_TRANSFER_WRITE_BIT,
    destination_image_current_layout,
    VK_IMAGE_LAYOUT_TRANSFER_DST_OPTIMAL,
    VK_QUEUE_FAMILY_IGNORED,
    VK_QUEUE_FAMILY_IGNORED,
    destination_image_aspect
} } );
```

```
CopyDataFromBufferToImage( command_buffer, staging_buffer,
destination_image, VK_IMAGE_LAYOUT_TRANSFER_DST_OPTIMAL,
{
  {
    0,
    0,
    0,
    destination_image_subresource,
    destination_image_offset,
    destination_image_size,
} } );
```

Next, we record another barrier that changes the image's usage from being the target of the copy operation to the one that is valid for the purpose for which the image will be used next. We also end the command buffer recording operation:

```
SetImageMemoryBarrier( command_buffer, VK_PIPELINE_STAGE_TRANSFER_BIT,
destination_image_consuming_stages,
{
  {
    destination_image,
    VK_ACCESS_TRANSFER_WRITE_BIT,
    destination_image_new_access,
    VK_IMAGE_LAYOUT_TRANSFER_DST_OPTIMAL,
    destination_image_new_layout,
    VK_QUEUE_FAMILY_IGNORED,
    VK_QUEUE_FAMILY_IGNORED,
    destination_image_aspect
} } );

if( !EndCommandBufferRecordingOperation( command_buffer ) ) {
  return false;
}
```

After that, we create a fence and submit a command buffer to the queue. We then wait on the fence to know the moment when we can safely delete the staging buffer and its memory object. We do it afterwards:

```
VkFence fence;
if( !CreateFence( logical_device, false, fence ) ) {
  return false;
}

if( !SubmitCommandBuffersToQueue( queue, {}, { command_buffer },
signal_semaphores, fence ) ) {
  return false;
}
```

Resources and Memory

```
if( !WaitForFences( logical_device, { fence }, VK_FALSE, 500000000 ) ) {
  return false;
}

DestroyBuffer( logical_device, staging_buffer );
FreeMemoryObject( logical_device, memory_object );

return true;
```

If we are reusing the existing buffer as a staging resource, we don't need the fence, because the buffer will live much longer, maybe for the whole lifetime of the application. This way, we can avoid frequent and unnecessary buffer creation and deletion, and memory object allocation and freeing.

See also

In `Chapter 3`, *Command Buffer and Synchronization*, see the following recipes:

- *Beginning a command buffer recording operation*
- *Ending a command buffer recording operation*
- *Creating a fence*
- *Waiting for fences*
- *Submitting command buffers to the queue*

See the following recipes in this chapter:

- *Creating a buffer*
- *Allocating and binding a memory object to a buffer*
- *Setting an image memory barrier*
- *Mapping, updating, and unmapping host-visible memory*
- *Copying data from a buffer to an image*
- *Using a staging buffer to update an image with a device-local memory bound*
- *Freeing a memory object*
- *Destroying a buffer*

Destroying an image view

When we don't need an image view any more, we should destroy it.

How to do it...

1. Take the handle of a logical device and store it in a variable of type `VkDevice` named `logical_device`.
2. Take the handle of an image view stored in a variable of type `VkImageView` named `image_view`.
3. Call `vkDestroyImageView( logical_device, image_view, nullptr )` and provide the handle of the logical device, the handle of the image view, and a `nullptr` value.
4. For safety reasons, assign a `VK_NULL_HANDLE` value to the `image_view` variable.

How it works...

Destroying an image view requires us to use its handle and the handle of the logical device on which the image view was created. It is performed in the following way:

```
if( VK_NULL_HANDLE != image_view ) {
  vkDestroyImageView( logical_device, image_view, nullptr );
  image_view = VK_NULL_HANDLE;
}
```

First, we check whether the handle is not empty. We don't need to do it--destroying a null handle is silently ignored. But it's good to skip unnecessary function calls. Next, we destroy the image view and assign a null handle to the variable in which the handle was stored.

See also

- *Creating an image view* recipe in this chapter

Destroying an image

Images that won't be used any more should be destroyed to release their resources.

How to do it...

1. Take a logical device and store its handle in a variable of type `VkDevice` named `logical_device`.
2. Use the image's handle to initialize a variable of type `VkImage` named `image`.
3. Call `vkDestroyImage( logical_device, image, nullptr )`. Provide the handle of the logical device, the handle of the image, and a `nullptr` value.
4. For safety reasons, assign a `VK_NULL_HANDLE` value to the `image` variable.

How it works...

Images are destroyed through a single call of the `vkDestroyImage()` function. For it, we provide the handle of the logical device, the handle of the image, and a `nullptr` value, like this:

```
if( VK_NULL_HANDLE != image ) {
  vkDestroyImage( logical_device, image, nullptr );
  image = VK_NULL_HANDLE;
}
```

We also try to avoid unnecessary function calls by checking whether the image's handle is not empty.

See also

- *Creating an image* recipe in this chapter

Destroying a buffer view

When we don't need a buffer view any more, we should destroy it.

Chapter 4

How to do it...

1. Take a logical device and store its handle in a variable of type `VkDevice` named `logical_device`.
2. Use the buffer's view handle and initialize a variable of type `VkBufferView` named `buffer_view` with it.
3. Call `vkDestroyBufferView( logical_device, buffer_view, nullptr )`. Provide the handle of the logical device, the handle of the buffer view, and a `nullptr` value.
4. For safety reasons, assign the `VK_NULL_HANDLE` value to the `buffer_view` variable.

How it works...

Buffer views are destroyed using the `vkDestroyBufferView()` function:

```
if( VK_NULL_HANDLE != buffer_view ) {
  vkDestroyBufferView( logical_device, buffer_view, nullptr );
  buffer_view = VK_NULL_HANDLE;
}
```

To avoid unnecessary function calls, we check whether the buffer view's handle is not empty before we call a buffer view destroying function.

See also

- *Creating a buffer view* recipe in this chapter

Freeing a memory object

In Vulkan, when we create resources, we later destroy them. On the other hand, resources that represent different memory objects or pools are allocated and freed. Memory objects bound to images and buffers are also freed. We should free them when we no longer need them.

[229]

How to do it...

1. Take the logical device's handle and store it in a variable of type `VkDevice` named `logical_device`.
2. Take the variable of type `VkDeviceMemory` named `memory_object`, in which the handle of the memory object is stored.
3. Call `vkFreeMemory( logical_device, memory_object, nullptr )`. Use the handle of the logical device, the handle of the memory object, and a `nullptr` value.
4. For safety reasons, assign the `VK_NULL_HANDLE` value to the `memory_object` variable.

How it works...

Memory objects can be freed before resources that were using them are destroyed. But we can't use these resources any more, we can only destroy them. In general, we can't bind one memory object to the resource, free it, and then bind another memory object to the same resource.

To free a memory object, we can write the following code:

```
if( VK_NULL_HANDLE != memory_object ) {
  vkFreeMemory( logical_device, memory_object, nullptr );
  memory_object = VK_NULL_HANDLE;
}
```

Memory objects must have been allocated from a logical device represented by the `logical_device` variable.

See also

The following recipes in this chapter:

- *Allocating and binding a memory object to a buffer*
- *Allocating and binding a memory object to an image*

Destroying a buffer

When a buffer is no longer used, we should destroy it.

How to do it...

1. Take the handle of a logical device and store it in a variable of type `VkDevice` named `logical_device`.
2. Store the buffer's handle in a variable of type `VkBuffer` named `buffer`.
3. Call `vkDestroyBuffer( logical_device, buffer, nullptr )` and provide the handle of the logical device, the handle of the buffer, and a `nullptr` value.
4. For safety reasons, assign the `VK_NULL_HANDLE` value to the `buffer` variable.

How it works...

Buffers are destroyed using the `vkDestroyBuffer()` function like this:

```
if( VK_NULL_HANDLE != buffer ) {
  vkDestroyBuffer( logical_device, buffer, nullptr );
  buffer = VK_NULL_HANDLE;
}
```

`logical_device` is a variable representing the logical device on which the buffer was created. When we destroy a buffer, we assign an empty handle to the variable representing this buffer, so we won't try to destroy the same resource twice.

See also

- *Creating a buffer view* recipe in this chapter

5
Descriptor Sets

In this chapter, we will cover the following recipes:

- Creating a sampler
- Creating a sampled image
- Creating a combined image sampler
- Creating a storage image
- Creating a uniform texel buffer
- Creating a storage texel buffer
- Creating a uniform buffer
- Creating a storage buffer
- Creating an input attachment
- Creating a descriptor set layout
- Creating a descriptor pool
- Allocating descriptor sets
- Updating descriptor sets
- Binding descriptor sets
- Creating descriptors with a texture and a uniform buffer
- Freeing descriptor sets
- Resetting a descriptor pool
- Destroying a descriptor pool
- Destroying a descriptor set layout
- Destroying a sampler

Introduction

In modern computer graphics, most of the rendering and processing of image data (such as vertices, pixels, or fragments) is done with a programmable pipeline and shaders. Shaders, to operate properly and to generate appropriate results, need to access additional data sources such as textures, samplers, buffers, or uniform variables. In Vulkan, these are provided through sets of descriptors.

Descriptors are opaque data structures that represent shader resources. They are organized into groups or sets and their contents are specified by descriptor set layouts. To provide resources to shaders, we bind descriptor sets to pipelines. We can bind multiple sets at once. To access resources from within shaders, we need to specify from which set and from which location within a set (called a **binding**) the given resource is acquired.

In this chapter, we will learn about the various descriptor types. We will see how to prepare resources (samplers, buffers, and images) so they can be used inside shaders. We will also look at how to set up an interface between an application and shaders and use resources inside shaders.

Creating a sampler

Samplers define a set of parameters that control how image data is loaded inside shaders (sampled). These parameters include address calculations (that is, wrapping or repeating), filtering (linear or nearest), or using mipmaps. To use samplers from within shaders, we first need to create them.

How to do it...

1. Take a handle of a logical device and store it in a variable of type `VkDevice` named `logical_device`.
2. Create a variable of type `VkSamplerCreateInfo` named `sampler_create_info` and use the following values for its members:
    - `VK_STRUCTURE_TYPE_SAMPLER_CREATE_INFO` value for `sType`
    - `nullptr` value for `pNext`
    - `0` value for `flags`
    - The desired magnification and minification filtering mode (`VK_FILTER_NEAREST` or `VK_FILTER_LINEAR`) for `magFilter` and `minFilter`

- The selected mipmap filtering mode
  (`VK_SAMPLER_MIPMAP_MODE_NEAREST` or
  `VK_SAMPLER_MIPMAP_MODE_LINEAR`) for `mipmapMode`
- The selected image addressing mode for image U, V, and W coordinates outside of the `0.0 - 1.0` range
  (`VK_SAMPLER_ADDRESS_MODE_REPEAT`,
  `VK_SAMPLER_ADDRESS_MODE_MIRRORED_REPEAT`,
  `VK_SAMPLER_ADDRESS_MODE_CLAMP_TO_EDGE``VK_SAMPLER_ADDRESS_MODE_CLAMP_TO_BORDER`, or
  `VK_SAMPLER_ADDRESS_MODE_MIRROR_CLAMP_TO_EDGE`) for `addressModeU`, `addressModeV` and `addressModeW`
- The desired value to be added to the mipmap level of detail calculations for `mipLodBias`
- `true` value if anisotropic filtering should be enabled or otherwise `false` for `anisotropyEnable`
- The maximal value of the anisotropy for `maxAnisotropy`
- `true` value if comparison against a reference value should be enabled during image lookups or, otherwise `false` for `compareEnable`
- The selected comparison function applied to the fetched data
  (`VK_COMPARE_OP_NEVER`, `VK_COMPARE_OP_LESS`,
  `VK_COMPARE_OP_EQUAL`, `VK_COMPARE_OP_LESS_OR_EQUAL`,
  `VK_COMPARE_OP_GREATER`, `VK_COMPARE_OP_NOT_EQUAL`,
  `VK_COMPARE_OP_GREATER_OR_EQUAL`, or `VK_COMPARE_OP_ALWAYS`)
  for `compareOp`
- The minimal and maximal values to clamp the calculated image's level of detail value (mipmap number) for `minLod` and `maxLod`
- One of the predefined border color values
  (`VK_BORDER_COLOR_FLOAT_TRANSPARENT_BLACK`,
  `VK_BORDER_COLOR_INT_TRANSPARENT_BLACK`,
  `VK_BORDER_COLOR_FLOAT_OPAQUE_BLACK`,
  `VK_BORDER_COLOR_INT_OPAQUE_BLACK`,
  `VK_BORDER_COLOR_FLOAT_OPAQUE_WHITE`, or
  `VK_BORDER_COLOR_INT_OPAQUE_WHITE`) for `borderColor`
- The `true` value if addressing should be performed using the image's dimensions or `false` if addressing should use normalized coordinates (in the `0.0-1.0` range) for `unnormalizedCoordinates`

3. Create a variable of type `VkSampler` named `sampler` in which the created sampler will be stored.
4. Call `vkCreateSampler( logical_device, &sampler_create_info, nullptr, &sampler )` and provide the `logical_device` variable, a pointer to the `sampler_create_info` variable, a `nullptr` value, and a pointer to the `sampler` variable.
5. Make sure the call was successful by checking whether the returned value was equal to `VK_SUCCESS`.

How it works...

Samplers control the way images are read inside shaders. They can be used separately or combined with a sampled image.

> Samplers are used for a `VK_DESCRIPTOR_TYPE_SAMPLER` descriptor type.

Sampling parameters are specified with a variable of type `VkSamplerCreateInfo` like this:

```
VkSamplerCreateInfo sampler_create_info = {
  VK_STRUCTURE_TYPE_SAMPLER_CREATE_INFO,
  nullptr,
  0,
  mag_filter,
  min_filter,
  mipmap_mode,
  u_address_mode,
  v_address_mode,
  w_address_mode,
  lod_bias,
  anisotropy_enable,
  max_anisotropy,
  compare_enable,
  compare_operator,
  min_lod,
  max_lod,
  border_color,
  unnormalized_coords
};
```

Chapter 5

This variable is then provided to the function that creates the sampler:

```
VkResult result = vkCreateSampler( logical_device, &sampler_create_info,
nullptr, &sampler );
if( VK_SUCCESS != result ) {
  std::cout << "Could not create sampler." << std::endl;
  return false;
}
return true;
```

 To specify a sampler inside shaders, we need to create a uniform variable with a `sampler` keyword.

An example of a GLSL code that uses a sampler, from which SPIR-V assembly can be generated, may look like this:

```
layout (set=m, binding=n) uniform sampler <variable name>;
```

See also

- See the following recipe in this chapter:
    - *Destroying a sampler*

Creating a sampled image

Sampled images are used to read data from images (textures) inside shaders. Usually, they are used together with samplers. And to be able to use an image as a sampled image, it must be created with a `VK_IMAGE_USAGE_SAMPLED_BIT` usage.

How to do it...

1. Take the handle of a physical device stored in a variable of type `VkPhysicalDevice` named `physical_device`.
2. Select a format that will be used for an image. Initialize a variable of type `VkFormat` named `format` with the selected image format.

[237]

Descriptor Sets

3. Create a variable of type `VkFormatProperties` named `format_properties`.
4. Call `vkGetPhysicalDeviceFormatProperties( physical_device, format, &format_properties )`, for which to provide the `physical_device` variable, the `format` variable, and a pointer to the `format_properties` variable.
5. Make sure the selected image format is suitable for a sampled image. Do that by checking whether the `VK_FORMAT_FEATURE_SAMPLED_IMAGE_BIT` bit of an `optimalTilingFeatures` member of the `format_properties` variable is set.
6. If the sampled image will be linearly filtered or if its mipmaps will be linearly filtered, make sure the selected format is suitable for a linearly filtered sampled image. Do that by checking whether the `VK_FORMAT_FEATURE_SAMPLED_IMAGE_FILTER_LINEAR_BIT` bit of an `optimalTilingFeatures` member of the `format_properties` variable is set.
7. Take the handle of the logical device created from the handle stored in the `physical_device` variable and use it to initialize a variable of type `VkDevice` named `logical_device`.
8. Create an image using the `logical_device` and `format` variables and choose the rest of the image parameters. Don't forget to provide a `VK_IMAGE_USAGE_SAMPLED_BIT` usage during the image creation. Store the image's handle in a variable of type `VkImage` named `sampled_image` (refer to the *Creating an image* recipe from `Chapter 4`, *Resources and Memory*).
9. Allocate a memory object with a `VK_MEMORY_PROPERTY_DEVICE_LOCAL_BIT` property (or use a range of an existing memory object) and bind it to the created image (refer to the *Allocating and binding memory object to an image* recipe from `Chapter 4`, *Resources and Memory*).
10. Create an image view using the `logical_device`, `sampled_image`, and `format` variables and select the rest of the view parameters. Store the image view's handle in a variable of type `VkImageView` named `sampled_image_view` (refer to the *Creating an image view* recipe from `Chapter 4`, *Resources and Memory*).

How it works...

Sampled images are used as a source of image data (textures) inside shaders. To fetch data from the image, usually we need a sampler object, which defines how the data should be read (refer to the *Creating a sampler* recipe).

 Sampled images are used for a `VK_DESCRIPTOR_TYPE_SAMPLED_IMAGE` descriptor type.

Inside shaders, we can use multiple samplers to read data from the same image in a different way. We can also use the same sampler with multiple images. But on some platforms, it may be more optimal to use combined image sampler objects, which gather a sampler and a sampled image in one object.

Not all image formats are supported for sampled images; this depends on the platform on which the application is executed. But there is a set of mandatory formats that can always be used for sampled images and linearly filtered sampled images. Examples of such formats include (but are not limited to) the following:

- `VK_FORMAT_B4G4R4A4_UNORM_PACK16`
- `VK_FORMAT_R5G6B5_UNORM_PACK16`
- `VK_FORMAT_A1R5G5B5_UNORM_PACK16`
- `VK_FORMAT_R8_UNORM` and `VK_FORMAT_R8_SNORM`
- `VK_FORMAT_R8G8_UNORM` and `VK_FORMAT_R8G8_SNORM`
- `VK_FORMAT_R8G8B8A8_UNORM`, `VK_FORMAT_R8G8B8A8_SNORM`, and `VK_FORMAT_R8G8B8A8_SRGB`
- `VK_FORMAT_B8G8R8A8_UNORM` and `VK_FORMAT_B8G8R8A8_SRGB`
- `VK_FORMAT_A8B8G8R8_UNORM_PACK32`, `VK_FORMAT_A8B8G8R8_SNORM_PACK32`, and `VK_FORMAT_A8B8G8R8_SRGB_PACK32`
- `VK_FORMAT_A2B10G10R10_UNORM_PACK32`
- `VK_FORMAT_R16_SFLOAT`
- `VK_FORMAT_R16G16_SFLOAT`
- `VK_FORMAT_R16G16B16A16_SFLOAT`
- `VK_FORMAT_B10G11R11_UFLOAT_PACK32`
- `VK_FORMAT_E5B9G9R9_UFLOAT_PACK32`

If we want to use some less typical format, we need to check whether it can be used for sampled images. This can be done like this:

```
VkFormatProperties format_properties;
vkGetPhysicalDeviceFormatProperties( physical_device, format,
&format_properties );
if( !(format_properties.optimalTilingFeatures &
VK_FORMAT_FEATURE_SAMPLED_IMAGE_BIT) ) {
```

Descriptor Sets

```
    std::cout << "Provided format is not supported for a sampled image." <<
std::endl;
    return false;
}
if( linear_filtering &&
    !(format_properties.optimalTilingFeatures &
VK_FORMAT_FEATURE_SAMPLED_IMAGE_FILTER_LINEAR_BIT) ) {
    std::cout << "Provided format is not supported for a linear image
filtering." << std::endl;
    return false;
}
```

If we are sure the selected format is suitable for our needs, we can create an image, a memory object for it, and an image view (in Vulkan, images are represented with image views most of the time). We need to specify a `VK_IMAGE_USAGE_SAMPLED_BIT` usage during the image creation:

```
if( !CreateImage( logical_device, type, format, size, num_mipmaps,
num_layers, VK_SAMPLE_COUNT_1_BIT, usage | VK_IMAGE_USAGE_SAMPLED_BIT,
false, sampled_image ) ) {
    return false;
}

if( !AllocateAndBindMemoryObjectToImage( physical_device, logical_device,
sampled_image, VK_MEMORY_PROPERTY_DEVICE_LOCAL_BIT, memory_object ) ) {
    return false;
}

if( !CreateImageView( logical_device, sampled_image, view_type, format,
aspect, sampled_image_view ) ) {
    return false;
}
return true;
```

When we want to use an image as a sampled image, before we load data from it inside shaders, we need to transition the image's layout to `VK_IMAGE_LAYOUT_SHADER_READ_ONLY_OPTIMAL`.

To create a uniform variable that represents a sampled image inside shaders, we need to use a `texture` keyword (possibly with a prefix) with an appropriate dimensionality.

Chapter 5

An example of a GLSL code from which SPIR-V assembly can be generated, that uses a sampled image, may look like this:

```
layout (set=m, binding=n) uniform texture2D <variable name>;
```

See also

- In Chapter 4, *Resources and Memory*, see the following recipes:
    - *Creating an image*
    - *Allocating and binding memory object to an image*
    - *Creating an image view*
    - *Destroying an image view*
    - *Destroying an image*
    - *Freeing a memory object*
- In this chapter, see the following recipe:
    - *Creating a sampler*

Creating a combined image sampler

From the application (API) perspective, samplers and sampled images are always separate objects. But inside shaders, they can be combined into one object. On some platforms, sampling from combined image samplers inside shaders may be more optimal than using separate samplers and sampled images.

How to do it...

1. Create a sampler object and store its handle in a variable of type `VkSampler` named `sampler` (refer to the *Creating a sampler* recipe).
2. Create a sampled image. Store the handle of the created image in a variable of type `VkImage` named `sampled_image`. Create an appropriate view for the sampled image and store its handle in a variable of type `VkImageView` named `sampled_image_view` (refer to the *Creating a sampled image* recipe).

How it works...

Combined image samplers are created in our application in the same way as normal samplers and sampled images. They are just used differently inside shaders.

> Combined image samplers can be bound to descriptors of a
> VK_DESCRIPTOR_TYPE_COMBINED_IMAGE_SAMPLER type.

The following code uses the *Creating a sampler* and *Creating a sampled image* recipes to create necessary objects:

```
if( !CreateSampler( logical_device, mag_filter, min_filter, mipmap_mode,
u_address_mode, v_address_mode, w_address_mode, lod_bias,
anisotropy_enable, max_anisotropy, compare_enable, compare_operator,
min_lod, max_lod, border_color, unnormalized_coords, sampler ) ) {
  return false;
}

bool linear_filtering = (mag_filter == VK_FILTER_LINEAR) || (min_filter ==
VK_FILTER_LINEAR) || (mipmap_mode == VK_SAMPLER_MIPMAP_MODE_LINEAR);
if( !CreateSampledImage( physical_device, logical_device, type, format,
size, num_mipmaps, num_layers, usage, view_type, aspect, linear_filtering,
sampled_image, sampled_image_view ) ) {
  return false;
}
return true;
```

The difference is inside the shaders.

> To create a variable that represents a combined image sampler inside GLSL shaders, we need to use a sampler keyword (possibly with a prefix) with an appropriate dimensionality.

Don't confuse samplers and combined image samplers--both use a sampler keyword inside shaders, but combined image samplers additionally have a dimensionality specified like in the following example:

```
layout (set=m, binding=n) uniform sampler2D <variable name>;
```

Combined image samplers deserve a separate treatment, because applications that use them may have a better performance on some platforms. So if there is no specific reason to use separate samplers and sampled images, we should try to combine them into single objects.

See also

In `Chapter 4`, *Resources and Memory*, see the following recipes:

- *Creating an image*
- *Allocating and binding memory object to an image*
- *Creating an image view*
- *Destroying an image view*
- *Destroying an image*
- *Freeing a memory object*

See the following recipes in this chapter:

- *Creating a sampler*
- *Creating a sampled image*
- *Destroying a sampler*

Creating a storage image

Storage images allow us to load (unfiltered) data from images bound to pipelines. But, what's more important, they also allow us to store data from shaders in the images. Such images must be created with a `VK_IMAGE_USAGE_STORAGE_BIT` usage flag specified.

How to do it...

1. Take the handle of a physical device and store it in a variable of type `VkPhysicalDevice` named `physical_device`.
2. Select a format that will be used for a storage image. Initialize a variable of type `VkFormat` named `format` with the selected format.

Descriptor Sets

3. Create a variable of type `VkFormatProperties` named `format_properties`.
4. Call `vkGetPhysicalDeviceFormatProperties( physical_device, format, &format_properties )` and provide the `physical_device` variable, the `format` variable, and a pointer to the `format_properties` variable.
5. Check whether the selected image format is suitable for a storage image. Do that by checking whether the `VK_FORMAT_FEATURE_STORAGE_IMAGE_BIT` bit of an `optimalTilingFeatures` member of the `format_properties` variable is set.
6. If atomic operations will be performed on the storage image, make sure the selected format supports them. Do that by checking whether the `VK_FORMAT_FEATURE_STORAGE_IMAGE_ATOMIC_BIT` bit of an `optimalTilingFeatures` member of the `format_properties` variable is set.
7. Take the handle of the logical device created from a `physical_device` and use it to initialize a variable of type `VkDevice` named `logical_device`.
8. Create an image using the `logical_device` and `format` variables and choose the rest of the image parameters. Make sure the `VK_IMAGE_USAGE_STORAGE_BIT` usage is specified during the image creation. Store the created handle in a variable of type `VkImage` named `storage_image` (refer to the *Creating an image* recipe from `Chapter 4, Resources and Memory`).
9. Allocate a memory object with a `VK_MEMORY_PROPERTY_DEVICE_LOCAL_BIT` property (or use a range of an existing memory object) and bind it to the image (refer to the *Allocating and binding memory object to an image* recipe from `Chapter 4, Resources and Memory`).
10. Create an image view using the `logical_device`, `storage_image`, and `format` variables and select the rest of the view parameters. Store the image view's handle in a variable of type `VkImageView` named `storage_image_view` (refer to the *Creating an image view* recipe from `Chapter 4, Resources and Memory`).

How it works...

When we want to store data in images from within shaders, we need to use storage images. We can also load data from such images, but these loads are unfiltered (we can't use samplers for storage images).

> Storage images correspond to descriptors of a `VK_DESCRIPTOR_TYPE_STORAGE_IMAGE` type.

Storage images are created with a VK_IMAGE_USAGE_STORAGE_BIT usage. We also can't forget about specifying a proper format. Not all formats may always be used for storage images. This depends on the platform our application is executed on. But there is a list of mandatory formats that all Vulkan drivers must support. It includes (but is not limited to) the following formats:

- VK_FORMAT_R8G8B8A8_UNORM, VK_FORMAT_R8G8B8A8_SNORM, VK_FORMAT_R8G8B8A8_UINT, and VK_FORMAT_R8G8B8A8_SINT
- VK_FORMAT_R16G16B16A16_UINT, VK_FORMAT_R16G16B16A16_SINT and VK_FORMAT_R16G16B16A16_SFLOAT
- VK_FORMAT_R32_UINT, VK_FORMAT_R32_SINT and VK_FORMAT_R32_SFLOAT
- VK_FORMAT_R32G32_UINT, VK_FORMAT_R32G32_SINT and VK_FORMAT_R32G32_SFLOAT
- VK_FORMAT_R32G32B32A32_UINT, VK_FORMAT_R32G32B32A32_SINT and VK_FORMAT_R32G32B32A32_SFLOAT

If we want to perform atomic operations on storage images, the list of mandatory formats is much shorter and includes only the following ones:

- VK_FORMAT_R32_UINT
- VK_FORMAT_R32_SINT

If another format is required for storage images or if we need to use another format to perform atomic operations on storage images, we must check whether the selected format is supported on a platform our application is executed on. This can be done with the following code:

```
VkFormatProperties format_properties;
vkGetPhysicalDeviceFormatProperties( physical_device, format,
&format_properties );
if( !(format_properties.optimalTilingFeatures &
VK_FORMAT_FEATURE_STORAGE_IMAGE_BIT) ) {
  std::cout << "Provided format is not supported for a storage image." <<
std::endl;
  return false;
}
if( atomic_operations &&
    !(format_properties.optimalTilingFeatures &
VK_FORMAT_FEATURE_STORAGE_IMAGE_ATOMIC_BIT) ) {
  std::cout << "Provided format is not supported for atomic operations on
storage images." << std::endl;
  return false;
}
```

Descriptor Sets

If the format is supported, we create images as usual, but we need to specify a
`VK_IMAGE_USAGE_STORAGE_BIT` usage. After the image is ready, we need to create a memory object, bind it to the image, and we also need an image view. These operations can be performed like this:

```
if( !CreateImage( logical_device, type, format, size, num_mipmaps,
num_layers, VK_SAMPLE_COUNT_1_BIT, usage | VK_IMAGE_USAGE_STORAGE_BIT,
false, storage_image ) ) {
  return false;
}

if( !AllocateAndBindMemoryObjectToImage( physical_device, logical_device,
storage_image, VK_MEMORY_PROPERTY_DEVICE_LOCAL_BIT, memory_object ) ) {
  return false;
}

if( !CreateImageView( logical_device, storage_image, view_type, format,
aspect, storage_image_view ) ) {
  return false;
}
return true;
```

Before we can load or store data in storage images from shaders, we must perform a transition to a `VK_IMAGE_LAYOUT_GENERAL` layout. It is the only layout in which these operations are supported.

Inside GLSL shaders, storage images are specified with an `image` keyword (possibly with a prefix) and an appropriate dimensionality. We also need to provide the image's format inside the `layout` qualifier.

An example of a storage image's definition in a GLSL shader is provided as follows:

```
layout (set=m, binding=n, r32f) uniform image2D <variable name>;
```

See also

In Chapter 4, *Resources and Memory*, see the following recipes:

- *Creating an image*
- *Allocating and binding memory object to an image*
- *Creating an image view*

- *Destroying an image view*
- *Destroying an image*
- *Freeing a memory object*

Creating a uniform texel buffer

Uniform texel buffers allow us to read data in a way similar to reading data from images-- their contents are interpreted not as an array of single (scalar) values but as formatted pixels (texel) with one, two, three, or four components. But through such buffers, we can access data that is much larger than the data provided through usual images.

We need to specify a VK_BUFFER_USAGE_UNIFORM_TEXEL_BUFFER_BIT usage when we want to use a buffer as a uniform texel buffer.

How to do it...

1. Take the handle of a physical device and store it in a variable of type VkPhysicalDevice named physical_device.
2. Select a format in which the buffer data will be stored. Use the format to initialize a variable of type VkFormat named format.
3. Create a variable of type VkFormatProperties named format_properties.
4. Call vkGetPhysicalDeviceFormatProperties(physical_device, format, &format_properties) and provide the handle of the physical device, the format variable, and a pointer to the format_properties variable.
5. Make sure the selected format is suitable for a uniform texel buffer by checking whether the bufferFeatures member of the format_properties variable has a VK_FORMAT_FEATURE_UNIFORM_TEXEL_BUFFER_BIT bit set.
6. Take the handle of a logical device created from the handle of the selected physical device. Store it in a variable of type VkDevice named logical_device.
7. Create a variable of type VkBuffer named uniform_texel_buffer.
8. Create a buffer, using the logical_device variable, with a desired size and usage. Don't forget to include a VK_BUFFER_USAGE_UNIFORM_TEXEL_BUFFER_BIT usage during the buffer's creation. Store the created handle in the uniform_texel_buffer variable (refer to the *Creating a buffer* recipe from Chapter 4, *Resources and Memory*).

Descriptor Sets

9. Allocate a memory object with a `VK_MEMORY_PROPERTY_DEVICE_LOCAL_BIT` property (or use an existing one) and bind it to the buffer. If the new memory object is allocated, store it in a variable of type `VkDeviceMemory` named `memory_object` (refer to the *Allocating and binding memory object to a buffer* recipe from `Chapter 4`, *Resources and Memory*).
10. Create a buffer view using the `logical_device`, `uniform_texel_buffer`, and `format` variables, and the desired offset and memory range. Store the resulting handle in a variable of type `VkBufferView` named `uniform_texel_buffer_view` (refer to the *Creating a buffer view* recipe from `Chapter 4`, *Resources and Memory*).

How it works...

Uniform texel buffers allow us to provide data interpreted as one-dimensional images. But this data may be much larger than typical images. Vulkan specification requires every driver to support 1D images of at least 4,096 texels. But for texel buffers, this minimal required limit goes up to 65,536 elements.

> Uniform texel buffers are bound to descriptors of a `VK_DESCRIPTOR_TYPE_UNIFORM_TEXEL_BUFFER` type.

Uniform texel buffers are created with a `VK_BUFFER_USAGE_UNIFORM_TEXEL_BUFFER_BIT` usage. But apart from that, we need to select an appropriate format. Not all formats are compatible with such buffers. The list of mandatory formats that can be used with uniform texel buffers includes (but is not limited to) the following ones:

- `VK_FORMAT_R8_UNORM`, `VK_FORMAT_R8_SNORM`, `VK_FORMAT_R8_UINT`, and `VK_FORMAT_R8_SINT`
- `VK_FORMAT_R8G8_UNORM`, `VK_FORMAT_R8G8_SNORM`, `VK_FORMAT_R8G8_UINT`, and `VK_FORMAT_R8G8_SINT`
- `VK_FORMAT_R8G8B8A8_UNORM`, `VK_FORMAT_R8G8B8A8_SNORM`, `VK_FORMAT_R8G8B8A8_UINT`, and `VK_FORMAT_R8G8B8A8_SINT`
- `VK_FORMAT_B8G8R8A8_UNORM`
- `VK_FORMAT_A8B8G8R8_UNORM_PACK32`, `VK_FORMAT_A8B8G8R8_SNORM_PACK32`, `VK_FORMAT_A8B8G8R8_UINT_PACK32`, and `VK_FORMAT_A8B8G8R8_SINT_PACK32`

- VK_FORMAT_A2B10G10R10_UNORM_PACK32 and VK_FORMAT_A2B10G10R10_UINT_PACK32
- VK_FORMAT_R16_UINT, VK_FORMAT_R16_SINT and VK_FORMAT_R16_SFLOAT
- VK_FORMAT_R16G16_UINT, VK_FORMAT_R16G16_SINT and VK_FORMAT_R16G16_SFLOAT
- VK_FORMAT_R16G16B16A16_UINT, VK_FORMAT_R16G16B16A16_SINT and VK_FORMAT_R16G16B16A16_SFLOAT
- VK_FORMAT_R32_UINT, VK_FORMAT_R32_SINT and VK_FORMAT_R32_SFLOAT
- VK_FORMAT_R32G32_UINT, VK_FORMAT_R32G32_SINT and VK_FORMAT_R32G32_SFLOAT
- VK_FORMAT_R32G32B32A32_UINT, VK_FORMAT_R32G32B32A32_SINT and VK_FORMAT_R32G32B32A32_SFLOAT
- VK_FORMAT_B10G11R11_UFLOAT_PACK32

To check whether other formats can be used with uniform texel buffers, we need to prepare the following code:

```
VkFormatProperties format_properties;
vkGetPhysicalDeviceFormatProperties( physical_device, format,
&format_properties );
if( !(format_properties.bufferFeatures &
VK_FORMAT_FEATURE_UNIFORM_TEXEL_BUFFER_BIT) ) {
  std::cout << "Provided format is not supported for a uniform texel
buffer." << std::endl;
  return false;
}
```

If the selected format is suitable for our needs, we can create a buffer, allocate a memory object for it, and bind it to the buffer. What is very important, is that we also need to create a buffer view:

```
if( !CreateBuffer( logical_device, size, usage |
VK_BUFFER_USAGE_UNIFORM_TEXEL_BUFFER_BIT, uniform_texel_buffer ) ) {
  return false;
}

if( !AllocateAndBindMemoryObjectToBuffer( physical_device, logical_device,
uniform_texel_buffer, VK_MEMORY_PROPERTY_DEVICE_LOCAL_BIT, memory_object )
) {
  return false;
}

if( !CreateBufferView( logical_device, uniform_texel_buffer, format, 0,
VK_WHOLE_SIZE, uniform_texel_buffer_view ) ) {
```

```
        return false;
    }
    return true;
```

From the API perspective, the structure of the buffer's contents doesn't matter. But in the case of uniform texel buffers, we need to specify a data format which will allow shaders to interpret the buffer's contents in an appropriate way. That's why a buffer view is required.

> In the GLSL shaders, uniform texel buffers are defined through variables of type `samplerBuffer` (possibly with a prefix).

An example of a uniform texel buffer variable defined in a GLSL shader is provided as follows:

```
layout (set=m, binding=n) uniform samplerBuffer <variable name>;
```

See also

In `Chapter 4`, *Resources and Memory*, see the following recipes:

- *Creating a buffer*
- *Allocating and binding memory object to a buffer*
- *Creating a buffer view*
- *Destroying a buffer view*
- *Freeing a memory object*
- *Destroying a buffer*

Creating a storage texel buffer

Storage texel buffers, like uniform texel buffers, are a way to provide large amount of image-like data to shaders. But they also allow us to store data in them and perform atomic operations on them. For this purpose, we need to create a buffer with a `VK_BUFFER_USAGE_STORAGE_TEXEL_BUFFER_BIT`.

How to do it...

1. Take the handle of a physical device. Store it in a variable of type `VkPhysicalDevice` named `physical_device`.
2. Select a format for the texel buffer's data and use it to initialize a variable of type `VkFormat` named `format`.
3. Create a variable of type `VkFormatProperties` named `format_properties`.
4. Call `vkGetPhysicalDeviceFormatProperties( physical_device, format, &format_properties )` and provide the handle of the selected physical device, the `format` variable, and a pointer to the `format_properties` variable.
5. Make sure the selected format is suitable for a storage texel buffer by checking whether the `bufferFeatures` member of the `format_properties` variable has a `VK_FORMAT_FEATURE_STORAGE_TEXEL_BUFFER_BIT` bit set.
6. If atomic operations will be performed on a created storage texel buffer, make sure the selected format is also suitable for atomic operations. For this purpose, check whether a `VK_FORMAT_FEATURE_STORAGE_TEXEL_BUFFER_ATOMIC_BIT` bit of the `bufferFeatures` member of the `format_properties` variable is set.
7. Take the handle of a logical device created from the handle of the selected physical device. Store it in a variable of type `VkDevice` named `logical_device`.
8. Create a variable of type `VkBuffer` named `storage_texel_buffer`.
9. Using the `logical_device` variable, create a buffer with the chosen size and usage. Make sure a `VK_BUFFER_USAGE_STORAGE_TEXEL_BUFFER_BIT` usage is specified during the buffer's creation. Store the buffer's handle in the `storage_texel_buffer` variable (refer to the *Creating a buffer* recipe from `Chapter 4`, *Resources and Memory*).
10. Allocate a memory object with a `VK_MEMORY_PROPERTY_DEVICE_LOCAL_BIT` property (or use an existing one) and bind it to the buffer. If a new memory object is allocated, store it in a variable of type `VkDeviceMemory` named `memory_object` (refer to the *Allocating and binding memory object to a buffer* recipe from `Chapter 4`, *Resources and Memory*).
11. Create a buffer view using the `logical_device`, `storage_texel_buffer`, and `format` variables, and the desired offset and memory range. Store the resulting handle in a variable of type `VkBufferView` named `storage_texel_buffer_view` (refer to the *Creating a buffer view* recipe from `Chapter 4`, *Resources and Memory*).

Descriptor Sets

How it works...

Storage texel buffers allow us to access and to store data in very large arrays. Data is interpreted as if it was read or stored inside one-dimensional images. Additionally, we can perform atomic operations on such buffers.

 Storage texel buffers can fill descriptors of a type equal to `VK_DESCRIPTOR_TYPE_STORAGE_TEXEL_BUFFER`.

To use a buffer as a storage texel buffer, it needs to be created with a `VK_BUFFER_USAGE_STORAGE_TEXEL_BUFFER_BIT` usage. A buffer view with an appropriate format is also required. For storage texel buffers, we can select one of the mandatory formats that include the following ones:

- `VK_FORMAT_R8G8B8A8_UNORM`, `VK_FORMAT_R8G8B8A8_SNORM`, `VK_FORMAT_R8G8B8A8_UINT`, and `VK_FORMAT_R8G8B8A8_SINT`
- `VK_FORMAT_A8B8G8R8_UNORM_PACK32`, `VK_FORMAT_A8B8G8R8_SNORM_PACK32`, `VK_FORMAT_A8B8G8R8_UINT_PACK32`, and `VK_FORMAT_A8B8G8R8_SINT_PACK32`
- `VK_FORMAT_R32_UINT`, `VK_FORMAT_R32_SINT`, and `VK_FORMAT_R32_SFLOAT`
- `VK_FORMAT_R32G32_UINT`, `VK_FORMAT_R32G32_SINT`, and `VK_FORMAT_R32G32_SFLOAT`
- `VK_FORMAT_R32G32B32A32_UINT`, `VK_FORMAT_R32G32B32A32_SINT`, and `VK_FORMAT_R32G32B32A32_SFLOAT`

For atomic operations, the list of mandatory formats is much shorter and includes only the following:

- `VK_FORMAT_R32_UINT` and `VK_FORMAT_R32_SINT`

Other formats may also be supported for storage texel buffers, but the support is not guaranteed and must be confirmed on the platform our application is executed on like this:

```
VkFormatProperties format_properties;
vkGetPhysicalDeviceFormatProperties( physical_device, format,
&format_properties );
if( !(format_properties.bufferFeatures &
VK_FORMAT_FEATURE_STORAGE_TEXEL_BUFFER_BIT) ) {
  std::cout << "Provided format is not supported for a uniform texel
buffer." << std::endl;
  return false;
```

```
}

if( atomic_operations &&
    !(format_properties.bufferFeatures &
  VK_FORMAT_FEATURE_STORAGE_TEXEL_BUFFER_ATOMIC_BIT) ) {
  std::cout << "Provided format is not supported for atomic operations on
storage texel buffers." << std::endl;
  return false;
}
```

For a storage texel buffer, we need to create a buffer, allocate and bind a memory object to the buffer, and also we need to create a buffer view that will define the format of the buffer's data:

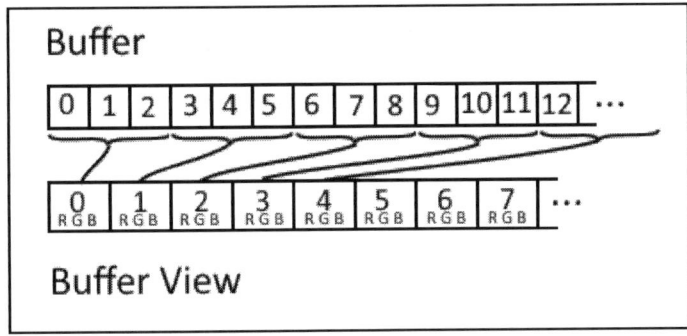

```
if( !CreateBuffer( logical_device, size, usage |
VK_BUFFER_USAGE_STORAGE_TEXEL_BUFFER_BIT, storage_texel_buffer ) ) {
  return false;
}

if( !AllocateAndBindMemoryObjectToBuffer( physical_device, logical_device,
storage_texel_buffer, VK_MEMORY_PROPERTY_DEVICE_LOCAL_BIT, memory_object )
) {
  return false;
}

if( !CreateBufferView( logical_device, storage_texel_buffer, format, 0,
VK_WHOLE_SIZE, storage_texel_buffer_view ) ) {
  return false;
}
return true;
```

Descriptor Sets

We can also use an existing memory object and bind a range of its memory to the storage texel buffer.

> From the GLSL perspective, storage texel buffer variables are defined using an `imageBuffer` (possibly with a prefix) keyword.

An example of a storage texel buffer defined in a GLSL shader looks like this:

```
layout (set=m, binding=n, r32f) uniform imageBuffer <variable name>;
```

See also

In Chapter 4, *Resources and Memory*, see the following recipes:

- *Creating a buffer*
- *Allocating and binding memory object to a buffer*
- *Creating a buffer view*
- *Destroying a buffer view*
- *Freeing a memory object*
- *Destroying a buffer*

Creating a uniform buffer

In Vulkan, uniform variables used inside shaders cannot be placed in a global namespace. They can be defined only inside uniform buffers. For these, we need to create buffers with a `VK_BUFFER_USAGE_UNIFORM_BUFFER_BIT` usage.

How to do it...

1. Take the created logical device and use its handle to initialize a variable of type `VkDevice` named `logical_device`.
2. Create a variable of type `VkBuffer` named `uniform_buffer`. It will hold the handle of the created buffer.

3. Create a buffer using a `logical_device` variable and specifying the desired size and usage. The latter must contain at least a `VK_BUFFER_USAGE_UNIFORM_BUFFER_BIT` flag. Store the handle of the buffer in the `uniform_buffer` variable (refer to the *Creating a buffer* recipe from Chapter 4, *Resources and Memory*).
4. Allocate a memory object with a `VK_MEMORY_PROPERTY_DEVICE_LOCAL_BIT` property (or use a range of an existing memory object) and bind it to the buffer (refer to the *Allocating and binding memory object to a buffer* recipe from Chapter 4, *Resources and Memory*).

How it works...

Uniform buffers are used to provide values for read-only uniform variables inside shaders.

Uniform buffers can be used for `VK_DESCRIPTOR_TYPE_UNIFORM_BUFFER` or `VK_DESCRIPTOR_TYPE_UNIFORM_BUFFER_DYNAMIC` descriptor types.

Typically, uniform buffers contain data for parameters that don't change too often, that is, matrices (for small amounts of data, **push constants** are recommended as updating them is usually much faster; information about push constants can be found in the *Providing data to shaders through push constants* recipe in Chapter 9, *Command Recording and Drawing*).

Creating a buffer in which data for uniform variables will be stored requires us to specify a `VK_BUFFER_USAGE_UNIFORM_BUFFER_BIT` flag during buffer creation. When the buffer is created, we need to prepare a memory object and bind it to the created buffer (we can also use an existing memory object and bind the part of its memory store to the buffer):

```
if( !CreateBuffer( logical_device, size, usage |
VK_BUFFER_USAGE_UNIFORM_BUFFER_BIT, uniform_buffer ) ) {
  return false;
}

if( !AllocateAndBindMemoryObjectToBuffer( physical_device, logical_device,
uniform_buffer, VK_MEMORY_PROPERTY_DEVICE_LOCAL_BIT, memory_object ) ) {
  return false;
}
return true;
```

Descriptor Sets

After the buffer and its memory objects are ready, we can upload data to them as we do with any other kinds of buffers. We just need to remember that uniform variables must be placed at appropriate offsets. These offsets are the same as in the std140 layout from the GLSL language and are defined as follows:

- A scalar variable of size N must be placed at offsets that are a multiple of N
- A vector with two components, where each component has a size of N, must be placed at offsets that are a multiple of 2N
- A vector with three or four components, where each component has a size of N, must be placed at offsets that are a multiple of 4N
- An array with elements of size N must be placed at offsets that are a multiple of N rounded up to the multiple of 16
- A structure must be placed at an offset that is the same as the biggest offset of its members, rounded up to a multiple of 16 (offset of a member with the biggest offset requirement, rounded up to the multiple of 16)
- A row-major matrix must be placed at an offset equal to the offset of a vector with the number of components equal to the number of columns in the matrix
- A column-major matrix must be placed at the same offsets as its columns

Dynamic uniform buffers differ from normal uniform buffers in the way their address is specified. During a descriptor set update, we specify the size of memory that should be used for a uniform buffer and an offset from the beginning of the buffer's memory. For normal uniform buffers, these parameters remain unchanged. For dynamic uniform buffers, the specified offset becomes a base offset that can be later modified by the dynamic offset which is added when a descriptor set is bound to a command buffer.

 Inside GLSL shaders, both uniform buffers and dynamic uniform buffers are defined with a `uniform` qualifier and a block syntax.

An example of a uniform buffer's definition in a GLSL shader is provided as follows:

```
layout (set=m, binding=n) uniform <variable name>
{
  vec4 <member 1 name>;
  mat4 <member 2 name>;
  // ...
};
```

[256]

See also

In `Chapter 4`, *Resources and Memory*, see the following recipes:

- *Creating a buffer*
- *Allocating and binding memory object to a buffer*
- *Freeing a memory object*
- *Destroying a buffer*

Creating a storage buffer

When we want to not only read data from a buffer inside shaders, but we would also like to store data in it, we need to use storage buffers. These are created with a `VK_BUFFER_USAGE_STORAGE_BUFFER_BIT` usage.

How to do it...

1. Take the handle of a logical device and store it in a variable of type `VkPhysicalDevice` named `physical_device`.
2. Create a variable of type `VkBuffer` named `storage_buffer` in which a handle of a created buffer will be stored.
3. Create a buffer of a desired size and usage using the `logical_device` variable. Specified usage must contain at least a `VK_BUFFER_USAGE_STORAGE_BUFFER_BIT` flag. Store the created handle in the `storage_buffer` variable (refer to the *Creating a buffer* recipe from `Chapter 4`, *Resources and Memory*).
4. Allocate a memory object with a `VK_MEMORY_PROPERTY_DEVICE_LOCAL_BIT` property (or use a range of an existing memory object) and bind it to the created buffer (refer to the *Allocating and binding memory object to a buffer* recipe from `Chapter 4`, *Resources and Memory*).

How it works...

Storage buffers support both read and write operations. We can also perform atomic operations on storage buffers' members which have unsigned integer formats.

Descriptor Sets

 Storage buffers correspond to VK_DESCRIPTOR_TYPE_STORAGE_BUFFER or VK_DESCRIPTOR_TYPE_STORAGE_BUFFER_DYNAMIC descriptor types.

Data for members of storage buffers must be placed at appropriate offsets. The easiest way to fulfill the requirements is to follow the rules for the std430 layout in the GLSL language. Base alignment rules for storage buffers are similar to the rules of uniform buffers with the exception of arrays and structures--their offsets don't need to be rounded up to a multiple of 16. For convenience, these rules are specified as follows:

- A scalar variable of size N must be placed at offsets that are a multiple of N
- A vector with two components, where each component has a size of N, must be placed at offsets that are a multiple of 2N
- A vector with three or four components, where each component has a size of N, must be placed at offsets that are a multiple of 4N
- An array with elements of size N must be placed at offsets that are a multiple of N
- A structure must be placed at offsets that are a multiple of the biggest offset of any of its members (a member with the biggest offset requirement)
- A row-major matrix must be placed at an offset equal to the offset of a vector with the number of components equal to the number of columns in the matrix
- A column-major matrix must be placed at the same offsets as its columns

Dynamic storage buffers differ in the way their base memory offset is defined. The offset and range specified during descriptor set updates remain unchanged for the normal storage buffers until the next update. In the case of their dynamic variations, the specified offset becomes a base address which is later modified by the dynamic offset specified when a descriptor set is bound to a command buffer.

 In GLSL shaders, storage buffers and dynamic storage buffers are defined identically with a buffer qualifier and a block syntax.

An example of a storage buffer used in a GLSL shader is provided as follows:

```
layout (set=m, binding=n) buffer <variable name>
{
  vec4 <member 1 name>;
  mat4 <member 2 name>;
  // ...
};
```

See also

In `Chapter 4`, *Resources and Memory*, see the following recipes:

- *Creating a buffer*
- *Allocating and binding memory object to a buffer*
- *Freeing a memory object*
- *Destroying a buffer*

Creating an input attachment

Attachments are images into which we render during drawing commands, inside render passes. In other words, they are render targets.

Input attachments are image resources from which we can read (unfiltered) data inside fragment shaders. We just need to remember that we can access only one location corresponding to a processed fragment.

Usually, for input attachments, resources that were previously color or depth/stencil attachments are used. But we can also use other images (and their image views). We just need to create them with a `VK_IMAGE_USAGE_INPUT_ATTACHMENT_BIT` usage.

How to do it...

1. Take the physical device on which operations are performed and store its handle in a variable of type `VkPhysicalDevice` named `physical_device`.
2. Select a format for an image and use it to initialize a variable of type `VkFormat` named `format`.
3. Create a variable of type `VkFormatProperties` named `format_properties`.
4. Call `vkGetPhysicalDeviceFormatProperties( physical_device, format, &format_properties )` and provide the `physical_device` and `format` variables, and a pointer to the `format_properties` variable.
5. If the image's color data will be read, make sure the selected format is suitable for such usage. For this, check whether a `VK_FORMAT_FEATURE_COLOR_ATTACHMENT_BIT` bit is set in an `optimalTilingFeatures` member of the `format_properties` variable.

6. If the image's depth or stencil data will be read, check whether the selected format can be used for reading depth or stencil data. Do that by making sure that a `VK_FORMAT_FEATURE_DEPTH_STENCIL_ATTACHMENT_BIT` bit is set in an `optimalTilingFeatures` member of the `format_properties` variable.
7. Take the handle of a logical device created from the used physical device. Store it in a variable of type `VkDevice` named `logical_device`.
8. Create an image using the `logical_device` and `format` variables, and select appropriate values for the rest of the image's parameters. Make sure the `VK_IMAGE_USAGE_INPUT_ATTACHMENT_BIT` usage is specified during the image creation. Store the created handle in a variable of type `VkImage` named `input_attachment` (refer to the *Creating an image* recipe from `Chapter 4`, *Resources and Memory*).
9. Allocate a memory object with a `VK_MEMORY_PROPERTY_DEVICE_LOCAL_BIT` property (or use a range of an existing memory object) and bind it to the image (refer to the *Allocating and binding memory object to an image* recipe from Chapter 4, *Resources and Memory*).
10. Create an image view using the `logical_device`, `input_attachment`, and `format` variables, and choose the rest of the image view's parameters. Store the created handle in a variable of type `VkImageView` named `input_attachment_image_view` (refer to the *Creating an image view* recipe from `Chapter 4`, *Resources and Memory*).

How it works...

Input attachments allow us to read data inside fragment shaders from images used as render pass attachments (typically, for input attachments, images that were previously color or depth stencil attachments will be used).

> Input attachments are used for descriptors of a `VK_DESCRIPTOR_TYPE_INPUT_ATTACHMENT` type.

In Vulkan, rendering operations are gathered into render passes. Each render pass has at least one subpass, but can have more. If we render to an attachment in one subpass, we can then use it as an input attachment and read data from it in subsequent subpasses of the same render pass. It is in fact the only way to read data from attachments in a given render pass--images serving as attachments in a given render pass can only be accessed through input attachments inside shaders (they cannot be bound to descriptor sets for purposes other than input attachments).

When reading data from input attachments, we are confined only to the location corresponding to the location of a processed fragment. But such an approach may be more optimal than rendering into an attachment, ending a render pass, binding an image to a descriptor set as a sampled image (texture), and starting another render pass which doesn't use the given image as any of its attachments.

For input attachments, we can also use other images (we don't have to use them as color or depth/stencil attachments). We just need to create them with a VK_IMAGE_USAGE_INPUT_ATTACHMENT_BIT usage and a proper format. The following formats are mandatory for input attachments from which color data will be read:

- VK_FORMAT_R5G6B5_UNORM_PACK16
- VK_FORMAT_A1R5G5B5_UNORM_PACK16
- VK_FORMAT_R8_UNORM, VK_FORMAT_R8_UINT and VK_FORMAT_R8_SINT
- VK_FORMAT_R8G8_UNORM, VK_FORMAT_R8G8_UINT, and VK_FORMAT_R8G8_SINT
- VK_FORMAT_R8G8B8A8_UNORM, VK_FORMAT_R8G8B8A8_UINT, VK_FORMAT_R8G8B8A8_SINT, and VK_FORMAT_R8G8B8A8_SRGB
- VK_FORMAT_B8G8R8A8_UNORM and VK_FORMAT_B8G8R8A8_SRGB
- VK_FORMAT_A8B8G8R8_UNORM_PACK32, VK_FORMAT_A8B8G8R8_UINT_PACK32, VK_FORMAT_A8B8G8R8_SINT_PACK32, and VK_FORMAT_A8B8G8R8_SRGB_PACK32
- VK_FORMAT_A2B10G10R10_UNORM_PACK32 and VK_FORMAT_A2B10G10R10_UINT_PACK32
- VK_FORMAT_R16_UINT, VK_FORMAT_R16_SINT and VK_FORMAT_R16_SFLOAT
- VK_FORMAT_R16G16_UINT, VK_FORMAT_R16G16_SINT and VK_FORMAT_R16G16_SFLOAT
- VK_FORMAT_R16G16B16A16_UINT, VK_FORMAT_R16G16B16A16_SINT, and VK_FORMAT_R16G16B16A16_SFLOAT
- VK_FORMAT_R32_UINT, VK_FORMAT_R32_SINT, and VK_FORMAT_R32_SFLOAT

Descriptor Sets

- VK_FORMAT_R32G32_UINT, VK_FORMAT_R32G32_SINT, and VK_FORMAT_R32G32_SFLOAT
- VK_FORMAT_R32G32B32A32_UINT, VK_FORMAT_R32G32B32A32_SINT, and VK_FORMAT_R32G32B32A32_SFLOAT

For input attachments from which depth/stencil data will be read, the following formats are mandatory:

- VK_FORMAT_D16_UNORM
- VK_FORMAT_X8_D24_UNORM_PACK32 or VK_FORMAT_D32_SFLOAT (at least one of these two formats must be supported)
- VK_FORMAT_D24_UNORM_S8_UINT or VK_FORMAT_D32_SFLOAT_S8_UINT (at least one of these two formats must be supported)

Other formats may also be supported but support for them is not guaranteed. We can check whether a given format is supported on the platform on which our application is executed like this:

```
VkFormatProperties format_properties;
vkGetPhysicalDeviceFormatProperties( physical_device, format,
&format_properties );
if( (aspect & VK_IMAGE_ASPECT_COLOR_BIT) &&
   !(format_properties.optimalTilingFeatures &
VK_FORMAT_FEATURE_COLOR_ATTACHMENT_BIT) ) {
  std::cout << "Provided format is not supported for an input attachment."
<< std::endl;
  return false;
}
if( (aspect & (VK_IMAGE_ASPECT_DEPTH_BIT | VK_IMAGE_ASPECT_DEPTH_BIT)) &&
   !(format_properties.optimalTilingFeatures &
VK_FORMAT_FEATURE_DEPTH_STENCIL_ATTACHMENT_BIT) ) {
  std::cout << "Provided format is not supported for an input attachment."
<< std::endl;
  return false;
}
```

Next, we just need to create an image, allocate a memory object (or use an existing one) and bind it to the image, and create an image view. We can do it like this:

```
if( !CreateImage( logical_device, type, format, size, 1, 1,
VK_SAMPLE_COUNT_1_BIT, usage | VK_IMAGE_USAGE_INPUT_ATTACHMENT_BIT, false,
input_attachment ) ) {
  return false;
}
```

```
if( !AllocateAndBindMemoryObjectToImage( physical_device, logical_device,
input_attachment, VK_MEMORY_PROPERTY_DEVICE_LOCAL_BIT, memory_object ) ) {
  return false;
}

if( !CreateImageView( logical_device, input_attachment, view_type, format,
aspect, input_attachment_image_view ) ) {
  return false;
}
return true;
```

Images and their views that are created like this can be used as input attachments. For this, we need to prepare a proper description of a render pass, and include the image views in framebuffers (refer to the *Specifying subpass descriptions* and *Creating a framebuffer* recipes from Chapter 6, *Render Passes and Framebuffers*).

Inside the GLSL shader code, variables that refer to input attachments are defined with a subpassInput (possibly with a prefix) keyword.

An example of an input attachment defined in a GLSL is provided as follows:

```
layout (input_attachment_index=i, set=m, binding=n) uniform subpassInput
<variable name>;
```

See also

In Chapter 4, *Resources and Memory*, see the following recipes:

- *Creating an image*
- *Allocating and binding memory object to an image*
- *Creating an image view*
- *Destroying an image view*
- *Destroying an image*
- *Freeing a memory object*

In Chapter 6, *Render Passes and Framebuffers*, see the following recipes:

- *Specifying subpass descriptions*
- *Creating a framebuffer*

Creating a descriptor set layout

Descriptor sets gather many resources (descriptors) in one object. They are later bound to a pipeline to establish an interface between our application and the shaders. But for the hardware to know what resources are grouped in a set, how many resources of each type there are, and what their order is, we need to create a descriptor set layout.

How to do it...

1. Take the handle of a logical device and assign it to a variable of type `VkDevice` named `logical_device`.
2. Create a vector variable with elements of type `VkDescriptorSetLayoutBinding` and call it `bindings`.
3. For each resource you want to create and assign later to a given descriptor set, add an element to the `bindings` vector. Use the following values for members of each new element:
    - The selected index of the given resource within a descriptor set for `binding`.
    - Desired type of a given resource for `descriptorType`
    - The number of resources of a specified type accessed through an array inside the shader (or 1 if the given resource is not accessed through an array) for `descriptorCount`
    - The logical OR of all shader stages in which the resource will be accessed for `stageFlags`
    - The `nullptr` value for `pImmutableSamplers`
4. Create a variable of type `VkDescriptorSetLayoutCreateInfo` named `descriptor_set_layout_create_info`. Initialize its members with the following values:
    - `VK_STRUCTURE_TYPE_DESCRIPTOR_SET_LAYOUT_CREATE_INFO` value for `sType`
    - `nullptr` value for `pNext`
    - 0 value for `flags`
    - The number of elements in the `bindings` vector for `bindingCount`
    - The pointer to the first element of the `bindings` vector for `pBindings`

5. Create a variable of type `VkDescriptorSetLayout` named `descriptor_set_layout`, in which the created layout will be stored.
6. Call `vkCreateDescriptorSetLayout( logical_device, &descriptor_set_layout_create_info, nullptr, &descriptor_set_layout )` and provide the handle of the logical device, a pointer to the `descriptor_set_layout_create_info` variable, a `nullptr` value, and a pointer to the `descriptor_set_layout variable`.
7. Make sure the call was successful by checking whether the return value is equal to `VK_SUCCESS`.

How it works...

The descriptor set layout specifies the internal structure of a descriptor set and, at the same time, strictly defines what resources can be bound to the descriptor set (we can't use resources other than those specified in the layout).

When we want to create layouts, we need to know what resources (descriptor types) will be used and what their order will be. The order is specified through bindings--they define the index (position) of a resource within a given set and are also used inside shaders (with a set number through a `layout` qualifier) to specify a resource we want to access:

```
layout (set=m, binding=n) // variable definition
```

We can choose any values for bindings, but we should keep in mind that unused indices may consume memory and impact the performance of our application.

To avoid unnecessary memory overhead and a negative performance impact, we should keep descriptor bindings as compact and as close to 0 as possible.

To create a descriptor set layout, we first need to specify a list of all the resources used in a given set:

```
VkDescriptorSetLayoutCreateInfo descriptor_set_layout_create_info = {
  VK_STRUCTURE_TYPE_DESCRIPTOR_SET_LAYOUT_CREATE_INFO,
  nullptr,
  0,
  static_cast<uint32_t>(bindings.size()),
  bindings.data()
};
```

Descriptor Sets

Next, we can create the layout like this:

```
VkResult result = vkCreateDescriptorSetLayout( logical_device,
&descriptor_set_layout_create_info, nullptr, &descriptor_set_layout );
if( VK_SUCCESS != result ) {
  std::cout << "Could not create a layout for descriptor sets." << std::endl;
  return false;
}
return true;
```

Descriptor set layouts (along with push constant ranges) also form a pipeline layout, which defines what type of resources can be accessed by a given pipeline. Created layouts, apart from pipeline layout creation, are also required during descriptor set allocation.

See also

- In Chapter 8, *Graphics and Compute Pipelines*, see the following recipe:
    - *Creating a pipeline layout*
- In this chapter, see the following recipe:
    - *Allocating descriptor sets*

Creating a descriptor pool

Descriptors, gathered into sets, are allocated from descriptor pools. When we create a pool, we must define which descriptors, and how many of them, can be allocated from the created pool.

How to do it...

1. Take the handle of a logical device on which the descriptor pool should be created. Store it in a variable of type VkDevice named logical_device.
2. Create a vector variable named descriptor_types with elements of type VkDescriptorPoolSize. For each type of descriptor that will be allocated from the pool, add a new element to the descriptor_types variable defining the specified type of descriptor and the number of descriptors of a given type that will be allocated from the pool.

3. Create a variable of type `VkDescriptorPoolCreateInfo` named `descriptor_pool_create_info`. Use the following values for members of this variable:
   - `VK_STRUCTURE_TYPE_DESCRIPTOR_POOL_CREATE_INFO` value for `sType`
   - `nullptr` value for `pNext`
   - `VK_DESCRIPTOR_POOL_CREATE_FREE_DESCRIPTOR_SET_BIT` value if it should be possible to free individual sets allocated from this pool or a `0` value to only allow for freeing all the sets at once (through a pool reset operation) for `flags`
   - The maximal number of sets that can be allocated from the pool for `maxSets`
   - Number of elements in the `descriptor_types` vector for `poolSizeCount`
   - Pointer to the first element of the `descriptor_types` vector for `pPoolSizes`
4. Create a variable of type `VkDescriptorPool` named `descriptor_pool` in which the handle of the created pool will be stored.
5. Call `vkCreateDescriptorPool( logical_device, &descriptor_pool_create_info, nullptr, &descriptor_pool )` and provide the `logical_device` variable, a pointer to the `descriptor_pool_create_info` variable, a `nullptr` value, and a pointer to the `descriptor_pool` variable.
6. Make sure the pool was successfully created by checking whether the call returned a `VK_SUCCESS` value.

How it works...

Descriptor pools manage the resources used for allocating descriptor sets (in a similar way to how command pools manage memory for command buffers). During descriptor pool creation, we specify the maximal amount of sets that can be allocated from a given pool and the maximal number of descriptors of a given type that can be allocated across all sets. This information is provided through a variable of type `VkDescriptorPoolCreateInfo` like this:

```
VkDescriptorPoolCreateInfo descriptor_pool_create_info = {
  VK_STRUCTURE_TYPE_DESCRIPTOR_POOL_CREATE_INFO,
  nullptr,
  free_individual_sets ?
```

Descriptor Sets

```
    VK_DESCRIPTOR_POOL_CREATE_FREE_DESCRIPTOR_SET_BIT : 0,
  max_sets_count,
  static_cast<uint32_t>(descriptor_types.size()),
  descriptor_types.data()
};
```

In the preceding example, the types of descriptors and their total number are provided through a `descriptor_types` vector variable. It may contain multiple elements and the created pool will be big enough to allow for allocation of all the specified descriptors.

The pool itself is created like this:

```
VkResult result = vkCreateDescriptorPool( logical_device,
&descriptor_pool_create_info, nullptr, &descriptor_pool );
if( VK_SUCCESS != result ) {
  std::cout << "Could not create a descriptor pool." << std::endl;
  return false;
}
return true;
```

When we have created a pool, we can allocate descriptor sets from it. But we must remember that we can't do this in multiple threads at the same time.

> We can't allocate descriptor sets from a given pool simultaneously in multiple threads.

See also

See the following recipes in this chapter:

- *Allocating descriptor sets*
- *Freeing descriptor sets*
- *Resetting a descriptor pool*
- *Destroying a descriptor pool*

Allocating descriptor sets

Descriptor sets gather shader resources (descriptors) in one container object. Its contents, types, and number of resources are defined by a descriptor set layout; storage is taken from pools, from which we can allocate descriptor sets.

How to do it...

1. Take the logical device and store its handle in a variable of type `VkDevice` named `logical_device`.
2. Prepare a descriptor pool from which descriptor sets should be allocated. Use the pool's handle to initialize a variable of type `VkDescriptorPool` named `descriptor_pool`.
3. Create a variable of type `std::vector<VkDescriptorSetLayout>` named `descriptor_set_layouts`. For each descriptor set that should be allocated from the pool, add a handle of a descriptor set layout that defines the structure of a corresponding descriptor set.
4. Create a variable of type `VkDescriptorSetAllocateInfo` named `descriptor_set_allocate_info` and use the following values for its members:
   - `VK_STRUCTURE_TYPE_DESCRIPTOR_SET_ALLOCATE_INFO` value for `sType`
   - `nullptr` value for `pNext`
   - The `descriptor_pool` variable for `descriptorPool`
   - The number of elements in the `descriptor_set_layouts` vector for `descriptorSetCount`
   - The pointer to the first element of the `descriptorSetCount` vector for `pSetLayouts`
5. Create a vector variable of type `std::vector<VkDescriptorSet>` named `descriptor_sets` and resize it to match the size of the `descriptor_set_layouts` vector.
6. Call `vkAllocateDescriptorSets( logical_device, &descriptor_set_allocate_info, &descriptor_sets[0] )` and provide the `logical_device` variable, a pointer to the `descriptor_set_allocate_info` variable, and a pointer to the first element of the `descriptor_sets` vector.
7. Make sure the call was successful and the `VK_SUCCESS` value was returned.

How it works...

Descriptor sets are used to provide resources to shaders. They form an interface between the application and programmable pipeline stages. The structure of this interface is defined by the descriptor set layouts. And the actual data is provided when we update descriptor sets with image or buffer resources and later bind these descriptor sets to the command buffer during the recording operation.

Descriptor sets are allocated from pools. When we create a pool, we specify how many descriptors (resources) and of what type we can allocate from it across all descriptor sets that will be allocated from the pool. We also specify the maximum number of descriptor sets that can be allocated from the pool.

When we want to allocate descriptor sets, we need to specify layouts that will describe their internal structure--one layout for each descriptor set. This information is specified like this:

```
VkDescriptorSetAllocateInfo descriptor_set_allocate_info = {
  VK_STRUCTURE_TYPE_DESCRIPTOR_SET_ALLOCATE_INFO,
  nullptr,
  descriptor_pool,
  static_cast<uint32_t>(descriptor_set_layouts.size()),
  descriptor_set_layouts.data()
};
```

Next, we allocate descriptor sets in the following way:

```
descriptor_sets.resize( descriptor_set_layouts.size() );

VkResult result = vkAllocateDescriptorSets( logical_device,
  &descriptor_set_allocate_info, descriptor_sets.data() );
if( VK_SUCCESS != result ) {
  std::cout << "Could not allocate descriptor sets." << std::endl;
  return false;
}
return true;
```

Unfortunately, the pool's memory may become fragmented when we allocate and free separate descriptor sets. In such situations, we may not be able to allocate new sets from a given pool, even if we haven't reached the specified limits. This situation is presented in the following diagram:

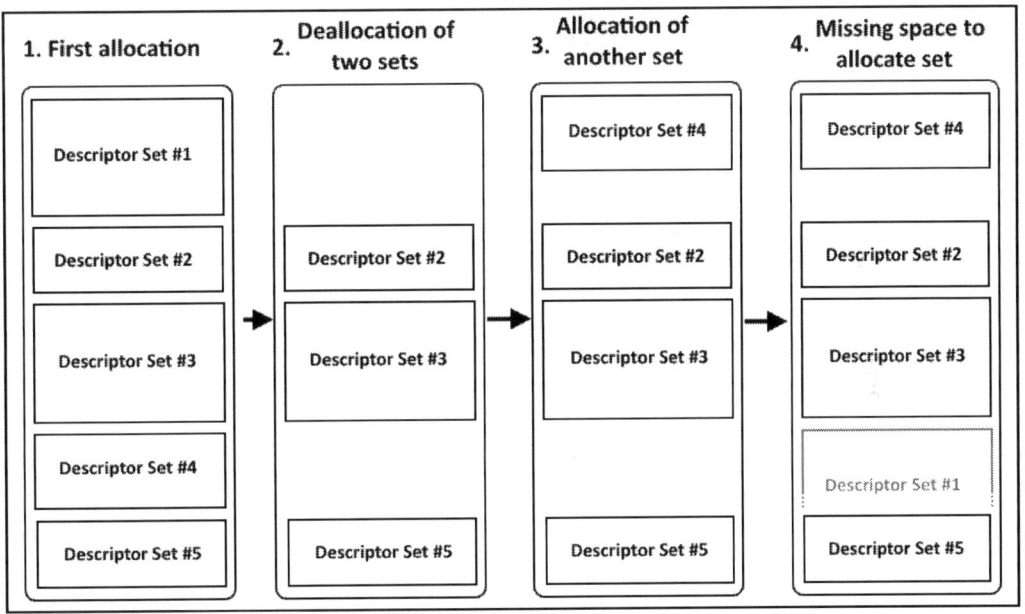

When we first allocate descriptors sets, the fragmentation problem will not occur. Additionally, if all descriptor sets use the same number of resources of the same type, it is guaranteed that this problem won't appear either.

To avoid problems with pool fragmentation, we can free all descriptor sets at once (by resetting a pool). Otherwise, if we can't allocate a new descriptor set and we don't want to reset the pool, we need to create another pool.

See also

See the following recipes in this chapter:

- *Creating a descriptor set layout*
- *Creating a descriptor pool*
- *Freeing descriptor sets*
- *Resetting a descriptor pool*

Updating descriptor sets

We have created a descriptor pool and allocated descriptor sets from it. We know their internal structure thanks to created layouts. Now we want to provide specific resources (samplers, image views, buffers, or buffer views) that should be later bound to the pipeline through descriptor sets. Defining resources that should be used is done through a process of updating descriptor sets.

Getting ready

Updating descriptor sets requires us to provide a considerable amount of data for each descriptor involved in the process. What's more, the provided data depends on the type of descriptor. To simplify the process and lower the number of parameters that need to be specified, and also to improve error checking, custom structures are introduced in this recipe.

For samplers and all kinds of image descriptors, an `ImageDescriptorInfo` type is used which has the following definition:

```
struct ImageDescriptorInfo {
  VkDescriptorSet                    TargetDescriptorSet;
  uint32_t                           TargetDescriptorBinding;
  uint32_t                           TargetArrayElement;
  VkDescriptorType                   TargetDescriptorType;
  std::vector<VkDescriptorImageInfo> ImageInfos;
};
```

For uniform and storage buffers (and their dynamic variations), a `BufferDescriptorInfo` type is used. It has the following definition:

```
struct BufferDescriptorInfo {
  VkDescriptorSet                     TargetDescriptorSet;
  uint32_t                            TargetDescriptorBinding;
  uint32_t                            TargetArrayElement;
  VkDescriptorType                    TargetDescriptorType;
  std::vector<VkDescriptorBufferInfo> BufferInfos;
};
```

For uniform and storage texel buffers, a `TexelBufferDescriptorInfo` type is introduced with the following definition:

```
struct TexelBufferDescriptorInfo {
    VkDescriptorSet                 TargetDescriptorSet;
    uint32_t                        TargetDescriptorBinding;
    uint32_t                        TargetArrayElement;
    VkDescriptorType                TargetDescriptorType;
    std::vector<VkBufferView>       TexelBufferViews;
};
```

The preceding structures are used when we want to update descriptor sets with handles of new descriptors (that haven't been bound yet). It is also possible to copy descriptor data from other, already updated, sets. For this purpose, a `CopyDescriptorInfo` type is used that is defined like this:

```
struct CopyDescriptorInfo {
    VkDescriptorSet     TargetDescriptorSet;
    uint32_t            TargetDescriptorBinding;
    uint32_t            TargetArrayElement;
    VkDescriptorSet     SourceDescriptorSet;
    uint32_t            SourceDescriptorBinding;
    uint32_t            SourceArrayElement;
    uint32_t            DescriptorCount;
};
```

All the preceding structures define the handle of a descriptor set that should be updated, an index of a descriptor within the given set, and an index into an array if we want to update descriptors accessed through arrays. The rest of the parameters are type-specific.

How to do it...

1. Use the handle of a logical device to initialize a variable of type `VkDevice` named `logical_device`.
2. Create a variable of type `std::vector<VkWriteDescriptorSet>` named `write_descriptors`. For each new descriptor that should be updated, add a new element to the vector and use the following values for its members:
    - `VK_STRUCTURE_TYPE_WRITE_DESCRIPTOR_SET` value for `sType`
    - `nullptr` value for `pNext`
    - The handle of a descriptor set that should be updated for `dstSet`

- Index (binding) of a descriptor within a specified set for `dstBinding`
- The beginning index into an array from which descriptors should be updated if the given descriptor is accessed through an array inside shaders (or 0 value otherwise) for `dstArrayElement`
- The number of descriptors to be updated (number of elements in `pImageInfo`, `pBufferInfo` or `pTexelBufferView` arrays) for `descriptorCount`
- The type of descriptor for `descriptorType`
- In the case of sampler or image descriptors, specify an array with the `descriptorCount` elements and provide a pointer to its first element in `pImageInfo` (set `pBufferInfo` and `pTexelBufferView` members to `nullptr`). Use the following values for each array element:
    - The sampler handle in the case of sampler and combined image sampler descriptors for `sampler`
    - The image view handle in the case of the sampled image, storage image, combined image sampler, and input attachment descriptors for `imageView`
    - The layout the given image will be in when a descriptor is accessed through shaders in the case of image descriptors for `imageLayout`
- In the case of uniform or storage buffers (and their dynamic variations), specify an array with the `descriptorCount` elements and provide a pointer to its first element in `pBufferInfo` (set `pImageInfo` and `pTexelBufferView` members to `nullptr`), and use the following values for each array element:
    - The buffer's handle for `buffer`
    - The memory offset (or base offset for dynamic descriptors) within a buffer for `offset`
    - The buffer's memory size that should be used for a given descriptor for `range`
- In the case of uniform texel buffers or storage texel buffers, specify an array with the `descriptorCount` number of texel view handles, and provide a pointer to its first element in `pTexelBufferView` (set `pImageInfo` and `pBufferInfo` members to `nullptr`).

3. Create a variable of type `std::vector<VkCopyDescriptorSet>` named `copy_descriptors`. Add an element to this vector for each descriptor data that should be copied from another, already updated, descriptor. Use the following values for the members of each new element:
   - `VK_STRUCTURE_TYPE_COPY_DESCRIPTOR_SET` value for `sType`
   - `nullptr` value for `pNext`
   - The handle of a descriptor set from which data should be copied for `srcSet`
   - The binding number from within a source descriptor set for `srcBinding`
   - The index into an array in the source descriptor set for `srcArrayElement`
   - The handle of a descriptor set in which data should be updated for `dstSet`
   - The binding number in the target descriptor set for `dstBinding`
   - The array index in the target descriptor set for `dstArrayElement`
   - The number of descriptors that should be copied from the source set and updated in the target set for `descriptorCount`

4. Call `vkUpdateDescriptorSets( logical_device, static_cast<uint32_t>(write_descriptors.size()), &write_descriptors[0], static_cast<uint32_t>(copy_descriptors.size()), &copy_descriptors[0] )` and provide the `logical_device` variable, the number of elements in the `write_descriptors` vector, a pointer to the first element of the `write_descriptors`, the number of elements in the `copy_descriptors` vector, and a pointer to the first element of the `copy_descriptors` vector.

How it works...

Updating descriptor sets causes specified resources (samplers, image views, buffers, or buffer views) to populate entries in the indicated sets. When the updated set is bound to a pipeline, such resources can be accessed through shaders.

We can write new (not used yet) resources to a descriptor set. In the following example, we do this by using the custom structures mentioned in the *Getting ready* section:

```
std::vector<VkWriteDescriptorSet> write_descriptors;
```

Descriptor Sets

```cpp
for( auto & image_descriptor : image_descriptor_infos ) {
  write_descriptors.push_back( {
    VK_STRUCTURE_TYPE_WRITE_DESCRIPTOR_SET,
    nullptr,
    image_descriptor.TargetDescriptorSet,
    image_descriptor.TargetDescriptorBinding,
    image_descriptor.TargetArrayElement,
    static_cast<uint32_t>(image_descriptor.ImageInfos.size()),
    image_descriptor.TargetDescriptorType,
    image_descriptor.ImageInfos.data(),
    nullptr,
    nullptr
  } );
}

for( auto & buffer_descriptor : buffer_descriptor_infos ) {
  write_descriptors.push_back( {
    VK_STRUCTURE_TYPE_WRITE_DESCRIPTOR_SET,
    nullptr,
    buffer_descriptor.TargetDescriptorSet,
    buffer_descriptor.TargetDescriptorBinding,
    buffer_descriptor.TargetArrayElement,
    static_cast<uint32_t>(buffer_descriptor.BufferInfos.size()),
    buffer_descriptor.TargetDescriptorType,
    nullptr,
    buffer_descriptor.BufferInfos.data(),
    nullptr
  } );
}

for( auto & texel_buffer_descriptor : texel_buffer_descriptor_infos ) {
  write_descriptors.push_back( {
    VK_STRUCTURE_TYPE_WRITE_DESCRIPTOR_SET,
    nullptr,
    texel_buffer_descriptor.TargetDescriptorSet,
    texel_buffer_descriptor.TargetDescriptorBinding,
    texel_buffer_descriptor.TargetArrayElement,
    static_cast<uint32_t>(texel_buffer_descriptor.TexelBufferViews.size()),
    texel_buffer_descriptor.TargetDescriptorType,
    nullptr,
    nullptr,
    texel_buffer_descriptor.TexelBufferViews.data()
  } );
}
```

We can also reuse descriptors from other sets. Copying already populated descriptors should be faster than writing new ones. This can be done like this:

```
std::vector<VkCopyDescriptorSet> copy_descriptors;

for( auto & copy_descriptor : copy_descriptor_infos ) {
  copy_descriptors.push_back( {
    VK_STRUCTURE_TYPE_COPY_DESCRIPTOR_SET,
    nullptr,
    copy_descriptor.SourceDescriptorSet,
    copy_descriptor.SourceDescriptorBinding,
    copy_descriptor.SourceArrayElement,
    copy_descriptor.TargetDescriptorSet,
    copy_descriptor.TargetDescriptorBinding,
    copy_descriptor.TargetArrayElement,
    copy_descriptor.DescriptorCount
  } );
}
```

The operation of updating descriptor sets is performed through a single function call:

```
vkUpdateDescriptorSets( logical_device,
static_cast<uint32_t>(write_descriptors.size()), write_descriptors.data(),
static_cast<uint32_t>(copy_descriptors.size()), copy_descriptors.data() );
```

See also

See the following recipes in this chapter:

- *Allocating descriptor sets*
- *Binding descriptor sets*
- *Creating descriptors with a texture and a uniform buffer*

Binding descriptor sets

When a descriptor set is ready (we have updated it with all the resources that will be accessed in shaders), we need to bind it to a command buffer during the recording operation.

How to do it...

1. Take the handle of a command buffer that is being recorded. Store the handle in a variable of type `VkCommandBuffer` named `command_buffer`.
2. Create a variable of type `VkPipelineBindPoint` named `pipeline_type` that will represent the type of a pipeline (graphics or compute) in which descriptor sets will be used.
3. Take the pipeline's layout and store its handle in a variable of type `VkPipelineLayout` named `pipeline_layout` (refer to the *Creating a pipeline layout* recipe from Chapter 8, *Graphics and Compute Pipelines*).
4. Create a variable of type `std::vector<VkDescriptorSet>` named `descriptor_sets`. For each descriptor set that should be bound to the pipeline, add a new element to the vector and initialize it with the descriptor set's handle.
5. Select an index to which the first set from the provided list should be bound. Store the index in a variable of type `uint32_t` named `index_for_first_set`.
6. If dynamic uniform or storage buffers are used in any of the sets being bound, create a variable of type `std::vector<uint32_t>` named `dynamic_offsets`, through which provide memory offset values for each dynamic descriptor defined in all the sets being bound. Offsets must be defined in the same order in which their corresponding descriptors appear in the layouts of each set (in order of increasing bindings).
7. Make the following call:

   ```
   vkCmdBindDescriptorSets( command_buffer, pipeline_type,
   pipeline_layout, index_for_first_set, static_cast<uint32_t>
   (descriptor_sets.size()), descriptor_sets.data(),
   static_cast<uint32_t>(dynamic_offsets.size()),
   dynamic_offsets.data() )
   ```

For this call, provide the `command_buffer`, `pipeline_type`, `pipeline_layout`, and `index_for_first_set` variables, the number of elements and a pointer to the first element of the `descriptor_sets` vector, and the number of elements and a pointer to the first element of the `dynamic_offsets` vector.

How it works...

When we start recording a command buffer, its state is (almost entirely) undefined. So before we can record drawing operations that reference image or buffer resources, we need to bind appropriate resources to the command buffer. This is done by binding descriptor sets with the `vkCmdBindDescriptorSets()` function call like this:

```
vkCmdBindDescriptorSets( command_buffer, pipeline_type, pipeline_layout,
  index_for_first_set, static_cast<uint32_t>(descriptor_sets.size()),
  descriptor_sets.data(), static_cast<uint32_t>(dynamic_offsets.size()),
  dynamic_offsets.data() )
```

See also

See the following recipes in this chapter:

- *Creating a descriptor set layout*
- *Allocating descriptor sets*
- *Updating descriptor sets*

Creating descriptors with a texture and a uniform buffer

In this sample recipe, we will see how to create the most commonly used resources: a combined image sampler and a uniform buffer. We will prepare a descriptor set layout for them, create a descriptor pool, and allocate a descriptor set from it. Then we will update the allocated set with the created resources. This way, we can later bind the descriptor set to a command buffer and access resources in shaders.

Descriptor Sets

How to do it...

1. Create a combined image sampler (an image, image view, and a sampler) with the selected parameters--the most commonly used are `VK_IMAGE_TYPE_2D` image type, `VK_FORMAT_R8G8B8A8_UNORM` format, `VK_IMAGE_VIEW_TYPE_2D` view type, `VK_IMAGE_ASPECT_COLOR_BIT` aspect, `VK_FILTER_LINEAR` filter mode, and `VK_SAMPLER_ADDRESS_MODE_REPEAT` addressing mode for all texture coordinates. Store the created handles in a variable of type `VkSampler` named `sampler`, of type `VkImage` named `sampled_image`, and another one of type `VkImageView` named `sampled_image_view` (refer to the *Creating a combined image sampler* recipe).
2. Create a uniform buffer with selected parameters and store the buffer's handle in a variable of type `VkBuffer` named `uniform_buffer` (refer to the *Creating a uniform buffer* recipe).
3. Create a variable named `bindings` of type `std::vector<VkDescriptorSetLayoutBinding>`.
4. Add one element with the following values to the `bindings` variable:
   - 0 value for `binding`
   - `VK_DESCRIPTOR_TYPE_COMBINED_IMAGE_SAMPLER` value for `descriptorType`
   - 1 value for `descriptorCount`
   - The `VK_SHADER_STAGE_FRAGMENT_BIT` value for `stageFlags`
   - The `nullptr` value for `stageFlags`
5. Add another element to the `bindings` vector and use the following values for its members:
   - 1 value for `binding`
   - `VK_DESCRIPTOR_TYPE_UNIFORM_BUFFER` value for `descriptorType`
   - 1 value for `descriptorCount`
   - The `VK_SHADER_STAGE_VERTEX_BIT | VK_SHADER_STAGE_FRAGMENT_BIT` value for `stageFlags`
   - The `nullptr` value for `pImmutableSamplers`
6. Create a descriptor set layout using the `bindings` variable and store its handle in a variable of type `VkDescriptorSetLayout` named `descriptor_set_layout` (refer to the *Creating a descriptor set layout* recipe).

7. Create a variable of type `std::vector<VkDescriptorPoolSize>` named `descriptor_types`. Add two elements to the created vector: one with `VK_DESCRIPTOR_TYPE_COMBINED_IMAGE_SAMPLER` and 1 values, the second with `VK_DESCRIPTOR_TYPE_UNIFORM_BUFFER` and 1 values.
8. Create a descriptor pool in which separate descriptor sets cannot be freed individually and only one descriptor set can be allocated. Use the `descriptor_types` variable during pool creation and store its handle in a variable of type `VkDescriptorPool` named `descriptor_pool` (refer to the *Creating a descriptor pool* recipe).
9. Allocate one descriptor set from `descriptor_pool` using the `descriptor_set_layout` layout variable. Store the created handle in a one-element vector of type `std::vector<VkDescriptorSet>` named `descriptor_sets` (refer to the *Allocating descriptor sets* recipe).
10. Create a variable of type `std::vector<ImageDescriptorInfo>` named `image_descriptor_infos`. Add one element to this vector with the following values:
    - The `descriptor_sets[0]` for `TargetDescriptorSet`
    - 0 value for `TargetDescriptorBinding`
    - 0 value for `TargetArrayElement`
    - `VK_DESCRIPTOR_TYPE_COMBINED_IMAGE_SAMPLER` value for `TargetDescriptorType`
    - Add one element to the `ImageInfos` member vector with the following values:
        - The `sampler` variable for `sampler`
        - The `sampled_image_view` variable for `imageView`
        - The `VK_IMAGE_LAYOUT_SHADER_READ_ONLY_OPTIMAL` value for `imageLayout`
11. Create a variable of type `std::vector<BufferDescriptorInfo>` named `buffer_descriptor_infos` with one element initialized with the following values:
    - The `descriptor_sets[0]` for `TargetDescriptorSet`
    - 1 value for `TargetDescriptorBinding`
    - 0 value for `TargetArrayElement`

Descriptor Sets

- `VK_DESCRIPTOR_TYPE_UNIFORM_BUFFER` value for `TargetDescriptorType`
- Add one element to the `BufferInfos` member vector and use the following values to initialize its members:
  - The `uniform_buffer` variable for `buffer`
  - The 0 for `offset`
  - The `VK_WHOLE_SIZE` value for `range`

8. Update the descriptor sets using the `image_descriptor_infos` and `buffer_descriptor_infos` vectors.

How it works...

To prepare the typically used descriptors, a combined image sampler and a uniform buffer, we first need to create them:

```
if( !CreateCombinedImageSampler( physical_device, logical_device,
VK_IMAGE_TYPE_2D, VK_FORMAT_R8G8B8A8_UNORM, sampled_image_size, 1, 1,
VK_IMAGE_USAGE_TRANSFER_DST_BIT,
  VK_IMAGE_VIEW_TYPE_2D, VK_IMAGE_ASPECT_COLOR_BIT, VK_FILTER_LINEAR,
VK_FILTER_LINEAR, VK_SAMPLER_MIPMAP_MODE_NEAREST,
VK_SAMPLER_ADDRESS_MODE_REPEAT,
  VK_SAMPLER_ADDRESS_MODE_REPEAT, VK_SAMPLER_ADDRESS_MODE_REPEAT, 0.0f,
false, 1.0f, false, VK_COMPARE_OP_ALWAYS, 0.0f, 0.0f,
VK_BORDER_COLOR_FLOAT_OPAQUE_BLACK, false,
  sampler, sampled_image, sampled_image_memory_object, sampled_image_view )
) {
  return false;
}

if( !CreateUniformBuffer( physical_device, logical_device,
uniform_buffer_size, VK_BUFFER_USAGE_TRANSFER_DST_BIT, uniform_buffer,
uniform_buffer_memory_object ) ) {
  return false;
}
```

Next, we prepare a layout that will define the internal structure of a descriptor set:

```
std::vector<VkDescriptorSetLayoutBinding> bindings = {
  {
    0,
    VK_DESCRIPTOR_TYPE_COMBINED_IMAGE_SAMPLER,
    1,
    VK_SHADER_STAGE_FRAGMENT_BIT,
```

```
          nullptr
      },
      {
        1,
        VK_DESCRIPTOR_TYPE_UNIFORM_BUFFER,
        1,
        VK_SHADER_STAGE_VERTEX_BIT | VK_SHADER_STAGE_FRAGMENT_BIT,
        nullptr
      }
    };
    if( !CreateDescriptorSetLayout( logical_device, bindings,
    descriptor_set_layout ) ) {
      return false;
    }
```

After that, we create a descriptor pool and allocate a descriptor set from it:

```
    std::vector<VkDescriptorPoolSize> descriptor_types = {
      {
        VK_DESCRIPTOR_TYPE_COMBINED_IMAGE_SAMPLER,
        1
      },
      {
        VK_DESCRIPTOR_TYPE_UNIFORM_BUFFER,
        1
      }
    };
    if( !CreateDescriptorPool( logical_device, false, 1, descriptor_types,
    descriptor_pool ) ) {
      return false;
    }

    if( !AllocateDescriptorSets( logical_device, descriptor_pool, {
    descriptor_set_layout }, descriptor_sets ) ) {
      return false;
    }
```

The last thing to do is to update the descriptor set with the resources created at the beginning:

```
    std::vector<ImageDescriptorInfo> image_descriptor_infos = {
      {
        descriptor_sets[0],
        0,
        0,
        VK_DESCRIPTOR_TYPE_COMBINED_IMAGE_SAMPLER,
        {
          {
```

Descriptor Sets

```
        sampler,
        sampled_image_view,
        VK_IMAGE_LAYOUT_SHADER_READ_ONLY_OPTIMAL
      }
    }
  }
};

std::vector<BufferDescriptorInfo> buffer_descriptor_infos = {
  {
    descriptor_sets[0],
    1,
    0,
    VK_DESCRIPTOR_TYPE_UNIFORM_BUFFER,
    {
      {
        uniform_buffer,
        0,
        VK_WHOLE_SIZE
      }
    }
  }
};

UpdateDescriptorSets( logical_device, image_descriptor_infos,
buffer_descriptor_infos, {}, {} );
return true;
```

See also

See the following recipes in this chapter:

- *Creating a combined image sampler*
- *Creating a uniform buffer*
- *Creating a descriptor set layout*
- *Creating a descriptor pool*
- *Allocating descriptor sets*
- *Updating descriptor sets*

Freeing descriptor sets

If we want to return memory allocated by a descriptor set and give it back to the pool, we can free a given descriptor set.

How to do it...

1. Use the handle of a logical device to initialize a variable of type `VkDevice` named `logical_device`.
2. Take the descriptor pool that was created with a `VK_DESCRIPTOR_POOL_CREATE_FREE_DESCRIPTOR_SET_BIT` flag. Store its handle in a variable of type `VkDescriptorPool` named `descriptor_pool`.
3. Create a vector of type `std::vector<VkDescriptorSet>` named `descriptor_sets`. Add all the descriptor sets that should be freed to the vector.
4. Call `vkFreeDescriptorSets( logical_device, descriptor_pool, static_cast<uint32_t>(descriptor_sets.size()), descriptor_sets.data() )`. For the call provide the `logical_device` and `descriptor_pool` variables, the number of elements in the `descriptor_sets` vector, and a pointer to the first element of the `descriptor_sets` vector.
5. Make sure the call was successful by checking whether it returns a `VK_SUCCESS` value.
6. Clear the `descriptor_sets` vector as we can't use the handles of freed descriptor sets any more.

How it works...

Freeing a descriptor set releases memory used by it and gives it back to the pool. It should be possible to allocate another set of the same type from the pool but it may not be possible due to the pool's memory fragmentation (in such a situation, we may need to create another pool or reset the one from which the set was allocated).

Descriptor Sets

We can free multiple descriptor sets at once, but all of them must come from the same pool. It is done like this:

```
VkResult result = vkFreeDescriptorSets( logical_device, descriptor_pool,
static_cast<uint32_t>(descriptor_sets.size()), descriptor_sets.data() );
if( VK_SUCCESS != result ) {
  std::cout << "Error occurred during freeing descriptor sets." << std::endl;
  return false;
}

descriptor_sets.clear();
return true;
```

We cannot free descriptor sets allocated from the same pool from multiple threads at the same time.

See also

See the following recipes in this chapter:

- *Creating a descriptor pool*
- *Allocating descriptor sets*
- *Resetting a descriptor pool*
- *Destroying a descriptor pool*

Resetting a descriptor pool

We can free all descriptor sets allocated from a given pool at once without destroying the pool itself. To do that, we can reset a descriptor pool.

How to do it...

1. Take the descriptor pool that should be reset and use its handle to initialize a variable of type `VkDescriptorPool` named `descriptor_pool`.
2. Take the handle of a logical device on which the descriptor pool was created. Store its handle in a variable of type `VkDevice` named `logical_device`.

3. Make the following call: `vkResetDescriptorPool( logical_device, descriptor_pool, 0 )`, for which use the `logical_device` and `descriptor_pool` variables and a `0` value.
4. Check for any error returned by the call. As successful operation should return `VK_SUCCESS`.

How it works...

Resetting a descriptor pool returns all the descriptor sets allocated from it back to the pool. All descriptor sets allocated from the pool are implicitly freed and they can't be used any more (their handles become invalid).

If the pool is created without a `VK_DESCRIPTOR_POOL_CREATE_FREE_DESCRIPTOR_SET_BIT` flag set, it is the only way to free descriptor sets allocated from it (apart from destroying the pool), as in such a situation, we can't free them individually.

To reset the pool, we can write code similar to the following:

```
VkResult result = vkResetDescriptorPool( logical_device, descriptor_pool, 0 );
if( VK_SUCCESS != result ) {
  std::cout << "Error occurred during descriptor pool reset." << std::endl;
  return false;
}
return true;
```

See also

See the following recipes in this chapter:

- *Creating a descriptor pool*
- *Allocating descriptor sets*
- *Freeing descriptor sets*
- *Destroying a descriptor pool*

Destroying a descriptor pool

When we don't need a descriptor pool any more, we can destroy it (with all descriptor sets allocated from the pool).

How to do it...

1. Take the handle of a created logical device and store it in a variable of type `VkDevice` named `logical_device`.
2. Provide the handle of the descriptor pool through a variable of type `VkDescriptorPool` named `descriptor_pool`.
3. Call `vkDestroyDescriptorPool( logical_device, descriptor_pool, nullptr )` and provide the `logical_device` and `descriptor_pool` variables and a `nullptr` value.
4. For safety, assign the `VK_NULL_HANDLE` value to the `descriptor_pool` variable.

How it works...

Destroying a descriptor pool implicitly frees all descriptor sets allocated from it. We don't need to free individual descriptor sets first. But because of this, we need to make sure that none of the descriptor sets allocated from the pool are referenced by the commands that are currently processed by the hardware.

When we are ready, we can destroy a descriptor pool like this:

```
if( VK_NULL_HANDLE != descriptor_pool ) {
  vkDestroyDescriptorPool( logical_device, descriptor_pool, nullptr );
  descriptor_pool = VK_NULL_HANDLE;
}
```

See also

See the following recipe in this chapter:

- *Creating a descriptor pool*

Destroying a descriptor set layout

Descriptor set layouts that are no longer used should be destroyed.

How to do it...

1. Provide a logical device's handle using a variable of type `VkDevice` named `logical_device`.
2. Take the handle of a created descriptor set layout and use it to initialize a variable of type `VkDescriptorSetLayout` named `descriptor_set_layout`.
3. Call `vkDestroyDescriptorSetLayout( logical_device, descriptor_set_layout, nullptr )` and provide handles of the logical device and descriptor set layout, and a `nullptr` value.
4. For safety, assign the `VK_NULL_HANDLE` value to the `descriptor_set_layout` variable.

How it works...

Descriptor set layouts are destroyed with the `vkDestroyDescriptorSetLayout()` function like this:

```
if( VK_NULL_HANDLE != descriptor_set_layout ) {
  vkDestroyDescriptorSetLayout( logical_device, descriptor_set_layout, nullptr );
  descriptor_set_layout = VK_NULL_HANDLE;
}
```

See also

See the following recipe in this chapter:

- *Creating a descriptor set layout*

Destroying a sampler

When we no longer need a sampler and we are sure it is not used anymore by the pending commands, we can destroy it.

How to do it...

1. Take the handle of a logical device on which the sampler was created and store it in a variable of type `VkDevice` named `logical_device`.
2. Take the handle of the sampler that should be destroyed. Provide it through a variable of type `VkSampler` named `sampler`.
3. Call `vkDestroySampler( logical_device, sampler, nullptr )` and provide the `logical_device` and `sampler` variables, and a `nullptr` value.
4. For safety, assign the `VK_NULL_HANDLE` value to the `sampler` variable.

How it works...

Samplers are destroyed like this:

```
if( VK_NULL_HANDLE != sampler ) {
  vkDestroySampler( logical_device, sampler, nullptr );
  sampler = VK_NULL_HANDLE;
}
```

We don't have to check whether the sampler's handle is not empty, because a deletion of a `VK_NULL_HANDLE` is ignored. We do this just to avoid an unnecessary function call. But when we delete a sampler, we must be sure that the handle (if not empty) is valid.

See also

See the following recipe in this chapter:

- *Creating a sampler*

6
Render Passes and Framebuffers

In this chapter, we will cover the following recipes:

- Specifying attachment descriptions
- Specifying subpass descriptions
- Specifying dependencies between subpasses
- Creating a render pass
- Creating a framebuffer
- Preparing a render pass for geometry rendering and postprocess subpasses
- Preparing a render pass and a framebuffer with color and depth attachments
- Beginning a render pass
- Progressing to the next subpass
- Ending a render pass
- Destroying a framebuffer
- Destroying a render pass

Introduction

In Vulkan, drawing commands are organized into render passes. A render pass is a collection of subpasses that describes how image resources (color, depth/stencil, and input attachments) are used: what their layouts are and how these layouts should be transitioned between subpasses, when we render into attachments or when we read data from them, if their contents are needed after the render pass, or if their usage is limited only to the scope of a render pass.

Render Passes and Framebuffers

The aforementioned data stored in render passes is just a general description, or a metadata. The actual resources involved in the rendering process are specified with framebuffers. Through them, we define which image views are used for which rendering attachments.

We need to prepare all this information in advance, before we can issue (record) rendering commands. With that knowledge, drivers can greatly optimize the drawing process, limit the amount of memory needed for the rendering, or even use a very fast cache for some of the attachments, improving the performance even more.

In this chapter, we will learn how to organize drawing operations into a set of render passes and subpasses, which are required to draw anything with Vulkan. We will also learn how to prepare a description of render target attachments used during rendering (drawing) and how to create framebuffers, which define actual image views that will be used as these attachments.

Specifying attachments descriptions

A render pass represents a set of resources (images) called attachments, which are used during rendering operations. These are divided into color, depth/stencil, input, or resolve attachments. Before we can create a render pass, we need to describe all the attachments used in it.

How to do it...

1. Create a vector with elements of type `VkAttachmentDescription`. Call the vector `attachments_descriptions`. For each attachment used in a render pass, add an element to the `attachments_descriptions` vector and use the following values for its members:
    - 0 value for `flags`
    - The selected format of a given attachment for `format`
    - The number of per pixel samples for `samples`

- For `loadOp`, specify the type of operation that should be performed on an attachment's contents when a render pass is started--a `VK_ATTACHMENT_LOAD_OP_CLEAR` value if the attachment contents should be cleared, a `VK_ATTACHMENT_LOAD_OP_LOAD` value if its current contents should be preserved or a `VK_ATTACHMENT_LOAD_OP_DONT_CARE` value if we intend to overwrite the whole attachment by ourselves and we don't care about its current contents (this parameter is used for color attachments or for the depth aspect of depth/stencil attachments.)
- For `storeOp`, specify how an attachment's contents should be treated after the render pass--use a `VK_ATTACHMENT_STORE_OP_STORE` value if they should be preserved or a `VK_ATTACHMENT_STORE_OP_DONT_CARE` value if we don't need the contents after the rendering (this parameter is used for color attachments or for the depth aspect of depth/stencil attachments)
- Specify how the stencil aspect (component) of an attachment should be treated at the beginning of a render pass for `stencilLoadOp` (the same as for the `loadOp` member but for a stencil aspect of depth/stencil attachments)
- Specify how the stencil aspect (component) of an attachment should be treated after a render pass for `stencilStoreOp` (the same as for the `storeOp` but for a stencil aspect of depth/stencil attachments)
- Specify what layout image will have when a render pass begins for `initialLayout`
- Specify the layout to which image should be automatically transitioned to after a render pass for `finalLayout`

How it works...

When we create a render pass, we have to create an array of attachment descriptions. This a general list of all the attachments used in a render pass. Indices into this array are then used for the subpass descriptions (refer to the *Specifying subpass descriptions* recipe). Similarly, when we create a framebuffer and specify exactly what image resource should be used for each attachment, we define a list where each element corresponds to the element of the attachment descriptions array.

Render Passes and Framebuffers

Usually, when we draw a geometry, we render it into at least one color attachment. Probably, we also want a depth test to be enabled, so we need a depth attachment too. Attachment descriptions for such a common scenario are presented here:

```
std::vector<VkAttachmentDescription> attachments_descriptions = {
  {
    0,
    VK_FORMAT_R8G8B8A8_UNORM,
    VK_SAMPLE_COUNT_1_BIT,
    VK_ATTACHMENT_LOAD_OP_CLEAR,
    VK_ATTACHMENT_STORE_OP_STORE,
    VK_ATTACHMENT_LOAD_OP_DONT_CARE,
    VK_ATTACHMENT_STORE_OP_DONT_CARE,
    VK_IMAGE_LAYOUT_UNDEFINED,
    VK_IMAGE_LAYOUT_PRESENT_SRC_KHR,
  },
  {
    0,
    VK_FORMAT_D16_UNORM,
    VK_SAMPLE_COUNT_1_BIT,
    VK_ATTACHMENT_LOAD_OP_CLEAR,
    VK_ATTACHMENT_STORE_OP_STORE,
    VK_ATTACHMENT_LOAD_OP_DONT_CARE,
    VK_ATTACHMENT_STORE_OP_DONT_CARE,
    VK_IMAGE_LAYOUT_UNDEFINED,
    VK_IMAGE_LAYOUT_DEPTH_STENCIL_ATTACHMENT_OPTIMAL,
  }
};
```

In the preceding example, we specify two attachments: one with a R8G8B8A8_UNORM and the other with a D16_UNORM format. Both attachments should be cleared at the beginning of a render pass (similarly to calling the OpenGL's glClear() function at the beginning of a frame). We also want to keep the contents of the first attachment, when the render pass is finished, but we don't need the contents of the second attachment. For both, we also specify an UNDEFINED initial layout. An UNDEFINED layout can always be used for an initial/old layout--it means that we don't need images content when a memory barrier is set up.

The value for the final layout depends on how we intend to use an image after the render pass. If we are rendering directly into a swapchain image and we want to display it on screen, we should use a PRESENT_SRC layout (as shown previously). For a depth attachment, if we don't intend to use a depth component after the render pass (which usually is true), we should set the same layout value as specified in the last subpass of a render pass.

It's also possible that a render pass does not use any attachments. In such a case, we don't need to specify attachment descriptions, but such a situation is rare.

See also

The following recipes in this chapter:

- *Specifying subpass descriptions*
- *Creating a render pass*
- *Creating a framebuffer*
- *Preparing a render pass and a framebuffer with color and depth attachments*

Specifying subpass descriptions

Operations performed in a render pass are grouped into subpasses. Each subpass represents a stage or a phase of our rendering commands in which a subset of render pass's attachments are used (into which we render or from which we read data).

A render pass always requires at least one subpass that is automatically started when we begin a render pass. And for each subpass, we need to prepare a description.

Getting ready

To lower the number of parameters required to prepare for each subpass, a custom structure type is introduced for this recipe. It is a simplified version of a `VkSubpassDescription` structure defined in the Vulkan header. It has the following definition:

```
struct SubpassParameters {
  VkPipelineBindPoint                    PipelineType;
  std::vector<VkAttachmentReference>     InputAttachments;
  std::vector<VkAttachmentReference>     ColorAttachments;
  std::vector<VkAttachmentReference>     ResolveAttachments;
  VkAttachmentReference const          * DepthStencilAttachment;
  std::vector<uint32_t>                  PreserveAttachments;
};
```

The `PipelineType` member defines a type of a pipeline (graphics or compute, though only graphics pipelines are supported inside render passes at this point) that will be used during the subpass. `InputAttachments` is a collection of attachments from which we will read data during the subpass. `ColorAttachments` specifies all attachments that will be used as color attachments (into which we will render during the subpass). `ResolveAttachments` specifies which color attachments should be resolved (changed from a multisampled image to a non-multisampled/single sampled image) at the end of the subpass. `DepthStencilAttachment`, if used, specifies which attachment is used as a depth and/or stencil attachment during the subpass. `PreserveAttachments` is a set of attachments that are not used in the subpass but whose contents must be preserved during the whole subpass.

How to do it...

1. Create a vector variable of type `std::vector<VkSubpassDescription>` named `subpass_descriptions`. For each subpass defined in a render pass, add an element to the `subpass_descriptions` vector and use the following values for its members:
    - 0 value for `flags`
    - `VK_PIPELINE_BIND_POINT_GRAPHICS` value for `pipelineBindPoint` (currently only graphics pipelines are supported inside render passes)
    - The number of input attachments used in the subpass for `inputAttachmentCount`
    - A pointer to the first element of an array with parameters of input attachments (or a `nullptr` value if no input attachments are used in the subpass) for `pInputAttachments`; use the following values for each member of the `pInputAttachments` array:
        - Index of the attachment in the list of all render pass attachments for `attachment`
        - A layout given image should be automatically transitioned to at the beginning of the subpass for `layout`

- The number of color attachments used in the subpass for `colorAttachmentCount`
- A pointer to the first element of the array with parameters of the subpass's color attachments (or a `nullptr` value if no color attachments are used in the subpass) for `pColorAttachments`; for each member of the array, specify values as described in points 4a and 4b.
- If any of the color attachments should be resolved (changed from multisampled to single-sampled) for `pResolveAttachments`, specify a pointer to the first element of the array with same number of elements as `pColorAttachments` or use a `nullptr` value if no color attachments need to be resolved; each member of the `pResolveAttachments` array corresponds to the color attachment at the same index and specifies to which attachment a given color attachment should be resolved at the end of the subpass; for each member of the array use specified values as described in points 4a and 4b; use a `VK_ATTACHMENT_UNUSED` value for the attachment index if the given color attachment should not be resolved.
- For `pDepthStencilAttachment` provide a pointer to the variable of type `VkAttachmentReference` if a depth/stencil attachment is used (or a `nullptr` value if no depth/stencil attachment is used in the subpass); for members of this variable, specify values as described in points 4a and 4b
- The number of attachments that are not used but whose contents should be preserved for `preserveAttachmentCount`.
- A pointer to the first element of an array with indices of attachments whose contents should be preserved in the subpass (or a `nullptr` value if there are no attachments to be preserved) for `pPreserveAttachments`.

How it works...

Vulkan render passes must have at least one subpass. Subpass parameters are defined in an array of `VkSubpassDescription` elements. Each such element describes how attachments are used in a corresponding subpass. There are separate lists of input, color, resolve, and preserved attachments and a single entry for depth/stencil attachments. Each of these members may be empty (or null). In this case, attachments of a corresponding type are not used in a subpass.

Each entry in one of the lists just described is a reference to the list of all attachments specified for a render pass in attachment descriptions (refer to the *Specifying attachments descriptions* recipe). Additionally, each entry specifies a layout in which an image should be during a subpass. Transitions to specified layouts are performed automatically by the driver.

Here is a code sample that uses a custom structure of a `SubpassParameters` type to specify a subpass definition:

```
subpass_descriptions.clear();

for( auto & subpass_description : subpass_parameters ) {
  subpass_descriptions.push_back( {
    0,
    subpass_description.PipelineType,
    static_cast<uint32_t>(subpass_description.InputAttachments.size()),
    subpass_description.InputAttachments.data(),
    static_cast<uint32_t>(subpass_description.ColorAttachments.size()),
    subpass_description.ColorAttachments.data(),
    subpass_description.ResolveAttachments.data(),
    subpass_description.DepthStencilAttachment,
    static_cast<uint32_t>(subpass_description.PreserveAttachments.size()),
    subpass_description.PreserveAttachments.data()
  } );
}
```

And here is a code sample defining one subpass that corresponds to an example with one color attachment: a depth/stencil attachment:

```
VkAttachmentReference depth_stencil_attachment = {
  1,
  VK_IMAGE_LAYOUT_DEPTH_STENCIL_ATTACHMENT_OPTIMAL,
};

std::vector<SubpassParameters> subpass_parameters = {
  {
    VK_PIPELINE_BIND_POINT_GRAPHICS,
    {},
    {
      {
        0,
        VK_IMAGE_LAYOUT_COLOR_ATTACHMENT_OPTIMAL
      }
    },
    {},
    &depth_stencil_attachment,
    {}
  }
};
```

First we specify a `depth_stencil_attachment` variable for a description of a depth/stencil attachment. For a depth data, the second attachment from the list of attachment descriptions is used; that's why we specify a value of 1 for its index (refer to the *Specifying attachment descriptions* recipe). And as we want to render into this attachment, we provide a `VK_IMAGE_LAYOUT_DEPTH_STENCIL_ATTACHMENT_OPTIMAL` value for its layout (the driver will automatically perform a transition, if needed).

In the example, we use just one color attachment. It is the first attachment from the list of attachment descriptions, so we use a 0 value for its index. When we render into a color attachment, we should specify a `VK_IMAGE_LAYOUT_COLOR_ATTACHMENT_OPTIMAL` value for its layout.

One last thing--as we want to render a geometry, we need to use a graphics pipeline. This is done through a `VK_PIPELINE_BIND_POINT_GRAPHICS` value provided for a `PipelineType` member.

As we don't use input attachments and we don't want to resolve any color attachments, their corresponding vectors are empty.

Render Passes and Framebuffers

See also

The following recipes in this chapter:

- *Specifying attachment descriptions*
- *Creating a render pass*
- *Creating a framebuffer*
- *Preparing a render pass for geometry rendering and postprocess subpasses*
- *Preparing a render pass and a framebuffer with color and depth attachments*

Specifying dependencies between subpasses

When operations in a given subpass depend on the results of operations in one of the earlier subpasses in the same render pass, we need to specify subpass dependencies. This is also required if there are dependencies between operations recorded within a render pass and those performed before it, or between operations that are executed after a render pass and those performed within the render pass. It is also possible to define dependencies within a single subpass.

> Defining subpass dependencies is similar to setting up memory barriers.

How to do it...

1. Create a variable of type `std::vector<VkSubpassDependency>` named `subpass_dependencies`. For each dependency, add a new element to the `subpass_dependencies` vector and use the following values for its members:
    - The index of a subpass from which ("producing") operations should be finished before the second set of ("consuming") operations (or a `VK_SUBPASS_EXTERNAL` value for commands before the render pass) for `srcSubpass`

- The index of a subpass whose operations depend on the previous set of commands (or a `VK_SUBPASS_EXTERNAL` value for operations after the render pass) for `dstSubpass`
- The set of pipeline stages which produce the result read by the "consuming" commands for `srcStageMask`
- The set of pipeline stages which depend on the data generated by the "producing" commands for `dstStageMask`
- The types of memory operations that occurred for the "producing" commands for `srcAccessMask`
- The types of memory operations that will be performed in "consuming" commands for `dstAccessMask`
- For `dependencyFlags`, use a `VK_DEPENDENCY_BY_REGION_BIT` value if the dependency is defined by region--it means that operations generating data for a given memory region must finish before operations reading data from the same region can be executed; if this flag is not specified, dependency is global, which means that data for the whole image must be generated before "consuming" commands can be executed.

How it works...

Specifying dependencies between subpasses (or between subpasses and commands before or after a render pass) is very similar to setting an image memory barrier and serves a similar purpose. We do this when we want to specify that commands from one subpass (or commands after the render pass) depend on results of operations performed in another subpass (or on commands executed before the render pass). We don't need to set up dependencies for the layout transitions--these are performed automatically based on the information provided for the render pass attachment and subpass descriptions. What's more, when we specify different attachment layouts for different subpasses, but in both subpasses the given attachment is used only for reading, we also don't need to specify a dependency.

Subpass dependencies are also required when we want to set up image memory barriers inside a render pass. Without specifying a so-called "self-dependency" (the source and destination subpass have the same index), we can't do that. However, if we define such a dependency for a given subpass, we can record a memory barrier in it. In other situations, the source subpass index must be lower than the target subpass index (excluding a `VK_SUBPASS_EXTERNAL` value).

There follows an example in which we prepare a dependency between two subpasses--the first draws geometry into color and depth attachments, and the second uses color data for postprocessing (it reads from the color attachment):

```
std::vector<VkSubpassDependency> subpass_dependencies = {
  {
    0,
    1,
    VK_PIPELINE_STAGE_COLOR_ATTACHMENT_OUTPUT_BIT,
    VK_PIPELINE_STAGE_FRAGMENT_SHADER_BIT,
    VK_ACCESS_COLOR_ATTACHMENT_WRITE_BIT,
    VK_ACCESS_INPUT_ATTACHMENT_READ_BIT,
    VK_DEPENDENCY_BY_REGION_BIT
  }
};
```

The aforementioned dependency is set between the first and second subpasses (indices with values of 0 and 1). Writes to the color attachment are performed in the `COLOR_ATTACHMENT_OUTPUT` stage. Postprocessing is done in a fragment shader and this stage is defined as a "consuming" stage. When we draw a geometry, we perform writes to a color attachment (access mask with value of `COLOR_ATTACHMENT_WRITE`). Then the color attachment is used as an input attachment and in the postprocess subpass we read from it (so we use an access mask with a value of `INPUT_ATTACHMENT_READ`). As we don't need to read data from other parts of an image, we can specify dependency by-region (a fragment stores a color value at given coordinates in the first subpass and the same value is read in the next subpass by a fragment with the same coordinates). When we do this, we should not assume that regions are larger than the single pixel, because the size of a region may be different on various hardware platforms.

See also

The following recipes in this chapter:

- *Specifying attachment descriptions*
- *Specifying subpass descriptions*
- *Creating a render pass*
- *Preparing a render pass for geometry rendering and postprocess subpasses*

Creating a render pass

Rendering (drawing a geometry) can only be performed inside render passes. When we also want to perform other operations such as image postprocessing or preparing geometry and light prepass data, we need to order these operations into subpasses. For this, we specify descriptions of all the required attachments, all subpasses into which operations are grouped, and the necessary dependencies between those operations. When this data is prepared, we can create a render pass.

Getting ready

To lower the number of parameters that need to be provided, in this recipe, we use a custom structure of type `SubpassParameters` (refer to the *Specifying subpass descriptions* recipe).

How to do it...

1. Create a variable of type `std::vector<VkAttachmentDescription>` named `attachments_descriptions` in which we specify descriptions of all render pass attachments (refer to the *Specifying attachment descriptions recipe*).
2. Prepare a variable of type `std::vector<VkSubpassDescription>` named `subpass_descriptions` and use it to define descriptions of subpasses (refer to the *Specifying subpass descriptions* recipe).

3. Create a variable of type `std::vector<VkSubpassDependency>` named `subpass_dependencies`. Add a new member to this vector for each dependency that needs to be defined in the render pass (refer to the *Specifying dependencies between subpasses* recipe).
4. Create a variable of type `VkRenderPassCreateInfo` named `render_pass_create_info` and initialize its member with the following values:
   - `VK_STRUCTURE_TYPE_RENDER_PASS_CREATE_INFO` value for `sType`
   - `nullptr` value for `pNext`
   - `0` value for `flags`
   - The number of elements in the `attachments_descriptions` vector for `attachmentCount`
   - A pointer to the first element of the `attachments_descriptions` vector (or a `nullptr` value if it is empty) for `pAttachments`
   - The number of elements in the `subpass_descriptions` vector for `subpassCount`
   - A pointer to the first element of the `subpass_descriptions` vector for `pSubpasses`
   - The number of elements in the `subpass_dependencies` vector for `dependencyCount`
   - A pointer to the first element of the `subpass_dependencies` vector (or a `nullptr` value if it is empty) for `pDependencies`
5. Take the handle of a logical device for which the render pass should be created. Store it in a variable of type `VkDevice` named `logical_device`.
6. Create a variable of type `VkRenderPass` named `render_pass` in which the handle of the created render pass will be stored.
7. Call `vkCreateRenderPass( logical_device, &render_pass_create_info, nullptr, &render_pass )`. For the call, provide the `logical_device` variable, a pointer to the `render_pass_create_info` variable, a `nullptr` value, and a pointer to the `render_pass` variable.
8. Make sure the call was successful by checking if it returned a `VK_SUCCESS` value.

How it works...

A render pass defines general information about how attachments are used by operations performed in all its subpasses. This allows the driver to optimize work and improve the performance of our application.

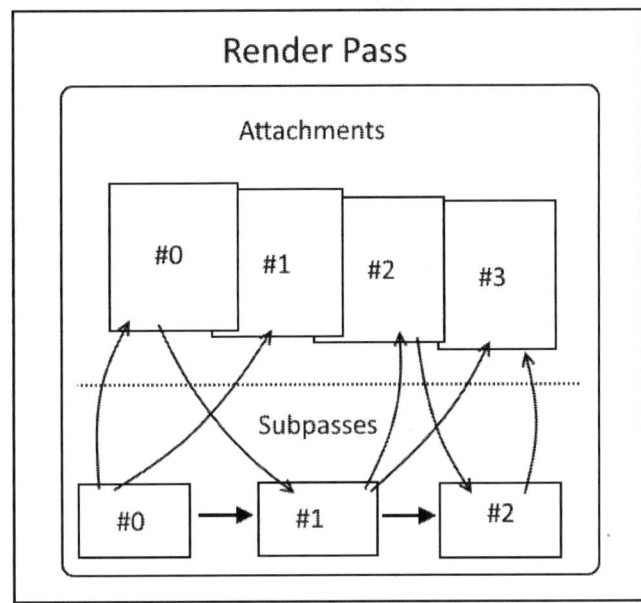

The most important parts of a render pass creation is a preparation of data--descriptions of all the used attachments and subpasses and a specification of dependencies between subpasses (refer to the *Specifying attachment descriptions*, *Specifying subpass descriptions*, and *Specifying dependencies between subpasses* recipes in this chapter). These steps can be presented in short as follows:

```
SpecifyAttachmentsDescriptions( attachments_descriptions );

std::vector<VkSubpassDescription> subpass_descriptions;
SpecifySubpassDescriptions( subpass_parameters, subpass_descriptions );

SpecifyDependenciesBetweenSubpasses( subpass_dependencies );
```

This data is then used when we specify parameter for a function creating a render pass:

```
VkRenderPassCreateInfo render_pass_create_info = {
  VK_STRUCTURE_TYPE_RENDER_PASS_CREATE_INFO,
  nullptr,
  0,
  static_cast<uint32_t>(attachments_descriptions.size()),
  attachments_descriptions.data(),
  static_cast<uint32_t>(subpass_descriptions.size()),
  subpass_descriptions.data(),
  static_cast<uint32_t>(subpass_dependencies.size()),
  subpass_dependencies.data()
};

VkResult result = vkCreateRenderPass( logical_device,
  &render_pass_create_info, nullptr, &render_pass );
if( VK_SUCCESS != result ) {
  std::cout << "Could not create a render pass." << std::endl;
  return false;
}
return true;
```

But for the drawing operations to be performed correctly, the render pass is not enough as it only specifies how operations are ordered into subpasses and how attachments are used. There is no information about what images are used for these attachments. Such information about specific resources used for all defined attachments is stored in framebuffers.

See also

The following recipes in this chapter:

- *Specifying attachment descriptions*
- *Specifying subpass descriptions*
- *Specifying dependencies between subpasses*
- *Creating a framebuffer*
- *Beginning a render pass*
- *Progressing to the next subpass*
- *Ending a render pass*
- *Destroying a render pass*

Creating a framebuffer

Framebuffers are used along with render passes. They specify what image resources should be used for corresponding attachments defined in a render pass. They also define the size of a renderable area. That's why when we want to record drawing operations, we not only need to create a render pass, but also a framebuffer.

How to do it...

1. Take the handle of a render pass that should be compatible with the framebuffer and use it to initialize a variable of type `VkRenderPass` named `render_pass`.
2. Prepare a list of image view handles that represent the images' subresources, which should be used for the render pass attachments. Store all the prepared image views in a variable of type `std::vector<VkImageView>` named `attachments`.
3. Create a variable of type `VkFramebufferCreateInfo` named `framebuffer_create_info`. Use the following values to initialize its members:
    - `VK_STRUCTURE_TYPE_FRAMEBUFFER_CREATE_INFO` value for `sType`
    - `nullptr` value for `pNext`
    - 0 value for `flags`
    - `render_pass` variable for `renderPass`
    - The number of elements in the `attachments` vector for `attachmentCount`
    - A pointer to the first element of the `attachments` vector (or a `nullptr` value if it is empty) for `pAttachments`
    - The selected width of a renderable area for `width`
    - The selected framebuffer's height for `height`
    - The number of framebuffer layers for `layers`
4. Take the handle of a logical device for which the framebuffer should be created and store in a variable of type `VkDevice` named `logical_device`.
5. Create a variable of type `VkFramebuffer` named `framebuffer` that will be initialized with a handle of a created framebuffer.

Render Passes and Framebuffers

6. Call `vkCreateFramebuffer( logical_device, &framebuffer_create_info, nullptr, &framebuffer )` for which we provide the `logical_device` variable, a pointer to the `framebuffer_create_info` variable, a `nullptr` value, and a pointer to the `framebuffer` variable.
7. Make sure the framebuffer was properly created by checking if the call returned a `VK_SUCCESS` value.

How it works...

Framebuffers are always created in conjunction with render passes. They define specific image subresources that should be used for attachments specified in render passes, so both of these object types should correspond to each other.

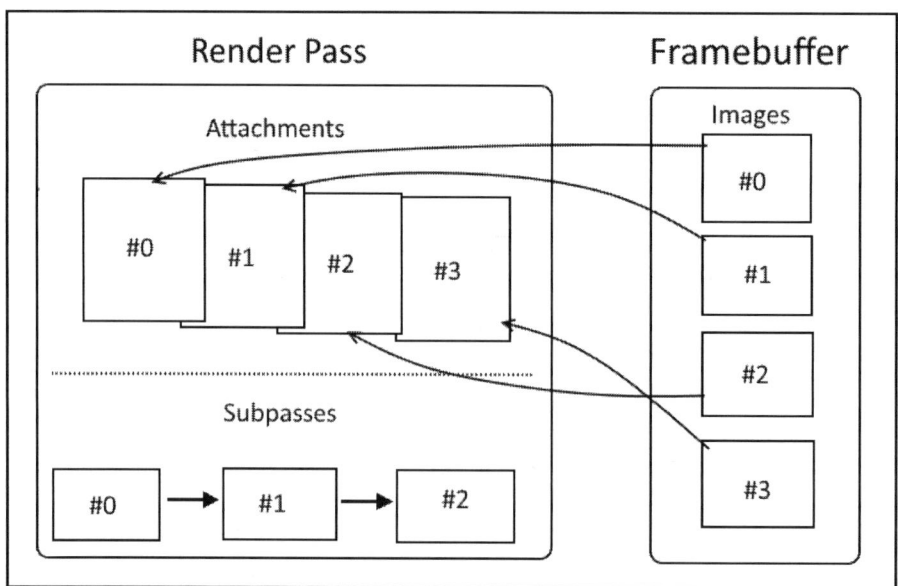

When we create a framebuffer, we provide a render pass object with which we can use the given framebuffer. However, we are not limited to using it only with the specified render pass. We can use the framebuffer also with all render passes that are compatible with the one provided.

What are compatible render passes? First, they must have the same number of subpasses. And each subpass must have a compatible set of input, color, resolve, and depth/stencil attachments. This means that formats and the number of samples of corresponding attachments must be the same. However, it is possible for the attachments to have different initial, subpasses and final layouts and different load and store operations.

Apart from that, framebuffers also define the size of a renderable area--the dimensions into which all rendering will be confined. However, what we need to remember is that it is up to us to make sure that the pixels/fragments outside of the specified range are not modified. For this purpose, we need to specify the appropriate parameters (viewport and scissor test) during the pipeline creation or when setting corresponding dynamic states (refer to the *Preparing viewport and scissor test state* recipe from Chapter 8, *Graphics and Compute Pipelines* and to the *Setting a dynamic viewport and scissors state* recipe from Chapter 9, *Command Recording and Drawing*).

We must ensure that rendering occurs only in the dimensions specified during the framebuffer creation.

When we begin a render pass in a command buffer and use the given framebuffer, we also need to make sure that the images' subresources specified in that framebuffer are not used for any other purpose. In other words, if we use a given portion of an image as a framebuffer attachment, we can't use it in any other way during the render pass.

Image subresources specified for render pass attachments cannot be used for any other (non-attachment) purpose between the beginning and the end of the render pass.

Here is a code sample responsible for creating a framebuffer:

```
VkFramebufferCreateInfo framebuffer_create_info = {
  VK_STRUCTURE_TYPE_FRAMEBUFFER_CREATE_INFO,
  nullptr,
  0,
  render_pass,
  static_cast<uint32_t>(attachments.size()),
  attachments.data(),
  width,
  height,
  layers
};

VkResult result = vkCreateFramebuffer( logical_device,
```

```
    &framebuffer_create_info, nullptr, &framebuffer );
if( VK_SUCCESS != result ) {
  std::cout << "Could not create a framebuffer." << std::endl;
  return false;
}
return true;
```

See also

In Chapter 4, *Resources and Memory*, see the following recipes:

- *Creating an image*
- *Creating an image view*

The following recipes in this chapter:

- *Specifying attachment descriptions*
- *Creating a framebuffer*

Preparing a render pass for geometry rendering and postprocess subpasses

When developing applications such as games or CAD tools there are often situations in which we need to draw a geometry and then, when the whole scene is rendered, we apply additional image effects called postprocessing.

In this sample recipe, we will see how to prepare a render pass in which we will have two subpasses. The first subpass renders into two attachments--color and depth. The second subpass reads data from the first color attachment and renders into another color attachment--a swapchain image that can be presented (displayed on screen) after the render pass.

Getting ready

To lower the number of parameters that need to be provided, in this recipe we use a custom structure of type SubpassParameters (refer to the *Specifying subpass descriptions* recipe).

Chapter 6

How to do it...

1. Create a variable of type `std::vector<VkAttachmentDescription>` named `attachments_descriptions`. Add an element to the `attachments_descriptions` vector that describes the first color attachment. Initialize it with the following values:
    - 0 value for `flags`
    - VK_FORMAT_R8G8B8A8_UNORM value for `format`
    - VK_SAMPLE_COUNT_1_BIT value for `samples`
    - VK_ATTACHMENT_LOAD_OP_CLEAR value for `loadOp`
    - VK_ATTACHMENT_STORE_OP_DONT_CARE value for `storeOp`
    - VK_ATTACHMENT_LOAD_OP_DONT_CARE value for `stencilLoadOp`
    - VK_ATTACHMENT_STORE_OP_DONT_CARE value for `stencilStoreOp`
    - VK_IMAGE_LAYOUT_UNDEFINED value for `initialLayout`
    - VK_IMAGE_LAYOUT_SHADER_READ_ONLY_OPTIMAL value for `finalLayout`

2. Add another element to the `attachments_descriptions` vector that specifies the depth/stencil attachment. Use the following values to initialize its members:
    - 0 value for `flags`
    - VK_FORMAT_D16_UNORM value for `format`
    - VK_SAMPLE_COUNT_1_BIT value for `samples`
    - VK_ATTACHMENT_LOAD_OP_CLEAR value for `loadOp`
    - VK_ATTACHMENT_STORE_OP_DONT_CARE value for `storeOp`
    - VK_ATTACHMENT_LOAD_OP_DONT_CARE value for `stencilLoadOp`
    - VK_ATTACHMENT_STORE_OP_DONT_CARE value for `stencilStoreOp`
    - VK_IMAGE_LAYOUT_UNDEFINED value for `initialLayout`
    - VK_IMAGE_LAYOUT_DEPTH_STENCIL_ATTACHMENT_OPTIMAL value for `finalLayout`

3. Add a third element to the `attachments_descriptions` vector. This time it will specify another color attachment. Initialize it with the following values:
    - 0 value for `flags`
    - VK_FORMAT_R8G8B8A8_UNORM value for `format`
    - VK_SAMPLE_COUNT_1_BIT value for `samples`

[311]

Render Passes and Framebuffers

- `VK_ATTACHMENT_LOAD_OP_CLEAR` value for `loadOp`
- `VK_ATTACHMENT_STORE_OP_STORE` value for `storeOp`
- `VK_ATTACHMENT_LOAD_OP_DONT_CARE` value for `stencilLoadOp`
- `VK_ATTACHMENT_STORE_OP_DONT_CARE` value for `stencilStoreOp`
- `VK_IMAGE_LAYOUT_UNDEFINED` value for `initialLayout`
- `VK_IMAGE_LAYOUT_PRESENT_SRC_KHR` value for `finalLayout`

4. Create a variable of type `VkAttachmentReference` named `depth_stencil_attachment` and initialize it with the following values:
   - 1 value for `attachment`
   - `VK_IMAGE_LAYOUT_DEPTH_STENCIL_ATTACHMENT_OPTIMAL` value for `layout`

5. Create a variable of type `std::vector<SubpassParameters>` named `subpass_parameters` and add one element with the following values to this vector:
   - `VK_PIPELINE_BIND_POINT_GRAPHICS` value for `PipelineType`
   - An empty vector for `InputAttachments`
   - A vector with one element and the following values for `ColorAttachments`:
     - 0 value for `attachment`
     - `VK_IMAGE_LAYOUT_COLOR_ATTACHMENT_OPTIMAL` value for `layout`
   - An empty vector for `ResolveAttachments`
   - A pointer to the `depth_stencil_attachment` variable for `DepthStencilAttachment`
   - An empty vector for `PreserveAttachments`

6. Add the second element to the `subpass_parameters` that describes the second subpass. Initialize its member using the following values:
   - `VK_PIPELINE_BIND_POINT_GRAPHICS` value for `PipelineType`
   - A vector with one element with the following values for `InputAttachments`:
     - 0 value for `attachment`
     - `VK_IMAGE_LAYOUT_SHADER_READ_ONLY_OPTIMAL` value for `layout`

- A vector with one element with the following values for `ColorAttachments`:
    - 2 value for `attachment`
    - `VK_IMAGE_LAYOUT_COLOR_ATTACHMENT_OPTIMAL` value for `layout`
- An empty vector for `ResolveAttachments`
- `nullptr` value for `DepthStencilAttachment`
- An empty vector for `PreserveAttachments`

5. Create a variable of type `std::vector<VkSubpassDependency>` named `subpass_dependencies` with a single element that uses the following values for its members:
    - 0 value for `srcSubpass`
    - 1 value for `dstSubpass`
    - `VK_PIPELINE_STAGE_COLOR_ATTACHMENT_OUTPUT_BIT` value for `srcStageMask`
    - `VK_PIPELINE_STAGE_FRAGMENT_SHADER_BIT` value for `dstStageMask`
    - `VK_ACCESS_COLOR_ATTACHMENT_WRITE_BIT` value for `srcAccessMask`
    - `VK_ACCESS_INPUT_ATTACHMENT_READ_BIT` value for `dstAccessMask`
    - `VK_DEPENDENCY_BY_REGION_BIT` value for `dependencyFlags`

6. Create the render pass using `attachments_descriptions`, `subpass_parameters` and `subpass_dependencies` variables. Store its handle in a variable of type `VkRenderPass` named `render_pass` (refer to the *Creating a render pass* recipe in this chapter).

How it works...

In this recipe, we create a render pass with the three attachments. They are specified as follows:

```
std::vector<VkAttachmentDescription> attachments_descriptions = {
  {
    0,
    VK_FORMAT_R8G8B8A8_UNORM,
    VK_SAMPLE_COUNT_1_BIT,
    VK_ATTACHMENT_LOAD_OP_CLEAR,
```

```
            VK_ATTACHMENT_STORE_OP_DONT_CARE,
            VK_ATTACHMENT_LOAD_OP_DONT_CARE,
            VK_ATTACHMENT_STORE_OP_DONT_CARE,
            VK_IMAGE_LAYOUT_UNDEFINED,
            VK_IMAGE_LAYOUT_SHADER_READ_ONLY_OPTIMAL,
        },
        {
            0,
            VK_FORMAT_D16_UNORM,
            VK_SAMPLE_COUNT_1_BIT,
            VK_ATTACHMENT_LOAD_OP_CLEAR,
            VK_ATTACHMENT_STORE_OP_DONT_CARE,
            VK_ATTACHMENT_LOAD_OP_DONT_CARE,
            VK_ATTACHMENT_STORE_OP_DONT_CARE,
            VK_IMAGE_LAYOUT_UNDEFINED,
            VK_IMAGE_LAYOUT_DEPTH_STENCIL_ATTACHMENT_OPTIMAL,
        },
        {
            0,
            VK_FORMAT_R8G8B8A8_UNORM,
            VK_SAMPLE_COUNT_1_BIT,
            VK_ATTACHMENT_LOAD_OP_CLEAR,
            VK_ATTACHMENT_STORE_OP_STORE,
            VK_ATTACHMENT_LOAD_OP_DONT_CARE,
            VK_ATTACHMENT_STORE_OP_DONT_CARE,
            VK_IMAGE_LAYOUT_UNDEFINED,
            VK_IMAGE_LAYOUT_PRESENT_SRC_KHR,
        },
    };
```

First there is a color attachment into which we render in the first subpass and from which we read in the second subpass. The second attachment is used for a depth data; and the third is another color attachment into which we render in the second subpass. As we don't need the contents of the first and second attachments after the render pass (we need the contents of the first attachment only in the second subpass), we specify a VK_ATTACHMENT_STORE_OP_DONT_CARE value for their store operations. We also don't need their contents at the beginning of the render pass, so we specify an UNDEFINED initial layout. We also clear all three attachments.

Next we define two subpasses:

```
VkAttachmentReference depth_stencil_attachment = {
  1,
  VK_IMAGE_LAYOUT_DEPTH_STENCIL_ATTACHMENT_OPTIMAL,
};

std::vector<SubpassParameters> subpass_parameters = {
  // #0 subpass
  {
    VK_PIPELINE_BIND_POINT_GRAPHICS,
    {},
    {
      {
        0,
        VK_IMAGE_LAYOUT_COLOR_ATTACHMENT_OPTIMAL
      }
    },
    {},
    &depth_stencil_attachment,
    {}
  },
  // #1 subpass
  {
    VK_PIPELINE_BIND_POINT_GRAPHICS,
    {
      {
        0,
        VK_IMAGE_LAYOUT_SHADER_READ_ONLY_OPTIMAL
      }
    },
    {
      {
        2,
        VK_IMAGE_LAYOUT_COLOR_ATTACHMENT_OPTIMAL
      }
    },
    {},
    nullptr,
    {}
  }
};
```

The first subpass uses a color attachment and a depth attachment. The second subpass reads from the first attachment (used here as an input attachment) and renders into the third attachment.

The last thing is to define a dependency between two subpasses for the first attachment, which is once a color attachment (we write data to it) and once an input attachment (we read data from it). After that we can create the render pass like this:

```
std::vector<VkSubpassDependency> subpass_dependencies = {
  {
    0,
    1,
    VK_PIPELINE_STAGE_COLOR_ATTACHMENT_OUTPUT_BIT,
    VK_PIPELINE_STAGE_FRAGMENT_SHADER_BIT,
    VK_ACCESS_COLOR_ATTACHMENT_WRITE_BIT,
    VK_ACCESS_INPUT_ATTACHMENT_READ_BIT,
    VK_DEPENDENCY_BY_REGION_BIT
  }
};

if( !CreateRenderPass( logical_device, attachments_descriptions,
subpass_parameters, subpass_dependencies, render_pass ) ) {
  return false;
}
return true;
```

See also

The following recipes in this chapter:

- *Specifying attachment descriptions*
- *Specifying subpass descriptions*
- *Specifying dependencies between subpasses*
- *Creating a render pass*

Preparing a render pass and a framebuffer with color and depth attachments

Rendering a 3D scene usually involves not only a color attachment, but also a depth attachment used for depth testing (we want further objects to be occluded by the objects closer to the camera).

In this sample recipe, we will see how to create images for color and depth data and a render pass with a single subpass that renders into color and depth attachments. We will also create a framebuffer that will use both images for the render pass attachments.

Getting ready

As in earlier recipes from this chapter, in this recipe we will use a custom structure of type SubpassParameters (refer to the *Specifying subpass descriptions* recipe).

How to do it...

1. Create a 2D image and image view for it with a VK_FORMAT_R8G8B8A8_UNORM format, VK_IMAGE_USAGE_COLOR_ATTACHMENT_BIT | VK_IMAGE_USAGE_SAMPLED_BIT usage and a VK_IMAGE_ASPECT_COLOR_BIT aspect. Choose the rest of the image's parameters. Store the created handles in variables of type VkImage named color_image, of type VkDeviceMemory named color_image_memory_object, and of type VkImageView named color_image_view (refer to the *Creating a 2D image and view* recipe from Chapter 4, *Resources and Memory*).
2. Create a second 2D image and image view for it with a VK_FORMAT_D16_UNORM format, VK_IMAGE_USAGE_DEPTH_STENCIL_ATTACHMENT_BIT | VK_IMAGE_USAGE_SAMPLED_BIT usage, VK_IMAGE_ASPECT_DEPTH_BIT aspect, and the same size as the image whose handle is stored in the color_image variable. Choose the rest of the image's parameters. Store the created handles in variables of type VkImage named depth_image, of type VkDeviceMemory named depth_image_memory_object, and of type VkImageView named depth_image_view (refer to the *Creating a 2D image and view* recipe from Chapter 4, *Resources and Memory*).

Render Passes and Framebuffers

3. Create a variable of type `std::vector<VkAttachmentDescription>` named `attachments_descriptions` and add two elements to the vector. Initialize the first element with the following values:
    - 0 value for `flags`
    - `VK_FORMAT_R8G8B8A8_UNORM` value for `format`
    - `VK_SAMPLE_COUNT_1_BIT` value for `samples`
    - `VK_ATTACHMENT_LOAD_OP_CLEAR` value for `loadOp`
    - `VK_ATTACHMENT_STORE_OP_STORE` value for `storeOp`
    - `VK_ATTACHMENT_LOAD_OP_DONT_CARE` value for `stencilLoadOp`
    - `VK_ATTACHMENT_STORE_OP_DONT_CARE` value for `stencilStoreOp`
    - `VK_IMAGE_LAYOUT_UNDEFINED` value for `initialLayout`
    - `VK_IMAGE_LAYOUT_SHADER_READ_ONLY_OPTIMAL` value for `finalLayout`

4. Use these values to initialize members of the second element of the `attachments_descriptions` vector:
    - 0 value for `flags`
    - `VK_FORMAT_D16_UNORM` value for `format`
    - `VK_SAMPLE_COUNT_1_BIT` value for `samples`
    - `VK_ATTACHMENT_LOAD_OP_CLEAR` value for `loadOp`
    - `VK_ATTACHMENT_STORE_OP_STORE` value for `storeOp`
    - `VK_ATTACHMENT_LOAD_OP_DONT_CARE` value for `stencilLoadOp`
    - `VK_ATTACHMENT_STORE_OP_DONT_CARE` value for `stencilStoreOp`
    - `VK_IMAGE_LAYOUT_UNDEFINED` value for `initialLayout`
    - `VK_IMAGE_LAYOUT_DEPTH_STENCIL_READ_ONLY_OPTIMAL` value for `finalLayout`

5. Create a variable of type `VkAttachmentReference` named `depth_stencil_attachment` and initialize it using the following values:
    - 1 value for `attachment`
    - `VK_IMAGE_LAYOUT_DEPTH_STENCIL_ATTACHMENT_OPTIMAL` value for `layout`

6. Create a vector of type `std::vector<SubpassParameters>` named `subpass_parameters`. Add a single element to this vector and use the following values to initialize it:
   - `VK_PIPELINE_BIND_POINT_GRAPHICS` value for `PipelineType`
   - An empty vector for `InputAttachments`
   - A vector with just one element with these values for `ColorAttachments`:
     1. `0` value for `attachment`
     2. `VK_IMAGE_LAYOUT_COLOR_ATTACHMENT_OPTIMAL` value for `layout`
   - An empty vector for `ResolveAttachments`
   - A pointer to the `depth_stencil_attachment` variable for `DepthStencilAttachment`
   - An empty vector for `PreserveAttachments`
7. Create a vector of type `std::vector<VkSubpassDependency>` named `subpass_dependencies` with a single element initialized using these values:
   - `0` value for `srcSubpass`
   - `VK_SUBPASS_EXTERNAL` value for `dstSubpass`
   - `VK_PIPELINE_STAGE_COLOR_ATTACHMENT_OUTPUT_BIT` value for `srcStageMask`
   - `VK_PIPELINE_STAGE_FRAGMENT_SHADER_BIT` value for `dstStageMask`
   - `VK_ACCESS_COLOR_ATTACHMENT_WRITE_BIT` value for `srcAccessMask`
   - `VK_ACCESS_SHADER_READ_BIT` value for `dstAccessMask`
   - `0` value for `dependencyFlags`
8. Create a render pass using `attachments_descriptions`, `subpass_parameters` and `subpass_dependencies` vectors. Store the created render pass handle in a variable of type `VkRenderPass` named `render_pass` (refer to the *Creating a render pass* recipe in this chapter).
9. Create a framebuffer using the `render_pass` variable and the `color_image_view` variable for its first attachment and the `depth_image_view` variable for the second attachment. Specify the same dimensions as used for the `color_image` and `depth_image` variables. Store the created framebuffer handle in a variable of type `VkFramebuffer` named `framebuffer`.

How it works...

In this sample recipe, we want to render into two images--one for color data, and another for the depth data. We imply that after the render pass they will be used as textures (we will sample them in shaders in another render pass); that's why they are created with COLOR_ATTACHMENT / DEPTH_STENCIL_ATTACHMENT usages (so we can render into them) and SAMPLED usage (so they both can be sampled from in shaders):

```
if( !Create2DImageAndView( physical_device, logical_device,
VK_FORMAT_R8G8B8A8_UNORM, { width, height }, 1, 1, VK_SAMPLE_COUNT_1_BIT,

  VK_IMAGE_USAGE_COLOR_ATTACHMENT_BIT | VK_IMAGE_USAGE_SAMPLED_BIT,
VK_IMAGE_ASPECT_COLOR_BIT, color_image, color_image_memory_object,
color_image_view ) ) {

  return false;
}

if( !Create2DImageAndView( physical_device, logical_device,
VK_FORMAT_D16_UNORM, { width, height }, 1, 1, VK_SAMPLE_COUNT_1_BIT,

  VK_IMAGE_USAGE_DEPTH_STENCIL_ATTACHMENT_BIT | VK_IMAGE_USAGE_SAMPLED_BIT,
VK_IMAGE_ASPECT_DEPTH_BIT, depth_image, depth_image_memory_object,
depth_image_view ) ) {
  return false;
}
```

Next we specify two attachments for the render pass. They are both cleared at the beginning of the render pass and their contents are preserved after the render pass:

```
std::vector<VkAttachmentDescription> attachments_descriptions = {
  {
    0,
    VK_FORMAT_R8G8B8A8_UNORM,
    VK_SAMPLE_COUNT_1_BIT,
    VK_ATTACHMENT_LOAD_OP_CLEAR,
    VK_ATTACHMENT_STORE_OP_STORE,
    VK_ATTACHMENT_LOAD_OP_DONT_CARE,
    VK_ATTACHMENT_STORE_OP_DONT_CARE,
    VK_IMAGE_LAYOUT_UNDEFINED,
    VK_IMAGE_LAYOUT_SHADER_READ_ONLY_OPTIMAL,
  },
  {
    0,
    VK_FORMAT_D16_UNORM,
    VK_SAMPLE_COUNT_1_BIT,
    VK_ATTACHMENT_LOAD_OP_CLEAR,
```

```
      VK_ATTACHMENT_STORE_OP_STORE,
      VK_ATTACHMENT_LOAD_OP_DONT_CARE,
      VK_ATTACHMENT_STORE_OP_DONT_CARE,
      VK_IMAGE_LAYOUT_UNDEFINED,
      VK_IMAGE_LAYOUT_DEPTH_STENCIL_READ_ONLY_OPTIMAL,
    }
};
```

The next step is to define a single subpass. It uses the first attachment for color writes and the second attachment for depth/stencil data:

```
VkAttachmentReference depth_stencil_attachment = {
  1,
  VK_IMAGE_LAYOUT_DEPTH_STENCIL_ATTACHMENT_OPTIMAL,
};

std::vector<SubpassParameters> subpass_parameters = {
  {
    VK_PIPELINE_BIND_POINT_GRAPHICS,
    {},
    {
      {
        0,
        VK_IMAGE_LAYOUT_COLOR_ATTACHMENT_OPTIMAL
      }
    },
    {},
    &depth_stencil_attachment,
    {}
  }
};
```

Finally, we define a dependency between the subpass and the commands that will be performed after the render pass. This is required, because we don't want other commands to start reading our images before their contents are fully written in the render pass. We also create the render pass and a framebuffer:

```
std::vector<VkSubpassDependency> subpass_dependencies = {
  {
    0,
    VK_SUBPASS_EXTERNAL,
    VK_PIPELINE_STAGE_COLOR_ATTACHMENT_OUTPUT_BIT,
    VK_PIPELINE_STAGE_FRAGMENT_SHADER_BIT,
    VK_ACCESS_COLOR_ATTACHMENT_WRITE_BIT,
    VK_ACCESS_SHADER_READ_BIT,
    0
  }
};
```

Render Passes and Framebuffers

```
if( !CreateRenderPass( logical_device, attachments_descriptions,
subpasses_parameters, subpasses_dependencies, render_pass ) ) {
  return false;
}

if( !CreateFramebuffer( logical_device, render_pass, { color_image_view,
depth_image_view }, width, height, 1, framebuffer ) ) {
  return false;
}
return true;
```

See also

- In `Chapter 4`, *Resources and Memory*, see the following recipe:
    - *Creating a 2D image and view*
- The following recipes in this chapter:
    - *Specifying attachment descriptions*
    - *Specifying subpass descriptions*
    - *Specifying dependencies between subpasses*
    - *Creating a render pass*
    - *Creating a framebuffer*

Beginning a render pass

When we have created a render pass and a framebuffer and we are ready to start recording commands needed to render a geometry, we must record an operation that begins the render pass. This also automatically starts its first subpass.

How to do it...

1. Take the handle of a command buffer stored in a variable of type `VkCommandBuffer` named `command_buffer`. Make sure the command buffer is in the recording state.
2. Use the handle of the render pass to initialize a variable of type `VkRenderPass` named `render_pass`.

3. Take the framebuffer that is compatible with the `render_pass`. Store its handle in a variable of type `VkFramebuffer` named `framebuffer`.
4. Specify the dimensions of the render area into which rendering will be confined during the render pass. This area cannot be larger than the size specified for the framebuffer. Store the dimensions in a variable of type `VkRect2D` named `render_area`.
5. Create a variable of type `std::vector<VkClearValue>` named `clear_values` with the number of elements equal to the number of attachments in the render pass. For each render pass attachment that uses a clear `loadOp`, provide the corresponding clear value at the same index as the attachment index.
6. Prepare a variable of type `VkSubpassContents` named `subpass_contents` describing how operations in the first subpass are recorded. Use a `VK_SUBPASS_CONTENTS_INLINE` value if commands are recorded directly and no secondary command buffer will be executed, or a `VK_SUBPASS_CONTENTS_SECONDARY_COMMAND_BUFFERS` value to specify that commands for the subpass are stored in the secondary command buffer and only executing a secondary command buffer command will be used (refer to the *Executing a secondary command buffer inside a primary command buffer* recipe from `Chapter 9`, *Command Recording and Drawing*).
7. Create a variable of type `VkRenderPassBeginInfo` named `render_pass_begin_info` and initialize its members using these values:
    - `VK_STRUCTURE_TYPE_RENDER_PASS_BEGIN_INFO` value for `sType`
    - `nullptr` value for `pNext`
    - `render_pass` variable for `renderPass`
    - `framebuffer` variable for `framebuffer`
    - `render_area` variable for `renderArea`
    - Number of elements in the `clear_values` vector for `clearValueCount`
    - Pointer to the first element of the `clear_values` vector (or a `nullptr` value if it is empty) for `pClearValues`
8. Call `vkCmdBeginRenderPass( command_buffer, &render_pass_begin_info, subpass_contents )`, providing the `command_buffer` variable, pointer to the `render_pass_begin_info` variable and the `subpass_contents` variable.

How it works...

Starting a render pass automatically starts its first subpass. Before this is done, all attachments, for which a clear `loadOp` was specified, are cleared--filled with a single color. Values used for clearing (and the rest of the parameters required to start a render pass) are specified in a variable of type `VkRenderPassBeginInfo`:

```
VkRenderPassBeginInfo render_pass_begin_info = {
  VK_STRUCTURE_TYPE_RENDER_PASS_BEGIN_INFO,
  nullptr,
  render_pass,
  framebuffer,
  render_area,
  static_cast<uint32_t>(clear_values.size()),
  clear_values.data()
};
```

An array with clearing values must have at least as many elements so they can correspond to attachments from the start to the last cleared attachment (the attachment with the greatest index that is being cleared). It is safer to have the same number of clear values as there are attachments in the render pass, but we only need to provide values for the cleared ones. If no attachments are cleared, we can provide a `nullptr` value for the clear values array.

When we start a render pass, we also need to provide the dimensions of the render area. It can be as large as the dimensions of the framebuffer, but can be smaller. It is up to us to make sure that the rendering will be confined to the specified area, or the pixels outside of this range may become undefined.

To begin the render pass we need to call:

```
vkCmdBeginRenderPass( command_buffer, &render_pass_begin_info,
  subpass_contents );
```

See also

- In Chapter 3, *Command Buffers and Synchronization*, see the following recipe:
    - *Beginning a command buffer recording operation*
- In Chapter 9, *Command Recording and Drawing*, see the following recipe:
    - *Executing a secondary command buffer inside a primary command buffer*
- The following recipes in this chapter:
    - *Creating a render pass*
    - *Creating a framebuffer*

Progressing to the next subpass

Commands that are recorded inside a render pass are divided into subpasses. When a set of commands from a given subpass is already recorded and we want to record commands for another subpass, we need to switch (or progress) to the next subpass.

How to do it...

1. Take the handle of a command buffer that's being recorded and store it in a variable of type `VkCommandBuffer` named `command_buffer`. Make sure the operation of beginning a render pass was already recorded in the `command_buffer`.
2. Specify how subpass commands are recorded: directly or through a secondary command buffer. Store the appropriate value in a variable of type `VkSubpassContents` named `subpass_contents` (refer to the *Beginning a render pass* recipe).
3. Call `vkCmdNextSubpass( command_buffer, subpass_contents )`. For the call, provide the `command_buffer` and `subpass_contents` variables.

How it works...

Progressing to the next subpass switches from the current to the next subpass in the same render pass. During this operation appropriate layout transitions are performed and memory and execution dependencies are introduced (similar to those in memory barriers). All this is performed automatically by the driver, if needed, so the attachments in the new subpass can be used in the way specified during the render pass creation. Moving to the next subpass also performs multisample resolve operations on specified color attachments.

Commands in the subpass can be recorded directly, by inlining them in the command buffer, or indirectly by executing a secondary command buffer.

To record an operation that switches from one subpass to another, we need to call a single function:

```
vkCmdNextSubpass( command_buffer, subpass_contents );
```

See also

The following recipes in this chapter:

- *Specifying subpass descriptions*
- *Creating a render pass*
- *Beginning a render pass*
- *Ending a render pass*

Ending a render pass

When all commands from all subpasses are already recorded, we need to end (stop or finish) a render pass.

How to do it...

1. Take the handle of a command buffer and store it in a variable of type `VkCommandBuffer` named `command_buffer`. Make sure the command buffer is in a recording state and that the operation of beginning a render pass was already recorded in it.
2. Call `vkCmdEndRenderPass( command_buffer )` for which provide the `command_buffer` variable.

How it works...

To end a render pass, we need to call a single function:

```
vkCmdEndRenderPass( command_buffer );
```

Recording this function in a command buffer performs multiple operations. Execution and memory dependencies are introduced (like the ones in memory barriers) and image layout transitions are performed--images are transitioned from layouts specified for the last subpass to the value of a final layout (refer to the *Specifying attachment descriptions* recipe). Also multisample resolving is performed on color attachments for which resolving was specified in the last subpass. Additionally, for attachments whose contents should be preserved after the render pass, attachment data may be transferred from the cache to the image's memory.

See also

The following recipes in this chapter:

- *Specifying subpass descriptions*
- *Creating a render pass*
- *Beginning a render pass*
- *Progressing to the next subpass*

Destroying a framebuffer

When a framebuffer is no longer used by the pending commands and we don't need it anymore, we can destroy it.

How to do it...

1. Initialize a variable of type `VkDevice` named `logical_device` with the handle of a logical device on which the framebuffer was created.
2. Take the framebuffer's handle and store it in a variable of type `VkFramebuffer` named `framebuffer`.
3. Make the following call: `vkDestroyFramebuffer( logical_device, framebuffer, nullptr )`, for which we provide the `logical_device` and `framebuffer` variables and a `nullptr` value.
4. For safety reasons, store a `VK_NULL_HANDLE` value in the `framebuffer` variable.

How it works...

The framebuffer is destroyed with the `vkDestroyFramebuffer()` function call. However, before we can destroy it, we must make sure that commands referencing the given framebuffer are no longer executed on the hardware.

The following code destroys a framebuffer:

```
if( VK_NULL_HANDLE != framebuffer ) {
  vkDestroyFramebuffer( logical_device, framebuffer, nullptr );
  framebuffer = VK_NULL_HANDLE;
}
```

See also

The following recipe in this chapter:

- *Creating a framebuffer*

Destroying a render pass

If a render pass is not needed and it is not used anymore by commands submitted to the hardware, we can destroy it.

How to do it...

1. Use the handle of a logical device, on which the render pass was created, to initialize a variable of type `VkDevice` named `logical_device`.
2. Store the handle of the render pass that should be destroyed in a variable of type `VkRenderPass` named `render_pass`.
3. Call `vkDestroyRenderPass( logical_device, render_pass, nullptr )` and provide the `logical_device` and `render_pass` variables and a `nullptr` value.
4. For safety reasons, assign a `VK_NULL_HANDLE` value to the `render_pass` variable.

How it works...

Destroying a render pass is performed with just a single function call like this:

```
if( VK_NULL_HANDLE != render_pass ) {
  vkDestroyRenderPass( logical_device, render_pass, nullptr );
  render_pass = VK_NULL_HANDLE;
}
```

See also

The following recipe in this chapter:

- *Creating a render pass*

7
Shaders

In this chapter, we will cover the following recipes:

- Converting GLSL shaders to SPIR-V assemblies
- Writing vertex shaders
- Writing tessellation control shaders
- Writing tessellation evaluation shaders
- Writing geometry shaders
- Writing fragment shaders
- Writing compute shaders
- Writing a vertex shader that multiplies a vertex position by a projection matrix
- Using push constants in shaders
- Writing a texturing vertex and fragment shaders
- Displaying polygon normals with a geometry shader

Introduction

Most modern graphics hardware platforms render images using programmable pipeline. 3D graphics data, such as vertices and fragments/pixels, are processed in a series of steps called stages. Some stages always perform the same operations, which we can only configure to a certain extent. However, there are other stages that need to be programmed. Small programs that control the behavior of these stages are called shaders.

Shaders

In Vulkan, there are five programmable graphics pipeline stages--vertex, tessellation control, evaluation, geometry, and fragment. We can also write compute shader programs for a compute pipeline. In the core Vulkan API, we control these stages with programs written in a SPIR-V. It is an intermediate language that allows us to process graphics data and perform mathematical calculation on vectors, matrices, images, buffers, or samplers. The low-level nature of this language improves compilation times. However, it also makes writing shaders harder. That's why the Vulkan SDK contains a tool called glslangValidator.

glslangValidator allows us to convert shader programs written in an OpenGL Shading Language (in short GLSL) into SPIR-V assemblies. This way, we can write shaders in a much more convenient high-level shading language, we can also easily validate them and then convert to a representation accepted by the Vulkan API, before we ship them with our Vulkan application.

In this chapter, we will learn how to write shaders using GLSL. We will see how to implement shaders for all programmable stages, how to implement tessellation or texturing, and how to use geometry shaders for debugging purposes. We will also see how to convert shaders written in a GLSL into SPIR-V assemblies using the glslangValidator program distributed with the Vulkan SDK.

Converting GLSL shaders to SPIR-V assemblies

The Vulkan API requires us to provide shaders in the form of SPIR-V assemblies. It is a binary, intermediate representation, so writing it manually is a very hard and cumbersome task. It is much easier and quicker to write shader programs in a high-level shading language such as GLSL. After that we just need to convert them into a SPIR-V form using the glslangValidator tool.

How to do it...

1. Download and install the Vulkan SDK (refer to the *Downloading Vulkan SDK* recipe from `Chapter 1`, *Instance and Devices*).
2. Open the command prompt/terminal and go to the folder which contains shader files that should be converted.

3. To convert a GLSL shader stored in the `<input>` file into a SPIR-V assembly stored in the `<output>` file, run the following command:

   `glslangValidator -H -o <output> <input> > <output_txt>`

How it works...

The glslangValidator tool is distributed along with the Vulkan SDK. It is located in the `VulkanSDK/<version>/bin` (for 64-bit version) or `VulkanSDK/<version>/bin32` (for 32-bit version) subfolder of the SDK. It has many features, but one of its main functions is the ability to convert GLSL shaders into SPIR-V assemblies that can be consumed by the Vulkan applications.

> The glslangValidator tool that converts GLSL shaders into SPIR-V assemblies is distributed with the Vulkan SDK.

The tool automatically detects the shader stage based on the extension of the `<input>` file. The available options are:

- `vert` for the vertex shader stage
- `tesc` for the tessellation control shader stage
- `tese` for the tessellation evaluation shader stage
- `geom` for the geometry shader stage
- `frag` for the fragment shader stage
- `comp` for the compute shader

The tool may also display the SPIR-V assembly in a readable, text form. The command presented in this recipe, stores such form in the selected `<output_txt>` file.

After GLSL shaders are converted into SPIR-V, these can be loaded in the application and used to create shader modules (refer to the *Creating a shader module* recipe from `Chapter 8`, *Graphics and Compute Pipelines*).

See also

- In Chapter 1, *Instances and Devices*, see the following recipe:
    - *Downloading Vulkan SDK*
- The following recipes in this chapter:
    - *Writing vertex shaders*
    - *Writing tessellation control shaders*
    - *Writing tessellation evaluation shaders*
    - *Writing geometry shaders*
    - *Writing fragment shaders*
    - *Writing compute shaders*
    - *Creating a shader module*

Writing vertex shaders

Vertex processing is a first graphics pipeline stage that can be programmed. Its main purpose is to convert positions of vertices, which form our geometry, from their local coordinate system into a coordinate system called a clip space. The clip coordinate system is used to allow graphics hardware to perform all following steps in a much easier and more optimal way. One of these steps is clipping, which clips processed vertices to only those that can be potentially visible, hence the name of the coordinate system. Apart from that, we can perform all the other operations, which are executed once per each vertex of drawn geometry.

How to do it...

1. Create a text file. Select a name for the file, but use a `vert` extension for it (for example, `shader.vert`).
2. Insert `#version 450` in the first line of the file.
3. Define a set of vertex input variables (attributes) that will be provided from the application for each vertex (unless otherwise specified). For each input variable:
    1. Define its location with a location layout qualifier and an index of the attribute:
       `layout( location = <index> )`
    2. Provide an `in` storage qualifier

3. Specify the type of input variable (such as `vec4`, `float`, `int3`)
4. Provide a unique name of the input variable

4. If necessary, define an output (varying) variable that will be passed (and interpolated, unless otherwise specified) to the later pipeline stages. To define each output variable:
    1. Provide the variable's location using a location layout qualifier and an index:
       `layout( location = <index> )`
    2. Specify an `out` storage qualifier
    3. Specify the type of output variable (such as `vec3` or `int`)
    4. Select a unique name of the output variable

5. If necessary, define uniform variables that correspond to descriptor resources created in the application. To define a uniform variable:
    1. Specify the number of descriptor set and a binding number in which a given resource can be accessed:
       `layout (set=<set index>, binding=<binding index>)`
    2. Provide a `uniform` storage qualifier
    3. Specify the type of the variable (such as `sampler2D`, `imageBuffer`)
    4. Define a unique name for the variable

6. Create a `void main()` function in which:
    1. Perform the desired operations
    2. Pass input variables into output variables (with or without transformations)
    3. Store the position of the processed vertex (possibly transformed) in the `gl_Position` built-in variable.

How it works...

The vertex processing (via the vertex shader) is the first programmable stage in a graphics pipeline. It is obligatory in every graphics pipeline that we create in Vulkan. Its main purpose is to transform positions of the vertices passed from the application from their local coordinate system into a clip space. How the transformation is done is up to us; we can omit it and provide coordinates that are already in the clip space. It is also possible for the vertex shader to do nothing at all, if later stages (tessellation or geometry shaders) calculate positions and pass them down the pipeline.

Shaders

Usually though, the vertex shader takes the position provided from the application as one of the input variables (coordinates) and multiplies it (on the left side) by a model-view-projection matrix.

The main purpose of the vertex shader is to take the position of a vertex, multiply a model-view-projection matrix by it, and store the result in the `gl_Position` built-in variable.

The vertex shader can also perform other operations, pass their results to later stages of the graphics pipeline, or store them in storage images or buffers. However, we must remember that all calculations are performed once per vertex of a drawn geometry.

In the following image, a single triangle is drawn with a wireframe rendering enabled in the pipeline object. To be able to draw nonsolid geometry, we need to enable a `fillModeNonSolid` feature during the logical device creation (refer to the *Getting features and properties of a physical device* and *Creating a logical device* recipes from `Chapter 1`, *Instance and Devices*).

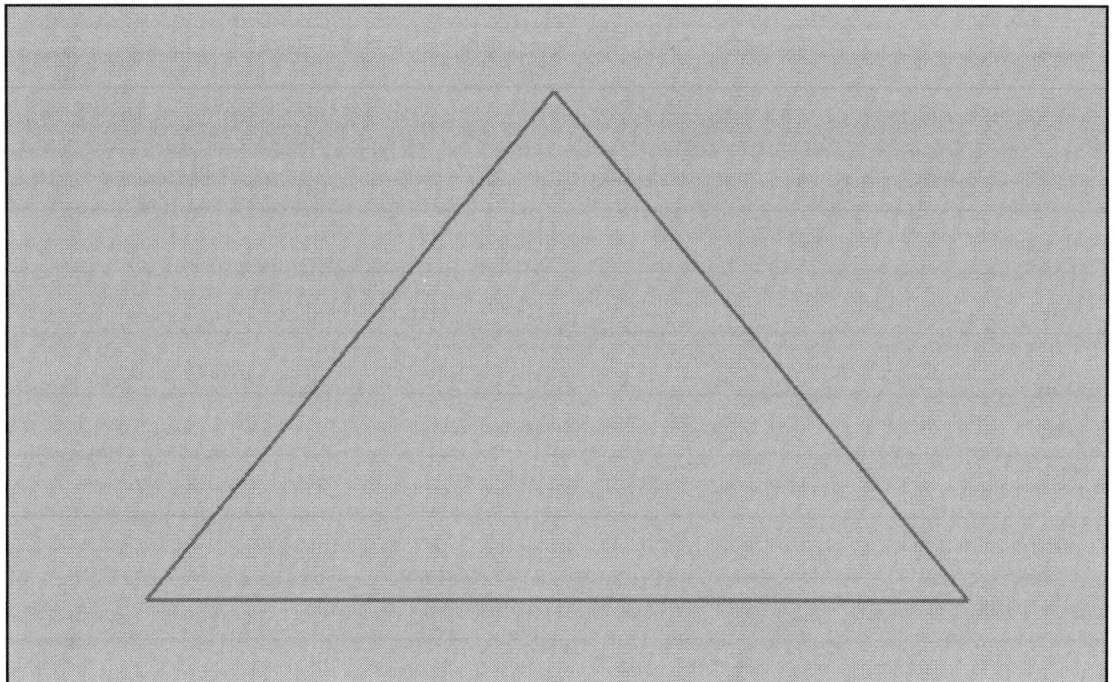

To draw this triangle, a simple vertex shader was used. Here's the source code of this shader written in a GLSL:

```
#version 450

layout( location = 0 ) in vec4 app_position;

void main() {
  gl_Position = app_position;
}
```

See also

- The following recipes in this chapter:
    - *Converting GLSL shaders to SPIR-V assemblies*
    - *Writing a vertex shader that multiplies a vertex position by a projection matrix*
- In Chapter 8, *Graphics and Compute Pipelines*, see the following recipes:
    - *Creating a shader module*
    - *Specifying pipeline vertex binding description, attribute description, and input state*
    - *Creating a graphics pipeline*

Writing tessellation control shaders

Tessellation is a process that divides geometry into much smaller parts. In graphics programming, it allows us to improve the number of details of rendered objects or to dynamically change their parameters, such as smoothness or shape, in much more flexible way.

Tessellation in Vulkan is optional. If enabled, it is performed after the vertex shader. It has three steps, of which two are programmable. The first programmable tessellation stage is used to set up parameters that control how the tessellation is performed. We do this by writing tessellation control shaders that specify values of tessellation factors.

How to do it...

1. Create a text file. Select a name for the file, but use a `tesc` extension for it (for example, `shader.tesc`).
2. Insert `#version 450` in the first line of the file.
3. Define the number of vertices that will form an output patch:

   `layout( vertices = <count> ) out;`

4. Define a set of input variables (attributes) that are provided from (written in) a vertex shader stage. For each input variable:
   1. Define its location with a location layout qualifier and an index of the attribute:
      `layout( location = <index> )`
   2. Provide an `in` storage qualifier
   3. Specify the type of input variable (such as `vec3`, `float`)
   4. Provide a unique name of the input variable
5. If necessary, define an output (varying) variable that will be passed (and interpolated, unless otherwise specified) to the later pipeline stages. To define each output variable:
   1. Provide the variable's location using a location layout qualifier and an index:
      `layout( location = <index> )`
   2. Specify an `out` storage qualifier
   3. Specify the type of output variable (such as `ivec2` or `bool`)
   4. Select a unique name of the output variable
   5. Make sure it is defined as an unsized array
6. If necessary, define uniform variables that correspond to descriptor resources created in the application, which can be accessed in the tessellation control stage. To define a uniform variable:
   1. Through a layout qualifier, specify the number of descriptor set and a binding number in which a given resource can be accessed:
      `layout (set=<set index>, binding=<binding index>)`
   2. Provide a `uniform` storage qualifier.
   3. Specify the type of the variable (such as `sampler`, `image1D`).
   4. Define a unique name of the variable.

7. Create a `void main()` function in which:
    1. Perform the desired operations.
    2. Pass input variables into output arrays of the variables (with or without transformations).
    3. Specify the inner tessellation level factor through a `gl_TessLevelInner` variable.
    4. Specify the outer tessellation level factor through a `gl_TessLevelOuter` variable.
    5. Store the position of the processed patch's vertex (possibly transformed) in a `gl_out[gl_InvocationID].gl_Position` variable.

How it works...

Tessellation shaders are optional in Vulkan; we don't have to use them. When we want to use them, we always need to use both tessellation control and tessellation evaluation shaders. We also need to enable a `tessellationShader` feature during the logical device creation.

> When we want to use tessellation in our application, we need to enable a `tessellationShader` feature during the logical device creation and we need to specify both tessellation control and evaluation shader stages during the graphics pipeline creation.

The tessellation stage operates on patches. Patches are formed from vertices, but (opposed to traditional polygons) each patch may have an arbitrary number of them--from 1 to at least 32.

The tessellation control shader, as the name suggests, specifies the way in which geometry formed from the patch is tessellated. This is done through inner and outer tessellation factors that must be specified in the shader code. An inner factor, represented by the built-in `gl_TessLevelInner[]` array, specifies how the internal part of the patch is tessellated. The outer factor, which corresponds to the `gl_TessLevelOuter[]` built-in array, defines how the outer edges of the patches are tessellated. Each array element corresponds to a given edge of the patch.

The tessellation control shader is executed once for each vertex in the output patch. The index of the current vertex is available in the built-in `gl_InvocationID` variable. Only a currently processed vertex (corresponding to the current invocation) can be written to, but the shader has access to all vertices of the input patch through a `gl_in[].gl_Position` variable.

An example of a tessellation control shader that specifies arbitrary tessellation factors and passes unmodified positions may look like this:

```
#version 450

layout( vertices = 3 ) out;

void main() {
  if( 0 == gl_InvocationID ) {
    gl_TessLevelInner[0] = 3.0;
    gl_TessLevelOuter[0] = 3.0;
    gl_TessLevelOuter[1] = 4.0;
    gl_TessLevelOuter[2] = 5.0;
  }
  gl_out[gl_InvocationID].gl_Position = gl_in[gl_InvocationID].gl_Position;
}
```

The same triangle as seen in the *Writing vertex shaders* recipe, drawn with the preceding tessellation control shader and with the tessellation evaluation shader from the *Writing tessellation evaluation shaders* recipe, should look like this:

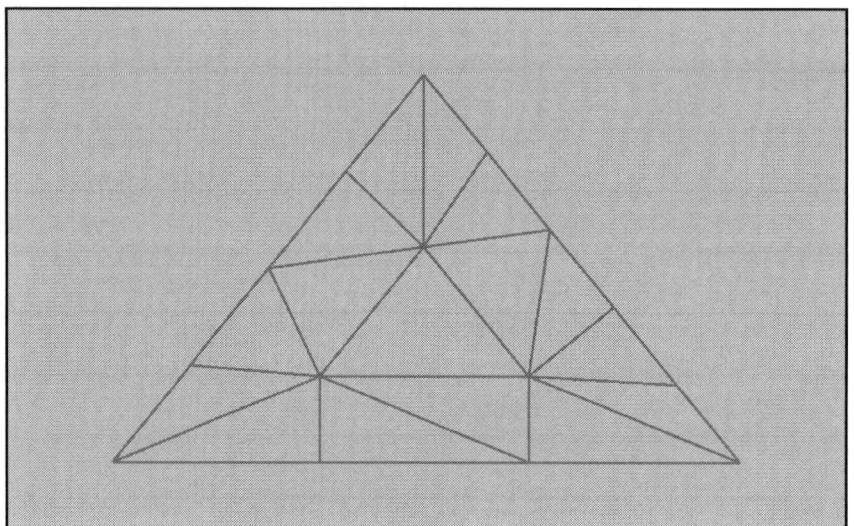

See also

- The following recipe in this chapter:
    - *Converting GLSL shaders to SPIR-V assemblies*
    - *Writing tessellation evaluation shaders*
- In Chapter 8, *Graphics and Compute Pipelines*, see the following recipes:
    - *Creating a shader module*
    - *Specifying pipeline tessellation state*
    - *Creating a graphics pipeline*

Writing tessellation evaluation shaders

Tessellation evaluation is the second programmable stage in the tessellation process. It is executed when the geometry is already tessellated (subdivided) and is used to gather results of the tessellation to form the new vertices and further modify them. When the tessellation is enabled, we need to write tessellation evaluation shaders to acquire the locations of generated vertices and provide them to the consecutive pipeline stages.

How to do it...

1. Create a text file. Select a name for the file and use a `tese` extension for it (for example, `shader.tese`).
2. Insert `#version 450` in the first line of the file.
3. Using the `in` layout qualifier, define the type of formed primitives (`isolines`, `triangles`, or `quads`), the spacing between formed vertices (`equal_spacing`, `fractional_even_spacing` or `fractional_odd_spacing`), and a winding order of generated triangles (`cw` to keep the winding provided in an application or `ccw` to reverse the winding provided in an application):

    ```
    layout( <primitive>, <spacing>, <winding> ) in;
    ```

Shaders

4. Define a set of input array variables that are provided from a tessellation control stage. For each input variable:
    1. Define its location with a location layout qualifier and an index of the attribute:
       `layout ( location = <index> )`
    2. Provide an `in` storage qualifier
    3. Specify the type of input variable (such as `vec2` or `int3`)
    4. Provide a unique name of the input variable
    5. Make sure it is defined as an array.

5. If necessary, define an output (varying) variable that will be passed (and interpolated, unless otherwise specified) to later pipeline stages. To define each output variable:
    1. Provide the variable's location using a location layout qualifier and an index:
       `layout ( location = <index> )`
    2. Specify an `out` storage qualifier
    3. Specify the type of output variable (such as `vec4`)
    4. Select a unique name of the output variable.

6. If necessary, define uniform variables that correspond to descriptor resources created in the application for which the tessellation evaluation stage can have access. To define a uniform variable:
    1. Specify the number of descriptor set and a binding number in which a given resource can be accessed:
       `layout (set=<set index>, binding=<binging index>)`
    2. Provide a `uniform` storage qualifier
    3. Specify the type of the variable (such as `sampler`, `image1D`)
    4. Define a unique name of the variable.

7. Create a `void main()` function in which:
    1. Perform the desired operations
    2. Use the built-in `gl_TessCoord` vector variable to generate a position of a new vertex using the positions of all the patch's vertices; modify the result to achieve the desired result, and store it in the `gl_Position` built-in variable
    3. In a similar way, use `gl_TessCoord` to generate interpolated values of all other input variables and store them in the output variables (with additional transformations if required).

How it works...

Tessellation control and evaluation shaders form two programmable stages required for the tessellation to work correctly. Between them is a stage that does the actual tessellation based on the parameters provided in the control stage. Results of the tessellation are acquired in the evaluation stage, where they are applied to form the new geometry.

Through tessellation evaluation we can control the way in which new primitives are aligned and formed: we specify their winding order and spacing between the generated vertices. We can also select whether we want the tessellation stage to create `isolines`, `triangles`, or `quads`.

New vertices are not created directly--the tessellator generates only barycentric tessellation coordinates for new vertices (weights), which are provided in the built-in `gl_TessCoord` variable. We can use these coordinates to interpolate between the original positions of vertices that formed a patch and place new vertices in the correct positions. That's why the evaluation shader, though executed once per generated vertex, has access to all vertices forming the patch. Their positions are provided through the `gl_Position` member of a built-in array variable, `gl_in[]`.

In case of commonly used triangles, the tessellation evaluation shader that just passes new vertices without further modifications may look like this:

```
#version 450

layout( triangles, equal_spacing, cw ) in;

void main() {
  gl_Position = gl_in[0].gl_Position * gl_TessCoord.x +
                gl_in[1].gl_Position * gl_TessCoord.y +
                gl_in[2].gl_Position * gl_TessCoord.z;
}
```

See also

- The following recipe in this chapter:
    - *Converting GLSL shaders to SPIR-V assemblies*
    - *Writing tessellation control shaders*
- In Chapter 8, *Graphics and Compute Pipelines*, see the following recipes:
    - *Creating a shader module*
    - *Specifying a pipeline tessellation state*
    - *Creating a graphics pipeline*

Writing geometry shaders

3D scenes are composed of objects called meshes. Mesh is a collection of vertices that form the external surface of an object. This surface is usually represented by triangles. When we render an object, we provide vertices and specify what type of primitives (`points`, `lines`, `triangles`) they build. After the vertices are processed by the vertex and optional tessellation stages, they are assembled into specified types of primitives. We can enable, also optional, the geometry stage and write geometry shaders that control or change the process of forming primitives from vertices. In geometry shaders, we can even create new primitives or destroy the existing ones.

How to do it...

1. Create a text file. Select a name for the file and use a `geom` extension for it (for example, `shader.geom`).
2. Insert `#version 450` in the first line of the file.
3. Using the `in` layout qualifier, define the type of primitives that are drawn in an application: `points`, `lines`, `lines_adjacency`, `triangles`, or `triangles_adjacency`:

    ```
    layout( <primitive type> ) in;
    ```

4. Using the `out` layout qualifier, define the type of primitives that are formed (output) by the geometry shader (`points`, `line_strip` or `triangle_strip`), and the maximal number of vertices that the shader may generate:

   ```
   layout ( <primitive type>, max_vertices = <count> ) out;
   ```

5. Define a set of input array variables that are provided from a vertex or tessellation evaluation stage. For each input variable:
   1. Define its location with a location layout qualifier and an index of the attribute:
      ```
      layout ( location = <index> )
      ```
   2. Provide an `in` storage qualifier
   3. Specify the type of input variable (such as `ivec4`, `int` or `float`)
   4. Provide a unique name of the input variable
   5. Make sure the variable is defined as an unsized array

6. If necessary, define an output (varying) variable that will be passed (and interpolated, unless otherwise specified) to the fragment shader stage. To define each output variable:
   1. Provide variable's location using a location layout qualifier and an index:
      ```
      layout ( location = <index> )
      ```
   2. Specify an `out` storage qualifier
   3. Specify the type of output variable (such as `vec3` or `uint`)
   4. Select a unique name of the output variable

7. If necessary, define uniform variables that correspond to descriptor resources created in the application for which the geometry stage may have access. To define a uniform variable:
   1. Specify the number of descriptor set and a binding number in which a given resource can be accessed:
      ```
      layout (set=<set index>, binding=<binging index>)
      ```
   2. Provide a `uniform` storage qualifier
   3. Specify the type of the variable (such as `image2D`, `sampler1DArray`)
   4. Define a unique name of the variable

Shaders

8. Create a `void main()` function in which:
    1. Perform the desired operations
    2. For each generated or passed vertex:
        - Write values to output variables
        - Store the position of the vertex (possibly transformed) in the built-in `gl_Position` variable
        - Call `EmitVertex()` to add a vertex to the primitive
    3. Finish the generation of the primitive by calling `EndPrimitive()` function (another primitive is implicitly started).

How it works...

Geometry is an optional stage in a graphics pipeline. Without it, when we draw geometry, primitives are automatically generated based on the type specified during the graphics pipeline creation. Geometry shaders allow us to create additional vertices and primitives, destroy the ones drawn in an application, or to change the type of primitives formed from vertices.

The geometry shader is executed once for each primitive in a geometry drawn by the application. It has access to all vertices that constitute the primitive, or even to the adjacent ones. With this data it can pass the same or create new vertices and primitives. We must remember that we shouldn't create too many vertices in a geometry shader. If we want to create many new vertices, tessellation shaders are better suited for this task (and have a better performance). Just increasing the maximal number of vertices the geometry shader may create, even if we don't always form them; may lower the performance of our application.

We should keep the number of vertices emitted by the geometry shader as low as possible.

[346]

Geometry shaders always generate strip primitives. If we want to create separate primitives that do not form a strip, we just need to end a primitive at an appropriate moment--vertices emitted after the primitive is ended are added to the next strip so we can create as many separate strips as we choose to. Here's an example which creates three separate triangles in the original triangle's corners:

```
#version 450

layout( triangles ) in;
layout( triangle_strip, max_vertices = 9 ) out;

void main() {
   for( int vertex = 0; vertex < 3; ++vertex ) {
     gl_Position = gl_in[vertex].gl_Position + vec4( 0.0, -0.2, 0.0, 0.0 );
     EmitVertex();

     gl_Position = gl_in[vertex].gl_Position + vec4( -0.2, 0.2, 0.0, 0.0 );
     EmitVertex();

     gl_Position = gl_in[vertex].gl_Position + vec4( 0.2, 0.2, 0.0, 0.0 );
     EmitVertex();

     EndPrimitive();
   }
}
```

When a single triangle is drawn with a simple pass-through vertex and fragment shaders, and with the preceding geometry shader, the result should look like this:

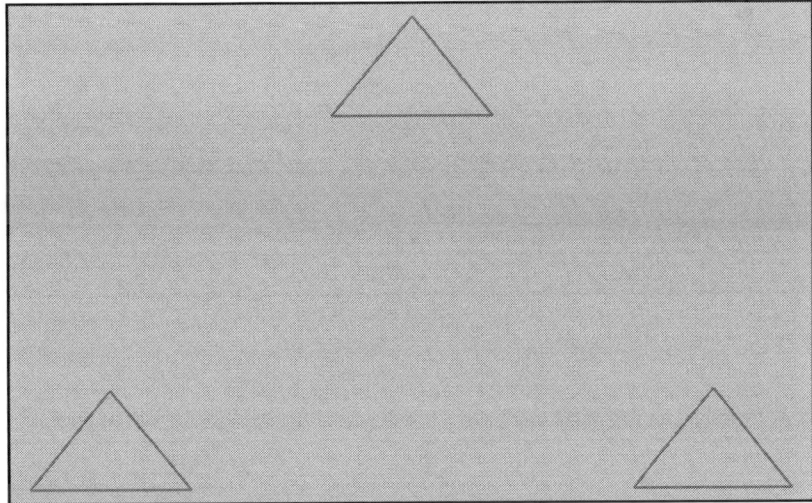

Shaders

See also

- The following recipes in this chapter:
    - *Converting GLSL shaders to SPIR-V assemblies*
    - *Displaying polygon normals with a geometry shader*
- In Chapter 8, *Graphics and Compute Pipelines*, see the following recipes:
    - *Creating a shader module*
    - *Specifying a pipeline input assembly state*
    - *Creating a graphics pipeline*

Writing fragment shaders

Fragments (or pixels) are parts of the image that can be potentially displayed on screen. They are created from geometry (drawn primitives) in a process called rasterization. They have specific screen space coordinates (x, y, and depth) but don't have any other data. We need to write a fragment shader to specify the color that needs to be displayed on screen. In the fragment shader, we can also select an attachment into which a given color should be written.

How to do it...

1. Create a text file. Select a name for the file, but use a `frag` extension for it (for example, `shader.frag`).
2. Insert `#version 450` in the first line of the file.
3. Define a set of input variables (attributes) that are provided from the earlier pipeline stages. For each input variable:
    1. Define its location with a location layout qualifier and an index of the attribute:
       `layout( location = <index> )`
    2. Provide an `in` storage qualifier
    3. Specify the type of input variable (such as `vec4`, `float`, `ivec3`)
    4. Provide a unique name of the input variable

4. Define an output variable for each attachment into which a color should be written. To define each output variable:
   1. Provide the variable's location (index of the attachment) using a location layout qualifier and a number:
      `layout( location = <index> )`
   2. Specify an `out` storage qualifier
   3. Specify the type of the output variable (such as `vec3` or `vec4`)
   4. Select a unique name of the output variable
5. If necessary, define uniform variables that correspond to descriptor resources created in the application. To define a uniform variable:
   1. Specify the number of descriptor set and a binding number in which a given resource can be accessed:
      `layout (set=<set index>, binding=<binding index>)`
   2. Provide a `uniform` storage qualifier
   3. Specify the type of the variable (such as `sampler1D`, `subpassInput`, or `imageBuffer`)
   4. Define a unique name of the variable
6. Create a `void main()` function in which:
   1. Perform the desired operations and calculations
   2. Store the color of the processed fragment in an output variable

How it works...

Geometry, which we draw in our application, is formed from primitives. These primitives are converted into fragments (pixels) in a process called rasterization. For each such fragment, a fragment shader is executed. Fragments may be discarded inside the shader or during framebuffer tests, such as depth, stencil, or scissor tests, so they won't even become pixels--that's why they are called fragments, not pixels.

Shaders

The main purpose of a fragment shader is to set a color that will be (potentially) written to an attachment. We usually use them to perform lighting calculations and texturing. Along with compute shaders, fragment shaders are often used for post-processing effects such as bloom or deferred shading/lighting. Also, only fragment shaders can access input attachments defined in a render pass (refer to the *Creating an input attachment* recipe from Chapter 5, *Descriptor Sets*).

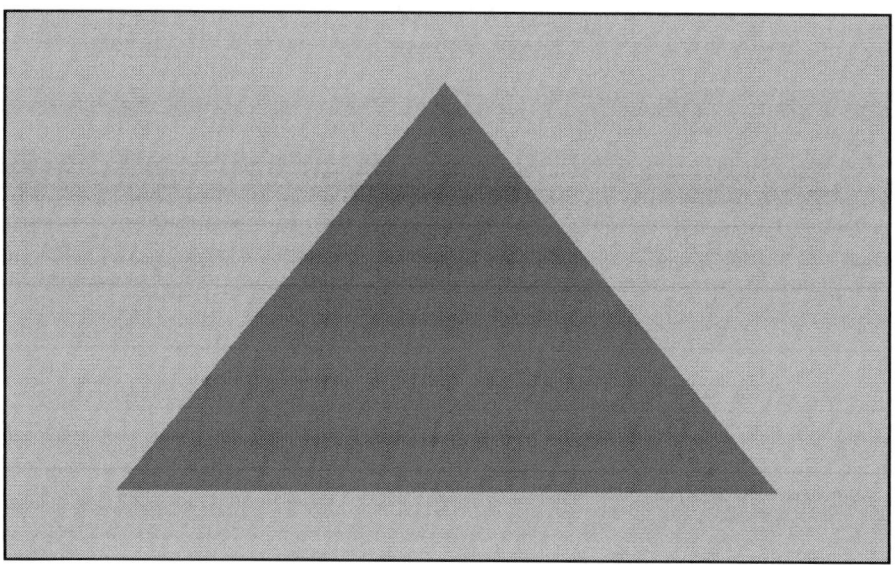

To draw the triangle in the preceding figure, a simple fragment shader is used, which stores a chosen, hardcoded color:

```
#version 450

layout( location = 0 ) out vec4 frag_color;

void main() {
   frag_color = vec4( 0.8, 0.4, 0.0, 1.0 );
}
```

See also

- The following recipes in this chapter:
  - *Converting GLSL shaders to SPIR-V assemblies*
  - *Writing a texturing vertex and fragment shaders*
- In Chapter 8, Graphics and Compute Pipelines, see the following recipes:
  - *Creating a shader module*
  - *Specifying a pipeline rasterization state*
  - *Creating a graphics pipeline*

Writing compute shaders

Compute shaders are used, as the name suggests, for general mathematical calculations. They are executed in (local) groups of a defined, three-dimensional size, which may have access to a common set of data. At the same time, many local groups can be executed to generate results faster.

How to do it...

1. Create a text file. Select a name for the file, but use a `comp` extension for it (for example, `shader.comp`).
2. Insert `#version 450` in the first line of the file.
3. Using an input layout qualifier, define the size of the local workgroup:

```
layout( local_size_x = <x size>, local_size_y = <y size>, local_size_z = <z size> ) in;
```

4. Define uniform variables that correspond to descriptor resources created in the application. To define a uniform variable:
    1. Specify the number of descriptor set and a binding number in which a given resource can be accessed:
       `layout (set=<set index>, binding=<binding index>)`
    2. Provide a `uniform` storage qualifier
    3. Specify the type of the variable (such as `image2D` or `buffer`)
    4. Define a unique name of the variable

Shaders

5. Create a `void main()` function in which:
   1. Perform the desired operations and calculations
   2. Store the results in selected uniform variables

How it works...

Compute shaders can be used only in a dedicated compute pipeline. They also cannot be executed (dispatched) inside render passes.

Compute shaders don't have any input nor output (user defined) variables passed from earlier or to later pipeline stages--it is the only stage in a compute pipeline. Uniform variables must be used for the source of compute shader data. Similarly, results of calculations performed in the compute shader can be stored only in the uniform variables.

There are some built-in input variables that provide information about the index of a given shader invocation within a local workgroup (through the `uvec3 gl_LocalInvocationID` variable), the number of workgroups dispatched at the same time (through the `uvec3 gl_NumWorkGroups` variable), or a number of the current workgroup (`uvec3 gl_WorkGroupID` variable). There is also a variable that uniquely identifies the current shader within all invocations in all workgroups--`uvec3 gl_GlobalInvocationID`. Its value is calculated like this:

```
gl_WorkGroupID * gl_WorkGroupSize + gl_LocalInvocationID
```

The size of the local workgroup is defined through the input layout qualifier. Inside the shader, the defined size is also available through the `uvec3 gl_WorkGroupSize` built-in variable.

In the following code, you can find a compute shader example that uses the `gl_GlobalInvocationID` variable to generate a simple, static fractal image:

```
#version 450

layout( local_size_x = 32, local_size_y = 32 ) in;

layout( set = 0, binding = 0, rgba8 ) uniform image2D StorageImage;

void main() {
  vec2 z = gl_GlobalInvocationID.xy * 0.001 - vec2( 0.0, 0.4 );
  vec2 c = z;

  vec4 color = vec4( 0.0 );
```

```
for( int i=0; i<50; ++I ) {
  z.x = z.x * z.x-- z.y * z.y + c.x;
  z.y = 2.0 * z.x * z.y + c.y;
  if( dot( z, z ) > 10.0 ) {
    color = i * vec4( 0.1, 0.15, 0.2, 0.0 );
    break;
  }
}

imageStore( StorageImage, ivec2( gl_GlobalInvocationID.xy ), color );
}
```

The preceding compute shader generates the following result when dispatched:

See also

- The following recipe in this chapter:
    - *Converting GLSL shaders to SPIR-V assemblies*
- In Chapter 8, *Graphics and Compute Pipelines*, see the following recipes:
    - *Creating a shader module*
    - *Creating a compute pipeline*

Writing a vertex shader that multiplies vertex position by a projection matrix

Transforming geometry from local to clip space is usually performed by the vertex shader, though any other vertex processing stage (tessellation or geometry) may accomplish this task. The transformation is done by specifying model, view, and projection matrices and providing them from the application to the shaders as three separate matrices, or as one, joined model-view-projection matrix (in short MVP). The most common and easy way is to use a uniform buffer through which we can provide such a matrix.

How to do it...

1. Create a vertex shader in a text file called `shader.vert` (refer to the *Writing vertex shaders* recipe).
2. Define an input variable (attribute) through which vertex positions will be provided to the vertex shader:

    ```
    layout(location = 0) in vec4 app_position;
    ```

3. Define a uniform buffer with a variable of type `mat4` through which data for the combined model-view-projection matrix will be provided:

    ```
    layout(set=0, binding=0) uniform UniformBuffer {
      mat4 ModelViewProjectionMatrix;
    };
    ```

4. Inside a `void main()` function, calculate vertex position in the clip space by multiplying the `ModelViewProjectionMatrix` uniform variable by the `app_position` input variable and storing the result in the `gl_Position` built-in variable like this:

    ```
    gl_Position = ModelViewProjectionMatrix * app_position;
    ```

How it works...

When we prepare a geometry that will be drawn in a 3D application, the geometry is usually modeled in the local coordinate system--the one in which it is more convenient for the artist to create the model. However, the graphics pipeline expects the vertices to be transformed to a clip space, as it is easier (and faster) to perform many operations in this coordinate system. Usually it is the vertex shader that performs this transformation. For this, we need to prepare a matrix that represents a perspective or orthogonal projection. Transformation from the local space to the clip space is performed by just multiplying the matrix by the position of a vertex.

The same matrix, apart from the projection, may also contain other operations, commonly referred to as model-view transformations. And because drawn geometry may contain hundreds or thousands of vertices, it is usually more optimal to multiply model, view, and projection matrices in the application, and provide a single, concatenated MVP matrix to the shader which needs to perform only a single multiplication:

```glsl
#version 450

layout(location = 0) in vec4 app_position;

layout(set=0, binding=0) uniform UniformBuffer {
  mat4 ModelViewProjectionMatrix;
};

void main() {
   gl_Position = ModelViewProjectionMatrix * app_position;
}
```

The preceding shader requires the application to prepare a buffer in which data for the matrix is stored (refer to the *Creating a uniform buffer* recipe from Chapter 5, *Descriptor Sets*). This buffer is then provided (in the current example) at a 0th binding to a descriptor set, which is later bound to the command buffer as the 0th set (refer to the *Updating descriptor sets* and *Binding descriptor sets* recipes from Chapter 5, *Descriptor Sets*).

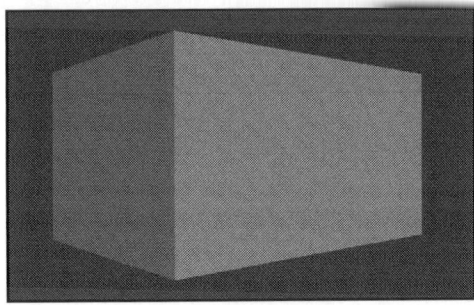

Shaders

See also

- In Chapter 5, *Descriptor Sets*, see the following recipes:
    - *Creating a uniform buffer*
    - *Updating descriptor sets*
    - *Binding descriptor sets*
- The following recipes in this chapter:
    - *Converting GLSL shaders to SPIR-V assemblies*
    - *Writing vertex shaders*
- In `Chapter 8`, *Graphics and Compute Pipelines*, see the following recipes:
    - *Creating a shader module*
    - *Creating a graphics pipeline*

Using push constants in shaders

When we provide data to shaders, we usually use uniform buffers, storage buffers, or other types of descriptor resources. Unfortunately, updating such resources may not be too convenient, especially when we need to provide data that changes frequently.

For this purpose, push constants were introduced. Through them we can provide data in a simplified and much faster way than by updating descriptor resources. However, we need to fit into a much smaller amount of available space.

Accessing push constants in GLSL shaders is similar to using uniform buffers.

How to do it...

1. Create a shader file.
2. Define a uniform block:
    1. Provide a `push_constant` layout qualifier:
       `layout( push_constant )`
    2. Use a `uniform` storage qualifier

3. Provide a unique name of the block
4. Inside the braces, define a set of uniform variables
5. Specify the name of the block instance `<instance name>`.

4. Inside the `void main()` function, access uniform variables using a block instance name:

`<instance name>.<variable name>`

How it works...

Push constants are defined and accessed in a way similar to uniform blocks are specified in GLSL shaders, but there are some differences we need to remember:

1. We need to use a `layout( push_constant )` qualifier before the definition of the block
2. We must specify an instance name for the block
3. We can define only one such block per shader
4. We access push constant variables by preceding their name with the instance name of the block:

`<instance name>.<variable name>`

Push constants are useful for providing small amounts of data that change frequently, such as the transformation matrix or current time value--updating the push constants block should be much faster than updating descriptor resources such as uniform buffers. We just need to remember about the data size which is much smaller than it is for descriptor resources. Specification requires push constants to store at least 128 bytes of data. Each hardware platform may allow for more storage, but it may not be considerably bigger.

 Push constants can store at least 128 bytes of data.

An example of defining and using push constants in a fragment shader through which a color is provided may look like this:

```
#version 450

layout( location = 0 ) out vec4 frag_color;

layout( push_constant ) uniform ColorBlock {
  vec4 Color;
} PushConstant;

void main() {
  frag_color = PushConstant.Color;
}
```

See also

- The following recipes in this chapter:
    - *Converting GLSL shaders to SPIR-V assemblies*
    - *Writing a vertex shader that multiplies a vertex position by a projection matrix*
- In Chapter 8, *Graphics and Compute Pipelines*, see the following recipes:
    - *Creating a shader module*
    - *Creating a pipeline layout*
- In Chapter 9, *Command Recording and Drawing*, see the following recipe:
    - *Providing data to shaders through push constants*

Writing texturing vertex and fragment shaders

Texturing is a common technique that significantly improves the quality of rendered images. It allows us to load an image and wrap it around the object like a wallpaper. It increases the memory usage, but saves the performance which would be wasted on processing much more complex geometry.

How to do it...

1. Create a vertex shader in a text file called `shader.vert` (refer to the *Writing vertex shaders* recipe).
2. Apart from the vertex position, define an additional input variable (attribute) in the vertex shader through which texture coordinates are provided from the application:

   `layout( location = 1 ) in vec2 app_tex_coordinates;`

3. In the vertex shader, define an output (varying) variable through which texture coordinates will be passed from the vertex shader to a fragment shader:

   `layout( location = 0 ) out vec2 vert_tex_coordinates;`

4. In the vertex shader's `void main()` function, assign the `app_tex_coordinates` variable to the `vert_tex_coordinates` variable:

   `vert_tex_coordinates = app_tex_coordinates;`

5. Create a fragment shader (refer to the *Writing fragment shaders* recipe).
6. In the fragment shader, define an input variable in which texture coordinates provided from the vertex shader will be passed:

   `layout( location = 0 ) in vec2 vert_tex_coordinates;`

7. Create a uniform `sampler2D` variable that will represent the texture which should be applied to the geometry:

   `layout( set=0, binding=0 ) uniform sampler2D TextureImage;`

8. Define an output variable in which the fragment's final color (read from the texture) will be stored:

   `layout( location = 0 ) out vec4 frag_color;`

9. In the fragment shader's `void main()` function, sample the texture and store the result in the `frag_color` variable:

   `frag_color = texture( TextureImage, vert_tex_coordinates );`

How it works...

To draw an object, we need all its vertices. To be able to use a texture and apply it to the model, apart from vertex positions, we also need texture coordinates specified for each vertex. These attributes (position and texture coordinate) are passed to the vertex shader. It takes the position and transforms it to the clip space (if necessary), and passes the texture coordinates to the fragment shader:

```
#version 450

layout( location = 0 ) in vec4 app_position;
layout( location = 1 ) in vec2 app_tex_coordinates;

layout( location = 0 ) out vec2 vert_tex_coordinates;

void main() {
  gl_Position = app_position;
  vert_tex_coordinates = app_tex_coordinates;
}
```

The texturing operation is performed in the fragment shader. The texture coordinates from all the vertices forming a polygon are interpolated and provided to the fragment shader. It uses these coordinates to read (sample) a color from the texture. This color is stored in the output and (potentially) in the attachment:

```
#version 450

layout( location = 0 ) in vec2 vert_tex_coordinates;

layout( set=0, binding=0 ) uniform sampler2D TextureImage;

layout( location = 0 ) out vec4 frag_color;

void main() {
   frag_color = texture( TextureImage, vert_tex_coordinates );
}
```

Apart from providing texture coordinates to shaders, the application also needs to prepare the texture itself. Usually, this is done by creating a combined image sampler (refer to the *Creating a combined image sampler* recipe from Chapter 5, *Descriptor Sets*) and providing it to a descriptor set at 0th binding (in this sample). The Descriptor set must be bound to a 0th set index.

See also

- In Chapter 5, *Descriptor Sets*, see the following recipes:
    - *Creating a combined image sampler*
    - *Updating descriptor sets*
    - *Binding descriptor sets*
- The following recipes in this chapter:
    - *Converting GLSL shaders to SPIR-V assemblies*
    - *Writing vertex shaders*
    - *Writing fragment shaders*
- In Chapter 8, *Graphics and Compute Pipelines*, see the following recipes:
    - *Creating a shader module*
    - *Creating a graphics pipeline*

Displaying polygon normals with a geometry shader

When rendering a geometry, we usually provide multiple attributes for each vertex--positions to draw the model, texture coordinates for texturing, and normal vectors for lighting calculation. Checking if all this data is correct may not be easy, but sometimes, when our rendering technique doesn't work as expected, it may be necessary.

In graphics programming, there are some debugging methods that are commonly used. Texture coordinates, which are usually two-dimensional, are displayed instead of the usual color. We can do the same with the normal vectors, but as they are three-dimensional, we can also display them in a form of lines. For this purpose, a geometry shader may be used.

How to do it...

1. Create a vertex shader called `normals.vert` (refer to the *Writing vertex shaders* recipe).
2. Define an input variable in which the vertex position will be provided to the vertex shader:

   ```
   layout( location = 0 ) in vec4 app_position;
   ```

3. Define a second input variable in which the vertex normal vector will be provided:

   ```
   layout( location = 1 ) in vec3 app_normal;
   ```

4. Define a uniform block with two matrices--one for a model-view transformation, the other for a projection matrix:

   ```
   layout( set = 0, binding = 0 ) uniform UniformBuffer {
     mat4 ModelViewMatrix;
     mat4 ProjectionMatrix;
   };
   ```

5. Define an output variable through which we will provide to a geometry shader a normal vector converted from a local space to a view space:

   ```
   layout( location = 0 ) out vec4 vert_normal;
   ```

6. Convert a vertex position to a view space by multiplying the `ModelViewMatrix` variable and storing the result in the `gl_Position` built-in variable:

   ```
   gl_Position = ModelViewMatrix * app_position;
   ```

7. In a similar way, convert the vertex normal to a view space, scale the result by a chosen value, and store the result in the `vert_normal` output variable:

   ```
   vert_normal = vec4( mat3( ModelViewMatrix ) * app_normal * <scale>, 0.0 );
   ```

8. Create a geometry shader called `normal.geom` (refer to the *Writing geometry shaders* recipe).

9. Define a `triangle` input primitive type:

   ```
   layout( triangles ) in;
   ```

10. Define an input variable through which the view-space vertex normal will be provided from the vertex shader:

    ```
    layout( location = 0 ) in vec4 vert_normal[];
    ```

11. Define a uniform block with two matrices--one for a model-view transformation, the other for a projection matrix:

    ```
    layout( set = 0, binding = 0 ) uniform UniformBuffer {
      mat4 ModelViewMatrix;
      mat4 ProjectionMatrix;
    };
    ```

12. Through an output layout qualifier, specify a `line_strip` as a generated primitive type with up to six vertices.

    ```
    layout( line_strip, max_vertices = 6 ) out;
    ```

13. Define an output variable through which a color will be provided from the geometry shader to a fragment shader:

    ```
    layout( location = 0 ) out vec4 geom_color;
    ```

Shaders

14. Inside the `void main()` function, use a variable of type `int` named `vertex` to loop over all the input vertices. Perform the following operations for each input vertex:
    1. Multiply `ProjectionMatrix` by an input vertex position and store the result in the `gl_Position` built-in variable:
       `gl_Position = ProjectionMatrix * gl_in[vertex].gl_Position;`
    2. In the `geom_color` output variable, store the desired color for the vertex normal at the contact point between geometry (vertex) and the vertex normal line:
       `geom_color = vec4( <chosen color> );`
    3. Generate a new vertex by calling the `EmitVertex()` function.
    4. Multiply `ProjectionMatrix` by the input vertex position offset by the `vert_normal` input variable. Store the result in the `gl_Position` built-in variable:
       `gl_Position = ProjectionMatrix * (gl_in[vertex].gl_Position + vert_normal[vertex]);`
    5. Store the color of the vertex normal's end point in the `geom_color` output variable:
       `geom_color = vec4( <chosen color> );`
    6. Generate a new vertex by calling the `EmitVertex()` function.
    7. Generate a primitive (a line with two points) by calling the `EndPrimitive()` function.
15. Create a fragment shader named `normals.frag` (refer to the *Writing fragment shaders* recipe).
16. Define an input variable through which a color, interpolated between two vertices of a line generated by the geometry shader, will be provided to the fragment shader:

    `layout( location = 0 ) in vec4 geom_color;`

17. Define an output variable for the fragment's color:

    `layout( location = 0 ) out vec4 frag_color;`

18. Inside the `void main()` function, store the value of the `geom_color` input variable in the `frag_color` output variable:

    `frag_color = geom_color;`

How it works...

Displaying vertex normal vectors from the application side is performed in two steps: first we draw geometry in a normal way with the usual set of shaders. The second step is to draw the same model but with a pipeline object that uses the vertex, geometry, and fragment shaders specified in this recipe.

The vertex shader just needs to pass a vertex position and a normal vector to the geometry shader. It may transform both to the view-space, but the same operation can be performed in the geometry shader. The sample source code of the vertex shader that does the transformation provided through a uniform buffer is presented in the following code:

```
#version 450

layout( location = 0 ) in vec4 app_position;
layout( location = 1 ) in vec3 app_normal;

layout( set = 0, binding = 0 ) uniform UniformBuffer {
  mat4 ModelViewMatrix;
  mat4 ProjectionMatrix;
};

layout( location = 0 ) out vec4 vert_normal;

void main() {
  gl_Position = ModelViewMatrix * app_position;
  vert_normal = vec4( mat3( ModelViewMatrix ) * app_normal * 0.2, 0.0 );
}
```

In the preceding code, the position and normal vector are both transformed to the view space with a model-view matrix. If we intend to scale a model non-uniformly (not the same scale for all dimensions), the normal vector must be transformed using an inverse transpose of the model-view matrix.

Shaders

The most important part of the code is performed inside geometry. It takes vertices that form the original primitive type (usually triangles), but outputs vertices forming line segments. It takes one input vertex, transforms it to a clip space and passes it further. The same vertex is used a second time, but this time it is offset by the vertex normal. After the translation, it is transformed to the clip space and passed to the output. These operations are performed for all vertices forming the original primitive. The source code for the whole geometry shader may look like this:

```
#version 450

layout( triangles ) in;

layout( location = 0 ) in vec4 vert_normal[];

layout( set = 0, binding = 0 ) uniform UniformBuffer {
  mat4 ModelViewMatrix;
  mat4 ProjectionMatrix;
};

layout( line_strip, max_vertices = 6 ) out;

layout( location = 0 ) out vec4 geom_color;

void main() {
  for( int vertex = 0; vertex < 3; ++vertex ) {
    gl_Position = ProjectionMatrix * gl_in[vertex].gl_Position;
    geom_color = vec4( 0.2 );
    EmitVertex();

    gl_Position = ProjectionMatrix * (gl_in[vertex].gl_Position + vert_normal[vertex]);
    geom_color = vec4( 0.6 );
    EmitVertex();

    EndPrimitive();
  }
}
```

The geometry shader takes vertices converted by the vertex shader to the view space and transforms them further to the clip space. This is done with a projection matrix provided through the same uniform buffer as the one used in a vertex shader. Why do we define two matrix variables in a single uniform buffer, if we use just one of them in the vertex shader and a second one in the geometry shader? Such an approach is more convenient, because we just need to create a single buffer and we need to bind only one descriptor set to the command buffer. In general, the less operations we perform or record in the command buffer, the more performance we achieve. So this approach should also be faster.

The fragment shader is simple as it only passes interpolated colors stored by the geometry shader:

```
#version 450

layout( location = 0 ) in vec4 geom_color;

layout( location = 0 ) out vec4 frag_color;

void main() {
   frag_color = geom_color;
}
```

The result of using the preceding shaders to draw a geometry, along with a model drawn in a normal way, can be seen in the following image:

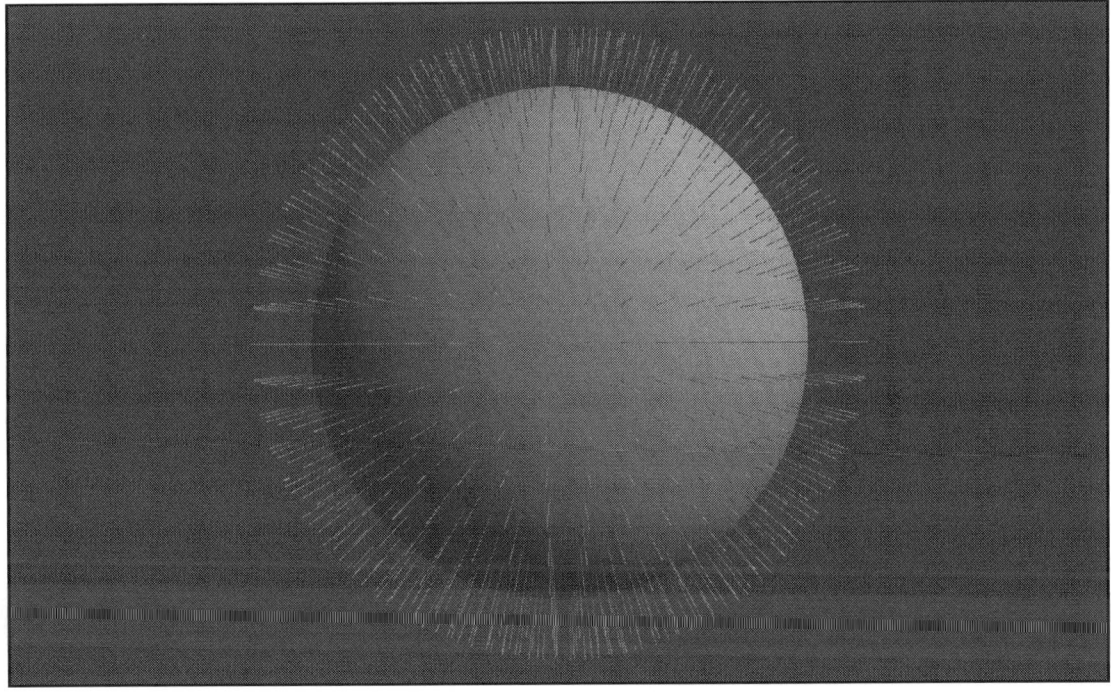

See also

- The following recipes in this chapter:
  - *Converting GLSL shaders to SPIR-V assemblies*
  - *Writing vertex shaders*
  - *Writing geometry shaders*
  - *Writing fragment shaders*
- In `Chapter 8`, *Graphics and Compute Pipelines,* see the following recipes:
  - *Creating a shader module*
  - *Creating a graphics pipeline*

8
Graphics and Compute Pipelines

In this chapter, we will cover the following recipes:

- Creating a shader module
- Specifying pipeline shader stages
- Specifying a pipeline vertex binding description, attribute description, and input state
- Specifying a pipeline input assembly state
- Specifying a pipeline tessellation state
- Specifying a pipeline viewport and scissor test state
- Specifying a pipeline rasterization state
- Specifying a pipeline multisample state
- Specifying a pipeline depth and stencil state
- Specifying a pipeline blend state
- Specifying pipeline dynamic states
- Creating a pipeline layout
- Specifying graphics pipeline creation parameters
- Creating a pipeline cache object
- Retrieving data from a pipeline cache
- Merging multiple pipeline cache objects
- Creating a graphics pipeline
- Creating a compute pipeline
- Binding a pipeline object

- Creating a pipeline layout with a combined image sampler, a buffer, and push constant ranges
- Creating a graphics pipeline with vertex and fragment shaders, depth test enabled, and with dynamic viewport and scissor tests
- Creating multiple graphics pipelines on multiple threads
- Destroying a pipeline
- Destroying a pipeline cache
- Destroying a pipeline layout
- Destroying a shader module

Introduction

Operations recorded in command buffers and submitted to queues are processed by the hardware. Processing is performed in a series of steps that form a pipeline. When we want to perform mathematical calculations, we use a compute pipeline. If we want to draw anything, we need a graphics pipeline.

Pipeline objects control the way in which geometry is drawn or computations are performed. They manage the behavior of the hardware on which our application is executed. And they are one of the biggest and most apparent differences between Vulkan and OpenGL. OpenGL used a state machine. It allowed us to change many rendering or computing parameters whenever we wanted. We could set up the state, activate a shader program, draw a geometry, then activate another shader program and draw another geometry. In Vulkan it is not possible because the whole rendering or computing state is stored in a single, monolithical object. When we want to use a different set of shaders, we need to prepare and use a separate pipeline. We can't just switch shaders.

This may be intimidating at first because many shader variations (not including the rest of the pipeline state) cause us to create multiple pipeline objects. But it serves two important goals. The first is the performance. Drivers that know the whole state in advance may optimize execution of the following operations. The second goal is the stability of the performance. Changing the state whenever we want may cause the driver to perform additional operations, such as shader recompilation, in unexpected and unpredictable moments. In Vulkan, all the required preparations, including shader compilation, are done only during the pipeline creation.

In this chapter, we will see how to set up all of the graphics or compute pipelines parameters to successfully create them. We will see how to prepare shader modules and define which shader stages are active, how to set up depth or stencil tests and how to enable blending. We will also specify what vertex attributes are used and how they are provided during drawing operations. Finally, we will see how to create multiple pipelines and how to improve the speed of their creation.

Creating a shader module

The first step in creating a pipeline object is to prepare shader modules. They represent shaders and contain their code written in a SPIR-V assembly. A single module may contain code for multiple shader stages. When we write shader programs and convert them into SPIR-V form, we need to create a shader module (or multiple modules) before we can use shaders in our application.

How to do it...

1. Take the handle of a logical device stored in a variable of type `VkDevice` named `logical_device`.
2. Load a binary SPIR-V assembly of a selected shader and store it in a variable of type `std::vector<unsigned char>` named `source_code`.
3. Create a variable of type `VkShaderModuleCreateInfo` named `shader_module_create_info`. Use the following values to initialize its members:
   - `VK_STRUCTURE_TYPE_SHADER_MODULE_CREATE_INFO` value for `sType`.
   - `nullptr` value for `pNext`
   - `0` value for `flags`
   - The number of elements in the `source_code` vector (size in bytes) for `codeSize`
   - A pointer to the first element of the `source_code` variable for `pCode`
4. Create a variable of type `VkShaderModule` named `shader_module` in which the handle of a created shader module will be stored.

Graphics and Compute Pipelines

5. Make the `vkCreateShaderModule( logical_device, &shader_module_create_info, nullptr, &shader_module )` function call for which provide the `logical_device` variable, a pointer to the `shader_module_create_info`, a `nullptr` value, and a pointer to the `shader_module` variable.
6. Make sure the `vkCreateShaderModule()` function call returned a `VK_SUCCESS` value which indicates that the shader module was properly created.

How it works...

Shader modules contain source code--a single SPIR-V assembly--of selected shader programs. It may represent multiple shader stages but a separate entry point must be associated with each stage. This entry point is then provided as one of the parameters when we create a pipeline object (refer to the *Specifying pipeline shader stages* recipe).

When we want to create a shader module, we need to load a file with the binary SPIR-V code or acquire it in any other way. Then we provide it to a variable of type `VkShaderModuleCreateInfo` like this:

```
VkShaderModuleCreateInfo shader_module_create_info = {
  VK_STRUCTURE_TYPE_SHADER_MODULE_CREATE_INFO,
  nullptr,
  0,
  source_code.size(),
  reinterpret_cast<uint32_t const *>(source_code.data())
};
```

Next, the pointer to such a variable is provided to the `vkCreateShaderModule()` function, which creates a module:

```
VkResult result = vkCreateShaderModule( logical_device,
&shader_module_create_info, nullptr, &shader_module );
if( VK_SUCCESS != result ) {
  std::cout << "Could not create a shader module." << std::endl;
  return false;
}
return true;
```

We just need to remember that shaders are not compiled when we create a shader module; this is done when we create a pipeline object.

 Shader compilation and linkage is performed during the pipeline object creation.

See also

The following recipes in this chapter:

- *Specifying pipeline shader stages*
- *Creating a graphics pipeline*
- *Creating a compute pipeline*
- *Destroying a shader module*

Specifying pipeline shader stages

In compute pipelines, we can use only compute shaders. But graphics pipelines may contain multiple shader stages--vertex (which is obligatory), geometry, tessellation control and evaluation, and fragment. So for the pipeline to be properly created, we need to specify what programmable shader stages will be active when a given pipeline is bound to a command buffer. And we also need to provide a source code for all the enabled shaders.

Getting ready

To simplify the recipe and lower the number of parameters needed to prepare descriptions of all enabled shader stages, a custom `ShaderStageParameters` type is introduced. It has the following definition:

```
struct ShaderStageParameters {
  VkShaderStageFlagBits       ShaderStage;
  VkShaderModule              ShaderModule;
  char const                * EntryPointName;
  VkSpecializationInfo const * SpecializationInfo;
};
```

Graphics and Compute Pipelines

In the preceding structure, `ShaderStage` defines a single pipeline stage for which the rest of the parameters are specified. `ShaderModule` is a module from which a SPIR-V source code for the given stage can be taken, associated with a function whose name is provided in the `EntryPointName` member. The `SpecializationInfo` parameter is a pointer to a variable of type `VkSpecializationInfo`. It allows values of the constant variables defined in the shader source code to be modified at runtime, during pipeline creation. But if we don't want to specify constant values, we can provide a `nullptr` value.

How to do it...

1. Create a shader module or modules containing source code for each shader stage that will be active in a given pipeline (refer to the *Creating a shader module* recipe).
2. Create a `std::vector` variable named `shader_stage_create_infos` with elements of type `VkPipelineShaderStageCreateInfo`.
3. For each shader stage that should be enabled in a given pipeline, add an element to the `shader_stage_create_infos` vector and use the following values to initialize its members:
    - VK_STRUCTURE_TYPE_PIPELINE_SHADER_STAGE_CREATE_INFO value for `sType`
    - `nullptr` value for `pNext`
    - 0 value for `flags`
    - The selected shader stage for `stage`
    - The shader module with a source code of a given shader stage for `module`
    - The name of the function that implements the given shader in the shader module (usually `main`) for `pName`
    - A pointer to a variable of type `VkSpecializationInfo` with a constant value specialization or a `nullptr` value if no specialization is required for `pSpecializationInfo`

How it works...

Defining a set of shader stages that will be active in a given pipeline requires us to prepare an array (or a vector) variable with elements of type `VkPipelineShaderStageCreateInfo`. Each shader stage requires a separate entry in which we need to specify a shader module and the name of the entry point that implements the behavior of a given shader in the provided module. We can also provide a pointer to the specialization info which allows us to modify values of shader constant variables during the pipeline creation (at runtime). This allows us to use the same shader code multiple times with slight variations.

> Specifying pipeline shader stages info is obligatory for both graphics and compute pipelines.

Let's imagine we want to use only vertex and fragment shaders. We can prepare a vector with elements of a custom `ShaderStageParameters` type like this:

```
std::vector<ShaderStageParameters>shader_stage_params = {
  {
    VK_SHADER_STAGE_VERTEX_BIT,
    *vertex_shader_module,
    "main",
     nullptr
  },
  {
    VK_SHADER_STAGE_FRAGMENT_BIT,
    *fragment_shader_module,
    "main",
    nullptr
  }
};
```

The implementation of the preceding recipe, which uses the data from the aforementioned vector, may look like this:

```
shader_stage_create_infos.clear();
for( auto & shader_stage : shader_stage_params ) {
  shader_stage_create_infos.push_back( {
    VK_STRUCTURE_TYPE_PIPELINE_SHADER_STAGE_CREATE_INFO,
    nullptr,
    0,
    shader_stage.ShaderStage,
    shader_stage.ShaderModule,
    shader_stage.EntryPointName,
    shader_stage.SpecializationInfo
  } );
}
```

Each shader stage provided in the array must be unique.

See also

The following recipes in this chapter:

- *Creating a shader module*
- *Creating a graphics pipeline*
- *Creating a compute pipeline*

Specifying a pipeline vertex binding description, attribute description, and input state

When we want to draw a geometry, we prepare vertices along with their additional attributes like normal vectors, colors, or texture coordinates. Such vertex data is chosen arbitrarily by us, so for the hardware to properly use them, we need to specify how many attributes there are, how are they laid out in memory, or where are they taken from. This information is provided through the vertex binding description and attribute description required to create a graphics pipeline.

How to do it...

1. Create a `std::vector` variable named `binding_descriptions` with elements of type `VkVertexInputBindingDescription`.
2. Add a separate entry to the `binding_descriptions` vector for each vertex binding (part of a buffer bound to a command buffer as a vertex buffer) used in a given pipeline. Use the following values to initialize its members:
   - The index of a binding (number which it represents) for `binding`
   - The number of bytes between two consecutive elements in a buffer for `stride`
   - Parameters indicating whether values of attributes read from a given binding should advance per vertex (`VK_VERTEX_INPUT_RATE_VERTEX`) or per instance (`VK_VERTEX_INPUT_RATE_INSTANCE`) for `inputRate`
3. Create a `std::vector` variable named `attribute_descriptions` with elements of type `VkVertexInputAttributeDescription`.

4. Add a separate entry to the `attribute_descriptions` vector variable for each attribute provided to a vertex shader in a given graphics pipeline. Use the following values to initialize its members:
   - The shader location through which a given attribute is read in a vertex shader for `location`
   - The index of a binding to which a vertex buffer with the source of this attribute's data will be bound for `binding`
   - The format of an attribute's data for `format`
   - The memory offset from the beginning of a given element in the binding for `offset`

5. Create a variable of type `VkPipelineVertexInputStateCreateInfo` named `vertex_input_state_create_info`. Use the following values to initialize its members:
   - `VK_STRUCTURE_TYPE_PIPELINE_VERTEX_INPUT_STATE_CREATE_INFO` value for `sType`
   - `nullptr` value for `pNext`
   - `0` value for `flags`
   - The number of elements in the `binding_descriptions` vector for `vertexBindingDescriptionCount`
   - A pointer to the first element of the `binding_descriptions` vector for `pVertexBindingDescriptions`
   - The number of elements in the `attribute_descriptions` vector for `vertexAttributeDescriptionCount`
   - A pointer to the first element of the `attribute_descriptions` vector for `pVertexAttributeDescriptions`

How it works...

Vertex binding defines a collection of data taken from a vertex buffer bound to a selected index. This binding is used as a numbered source of data for vertex attributes. We can use at least 16 separate bindings to which we can bind separate vertex buffers or different parts of memory of the same buffer.

The vertex input state is obligatory for a graphics pipeline creation.

[378]

Through a binding description, we specify where the data is taken from (from which binding), how it is laid out (what is the stride between consecutive elements in the buffer), and how this data is read (whether it should be fetched per vertex or per instance).

As an example, when we want to use three attributes--three element vertex positions, two element texture coordinates, and three element color values, which are read per vertex from the 0th binding--we can use the following code:

```
std::vector<VkVertexInputBindingDescription> binding_descriptions = {
  {
    0,
    8 * sizeof( float ),
    VK_VERTEX_INPUT_RATE_VERTEX
  }
};
```

Through a vertex input description we define the attributes taken from a given binding. For each attribute we need to provide a shader location (the same as in the shader source code defined through a `layout( location = <number> )` qualifier), a format of the data used for a given attribute, and a memory offset at which the given attribute starts (relative to the beginning of the data for the given element). The number of input description entries specifies the total number of attributes used during rendering.

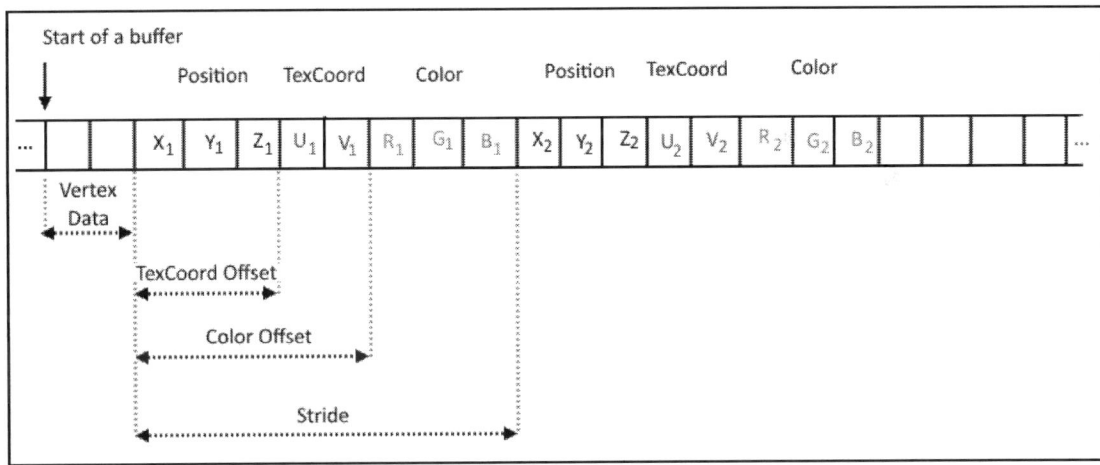

Graphics and Compute Pipelines

In the previous situation--with three component vertex positions, two component texture coordinates, and three component colors--we can use the following code to specify the vertex input description:

```
std::vector<VkVertexInputAttributeDescription> attribute_descriptions = {
    {
        0,
        0,
        VK_FORMAT_R32G32B32_SFLOAT,
        0
    },
    {
        1,
        0,
        VK_FORMAT_R32G32_SFLOAT,
        3 * sizeof( float )
    },
    {
        2,
        0,
        VK_FORMAT_R32G32B32_SFLOAT,
        5 * sizeof( float )
    }
};
```

All three attributes are taken from the 0th binding. Positions are provided to a vertex shader at the 0th location, texcoords through the first location, and color values through the second location. The position and color are three component vectors, and texcoords have two components. They all use floating-point signed values. The position is first, so it has no offset. The texture coordinate goes next, so it has an offset of three floating-point values. The color starts after the texture coordinate, so its offset is equal to five floating-point values.

The implementation of this recipe is provided in the following code:

```
vertex_input_state_create_info = {
    VK_STRUCTURE_TYPE_PIPELINE_VERTEX_INPUT_STATE_CREATE_INFO,
    nullptr,
    0,
    static_cast<uint32_t>(binding_descriptions.size()),
    binding_descriptions.data(),
    static_cast<uint32_t>(attribute_descriptions.size()),
    attribute_descriptions.data()
};
```

See also

- In Chapter 7, *Shaders*, see the recipe:
    - *Writing vertex shaders*
- In Chapter 9, *Command Recording and Drawing*, see the following recipe:
    - *Binding vertex buffers*
- The recipe *Creating a graphics pipeline* in this chapter

Specifying a pipeline input assembly state

Drawing geometry (3D models) involves specifying the type of primitives that are formed from provided vertices. This is done through an input assembly state.

How to do it...

1. Create a variable of type `VkPipelineInputAssemblyStateCreateInfo` named `input_assembly_state_create_info`. Use the following values to initialize its members:
    - `VK_STRUCTURE_TYPE_PIPELINE_INPUT_ASSEMBLY_STATE_CREATE_INFO` value for `sType`
    - `nullptr` value for `pNext`
    - `0` value for `flags`
    - The selected type of primitives to be formed from vertices (point list, line list, line strip, triangle list, triangle strip, triangle fan, line list with adjacency, line strip with adjacency, triangle list with adjacency, triangle strip with adjacency, or patch list) for `topology`
    - For the `primitiveRestartEnable` member, in cases of drawing commands that use vertex indices, specify whether a special index value should restart a primitive (`VK_TRUE`, can't be used for list primitives) or if a primitive restart should be disabled (`VK_FALSE`)

Graphics and Compute Pipelines

How it works...

Through an input assembly state, we define what types of polygons are formed from the drawn vertices. The most commonly used primitives are triangle strips or lists, but the used topology depends on the results we want to achieve.

 An input assembly state is required for the graphics pipeline creation.

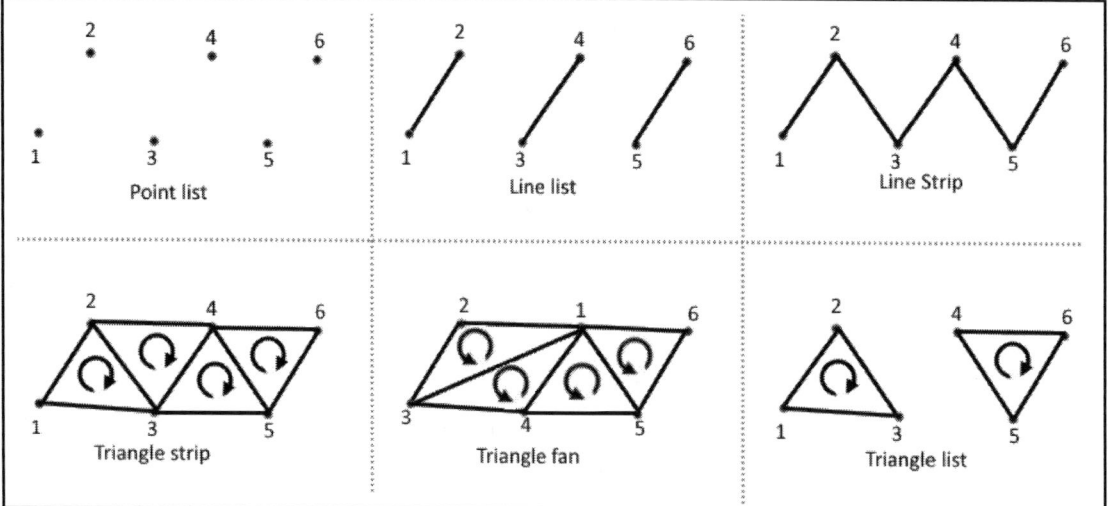

When selecting how vertices are assembled, we just need to bear in mind some requirements:

- We can't use list primitives with a primitive restart option.
- Primitives with adjacency can only be used with geometry shaders. For this to work correctly, a `geometryShader` feature must be enabled during the logical device creation.
- When we want to use tessellation shaders, we can only use patch primitives. In addition, we also need to remember that a `tessellationShader` feature must be enabled during the logical device creation.

Here is an example of a source code that initializes a variable of type
`VkPipelineInputAssemblyStateCreateInfo`:

```
input_assembly_state_create_info = {
    VK_STRUCTURE_TYPE_PIPELINE_INPUT_ASSEMBLY_STATE_CREATE_INFO,
    nullptr,
    0,
    topology,
    primitive_restart_enable
};
```

See also

- The following recipes in this chapter:
    - *Specifying pipeline rasterization state*
    - *Creating a graphics pipeline*

Specifying a pipeline tessellation state

Tessellation shaders are one of the optional, additional programmable shader stages that can be enabled in a graphics pipeline. But when we want to activate them, we also need to prepare a pipeline tessellation state.

How to do it...

1. Create a variable of type `VkPipelineTessellationStateCreateInfo` named `tessellation_state_create_info`. Use the following to initialize its members:
    - `VK_STRUCTURE_TYPE_PIPELINE_TESSELLATION_STATE_CREATE_INFO` value for `sType`
    - `nullptr` value for `pNext`
    - `0` value for `flags`
    - The number of control points (vertices) which form a patch for `patchControlPoints`

[383]

How it works...

To use tessellation shaders in our application, we need to enable a `tessellationShader` feature during a logical device creation, we need to write a source code for both tessellation control and evaluation shaders, we need to create a shader module (or two) for them, and we also need to prepare a pipeline tessellation state represented by a variable of type `VkPipelineTessellationStateCreateInfo`.

> The tessellation state is optional--we need to specify it only when we want to use tessellation shaders in a graphics pipeline.

In the tessellation state we only provide information about the number of control points (vertices) from which a patch is formed. The specification states that patches may have up to at least 32 vertices.

> The maximal supported number of control points (vertices) in a patch must be at least 32.

A patch is just a collection of points (vertices) that are used by the tessellation stages to generate typical points, lines, or polygons like triangles. It can be exactly the same as usual polygons. As an example, we can take vertices that form a triangle and draw them as patches. Results of such an operation are correct. But for the patch, we can use any other unusual order and number of vertices. This gives us much more flexibility in controlling the way new vertices are created by the tessellation engine.

To fill a variable of type `VkPipelineTessellationStateCreateInfo`, we can prepare the following code:

```
tessellation_state_create_info = {
  VK_STRUCTURE_TYPE_PIPELINE_TESSELLATION_STATE_CREATE_INFO,
  nullptr,
  0,
  patch_control_points_count
};
```

See also

- In Chapter 7, *Shaders*, see the following recipes:
    - *Writing tessellation control shaders*
    - *Writing tessellation evaluation shaders*
- The recipe *Creating a graphics pipeline* in this chapter

Specifying a pipeline viewport and scissor test state

Drawing an object on screen requires us to specify the screen parameters. Creating a swapchain is not enough--we don't always need to draw to the entire available image area. There are situations in which we just want to draw a smaller picture in the whole image, such as the reflection in the back mirror of a car or half of the image in split-screen multiplayer games. We define the area of the image to which we want to draw through a pipeline viewport and scissor test states.

Getting ready

Specifying parameters for a viewport and scissor states requires us to provide a separate set of parameters for both the viewport and scissor test, but the number of elements in both sets must be equal. To keep parameters for both states together, a custom `ViewportInfo` type is introduced in this recipe. It has the following definition:

```
struct ViewportInfo {
  std::vector<VkViewport>   Viewports;
  std::vector<VkRect2D>     Scissors;
};
```

The first member, as the name suggests, contains parameters for a set of viewports. The second is used to define the parameters for scissor tests corresponding to each viewport.

How to do it...

1. If rendering is to be performed to more than one viewport, create a logical device with the `multiViewport` feature enabled.

Graphics and Compute Pipelines

2. Create a variable of type `std::vector<VkViewport>` named `viewports`. Add a new element to the `viewports` vector for each viewport into which rendering will be done. Use the following values to initialize its members:
    - The position (in pixels) of the left side of the rendering area for `x`
    - The position (in pixels) of the top side of the rendering area for `y`
    - The width of the rendering area (in pixels) for `width`
    - The height of the rendering area (in pixels) for `height`
    - The value between `0.0` and `1.0` for the minimal depth of the viewport for `minDepth`
    - The value between `0.0` and `1.0` for the maximal depth of the viewport for `maxDepth`

3. Create a variable of type `std::vector<VkRect2D>` named `scissors`. Add a new element to the `scissors` vector variable for each viewport into which rendering will be done (the `scissors` vector must have the same number of elements as the `viewports` vector). Use the following values to initialize its members:
    - The position of the top left corner of the scissor rectangle for the `x` and `y` members of the `offset`
    - The width and height of the scissor rectangle for the `width` and `height` members of the `extent`

4. Create a variable of type `VkPipelineViewportStateCreateInfo` named `viewport_state_create_info`. Use the following values to initialize its members:
    - `VK_STRUCTURE_TYPE_PIPELINE_VIEWPORT_STATE_CREATE_INFO` value for `sType`
    - `nullptr` value for `pNext`
    - 0 value for `flags`
    - The number of elements in the `viewports` vector for `viewportCount`
    - A pointer to the first element of the `viewports` vector for `pViewports`
    - The number of elements in the `scissors` vector for `scissorCount`
    - A pointer to the first element of the `scissors` vector for `pScissors`

How it works...

Vertex positions are transformed (usually inside a vertex shader) from the local space into a clip space. The hardware then performs a perspective division which generates normalized device coordinates. Next, polygons are assembled and rasterized--this process generates fragments. Each fragment has its own position defined in a framebuffer's coordinates. Also, for this position to be correctly calculated, a viewport transformation is required. Parameters of this transformation are specified in a viewport state.

> The viewport and scissor test state is optional, though commonly used-- we don't need to provide it when rasterization is disabled.

Through a viewport state, we define the top-left corner and the width and height of the rendering area in a framebuffer's coordinates (pixels on screen). We also define the minimal and maximal viewport depth value (floating-point values between 0.0 and 1.0, inclusive). It is valid to specify the value of the maximal depth to be smaller than the value of the minimal depth.

A scissor test allows us to additionally clip the generated fragments to a rectangle specified in the scissor parameters. When we don't want to clip fragments, we need to specify an area equal to a viewport size.

> In Vulkan, the scissor test is always enabled.

The number of set of parameters for a viewport and scissor test must be equal. That's why it may be good to define a custom type with which we can keep the number of elements of both properties equal. The following is a sample code that specifies parameters for one viewport and one scissor test through a variable of a custom `ViewportInfo` type:

```
ViewportInfo viewport_infos = {
  {
    {
      0.0f,
      0.0f,
      512.0f,
      512.0f,
      0.0f,
      1.0f
    },
```

```
    },
    {
        {
            0,
            0
        },
        {
            512,
            512
        }
    }
};
```

The preceding variable can be used to create a viewport and scissor test as defined in this recipe. The implementation of the recipe may look like this:

```
uint32_t viewport_count =
static_cast<uint32_t>(viewport_infos.Viewports.size());
uint32_t scissor_count =
static_cast<uint32_t>(viewport_infos.Scissors.size());
viewport_state_create_info = {
  VK_STRUCTURE_TYPE_PIPELINE_VIEWPORT_STATE_CREATE_INFO,
  nullptr,
  0,
  viewport_count,
  viewport_infos.Viewports.data(),
  scissor_count,
  viewport_infos.Scissors.data()
};
```

If we want to change some of the viewport or scissor test parameters, we need to recreate a pipeline. But during the pipeline creation, we can specify that the viewport and scissor test parameters are dynamic. This way, we don't need to recreate a pipeline to change these parameters--we specify them during command buffer recording. But we need to remember that the number of viewports (and scissor tests) is always specified during the pipeline creation. We can't change it later.

It is possible to define a viewport and scissor test as dynamic states and specify their parameters during command buffer recording. The number of viewports (and scissor tests) is always specified during the graphics pipeline creation.

We also can't provide more than one viewport and scissor test, unless a `multiViewport` feature is enabled for a logical device. An index of a viewport transformation that will be used for rasterization can be changed only inside geometry shaders.

Changing the index of a viewport transformation used for rasterization requires us to use geometry shaders.

See also

- In `Chapter 1`, *Instances and Devices*, see the following recipes:
    - *Getting features and properties of a physical device*
    - *Creating a logical device*
- In `Chapter 7`, *Shaders*, see the recipe:
    - *Writing geometry shaders*
- The recipe *Creating a graphics pipeline*, in this chapter

Specifying a pipeline rasterization state

The rasterization process generates fragments (pixels) from the assembled polygons. The viewport state is used to specify where, in the framebuffer coordinates, fragments will be generated. To specify how (if at all) fragments are generated, we need to prepare a rasterization state.

Graphics and Compute Pipelines

How to do it...

1. Create a variable of type `VkPipelineRasterizationStateCreateInfo` named `rasterization_state_create_info`. Use the following values to initialize its members:
    - `VK_STRUCTURE_TYPE_PIPELINE_RASTERIZATION_STATE_CREATE_INFO` value for `sType`.
    - `nullptr` value for `pNext`.
    - 0 value for `flags`.
    - For `depthClampEnable` use a `true` value if a depth value for fragments whose depth is outside of the min/max range specified in a viewport state should be clamped within this range, or use a `false` value if fragments with depth outside of the this range should be clipped (discarded); when the `depthClampEnable` feature is not enabled only a `false` value can be specified.
    - For `rasterizerDiscardEnable` use a `false` value if fragments should be normally generated or `true` to disable rasterization.
    - For `polygonMode` specify how assembled polygons should be rendered--fully filled or if lines or points should be rendered (lines and points modes can only be used if a `fillModeNonSolid` feature is enabled).
    - The sides of the polygon--front, back, both or none--that should be culled for `cullMode`.
    - The side of the polygon--drawn on screen in clockwise or counterclockwise vertex order--that should be considered as a front side for `frontFace`.
    - For `depthBiasEnable` specify a `true` value if depth values calculated for fragments should be additionally offset or a `false` value if no such modification should be performed.
    - The constant value that should be added to a fragment's calculated depth value when depth bias is enabled for `depthBiasConstantFactor`.
    - The maximum (or minimum) value of a depth bias which can be added to a fragment's depth when depth bias is enabled for `depthBiasClamp`.
    - The value added to fragment's slope in depth bias calculations when depth bias is enabled for `depthBiasSlopeFactor`.

- The value specifying the width of rendered lines for `lineWidth`; if a `wideLines` feature is not enabled, only a `1.0` value can be specified; otherwise, values greater than `1.0` can also be provided.

How it works...

The rasterization state controls the parameters of a rasterization. First and foremost it defines if the rasterization is enabled or disabled. Through it we can specify which side of the polygon is the front--if it is the one in which vertices appear in a clockwise order on screen or if in a counterclockwise order. Next, we need to control if culling should be enabled for the front, back, both faces, or if it should be disabled. In OpenGL, by default, counterclockwise faces were considered front and culling was disabled. In Vulkan, there is no default state so how we define these parameters is up to us.

A rasterization state is always required during the graphics pipeline creation.

The rasterization state also controls the way polygons are drawn. Usually we want them to be fully rendered (filled). But we can specify if only their edges (lines) or points (vertices) should be drawn. Lines or points modes can only be used if the `fillModeNonSolid` feature is enabled during the logical device creation.

For the rasterization state, we also need to define how the depth value of generated fragments is calculated. We can enable depth bias--a process which offsets a generated depth value by a constant value and an additional slope factor. We also specify the maximal (or minimal) offset value that can be applied to the depth value when depth bias is enabled.

After that, we also need to define what to do with fragments whose depth value is outside the range specified in a viewport state. When the depth clamp is enabled, the depth value of such fragments is clamped to the defined range and the fragments are processed further. If the depth clamp is disabled, such fragments are discarded.

One last thing is to define the width of the rendered lines. Normally we can specify only a value of `1.0`. But if we enable the `wideLines` feature, we can provide values greater than `1.0`.

The rasterization state is defined through a variable of type `VkPipelineRasterizationStateCreateInfo`. A sample source code that fills such variable with values provided through other variables, is presented in the following code:

```
VkPipelineRasterizationStateCreateInfo rasterization_state_create_info = {
  VK_STRUCTURE_TYPE_PIPELINE_RASTERIZATION_STATE_CREATE_INFO,
  nullptr,
  0,
  depth_clamp_enable,
  rasterizer_discard_enable,
  polygon_mode,
  culling_mode,
  front_face,
  depth_bias_enable,
  depth_bias_constant_factor,
  depth_bias_clamp,
  depth_bias_slope_factor,
  line_width
};
```

See also

- The following recipes in this chapter:
    - *Specifying pipeline viewport and scissor test state*
    - *Creating a graphics pipeline*

Specifying a pipeline multisample state

Multisampling is a process that eliminates jagged edges of drawn primitives. In other words, it allows us to anti-alias polygons, lines and points. We define how multisampling is performed (and if at all) through a multisample state.

How to do it...

1. Create a variable of type `VkPipelineMultisampleStateCreateInfo` named `multisample_state_create_info`. Use the following values to initialize its members:
    - `VK_STRUCTURE_TYPE_PIPELINE_MULTISAMPLE_STATE_CREATE_INFO` value for `sType`

- `nullptr` value for `pNext`
- `0` value for `flags`
- The number of samples generated per pixel for `rasterizationSamples`
- A `true` value if per sample shading should be enabled (only if `sampleRateShading` feature is enabled) or `false` otherwise for `sampleShadingEnable`
- A minimum fraction of uniquely shaded samples, when sample shading is enabled, for `minSampleShading`
- A pointer to an array of bitmasks that controls a fragment's static coverage or a `nullptr` value to indicate that no coverage is removed from the fragments (all bits are enabled in the mask) for `pSampleMask`
- A `true` value if a fragment's coverage should be generated based on the fragment's alpha value or `false` otherwise for `alphaToCoverageEnable`
- A `true` value if an alpha component of the fragment's color should be replaced with a `1.0` value for floating-point formats or with a maximum available value of a given format for fixed-point formats (only when the `alphaToOne` feature is enabled) or `false` otherwise value for `alphaToOneEnable`

How it works...

The multisample state allows us to enable anti-aliasing of drawn primitives. Through it we can define the number of samples generated per fragment, enable per sample shading and specify the minimal number of uniquely shaded samples, and define a fragment's coverage parameters --the sample coverage mask, whether the coverage should be generated from an alpha component of the fragment's color. We can also specify if an alpha component should be replaced with a `1.0` value.

A multisample state is required only when rasterization is enabled.

To prepare a multisample state, we need to create a variable of a `VkPipelineMultisampleStateCreateInfo` **type like this:**

```
multisample_state_create_info = {
  VK_STRUCTURE_TYPE_PIPELINE_MULTISAMPLE_STATE_CREATE_INFO,
  nullptr,
  0,
  sample_count,
  per_sample_shading_enable,
  min_sample_shading,
  sample_masks,
  alpha_to_coverage_enable,
  alpha_to_one_enable
};
```

In the preceding code, the function's parameters are used to initialize members of a `multisample_state_create_info` variable.

See also

The following recipes in this chapter:

- *Specifying pipeline rasterization state*
- *Creating a graphics pipeline*

Specifying a pipeline depth and stencil state

Usually, when we render a geometry, we want to mimic the way we see the world--objects further away are smaller, objects closer to us are larger and they cover the objects behind them (obscure our view). In modern 3D graphics, this last effect (objects further away being obscured by objects being nearer) is achieved through a depth test. The way in which a depth test is performed, is specified through a depth and stencil state of a graphics pipeline.

How to do it...

1. Create a variable of type `VkPipelineDepthStencilStateCreateInfo` named `depth_and_stencil_state_create_info`. Use the following values to initialize its members:
    - `VK_STRUCTURE_TYPE_PIPELINE_DEPTH_STENCIL_STATE_CREATE_INFO` value for `sType`
    - `nullptr` value for `pNext`
    - `0` value for `flags`
    - A `true` value if we want to enable a depth test or otherwise `false` for `depthTestEnable`
    - A `true` value if we want to store the depth value in a depth buffer and otherwise `false` for `depthWriteEnable`
    - A chosen compare operator (`never`, `less`, `less and equal`, `equal`, `greater and equal`, `greater`, `not equal`, `always`) controlling how the depth test is performed for `depthCompareOp`
    - A `true` value if we want to enable additional depth bounds tests (only if `depthBounds` feature is enabled) or otherwise `false` for `depthBoundsTestEnable`
    - A `true` value if we want to use a stencil test or `false` if we want to disable it for `stencilTestEnable`
    - Use the following values to initialize members of a `front` field through which we set up stencil test parameters performed for front-facing polygons:
        - Function performed when samples fail the stencil test for `failOp`.
        - Action performed when samples pass the stencil test for `passOp`.
        - Action taken when samples pass the stencil test but fail the depth test for `depthFailOp`.
        - Operator (`never`, `less`, `less and equal`, `equal`, `greater and equal`, `greater`, `not equal`, `always`) used to perform the stencil test for `compareOp`.
        - Mask selecting the bits of stencil values that take part in the stencil test for `compareMask`.
        - Mask selecting which bits of a stencil value should be updated in a framebuffer for `writeMask`.

- Reference value used for stencil test comparison for `reference`.
- For `back` member setup stencil test parameters as described previously for front-facing polygons but, this time, for back-facing polygons.
- The value between `0.0` and `1.0` (inclusive) describing the minimal value of a depth bounds test for `minDepthBounds`.
- The value from `0.0` to `1.0` (inclusive) describing the maximal value of a depth bounds test for `maxDepthBounds`.

How it works...

The depth and stencil state specifies whether a depth and/or stencil test should be performed. If any of them are enabled, we also define parameters for each of these tests.

 A depth and stencil state is not required when rasterization is disabled or if a given subpass in a render pass does not use any depth/stencil attachments.

We need to specify how the depth test is performed (how depth values are compared) and if the depth value of a processed fragment should be written to a depth attachment when the fragment passes the test.

When the `depthBounds` feature is enabled, we can also activate an additional depth bounds test. This test checks whether the depth value of a processed fragment is inside a specified `minDepthBounds` - `maxDepthBounds` range. If it is not, the processed fragment is discarded as if it failed the depth test.

The stencil test allows us to perform additional tests on integer values associated with each fragment. It can be used for various purposes. As an example, we can define an exact part of the screen which can be updated during drawing, but, contrary to the scissor test, this area may have any shape, even if it is very complicated. Such an approach is used in deferred shading/lighting algorithms to restrict image areas that can be lit by a given light source. Another example of a stencil test is using it to show silhouettes of objects that are hidden behind other objects or highlighting objects selected by a mouse pointer.

In the case of an enabled stencil test, we need to define its parameters separately for front- and back-facing polygons. These parameters include actions performed when a given fragment fails the stencil test, passes it but fails the depth test, and passes both the stencil and depth test. For each situation, we define that current value in a stencil attachment should be kept intact, reset to 0, replaced with a reference value, incremented or decremented with clamping (saturation) or with wrapping, or if the current value should be inverted bitwise. We also specify how the test is performed by setting the comparison operator (similar to the operator defined in the depth test), comparison and write masks which select the stencil value's bits that should take part in the test or which should be updated in a stencil attachment, and a reference value.

The sample source code that prepares a variable of a `VkPipelineDepthStencilStateCreateInfo` type, through which the depth and stencil test is defined, is presented in the following code:

```
VkPipelineDepthStencilStateCreateInfo depth_and_stencil_state_create_info =
{
  VK_STRUCTURE_TYPE_PIPELINE_DEPTH_STENCIL_STATE_CREATE_INFO,
  nullptr,
  0,
  depth_test_enable,
  depth_write_enable,
  depth_compare_op,
  depth_bounds_test_enable,
  stencil_test_enable,
  front_stencil_test_parameters,
  back_stencil_test_parameters,
  min_depth_bounds,
  max_depth_bounds
};
```

See also

- In Chapter 6, *Render Passes and Framebuffers*, see the following recipes:
    - *Specifying subpass descriptions*
    - *Creating a framebuffer*
- The following recipes in this chapter:
    - *Specifying pipeline rasterization state*
    - *Creating a graphics pipeline*

Specifying a pipeline blend state

Transparent objects are very common in the environment we see every day around us. Such objects are also common in 3D applications. To simulate transparent materials and simplify operations that the hardware needs to perform to render transparent objects, blending was introduced. It mixes the color of a processed fragment with a color that is already stored in a framebuffer. Parameters for this operation are prepared through a graphics pipeline's blend state.

How to do it...

1. Create a variable of type `VkPipelineColorBlendAttachmentState` named `attachment_blend_states`.
2. For each color attachment used in a subpass in which a given graphics pipeline is bound, add a new element to the `attachment_blend_states` vector. If the `independentBlend` feature is not enabled, all elements added to the `attachment_blend_states` vector must be exactly the same. If this feature is enabled, elements may be different. Either way, use the following values to initialize members of each added element:
    - A `true` value whether blending should be enabled and otherwise `false` for `blendEnable`
    - The selected blend factor for the color of the processed (source) fragment for `srcColorBlendFactor`
    - The selected blend factor for the color already stored in an (destination) attachment for `dstColorBlendFactor`
    - The operator used to perform the blending operation on color components for `colorBlendOp`
    - The selected blend factor for the alpha value of an incoming (source) fragment for `srcAlphaBlendFactor`
    - The selected blend factor for the alpha value already stored in a destination attachment for `dstAlphaBlendFactor`
    - The function used to perform the blending operation on alpha components for `alphaBlendOp`
    - The color mask used to select which components should be written to in an attachment (no matter if blending is enabled or disabled) for `colorWriteMask`

3. Create a variable of type `VkPipelineColorBlendStateCreateInfo` named `blend_state_create_info`. Use these values to initialize its members:
    - `VK_STRUCTURE_TYPE_PIPELINE_COLOR_BLEND_STATE_CREATE_INFO` value for `sType`
    - `nullptr` value for `pNext`
    - 0 value for `flags`
    - A `true` value if a logical operation should be performed between a fragment's color and a color already stored in an attachment (which disables blending) or `false` otherwise for `logicOpEnable`.
    - The type of the logical operation to be performed (if logical operation is enabled) for `logicOp`
    - A number of elements in the `attachment_blend_states` vector for `attachmentCount`
    - A pointer to the first element of the `attachment_blend_states` vector for `pAttachments`
    - Four floating-point values defining red, green, blue, and alpha components of a blend constant used for some of the blending factors for `blendConstants[4]`

How it works...

The blending state is optional and is not required if rasterization is disabled or when there are no color attachments in a subpass, in which a given graphics pipeline is used.

The blending state is used mainly to define the parameters of a blending operation. But it also serves other purposes. In it we specify a color mask which selects which color components are updated (written to) during rendering. It also controls the state of a logical operation. When enabled, one of the specified logical operations is performed between a fragment's color and a color already written in a framebuffer.

A logical operation is performed only for attachments with integer and normalized integer formats.

Graphics and Compute Pipelines

Supported logical operations include:

- `CLEAR`: Setting the color to zero
- `AND`: Bitwise `AND` operation between the source (fragment's) color and a destination color (already stored in an attachment)
- `AND_REVERSE`: Bitwise `AND` operation between source and inverted destination colors
- `COPY`: Copying the source (fragment's) color without any modifications
- `AND_INVERTED`: Bitwise `AND` operation between destination and inverted source colors
- `NO_OP`: Leaving the already stored color intact
- `XOR`: Bitwise excluded `OR` between source and destination colors
- `OR`: Bitwise `OR` operation between the source and destination colors
- `NOR`: Inverted bitwise `OR`
- `EQUIVALENT`: Inverted `XOR`
- `INVERT`: Inverted destination color
- `OR_REVERSE`: Bitwise `OR` between the source color and inverted destination color
- `COPY_INVERTED`: Copying bitwise inverted source color
- `OR_INVERTED`: Bitwise `OR` operation between destination and inverted source color
- `NAND`: Inverted bitwise `AND` operation
- `SET`: Setting all color bits to ones

Blending is controlled separately for each color attachment used during rendering in a subpass in which a given graphics pipeline is bound. This means that we need to specify blending parameters for each color attachment used in rendering. But we need to remember that if the `independentBlend` feature is not enabled, blending parameters for each attachment must be exactly the same.

For blending, we specify the source and destination factors separately for color components and an alpha component. Supported blend factors include:

- `ZERO`: 0
- `ONE`: 1
- `SRC_COLOR`: `<source component>`
- `ONE_MINUS_SRC_COLOR`: 1 - `<source component>`
- `DST_COLOR`: `<destination component>`

- `ONE_MINUS_DST_COLOR`: 1 - <destination component>
- `SRC_ALPHA`: <source alpha>
- `ONE_MINUS_SRC_ALPHA`: 1 - <source alpha>
- `DST_ALPHA`: <destination alpha>
- `ONE_MINUS_DST_ALPHA`: 1 - <destination alpha>
- `CONSTANT_COLOR`: <constant color component>
- `ONE_MINUS_CONSTANT_COLOR`: 1 - <constant color component>
- `CONSTANT_ALPHA`: <alpha value of a constant color>
- `ONE_MINUS_CONSTANT_ALPHA`: 1 - <alpha value of a constant color>
- `SRC_ALPHA_SATURATE`: min(<source alpha>, 1 - <destination alpha>)
- `SRC1_COLOR`: <component of a source's second color> (used in dual source blending)
- `ONE_MINUS_SRC1_COLOR`: 1 - <component of a source's second color> (from dual source blending)
- `SRC1_ALPHA`: <alpha component of a source's second color> (in dual source blending)
- `ONE_MINUS_SRC1_ALPHA`: 1 - <alpha component of a source's second color> (from dual source blending)

Some of the blending factors use constant color instead of a fragment's (source) color or color already stored in an attachment (destination). This constant color may be specified statically during the pipeline creation or dynamically (as one of the dynamic pipeline states) by the `vkCmdSetBlendConstants()` function call during command buffer recording.

Blending factors that use the source's second color (SRC1) may be used only when the `dualSrcBlend` feature is enabled.

The blending function that controls how blending is performed is also specified separately for color and alpha components. Blending operators include:

- ADD: <src component> * <src factor> + <dst component> * <dst factor>
- SUBTRACT: <src component> * <src factor> - <dst component> * <dst factor>

Graphics and Compute Pipelines

- REVERSE_SUBTRACT: `<dst component> * <dst factor> - <src component> * <src factor>`
- MIN: `min( <src component>, <dst component> )`
- MAX: `max( <src component>, <dst component> )`

Enabling a logical operation disables blending.

The following is an example of setting up a blend state with both disabled logical operation and blending:

```
std::vector<VkPipelineColorBlendAttachmentState> attachment_blend_states =
{
  {
    false,
    VK_BLEND_FACTOR_ONE,
    VK_BLEND_FACTOR_ONE,
    VK_BLEND_OP_ADD,
    VK_BLEND_FACTOR_ONE,
    VK_BLEND_FACTOR_ONE,
    VK_BLEND_OP_ADD,
    VK_COLOR_COMPONENT_R_BIT |
    VK_COLOR_COMPONENT_G_BIT |
    VK_COLOR_COMPONENT_B_BIT |
    VK_COLOR_COMPONENT_A_BIT
  }
};
VkPipelineColorBlendStateCreateInfo blend_state_create_info;
SpecifyPipelineBlendState( false, VK_LOGIC_OP_COPY,
attachment_blend_states, { 1.0f, 1.0f, 1.0f, 1.0f },
blend_state_create_info );
```

The implementation of this recipe that fills a variable of the `VkPipelineColorBlendStateCreateInfo` type may look like this:

```
blend_state_create_info = {
  VK_STRUCTURE_TYPE_PIPELINE_COLOR_BLEND_STATE_CREATE_INFO,
  nullptr,
  0,
  logic_op_enable,
  logic_op,
  static_cast<uint32_t>(attachment_blend_states.size()),
  attachment_blend_states.data(),
  {
```

```
      blend_constants[0],
      blend_constants[1],
      blend_constants[2],
      blend_constants[3]
   }
};
```

See also

- In `Chapter` 6, *Render Passes and Framebuffers*, see the following recipes:
    - *Specifying subpass descriptions*
    - *Creating a framebuffer*
- In `Chapter` 9, *Command Recording and Drawing*, see the following recipe
    - *Setting blend constants states dynamically*
- The following recipes in this chapter:
    - *Specifying pipeline rasterization state*
    - *Creating a graphics pipeline*

Specifying pipeline dynamic states

Creating a graphics pipeline requires us to provide lots of parameters. What's more, once set, these parameters can't be changed. Such an approach was taken to improve the performance of our application and present a stable and predictable environment to the driver. But, unfortunately, it is also uncomfortable for developers as they may need to create many pipeline objects with almost identical states that differ only in small details.

To circumvent this problem, dynamic states were introduced. They allow us to control some of the pipeline's parameters dynamically by recording specific functions in command buffers. And in order to do that, we need to specify which parts of the pipeline are dynamic. This is done by specifying pipeline dynamic states.

How to do it...

1. Create a variable of type `std::vector<VkDynamicState>` named `dynamic_states`. For each (unique) pipeline state that should be set dynamically, add a new element to the `dynamic_states` vector. The following values can be used:
    - `VK_DYNAMIC_STATE_VIEWPORT`
    - `VK_DYNAMIC_STATE_SCISSOR`
    - `VK_DYNAMIC_STATE_LINE_WIDTH`
    - `VK_DYNAMIC_STATE_DEPTH_BIAS`
    - `VK_DYNAMIC_STATE_BLEND_CONSTANTS`
    - `VK_DYNAMIC_STATE_DEPTH_BOUNDS`
    - `VK_DYNAMIC_STATE_STENCIL_COMPARE_MASK`
    - `VK_DYNAMIC_STATE_STENCIL_WRITE_MASK`
    - `VK_DYNAMIC_STATE_STENCIL_REFERENCE`

2. Create a variable of type `VkPipelineDynamicStateCreateInfo` named `dynamic_state_creat_info`. Use the following values to initialize its members:
    - `VK_STRUCTURE_TYPE_PIPELINE_DYNAMIC_STATE_CREATE_INFO` value for `sType`
    - `nullptr` value for `pNext`
    - 0 value for `flags`
    - The number of elements in the `dynamic_states` vector for `dynamicStateCount`
    - A pointer to the first element of the `dynamic_states` vector for `pDynamicStates`

How it works...

Dynamic pipeline states were introduced to allow for some flexibility in setting the state of pipeline objects. There may not be too many different parts of the pipeline that can be set during command buffer recording, but the selection is a compromise between the performance, the simplicity of a driver, the capabilities of modern hardware, and the API's ease of use.

A dynamic state is optional. If we don't want to set any part of the pipeline dynamically, we don't need to do it.

The following parts of the graphics pipeline can be set dynamically:

- **Viewport**: Parameters for all viewports are set through the vkCmdSetViewport() function call, but the number of viewports is still defined during the pipeline creation (refer to the *Specifying pipeline viewport and scissor test state* recipe)
- **Scissor**: Parameters controlling the scissor test are set through the vkCmdSetScissor() function call, though the number of rectangles used for the scissor test are defined statically during the pipeline creation and must be the same as the number of viewports (refer to the *Specifying pipeline viewport and scissor test state* recipe)
- **Line width**: The width of drawn lines is specified not in a graphics pipeline's state but through the vkCmdSetLineWidth() function (refer to the *Specifying pipeline rasterization state* recipe)
- **Depth bias**: When enabled, the depth bias constant factor, slope factor, and maximum (or minimum) bias applied to a fragment's calculated depth value are defined through recording the vkCmdSetDepthBias() function (refer to the *Specifying pipeline depth and stencil state* recipe)
- **Depth bounds**: When the depth bounds test is enabled, minimum and maximum values used during the test are specified with the vkCmdSetDepthBounds() function (refer to the *Specifying pipeline depth and stencil state* recipe)
- **Stencil compare mask**: Specific bits of stencil values used during the stencil test are defined with the vkCmdSetStencilCompareMask() function call (refer to the *Specifying pipeline depth and stencil state* recipe)
- **Stencil write mask**: Specifying which bits may be updated in a stencil attachment is done through the vkCmdSetStencilWriteMask() function (refer to the *Specifying pipeline depth and stencil state* recipe)

- **Stencil reference value**: Setting the reference value used during the stencil test is performed with the vkCmdSetStencilReference() function call (refer to the *Specifying pipeline depth and stencil state* recipe)
- **Blend constants**: Four floating-point values for red, green, blue, and alpha components of a blend constant are specified by recording a vkCmdSetBlendConstants() function (refer to the *Specifying pipeline blend state* recipe)

Specifying that a given state is set dynamically is done by creating an array (or a vector) of VkDynamicState enums with values corresponding to the chosen states and providing the array (named dynamic_states in the following code) to the variable of a VkPipelineDynamicStateCreateInfo type like this:

```
VkPipelineDynamicStateCreateInfo dynamic_state_creat_info = {
  VK_STRUCTURE_TYPE_PIPELINE_DYNAMIC_STATE_CREATE_INFO,
  nullptr,
  0,
  static_cast<uint32_t>(dynamic_states.size()),
dynamic_states.data()
};
```

See also

- The following recipes in this chapter:
    - *Specifying pipeline viewport and scissor test state*
    - *Specifying pipeline rasterization state*
    - *Specifying pipeline depth and stencil state*
    - *Specifying pipeline blend state*
    - *Creating a graphics pipeline*
- In Chapter 9, *Command Recording and Drawing*, see the following recipes:
    - *Setting viewport state dynamically*
    - *Setting scissors state dynamically*
    - *Setting depth bias state dynamically*
    - *Setting blend constants state dynamically*

Creating a pipeline layout

Pipeline layouts are similar to descriptor set layouts. Descriptor set layouts are used to define what types of resources form a given descriptor set. Pipeline layouts define what types of resources can be accessed by a given pipeline. They are created from descriptor set layouts and, additionally, push constant ranges.

Pipeline layouts are needed for the pipeline creation as they specify the interface between shader stages and shader resources through a set, binding, array element address. The same address needs to be used in shaders (through a layout qualifier) so they can successfully access a given resource. But even if a given pipeline doesn't use any descriptor resources, we need to create a pipeline layout to inform the driver that no such interface is needed.

How to do it...

1. Take the handle of a logical device stored in a variable of type `VkDevice` named `logical_device`.
2. Create a `std::vector` variable named `descriptor_set_layouts` with elements of type `VkDescriptorSetLayout`. For each descriptor set, through which resources will be accessed from shaders in a given pipeline, add a descriptor set layout to the `descriptor_set_layouts` vector.
3. Create a `std::vector<VkPushConstantRange>` variable named `push_constant_ranges`. Add new elements to this vector for each separate range (a unique set of push constants used by different shader stages) and use the following values to initialize its members:
    - A logical OR of all shader stages that access a given push constant for `stageFlags`
    - The value that is a multiple of 4 for the offset at which a given push constant starts in memory for `offset`
    - The value that is a multiple of 4 for the size of a memory for a given push constant for `size`

4. Create a variable of type `VkPipelineLayoutCreateInfo` named `pipeline_layout_create_info`. Use the following values to initialize its members:
    - `VK_STRUCTURE_TYPE_PIPELINE_LAYOUT_CREATE_INFO` value for `sType`
    - `nullptr` value for `pNext`
    - `0` value for `flags`
    - The number of elements in the `descriptor_set_layouts` vector for `setLayoutCount`
    - A pointer to the first element of the `descriptor_set_layouts` vector for `pSetLayouts`
    - The number of elements in the `push_constant_ranges` vector for `pushConstantRangeCount`
    - A pointer to the first element of the `push_constant_ranges` for `pPushConstantRanges`
5. Create a variable of type `VkPipelineLayout` named `pipeline_layout`, in which the handle of the created pipeline layout will be stored.
6. Make the following call: `vkCreatePipelineLayout( logical_device, &pipeline_layout_create_info, nullptr, &pipeline_layout )` for which provide the `logical_device` variable, a pointer to the `pipeline_layout_create_info` variable, a `nullptr` value, and a pointer to the `pipeline_layout` variable.
7. Make sure the call was successful by checking if it returned the `VK_SUCCESS` value.

How it works...

A pipeline layout defines the set of resources that can be accessed from shaders of a given pipeline. When we record command buffers, we bind descriptor sets to selected indices (refer to the *Binding descriptor sets* recipe). This index corresponds to a descriptor set layout at the same index in the array used during the pipeline layout creation (the `descriptor_set_layouts` vector from this recipe). The same index needs to be specified inside shaders through a `layout( set = <index>, binding = <number> )` qualifier for the given resource to be properly accessed.

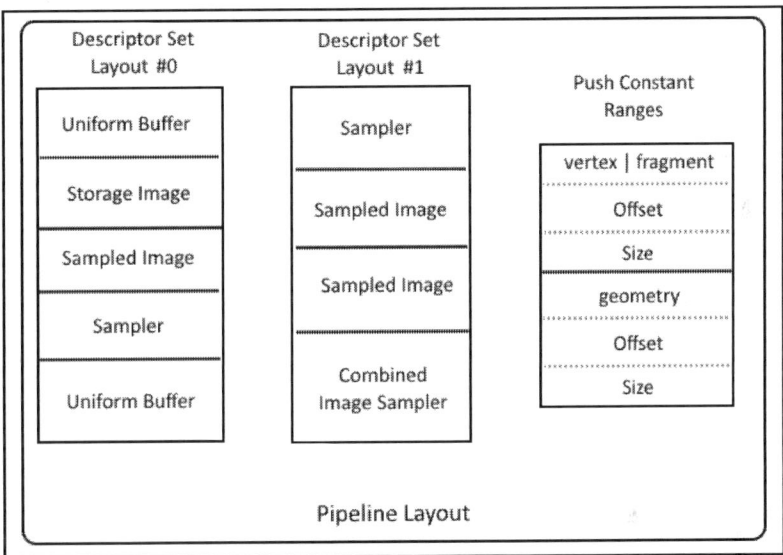

Usually, multiple pipelines will access different resources. During command buffer recording, we bind a given pipeline and descriptor sets. Only after that can we issue drawing commands. When we switch from one pipeline to another, we need to bind new descriptor sets according to the pipeline's needs. But frequently binding different descriptor sets may impact the performance of our application. That's why it is good to create pipelines with similar (or compatible) layouts and bind descriptor sets that do not change too often (that are common for many pipelines) to indices near the 0 (or near the start of a layout). This way, when we switch pipelines, descriptor sets near the start of the pipeline layout (from index 0 to some index N) can still be used and don't need to be updated. It is only necessary to bind the different descriptor sets--those that are placed at greater indices (after the given index N). But one additional condition must be met-- to be similar (or compatible), the pipeline layouts must use the same push constant ranges.

Graphics and Compute Pipelines

We should bind descriptor sets that are common for many pipelines near the start of a pipeline layout (near the 0th index).

Pipeline layouts also define the ranges of push constants. They allow us to provide a small set of constant values to shaders. They are much faster than updating descriptor sets, but memory that can be consumed by push constants is also much smaller--it is at least 128 bytes for all ranges defined in a pipeline layout. Different hardware may offer more memory for push constants, but we can't rely on it if we target hardware from various vendors.

As an example, when we want to define a different range for each stage in a graphics pipeline, we have more or less 128 / 5 = 26 bytes per stage for a push constant. Of course, we can define ranges that are common for multiple shader stages. But each shader stage may have access to only one push constant range.

The preceding example is the worst case. Usually not all stages will use different push constant ranges. Quite commonly, stages won't require access to a push constant range at all. So there should be enough memory for several 4-component vectors or a matrix or two.

Each pipeline stage can access only one push constant range.

We also need to remember that the size and an offset of a push constant range must be a multiple of 4.

In the following code, we can see a source code that implements this recipe. Descriptor set layouts and ranges of push constants are provided through `descriptor_set_layouts` and `push_constant_ranges` variables, respectively:

```
VkPipelineLayoutCreateInfo pipeline_layout_create_info = {
  VK_STRUCTURE_TYPE_PIPELINE_LAYOUT_CREATE_INFO,
  nullptr,
  0,
  static_cast<uint32_t>(descriptor_set_layouts.size()),
  descriptor_set_layouts.data(),
  static_cast<uint32_t>(push_constant_ranges.size()),
  push_constant_ranges.data()
};

VkResult result = vkCreatePipelineLayout( logical_device,
  &pipeline_layout_create_info, nullptr, &pipeline_layout );
```

```
if( VK_SUCCESS != result ) {
  std::cout << "Could not create pipeline layout." << std::endl;
  return false;
}
return true;
```

See also

- In `Chapter 5`, *Descriptor Sets*, see the following recipe:
    - *Binding descriptor sets*
- In `Chapter 7`, *Shaders*, see the following recipes:
    - *Writing a vertex shader that multiplies vertex position by a projection matrix*
    - *Using push constants in shaders*
- The following recipes in this chapter:
    - *Creating a graphics pipeline*
    - *Creating a compute pipeline*
    - *Creating a pipeline layout with push constants, sampled image, and a buffer*
    - *Destroying a pipeline layout*
- In `Chapter 9`, *Command Recording and Drawing*, see the following recipe:
    - *Providing data to shaders through push constants*

Specifying graphics pipeline creation parameters

Creating a graphics pipeline requires us to prepare many parameters controlling its many different aspects. All these parameters are grouped into a variable of type `VkGraphicsPipelineCreateInfo` which needs to be properly initialized before we can use it to create a pipeline.

How to do it...

1. Create a variable of a bitfield type `VkPipelineCreateFlags` named `additional_options` through which provide additional pipeline creation options:
    - **Disable optimization**: specifies that the created pipeline won't be optimized, but the creation process may be faster
    - **Allow derivatives**: specifies that other pipelines may be created from it
    - **Derivative**: specifies that this pipeline will be created based on another, already created pipeline
2. Create a variable of type `std::vector<VkPipelineShaderStageCreateInfo>` named `shader_stage_create_infos`. For each shader stage enabled in a given pipeline, add a new element to the `shader_stage_create_infos` vector, specifying the stage's parameters. At least the vertex shader stage must be present in the `shader_stage_create_infos` vector (refer to the *Specifying pipeline shader stages* recipe).
3. Create a variable of type `VkPipelineVertexInputStateCreateInfo` named `vertex_input_state_create_info` through which vertex bindings, attributes, and input state are specified (refer to the *Specifying pipeline vertex binding description, attribute description, and input state* recipe).
4. Create a variable of type `VkPipelineInputAssemblyStateCreateInfo` named `input_assembly_state_create_info`. Use it to define how drawn vertices are assembled into polygons (refer to the *Specifying pipeline input assembly state* recipe).
5. If a tessellation should be enabled in a given pipeline, create a variable of type `VkPipelineTessellationStateCreateInfo` named `tessellation_state_create_info` in which the number of control points forming a patch is defined (refer to the *Specifying pipeline tessellation state* recipe).
6. If a rasterization process won't be disabled in a given pipeline, create a variable of type `VkPipelineViewportStateCreateInfo` named `viewport_state_create_info`. In the variable, specify viewport and scissor test parameters (refer to the *Specifying pipeline viewport and scissor test state* recipe).
7. Create a variable of type `VkPipelineRasterizationStateCreateInfo` named `rasterization_state_create_info` that defines the properties of a rasterization (refer to the *Specifying pipeline rasterization state* recipe).

8. If rasterization is enabled in a given pipeline, create a variable of type `VkPipelineMultisampleStateCreateInfo` named `multisample_state_create_info` that defines multisampling (anti-aliasing) parameters (refer to the *Specifying pipeline multisample state* recipe).
9. If rasterization is active and depth and/or stencil attachments are used during drawing with a given pipeline bound, create a variable of type `VkPipelineDepthStencilStateCreateInfo` named `depth_and_stencil_state_create_info`. Use it to define parameters of depth and stencil tests (refer to the *Specifying pipeline depth and stencil state* recipe).
10. If rasterization is not disabled, create a variable of type `VkPipelineColorBlendStateCreateInfo` named `blend_state_create_info` through which to specify parameters of operations performed on fragments (refer to the *Specifying pipeline blend state* recipe).
11. If there are parts of the pipeline which should be set dynamically, create a variable of type `VkPipelineDynamicStateCreateInfo` named `dynamic_state_creat_info` that defines those dynamically set parts (refer to the *Specifying pipeline dynamic states* recipe).
12. Create a pipeline layout and store its handle in a variable of type `VkPipelineLayout` named `pipeline_layout`.
13. Take the handle of a render pass in which drawing with a given pipeline bound will be performed. Use the render pass handle to initialize a variable of type `VkRenderPass` named `render_pass` (refer to the *Creating a render pass* recipe from Chapter 6, *Render Passes and Framebuffers*).
14. Create a variable of type `uint32_t` named `subpass`. Store the index of the render pass's subpass in which a given pipeline will be used during drawing operations (refer to the *Specifying subpass descriptions* recipe from Chapter 6, *Render Passes and Framebuffers*).
15. Create a variable of type `VkGraphicsPipelineCreateInfo` named `graphics_pipeline_create_info`. Use the following values to initialize its members:
    - `VK_STRUCTURE_TYPE_GRAPHICS_PIPELINE_CREATE_INFO` value for `sType`
    - `nullptr` value for `pNext`
    - `additional_options` variable for `flags`
    - The number of elements in the `shader_stage_create_infos` vector for `stageCount`

- A pointer to the first element of the `shader_stage_create_infos` vector for `pStages`
- A pointer to the `vertex_input_state_create_info` variable for `pVertexInputState`
- A pointer to the `input_assembly_state_create_info` variable for `pInputAssemblyState`
- A pointer to the `tessellation_state_create_info` variable if tessellation should be active or a `nullptr` value if tessellation should be disabled for `pTessellationState`
- A pointer to the `viewport_state_create_info` variable if rasterization is active or a `nullptr` value if rasterization is disabled for `pViewportState`
- A pointer to the `rasterization_state_create_info` variable for `pRasterizationState`
- A pointer to the `multisample_state_create_info` variable if rasterization is enabled and a `nullptr` value otherwise for `pMultisampleState`
- A pointer to the `depth_and_stencil_state_create_info` variable if rasterization is enabled and there is a depth and/or stencil attachment used in the `subpass` or a `nullptr` value otherwise for `pDepthStencilState`
- A pointer to the `blend_state_create_info` variable if rasterization is enabled and there is a color attachment used in the `subpass` or a `nullptr` value otherwise for `pColorBlendState`
- A pointer to the `dynamic_state_creat_info` variable if there are parts of the pipeline that should be setup dynamically, or a `nullptr` value if the whole pipeline is prepared statically for `pDynamicState`
- The `pipeline_layout` variable for `layout`
- The `render_pass` variable for `renderPass`
- The `subpass` variable for `subpass`
- If the pipeline should derive from another, already created pipeline, provide the handle of the parent pipeline, otherwise provide a `VK_NULL_HANDLE` for `basePipelineHandle`
- If a pipeline should derive from another pipeline that is created within the same batch of pipelines, provide the index of a parent pipeline, otherwise provide a `-1` value for `basePipelineIndex`

How it works...

Preparing data for a graphics pipeline creation is performed in multiple steps and each step specifies different parts of a graphics pipeline. All of these parameters are gathered in a variable of type `VkGraphicsPipelineCreateInfo`.

During the pipeline creation, we can provide many parameters of type `VkGraphicsPipelineCreateInfo`, each one specifying attributes of a single pipeline that will be created.

When a graphics pipeline is created, we can use it for drawing by binding it to the command buffer before recording a drawing command. Graphics pipelines can be bound to command buffers only inside render passes (after the beginning of a render pass is recorded). During the pipeline creation, we specify inside which render pass a given pipeline will be used. However, we are not limited only to the provided render pass. We can also use the same pipeline with other render passes if they are compatible with the specified one (refer to the Creating a render pass recipe from `Chapter 6`, *Render Passes and Framebuffers*).

It is a rare situation when each created pipeline doesn't have any common state with other pipelines. That's why, to speed up the pipeline creation, it is possible to specify that a pipeline can be a parent of other pipelines (allow derivatives) or that the pipeline will be a child of (derived from) another pipeline. To use this feature and shorten the time needed to create a pipeline, we can use `basePipelineHandle` or `basePipelineIndex` members of variables of type `VkGraphicsPipelineCreateInfo` (the `graphics_pipeline_create_info` variable in this recipe).

The `basePipelineHandle` member allows us to specify a handle of an already created pipeline, which should be a parent of the newly created one.

The `basePipelineIndex` member is used when we create multiple pipelines at once. Through it we specify an index into the array with elements of type `VkGraphicsPipelineCreateInfo` provided to the `vkCreateGraphicsPipelines()` function. This index points to a parent pipeline that will be created along with the child pipeline in the same, single function call. As they are created together, we can't provide a handle, that's why there is a separate field for an index. One requirement is that the index of a parent pipeline must be smaller than the index of a child pipeline (it must appear earlier in the list of `VkGraphicsPipelineCreateInfo` elements, before the element that describes the derived pipeline).

Graphics and Compute Pipelines

We can't use both `basePipelineHandle` and `basePipelineIndex` members; we can provide value only for one of them. If we want to specify a handle, we must provide a -1 value for the `basePipelineIndex` field. If we want to specify an index, we need to provide a `VK_NULL_HANDLE` value for the `basePipelineHandle` member.

The rest of the parameters are described in earlier recipes of this chapter. The following is an example of how to use them to initialize the members of the variable of type `VkGraphicsPipelineCreateInfo`:

```
VkGraphicsPipelineCreateInfo graphics_pipeline_create_info = {
  VK_STRUCTURE_TYPE_GRAPHICS_PIPELINE_CREATE_INFO,
  nullptr,
  additional_options,
  static_cast<uint32_t>(shader_stage_create_infos.size()),
  shader_stage_create_infos.data(),
  &vertex_input_state_create_info,
  &input_assembly_state_create_info,
  &tessellation_state_create_info,
  &viewport_state_create_info,
  &rasterization_state_create_info,
  &multisample_state_create_info,
  &depth_and_stencil_state_create_info,
  &blend_state_create_info,
  &dynamic_state_creat_info,
  pipeline_layout,
  render_pass,
  subpass,
  base_pipeline_handle,
  base_pipeline_index
};
```

See also

The following recipes in this chapter:

- *Specifying pipeline shader stages*
- *Specifying pipeline vertex binding description, attribute description, and input state*
- *Specifying pipeline input assembly state*
- *Specifying pipeline tessellation state*
- *Specifying pipeline viewport and scissor test state*
- *Specifying pipeline rasterization state*

- *Specifying pipeline multisample state*
- *Specifying pipeline depth and stencil state*
- *Specifying pipeline blend state*
- *Specifying pipeline dynamic states*
- *Creating a pipeline layout*

Creating a pipeline cache object

Creating a pipeline object is a complicated and time-consuming process from the driver's perspective. A pipeline object is not a simple wrapper for parameters set during the creation. It involves preparing the states of all programmable and fixed pipeline stages, setting an interface between shaders and descriptor resources, compiling and linking shader programs, and performing error checking (that is, checking if shaders are linked properly). Results of these operations may be stored in a cache. This cache can then be reused to speed up the creation of pipeline objects with similar properties. To be able to use a pipeline cache object, we first need to create it.

How to do it...

1. Take the handle of a logical device and store it in a variable of type `VkDevice` named `logical_device`.
2. If available (that is, retrieved from other caches), prepare data to initialize a newly created cache object. Store the data in a variable of type `std::vector<unsigned char>` named `cache_data`.
3. Create a variable of type `VkPipelineCacheCreateInfo` named `pipeline_cache_create_info`. Use the following values to initialize its members:
   - VK_STRUCTURE_TYPE_PIPELINE_CACHE_CREATE_INFO value for `sType`.
   - `nullptr` value for `pNext`.
   - 0 value for `flags`.
   - The number of elements in the `cache_data` vector (size of the initialization data in bytes) for `initialDataSize`.
   - A pointer to the first element of the `cache_data` vector for `pInitialData`.

[417]

Graphics and Compute Pipelines

4. Create a variable of type `VkPipelineCache` named `pipeline_cache` in which the handle of the created cache object will be stored.
5. Make the following function call: `vkCreatePipelineCache( logical_device, &pipeline_cache_create_info, nullptr, &pipeline_cache )`. For the call, provide the `logical_device` variable, a pointer to the `pipeline_cache_create_info` variable, a `nullptr` value, and a pointer to the `pipeline_cache` variable.
6. Make sure the call was successful by checking if it returned a `VK_SUCCESS` value.

How it works...

A pipeline cache, as the name suggests, stores the results of a pipeline preparation process. It is optional and can be omitted, but when used, can significantly speed up the creation of pipeline objects.

To use a cache during the pipeline creation, we just need to create a cache object and provide it to the pipeline creating function. The driver automatically caches the results in the provided object. Also, if the cache contains any data, the driver automatically tries to use it for the pipeline creation.

The most common scenario of using a pipeline cache object, is to store its contents in a file and reuse them between separate executions of the same application. The first time we run our application, we create an empty cache and all the pipelines we need. Next, we retrieve the cache data and save it to a file. Next time the application is executed, we also create the cache, but this time we initialize it with the contents read from a previously created file. From now on, each time we run our application, the process of creating pipelines should be much shorter. Of course, when we create only small number of pipelines, we probably won't notice any improvement. But modern 3D applications, especially games, may have tens, hundreds, or sometimes even thousands of different pipelines (due to shader variations). In such situations, the cache can significantly boost the process of creating all of them.

Let's assume the cache data is stored in a vector variable named `cache_data`. It may be empty or initialized with contents retrieved from previous pipeline creations. The process of creating a pipeline cache that uses this data is presented in the following code:

```
VkPipelineCacheCreateInfo pipeline_cache_create_info = {
  VK_STRUCTURE_TYPE_PIPELINE_CACHE_CREATE_INFO,
  nullptr,
  0,
  static_cast<uint32_t>(cache_data.size()),
```

```
    cache_data.data()
};

VkResult result = vkCreatePipelineCache( logical_device,
&pipeline_cache_create_info, nullptr, &pipeline_cache );
if( VK_SUCCESS != result ) {
   std::cout << "Could not create pipeline cache." << std::endl;
   return false;
}
return true;
```

See also

The following recipes in this chapter:

- *Retrieving data from a pipeline cache*
- *Merging multiple pipeline cache objects*
- *Creating a graphics pipeline*
- *Creating a compute pipeline*
- *Creating multiple graphics pipelines on multiple threads*
- *Destroying a pipeline cache*

Retrieving data from a pipeline cache

A cache allows us to improve the performance of creating multiple pipeline objects. But for us to be able to use the cache each time we execute our application, we need a way to store the contents of the cache and reuse it any time we want. To do that, we can retrieve the data gathered in a cache.

How to do it...

1. Take the handle of a logical device and use it to initialize a variable of type `VkDevice` named `logical_device`.
2. Store the handle of a pipeline cache, from which data should be retrieved, in a variable of type `VkPipelineCache` named `pipeline_cache`.

Graphics and Compute Pipelines

3. Prepare a variable of type `size_t` named `data_size`.
4. Call `vkGetPipelineCacheData( logical_device, pipeline_cache, &data_size, nullptr )` providing the `logical_device` and `pipeline_cache` variables, a pointer to the `data_size` variable, and a `nullptr` value.
5. If a function call was successful (a `VK_SUCCESS` value was returned), the size of memory that can hold the cache contents is stored in the `data_size` variable.
6. Prepare a storage space for the cache contents. Create a variable of type `std::vector<unsigned char>` named `pipeline_cache_data`.
7. Resize the `pipeline_cache_data` vector to be able to hold at least `data_size` number of elements.
8. Call `vkGetPipelineCacheData( logical_device, pipeline_cache, &data_size, pipeline_cache_data.data() )` but this time, apart from the previously used parameters, additionally provide a pointer to the first element of the `pipeline_cache_data` vector as the last parameter.
9. If the function returns successfully, cache contents are stored in the `pipeline_cache_data` vector.

How it works...

Retrieving pipeline cache contents is performed in a typical Vulkan double-call of a single function. The first call of the `vkGetPipelineCacheData()` function, stores the total number of bytes required to hold the entire data retrieved from the pipeline cache. This allows us to prepare enough storage for the data:

```
size_t data_size = 0;
VkResult result = VK_SUCCESS;

result = vkGetPipelineCacheData( logical_device, pipeline_cache,
&data_size, nullptr );
if( (VK_SUCCESS != result) ||
    (0 == data_size) ) {
  std::cout << "Could not get the size of the pipeline cache." <<
  std::endl;
  return false;
}
pipeline_cache_data.resize( data_size );
```

Now, when we are ready to acquire the cache contents, we can call the `vkGetPipelineCacheData()` function once more. This time the last parameter must point to the beginning of the prepared storage. A successful call writes the provided number of bytes to the indicated memory:

```
result = vkGetPipelineCacheData( logical_device, pipeline_cache,
&data_size, pipeline_cache_data.data());
if( (VK_SUCCESS != result) ||
    (0 == data_size) ) {
  std::cout << "Could not acquire pipeline cache data." << std::endl;
  return false;
}

return true;
```

Data retrieved in this way can be used directly to initialize the contents of any other newly created cache object.

See also

The following recipes in this chapter:

- *Creating a pipeline cache object*
- *Merging multiple pipeline cache objects*
- *Creating a graphics pipeline*
- *Creating a compute pipeline*
- *Destroying a pipeline cache*

Merging multiple pipeline cache objects

It may be a common scenario that we will have to create multiple pipelines in our application. To shorten the time needed to create them all, it may be a good idea to split the creation into multiple threads executed simultaneously. Each such thread should use a separate pipeline cache. After all the threads are finished, we would like to reuse the cache next time our application is executed. For this purpose, it is best to merge multiple cache objects into one.

How to do it...

1. Store the handle of a logical device in a variable of type `VkDevice` named `logical_device`.
2. Take the cache object into which other caches will be merged. Using its handle, initialize a variable of type `VkPipelineCache` named `target_pipeline_cache`.
3. Create a variable of type `std::vector<VkPipelineCache>` named `source_pipeline_caches`. Store the handles of all pipelines caches that should be merged in the `source_pipeline_caches` vector (make sure none of the cache objects is the same as the `target_pipeline_cache` cache).
4. Make the following call: `vkMergePipelineCaches( logical_device, target_pipeline_cache, static_cast<uint32_t>(source_pipeline_caches.size()), source_pipeline_caches.data() )`. For the call, provide the `logical_device` and `target_pipeline_cache` variables, the number of elements in the `source_pipeline_caches` vector, and a pointer to the first element of the `source_pipeline_caches` vector.
5. Make sure the call was successful and that it returned a `VK_SUCCESS` value.

How it works...

Merging pipeline caches allows us to combine separate cache objects into one. This way it is possible to perform multiple pipeline creations that use separate caches in multiple threads and then merge the results into one, common cache object. Separate threads may also use the same pipeline cache object, but access to the cache may be guarded by a mutex in the driver, thus making splitting the job into multiple threads quite useless. Saving one cache data in a file is simpler than managing multiple ones. And, during the merging operation, duplicate entries should be removed by the driver, thus saving us some additional space and memory.

Merging multiple pipeline cache objects is performed like this:

```
VkResult result = vkMergePipelineCaches( logical_device,
target_pipeline_cache,
static_cast<uint32_t>(source_pipeline_caches.size()),
source_pipeline_caches.data() );
if( VK_SUCCESS != result ) {
  std::cout << "Could not merge pipeline cache objects." << std::endl;
  return false;
}
return true;
```

We need to remember that a cache, into which we merge other cache objects, cannot appear in the list of (source) caches to be merged.

See also

The following recipes in this chapter:

- *Creating a pipeline cache object*
- *Retrieving data from a pipeline cache*
- *Creating a graphics pipeline*
- *Creating a compute pipeline*
- *Creating multiple graphics pipelines on multiple threads*
- *Destroying a pipeline cache*

Creating a graphics pipeline

A graphics pipeline is the object that allows us to draw anything on screen. It controls how the graphics hardware performs all the drawing-related operations, which transform vertices provided by the application into fragments appearing on screen. Through it we specify shader programs used during drawing, the state and parameters of tests such as depth and stencil, or how the final color is calculated and written to any of the subpass attachments. It is one of the most important objects used by our application. Before we can draw anything, we need to create a graphics pipeline. If we want, we can create multiple pipelines at once.

How to do it...

1. Take the handle of a logical device and store it in a variable of type `VkDevice` named `logical_device`.
2. Create a variable of type `std::vector<VkGraphicsPipelineCreateInfo>` named `graphics_pipeline_create_infos`. For each pipeline that should be created, add an element to the `graphics_pipeline_create_infos` vector describing the pipeline's parameters (refer to the *Specifying graphics pipeline creation parameters* recipe).
3. If a pipeline cache should be used during the creation process, store its handle in a variable of type `VkPipelineCache` named `pipeline_cache`.
4. Create a variable of type `std::vector<VkPipeline>` named `graphics_pipelines`, in which handles of the created `pipeline` will be stored. Resize the vector to hold the same number of elements as the `graphics_pipeline_create_infos` vector.
5. Call `vkCreateGraphicsPipelines( logical_device, pipeline_cache, static_cast<uint32_t>(graphics_pipeline_create_infos.size()), graphics_pipeline_create_infos.data(), nullptr, graphics_pipelines.data() )` and provide the `logical_device` variable, the `pipeline_cache` variable or a `nullptr` value if no cache is used during the pipeline creation, the number of elements in the `graphics_pipeline_create_infos` vector, a pointer to the first element of the `graphics_pipeline_create_info` vector, a `nullptr` value, and a pointer to the first element of the `graphics_pipeline` vector.
6. Make sure all the pipelines were successfully created by checking whether the call returned a `VK_SUCCESS` value. If any of the pipelines weren't created successfully, other values will be returned.

How it works...

A graphics pipeline allows us to draw anything on screen. It controls the parameters of all programmable and fixed stages of the pipeline realized by the graphics hardware. A simplified diagram of a graphics pipeline is presented in the following image. White blocks represent programmable stages, gray ones are the fixed parts of the pipeline:

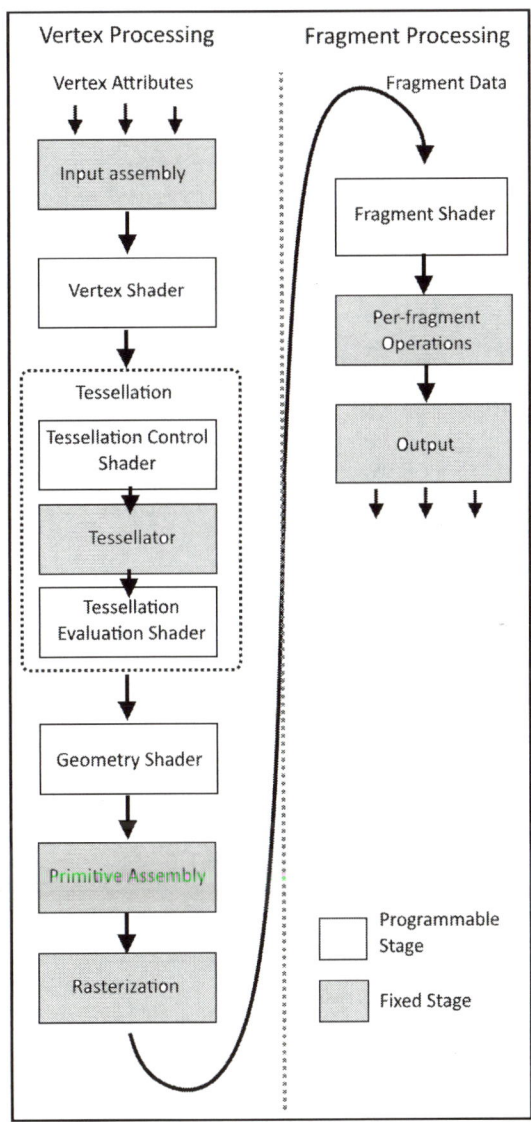

Programmable stages consist of vertex, tessellation control and evaluation, and geometry and fragment shaders, of which only the vertex stage is obligatory. The rest are optional and enabling them depends on the parameters specified during the pipeline creation. As an example, if rasterization is disabled, there is no fragment shader stage. If we enable the tessellation stage, we need to provide both tessellation control and evaluation shaders.

A graphics pipeline is created with a `vkCreateGraphicsPipelines()` function. It allows us to create multiple pipelines at once. We need to provide an array of variables of type `VkGraphicsPipelineCreateInfo`, a number of elements in this array, and a pointer to an array with elements of type `VkPipeline`. This array must be large enough to hold the same number of elements as the input array with elements of type `VkGraphicsPipelineCreateInfo` (the `graphics_pipeline_create_infos` vector). When we prepare elements to the `graphics_pipeline_create_infos` vector and want to use its `basePipelineIndex` member to specify a parent pipeline created within the same function call, we provide an index into the `graphics_pipeline_create_infos` vector.

The implementation of this recipe is presented in the following code:

```
graphics_pipelines.resize( graphics_pipeline_create_infos.size() );
VkResult result = vkCreateGraphicsPipelines( logical_device,
  pipeline_cache,
  static_cast<uint32_t>(graphics_pipeline_create_infos.size()),
  graphics_pipeline_create_infos.data(), nullptr, graphics_pipelines.data()
);
if( VK_SUCCESS != result ) {
  std::cout << "Could not create a graphics pipeline." << std::endl;
  return false;
}
return true;
```

See also

The following recipe in this chapter:

- *Specifying graphics pipeline creation parameters*
- *Creating a pipeline cache object*
- *Binding a pipeline object*
- *Creating a graphics pipeline with vertex and fragment shaders, depth test enabled, and with dynamic viewport and scissor tests*
- *Creating multiple graphics pipelines on multiple threads*
- *Destroying a pipeline*

Creating a compute pipeline

A compute pipeline is the second type of pipeline available in the Vulkan API. It is used for dispatching compute shaders, which can perform any mathematical operations. And as the compute pipeline is much simpler than the graphics pipeline, we create it by providing far fewer parameters.

How to do it...

1. Take the handle of a logical device and initialize a variable of type `VkDevice` named `logical_device` with it.
2. Create a variable of a bitfield type `VkPipelineCreateFlags` named `additional_options`. Initialize it with any combination of these additional pipeline creation options:
   - **Disable optimization**: specifies that the created pipeline won't be optimized, but the creation process may be faster
   - **Allow derivatives**: specifies that other pipelines may be created from it
   - **Derivative**: specifies that this pipeline will be created based on another, already created pipeline
3. Create a variable of type `VkPipelineShaderStageCreateInfo` named `compute_shader_stage` through which specify a single compute shader stage (refer to the *Specifying pipeline shader stages* recipe).
4. Create a pipeline layout and store its handle in a variable of type `VkPipelineLayout` named `pipeline_layout`.
5. If a pipeline cache should be used during the pipeline creation, store the handle of a created cache object in a variable of type `VkPipelineCache` named `pipeline_cache`.
6. Create a variable of type `VkComputePipelineCreateInfo` named `compute_pipeline_create_info`. Use the following values to initialize its members:
   - `VK_STRUCTURE_TYPE_COMPUTE_PIPELINE_CREATE_INFO` value for `sType`
   - `nullptr` value for `pNext`
   - `additional_options` variable for `flags`
   - `compute_shader_stage` variable for `stage`
   - `pipeline_layout` variable for `layout`

- If the pipeline should be a child of another pipeline, provide the handle of a parent pipeline or otherwise a `VK_NULL_HANDLE` value for `basePipelineHandle`
- `-1` value for `basePipelineIndex`

7. Create a variable of type `VkPipeline` named `compute_pipeline` in which a handle of the created compute pipeline will be stored.
8. Call `vkCreateComputePipelines( logical_device, pipeline_cache, 1, &compute_pipeline_create_info, nullptr, &compute_pipeline )` and provide the `logical_device` variable, the `pipeline_cache` variable if caching should be enabled or a `VK_NULL_HANDLE` value otherwise, 1 value, a pointer to the `compute_pipeline_create_info` variable, a `nullptr` value, and a pointer to the `compute_pipeline` variable.
9. Make sure the call was successful by checking if it returned a `VK_SUCCESS` value.

How it works...

We use compute pipelines when we want to dispatch compute shaders. A compute pipeline consists of only a single compute shader stage (though the hardware may implement additional stages if needed).

Compute pipelines cannot be used inside render passes.

Compute shaders don't have any input or output variables, apart from some built-in values. For the input and output data, only uniform variables (buffers or images) can be used (refer to the *Writing compute shaders* recipe from `Chapter 7, Shaders`). That's why, though the compute pipeline is simpler, compute shaders are more universal and can be used to perform mathematical operations or operations that operate on images.

Compute pipelines, similar to graphics pipelines, can be created in bulks and multiple variables of type `VkComputePipelineCreateInfo` just need to be provided to the compute pipeline creating function. Also, compute pipelines can be parents of other compute pipelines and can derive from other parent pipelines. All this speeds up the creation process. To use this ability, we need to provide appropriate values for `basePipelineHandle` or `basePipelineIndex` members of variables of type `VkComputePipelineCreateInfo` (refer to the *Creating a graphics pipeline* recipe).

The simplified process of creating a single compute pipeline is presented in the following code:

```
VkComputePipelineCreateInfo compute_pipeline_create_info = {
  VK_STRUCTURE_TYPE_COMPUTE_PIPELINE_CREATE_INFO,
  nullptr,
  additional_options,
  compute_shader_stage,
  pipeline_layout,
  base_pipeline_handle,
  -1
};

VkResult result = vkCreateComputePipelines( logical_device, pipeline_cache,
1, &compute_pipeline_create_info, nullptr, &compute_pipeline );
if( VK_SUCCESS != result ) {
  std::cout << "Could not create compute pipeline." << std::endl;
  return false;
}
return true;
```

See also

- In Chapter 7, *Shaders*, see the following recipe:
    - *Writing compute shaders*
- The following recipes in this chapter:
    - *Specifying pipeline shader stages*
    - *Creating a pipeline layout*
    - *Creating a pipeline cache object*
    - *Destroying a pipeline*

Binding a pipeline object

Before we can issue drawing commands or dispatch computational work, we need to set up all the required states for the command to be successfully performed. One of the required states is binding a pipeline object to the command buffer--a graphics pipeline if we want to draw objects on screen or a compute pipeline if we want to perform computational work.

How to do it...

1. Take the handle of a command buffer and store it in a variable of type `VkCommandBuffer` named `command_buffer`. Make sure the command buffer is in the recording state.
2. If a graphics pipeline needs to be bound, make sure the beginning of a render pass has already been recorded in the `command_buffer`. If a compute pipeline should be bound, make sure no render pass is started or any render passes are finished in the `command_buffer`.
3. Take the handle of a pipeline object. Use it to initialize a variable of type `VkPipeline` named `pipeline`.
4. Call `vkCmdBindPipeline( command_buffer, pipeline_type, pipeline )`. Provide the `command_buffer` variable, the type of the pipeline (graphics or compute) that is being bound to the command buffer, and the `pipeline` variable.

How it works...

A pipeline needs to be bound before we can draw or dispatch computational work in a command buffer. Graphics pipelines can be bound only inside render passes--the one specified during pipeline creation or a compatible one. Compute pipelines cannot be used inside render passes. If we want to use them, any started render pass needs to be finished.

Binding a pipeline object is achieved with a single function call like this:

```
vkCmdBindPipeline( command_buffer, pipeline_type, pipeline );
```

See also

- In `Chapter 3`, *Command Buffers and Synchronization*, see the recipe:
    - *Beginning a command buffer recording operation*
- In `Chapter 6`, *Render Passes and Framebuffers*, see the following recipes:
    - *Beginning a render pass*
    - *Ending a render pass*
- The following recipes in this chapter:
    - *Creating a graphics pipeline*
    - *Creating a compute pipeline*

Creating a pipeline layout with a combined image sampler, a buffer, and push constant ranges

We know how to create descriptor set layouts and use them to create a pipeline layout. Here, in this sample recipe, we will have a look at how to create a specific pipeline layout-- one which allows a pipeline to access a combined image sampler, a uniform buffer, and a selected number of push constant ranges.

How to do it...

1. Take the handle of a logical device and store it in a variable of type `VkDevice` named `logical_device`.
2. Create a variable of type `std::vector<VkDescriptorSetLayoutBinding>` named `descriptor_set_layout_bindings`.
3. Add a new element to the `descriptor_set_layout_bindings` vector and use the following values to initialize its members:
    - 0 value for `binding`.
    - `VK_DESCRIPTOR_TYPE_SAMPLED_IMAGE` value for `descriptorType`.
    - 1 value for `descriptorCount`.
    - `VK_SHADER_STAGE_FRAGMENT_BIT` value for `stageFlags`.
    - `nullptr` value for `pImmutableSamplers`.
4. Add a second member to the `descriptor_set_layout_bindings` vector and use the following values to initialize its members:
    - 1 value for `binding`.
    - `VK_DESCRIPTOR_TYPE_UNIFORM_BUFFER` value for `descriptorType`.
    - 1 value for `descriptorCount`.
    - `VK_SHADER_STAGE_VERTEX_BIT` value for `stageFlags`.
    - `nullptr` value for `pImmutableSamplers`.

Graphics and Compute Pipelines

5. Create a descriptor set layout using the `logical_device` and `descriptor_set_layout_bindings` variables and store it in a variable of type `VkDescriptorSetLayout` named `descriptor_set_layout` (refer to the *Creating a descriptor set layout* recipe from Chapter 5, *Descriptor Sets*).
6. Create a variable of type `std::vector<VkPushConstantRange>` named `push_constant_ranges` and initialize it with the desired number of push constant ranges, each with desired values (refer to the *Creating a pipeline layout* recipe).
7. Create a variable of type `VkPipelineLayout` named `pipeline_layout` in which the handle of the created pipeline layout will be stored.
8. Create the pipeline layout using the `logical_device`, `descriptor_set_layout` and `push_constant_ranges` variables. Store the created handle in the `pipeline_layout` variable (refer to the *Creating a pipeline layout* recipe).

How it works...

In this recipe, we assume that we want to create a graphics pipeline that needs access to a uniform buffer and a combined image sampler. This is a common situation--we use the uniform buffer in a vertex shader to transform vertices from the local space to the clip space. A fragment shader is used for texturing so it needs access to a combined image sampler descriptor.

We need to create a descriptor set that contains these two types of resources. For this purpose, we create a layout for it, which defines a uniform buffer used in a vertex shader and a combined image sampler accessed in a fragment shader:

```
std::vector<VkDescriptorSetLayoutBinding> descriptor_set_layout_bindings =
{
  {
    0,
    VK_DESCRIPTOR_TYPE_SAMPLED_IMAGE,
    1,
    VK_SHADER_STAGE_FRAGMENT_BIT,
    nullptr
  },
  {
    1,
    VK_DESCRIPTOR_TYPE_UNIFORM_BUFFER,
    1,
    VK_SHADER_STAGE_VERTEX_BIT,
    nullptr
```

```
    }
  };

  if( !CreateDescriptorSetLayout( logical_device,
  descriptor_set_layout_bindings, descriptor_set_layout ) ) {
    return false;
  }
```

Using such a descriptor set layout, we can create a pipeline layout using an additional vector with information for ranges of push constants:

```
  if( !CreatePipelineLayout( logical_device, { descriptor_set_layout },
  push_constant_ranges, pipeline_layout ) ) {
    return false;
  }
  return true;
```

Now, when we create a pipeline with such a layout, we can bind one descriptor set to index 0. This descriptor set must have two descriptor resources--a combined image sampler at binding 0 and a uniform buffer at binding 1.

See also

- In `Chapter 5`, *Descriptor Sets*, see the recipe:
    - *Creating a descriptor set layout*
- *Creating a pipeline layout*, in this chapter.

Creating a graphics pipeline with vertex and fragment shaders, depth test enabled, and with dynamic viewport and scissor tests

In this recipe, we will see how to create a commonly used graphics pipeline, in which vertex and fragment shaders are active and a depth test is enabled. We will also specify that viewport and scissor tests are set up dynamically.

Graphics and Compute Pipelines

How to do it...

1. Take the handle of a logical device. Use it to initialize a variable of type `VkDevice` named `logical_device`.
2. Take the SPIR-V assembly of a vertex shader and use it, along with the `logical_device` variable, to create a shader module. Store it in a variable of type `VkShaderModule` named `vertex_shader_module` (refer to the *Creating a shader module* recipe).
3. Take the SPIR-V assembly of a fragment shader and using it, along with the `logical_device` variable, create a second shader module. Store its handle in a variable of type `VkShaderModule` named `fragment_shader_module` (refer to the *Creating a shader module* recipe).
4. Create a variable of type `std::vector` named `shader_stage_params` with elements of a custom `ShaderStageParameters` type (refer to the *Specifying pipeline shader stages* recipe).
5. Add an element to the `shader_stage_params` vector and use the following values to initialize its members:
    - VK_SHADER_STAGE_VERTEX_BIT value for `ShaderStage`.
    - `vertex_shader_module` variable for `ShaderModule`.
    - `main` string for `EntryPointName`.
    - `nullptr` value for `SpecializationInfo`.
6. Add a second element to the `shader_stage_params` vector and use the following values to initialize its members:
    - VK_SHADER_STAGE_FRAGMENT_BIT value for `ShaderStage`.
    - `fragment_shader_module` variable for `ShaderModule`.
    - `main` string for `EntryPointName`.
    - `nullptr` value for `SpecializationInfo`.
7. Create a variable of type `std::vector<VkPipelineShaderStageCreateInfo>` named `shader_stage_create_infos` and initialize it using the members of the `shader_stage_params` vector (refer to the *Specifying pipeline shader stages* recipe).
8. Create a variable of type `VkPipelineVertexInputStateCreateInfo` named `vertex_input_state_create_info`. Initialize it with the desired parameters of vertex input bindings and vertex attributes (refer to the *Specifying pipeline vertex binding description, attribute description, and input state* recipe).

[434]

9. Create a variable of type `VkPipelineInputAssemblyStateCreateInfo` named `input_assembly_state_create_info` and initialize it using the desired primitive topology (triangle list or triangle strip, or line list, and so on) and decide whether the primitive restart should be enabled or disabled (refer to the *Specifying pipeline input assembly state* recipe).
10. Create a variable of type `VkPipelineViewportStateCreateInfo` named `viewport_state_create_info`. Initialize it using a variable of the `ViewportInfo` type with one-element vectors for both viewport and scissor test vectors. Values stored in these vectors don't matter as viewport and stencil parameters will be defined dynamically during command buffer recording. But as the number of viewports (and scissor test states) are defined statically, both vectors need to have one element (refer to the *Specifying pipeline viewport and scissor test state* recipe).
11. Create a variable of type `VkPipelineRasterizationStateCreateInfo` named `rasterization_state_create_info` and initialize it with selected values. Remember to provide a false value for the `rasterizerDiscardEnable` member (refer to the *Specifying pipeline rasterization state* recipe).
12. Create a variable of type `VkPipelineMultisampleStateCreateInfo` named `multisample_state_create_info`. Specify the desired parameters of a multisampling (refer to the *Specifying pipeline multisample state* recipe).
13. Create a variable of type `VkPipelineDepthStencilStateCreateInfo` named `depth_and_stencil_state_create_info`. Remember to enable depth writes and a depth test and to specify a `VK_COMPARE_OP_LESS_OR_EQUAL` operator for a depth test. Define the rest of the depth and stencil parameters as required (refer to the *Specifying pipeline depth and stencil state* recipe).
14. Create a variable of type `VkPipelineColorBlendStateCreateInfo` named `blend_state_create_info` and initialize it with the desired set of values (refer to the *Specifying pipeline blend state* recipe).
15. Create a variable of type `std::vector<VkDynamicState>` named `dynamic_states`. Add two elements to the vector, one with a `VK_DYNAMIC_STATE_VIEWPORT` value, and a second with a `VK_DYNAMIC_STATE_SCISSOR` value.
16. Create a variable of type `VkPipelineDynamicStateCreateInfo` named `dynamic_state_create_info`. Prepare its contents using the `dynamic_states` vector (refer to the *Specifying pipeline dynamic states* recipe).

Graphics and Compute Pipelines

17. Create a variable of type `VkGraphicsPipelineCreateInfo` named `graphics_pipeline_create_info`. Initialize it using the `shader_stage_create_infos`, `vertex_input_state_create_info`, `input_assembly_state_create_info`, `viewport_state_create_info`, `rasterization_state_create_info`, `multisample_state_create_info`, `depth_and_stencil_state_create_info`, `blend_state_create_info` and `dynamic_state_create_info` variables. Provide the created pipeline layout, the selected render pass, and its subpass. Use the handle or index of a parent pipeline. Provide a `nullptr` value for the tessellation state info.
18. Create a graphics pipeline using the `logical_device` and `graphics_pipeline_create_info` variables. Provide the handle of a pipeline cache, if needed. Store the handle of the created pipeline in the one element vector variable of type `std::vector<VkPipeline>` named `graphics_pipeline`.

How it works...

One of the most commonly used pipelines is a pipeline with only vertex and fragment shaders. To prepare parameters of vertex and fragment shader stages we can use the following code:

```
std::vector<unsigned char> vertex_shader_spirv;
if( !GetBinaryFileContents( vertex_shader_filename, vertex_shader_spirv ) )
{
  return false;
}

VkDestroyer<VkShaderModule> vertex_shader_module( logical_device );
if( !CreateShaderModule( logical_device, vertex_shader_spirv,
*vertex_shader_module ) ) {
  return false;
}

std::vector<unsigned char> fragment_shader_spirv;
if( !GetBinaryFileContents( fragment_shader_filename, fragment_shader_spirv
) ) {
  return false;
}
VkDestroyer<VkShaderModule> fragment_shader_module( logical_device );
if( !CreateShaderModule( logical_device, fragment_shader_spirv,
*fragment_shader_module ) ) {
  return false;
}
```

Chapter 8

```
std::vector<ShaderStageParameters> shader_stage_params = {
  {
    VK_SHADER_STAGE_VERTEX_BIT,
    *vertex_shader_module,
    "main",
    nullptr
  },
  {
    VK_SHADER_STAGE_FRAGMENT_BIT,
    *fragment_shader_module,
    "main",
    nullptr
  }
};

std::vector<VkPipelineShaderStageCreateInfo> shader_stage_create_infos;
SpecifyPipelineShaderStages( shader_stage_params, shader_stage_create_infos
);
```

In the preceding code, we load source codes of vertex and fragment shaders, create shader modules for them, and specify parameters of the shader stages.

Next we need to select whatever parameters we would like for vertex bindings and vertex attributes:

```
VkPipelineVertexInputStateCreateInfo vertex_input_state_create_info;
SpecifyPipelineVertexInputState( vertex_input_binding_descriptions,
vertex_attribute_descriptions, vertex_input_state_create_info );

VkPipelineInputAssemblyStateCreateInfo input_assembly_state_create_info;
SpecifyPipelineInputAssemblyState( primitive_topology,
primitive_restart_enable, input_assembly_state_create_info );
```

Viewport and scissor test parameters are important. But as we want to define them dynamically, only the number of viewports matters during the pipeline creation. That's why here we can specify whatever values we want:

```
ViewportInfo viewport_infos = {
  {
    {
      0.0f,
      0.0f,
      500.0f,
      500.0f,
      0.0f,
      1.0f
    }
  },
```

[437]

Graphics and Compute Pipelines

```
      {
        {
          {
            0,
            0
          },
          {
            500,
            500
          }
        }
      }
    };
    VkPipelineViewportStateCreateInfo viewport_state_create_info;
    SpecifyPipelineViewportAndScissorTestState( viewport_infos,
    viewport_state_create_info );
```

Next we need to prepare parameters for rasterization and multisample states (rasterization must be enabled if we want to use a fragment shader):

```
    VkPipelineRasterizationStateCreateInfo rasterization_state_create_info;
    SpecifyPipelineRasterizationState( false, false, polygon_mode,
    culling_mode, front_face, false, 0.0f, 1.0f, 0.0f, 1.0f,
    rasterization_state_create_info );

    VkPipelineMultisampleStateCreateInfo multisample_state_create_info;
    SpecifyPipelineMultisampleState( VK_SAMPLE_COUNT_1_BIT, false, 0.0f,
    nullptr, false, false, multisample_state_create_info );
```

We also want to enable a depth test (and depth writes). Usually we want to simulate how people or cameras observe the world, where objects near the viewer block the view, and obscure objects that are further away. That's why for the depth test, we specify a `VK_COMPARE_OP_LESS_OR_EQUAL` operator which defines that samples with lower or equal depth values pass and those with greater depth values fail the depth test. Other depth-related parameters and parameters for the stencil test can be set as we want, but here we assume the stencil test is disabled (so the values of the stencil test parameters don't matter here):

```
    VkStencilOpState stencil_test_parameters = {
      VK_STENCIL_OP_KEEP,
      VK_STENCIL_OP_KEEP,
      VK_STENCIL_OP_KEEP,
      VK_COMPARE_OP_ALWAYS,
      0,
      0,
      0
    };
```

```
VkPipelineDepthStencilStateCreateInfo depth_and_stencil_state_create_info;
SpecifyPipelineDepthAndStencilState( true, true,
VK_COMPARE_OP_LESS_OR_EQUAL, false, 0.0f, 1.0f, false,
stencil_test_parameters, stencil_test_parameters,
depth_and_stencil_state_create_info );
```

Blending parameters can be set as we want:

```
VkPipelineColorBlendStateCreateInfo blend_state_create_info;
SpecifyPipelineBlendState( logic_op_enable, logic_op,
attachment_blend_states, blend_constants, blend_state_create_info );
```

One last thing is to prepare a list of dynamic states:

```
std::vector<VkDynamicState> dynamic_states = {
  VK_DYNAMIC_STATE_VIEWPORT,
  VK_DYNAMIC_STATE_SCISSOR
};
VkPipelineDynamicStateCreateInfo dynamic_state_create_info;
SpecifyPipelineDynamicStates( dynamic_states, dynamic_state_create_info );
```

Now we can create a pipeline:

```
VkGraphicsPipelineCreateInfo graphics_pipeline_create_info;
SpecifyGraphicsPipelineCreationParameters( additional_options,
shader_stage_create_infos, vertex_input_state_create_info,
input_assembly_state_create_info, nullptr, &viewport_state_create_info,
rasterization_state_create_info, &multisample_state_create_info,
&depth_and_stencil_state_create_info, &blend_state_create_info,
&dynamic_state_create_info, pipeline_layout, render_pass,
subpass, base_pipeline_handle, -1, graphics_pipeline_create_info );

if( !CreateGraphicsPipelines( logical_device, {
graphics_pipeline_create_info }, pipeline_cache, graphics_pipeline ) ) {
  return false;
}
return true;
```

See also

The following recipes in this chapter:

- *Specifying pipeline shader stages*
- *Specifying pipeline vertex binding description, attribute description, and input state*
- *Specifying pipeline input assembly state*

- *Specifying pipeline viewport and scissor test state*
- *Specifying pipeline rasterization state*
- *Specifying pipeline multisample state*
- *Specifying pipeline depth and stencil state*
- *Specifying pipeline blend state*
- *Specifying pipeline dynamic states*
- *Creating a pipeline layout*
- *Specifying graphics pipeline creation parameters*
- *Creating a pipeline cache object*
- *Creating a graphics pipeline*

Creating multiple graphics pipelines on multiple threads

The process of creating a graphics pipeline may take a (relatively) long time. Shader compilation takes place during the pipeline creation, the driver checks if compiled shaders can be properly linked together and if a state is properly specified for the shaders to work correctly. That's why, especially when we have lots of pipelines to create, it is good to split this process into multiple threads.

But when we have lots of pipelines to create, we should use a cache to speed up the creation even further. Here we will see how to use a cache for multiple concurrent pipeline creations and how to merge the cache afterwards.

Getting ready

In this recipe we use a custom template wrapper class of a `VkDestroyer<>` class. It is used to automatically destroy unused resources.

How to do it...

1. Store the name of the file from which cache contents should be read, and into which cache contents should be written, in a variable of type `std::string` named `pipeline_cache_filename`.

2. Create a variable of type `std::vector<unsigned char>` named `cache_data`. If the file named `pipeline_cache_filename` exists, load its contents into the `cache_data` vector.
3. Take the handle of a logical device and store it in a variable of type `VkDevice` named `logical_device`.
4. Create a variable of type `std::vector<VkPipelineCache>` named `pipeline_caches`. For each separate thread, create a pipeline cache object and store its handle in the `pipeline_caches` vector (refer to the *Creating a pipeline cache object* recipe).
5. Create a variable of type `std::vector<std::thread>` named `threads`. Resize it to store the desired number of threads.
6. Create a variable of type `std::vector<std::vector<VkGraphicsPipelineCreateInfo>>` named `graphics_pipelines_create_infos`. For each thread, add new vector to the `graphics_pipelines_create_infos` variable containing variables of type `VkGraphicsPipelineCreateInfo`, where the number of these variables should be equal to the number of pipelines that should be created on a given thread.
7. Create a variable of type `std::vector<std::vector<VkPipeline>>` named `graphics_pipelines`. Resize each member vector that corresponds to each thread to hold the same number of pipelines created on a given thread.
8. Create the desired number of threads where each thread creates the selected number of pipelines using the `logical_device` variable, a cache corresponding to this thread (`pipeline_caches[<thread number>]`), and a corresponding vector with elements of type `VkGraphicsPipelineCreateInfo` (`graphics_pipelines_create_infos[<thread number>]` vector variable).
9. Wait for all threads to finish.
10. Create new cache in a variable of type `VkPipelineCache` named `target_cache`.
11. Merge pipeline caches stored in the `pipeline_caches` vector into the `target_cache` variable (refer to the *Merging multiple pipeline cache objects* recipe).
12. Retrieve the cache contents of the `target_cache` variable and store it in the `cache_data` vector.
13. Save the contents of the `cache_data` vector into the file named `pipeline_cache_filename` (replace the file's contents with the new data).

How it works...

Creating multiple graphics pipelines requires us to provide lots of parameters for many different pipelines. But using separate threads, where each thread creates multiple pipelines, should reduce the time needed to create all the pipelines.

To speed things even more, it is good to use a pipeline cache. First we need to read the previously stored cache contents from the file, if it was created. Next we need to create the cache for each separate thread. Each cache should be initialized with the cache contents loaded from the file (if it was found):

```
std::vector<unsigned char> cache_data;
GetBinaryFileContents( pipeline_cache_filename, cache_data );

std::vector<VkDestroyer<VkPipelineCache>> pipeline_caches(
graphics_pipelines_create_infos.size() );
for( size_t i = 0; i < graphics_pipelines_create_infos.size(); ++i ) {
  pipeline_caches[i] = VkDestroyer< VkPipelineCache >( logical_device );
  if( !CreatePipelineCacheObject( logical_device, cache_data,
*pipeline_caches[i] ) ) {
    return false;
  }
}
```

The next step is to prepare storage space in which handles of pipelines created on each thread will be stored. We also start all the threads that create multiple pipelines using the corresponding cache object:

```
std::vector<std::thread>threads( graphics_pipelines_create_infos.size() );
for( size_t i = 0; i < graphics_pipelines_create_infos.size(); ++i ) {
  graphics_pipelines[i].resize( graphics_pipelines_create_infos[i].size()
);
  threads[i] = std::thread::thread( CreateGraphicsPipelines,
logical_device, graphics_pipelines_create_infos[i], *pipeline_caches[i],
graphics_pipelines[i] );
}
```

Now we need to wait until all the threads are finished. After that we can merge different cache objects (from each thread) into one, from which we retrieve the contents. These new contents we can store in the same file from which we loaded the contents at the beginning (we should replace the contents):

```
for( size_t i = 0; i < graphics_pipelines_create_infos.size(); ++i ) {
  threads[i].join();
}
```

```
VkPipelineCache target_cache = *pipeline_caches.back();
std::vector<VkPipelineCache> source_caches( pipeline_caches.size() - 1 );
for( size_t i = 0; i < pipeline_caches.size() - 1; ++i ) {
  source_caches[i] = *pipeline_caches[i];
}

if( !MergeMultiplePipelineCacheObjects( logical_device, target_cache,
source_caches ) ) {
  return false;
}

if( !RetrieveDataFromPipelineCache( logical_device, target_cache,
cache_data ) ) {
  return false;
}

if( !SaveBinaryFile( pipeline_cache_filename, cache_data ) ) {
  return false;
}

return true;
```

See also

The following recipes in this chapter:

- *Specifying graphics pipeline creation parameters*
- *Creating a pipeline cache object*
- *Retrieving data from a pipeline cache*
- *Merging multiple pipeline cache objects*
- *Creating a graphics pipeline*
- *Destroying a pipeline cache*

Destroying a pipeline

When a pipeline object is no longer needed and we are sure that it is not being used by the hardware in any of the submitted command buffers, we can safely destroy it.

How to do it...

1. Take the handle of a logical device. Use it to initialize a variable of type `VkDevice` named `logical_device`.
2. Take the handle of a pipeline object that should be destroyed. Store it in a variable of type `VkPipeline` named `pipeline`. Make sure it is not being referenced by any commands submitted to any of the available queues.
3. Call `vkDestroyPipeline( logical_device, pipeline, nullptr )` for which provide the `logical_device` and `pipeline` variables and a `nullptr` value.
4. For safety reasons, assign a `VK_NULL_HANDLE` value to the `pipeline` variable.

How it works...

When a pipeline is no longer needed, we can destroy it by calling the `vkDestroyPipeline()` function like this:

```
if( VK_NULL_HANDLE != pipeline ) {
  vkDestroyPipeline( logical_device, pipeline, nullptr );
  pipeline = VK_NULL_HANDLE;
}
```

Pipeline objects are used during rendering. So before we can destroy them, we must make sure all the rendering commands that used them are already finished. This is best done by associating a fence object with a submission of a given command buffer. After that we need to wait for the fence before we destroy pipeline objects referenced in that command buffer (refer to the *Waiting for fences* recipe). However, other synchronization methods are also valid.

See also

- In `Chapter 3`, *Command Buffers and Synchronization*, see the following recipes:
    - *Waiting for fences*
    - *Waiting for all submitted commands to be finished*
- The following recipes in this chapter:
    - *Creating a graphics pipeline*
    - *Creating a compute pipeline*

Destroying a pipeline cache

A pipeline cache is not used in any commands recorded in a command buffer. That's why, when we have created all the pipelines we wanted, merged cache data, or retrieved its contents, we can destroy the cache.

How to do it...

1. Store the handle of a logical device in a variable of type `VkDevice` named `logical_device`.
2. Take the handle of a pipeline cache object that should be destroyed. Use the handle to initialize a variable of type `VkPipelineCache` named `pipeline_cache`.
3. Call `vkDestroyPipelineCache( logical_device, pipeline_cache, nullptr )` and provide the `logical_device` and `pipeline_cache` variables, and a `nullptr` value.
4. For safety reasons, store the `VK_NULL_HANDLE` value in the `pipeline_cache` variable.

How it works...

Pipeline cache objects can be used only during the creation of pipelines, for retrieving data from it, and for merging multiple caches into one. None of these operations are recorded in the command buffers, so as soon as any function performing one the mentioned operations has finished, we can destroy the cache like this:

```
if( VK_NULL_HANDLE != pipeline_cache ) {
  vkDestroyPipelineCache( logical_device, pipeline_cache, nullptr );
  pipeline_cache = VK_NULL_HANDLE;
}
```

See also

The following recipes in this chapter:

- *Creating a pipeline cache object*
- *Retrieving data from a pipeline cache*
- *Merging multiple pipeline cache objects*
- *Creating a graphics pipeline*
- *Creating a compute pipeline*

Destroying a pipeline layout

When we don't need a pipeline layout anymore, and we don't intend to create more pipelines with it, bind descriptor sets or update push constants that used the given layout, and all operations using the pipeline layout are already finished, we can destroy the layout.

How to do it...

1. Take the handle of a logical device. Use it to initialize a variable of type `VkDevice` named `logical_device`.
2. Take the handle of a pipeline layout stored in a variable of type `VkPipelineLayout` named `pipeline_layout`.
3. Call `vkDestroyPipelineLayout( logical_device, pipeline_layout, nullptr )`. For the call, provide the `logical_device` and `pipeline_layout` variables and a `nullptr` value.
4. For safety reasons, assign a `VK_NULL_HANDLE` to the `pipeline_layout` variable.

How it works...

Pipeline layouts are used only in three situations--creating pipelines, binding descriptor sets, and updating push constants. When a given pipeline layout was used only to create a pipeline, it may be destroyed immediately after the pipeline is created. If we are using it to bind descriptor sets or update push constants, we need to wait until the hardware stops processing command buffers, in which these operations were recorded. Then, we can safely destroy the pipeline layout using the following code:

```
if( VK_NULL_HANDLE != pipeline_layout ) {
  vkDestroyPipelineLayout( logical_device, pipeline_layout, nullptr );
  pipeline_layout = VK_NULL_HANDLE;
}
```

See also

- In Chapter 3, *Command Buffers and Synchronization*, see the following recipes:
    - *Waiting for fences*
    - *Waiting for all submitted commands to be finished*
- In Chapter 5, *Descriptor Sets*, see the following recipe:
    - *Binding descriptor sets*
- The following recipes in this chapter:
    - *Creating a pipeline layout*
    - *Creating a graphics pipeline*
    - *Creating a compute pipeline*
    - *Providing data to shaders through push constants*

Destroying a shader module

Shader modules are used only for creating pipeline objects. After they are created, we can immediately destroy them, if we don't intend to use them anymore.

How to do it...

1. Use the handle of a logical device to initialize a variable of type `VkDevice` named `logical_device`.
2. Take the shader module's handle stored in a variable of type `VkShaderModule` named `shader_module`.
3. Call `vkDestroyShaderModule( logical_device, shader_module, nullptr )` providing the `logical_device` variable, the `shader_module` variable, and a `nullptr` value.
4. Assign a `VK_NULL_HANDLE` value to the `shader_module` variable for safety reasons.

How it works...

Shader modules are used only during the pipeline creation. They are provided as part of a shader stages state. When pipelines that use given modules are already created, we can destroy the modules (immediately after the pipeline creating functions have finished), as they are not needed for the pipeline objects to be correctly used by the driver.

> Created pipelines don't need shader modules anymore to be successfully used.

To destroy a shader module, use the following code:

```
if( VK_NULL_HANDLE != shader_module ) {
  vkDestroyShaderModule( logical_device, shader_module, nullptr );
  shader_module = VK_NULL_HANDLE;
}
```

See also

The following recipes in this chapter:

- *Creating a shader module*
- *Specifying pipeline shader stages*
- *Creating a graphics pipeline*
- *Creating a compute pipeline*

9
Command Recording and Drawing

In this chapter, we will cover the following recipes:

- Clearing a color image
- Clearing a depth-stencil image
- Clearing render pass attachments
- Binding vertex buffers
- Binding an index buffer
- Providing data to shaders through push constants
- Setting viewport state dynamically
- Setting scissor state dynamically
- Setting line width state dynamically
- Setting depth bias state dynamically
- Setting blend constants state dynamically
- Drawing a geometry
- Drawing an indexed geometry
- Dispatching compute work
- Executing a secondary command buffer inside a primary command buffer
- Recording a command buffer that draws a geometry with a dynamic viewport and scissor states
- Recording command buffers on multiple threads
- Preparing a single frame of animation
- Increasing performance through increasing the number of separately rendered frames

Introduction

Vulkan was designed as a graphics and compute API. Its main purpose is to allow us to generate dynamic images using a graphics hardware produced by various vendors. We already know how to create and manage resources and use them as a source of data for shaders. We learned about different shader stages and pipeline objects controlling the state of rendering or dispatching computational work. We also know how to record command buffers and order operations into render passes. One last step we must learn about is how to utilize this knowledge to render images.

In this chapter, we will see what additional commands we can record and what commands need to be recorded so we can properly render a geometry or issue computational operations. We will also learn about the drawing commands and organizing them in our source code in such a way so that it maximizes the performance of our application. Finally, we will utilize one of the greatest strengths of the Vulkan API--the ability to record command buffers in multiple threads.

Clearing a color image

In traditional graphics APIs, we start rendering a frame by clearing a render target or a back buffer. In Vulkan, we should perform the clearing by specifying a `VK_ATTACHMENT_LOAD_OP_CLEAR` value for a `loadOp` member of the render pass's attachment description (refer to the *Specifying attachment descriptions* recipe from Chapter 6, *Render Passes and Framebuffers*). But sometimes, we can't clear an image inside a render pass and we need to do it implicitly.

How to do it...

1. Take the handle of a command buffer stored in a variable of type `VkCommandBuffer` named `command_buffer`. Make sure the command buffer is in the recording state and no render pass has started.
2. Take the handle of an image that should be cleared. Provide it through a variable of type `VkImage` named `image`.
3. Store the layout, in which the `image` will have during clearing, in a variable of type `VkImageLayout` named `image_layout`.

4. Prepare a list of all mipmap levels of the `image` and array layers that should be cleared in a variable of type `std::vector<VkImageSubresourceRange>` named `image_subresource_ranges`. For each range of sub-resources of the `image`, add a new element to the `image_subresource_ranges` vector and use the following values to initialize its members:
    - The image's aspect (color, depth, and/or stencil aspect cannot be provided) for `aspectMask`
    - The first mipmap level to be cleared in a given range for `baseMipLevel`
    - The number of continuous mipmap levels that should be cleared in a given range for `levelCount`
    - The number of a first array layer that should be cleared in a given range for `baseArrayLayer`
    - The number of continuous array layers to be cleared for `layerCount`
5. Provide a color to which the image should be cleared using the following members of a variable type `VkClearColorValue` named `clear_color`:
    - `int32`: When the image has a signed integer format
    - `uint32`: When the image has an unsigned integer format
    - `float32`: For the rest of the formats
6. Call the `vkCmdClearColorImage( command_buffer, image, image_layout, &clear_color, static_cast<uint32_t>(image_subresource_ranges.size()), image_subresource_ranges.data() )` command for which it provides the `command_buffer, image, image_layout` variables, a pointer to the `clear_color` variable, the number of elements in the `image_subresource_ranges` vector, and a pointer to the first element of the `image_subresource_ranges` vector.

How it works...

Clearing color images is performed by recording the `vkCmdClearColorImage()` function in a command buffer. The `vkCmdClearColorImage()` command cannot be recorded inside a render pass.

Command Recording and Drawing

It requires us to provide the image's handle, its layout, and an array of its sub-resources (mipmap levels and/or array layers) that should be cleared. We must also specify the color to which the image should be cleared. These parameters can be used like this:

```
vkCmdClearColorImage( command_buffer, image, image_layout, &clear_color,
static_cast<uint32_t>(image_subresource_ranges.size()),
image_subresource_ranges.data() );
```

Remember that by using this function, we can clear only color images (with a color aspect and one of the color formats).

 The vkCmdClearColorImage() function can be used only for images created with **transfer dst** usage.

See also

- In Chapter 3, *Command Buffers and Synchronization*, see the recipe:
    - *Beginning a command buffer recording operation*
- In Chapter 4, *Resources and Memory*, see the recipe:
    - *Creating an image*
- In Chapter 6, *Render Passes and Framebuffers*, see the following recipes:
    - *Specifying attachment descriptions*
    - *Clearing render pass attachments*
    - *Clearing a depth-stencil image*

Clearing a depth-stencil image

Similarly to color images, we sometimes need to manually clear a depth-stencil image outside of a render pass.

How to do it...

1. Take the command buffer that is in a recording state and has no render pass currently started in it. Using its handle, initialize a variable of type `VkCommandBuffer` named `command_buffer`.
2. Take the handle of a depth-stencil image and store it in a variable of type `VkImage` named `image`.
3. Store the value representing the layout, in which the `image` will have during clearing, in a variable of type `VkImageLayout` named `image_layout`.
4. Create a variable of type `std::vector<VkImageSubresourceRange>` named `image_subresource_ranges`, which will contain a list of mipmap levels of all the `image`'s and array layers, which should be cleared. For each such range, add a new element to the `image_subresource_ranges` vector and use the following values to initialize its members:
   - The depth and/or stencil aspect for `aspectMask`
   - The first mipmap level to be cleared in a given range for `baseMipLevel`
   - The number of continuous mipmap levels in a given range for `levelCount`
   - The number of a first array layer that should be cleared for `baseArrayLayer`
   - The number of continuous array layers to be cleared in a range for `layerCount`
5. Provide a value which should be used to clear (fill) the image using the following members of a variable of type `VkClearDepthStencilValue` named `clear_value`:
   - `depth` when a depth aspect should be cleared
   - `stencil` for a value used to clear the stencil aspect
6. Call `vkCmdClearDepthStencilImage( command_buffer, image, image_layout, &clear_value, static_cast<uint32_t>(image_subresource_ranges.size()), image_subresource_ranges.data() )` and provide the `command_buffer`, `image`, and `image_layout` variables, a pointer to the `clear_value` variable, the number of elements in the `image_subresource_ranges` vector, and a pointer to the first element of the `image_subresource_ranges` vector.

How it works...

Clearing the depth-stencil image outside of a render pass is performed like this:

```
vkCmdClearDepthStencilImage( command_buffer, image, image_layout,
  &clear_value, static_cast<uint32_t>(image_subresource_ranges.size()),
  image_subresource_ranges.data() );
```

We can use this function only for images created with a transfer dst usage (clearing is considered as a transfer operation).

See also

- In `Chapter 3`, *Command Buffers and Synchronization*, see the recipe:
    - *Beginning a command buffer recording operation*
- In `Chapter 4`, *Resources and Memory*, see the recipe:
    - *Creating an image*
- In `Chapter 6`, *Render Passes and Framebuffers*, see the following recipes:
    - *Specifying attachment descriptions*
    - *Clearing render pass attachments*
- The *Clearing a color image* recipe, in this chapter

Clearing render pass attachments

There are situations in which we cannot rely only on implicit attachment clearings performed as initial render pass operations, and we need to clear attachments explicitly in one of the sub-passes. We can do this by calling a `vkCmdClearAttachments()` function.

How to do it...

1. Take a command buffer that is in a recording state and store its handle in a variable of type `VkCommandBuffer` named `command_buffer`.
2. Create a vector variable of type `std::vector<VkClearAttachment>` named `attachments`. For each `framebuffer` attachment that should be cleared inside a current sub-pass of a render pass, add an element to the vector and initialize it with the following values:

- The attachment's aspect (color, depth, or stencil) for `aspectMask`
- If `aspectMask` is set to `VK_IMAGE_ASPECT_COLOR_BIT`, specify an index of a color attachment in the current sub-pass for `colorAttachment`; otherwise, this parameter is ignored
- A desired clear value for a color, depth, or stencil aspect for `clearValue`

3. Create a variable of type `std::vector<VkClearRect>` named `rects`. For each area that should be cleared in all the specified attachments, add an element to the vector and initialize it with the following values:
   - The rectangle to be cleared (top-left corner and a width and height) for `rect`
   - The index of a first layer to be cleared for `baseArrayLayer`
   - The number of layers to be cleared for `layerCount`
4. Call `vkCmdClearAttachments( command_buffer, static_cast<uint32_t>(attachments.size()), attachments.data(), static_cast<uint32_t>(rects.size()), rects.data() )`. For the function call, provide the handle of the command buffer, the number of elements in the `attachments` vector, a pointer to its first element, the number of elements in the `rects` vector, and a pointer to its first element.

How it works...

When we want to explicitly clear an image that is used as a framebuffer's attachment inside a started render pass, we cannot use the usual image clearing functions. We can do this only by selecting which attachments should be cleared. This is done through the `vkCmdClearAttachments()` function like this:

```
vkCmdClearAttachments( command_buffer,
static_cast<uint32_t>(attachments.size()), attachments.data(),
static_cast<uint32_t>(rects.size()), rects.data() );
```

Using this function, we can clear multiple regions of all the indicated attachments.

 We can call the `vkCmdClearAttachments()` function only inside a render pass.

See also

- In `Chapter 3`, *Command Buffers and Synchronization*, see the recipe:
    - *Beginning a command buffer recording operation*
- In `Chapter 6`, *Render Passes and Framebuffers*, see the recipes:
    - *Specifying attachment descriptions*
    - *Specifying sub-pass descriptions*
    - *Beginning a render pass*
- The following recipes from this chapter:
    - *Clearing a color image*
    - *Clearing a depth-stencil image*

Binding vertex buffers

When we draw a geometry, we need to specify data for vertices. At the very least, vertex positions are required, but we can specify other attributes such as normal, tangent or bitangent vectors, colors, or texture coordinates. This data comes from buffers created with a **vertex buffer** usage. We need to bind these buffers to specified bindings before we can issue drawing commands.

Getting ready

In this recipe, a custom `VertexBufferParameters` type is introduced. It has the following definition:

```
struct VertexBufferParameters {
  VkBuffer      Buffer;
  VkDeviceSize  MemoryOffset;
};
```

This type is used to specify the buffer's parameters: its handle (in the `Buffer` member) and an offset from the start of the buffer's memory from which data should be taken (in the `MemoryOffset` member).

How to do it...

1. Take the handle of a command buffer that is in a recording state and use it to initialize a variable of type `VkCommandBuffer` named `command_buffer`.
2. Create a variable of type `std::vector<VkBuffer>` named `buffers`. For each buffer that should be bound to a specific binding in the command buffer, add the buffer's handle to the `buffers` vector.
3. Create a variable of type `std::vector<VkDeviceSize>` named `offsets`. For each buffer in the `buffers` vector, add a new member to the `offsets` vector with an offset value from the start of the corresponding buffer's memory (the buffer at the same index in the `buffers` vector).
4. Call `vkCmdBindVertexBuffers( command_buffer, first_binding, static_cast<uint32_t>(buffers_parameters.size()), buffers.data(), offsets.data() )`, providing the handle of the command buffer, the number of the first binding to which the first buffer from the list should be bound, the number of elements in the `buffers` (and `offsets`) vector, and a pointer to the first element of the `buffers` vector and to the first element of the `offsets` vector.

How it works...

During the graphics pipeline creation, we specify the vertex attributes that will be used (provided to shaders) during drawing. This is done through vertex binding and attributes descriptions (refer to the *Specifying a pipeline vertex binding description, attribute description, and input state* recipe from `Chapter 8`, *Graphics and Compute Pipelines*). Through them, we define the number of attributes, their formats, the location through which the shader will be able to access them, and the memory properties, such as offset and stride. We also provide the binding index from which a given attribute should be read. With this binding, we need to associate a selected buffer, in which data for a given attribute (or attributes) is stored. The association is made by binding a buffer to the selected binding index in a given command buffer, like this:

```
std::vector<VkBuffer>     buffers;
std::vector<VkDeviceSize> offsets;
for( auto & buffer_parameters : buffers_parameters ) {
  buffers.push_back( buffer_parameters.Buffer );
  offsets.push_back( buffer_parameters.MemoryOffset );
}
vkCmdBindVertexBuffers( command_buffer, first_binding,
  static_cast<uint32_t>(buffers_parameters.size()), buffers.data(),
```

Command Recording and Drawing

```
offsets.data() );
```

In the preceding code, the handles of all the buffers that should be bound and their memory offsets are provided through a variable of type `std::vector<VertexBufferParameters>` named `buffers_parameters`.

Remember that we can only bind buffers created with a vertex buffer usage.

See also

- In `Chapter 3`, *Command Buffers and Synchronization*, see the recipe:
  - *Beginning a command buffer recording operation*
- In `Chapter 4`, *Resources and Memory*, see the recipe:
  - *Creating a buffer*
- In `Chapter 8`, *Graphics and Compute Pipelines*, see the following recipes:
  - *Specifying a pipeline vertex binding description*
  - *Attribute description and input state*
- The following recipes in this chapter:
  - *Drawing a geometry*
  - *Drawing an indexed geometry*

Binding an index buffer

To draw a geometry, we can provide the list of vertices (and their attributes) in two ways. The first way is a typical list, in which vertices are read one after another. The second method requires us to provide additional indices that indicate which vertices should be read to form polygons. This feature is known as indexed drawing. It allows us to reduce the memory consumption as we don't need to specify the same vertices multiple times. It is especially important when we have multiple attributes associated with each vertex, and when each such vertex is used across many polygons.

Indices are stored in a buffer called an **index buffer**, which must be bound before we can draw an indexed geometry.

How to do it...

1. Store the command buffer's handle in a variable of type `VkCommandBuffer` named `command_buffer`. Make sure it is in a recording state.
2. Take the handle of the buffer in which the indices are stored. Use its handle to initialize a variable of type `VkBuffer` named `buffer`.
3. Take an offset value (from the start of the buffer's memory) that indicates the beginning of the indice's data. Store the offset in a variable of type `VkDeviceSize` named `memory_offset`.
4. Provide the type of data used for the indices. Use a `VK_INDEX_TYPE_UINT16` value for 16-bit unsigned integers or a `VK_INDEX_TYPE_UINT32` value for 32-bit unsigned integers. Store the value in a variable of type `VkIndexType` named `index_type`.
5. Call `vkCmdBindIndexBuffer( command_buffer, buffer, memory_offset, index_type )`, and provide the handles of the command buffer and the buffer, the memory offset value, and the type of data used for the indices (the `index_type` variable as the last argument).

How it works...

To use a buffer as a source of vertex indices, we need to create it with an *index buffer* usage and fill it with proper data--indices indicating what vertices should be used for drawing. Indices must be tightly packed (one after another) and they should just point to a given index in an array of vertex data, hence the name. This is shown in the following diagram:

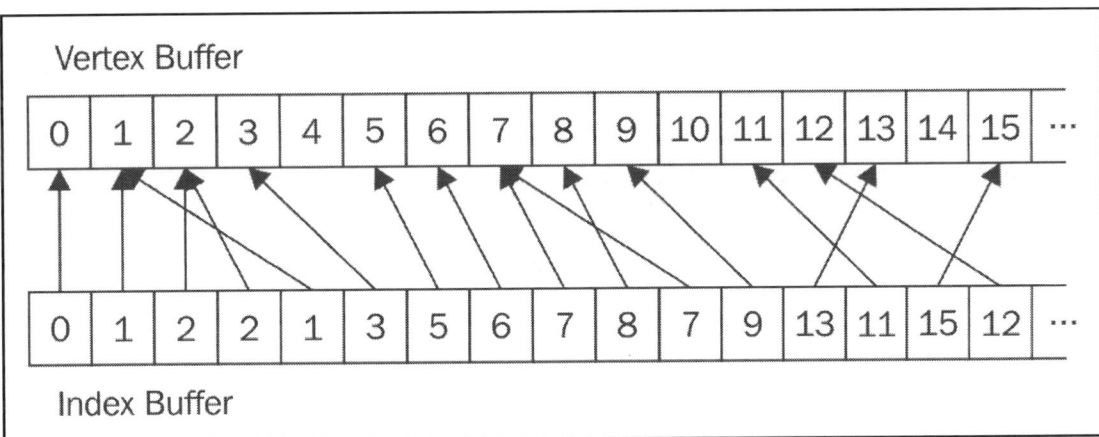

Before we can record an indexed drawing command, we need to bind an index buffer, like this:

```
vkCmdBindIndexBuffer( command_buffer, buffer, memory_offset, index_type );
```

For the call, we need to provide a command buffer, to which we record the function and the buffer that should act as an index buffer. Also, the memory offset from the start of the buffer's memory is required. It shows from which parts of the buffer's memory the driver should start reading the indices. The last parameter, the `index_type` variable in the preceding example, specifies the data type of the indices stored in the buffer--if they are specified as unsigned integers with 16 or 32 bits.

See also

- In `Chapter 3`, *Command Buffers and Synchronization*, see the recipe:
    - *Beginning a command buffer recording operation*
- In `Chapter 4`, *Resources and Memory*, see the recipe:
    - *Creating a buffer*
- The following recipes in this chapter:
    - *Binding vertex buffers*
    - *Drawing an indexed geometry*

Providing data to shaders through push constants

During drawing or dispatching computational work, specific shader stages are executed-- the ones defined during the pipeline creation. So the shaders can perform their job, we need to provide data to them. Most of the time we use descriptor sets, as they allow us to provide kilobytes or even megabytes of data through buffers or images. But using them is quite complicated. And, what's more important, frequent changes of descriptor sets may impact the performance of our application. But sometimes, we need to provide a small amount of data in a fast and easy way. We can do this using push constants.

How to do it...

1. Store the handle of a command buffer in a variable of type `VkCommandBuffer` named `command_buffer`. Make sure it is in a recording state.
2. Take the layout of a pipeline that uses a range of push constants. Store the handle of the layout in a variable of type `VkPipelineLayout` named `pipeline_layout`.
3. Through a variable of type `VkShaderStageFlags` named `pipeline_stages`, define the shader stages that will access a given range of push constant data.
4. In a variable of type `uint32_t` named `offset`, specify an offset (in bytes) from which the push constant memory should be updated. The `offset` must be a multiple of 4.
5. Define the size (in bytes) of the part of the updated memory in a variable of type `uint32_t` named `size`. The `size` must be a multiple of 4.
6. Using a variable of type `void *` named `data`, provide a pointer to a memory from which the data should be copied to push the constant memory.
7. Make the following call:

```
vkCmdPushConstants( command_buffer, pipeline_layout,
    pipeline_stages, offset, size, data )
```

8. For the call, provide (in the same order) the variables described in bullets from 1 to 6.

How it works...

Push constants allow us to quickly provide a small amount of data to shaders (refer to the *Using push constants in shaders* recipe from Chapter 7, *Shaders*). Drivers are required to offer at least 128 bytes of memory for push constant data. This is not much, but it is expected that push constants are much faster than updating data in a descriptor resource. This is the reason we should use them to provide data that changes very frequently, even with each drawing or dispatching of compute shaders.

Command Recording and Drawing

Data to push constants is copied from the provided memory address. Remember that we can update only data whose size is a multiple of 4. The offset within a push constant memory (to which we copy the data) must also be a multiple of 4. As an example, to copy four floating-point values, we can use the following code:

```
std::array<float, 4> color = { 0.0f, 0.7f, 0.4f, 0.1f };
ProvideDataToShadersThroughPushConstants( CommandBuffer, *PipelineLayout,
VK_SHADER_STAGE_FRAGMENT_BIT, 0, static_cast<uint32_t>(sizeof( color[0] ) *
color.size()), &color[0] );
```

`ProvideDataToShadersThroughPushConstants()` is a function that implements this recipe in the following way:

```
vkCmdPushConstants( command_buffer, pipeline_layout, pipeline_stages,
offset, size, data );
```

See also

- In Chapter 7, *Shaders*, see the recipe:
  - *Using push constants in shaders*
- In Chapter 8, *Graphics and Compute Pipelines*, see the recipe:
  - *Creating a pipeline layout*

Setting viewport states dynamically

The graphics pipeline defines parameters of lots of different states used during rendering. Creating separate pipeline objects every time we need to use slightly different values of some of these parameters would be cumbersome and very impractical. That's why dynamic states are available in Vulkan. We can define a viewport transformation to be one of them. In such a situation, we specify its parameters through a function call recorded in command buffers.

How to do it...

1. Take the handle of a command buffer that is in a recording state. Using its handle, initialize a variable of type `VkCommandBuffer` named `command_buffer`.

2. Specify the number of the first viewport whose parameters should be set. Store the number in a variable of type `uint32_t` named `first_viewport`.
3. Create a variable of type `std::vector<VkViewport>` named `viewports`. For each viewport that was defined during the pipeline creation, add a new element to the `viewports` vector. Through it, specify the parameters of a corresponding viewport using the following values:
   - The left side (in pixels) of the upper left corner for `x`
   - The top side (in pixels) of the upper left corner for `y`
   - The width of the viewport for `width`
   - The height of the viewport for `height`
   - The minimal depth value used during a fragment's depth calculations for `minDepth`
   - The maximal value of a fragment's calculated depth for `maxDepth`
4. Call `vkCmdSetViewport( command_buffer, first_viewport, static_cast<uint32_t>(viewports.size()), viewports.data() )` and provide the handle of the `command buffer`, the `first_viewport` variable, the number of elements in the viewports vector, and a pointer to the first element of the `viewports` vector.

How it works...

The viewport state can be specified to be one of the dynamic pipeline states. We do this during the pipeline creation (refer to the *Specifying pipeline dynamic states* recipe from Chapter 8, *Graphics and Compute Pipelines*). Here, dimensions of the viewport are specified with a function call like this:

```
vkCmdSetViewport( command_buffer, first_viewport,
    static_cast<uint32_t>(viewports.size()), viewports.data() );
```

Parameters defining the dimensions of each viewport used during rendering (refer to the *Specifying a pipeline viewport and scissor test state* recipe from Chapter 8, *Graphics and Compute Pipelines*) are specified through an array, where each element of the array corresponds to a given viewport (offset by the value specified in the `firstViewport` function parameter-- `first_viewport` variable in the preceding code).

We just need to remember that the number of viewports used during rendering is always specified statically in a pipeline, no matter if the viewport state is specified as dynamic or not.

See also

- In `Chapter 3`, *Command Buffers and Synchronization*, see the recipe:
    - *Beginning a command buffer recording operation*
- In `Chapter 8`, *Graphics and Compute Pipelines*, see the following recipes:
    - *Specifying a pipeline viewport and scissor test state*
    - *Specifying pipeline dynamic states*

Setting scissor states dynamically

The viewport defines a part of an attachment (image) to which the clip's space will be mapped. The scissor test allows us to additionally confine a drawing to the specified rectangle within the specified viewport dimensions. The scissor test is always enabled; we can only set up various values for its parameters. This can be done statically during the pipeline creation, or dynamically. The latter is done with a function call recorded in a command buffer.

How to do it...

1. Store the handle of a command buffer that is in a recording state in a variable of type `VkCommandBuffer` named `command_buffer`.
2. Specify the number of the first scissor rectangle in a variable of type `uint32_t` named `first_scissor`. Remember that the number of scissor rectangles corresponds to the number of viewports.
3. Create a variable of type `std::vector<VkRect2D>` named `scissors`. For each scissor rectangle we want to specify, add an element to the `scissors` variable. Use the following values to specify its members:
    - The horizontal offset (in pixels) from the upper left corner of the viewport for the x member of the `offset`
    - The vertical offset (in pixels) from the upper left corner of the viewport for the y member of the `offset`
    - The width (in pixels) of the scissor rectangle for the `width` member of the `extent`
    - The height (in pixels) of the scissor rectangle for the `height` member of the `extent`

4. Call `vkCmdSetScissor( command_buffer, first_scissor, static_cast<uint32_t>(scissors.size()), scissors.data() )` and provide the `command_buffer` and `first_scissor` variables, the number of elements in the `scissors` vector, and a pointer to the first element of the `scissors` vector.

How it works...

The scissor test allows us to restrict rendering to a rectangle area specified anywhere inside the viewport. This test is always enabled and must be specified for all viewports defined during the pipeline creation. In other words, the number of specified scissor rectangles must be the same as the number of viewports. If we are providing parameters for a scissor test dynamically, we don't need to do it in a single function call. But before the drawing command is recorded, scissor rectangles for all the viewports must be defined.

To define a set of rectangles for the scissor test, we need to use the following code:

```
vkCmdSetScissor( command_buffer, first_scissor,
    static_cast<uint32_t>(scissors.size()), scissors.data() );
```

The `vkCmdSetScissor()` function allows us to define scissor rectangles for only a subset of viewports. Parameters specified at index `i` in the `scissors` array (vector) correspond to a viewport at index `first_scissor + i`.

See also

- In Chapter 3, *Command Buffers and Synchronization*, see the recipe:
    - *Beginning a command buffer recording operation*
- In Chapter 8, *Graphics and Compute Pipelines*, see the following recipes:
    - *Specifying a pipeline viewport and scissor test state*
    - *Specifying pipeline dynamic states*
- *Setting viewport states dynamically*, in this chapter

Setting line width states dynamically

One of the parameters defined during the graphics pipeline creation is the width of drawn lines. We can define it statically. But if we intend to draw multiple lines with different widths, we should specify line width as one of the dynamic states. This way, we can use the same pipeline object and specify the width of the drawn lines with a function call.

How to do it...

1. Take the handle of a command buffer that is being recorded and use it to initialize a variable of type `VkCommandBuffer` named `command_buffer`.
2. Create a variable of type `float` named `line_width` through which the width of drawn lines will be provided.
3. Call `vkCmdSetLineWidth( command_buffer, line_width )` providing the `command_buffer` and `line_width` variables.

How it works...

Setting the width of lines dynamically for a given graphics pipeline is performed with the `vkCmdSetLineWidth()` function call. We just need to remember that to use various widths, we must enable the `wideLines` feature during the logical device creation. Otherwise, we can only specify a value of `1.0f`. In such a case, we shouldn't create a pipeline with a dynamic line width state. But, if we have enabled the mentioned feature and we want to specify various values for line widths, we can do it like this:

```
vkCmdSetLineWidth( command_buffer, line_width );
```

See also

- In Chapter 3, *Command Buffers and Synchronization,* see the following recipe:
    - *Beginning a command buffer recording operation*
- In Chapter 8, *Graphics and Compute Pipelines,* see the following recipes:
    - *Specifying a pipeline input assembly state*
    - *Specifying a pipeline rasterization state*
    - *Specifying pipeline dynamic states*

Setting depth bias states dynamically

When rasterization is enabled, each fragment that is generated during this process has its own coordinates (position on screen) and a depth value (distance from the camera). Depth value is used for the depth test, allowing for some opaque objects to cover other objects.

Enabling depth bias allows us to modify the fragment's calculated depth value. We can provide parameters for biasing a fragment's depth during the pipeline creation. But when depth bias is specified as one of the dynamic states, we do it through a function call.

How to do it...

1. Take the handle of a command buffer that is being recorded. Use the handle to initialize a variable of type `VkCommandBuffer` named `command_buffer`.
2. Store the value for the constant offset added to the fragment's depth in a variable of type `float` named `constant_factor`.
3. Create a variable of type `float` named `clamp`. Use it to provide the maximal (or minimal) depth bias that can be applied to an unmodified depth.
4. Prepare a variable of type `float` named `slope_factor`, in which store a value applied to the fragment's slope used during depth bias calculations.
5. Call the `vkCmdSetDepthBias( command_buffer, constant_factor, clamp, slope_factor )` function providing the prepared `command_buffer`, `constant_factor`, `clamp` and `slope_factor` variables, which are mentioned in the previous steps.

How it works...

Depth bias is used to offset a depth value of a given fragment (or rather, all fragments generated from a given polygon). Commonly, it is used when we want to draw objects that are very near other objects; for example, pictures or posters on walls. Due to the nature of depth calculations, such objects may be incorrectly drawn (partially hidden) when viewed from a distance. This issue is known as depth-fighting or Z-fighting.

Depth bias modifies the calculated depth value--the value used during the depth test and stored in a depth attachment--but does not affect the rendered image in any way (that is, it does not increase the visible distance between the poster and the wall it is attached to). Modifications are performed based on a constant factor and fragment's slope. We also specify the maximal or minimal value of the depth bias (`clamp`) which can be applied. These parameters are provided like this:

```
vkCmdSetDepthBias( command_buffer, constant_factor, clamp, slope_factor );
```

See also

- In Chapter 3, *Command Buffers and Synchronization*, see the following recipe:
    - *Beginning a command buffer recording operation*
- In Chapter 8, *Graphics and Compute Pipelines*, see the following recipes:
    - *Specifying pipeline rasterization states*
    - *Specifying pipeline depth and stencil states*
    - *Specifying pipeline dynamic states*

Setting blend constants states dynamically

Blending is a process that mixes a color stored in a given attachment with a color of a processed fragment. It is often used to simulate transparent objects.

There are multiple ways in which a fragment's color and a color stored in an attachment can be combined--for the blending, we specify factors (weights) and operations, which generate the final color. It is also possible that an additional, constant color is used by these calculations. During the pipeline creation, we can specify that components of the constant color are provided dynamically. In such a case, we set them with a function recorded in a command buffer.

How to do it...

1. Take the handle of a command buffer and use it to initialize a variable of type `VkCommandBuffer` named `command_buffer`.
2. Create a variable of type `std::array<float, 4>` named `blend_constants`. In the array's four elements, store the red, green, blue, and alpha components of the constant color used during the blending calculations.
3. Call `vkCmdSetBlendConstants( command_buffer, blend_constants.data() )` and provide the `command_buffer` variable and a pointer to the first element of the `blend_constants` array.

How it works...

Blending is enabled (statically) during graphics pipeline creation. When we enable it, we must provide multiple parameters that define the behavior of this process (refer to the *Specifying pipeline blend state* recipe from `Chapter 8`, *Graphics and Compute Pipelines*). Among these parameters are blend constants--four components of a constant color used during blending calculations. Normally, they are defined statically during the pipeline creation. But, if we enable blending and intend to use multiple different values for the blend constants, we should specify that we will provide them dynamically (refer to the *Specifying pipeline dynamic states* recipe from `Chapter 8`, *Graphics and Compute Pipelines*). This will allow us to avoid creating multiple similar graphics pipeline objects.

Values for the blend constants are provided with a single function call, like this:

```
vkCmdSetBlendConstants( command_buffer, blend_constants.data() );
```

See also

- In `Chapter 3`, *Command Buffers and Synchronization*, see the following recipe:
    - *Beginning a command buffer recording operation*
- In `Chapter 8`, *Graphics and Compute Pipelines*, see the following recipes:
    - *Specifying pipeline blend states*
    - *Specifying pipeline dynamic states*

Drawing a geometry

Drawing is the operation we usually want to perform using graphics APIs such as OpenGL or Vulkan. It sends the geometry (vertices) provided by the application through a vertex buffer down the graphics pipeline, where it is processed step by step by programmable shaders and fixed-function stages.

Drawing requires us to provide the number of vertices we would like to process (display). It also allows us to display multiple instances of the same geometry at once.

How to do it...

1. Store the handle of a command buffer in a variable of type `VkCommandBuffer` named `command_buffer`. Make sure the command buffer is currently being recorded and that the parameters of all the states used during rendering are already set in it (bound to it). Also, make sure that the render pass is started in the command buffer.
2. Use a variable of type `uint32_t` named `vertex_count` to hold the number of vertices we would like to draw.
3. Create a variable of type `uint32_t` named `instance_count` and initialize it with the number of geometry instances that should be displayed.
4. Prepare a variable of type `uint32_t` named `first_vertex`. Store the number of the first vertex from which the drawing should be performed.
5. Create a variable of type `uint32_t` named `first_instance` in which the number of the first instance (instance offset) should be stored.
6. Call the following function: `vkCmdDraw( command_buffer, vertex_count, instance_count, first_vertex, first_instance )`. For the call, provide all of the preceding variables in the same order.

How it works...

Drawing is performed with a call of the `vkCmdDraw()` function:

```
vkCmdDraw( command_buffer, vertex_count, instance_count, first_vertex,
    first_instance );
```

It allows us to draw any number of vertices, where vertices (and their attributes) are stored one after another in a vertex buffer (no index buffer is used). During the call we need to provide an offset--the number of the first vertex from which drawing should be started. This can be used when we have multiple models stored in one vertex buffer (for example, compounds of a model) and we want to draw only one of them.

The preceding function allows us to draw a single mesh (model), and also multiple instances of the same mesh. This is particularly useful when we have specified that some of the attributes change per instance, not per vertex (refer to the *Specifying pipeline vertex binding description, attribute description, and input state* recipe from `Chapter 8`, *Graphics and Compute Pipelines*). This way, each drawn instance of the same model may be a little bit different.

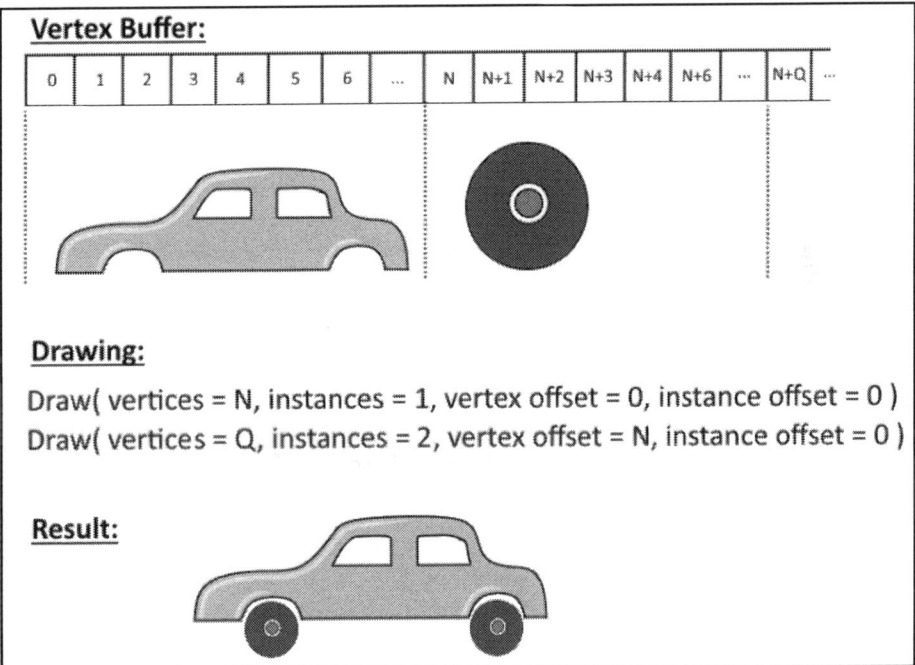

Command Recording and Drawing

Almost everything we do in Vulkan is used during drawing. So before we record a drawing command in a command buffer, we must be sure all the required data and parameters are properly set. Remember that each time we record a command buffer, it doesn't have any state. So before we can draw anything, we must set up the state accordingly.

There is no such thing as default state in Vulkan.

An example can be descriptor sets or dynamic pipeline states. Each time we start recording a command buffer, before we can draw anything, all the required descriptor sets (those used by shaders) must be bound to the command buffer. Similarly, every pipeline state that is specified as dynamic must have its parameters provided through corresponding functions. Another thing to remember is the render pass, which must be started in a command buffer for the drawing to be properly executed.

Drawing can be performed only inside the render pass.

See also

- In Chapter 3, *Command Buffers and Synchronization*, see the recipe:
    - *Beginning a command buffer recording operation*
- In Chapter 4, *Resources and Memory*, see the recipe:
    - *Creating a buffer*
- In Chapter 5, *Descriptor Sets*, see the recipe:
    - *Binding descriptor sets*
- In Chapter 6, *Render Passes and Framebuffers*, see the following recipes:
    - *Creating a render pass*
    - *Creating a framebuffer*
    - *Beginning a render pass*
- In Chapter 8, *Graphics and Compute Pipelines*, see the following recipes:
    - *Creating a graphics pipeline*
    - *Binding a pipeline object*

- The following recipes in this chapter:
    - *Binding vertex buffers*
    - *Setting viewport states dynamically*
    - *Setting scissor states dynamically*

Drawing an indexed geometry

Quite often it is more convenient to reuse vertices stored in a vertex buffer. Like the corners of a cube which belong to multiple sides, vertices in arbitrary geometry may belong to many parts of the whole model.

Drawing the object one vertex after another would require us to store the same vertex (along with all its attributes) multiple times. A better solution is to indicate which vertices should be used for drawing, no matter how they are ordered in the vertex buffer. For this purpose, indexed drawing was introduced in the Vulkan API. To draw geometry using indices stored in an index buffer, we need to call the `vkCmdDrawIndexed()` function.

How to do it...

1. Create a variable of type `VkCommandBuffer` named `command_buffer`, in which store the handle of a command buffer. Make sure the command buffer is in the recording state.
2. Initialize a variable of type `uint32_t` named `index_count` with the number of indices (and vertices) that should be drawn.
3. Use the number of instances (of the same geometry) to be drawn to initialize a variable of type `uint32_t` named `instance_count`.
4. Store the offset (in the number of indices) from the beginning of an index buffer in a variable of type `uint32_t` named `first_index`. From this index, drawing will be started.
5. Prepare a variable of type `uint32_t` named `vertex_offset`, in which the vertex offset (the value added to each index) should be stored.
6. Create a variable of type `uint32_t` named `first_instance` that should hold the number of the first geometry instance to be drawn.
7. Make the following call: `vkCmdDrawIndexed( command_buffer, index_count, instance_count, first_index, vertex_offset, first_instance )`. For the call, provide all of the preceding variables, in the same order.

Command Recording and Drawing

How it works...

Indexed drawing is the way to reduce the memory consumption. It allows us to remove duplicate vertices from vertex buffers, so we can allocate smaller vertex buffers. An additional index buffer is required, but usually vertex data requires much more memory space. This is especially the case in situations when each vertex has more attributes than just one position, such as normal, tangent, and bitangent vectors and two texture coordinates, which are used very often.

Indexed drawing also allows graphics hardware to reuse data from the already processed vertices through a form of vertex caching. With normal (non-indexed) drawing, hardware needs to process each vertex. When indices are used, hardware has additional information about processed vertices and knows if a given vertex was recently processed or not. If the same vertex was recently used (the last several dozens of processed vertices), in many situations the hardware may reuse the results of this vertex's previous processing.

To draw a geometry using vertex indices, we need to bind an index buffer before we record an indexed drawing command (refer to the *Binding an index buffer* recipe). We must also start a render pass, as indexed drawing (similarly to normal drawing) can be recorded only inside render passes. We also need to bind a graphics pipeline and all other required states (depending on the resources used by the graphics pipeline), and we are then good to call the following function:

```
vkCmdDrawIndexed( command_buffer, index_count, instance_count, first_index,
vertex_offset, first_instance );
```

Indexed drawing, similarly to normal drawing, can only be performed inside a render pass.

See also

- In Chapter 3, *Command Buffers and Synchronization*, see the recipe:
    - *Beginning a command buffer recording operation*
- In Chapter 4, *Resources and Memory*, see the recipe:
    - *Creating a buffer*
- In Chapter 5, *Descriptor Sets*, see the recipe:
    - *Binding descriptor sets*

Chapter 9

- In `Chapter` 6, *Render Passes and Framebuffers*, see the following recipes:
    - *Creating a render pass*
    - *Creating a framebuffer*
    - *Beginning a render pass*
- In `Chapter` 8, *Graphics and Compute Pipelines*, see the following recipes:
    - *Creating a graphics pipeline*
    - *Binding a pipeline object*
- The following recipes in this chapter:
    - *Binding vertex buffers*
    - *Binding an index buffer*
    - *Setting viewport states dynamically*
    - *Setting scissor states dynamically*

Dispatching compute work

Apart from drawing, Vulkan can be used to perform general computations. For this purpose, we need to write compute shaders and execute them--this is called dispatching. When we want to issue computational work to be performed, we need to specify how many separate compute shader instances should be executed and how they are divided into workgroups.

How to do it...

1. Take the handle of a command buffer and store it in a variable of type `VkCommandBuffer` named `command_buffer`. Make sure the command buffer is in the recording state and no render pass is currently started.
2. Store the number of local workgroups along the *x* dimension in a variable of type `uint32_t` named `x_size`.
3. The number of local workgroups in the *y* dimensions should be stored in a variable of type `uint32_t` named `y_size`.

Command Recording and Drawing

4. Use the number of local workgroups along the z dimension to initialize a variable of type `uint32_t` named `z_size`.
5. Record the `vkCmdDispatch( command_buffer, x_size, y_size, z_size )` function using the preceding variables as its arguments.

How it works...

When we dispatch compute work, we use compute shaders from the bound compute pipeline to perform the task they are programmed to do. Compute shaders use resources provided through descriptor sets. Results of their computations can also be stored only in resources provided through descriptor sets.

Compute shaders don't have a specific goal or use case scenario which they must fulfil. They can be used to perform any computations that operate on data read from descriptor resources. We can use them to perform image post-processing, such as color correction or blur. We can perform physical calculations and store transformation matrices in buffers or calculate new positions of a morphing geometry. The possibilities are limited only by the desired performance and hardware capabilities.

Compute shaders are dispatched in groups. The number of local invocations in x, y, and z dimensions are specified inside the shader source code (refer to the *Writing compute shaders* recipe from `Chapter 7, Shaders`). The collection of these invocations is called a workgroup. During dispatching the compute shaders, we specify how many such workgroups should be executed in each x, y, and z dimension. This is done through the parameters of the `vkCmdDispatch()` function:

```
vkCmdDispatch( command_buffer, x_size, y_size, z_size );
```

We just need to remember that the number of workgroups in a given dimension cannot be larger than the value in the corresponding index of the `maxComputeWorkGroupCount[3]` physical device's limit. Currently, the hardware must allow to dispatch at least 65,535 workgroups in a given dimension.

Dispatching compute workgroups cannot be done inside render passes. In Vulkan, render passes can be used only for drawing. If we want to bind compute pipelines and perform some computations inside compute shaders, we must end a render pass.

Compute shaders cannot be dispatched inside render passes.

[476]

See also

- In `Chapter` 3, *Command Buffers and Synchronization,* see the recipe:
  - *Beginning a command buffer recording operation*
- In `Chapter` 5, *Descriptor Sets,* see the recipe:
  - *Binding descriptor sets*
- In `Chapter` 6, *Render Passes and Framebuffers,* see the recipe:
  - *Ending a render pass*
- In `Chapter` 7, *Shaders,* see the following recipes:
  - *Writing compute shaders*
  - *Creating a compute pipeline*
  - *Binding a pipeline object*

Executing a secondary command buffer inside a primary command buffer

In Vulkan we can record two types of command buffers--primary and secondary. Primary command buffers can be submitted to queues directly. Secondary command buffers can be executed only from within primary command buffers.

How to do it...

1. Take a command buffer's handle. Store it in a variable of type `VkCommandBuffer` named `command_buffer`. Make sure the command buffer is in the recording state.
2. Prepare a variable of type `std::vector<VkCommandBuffer>` named `secondary_command_buffers` containing secondary command buffers that should be executed from within the `command_buffer`.

3. Record the following command: `vkCmdExecuteCommands( command_buffer, static_cast<uint32_t>(secondary_command_buffers.size()), secondary_command_buffers.data() )`. Provide the handle of the primary command buffer, the number of elements in the `secondary_command_buffers` vector, and a pointer to its first element.

How it works...

Secondary command buffers are recorded in a similar way to primary command buffers. In most cases, primary command buffers should be enough to perform rendering or computing work. But there may be situations in which we need to divide work into two command buffer types. When we have recorded secondary command buffers and we want the graphics hardware to process them, we can execute them from within a primary command buffer like this:

```
vkCmdExecuteCommands( command_buffer,
static_cast<uint32_t>(secondary_command_buffers.size()),
secondary_command_buffers.data() );
```

See also

- In `Chapter 3`, *Command Buffers and Synchronization*, see the recipe:
    - *Beginning a command buffer recording operation*

Recording a command buffer that draws a geometry with dynamic viewport and scissor states

Now we have all the knowledge required to draw images using the Vulkan API. In this sample recipe, we will aggregate some of the previous recipes and see how to use them to record a command buffer that displays a geometry.

Getting ready

To draw a geometry, we will use a custom structure type that has the following definition:

```
struct Mesh {
  std::vector<float>     Data;
  std::vector<uint32_t> VertexOffset;
  std::vector<uint32_t> VertexCount;
};
```

The `Data` member contains values for all the attributes of a given vertex, one vertex after another. For example, there are three components of position attribute, three components of a normal vector and two texture coordinates of a first vertex. After that, there is data for the position, normal, and **TexCoords** of a second vertex, and so on.

The `VertexOffset` member is used to store vertex offsets of separate parts of a geometry. The `VertexCount` vector contains a number of vertices in each such part.

Before we can draw a model whose data is stored in a variable of the preceding type, we need to copy the contents of a `Data` member to a buffer that will be bound to a command buffer as a vertex buffer.

How to do it...

1. Take the handle of a primary command buffer and store it in a variable of type `VkCommandBuffer` named `command_buffer`.
2. Start recording the `command_buffer` (refer to the *Beginning a command buffer recording operation* recipe from `Chapter 3`, *Command Buffers and Synchronization*).
3. Take the handle of an acquired swapchain image and use it to initialize a variable of type `VkImage` named `swapchain_image` (refer to the *Getting handles of swapchain images* and *Acquiring a swapchain image* recipes from `Chapter 2`, *Image Presentation*).
4. Store the index of a queue family that is used for swapchain image presentation in a variable of type `uint32_t` named `present_queue_family_index`.
5. Store the index of a queue family used for performing graphics operations in a variable of type `uint32_t` named `graphics_queue_family_index`.

Command Recording and Drawing

6. If values stored in the `present_queue_family_index` and `graphics_queue_family_index` variables are different, set up an image memory barrier in the `command_buffer` (refer to the *Setting an image memory barrier* recipe from `Chapter 4, Resources and Memory`). Use a `VK_PIPELINE_STAGE_TOP_OF_PIPE_BIT` value for the `generating_stages` parameter and a `VK_PIPELINE_STAGE_COLOR_ATTACHMENT_OUTPUT_BIT` value for the `consuming_stages` parameters. For the barrier, provide a single variable of type `ImageTransition` and use the following values to initialize its members:
    - The `swapchain_image` variable for `Image`
    - The `VK_ACCESS_MEMORY_READ_BIT` value for `CurrentAccess`
    - The `VK_ACCESS_COLOR_ATTACHMENT_WRITE_BIT` value for `NewAccess`
    - The `VK_IMAGE_LAYOUT_PRESENT_SRC_KHR` value for `CurrentLayout`
    - The `VK_IMAGE_LAYOUT_PRESENT_SRC_KHR` value for `NewLayout`
    - The `present_queue_family_index` variable for `CurrentQueueFamily`
    - The `graphics_queue_family_index` variable for `NewQueueFamily`
    - The `VK_IMAGE_ASPECT_COLOR_BIT` value for `Aspect`
7. Take the handle of a `render pass` and store it in a variable of type `VkRenderPass` named `render_pass`.
8. Store the handle of a framebuffer compatible with the `render_pass` in a variable of type `VkFramebuffer` named `framebuffer`.
9. Store the size of the `framebuffer` in a variable of type `VkExtent2D` named `framebuffer_size`.
10. Create a variable of type `std::vector<VkClearValue>` named `clear_values`. For each attachment used in the `render_pass` (and the `framebuffer`), add an element to the `clear_values` variable with values, to which corresponding attachments should be cleared.
11. Record a `render pass` beginning operation in the `command_buffer`. Use the `render_pass, framebuffer, framebuffer_size,` and `clear_values` variables and a `VK_SUBPASS_CONTENTS_INLINE` value (refer to *Beginning a render pass* recipe from `Chapter 6, Render Passes and Framebuffers`).

12. Take the handle of a graphics pipeline and use it to initialize a variable of type `VkPipeline` named `graphics_pipeline`. Make sure the pipeline was created with dynamic viewport and scissor states.
13. Bind the pipeline to the `command_buffer`. Provide a `VK_PIPELINE_BIND_POINT_GRAPHICS` value and the `graphics_pipeline` variable (refer to the *Binding a pipeline object* recipe from Chapter 8, *Graphics and Compute Pipelines*).
14. Create a variable of type `VkViewport` named `viewport`. Use the following values to initialize its members:
    - The `0.0f` value for x
    - The `0.0f` value for y
    - The `width` member of the `framebuffer_size` variable for `width`
    - The `height` member of the `framebuffer_size` variable for `height`
    - The `0.0f` value for `minDepth`
    - The `1.0f` value for `maxDepth`
15. Set the viewport state dynamically in the `command_buffer`. Use a 0 value for the `first_viewport` parameter and a vector of type `std::vector<VkViewport>` with a single element containing the `viewport` variable for the `viewports` parameter (refer to the *Setting viewport state dynamically* recipe).
16. Create a variable of type `VkRect2D` named `scissor`. Use the following values to initialize its members:
    - The 0 value for the x member of the `offset`
    - The 0 value for the y member of the `offset`
    - The `framebuffer_size.width` member variable for the `width` member of the `extent`
    - The `framebuffer_size.height` member variable for the `height` member of the `extent`
17. Set the scissor state dynamically in the `command_buffer`. Use a 0 value for the `first_scissor` parameter and a vector of type `std::vector<VkRect2D>` with a single element containing the `scissor` variable as the `scissors` parameter (refer to the *Setting scissor states dynamically* recipe in this chapter).

18. Create a variable of type `std::vector<VertexBufferParameters>` named `vertex_buffers_parameters`. For each buffer that should be bound to the `command_buffer` as a vertex buffer, add an element to the `vertex_buffers_parameters` vector. Use the following values to initialize the members of the new element:
    - The handle of a buffer that should be used as the vertex buffer for `Buffer`
    - The offset in bytes from the beginning of the buffer's memory (the memory part that should be bound for the vertex buffer) for `memoryoffset`
19. Store the value of the first binding, to which the first vertex buffer should be bound, in a variable of type `uint32_t` named `first_vertex_buffer_binding`.
20. Bind vertex buffers to the `command_buffer` using the `first_vertex_buffer_binding` and `vertex_buffers_parameters` variables (refer to the *Binding vertex buffers* recipe).
21. Perform the following operations if any descriptor resources should be used during drawing:
    1. Take the handle of a pipeline's layout and store it in a variable of type `VkPipelineLayout` named `pipeline_layout` (refer to *Creating a pipeline layout* recipe from Chapter 8, *Graphics and Compute Pipelines*).
    2. Add each descriptor set to be used during drawing to a vector variable of type `std::vector<VkDescriptorSet>` named `descriptor_sets`.
    3. Store an index, to which the first descriptor set should be bound, in a variable of type `uint32_t` named `index_for_first_descriptor_set`.
    4. Bind descriptor sets to the `command_buffer` using a `VK_PIPELINE_BIND_POINT_GRAPHICS` value and the `pipeline_layout`, `index_for_first_descriptor_set` and `descriptor_sets` variables.
22. Draw a geometry in the `command_buffer` specifying the desired values for the `vertex_count`, `instance_count`, `first_vertex`, and `first_instance` parameters (refer to the *Drawing a geometry* recipe).
23. End a render pass in the `command_buffer` (refer to the *Ending a render pass* recipe from Chapter 6, *Render Passes and Framebuffers*).

24. If values stored in the `present_queue_family_index` and `graphics_queue_family_index` variables are different, set up another image memory barrier in the `command_buffer` (refer to the *Setting an image memory barrier* recipe from `Chapter 4, Resources and Memory`). Use the `VK_PIPELINE_STAGE_COLOR_ATTACHMENT_OUTPUT_BIT` value for the `generating_stages` parameter and the `VK_PIPELINE_STAGE_BOTTOM_OF_PIPE_BIT` value for the `consuming_stages` parameter. For the barrier, provide a single variable of type `ImageTransition` initialized with the following values:
    - The `swapchain_image` variable for `Image`
    - The `VK_ACCESS_COLOR_ATTACHMENT_WRITE_BIT` value for `CurrentAccess`
    - The `VK_ACCESS_MEMORY_READ_BIT` value for `NewAccess`
    - The `VK_IMAGE_LAYOUT_PRESENT_SRC_KHR` value for `CurrentLayout`
    - The `VK_IMAGE_LAYOUT_PRESENT_SRC_KHR` value for `NewLayout`
    - The `graphics_queue_family_index` variable for `CurrentQueueFamily` and the `present_queue_family_index` variable for `NewQueueFamily`
    - The `VK_IMAGE_ASPECT_COLOR_BIT` value for `Aspect`
25. Stop recording the `command_buffer` (refer to the *Ending a command buffer recording operation* recipe from `Chapter 3, Command Buffers and Synchronization`).

How it works...

Assume we want to draw a single object. We want the object to appear directly on screen so, before we begin, we must acquire a swapchain image (refer to the *Acquiring a swapchain image* recipe from `Chapter 2, Image Presentation`). Next, we start recording the command buffer (refer to the *Beginning a command buffer recording operation* recipe from `Chapter 3, Command Buffers and Synchronization`):

```
if( !BeginCommandBufferRecordingOperation( command_buffer,
VK_COMMAND_BUFFER_USAGE_ONE_TIME_SUBMIT_BIT, nullptr ) ) {
  return false;
}
```

Command Recording and Drawing

The first thing we need to record is to change the swapchain image's layout to a VK_IMAGE_LAYOUT_COLOR_ATTACHMENT_OPTIMAL layout. This operation should be performed implicitly using appropriate render pass parameters (initial and sub-pass layouts). But if queues used for the presentation and graphics operations come from two different families, we must perform ownership transfer. This cannot be done implicitly--for this we need to set up an image memory barrier (refer to the *Setting an image memory barrier* recipe from Chapter 4, *Resources and Memory*):

```
if( present_queue_family_index != graphics_queue_family_index ) {
  ImageTransition image_transition_before_drawing = {
    swapchain_image,
    VK_ACCESS_MEMORY_READ_BIT,
    VK_ACCESS_COLOR_ATTACHMENT_WRITE_BIT,
    VK_IMAGE_LAYOUT_PRESENT_SRC_KHR,
    VK_IMAGE_LAYOUT_PRESENT_SRC_KHR,
    present_queue_family_index,
    graphics_queue_family_index,
    VK_IMAGE_ASPECT_COLOR_BIT
  };
  SetImageMemoryBarrier( command_buffer, VK_PIPELINE_STAGE_TOP_OF_PIPE_BIT, VK_PIPELINE_STAGE_COLOR_ATTACHMENT_OUTPUT_BIT, { image_transition_before_drawing } );
}
```

The next thing to do is to start a render pass (refer to the *Beginning a render pass* recipe from Chapter 6, *Render Passes and Framebuffers*). We also need to bind a pipeline object (refer to the *Binding a pipeline object* recipe from Chapter 8, *Graphics and Compute Pipelines*). We must do this before we can set up any pipeline related state:

```
BeginRenderPass( command_buffer, render_pass, framebuffer, { { 0, 0 }, framebuffer_size }, clear_values, VK_SUBPASS_CONTENTS_INLINE );

BindPipelineObject( command_buffer, VK_PIPELINE_BIND_POINT_GRAPHICS, graphics_pipeline );
```

When a pipeline is bound, we must set up any state that was marked as dynamic during the pipeline creation. Here, we set up viewport and scissor test states respectively (refer to the *Setting viewport states dynamically* and *Setting scissor states dynamically* recipes). We also bind a buffer that should be a source of vertex data (refer to the *Binding vertex buffers* recipe). This buffer must contain data copied from a variable of type Mesh:

```
VkViewport viewport = {
  0.0f,
  0.0f,
  static_cast<float>(framebuffer_size.width),
  static_cast<float>(framebuffer_size.height),
```

```
        0.0f,
        1.0f,
    };
    SetViewportStateDynamically( command_buffer, 0, { viewport } );

    VkRect2D scissor = {
        {
            0,
            0
        },
        {
            framebuffer_size.width,
            framebuffer_size.height
        }
    };
    SetScissorStateDynamically( command_buffer, 0, { scissor } );

    BindVertexBuffers( command_buffer, first_vertex_buffer_binding,
    vertex_buffers_parameters );
```

One last thing to do in this example is to bind the descriptor sets, which can be accessed inside shaders (refer to the *Binding descriptor sets* recipe from Chapter 5, *Descriptor Sets*):

```
    BindDescriptorSets( command_buffer, VK_PIPELINE_BIND_POINT_GRAPHICS,
    pipeline_layout, index_for_first_descriptor_set, descriptor_sets, {} );
```

Now we are ready to draw a geometry. Of course, in more advanced scenarios, we would need to set up parameters of other states and bind other resources. For example, we may need to use an index buffer and provide values for push constants. But, the preceding setup is also enough for many cases:

```
    for( size_t i = 0; i < geometry.Parts.size(); ++i ) {
        DrawGeometry( command_buffer, geometry.Parts[i].VertexCount,
        instance_count, geometry.Parts[i].VertexOffset, first_instance );
    }
```

To draw a geometry, we must provide the number of geometry instances we want to draw and an index of a first instance. Vertex offsets and the number of vertices to draw are taken from the members of variables of type `Mesh`.

Command Recording and Drawing

Before we can stop recording a command buffer, we need to end a render pass (refer to the *Ending a render pass* recipe from `Chapter 6`, *Render Passes and Framebuffers*). After that, another transition on a swapchain image is required. When we are done rendering a single frame of animation, we want to present (display) a swapchain image. For this, we need to change its layout to a `VK_IMAGE_LAYOUT_PRESENT_SRC_KHR` layout, because this layout is required for the presentation engine to correctly display an image. This transition should also be performed implicitly through render pass parameters (the final layout). But again, if the queues used for graphics operations and presentations are different, a queue ownership transfer is necessary. This is done with another image memory barrier. After that, we stop recording a command buffer (refer to the *Ending a command buffer recording operation* recipe from `Chapter 3`, *Command Buffers and Synchronization*):

```
EndRenderPass( command_buffer );

if( present_queue_family_index != graphics_queue_family_index ) {
  ImageTransition image_transition_before_present = {
    swapchain_image,
    VK_ACCESS_COLOR_ATTACHMENT_WRITE_BIT,
    VK_ACCESS_MEMORY_READ_BIT,
    VK_IMAGE_LAYOUT_PRESENT_SRC_KHR,
    VK_IMAGE_LAYOUT_PRESENT_SRC_KHR,
    graphics_queue_family_index,
    present_queue_family_index,
    VK_IMAGE_ASPECT_COLOR_BIT
  };
  SetImageMemoryBarrier( command_buffer,
  VK_PIPELINE_STAGE_COLOR_ATTACHMENT_OUTPUT_BIT,
  VK_PIPELINE_STAGE_BOTTOM_OF_PIPE_BIT, { image_transition_before_present }
  );
}

if( !EndCommandBufferRecordingOperation( command_buffer ) ) {
  return false;
}
return true;
```

This concludes the command buffer recording operation. We can use this command buffer and submit it to a (graphics) queue. It can be submitted only once, because it was recorded with a `VK_COMMAND_BUFFER_USAGE_ONE_TIME_SUBMIT_BIT` flag. But, of course, we can record a command buffer without this flag and submit it multiple times.

After submitting the command buffer, we can present a swapchain image, so it is displayed on screen. But, we must remember that submission and presentation operations should be synchronized (refer to the *Preparing a single frame of animation* recipe).

See also

- In Chapter 2, *Image Presentation*, see the following recipes:
    - *Acquiring a swapchain image*
    - *Presenting an image*
- In Chapter 3, *Command Buffers and Synchronization*, see the following recipes:
    - *Beginning a command buffer recording operation*
    - *Ending a command buffer recording operation*
- In Chapter 4, *Resources and Memory*, see the recipe:
    - *Setting an image memory barrier*
- In Chapter 5, *Descriptor Sets*, see the recipe:
    - *Binding descriptor sets*
- In Chapter 6, *Render Passes and Framebuffers*, see the following recipes:
    - *Beginning a render pass*
    - *Ending a render pass*
- In Chapter 8, *Graphics and Compute Pipelines*, see the recipe:
    - *Binding a pipeline object*
- The following recipes in this chapter:
    - *Binding vertex buffers*
    - *Setting viewport states dynamically*
    - *Setting scissor states dynamically*
    - *Drawing a geometry*
    - *Preparing a single frame of animation*

Recording command buffers on multiple threads

High level graphics APIs such as OpenGL are much easier to use, but they are also limited in many aspects. One such aspect is the lack of ability to render scenes on multiple threads. Vulkan fills this gap. It allows us to record command buffers on multiple threads, utilizing as much processing power of not only the graphics hardware, but also of the main processor.

[487]

Getting ready

For the purpose of this recipe, a new type is introduced. It has the following definition:

```
struct CommandBufferRecordingThreadParameters {
  VkCommandBuffer                          CommandBuffer;

  std::function<bool( VkCommandBuffer )>   RecordingFunction;

};
```

The preceding structure is used to store parameters specific for each thread used to record command buffers. The handle of a command buffer that will be recorded on a given thread is stored in the `CommandBuffer` member. The `RecordingFunction` member is used to define a function, inside which we will record the command buffer on a separate thread.

How to do it...

1. Create a variable of type `std::vector<CommandBufferRecordingThreadParameters>` named `threads_parameters`. For each thread used to record a command buffer, add a new element to the preceding vector. Initialize the element with the following values:
   - The handle of a command buffer to be recorded on a separate thread for `CommandBuffer`
   - The function (accepting a command buffer handle) used to record a given command buffer for `RecordingFunction`

2. Create a variable of type `std::vector<std::thread>` named `threads`. Resize it to be able to hold the same number of elements as the `threads_parameters` vector.

3. For each element in the `threads_parameters` vector, start a new thread that will use the `RecordingFunction` and provide the `CommandBuffer` as the function's argument. Store the handle of a created thread at the corresponding position in the `threads` vector.

4. Wait until all created threads finish their execution by joining with all elements in the `threads` vector.
5. Gather all recorded command buffers in a variable of type `std::vector<VkCommandBuffer>` named `command_buffers`.

How it works...

When we want to use Vulkan in a multithreaded application, we must keep in mind several rules. First, we shouldn't modify the same object on multiple threads. For example, we cannot allocate command buffers from a single pool or we cannot update a descriptor set from multiple threads.

We can access resources from multiple threads only if the access is read only or if we reference separate resources. But, as it may be hard to track which resources were created on which thread, in general, resource creation and modification should be performed only on a single *main* thread (which we can also call *the rendering thread*).

The most common scenario of utilizing multithreading in Vulkan is to concurrently record command buffers. This operation takes most of the processor time. It is also the most important operation performance-wise, so dividing it into multiple threads is very reasonable.

When we want to record multiple command buffers in parallel, we need to use not only a separate command buffer for each thread, but also a separate command pool.

> We need to use a separate command pool for each thread, on which command buffers will be recorded. In other words--a command buffer recorded on each thread must be allocated from a separate command pool.

Command buffer recording doesn't affect other resources (apart from the pool). We only prepare commands that will be submitted to a queue, so we can record any operations that use any resources. For example, we can record operations that access the same images or the same descriptor sets. The same pipelines can be bound to different command buffers at the same time during recording. We can also record operations that draw into the same attachments. We only record (prepare) operations.

Command Recording and Drawing

Recording command buffers on multiple threads may be performed like this:

```
std::vector<std::thread> threads( threads_parameters.size() );
for( size_t i = 0; i < threads_parameters.size(); ++i ) {
  threads[i] = std::thread::thread(
threads_parameters[i].RecordingFunction,
threads_parameters[i].CommandBuffer );
}
```

Here, each thread takes a separate `RecordingFunction` member, in which a corresponding command buffer is recorded. When all threads finish recording their command buffers, we need to gather the command buffers and submit them to a queue, when they are executed.

In real-life applications, we will probably want to avoid creating and destroying threads in this way. Instead, we should take an existing job/task system and use it to also record the necessary command buffers. But the presented example is easy to use and understand. And, it is also good at illustrating the steps that need to be performed to use Vulkan in multithreaded applications.

Submission can also be performed only from a single thread (queues, similarly to other resources, cannot be accessed concurrently), so we need to wait until all threads finish their jobs:

```
std::vector<VkCommandBuffer> command_buffers( threads_parameters.size() );
for( size_t i = 0; i < threads_parameters.size(); ++i ) {
  threads[i].join();
  command_buffers[i] = threads_parameters[i].CommandBuffer;
}

if( !SubmitCommandBuffersToQueue( queue, wait_semaphore_infos,
command_buffers, signal_semaphores, fence ) ) {
  return false;
}
return true;
```

 Submitting command buffers to a queue can be performed only from a single thread at a time.

[490]

Chapter 9

The preceding situation is presented in the following diagram:

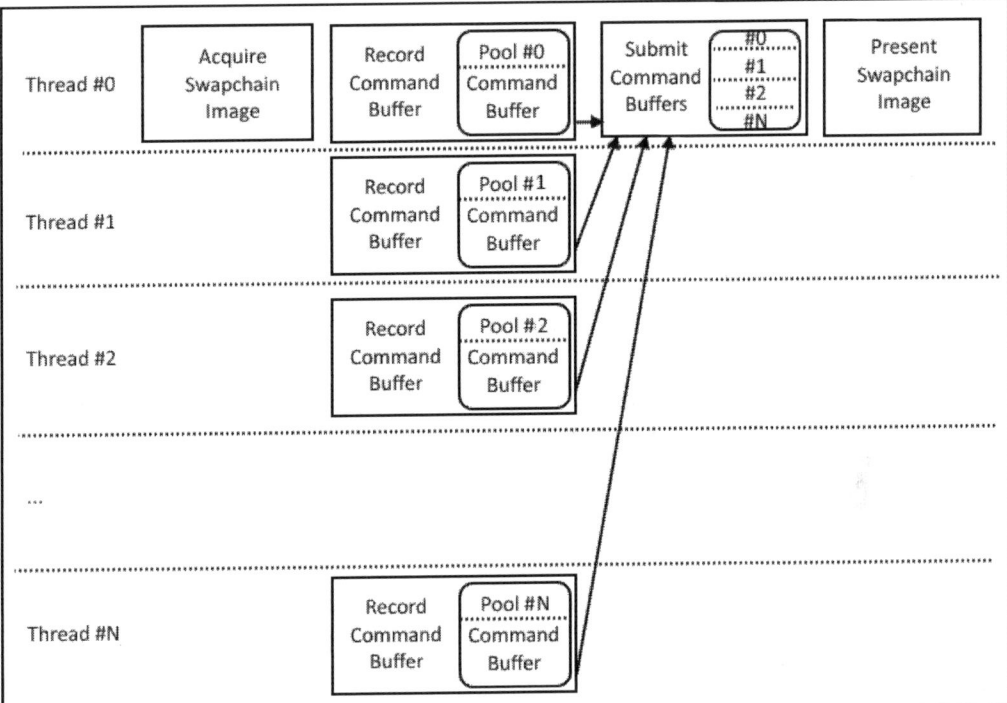

A similar situation occurs with a swapchain object. We can acquire and present swapchain images only from a single thread at a given moment. We cannot do this concurrently.

 A swapchain object cannot be accessed (modified) concurrently on multiple threads. Acquiring an image and presenting it should be done on a single thread.

But, it is a valid operation to acquire a swapchain image on a single thread and then concurrently record multiple command buffers that render into this swapchain image. We just need to make sure that the first submitted command buffer performs a layout transition away from the VK_IMAGE_LAYOUT_PRESENT_SRC_KHR (or the VK_IMAGE_LAYOUT_UNDEFINED) layout. Transition back to the VK_IMAGE_LAYOUT_PRESENT_SRC_KHR layout must be performed inside the command buffer that was submitted to the queue at the end. The order in which these command buffers were recorded doesn't matter; only the submission order is crucial.

[491]

Of course, when we want to record operations that modify resources (for example, store values in buffers), we must also record proper synchronization operations (such as pipeline barriers). This is necessary for the proper execution, but it doesn't matter from the recording perspective.

See also

- In `Chapter 2`, *Image Presentation*, see the following recipes:
    - *Acquiring a swapchain image*
    - *Presenting an image*
- In `Chapter 3`, *Command Buffers and Synchronization*, see the following recipes:
    - *Submitting command buffers to a queue*

Preparing a single frame of animation

Usually, when we create 3D applications that render images, we would like images to be displayed on screen. For this purpose, a swapchain object is created in Vulkan. We know how to acquire images from a swapchain. We have also learned how to present them. Here, we will see how to connect image acquiring and presentation, how to record a command buffer in between, and how we should synchronize all of these operations to render a single frame of animation.

How to do it...

1. Take the handle of a logical device and store it in a variable of type `VkDevice` named `logical_device`.
2. Use a handle of a created swapchain to initialize a variable of type `VkSwapchainKHR` named `swapchain`.
3. Prepare a semaphore handle in a variable of type `VkSemaphore` named `image_acquired_semaphore`. Make sure the semaphore is unsignaled or isn't being used in any previous submissions that haven't completed yet.

Chapter 9

4. Create a variable of type `uint32_t` named `image_index`.
5. Acquire an image from the `swapchain` using the `logical_device`, `swapchain`, and `image_acquired_semaphore` variables and store its index in the `image_index` variable (refer to the *Acquiring a swapchain image* recipe from `Chapter 2`, *Image Presentation*).
6. Prepare a handle of a render pass that will be used during recording drawing operations. Store it in a variable of type `VkRenderPass` named `render_pass`.
7. Prepare image views for all swapchain images. Store them in a variable of type `std::vector<VkImageView>` named `swapchain_image_views`.
8. Store the size of the swapchain images in a variable of type `VkExtent2D` named `swapchain_size`.
9. Create a variable of type `VkFramebuffer` named `framebuffer`.
10. Create a framebuffer for the `render_pass` (with at least an image view corresponding to the swapchain's image at the position `image_index`) using the `logical_device`, `swapchain_image_views[image_index]` and `swapchain_size` variables. Store the created handle in the framebuffer variable (refer to the *Creating a framebuffer* recipe from `Chapter 6`, *Render Passes and Framebuffers*).
11. Record a command buffer using the acquired swapchain image at the `image_index` position and the `framebuffer` variable. Store the handle of the recorded command buffer in a variable of type `VkCommandBuffer` named `command_buffer`.
12. Prepare a queue that will process commands recorded in the `command_buffer`. Store the queue's handle in a variable of type `VkQueue` named `graphics_queue`.
13. Take the handle of an unsignaled semaphore and store it in a variable of type `VkSemaphore` named `ready_to_present_semaphore`.
14. Prepare an unsignaled fence and store its handle in a variable of type `VkFence` named `finished_drawing_fence`.
15. Create a variable of type `WaitSemaphoreInfo` named `wait_semaphore_info` (refer to the *Submitting command buffers to a queue* recipe from `Chapter 3`, *Command Buffers and Synchronization*). Initialize members of this variable using the following values:
    - The `image_acquired_semaphore` variable for semaphore
    - The `VK_PIPELINE_STAGE_COLOR_ATTACHMENT_OUTPUT_BIT` value for `WaitingStage`

[493]

16. Submit the `command_buffer` to the `graphics_queue`, specifying one element vector with the `wait_semaphore_info` variable for the `wait_semaphore_infos` parameter, the `ready_to_present_semaphore` variable for the semaphore to be signaled, and the `finished_drawing_fence` variable for the fence to be signaled (refer to the *Submitting command buffers to the queue* recipe from `Chapter 3`, *Command Buffers and Synchronization*).
17. Prepare the handle of a queue used for presentation. Store it in a variable of type `VkQueue` named `present_queue`.
18. Create a variable of type `PresentInfo` named `present_info` (refer to the *Presenting an image* recipe from `Chapter 2`, *Image Presentation*). Initialize members of this variable with the following values:
    - The `swapchain` variable for `Swapchain`
    - The `image_index` variable for `ImageIndex`
19. Present the acquired swapchain image to the `present_queue` queue. Provide one element vector with the `ready_to_present_semaphore` variable as the `rendering_semaphores` parameter, and one element vector with the `present_info` variable as the `images_to_present` parameter (refer to the *Presenting an image* recipe from `Chapter 2`, *Image Presentation*).

How it works...

Preparing a single frame of animation can be divided into five steps:

1. Acquiring a swapchain image.
2. Creating a framebuffer.
3. Recording a command buffer.
4. Submitting the command buffer to the queue.
5. Presenting an image.

First, we must acquire a swapchain image into which we can render. Rendering is performed inside a render pass that defines the parameters of attachments. Specific resources used for these attachments are defined in a framebuffer.

Chapter 9

As we want to render into a swapchain image (to display the image on screen), this image must be specified as one of the attachments defined in a framebuffer. It may seem that creating a framebuffer earlier and reusing it during the rendering is a good idea. Of course, it is a valid approach but it has its drawbacks. The most important drawback is that it may be hard to maintain it during the lifetime of our application. We can render only into the image that was acquired from a swapchain. But as we don't know which image will be acquired, we need to prepare separate framebuffers for all swapchain images. What's more, we will need to recreate them each time a swapchain object is recreated. If our rendering algorithm requires more attachments to render into, we will start creating multiple variations of framebuffers for all combinations of swapchain images and images created by us. This becomes very cumbersome.

That's why it is much easier to create a framebuffer just before we start recording a command buffer. We create the framebuffer with only those resources that are needed to render this single frame. We just need to remember that we can destroy such a framebuffer only when the execution of a submitted command buffer is finished.

> A framebuffer cannot be destroyed until the queue stops processing a command buffer in which the framebuffer was used.

When an image is acquired and a framebuffer is created, we can record a command buffer. These operations may be performed like this:

```
uint32_t image_index;
if( !AcquireSwapchainImage( logical_device, swapchain,
image_acquired_semaphore, VK_NULL_HANDLE, image_index ) ) {
  return false;
}

std::vector<VkImageView> attachments = { swapchain_image_views[image_index]
};
if( VK_NULL_HANDLE != depth_attachment ) {
  attachments.push_back( depth_attachment );
}
if( !CreateFramebuffer( logical_device, render_pass, attachments,
swapchain_size.width, swapchain_size.height, 1, *framebuffer ) ) {
  return false;
}

if( !record_command_buffer( command_buffer, image_index, *framebuffer ) ) {
  return false;
}
```

[495]

Command Recording and Drawing

After that, we are ready to submit the command buffer to the queue. Operations recorded in the command buffer must wait until the presentation engine allows us to use the acquired image. For this purpose, we specify a semaphore when the image is acquired. This semaphore must also be provided as one of the wait semaphores during command buffer submission:

```
std::vector<WaitSemaphoreInfo> wait_semaphore_infos = wait_infos;
wait_semaphore_infos.push_back( {
  image_acquired_semaphore,
  VK_PIPELINE_STAGE_COLOR_ATTACHMENT_OUTPUT_BIT
} );
if( !SubmitCommandBuffersToQueue( graphics_queue, wait_semaphore_infos, {
command_buffer }, { ready_to_present_semaphore }, finished_drawing_fence )
) {
  return false;
}

PresentInfo present_info = {
  swapchain,
  image_index
};
if( !PresentImage( present_queue, { ready_to_present_semaphore }, {
present_info } ) ) {
  return false;
}
return true;
```

A rendered image can be presented (displayed on screen) when the queue stops processing the command buffer, but we don't want to wait and check when this happens. That's why we use an additional semaphore (the `ready_to_present_semaphore` variable in the preceding code) that will be signaled when the command buffer's execution is finished. The same semaphore is then provided when we present a swapchain image. This way, we synchronize operations internally on the GPU as this is much faster than synchronizing them on the CPU. If we weren't using the semaphore, we would need to wait until the fence is signaled and only then could we present an image. This would stall our application and hurt the performance considerably.

You may wonder why we need the fence (`finished_drawing_fence` in the preceding code), as it also gets signaled when the command buffer processing is finished. Isn't the semaphore enough? No, there are situations in which the application also needs to know when the execution of a given command buffer has ended. One such situation is when destroying the created framebuffer. We can't destroy it until the preceding fence is signaled. Only the application can destroy the resources it created, so it must know when it can safely destroy them (when they are not used anymore). Another example is re-recording of the command buffer. We can't record it again until its execution on a queue is finished. So we need to know when this happens. And, as the application cannot check the state of a semaphore, the fence must be used.

Using both a semaphore and a fence allows us to submit command buffers and present images immediately one after another, without unnecessary waits. And we can do these operations for multiple frames independently, increasing the performance even further.

See also

- In `Chapter 2`, *Image Presentation*, see the following recipes:
    - *Getting handles of swapchain images*
    - *Acquiring a swapchain image*
    - *Presenting an image*
- In `Chapter 3`, *Command Buffers and Synchronization*, see the following recipes:
    - *Creating a semaphore*
    - *Creating a fence*
    - *Submitting command buffers to a queue*
    - *Checking if processing of a submitted command buffer has finished*
- In `Chapter 6`, *Render Passes and Framebuffers*, see the following recipes:
    - *Creating a render pass*
    - *Creating a framebuffer*

Increasing the performance through increasing the number of separately rendered frames

Rendering a single frame of animation and submitting it to a queue is the goal of 3D graphics applications, such as games and benchmarks. But a single frame isn't enough. We want to render and display multiple frames or we won't achieve the effect of animation.

Unfortunately, we can't re-record the same command buffer immediately after we submit it; we must wait until the queue stops processing it. But, waiting until the command buffer processing is finished is a waste of time and it hurts the performance of our application. That's why we should render multiple frames of animation independently.

Getting ready

For the purpose of this recipe, we will use variables of a custom `FrameResources` type. It has the following definition:

```
struct FrameResources {
  VkCommandBuffer              CommandBuffer;
  VkDestroyer<VkSemaphore>     ImageAcquiredSemaphore;
  VkDestroyer<VkSemaphore>     ReadyToPresentSemaphore;
  VkDestroyer<VkFence>         DrawingFinishedFence;
  VkDestroyer<VkImageView>     DepthAttachment;
  VkDestroyer<VkFramebuffer>   Framebuffer;
};
```

The preceding type is used to define resources that manage the lifetime of a single frame of animation.

The `CommandBuffer` member stores a handle of a command buffer used to record operations of a single, independent frame of animation. In a real-life application, a single frame will be probably composed of multiple command buffers recorded in multiple threads. But for the purpose of a basic code sample, one command buffer is enough.

The `ImageAcquiredSemaphore` member is used to store a semaphore handle passed to the presentation engine when we acquire an image from a swapchain. This semaphore must then be provided as one of the wait semaphores when we submit the command buffer to a queue.

The `ReadyToPresentSemaphore` member indicates a semaphore that gets signaled when a queue stops processing our command buffer. We should use it during image presentation, so the presentation engine knows when the image is ready.

The `DrawingFinishedFence` member contains a fence handle. We provide it during the command buffer submission. Similarly to the `ReadyToPresentSemaphore` member, this fence gets signaled when the command buffer is no longer executed on a queue. But the fence is necessary to synchronize operations on the CPU side (the operations our application performs), not the GPU (and the presentation engine). When this fence is signaled, we know that we can both re-record the command buffer and destroy a framebuffer.

The `DepthAttachment` member is used to store an image view for an image serving as a depth attachment inside a sub-pass.

The `Framebuffer` member is used to store a temporary framebuffer handle created for the lifetime of a single frame of animation.

Most of the preceding members are wrapped into objects of a `VkDestroyer` type. This type is responsible for the implicit destruction of an owned object, when the object is no longer necessary.

How to do it...

1. Take the handle of a logical device and store it in a variable of type `VkDevice` named `logical_device`.
2. Create a variable of type `std::vector<FrameResources>` named `frame_resources`. Resize it to hold the resources for the desired number of independently rendered frames (the recommended size is three), and initialize each element using the following values (the values stored in each element must be unique):

    - The handle of a created command buffer for `commandbuffer`
    - Two handles of created semaphores for `ImageAcquiredSemaphore` and `ReadyToPresentSemaphore`
    - The handle of a fence created in an already signaled state for `DrawingFinishedFence`

- The handle of an image view for an image serving as a depth attachment for `DepthAttachment`
- The `VK_NULL_HANDLE` value for `Framebuffer`

3. Create a (potentially static) variable of type `uint32_t` named `frame_index`. Initialize it with a `0` value.
4. Create a variable of type `FrameResources` named `current_frame` that references an element of the `frame_resources` vector pointed to by the `frame_index` variable.
5. Wait until the `current_frame.DrawingFinishedFence` gets signaled. Provide the `logical_device` variable and a timeout value equal to `2000000000` (refer to the *Waiting for fences* recipe from `Chapter 3`, *Command Buffers and Synchronization*).
6. Reset the state of the `current_frame.DrawingFinishedFence` fence (refer to the *Resetting fences* recipe from `Chapter 3`, *Command Buffers and Synchronization*).
7. If the `current_frame.Framebuffer` member contains a handle of a created framebuffer, destroy it and assign a `VK_NULL_HANDLE` value to the member (refer to the *Destroying a framebuffer* recipe from `Chapter 6`, *Render Passes and Framebuffers*).
8. Prepare a single frame of animation using all the members of the `current_frame` variable (refer to the *Preparing a single frame of animation* recipe):
    1. Acquire a swapchain image providing the `current_frame.ImageAcquiredSemaphore` variable during this operation.
    2. Create a framebuffer and store its handle in the `current_frame.Framebuffer` member.
    3. Record a command buffer stored in the `current_frame.CommandBuffer` member.
    4. Submit the `current_frame.CommandBuffer` member to a selected queue, providing the `current_frame.ImageaAquiredSemaphore` semaphore as one of the waiting semaphores, the `current_frame.ReadyToPresentSemaphore` semaphore as the semaphore to be signaled, and the `current_frame.DrawingFinishedFence` fence as the fence to be signaled when the command buffer's execution is finished.

5. Present a swapchain image to a selected queue, providing the one element vector with the `current_frame.ReadyToPresentSemaphore` variable as the `rendering_semaphores` parameter.

9. Increment a value stored in the `frame_index` variable. If it is equal to the number of elements in the `frame_resources` vector, reset the variable to 0.

How it works...

Rendering animation is performed in a loop. One frame is rendered and an image is presented, then usually the operating system messages are processed. Next, another frame is rendered and presented, and so on.

When we have only one command buffer and other resources required to prepare, render, and display a frame, we can't reuse them immediately. Semaphores cannot be used for another submission until the previous submission, in which they were used, has been finished. This situation requires us to wait for the end of the command buffer processing. But such waits are highly undesirable. The more we wait on the CPU, the more stalls we introduce to the graphics hardware and the worse performance we achieve.

To shorten the time we wait in our application (until a command buffer recorded for the previous frame is executed), we need to prepare several sets of resources required to render and present a frame. When we record and submit a command buffer for one frame and we want to prepare another frame, we just take another set of resources. For the next frame, we use yet another set of resources until we have used all of them. Then we just take the least recently used set--of course, we need to check if we can reuse it but, at this time, there is a high probability that it has already been processed by the hardware. The process of rendering animation using multiple sets of **Frame Resources** is presented in the following diagram:

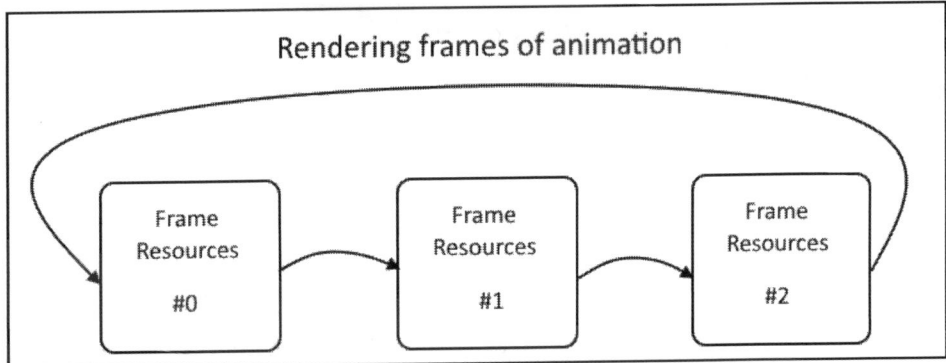

How many sets should we prepare? We may think that the more sets we have the better, because we won't need to wait at all. But unfortunately, the situation isn't that simple. First, we increase the memory footprint of our application. But, more importantly, we increase an input lag. Usually, we render animation based on the input from the user, who wants to rotate a virtual camera, view a model, or move a character. We want our application to respond to a user's input as quickly as possible. When we increase the number of independently rendered frames, we also increase the time between a user's input and the effect it has on the rendered image.

We need to balance the number of separately rendered frames, the performance of our application, its memory usage, and the input lag.

So, how many frame resources should we have? This of course depends on the complexity of the rendered scenes, the performance of the hardware on which the application is executed, and the type of rendering scenario it realizes (that is, the type of game we are creating--whether it is a fast **first-person perspective** (**FPP**) shooter or a racing game, or a more slow-paced tour based **role-playing game** (**RPG**)). So there is not one exact value that will fit all possible scenarios. Tests have shown that increasing the number of frame resources from one to two may increase the performance by 50%. Adding a third set increases the performance further, but the growth isn't as big this time. So, the performance gain is smaller with each additional set of frame resources. Three sets of rendering resources seems like a good choice, but we should perform our own tests and see what is best for our specific needs.

We can see three examples of recording and submitting command buffers with one, two, and three independent sets of resources needed to render frames of animations, as follows:

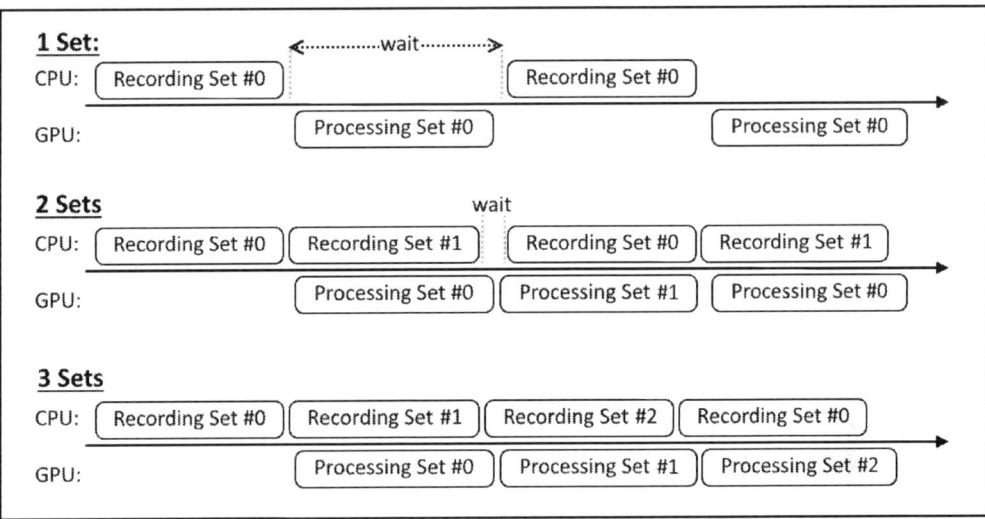

Now that we know why we should use several independent numbers of frame resources, we can see how to render a frame using them.

First, we start by checking if we can use a given set of resources to prepare a frame. We do this by checking the status of a fence. If it is signaled, we are good to go. You may wonder, what should we do when we render the very first frame--we didn't submit anything to a queue yet, so the fence didn't have an opportunity to be signaled. It's true, and that's why, for the purpose of preparing frame resources, we should create fences in an already signaled state:

```
static uint32_t frame_index = 0;
FrameResources & current_frame = frame_resources[frame_index];

if( !WaitForFences( logical_device, { *current_frame.DrawingFinishedFence
}, false, 2000000000 ) ) {
  return false;
}
if( !ResetFences( logical_device, { *current_frame.DrawingFinishedFence } )
) {
  return false;
}
```

We should also check if a framebuffer used for the frame was created. If it was, we should destroy it because it will be created later. For an acquired swapchain image, an `InitVkDestroyer()` function initializes the provided variable with a new, empty object handle and, if necessary, destroys the previously owned object. After that, we render the frame and present an image. To do this, we need a command buffer and two semaphores (refer to the *Preparing a single frame of animation* recipe):

```
InitVkDestroyer( logical_device, current_frame.Framebuffer );

if( !PrepareSingleFrameOfAnimation( logical_device, graphics_queue,
present_queue, swapchain, swapchain_size, swapchain_image_views,
*current_frame.DepthAttachment, wait_infos,
*current_frame.ImageAcquiredSemaphore,
*current_frame.ReadyToPresentSemaphore,
*current_frame.DrawingFinishedFence, record_command_buffer,
current_frame.CommandBuffer, render_pass, current_frame.Framebuffer ) ) {
   return false;
}

frame_index = (frame_index + 1) % frame_resources.size();
return true;
```

One last thing is to increase the index of the currently used set of frame resources. For the next frame of animation we will use another set, until we have used all of them, and we start from the beginning:

```
frame_index = (frame_index + 1) % frame_resources.size();
return true;
```

See also

- In Chapter 3, *Command Buffers and Synchronization*, see the following recipes:
  - *Waiting for fences*
  - *Resetting fences*
- In Chapter 6, *Render Passes and Framebuffers*, see the following recipe:
  - *Destroying a framebuffer*
- *Preparing a single frame of animation* recipe in this chapter

10
Helper Recipes

In this chapter, we will cover the following recipes:

- Preparing a translation matrix
- Preparing a rotation matrix
- Preparing a scaling matrix
- Preparing a perspective projection matrix
- Preparing an orthographic projection matrix
- Loading texture data from a file
- Loading a 3D model from an OBJ file

Introduction

In previous chapters, we have learned about the various aspects of the Vulkan API. We now know how to use the graphics library and how to create applications that render 3D images and perform mathematical calculations. But the sole knowledge about the Vulkan API may not be enough to generate more complicated scenes and to implement various rendering algorithms. There are several very useful operations that can aid us in creating, manipulating, and displaying 3D objects.

In this chapter, we will learn how to prepare transformation matrices that are used to move, rotate, and scale 3D meshes. We will also see how to generate projection matrices. Finally, we will use simple yet very powerful single-header libraries to load images and 3D models stored in files.

Preparing a translation matrix

Basic operations that can be performed on 3D models include moving the objects in a desired direction for a selected distance (number of units).

How to do it...

1. Prepare three variables of type `float` named x, y, and z, and initialize them with the amount of translation (movement distance) applied to the object along the x (right/left), y (up/down), and z (near/far) directions respectively.
2. Create a variable of type `std::array<float, 16>` named `translation_matrix` that will hold a matrix representing the desired operation. Initialize elements of the `translation_matrix` array with the following values:
   - All elements initialize with a `0.0f` value
   - 0th, 5th, 10th, and 15th elements (main diagonal) with a `1.0f` value
   - 12th element with a value stored in the x variable
   - 13th element with a value stored in the y variable
   - 14th element with a value stored in the z variable
3. Provide values of all elements of the `translation_matrix` variable to shaders (possibly via a uniform buffer or a push constant) or multiply it by another matrix to accumulate multiple operations in one matrix.

How it works...

Translation is one of three basic transformations that can be applied to an object (the rest are rotation and scaling). It allows us to move a 3D model in a desired direction for a desired distance:

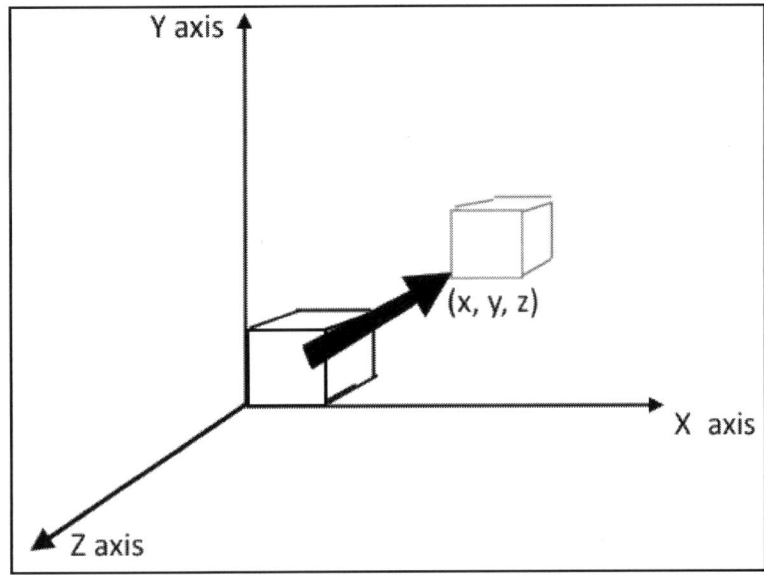

Movement can also be applied to the camera, thus changing the point from which we observe a whole rendered scene.

Creating a translation matrix is a simple process. We need an identity 4x4 matrix--all its elements must be initialized with zeros (0.0f) except for the elements on the main diagonal, which must be initialized with ones (1.0f). Now we initialize the first three elements of the fourth column with the distance we want to apply in the x, y, and z axes respectively, as follows:

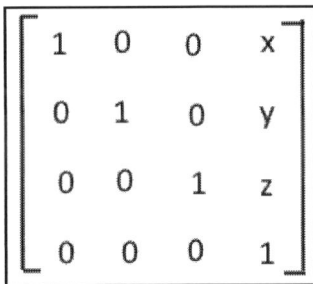

The following code creates a translation matrix:

```
std::array<float, 16> translation_matrix = {
  1.0f, 0.0f, 0.0f, 0.0f,
  0.0f, 1.0f, 0.0f, 0.0f,
  0.0f, 0.0f, 1.0f, 0.0f,
     x,    y,    z, 1.0f
};
return translation_matrix;
```

In the preceding code, we assume the matrix has a `column_major` order (first four elements compose a first column of the matrix, next four elements compose a second column, and so on), so it is transposed compared to the preceding figure. But the order of elements of the matrix provided to the shaders depends on a `row_major` or `column_major` **layout qualifier** specified in the shaders' source code.

> Keep in mind the order of elements of matrix defined in the shaders. It is specified through a `row_major` or `column_major` layout qualifier.

See also

- In Chapter 5, *Descriptor Sets*, see the following recipe:
    - *Creating a uniform buffer*
- In Chapter 7, *Shaders*, see the following recipes:
    - *Writing a vertex shader that multiplies vertex position by a projection matrix*
    - *Using push constants in shaders*
- In Chapter 9, *Command Recording and Drawing*, see the following recipe:
    - *Providing data to shaders through push constants*
- The following recipes in this chapter:
    - *Preparing a scaling matrix*
    - *Preparing a rotation matrix*

Chapter 10

Preparing a rotation matrix

When we create a 3D scene and manipulate its objects, we usually need to rotate them in order to properly place and orient them among other objects. Rotating an object is achieved with a rotation matrix. For it, we need to specify a vector, around which rotation will be performed, and an angle--how much rotation we want to apply.

How to do it...

1. Prepare three variables of type `float` named x, y, and z. Initialize them with values that define an arbitrary vector, around which rotation should be performed. Make sure the vector is normalized (has a length equal to `1.0f`).
2. Prepare a variable of type `float` named `angle` and store an angle of the rotation (in radians) in it.
3. Create a variable of type `float` named c. Store a cosine of the angle in it.
4. Create a variable of type `float` named s. Store a sine of the angle in it.
5. Create a variable of type `std::array<float, 16>` named `rotation_matrix` that will hold a matrix representing the desired operation. Initialize elements of the `rotation_matrix` array with the following values:
   - 0th element with a x * x * (1.0f - c) + c
   - 1st element with a y * x * (1.0f - c) - z * s
   - 2nd element with a z * x * (1.0f - c) + y * s
   - 4th element with a x * y * (1.0f - c) + z * s
   - 5th element with a y * y * (1.0f - c) + c
   - 6th element with a z * y * (1.0f - c) - x * s
   - 8th element with a x * z * (1.0f - c) - y * s
   - 9th element with a y * z * (1.0f - c) + x * s
   - 10th element with a z * z * (1.0f - c) + c
   - The rest of the elements initialize with a `0.0f` value
   - Except for the 15th element, which should contain a `1.0f` value
6. Provide values of all elements of the `rotation_matrix` variable to shaders (possibly via a uniform buffer or a push constant) or multiply it by another matrix to accumulate multiple operations in one matrix.

How it works...

Preparing a matrix that represents a general rotation transformation is quite complicated. It can be divided into three separate matrices--representing rotations around each of the x, y, and z axis--that are later multiplied to generate the same result. Each such rotation is much simpler to prepare, but all in all it requires more operations to be performed, thus it may have a worse performance.

That's why it is better to prepare a matrix that represents a rotation around a selected (arbitrary) vector. For this we need to specify an angle, which defines the amount of rotation to apply, and a vector. This vector should be normalized, or the amount of the applied rotation will be scaled proportionally to the length of the vector.

 Vector, around which rotation is performed, should be normalized.

The following figure shows a rotation matrix. Data needed to perform rotation transformation is placed in the upper-left 3x3 matrix. Each column of such matrix defines the directions of x, y, and z axes respectively after the rotation is performed. What's more, a transposed rotation matrix defines exactly the opposite transformation:

$$\begin{bmatrix} R_{xx} & R_{yx} & R_{zx} & 0 \\ R_{xy} & R_{yy} & R_{zy} & 0 \\ R_{xz} & R_{yz} & R_{zz} & 0 \\ 0 & 0 & 0 & 1 \end{bmatrix}$$

For example, if we want to rotate a camera to simulate that the character we control looks around left and right, or if we want to display a car that is turning left or right, we should specify a vector that points upwards (0.0f, 1.0f, 0.0f). We can also specify a vector that points downwards (0.0f, -1.0f, 0.0f). In this case, the object will be rotated for the same angle, but in the opposite direction. We need to choose which option is more convenient for us:

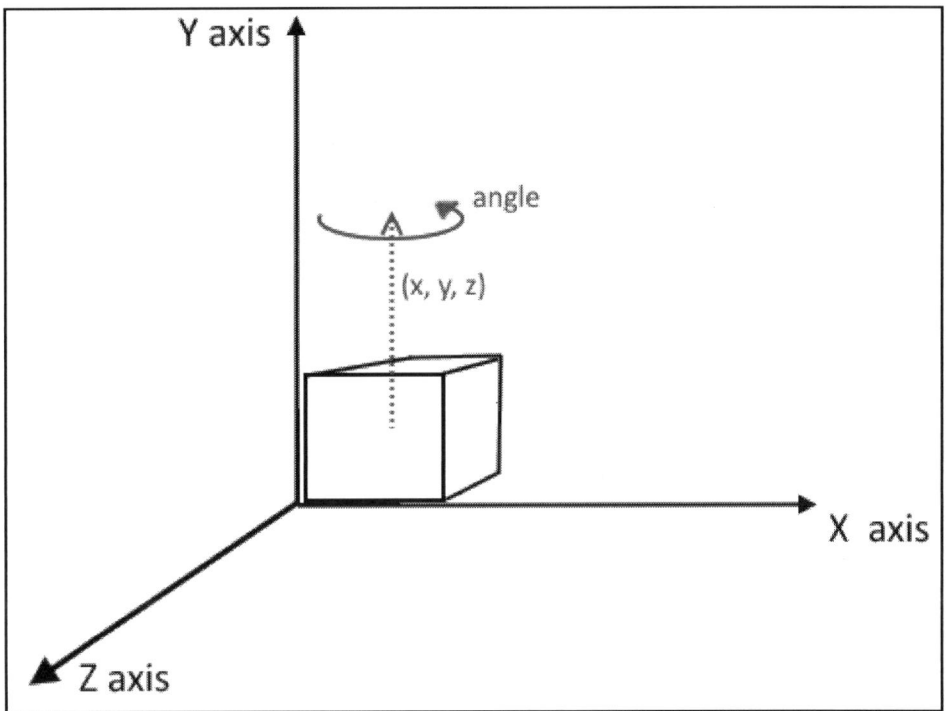

The following is the code that creates a rotation matrix. It first checks if we want to normalize the vector and modifies its components accordingly. Next, helper variables are prepared that store temporary results. Finally, all elements of the rotation matrix are initialized:

```
if( normalize ) {
    std::array<float, 3> normalized = Normalize( x, y, z );
    x = normalized[0];
    y = normalized[1];
    z = normalized[2];
}
const float c = cos( Deg2Rad( angle ) );
const float _1_c = 1.0f - c;
```

Helper Recipes

```
const float s = sin( Deg2Rad( angle ) );
std::array<float, 16> rotation_matrix = {
  x * x * _1_c + c,
  y * x * _1_c - z * s,
  z * x * _1_c + y * s,
  0.0f,
  x * y * _1_c + z * s,
  y * y * _1_c + c,
  z * y * _1_c - x * s,
  0.0f,
  x * z * _1_c - y * s,
  y * z * _1_c + x * s,
  z * z * _1_c + c,
  0.0f,
  0.0f,
  0.0f,
  0.0f,
  1.0f
};
return rotation_matrix;
```

We need to remember the order of elements in an array (application) and in the matrix defined in a shaders source code. Inside shaders, we control it with `row_major` or `column_major` layout qualifiers.

See also

- In Chapter 5, *Descriptor Sets*, see the following recipe:
  - *Creating a uniform buffer*
- In Chapter 7, *Shaders*, see the following recipes:
  - *Writing a vertex shader that multiplies vertex position by a projection matrix*
  - *Using push constants in shaders*
- In Chapter 9, *Command Recording and Drawing*, see the following recipe:
  - *Providing data to shaders through push constants*
- The following recipe in this chapter:
  - *Preparing a translation matrix*
  - *Preparing a scaling matrix*

Preparing a scaling matrix

The third transformation that can be performed on a 3D model is scaling. This allows us to change an object's size.

How to do it...

1. Prepare three variables of type `float` named x, y, and z that will hold the scaling factor applied to a model in x (width), y (height), and z (depth) dimensions, respectively.
2. Create a variable of type `std::array<float, 16>` named `scaling_matrix`, in which a matrix representing the desired operation will be stored. Initialize elements of the `scaling_matrix` array with the following values:
    - All elements initialize with a `0.0f` value
    - 0th element with a value stored in the x variable
    - 5th element with a value stored in the y variable
    - 10th element with a value stored in the z variable
    - 15th element with a `1.0f` value
3. Provide values of all elements of the `scaling_matrix` variable to shaders (possibly via a uniform buffer or a push constant) or multiply it by another matrix to accumulate multiple operations in one matrix.

How it works...

Sometimes we need to change an object's size (compared to other objects in the scene). For example, due to the effect of a magical incantation, our character shrinks to fit into a very small hole. This transformation is achieved with a scaling matrix that looks like this:

$$\begin{bmatrix} x & 0 & 0 & 0 \\ 0 & y & 0 & 0 \\ 0 & 0 & z & 0 \\ 0 & 0 & 0 & 1 \end{bmatrix}$$

Using the scaling matrix, we can resize the model differently in each dimension:

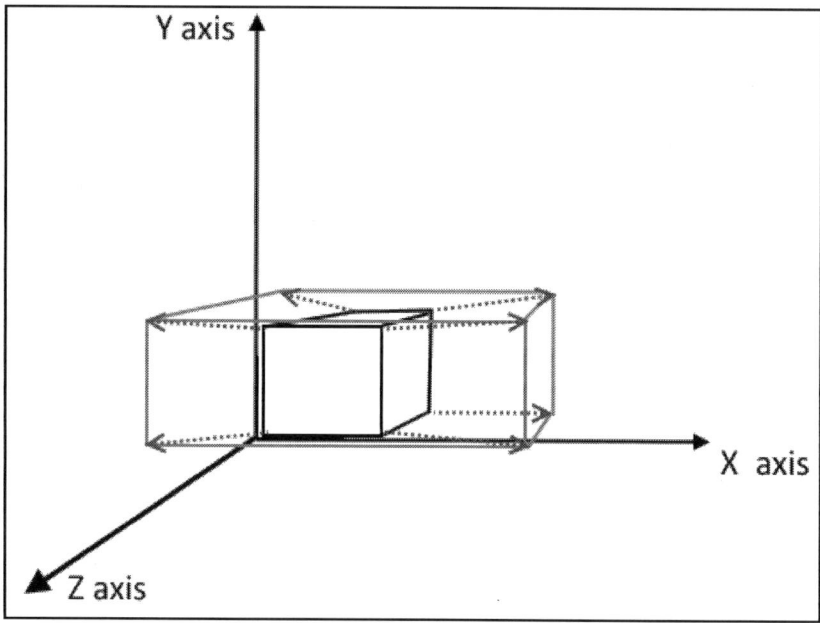

We must be cautious if we don't scale an object uniformly. Usually, to simplify the code and improve the performance, we provide a combined transformation matrix to a shader and use the same matrix to transform not only vertices, but also normal vectors. When we scale an object uniformly, we just need to normalize the normal vector in the shader after the transformation. But when we use a transformation that scales an object differently in each dimension, we cannot apply it to a normal vector, because lighting calculations will be incorrect (direction represented by the normal vector will be changed). If we really need to perform such scaling, we need to use an inverse transpose matrix for the normal vector transformation. We must prepare it separately and provide it to a shader.

 When an object is scaled differently in each dimension, a normal vector must be transformed by an inverse transformation matrix.

Preparing a scaling matrix can be performed with the following code:

```
std::array<float, 16> scaling_matrix = {
       x, 0.0f, 0.0f, 0.0f,
    0.0f,    y, 0.0f, 0.0f,
    0.0f, 0.0f,    z, 0.0f,
    0.0f, 0.0f, 0.0f, 1.0f
};
return scaling_matrix;
```

As with all other matrices, we need to remember about the order of elements defined in our application (CPU) and order of elements of the matrices defined in the shader source code (`column_major` versus `row_major` order).

See also

- In Chapter 5, *Descriptor Sets*, see the following recipe:
    - *Creating a uniform buffer*
- In Chapter 7, *Shaders*, see the following recipes:
    - *Writing a vertex shader that multiplies vertex position by a projection matrix*
    - *Using push constants in shaders*
- In Chapter 9, *Command Recording and Drawing*, see the following recipe:
    - *Providing data to shaders through push constants*
- The following recipes in this chapter:
    - *Preparing a translation matrix*
    - *Preparing a rotation matrix*

Preparing a perspective projection matrix

3D applications usually try to simulate the effect of how we perceive the world around us--objects in the distance seem smaller than the objects that are closer to us. To achieve this effect, we need to use a perspective projection matrix.

How to do it...

1. Prepare a variable of type `float` named `aspect_ratio` that will hold an aspect ratio of a renderable area (image's width divided by its height).
2. Create a variable of type `float` named `field_of_view`. Initialize it with an angle (in radians) of a vertical field of view of a camera.
3. Create a variable of type `float` named `near_plane` and initialize it with the distance from the camera's position to the near clipping plane.
4. Create a variable of type `float` named `far_plane`. Store the distance between a camera and the far clipping plane in the variable.
5. Calculate a value of `1.0f` divided by a tangent of the half of the `field_of_view` (`1.0f / tan(Deg2Rad(0.5f * field_of_view))`) and store the result in a variable of type `float` named `f`.
6. Create a variable of type `std::array<float, 16>` named `perspective_projection_matrix` that will hold a matrix representing the desired projection. Initialize elements of the `perspective_projection_matrix` array with the following values:
    - 0th element with a `f / aspect_ratio`
    - 5th element with a `-f`
    - 10th element with a `far_plane / (near_plane - far_plane)`
    - 11th element with a `-1.0f` value
    - 14th element with a `(near_plane * far_plane) / (near_plane - far_plane)`
    - The rest of the elements initialize with a `0.0f` value
7. Provide values of all elements of the `perspective_projection_matrix` variable to shaders (possibly via a uniform buffer or a push constant) or multiply it by another matrix to accumulate multiple operations in one matrix.

How it works...

A graphics pipeline operates on vertex positions defined in a so-called clip space. Usually, we specify vertices in a local (model) coordinate system and provide them directly to a vertex shader. That's why we need to transform provided vertex positions from their local space to a clip space in one of the vertex processing stages (vertex, tessellation control, tessellation evaluation, or a geometry shader). This transformation is performed with a projection matrix. If we want to simulate the effect of a perspective division, we need to use a perspective projection matrix and multiply it by a vertex position:

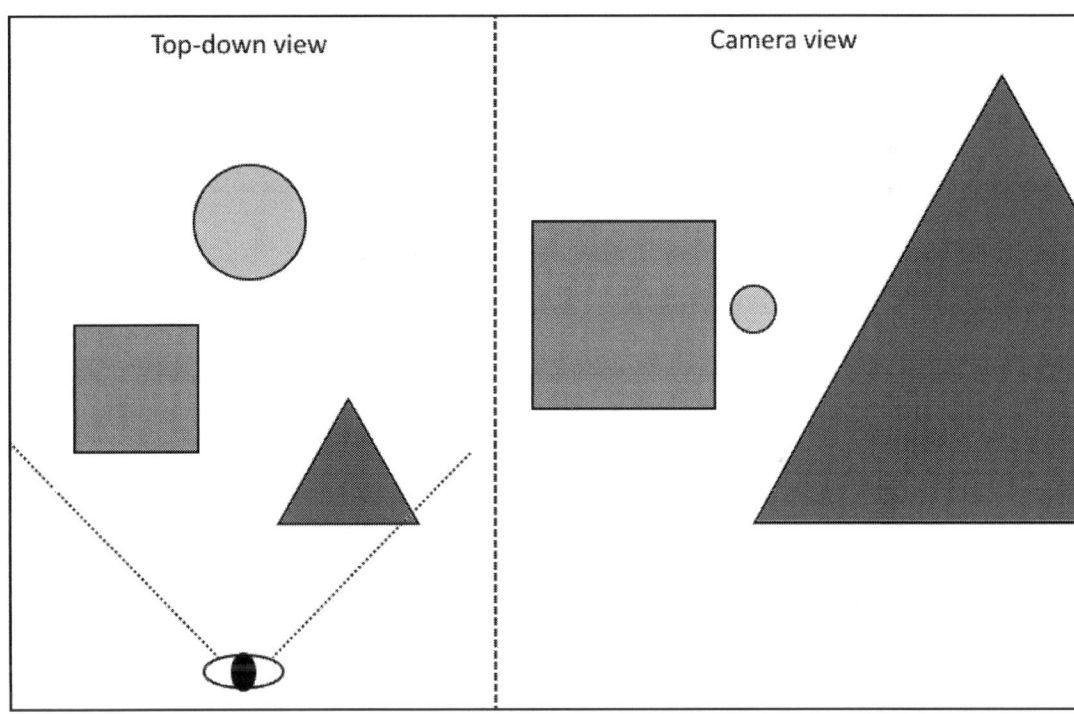

Helper Recipes

To create a perspective projection matrix, we need to know the dimensions of a renderable area, to calculate its aspect ratio (width divided by height). We also need to specify a (vertical) field of view, which we can think of as a zoom of a virtual camera:

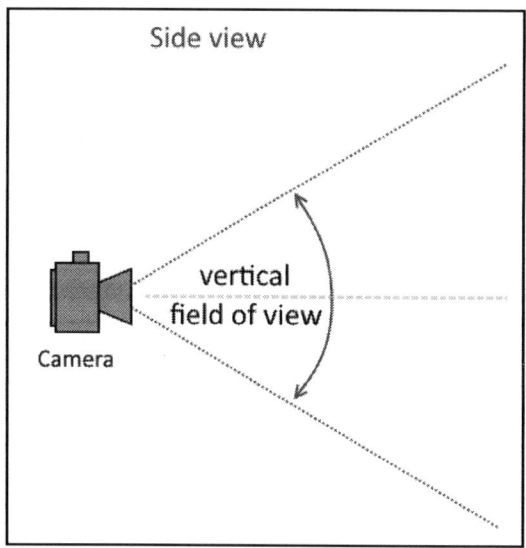

One last thing required to create a perspective projection matrix are two distances to near and far clipping planes. As they impact the depth calculations, they should be specified as close to the objects on the scene as possible. If we specify a large value for a near plane, and a small value for a far plane, our scene will be (in general) clipped--we will see how objects are popping in and out of the scene. On the other hand, if the near distance is too small, and the distance to the far plane is too big, we will lose the precision of a depth buffer and depth calculations may be incorrect.

 Near and far clipping planes should correspond to the scene being displayed.

Using the preceding described data, we can create a perspective projection matrix using the following code:

```
float f = 1.0f / tan( Deg2Rad( 0.5f * field_of_view ) );

Matrix4x4 perspective_projection_matrix = {
  f / aspect_ratio,
  0.0f,
  0.0f,
```

```
    0.0f,
    0.0f,
    -f,
    0.0f,
    0.0f,

    0.0f,
    0.0f,
    far_plane / (near_plane - far_plane),
    -1.0f,

    0.0f,
    0.0f,
    (near_plane * far_plane) / (near_plane - far_plane),
    0.0f
};
return perspective_projection_matrix;
```

See also

- In `Chapter 5`, *Descriptor Sets*, see the following recipe:
    - *Creating a uniform buffer*
- In `Chapter 7`, *Shaders*, see the following recipes:
    - *Writing a vertex shader that multiplies vertex position by a projection matrix*
    - *Using push constants in shaders*
- In `Chapter 9`, *Command Recording and Drawing*, see the following recipe:
    - *Providing data to shaders through push constants*
- The following recipe in this chapter:
    - *Preparing an orthographic projection matrix*

Preparing an orthographic projection matrix

Orthographic projection is another type of operation that transforms vertices from their local coordinate system to a clip space. But opposed to a perspective projection, it doesn't take a perspective division into account (doesn't simulate the way we perceive our surroundings). But similarly to a perspective projection, it is also represented by a 4x4 matrix, which we need to create in order to use this type of projection.

How to do it...

1. Create two variables of type `float` named `left_plane` and `right_plane`, and initialize them with the positions (on the x axis) of left and right clipping planes, respectively.
2. Prepare two variables of type `float` named `bottom_plane` and `top_plane`. Initialize them with positions of (on the y axis) of the bottom and top clipping planes, respectively.
3. Create two variables of type `float` named `near_plane` and `far_plane`. Use them to hold distances from the camera to the near and far clipping planes, respectively.
4. Create a variable of type `std::array<float, 16>` named `orthographic_projection_matrix`. It will hold a matrix representing the desired projection. Initialize elements of the `orthographic_projection_matrix` array with the following values:
    - All elements of the matrix initialize with a `0.0f` value
    - 0th element with a `2.0f / (right_plane - left_plane)`
    - 5th element with a `2.0f / (bottom_plane - top_plane)`
    - 10th element with a `1.0f / (near_plane - far_plane)`
    - 12th element with a `-(right_plane + left_plane) / (right_plane - left_plane)`
    - 13th element with a `-(bottom_plane + top_plane) / (bottom_plane - top_plane)`
    - 14th element with a `near_plane / (near_plane - far_plane)`
    - 15th element with a `1.0f` value
5. Provide values of all elements of the `orthographic_projection_matrix` variable to shaders (possibly via a uniform buffer or a push constant) or multiply it by another matrix to accumulate multiple operations in one matrix.

How it works...

When we use orthographic projection, all objects in the scene maintain their size and screen position no matter how far from the camera they are. That's why orthographic projection is very useful for drawing all kinds of **UIs** (**user interfaces**). We can define our virtual screen, we know all its sides (planes defined for the projection), and we can easily place and manipulate interface elements on screen. We can also use depth tests if needed.

Orthographic projection is also widely used in **CAD** programs (**Computer Aided Design**). These tools are used for designing buildings, ships, electronic circuits, or mechanical devices. In such situations, all sizes of all objects in the scene must be exactly the ones as defined by the designers and all directions must keep their relations (that is, all parallel lines must always stay parallel), no matter how far from the camera objects are and from which angle they are viewed.

The following code is used to create a matrix that represents an orthographic projection:

```
Matrix4x4 orthographic_projection_matrix = {
  2.0f / (right_plane - left_plane),
  0.0f,
  0.0f,
  0.0f,

  0.0f,
  2.0f / (bottom_plane - top_plane),
  0.0f,
  0.0f,

  0.0f,
  0.0f,
  1.0f / (near_plane - far_plane),
  0.0f,

  -(right_plane + left_plane) / (right_plane - left_plane),
  -(bottom_plane + top_plane) / (bottom_plane - top_plane),
  near_plane / (near_plane - far_plane),
  1.0f
};
return orthographic_projection_matrix;
```

See also

- In `Chapter 5`, *Descriptor Sets*, see the following recipe:
    - *Creating a uniform buffer*
- In `Chapter 7`, *Shaders*, see the following recipes:
    - *Writing a vertex shader that multiplies vertex position by a projection matrix*
    - *Using push constants in shaders*
- In `Chapter 9`, *Command Recording and Drawing*, see the following recipe:
    - *Providing data to shaders through push constants*
- The *Preparing a perspective projection matrix* recipe in this chapter

Loading texture data from a file

Texturing is a commonly used technique. It allows us to place an image on the surface of an object in a similar way to how we put wallpaper on walls. This way we don't need to increase the geometric complexity of a mesh, which would be both too complex for the hardware to process it, and would use too much memory. Texturing is simpler to handle and allows us to achieve better, more convincing results.

Textures can be generated procedurally (dynamically in code), but usually their contents are read from images or photos.

Getting ready

There are many different libraries allowing us to load contents of images. All of them have their own specific behaviors, usages, and licenses. In this recipe, we will use a `stb_image` library created by *Sean T. Barrett*. It is very simple to use, yet supports enough image formats to start developing a Vulkan application. And one of its main strengths is that it is a single header library, all its code is placed in just one header file. It doesn't depend on any other libraries, files, or resources. Another advantage is that we can use it in whatever way we want.

The `stb_image.h` file is available at `https://github.com/nothings/stb`.

To use the `stb_image` library in our application, we need to download a `stb_image.h` file from https://github.com/nothings/stb and include it in our project. This file can be included at many places in our code, but to create the library's implementation in only one of the source files we need to include the file and precede it with a `#define STB_IMAGE_IMPLEMENTATION` definition like this:

```
#include ...
#define STB_IMAGE_IMPLEMENTATION
#include "stb_image.h"
```

How to do it...

1. Store the name of a file, from which the texture image should be loaded, in a variable of type `char const *` named `filename`.
2. Create a variable of type `int` named `num_requested_components`. Initialize it with the desired number of components to be loaded from a file (a value from `1` to `4`) or with a `0` value to load all available components.
3. Create three variables of type `int` named `width`, `height`, and `num_components`, and initialize all of them with a `0` value.
4. Create a variable of type `unsigned char *` named `stbi_data`.
5. Call `stbi_load( filename, &width, &height, &num_components, num_requested_components )` and provide the `filename` variable, pointers to the `width`, `height`, and `num_components` variables, and the `num_requested_components` variable. Store the result of the function call in the `stbi_data` variable.
6. Make sure the call successfully loaded the contents of the specified file by checking if a value stored in the `stbi_data` variable is not equal to a `nullptr` value and if the values stored in the `width`, `height`, and `num_components` variables are greater than `0`.
7. Create a variable of type `int` named `data_size` and initialize it with a value calculated using the following formulae:

$$width * height * (0 < num\_requested\_components \;?\; num\_requested\_components : num\_components)$$

8. Create a variable of type `std::vector<unsigned char>` named `image_data`. Resize it to hold the `data_size` number of elements.
9. Copy `data_size` number of bytes from the `stbi_data` to a memory starting at the first element of the `image_data` vector using the following call:

   ```
   std::memcpy( image_data.data(), stbi_data.get(), data_size )
   ```

10. Call `stbi_image_free( stbi_data )`.

How it works...

Using the `stb_image` library comes down to calling the `stbi_load()` function. It takes the name of a file, the selected number of components to be loaded from the file, and returns a pointer to the memory containing the loaded data. The library always converts an image's contents to 8 bits per channel. The width and height of the image and the real number of components available in the image are stored in optional variables.

The code loading an image is presented as follows:

```
int width = 0;
int height = 0;
int num_components = 0;
std::unique_ptr<unsigned char, void(*)(void*)> stbi_data( stbi_load(
filename, &width, &height, &num_components, num_requested_components ),
stbi_image_free );

if( (!stbi_data) ||
    (0 >= width) ||
    (0 >= height) ||
    (0 >= num_components) ) {
  std::cout << "Could not read image!" << std::endl;
  return false;
}
```

The pointer returned by the `stbi_load()` function must be released by calling the `stbi_image_free()` function with a value returned by the former function provided as its only parameter. That's why it is good to copy loaded data to our own variable (that is, a vector) or directly to one of the Vulkan resources (image), so there are no memory leaks. This is presented as follows:

```
std::vector<unsigned char> image_data;
int data_size = width * height * (0 < num_requested_components ?
num_requested_components : num_components);
image_data.resize( data_size );
std::memcpy( image_data.data(), stbi_data.get(), data_size );
return true;
```

In the preceding code, the memory pointer returned by the `stbi_load()` function is released automatically, because we are storing it in a smart pointer of type `std::unique_ptr`. In the example, we copy the image's contents to a vector. This vector can be used later in our application as a source of texture data.

See also

- In `Chapter` 4, *Resources and Memory*, see the following recipes:
    - *Creating an image*
    - *Allocating and binding memory object to an image*
    - *Creating an image view*
- In `Chapter` 5, *Descriptor Sets*, see the following recipes:
    - *Creating a sampled image*
    - *Creating a combined image sampler*
- In `Chapter` 7, *Shaders*, see the following recipe:
    - *Writing a texturing vertex and fragment shaders*

Loading a 3D model from an OBJ file

Rendering 3D scenes requires us to draw objects, which are also called models or meshes. A mesh is a collection of vertices (points) with information about how these vertices form surfaces or faces (usually triangles).

Helper Recipes

Objects are prepared in modeling software or CAD programs. They can be stored in many various formats, which are later loaded in 3D applications, provided to graphics hardware, and then rendered. One of the simpler file types, which holds mesh data, is a **Wavefront OBJ**. We will learn how to load models stored in this format.

Getting ready

There are multiple libraries that allow us to load OBJ files (or other file types). One of the simpler, yet very fast and still being improved, libraries is a **tinyobjloader** developed by *Syoyo Fujita*. It is a single header library, so we don't need to include any other files or reference any other libraries.

 The tinyobjloader library can be downloaded from
`https://github.com/syoyo/tinyobjloader`.

To use the library, we need to download a `tiny_obj_loader.h` file from `https://github.com/syoyo/tinyobjloader`. We can include it at many places in our code, but to generate its implementation, we need to include it in one of our source files and precede the inclusion with a `#define TINYOBJLOADER_IMPLEMENTATION` definition like this:

```
#include ...
#define TINYOBJLOADER_IMPLEMENTATION
#include "tiny_obj_loader.h"
```

For the purpose of this recipe, we will also use a custom `Mesh` type that will hold the loaded data in a form that can be easily used with a Vulkan API. This type has the following definition:

```
struct Mesh {
  std::vector<float>  Data;
  struct Part {
    uint32_t  VertexOffset;
    uint32_t  VertexCount;
  };
  std::vector<Part>   Parts;
};
```

The `Data` member stores vertex attributes--positions, normals, and texture coordinates (normal vectors and texcoords are optional). Next there is a vector member named `Parts`, which defines separate parts of the model. Each such part needs to be drawn with a separate API call (such as the `vkCmdDraw()` function). The model part is defined by two parameters. `VertexOffset` defines where the given part starts (what is its offset in an array of vertex data). `VertexCount` defines the number of vertices the given part is composed of.

How to do it...

1. Prepare a variable of type `char const *` named `filename` and store a name of the file, from which model data will be loaded, in the variable.
2. Create the following variables:
    - Of type `tinyobj::attrib_t` named `attribs`
    - Of type `std::vector<tinyobj::shape_t>` named `shapes`
    - Of type `std::vector<tinyobj::material_t>` named `materials`
    - Of type `std::string` named `error`
3. Call `tinyobj::LoadObj( &attribs, &shapes, &materials, &error, filename )`, for which provide pointers to the `attribs`, `shapes`, `materials`, and `error` variables, and also the `filename` variable as the last parameter.
4. Make sure the call successfully loaded the model data from file by checking if the function call returned a `true` value.
5. Create a variable of type `Mesh` named `mesh` that will hold model data in a form suitable for a Vulkan API.
6. Create a variable of type `uint32_t` named `offset` and initialize it with a `0` value.
7. Iterate over all elements of the `shapes` vector. Assuming that the current element is stored in a variable of type `tinyobj::shape_t` named `shape`, do the following operations for each element:
    1. Create a variable of type `uint32_t` named `part_offset`. Initialize it with a value stored in the `offset` variable.

2. Iterate over all elements of the `shape.mesh.indices` vector, store currently processed elements in a variable of type `tinyobj::index_t` named `index`, and do the following operations for each element:
   - Copy three elements of an `attribs.vertices` vector, available at indices equal to (3 * `index.vertex_index`), (3 * `index.vertex_index + 1`), and (3 * `index.vertex_index + 2`), as new elements of the `mesh.Data` vector
   - If normal vectors should be loaded, copy three elements of an `attribs.normals` vector, which are indicated by indices equal to (3 * `index.normal_index`), (3 * `index.normal_index + 1`), and (3 * `index.normal_index + 2`), to the `mesh.Data` vector
   - If texture coordinates should also be loaded, add two elements to the `mesh.Data` vector and initialize them with values stored in an `attribs.texcoords` vector at positions (2 * `index.texcoord_index`) and (2 * `index.texcoord_index + 1`)
   - Increase the value of the `offset` variable by one
3. Store a calculated value of `offset - part_offset` in a variable of type `uint32_t` named `part_vertex_count`.
4. If the value of the `part_vertex_count` variable is greater than zero (a 0 value), add a new element to the `mesh.Parts` vector. Initialize its contents with the following values:
   - The `part_offset` variable for `VertexOffset`
   - The `part_vertex_count` variable for `VertexCount`

How it works...

3D models should be as small as possible to speed the loading process and lower the disk space required to store them. Usually, when we think about creating games, we should choose one of the binary formats, because most of them meet the mentioned requirements.

But when we start learning new APIs, it is good to choose a simpler format. OBJ files contain data stored in a text form, so we can easily view it or even modify it by ourselves. Most (if not all) commonly used modeling programs allow generated models to be exported to OBJ files. So it is a good format to get started with.

Here we will focus on loading only the vertex data. First we need to prepare storage for a model. After that we can load the model using the tinyobjloader library. If anything goes wrong, we check the error message and display it to a user:

```
tinyobj::attrib_t                   attribs;
std::vector<tinyobj::shape_t>       shapes;
std::vector<tinyobj::material_t>    materials;
std::string                         error;
bool result = tinyobj::LoadObj( &attribs, &shapes, &materials, &error,
filename.c_str() );
if( !result ) {
  std::cout << "Could not open '" << filename << "' file.";
  if( 0 < error.size() ) {
    std::cout << " " << error;
  }
  std::cout << std::endl;
  return false;
}
```

Theoretically, we could end our model-loading code here, but this data structure is not well suited for the Vulkan API. Though the normal vector and texture coordinates of a single vertex may be placed in separate arrays, they should be placed at the same index. Unfortunately, this may not be the case when it comes to an OBJ file format, which reuses the same values for multiple vertices. Because of that, we need to convert loaded data to a format that can be easily used by a graphics hardware:

```
Mesh mesh = {};
uint32_t offset = 0;
for( auto & shape : shapes ) {
  uint32_t part_offset = offset;

  for( auto & index : shape.mesh.indices ) {
    mesh.Data.emplace_back( attribs.vertices[3 * index.vertex_index + 0] );
    mesh.Data.emplace_back( attribs.vertices[3 * index.vertex_index + 1] );
    mesh.Data.emplace_back( attribs.vertices[3 * index.vertex_index + 2] );
    ++offset;

    if( (load_normals) &&
        (attribs.normals.size() > 0) ) {
      mesh.Data.emplace_back( attribs.normals[3*index.normal_index+0]);
      mesh.Data.emplace_back( attribs.normals[3*index.normal_index+1]);
      mesh.Data.emplace_back( attribs.normals[3*index.normal_index+2]);
```

```
    }

    if( (load_texcoords) &&
        (attribs.texcoords.size() > 0)) {
      mesh.Data.emplace_back( attribs.texcoords[2 * index.texcoord_index + 0] );
      mesh.Data.emplace_back( attribs.texcoords[2 * index.texcoord_index + 1] );
    }
  }

  uint32_t part_vertex_count = offset - part_offset;
  if( 0 < part_vertex_count ) {
    mesh.Parts.push_back( { part_offset, part_vertex_count } );
  }
}
```

After the preceding conversion, data stored in the `Data` member of the `mesh` variable can be directly copied to a vertex buffer. On the other hand, `VertexOffset` and `VertexCount` members of each part of the model are used during drawing--we can provide them to a `vkCmdDraw()` function.

When we create a graphics pipeline, which will be used to draw models loaded with the tinyobjloader library and stored in variables of a custom type `Mesh`, we need to specify a `VK_PRIMITIVE_TOPOLOGY_TRIANGLE_LIST` topology for an input assembly state (refer to the *Specifying pipeline input assembly state* recipe from `Chapter 8`, *Graphics and Compute Pipelines*). We also need to remember that each vertex is composed of three floating point values defining its position. When vertex normals are also loaded, they are also described by three floating point values. Texture coordinates, which are also optional, contain two floating point values. Each of the position, normal, and texcoord attributes are placed one after another for the first vertex, and then there are the position, normal, and texcoord attributes of the second vertex, and so on. The preceding information is required to properly set up vertex binding and attribute descriptions specified during graphics pipeline creation (refer to the *Specifying pipeline vertex binding description, attribute description and input state* recipe from `Chapter 8`, *Graphics and Compute Pipelines*).

See also

- In Chapter 4, *Resources and Memory*, see the following recipes:
    - *Creating a buffer*
    - *Allocating and binding memory object to a buffer*
    - *Using staging buffer to update a buffer with a device-local memory bound*

- In Chapter 7, *Shaders*, see the following recipe:
    - *Writing vertex shaders*

- In Chapter 8, *Graphics and Compute Pipelines*, see the following recipes:
    - *Specifying pipeline vertex binding description, attribute description and input state*
    - *Specifying pipeline input assembly state*

- In Chapter 9, *Command Recording and Drawing*, see the following recipes:
    - *Binding vertex buffers*
    - *Drawing a geometry*

11
Lighting

In this chapter, we will cover the following recipes:

- Rendering a geometry with a vertex diffuse lighting
- Rendering a geometry with a fragment specular lighting
- Rendering a normal mapped geometry
- Drawing a reflective and refractive geometry using cubemaps
- Adding shadows to the scene

Introduction

Lighting is one of the most important factors influencing the way we perceive everything that surrounds us. Most of the information our brains gather about the world comes from our eyes. Human sight is very sensitive to even the slightest change in lighting conditions. That's why lighting is also very important for creators of 3D applications, games, and movies.

In the times when 3D graphics libraries supported only a fixed-function pipeline, lighting calculations were performed according to a predefined set of rules--developers could only select colors for a light source and a lit object. This led most games and applications that used a given library to have a similar look and feel. The next step in the evolution of graphics hardware was the introduction of fragment shaders: their main purpose was to calculate the final color of a fragment (pixel). Fragment shaders literally shaded the geometry, so the name shader was a natural choice. Their main advantage was that they were programmable. They could perform not only lighting calculations, but also realize almost any other algorithm.

Lighting

Nowadays, graphics hardware is much more sophisticated. There are other types of programmable parts of graphics hardware which have also adopted the term shaders for their names. There are many different algorithms and approaches which all use shaders to display interesting images in games, 3D applications, and movies. The basic purpose of shader programs is still very important even today--lighting calculations must be performed if we want to achieve interesting, eye-catching results.

In this chapter, we will learn about commonly used lighting techniques from simple object diffuse lighting calculations, to a shadow mapping algorithm.

Rendering a geometry with a vertex diffuse lighting

A basic diffuse lighting algorithm lies at the core of most lighting calculations. It is used to simulate the appearance of matte surfaces that reflect the light, scattering it in many different directions. In this recipe, we will see how to achieve geometry rendering using vertex and fragment shaders that implement the diffuse lighting algorithm.

An example of an image generated with this recipe looks like the following:

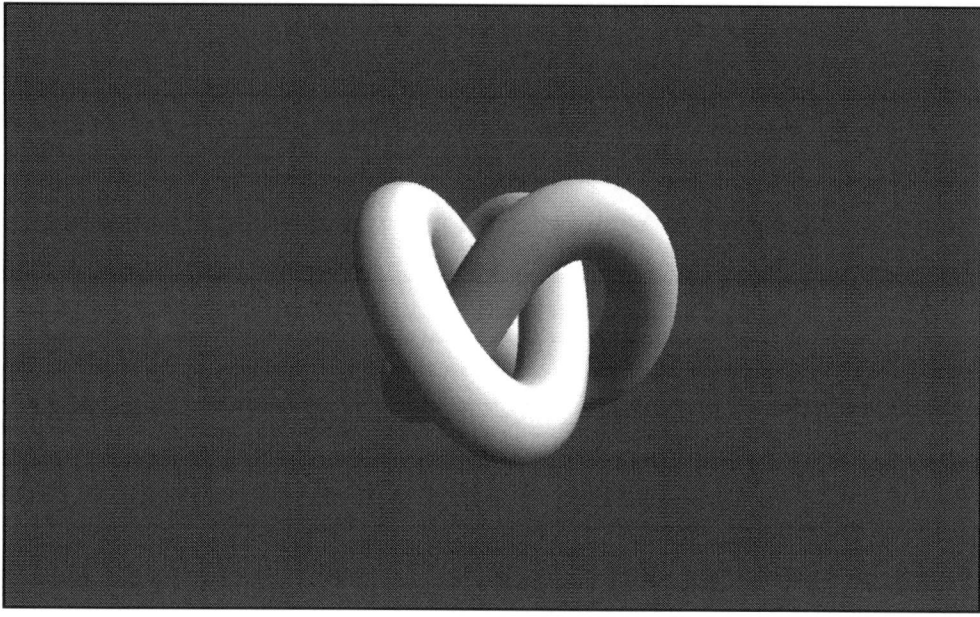

 The following recipe is very detailed so that you can understand and follow all the steps more easily. Further recipes will be based on the knowledge described here, so they are shorter but also more general.

Getting ready

Diffuse lighting is based on a **cosine law** introduced by **Johann Heinrich Lambert**. It says that the lighting intensity of an observed surface is proportional to the cosine of the angle between the direction from the surface to the source of light (a light vector) and the surface normal vector:

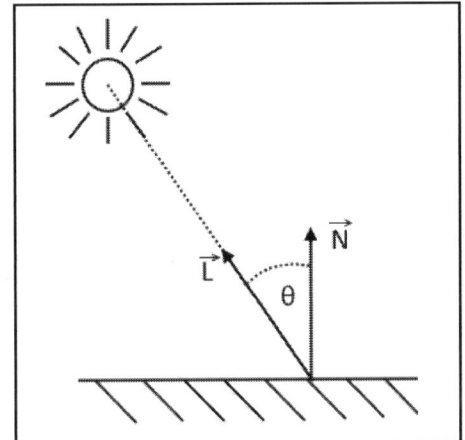

This law is easily implemented inside shaders. Normal vectors are provided from the application as one of the vertex attributes. The positions of all vertices are also known, so we only need to provide a light direction or the position of a light source to calculate the light vector inside shaders. Both normal and light vectors must be normalized (both must have a length equal to 1.0). The next step is to calculate a cosine of the angle between these two vectors. This is done with a single dot() function like this:

```
max( 0.0, dot( normal_vector, light_vector ) )
```

We must remember that a cosine can give negative results. This happens when we calculate lighting for points on a surface that point in the opposite direction to a light source. Such points cannot be lit by a given light source (they are in shadow from the perspective of a given light source), so we must disregard such results and clamp them to the 0 value.

Lighting

In all the following recipes we will use objects of a `VkDestroyer` class, which allow us to automatically destroy Vulkan resources. For convenience, a `InitVkDestroyer()` function is also introduced. Its purpose is to wrap a given resource in the `VkDestroyer` object and connect it to a created logical device.

How to do it...

1. Create a Vulkan instance and a logical device with a set of enabled swapchain extensions. Also store the handle of a physical device from which the logical device was created (refer to the *Creating a Vulkan Instance with WSI extensions enabled* and *Creating a logical device with WSI extensions enabled* recipes from `Chapter 2`, *Image Presentation*).
2. Acquire handles of graphics and presentation queues from the logical device (refer to the *Getting a device queue* recipe from `Chapter 1`, *Instance and Devices*).
3. Create a swapchain with a desired set of parameters. Store the swapchain's size (image dimensions) and format (refer to the *Creating a swapchain with R8G8B8A8 format and a MAILBOX present mode* recipe from `Chapter 2`, *Image Presentation*).
4. Get handles of all swapchain images (refer to the *Getting handles of swapchain images* recipe from `Chapter 2`, *Image Presentation*).
5. Create image views for all swapchain images (refer to the *Creating an image view* recipe from `Chapter 4`, *Resources and Memory*).
6. Create a set of resources required to generate frames of animation--command pool and command buffers, semaphores (at least two for acquiring a swapchain image and to indicate when a frame rendering is finished, which is required during swapchain image presentation), fences and framebuffers. Create at least one such set, but more can be created if we want to render more frames separately (refer to the *Increasing the performance through increasing the number of separately rendered frames* recipe from `Chapter 9`, *Command Recording and Drawing*).
7. Load a 3D model data with vertex positions and normal vectors into a variable of type `Mesh` named `Model` (refer to the *Loading a 3D model from an OBJ file* recipe from `Chapter 10`, *Helper Recipes*).
8. Create a buffer that will serve as a vertex buffer and will support `VK_BUFFER_USAGE_TRANSFER_DST_BIT` and `VK_BUFFER_USAGE_VERTEX_BUFFER_BIT` usages (refer to the *Creating a buffer* recipe from `Chapter 4`, *Resources and Memory*).

9. Allocate a memory object with a `VK_MEMORY_PROPERTY_DEVICE_LOCAL_BIT` property and bind it to the vertex buffer (refer to the *Allocating and binding memory object to a buffer* recipe from `Chapter 4`, *Resources and Memory*).
10. Copy vertex data from the `Data` member of the `Model` variable into the vertex buffer using a staging buffer (refer to the *Using staging buffer to update buffer with a device-local memory bound* recipe from `Chapter 4`, *Resources and Memory*).
11. Create a uniform buffer with `VK_BUFFER_USAGE_TRANSFER_DST_BIT` and `VK_BUFFER_USAGE_UNIFORM_BUFFER_BIT` usages that is big enough to hold data for two 16-element matrices of floating-point values (refer to the *Creating a uniform buffer* recipe from `Chapter 5`, *Descriptor Sets*).
12. Create a descriptor set layout with only one uniform buffer accessed by a vertex shader stage (refer to the *Creating a descriptor set layout* recipe from `Chapter 5`, *Descriptor Sets*).
13. Create a descriptor pool from which a descriptor for one uniform buffer can be allocated (refer to the *Creating a descriptor pool* recipe from `Chapter 5`, *Descriptor Sets*).
14. Allocate a descriptor set from the created pool using the prepared layout (refer to *Allocating descriptor sets* recipe from `Chapter 5`, *Descriptor Sets*).
15. Update the descriptor set with the uniform buffer's handle (refer to the *Updating descriptor sets* recipes from `Chapter 5`, *Descriptor Sets*).
16. Prepare parameters for a render pass creation. First, specify descriptions of two attachments (refer to the *Specifying attachments descriptions* recipe from `Chapter 6`, *Render Passes and Framebuffers*):
    - The first attachment should have the same format as the swapchain images. It should be cleared on a render pass start and its contents should be stored at the end of the render pass. Its initial layout can be undefined, but a final layout must be a `VK_IMAGE_LAYOUT_PRESENT_SRC_KHR`.
    - The second attachment should have one of the supported depth formats (`VK_FORMAT_D16_UNORM` format must always be supported, and at least one of `VK_FORMAT_X8_D24_UNORM_PACK32` or `VK_FORMAT_D32_SFLOAT` must be supported). It must be cleared on the render pass start, but its contents don't need to be preserved after the render pass. Its initial layout may be undefined and the final layout should be the same as a layout specified in a subpass (to avoid unnecessary layout transitions).

17. Specify one subpass for the render pass, in which the first render pass attachment will be provided as a color attachment with a `VK_IMAGE_LAYOUT_COLOR_ATTACHMENT_OPTIMAL` layout, and the second attachment will be used as a depth attachment with a `VK_IMAGE_LAYOUT_DEPTH_STENCIL_ATTACHMENT_OPTIMAL` layout (refer to the *Specifying subpass descriptions* recipe from `Chapter 6`, *Render Passes and Framebuffers*).

18. Specify two subpass dependencies for the render pass (refer to the *Specifying dependencies between subpasses* recipe from `Chapter 6`, *Render Passes and Framebuffers*). Use the following values for the first dependency:
    - `VK_SUBPASS_EXTERNAL` value for `srcSubpass`
    - 0 value for `dstSubpass`
    - `VK_PIPELINE_STAGE_TOP_OF_PIPE_BIT` value for `srcStageMask`
    - `VK_PIPELINE_STAGE_COLOR_ATTACHMENT_OUTPUT_BIT` value for `dstStageMask`
    - `VK_ACCESS_MEMORY_READ_BIT` value for `srcAccessMask`
    - `VK_ACCESS_COLOR_ATTACHMENT_WRITE_BIT` value for `dstAccessMask`
    - `VK_DEPENDENCY_BY_REGION_BIT` value for `dependencyFlags`

19. Use the following values for the second render pass dependency:
    - 0 value for `srcSubpass`
    - `VK_SUBPASS_EXTERNAL` value for `dstSubpass`
    - `VK_PIPELINE_STAGE_COLOR_ATTACHMENT_OUTPUT_BIT` value for `srcStageMask`
    - `VK_PIPELINE_STAGE_TOP_OF_PIPE_BIT` value for `dstStageMask`
    - `VK_ACCESS_COLOR_ATTACHMENT_WRITE_BIT` value for `srcAccessMask`
    - `VK_ACCESS_MEMORY_READ_BIT` value for `dstAccessMask`
    - `VK_DEPENDENCY_BY_REGION_BIT` value for `dependencyFlags`

20. Create the render pass using the prepared parameters (refer to the *Creating a render pass* recipe from `Chapter 6`, *Render Passes and Framebuffers*).

21. Create a pipeline layout using the prepared descriptor set layout with only a uniform buffer (refer to the *Creating a pipeline layout* recipe from `Chapter 8`, *Graphics and Compute Pipelines*).

22. Create a shader module for a vertex shader stage using a SPIR-V assembly generated from the following GLSL code (refer to the *Converting GLSL shaders to SPIR-V assemblies* recipe from Chapter 7, *Shaders* and to the *Creating a shader module* recipe from Chapter 8, *Graphics and Compute Pipelines*):

    ```
    #version 450
    layout( location = 0 ) in vec4 app_position;
    layout( location = 1 ) in vec3 app_normal;
    layout( set = 0, binding = 0 ) uniform UniformBuffer {
      mat4 ModelViewMatrix;
      mat4 ProjectionMatrix;
    };
    layout( location = 0 ) out float vert_color;
    void main() {
      gl_Position = ProjectionMatrix * ModelViewMatrix *
      app_position;
      vec3 normal = mat3( ModelViewMatrix ) * app_normal;

      vert_color = max( 0.0, dot( normal, vec3( 0.58, 0.58, 0.58 ) )
      ) + 0.1;
    }
    ```

23. Create a shader module for a fragment shader stage using a SPIR-V assembly generated from the following GLSL code:

    ```
    #version 450
    layout( location = 0 ) in float vert_color;
    layout( location = 0 ) out vec4 frag_color;
    void main() {
       frag_color = vec4( vert_color );
    }
    ```

24. Specify pipeline shader stages with vertex and fragment shaders, both using a `main` function from respective shader modules (refer to the *Specifying pipeline shader stages* recipe from Chapter 8, *Graphics and Compute Pipelines*).

25. Specify a pipeline vertex input state with two attributes that are read from the same 0 binding. Binding should be created with data read per vertex and a stride equal to 6 * `sizeof( float )` (refer to the *Specifying pipeline vertex input state* recipe from Chapter 8, *Graphics and Compute Pipelines*). The first attribute should have the following parameters:
    - 0 value for `location`
    - 0 value for `binding`
    - `VK_FORMAT_R32G32B32_SFLOAT` value for `format`
    - 0 value for `offset`

26. The second vertex attribute should be specified using the following values:
    - 1 value for `location`
    - 0 value for `binding`
    - `VK_FORMAT_R32G32B32_SFLOAT` value for `format`
    - `3 * sizeof( float)` value for `offset`
27. Specify a pipeline input assembly state with a `VK_PRIMITIVE_TOPOLOGY_TRIANGLE_LIST` topology and without primitive restart (refer to the *Specifying pipeline input assembly state* recipe from `Chapter 8`, *Graphics and Compute Pipelines*).
28. Specify a pipeline viewport and scissor test state with only one viewport and scissor test state. Initial values don't matter as they will be set dynamically (refer to the *Specifying pipeline viewport and scissor test state* recipe from `Chapter 8`, *Graphics and Compute Pipelines*).
29. Specify a pipeline rasterization state without depth clamp, with no rasterization discard, with a `VK_POLYGON_MODE_FILL`, `VK_CULL_MODE_BACK_BIT` and `VK_FRONT_FACE_COUNTER_CLOCKWISE`, without a depth bias and with line widths of `1.0f` (refer to the *Specifying pipeline rasterization state* recipe from `Chapter 8`, *Graphics and Compute Pipelines*).
30. Specify a pipeline multisample state with only a single sample and without sample shading, sample masks, alpha to coverage, or alpha to one (refer to the *Specifying pipeline multisample state* recipe from `Chapter 8`, *Graphics and Compute Pipelines*).
31. Specify a pipeline depth state with a depth test and depth writes enabled, with a `VK_COMPARE_OP_LESS_OR_EQUAL` operator and without depth bounds or stencil tests (refer to the *Specifying pipeline depth and stencil state* recipe from `Chapter 8`, *Graphics and Compute Pipelines*).
32. Specify a pipeline blend state with both logical operations and blending disabled (refer to the *Specifying pipeline blend state* recipe from `Chapter 8`, *Graphics and Compute Pipelines*).
33. Specify the viewport and scissor test as dynamic states of a pipeline (refer to the *Specifying pipeline dynamic states* recipe from `Chapter 8`, *Graphics and Compute Pipelines*).
34. Create a graphics pipeline using the prepared parameters (refer to the *Creating graphics pipelines* recipe from `Chapter 8`, *Graphics and Compute Pipelines*).

35. Create a staging buffer supporting a `VK_BUFFER_USAGE_TRANSFER_SRC_BIT` usage, which can hold data of two matrices, each with 16 floating-point elements. The buffer's memory object should be allocated on a memory that is host-visible (refer to the *Creating a buffer* and *Allocating and binding memory object to a buffer* recipes from `Chapter 4`, *Resources and Memory*).

36. Create a 2D image (with an appropriate memory object) and an image view with the same format as the render pass's depth attachment, with the same size as the size of swapchain images, with one mipmap level and array layer. The image must support a `VK_IMAGE_USAGE_DEPTH_STENCIL_ATTACHMENT_BIT` usage (refer to the *Creating a 2D image and view* recipe from `Chapter 4`, *Resources and Memory*). Remember that these resources (along with the swapchain) must be recreated each time the application's window is resized.

37. Prepare a model matrix, which can be a multiplication of rotation, scaling and translation matrices (refer to the *Preparing a translation matrix*, *Preparing a rotation matrix* and *Preparing a scaling matrix* recipes from `Chapter 10`, *Helper Recipes*). Copy the contents of the concatenated matrix to the staging buffer at a 0 offset (refer to the *Mapping, updating and unmapping host-visible memory* recipe from `Chapter 4`, *Resources and Memory*).

38. Prepare a perspective projection matrix based on the aspect ratio of swapchain's dimensions (refer to the *Preparing a perspective projection matrix recipe* from `Chapter 10`, *Helper Recipes*). Copy contents of the matrix to the staging buffer at an offset equal to the number of elements in the model matrix (16) multiplied by the size of a single element (`sizeof(float)`). Remember to recreate the projection matrix and copy it to the staging buffer each time the application's window is resized (refer to *Mapping, updating and unmapping host-visible memory* recipe from `Chapter 4`, *Resources and Memory*).

39. Inside a rendering loop, for each loop iteration, prepare a frame of animation by acquiring one of the swapchain images, creating a framebuffer with the acquired swapchain image and the image serving as a depth attachment, recording the command buffer as described below, submitting it to the graphics queue and presenting the acquired image (refer to the *Preparing a single frame of animation* recipe from `Chapter 9`, *Command Recording and Drawing*).

40. To record the command buffer:
    - Begin recording the command buffer specifying a `VK_COMMAND_BUFFER_USAGE_ONE_TIME_SUBMIT_BIT` usage (refer to the *Beginning a command buffer recording operation* recipe from `Chapter 3`, *Command Buffers and Synchronization*).

- If the staging buffer has been updated since the last frame, set a buffer memory barrier for the uniform buffer to inform the driver that the buffer's memory will be accessed in a different way, copy data from the staging buffer to the uniform buffer, and set up another buffer memory barrier (refer to the *Setting a buffer memory barrier* and *Copying data between buffers* recipes from Chapter 4, *Resources and Memory*).
- When graphics and presentation queues are different, transform the ownership for the acquired swapchain image from the presentation queue to the graphics queue using an image memory barrier (refer to the *Setting an image memory barrier* from Chapter 4, *Resources and Memory*).
- Begin the render pass (refer to the *Beginning a render pass* recipe from Chapter 6, *Render Passes and Framebuffers*).
- Set the viewport and scissor test states dynamically providing the current swapchain dimensions (refer to the *Setting viewport state dynamically* and *Setting scissors state dynamically* recipes from Chapter 9, *Command Recording and Drawing*).
- Bind the vertex buffer to the 0 binding (refer to the *Binding vertex buffers* recipe from Chapter 9, *Command Recording and Drawing*).
- Bind the descriptor set to the 0 index (refer to the *Binding descriptor sets* recipe from Chapter 5, *Descriptor Sets*).
- Bind the graphics pipeline (refer to the *Binding a pipeline object* recipe from Chapter 8, *Graphics and Compute Pipelines*).
- Draw the model geometry (refer to the *Drawing a geometry* recipe from Chapter 9, *Command Recording and Drawing*).
- End the render pass (refer to the *Ending a render pass* recipe from Chapter 6, *Render Passes and Framebuffers*).
- If the graphics and presentation queues are different, transform the ownership for the acquired swapchain image from the graphics queue to the presentation queue using an image memory barrier (refer to the *Setting an image memory barrier* from Chapter 4, *Resources and Memory*).
- End the command buffer's recording operation (refer to the *Ending a command buffer recording operation* recipe from Chapter 3, *Command Buffers and Synchronization*).

36. To increase the performance of an application, prepare multiple animation frames using separate sets of resources (refer to the *Increasing the performance through increasing the number of separately rendered frames* recipe from Chapter 9, *Command Recording and Drawing*).

How it works...

Assume we have created a Vulkan Instance and a logical device with enabled WSI extensions. We also created a swapchain object (the full source code for these operations can be found in the accompanying code samples).

To render any geometry, we need to first load a 3D model. Its data needs to be copied to a vertex buffer, so we also need to create a vertex buffer, allocate and bind a memory to it, and we need to copy the model data using a staging buffer:

```
if( !Load3DModelFromObjFile( "Data/Models/knot.obj", true, false, false,
true, Model ) ) {
  return false;
}
InitVkDestroyer( LogicalDevice, VertexBuffer );
if( !CreateBuffer( *LogicalDevice, sizeof( Model.Data[0] ) *
Model.Data.size(), VK_BUFFER_USAGE_TRANSFER_DST_BIT |
VK_BUFFER_USAGE_VERTEX_BUFFER_BIT, *VertexBuffer ) ) {
  return false;
}
InitVkDestroyer( LogicalDevice, VertexBufferMemory );
if( !AllocateAndBindMemoryObjectToBuffer( PhysicalDevice, *LogicalDevice,
*VertexBuffer, VK_MEMORY_PROPERTY_DEVICE_LOCAL_BIT, *VertexBufferMemory ) )
{
  return false;
}
if( !UseStagingBufferToUpdateBufferWithDeviceLocalMemoryBound(
PhysicalDevice, *LogicalDevice, sizeof( Model.Data[0] ) *
Model.Data.size(), &Model.Data[0], *VertexBuffer, 0, 0,
VK_ACCESS_TRANSFER_WRITE_BIT, VK_PIPELINE_STAGE_TOP_OF_PIPE_BIT,
VK_PIPELINE_STAGE_VERTEX_INPUT_BIT, GraphicsQueue.Handle,
FrameResources.front().CommandBuffer, {} ) ) {
  return false;
}
```

Next, a uniform buffer is required. Using the uniform buffer we will provide transformation matrices to the shaders:

```
InitVkDestroyer( LogicalDevice, UniformBuffer );
InitVkDestroyer( LogicalDevice, UniformBufferMemory );
if( !CreateUniformBuffer( PhysicalDevice, *LogicalDevice, 2 * 16 * sizeof(
float ), VK_BUFFER_USAGE_TRANSFER_DST_BIT |
VK_BUFFER_USAGE_UNIFORM_BUFFER_BIT,
  *UniformBuffer, *UniformBufferMemory ) ) {
  return false;
}
```

Lighting

The uniform buffer will be accessed in a vertex shader. For this purpose, we need a descriptor set layout, a descriptor pool, and a single descriptor set, which will be updated (populated) with the created uniform buffer:

```
VkDescriptorSetLayoutBinding descriptor_set_layout_binding = {
  0,
  VK_DESCRIPTOR_TYPE_UNIFORM_BUFFER,
  1,
  VK_SHADER_STAGE_VERTEX_BIT,
  nullptr
};
InitVkDestroyer( LogicalDevice, DescriptorSetLayout );
if( !CreateDescriptorSetLayout( *LogicalDevice, {
descriptor_set_layout_binding }, *DescriptorSetLayout ) ) {
  return false;
}
VkDescriptorPoolSize descriptor_pool_size = {
  VK_DESCRIPTOR_TYPE_UNIFORM_BUFFER,
  1
};
InitVkDestroyer( LogicalDevice, DescriptorPool );
if( !CreateDescriptorPool( *LogicalDevice, false, 1, { descriptor_pool_size
}, *DescriptorPool ) ) {
  return false;
}
if( !AllocateDescriptorSets( *LogicalDevice, *DescriptorPool, {
*DescriptorSetLayout }, DescriptorSets ) ) {
  return false;
}
BufferDescriptorInfo buffer_descriptor_update = {
  DescriptorSets[0],
  0,
  0,
  VK_DESCRIPTOR_TYPE_UNIFORM_BUFFER,
  {
    {
      *UniformBuffer,
      0,
      VK_WHOLE_SIZE
    }
  }
};
UpdateDescriptorSets( *LogicalDevice, {}, { buffer_descriptor_update }, {},
{} );
```

Rendering operations can only be performed inside render passes. We need a render pass with two attachments: the first is a swapchain image; and second is an image created by us that will serve as a depth attachment. As we will render only a single model without any postprocessing techniques, it is enough for the render pass to have just one subpass.

```
std::vector<VkAttachmentDescription> attachment_descriptions = {
  {
    0,
    Swapchain.Format,
    VK_SAMPLE_COUNT_1_BIT,
    VK_ATTACHMENT_LOAD_OP_CLEAR,
    VK_ATTACHMENT_STORE_OP_STORE,
    VK_ATTACHMENT_LOAD_OP_DONT_CARE,
    VK_ATTACHMENT_STORE_OP_DONT_CARE,
    VK_IMAGE_LAYOUT_UNDEFINED,
    VK_IMAGE_LAYOUT_PRESENT_SRC_KHR
  },
  {
    0,
    DepthFormat,
    VK_SAMPLE_COUNT_1_BIT,
    VK_ATTACHMENT_LOAD_OP_CLEAR,
    VK_ATTACHMENT_STORE_OP_DONT_CARE,
    VK_ATTACHMENT_LOAD_OP_DONT_CARE,
    VK_ATTACHMENT_STORE_OP_DONT_CARE,
    VK_IMAGE_LAYOUT_UNDEFINED,
    VK_IMAGE_LAYOUT_DEPTH_STENCIL_ATTACHMENT_OPTIMAL
  }
};
VkAttachmentReference depth_attachment = {
  1,
  VK_IMAGE_LAYOUT_DEPTH_STENCIL_ATTACHMENT_OPTIMAL
};
std::vector<SubpassParameters> subpass_parameters = {
  {
    VK_PIPELINE_BIND_POINT_GRAPHICS,
    {},
    {
      {
        0,
        VK_IMAGE_LAYOUT_COLOR_ATTACHMENT_OPTIMAL,
      }
    },
    {},
    &depth_attachment,
    {}
  }
};
```

```
std::vector<VkSubpassDependency> subpass_dependencies = {
  {
    VK_SUBPASS_EXTERNAL,
    0,
    VK_PIPELINE_STAGE_TOP_OF_PIPE_BIT,
    VK_PIPELINE_STAGE_COLOR_ATTACHMENT_OUTPUT_BIT,
    VK_ACCESS_MEMORY_READ_BIT,
    VK_ACCESS_COLOR_ATTACHMENT_WRITE_BIT,
    VK_DEPENDENCY_BY_REGION_BIT
  },
  {
    0,
    VK_SUBPASS_EXTERNAL,
    VK_PIPELINE_STAGE_COLOR_ATTACHMENT_OUTPUT_BIT,
    VK_PIPELINE_STAGE_TOP_OF_PIPE_BIT,
    VK_ACCESS_COLOR_ATTACHMENT_WRITE_BIT,
    VK_ACCESS_MEMORY_READ_BIT,
    VK_DEPENDENCY_BY_REGION_BIT
  }
};
InitVkDestroyer( LogicalDevice, RenderPass );
if( !CreateRenderPass( *LogicalDevice, attachment_descriptions,
subpass_parameters, subpass_dependencies, *RenderPass ) ) {
  return false;
}
```

We also need a staging buffer. It will be used to transfer data from the application to the uniform buffer:

```
InitVkDestroyer( LogicalDevice, StagingBuffer );
if( !CreateBuffer( *LogicalDevice, 2 * 16 * sizeof(float),
VK_BUFFER_USAGE_TRANSFER_SRC_BIT, *StagingBuffer ) ) {
  return false;
}
InitVkDestroyer( LogicalDevice, StagingBufferMemory );
if( !AllocateAndBindMemoryObjectToBuffer( PhysicalDevice, *LogicalDevice,
*StagingBuffer, VK_MEMORY_PROPERTY_HOST_VISIBLE_BIT, *StagingBufferMemory )
) {
  return false;
}
```

Before we can render a frame, we need to do one last thing: create a graphics pipeline. As the code required to create one is pretty straightforward, we will skip it (it can be seen in the code samples accompanying this book).

To see the model, we need to prepare model and projection matrices. A model matrix is used to place a model in a virtual world--it can be moved, scaled, or rotated. Such a matrix is usually combined with a view matrix, which is used to move a camera in our scene. Here, for simplicity, we won't use a view transformation; but we still need a projection matrix. Because the values in the projection matrix depend on the framebuffer's aspect ratio (in this case the size of the application's window), it must be recomputed every time the application window's dimensions are changed:

```
Matrix4x4 rotation_matrix = PrepareRotationMatrix( vertical_angle, { 1.0f,
0.0f, 0.0f } ) * PrepareRotationMatrix( horizontal_angle, { 0.0f, -1.0f,
0.0f } );
Matrix4x4 translation_matrix = PrepareTranslationMatrix( 0.0f, 0.0f, -4.0f
);
Matrix4x4 model_view_matrix = translation_matrix * rotation_matrix;
if( !MapUpdateAndUnmapHostVisibleMemory( *LogicalDevice,
*StagingBufferMemory, 0, sizeof( model_view_matrix[0] ) *
model_view_matrix.size(), &model_view_matrix[0], true, nullptr ) ) {
  return false;
}
Matrix4x4 perspective_matrix = PreparePerspectiveProjectionMatrix(
static_cast<float>(Swapchain.Size.width) /
static_cast<float>(Swapchain.Size.height),
  50.0f, 0.5f, 10.0f );
if( !MapUpdateAndUnmapHostVisibleMemory( *LogicalDevice,
*StagingBufferMemory, sizeof( model_view_matrix[0] ) *
model_view_matrix.size(),
  sizeof( perspective_matrix[0] ) * perspective_matrix.size(),
&perspective_matrix[0], true, nullptr ) ) {
  return false;
```

Finally, the last thing we need to do is to prepare an animation frame. This is usually performed inside a rendering loop, where for each loop iteration a separate (new) frame is rendered.

First, we need to check if the uniform buffer's contents need to be updated and whether the data needs to be copied from the staging buffer to the uniform buffer:

```
if( !BeginCommandBufferRecordingOperation( command_buffer,
VK_COMMAND_BUFFER_USAGE_ONE_TIME_SUBMIT_BIT, nullptr ) ) {
  return false;
}
if( UpdateUniformBuffer ) {
  UpdateUniformBuffer = false;
  BufferTransition pre_transfer_transition = {
    *UniformBuffer,
    VK_ACCESS_UNIFORM_READ_BIT,
    VK_ACCESS_TRANSFER_WRITE_BIT,
```

Lighting

```
    VK_QUEUE_FAMILY_IGNORED,
    VK_QUEUE_FAMILY_IGNORED
};
SetBufferMemoryBarrier( command_buffer,
VK_PIPELINE_STAGE_BOTTOM_OF_PIPE_BIT, VK_PIPELINE_STAGE_TRANSFER_BIT, {
pre_transfer_transition } );
  std::vector<VkBufferCopy> regions = {
    {
      0,
      0,
      2 * 16 * sizeof( float )
    }
  };
  CopyDataBetweenBuffers( command_buffer, *StagingBuffer, *UniformBuffer,
regions );
  BufferTransition post_transfer_transition = {
    *UniformBuffer,
    VK_ACCESS_TRANSFER_WRITE_BIT,
    VK_ACCESS_UNIFORM_READ_BIT,
    VK_QUEUE_FAMILY_IGNORED,
    VK_QUEUE_FAMILY_IGNORED
  };
  SetBufferMemoryBarrier( command_buffer, VK_PIPELINE_STAGE_TRANSFER_BIT,
VK_PIPELINE_STAGE_VERTEX_SHADER_BIT, { post_transfer_transition } );
}
```

Next, we transfer queue ownership for swapchain images (in a situation when graphics and present queues are different). After that, we start the render pass and set up all the states required to render a geometry: we set viewport and scissor test states, bind the vertex buffer, descriptor set and the graphics pipeline. After that, the geometry is drawn and the render pass is finished. Once again, we need to transfer the queue ownership back to the presentation queue (if the graphics queue is different) and we stop recording the command buffer. Now it can be submitted to the queue:

```
if( PresentQueue.FamilyIndex != GraphicsQueue.FamilyIndex ) {
  ImageTransition image_transition_before_drawing = {
    Swapchain.Images[swapchain_image_index],
    VK_ACCESS_MEMORY_READ_BIT,
    VK_ACCESS_COLOR_ATTACHMENT_WRITE_BIT,
    VK_IMAGE_LAYOUT_UNDEFINED,
    VK_IMAGE_LAYOUT_COLOR_ATTACHMENT_OPTIMAL,
    PresentQueue.FamilyIndex,
    GraphicsQueue.FamilyIndex,
    VK_IMAGE_ASPECT_COLOR_BIT
  };
  SetImageMemoryBarrier( command_buffer,
VK_PIPELINE_STAGE_COLOR_ATTACHMENT_OUTPUT_BIT,
```

```
VK_PIPELINE_STAGE_COLOR_ATTACHMENT_OUTPUT_BIT, {
image_transition_before_drawing } );
}
BeginRenderPass( command_buffer, *RenderPass, framebuffer, { { 0, 0 },
Swapchain.Size }, { { 0.1f, 0.2f, 0.3f, 1.0f },{ 1.0f, 0 } },
VK_SUBPASS_CONTENTS_INLINE );
VkViewport viewport = {
  0.0f,
  0.0f,
  static_cast<float>(Swapchain.Size.width),
  static_cast<float>(Swapchain.Size.height),
  0.0f,
  1.0f,
};
SetViewportStateDynamically( command_buffer, 0, { viewport } );
VkRect2D scissor = {
  {
    0,
    0
  },
  {
    Swapchain.Size.width,
    Swapchain.Size.height
  }
};
SetScissorsStateDynamically( command_buffer, 0, { scissor } );
BindVertexBuffers( command_buffer, 0, { { *VertexBuffer, 0 } } );
BindDescriptorSets( command_buffer, VK_PIPELINE_BIND_POINT_GRAPHICS,
*PipelineLayout, 0, DescriptorSets, {} );
BindPipelineObject( command_buffer, VK_PIPELINE_BIND_POINT_GRAPHICS,
*Pipeline );
for( size_t i = 0; i < Model.Parts.size(); ++i ) {
  DrawGeometry( command_buffer, Model.Parts[i].VertexCount, 1,
Model.Parts[i].VertexOffset, 0 );
}
EndRenderPass( command_buffer );
if( PresentQueue.FamilyIndex != GraphicsQueue.FamilyIndex ) {
  ImageTransition image_transition_before_present = {
    Swapchain.Images[swapchain_image_index],
    VK_ACCESS_COLOR_ATTACHMENT_WRITE_BIT,
    VK_ACCESS_MEMORY_READ_BIT,
    VK_IMAGE_LAYOUT_PRESENT_SRC_KHR,
    VK_IMAGE_LAYOUT_PRESENT_SRC_KHR,
    GraphicsQueue.FamilyIndex,
    PresentQueue.FamilyIndex,
    VK_IMAGE_ASPECT_COLOR_BIT
  };
  SetImageMemoryBarrier( command_buffer,
```

Lighting

```
            VK_PIPELINE_STAGE_COLOR_ATTACHMENT_OUTPUT_BIT,
            VK_PIPELINE_STAGE_BOTTOM_OF_PIPE_BIT, { image_transition_before_present }
        );
    }
    if( !EndCommandBufferRecordingOperation( command_buffer ) ) {
        return false;
    }
    return true;
```

When we prepare the preceding frame, normal vectors and vertex positions are automatically fetched from the vertex buffer. Positions are used, not only to display a geometry, but along with the normal vectors, they are also used for lighting calculations.

```
gl_Position = ProjectionMatrix * ModelViewMatrix * app_position;
vec3 normal = mat3( ModelViewMatrix ) * app_normal;
vert_color = max( 0.0, dot( normal, vec3( 0.58, 0.58, 0.58 ) ) ) + 0.1;
```

For simplicity, the light vector is hardcoded in the vertex shader, but normally it should be provided using a uniform buffer or a push constant. In this case, the light vector always points in the same direction (for all vertices), so it simulates a directional light, which usually represents the sun.

In the preceding code, all lighting calculations are performed in the view space. We can perform such calculations in any coordinate system we want, but all vectors (normal, light vectors, view vectors, and so on) must be transformed to the same space in order for the calculations to be correct.

After calculating the diffuse term, we also add a constant value to the calculated color. Usually this is referred to as ambient lighting, which is used to brighten up the scene (otherwise all shadows/unlit surfaces would be too dark).

Below we can see diffuse lighting calculated at each vertex applied to geometry with a different number of polygons: on the left, a detailed geometry (high-polygon); and, on the right model, with a much smaller amount of detail (low-polygon):

Chapter 11

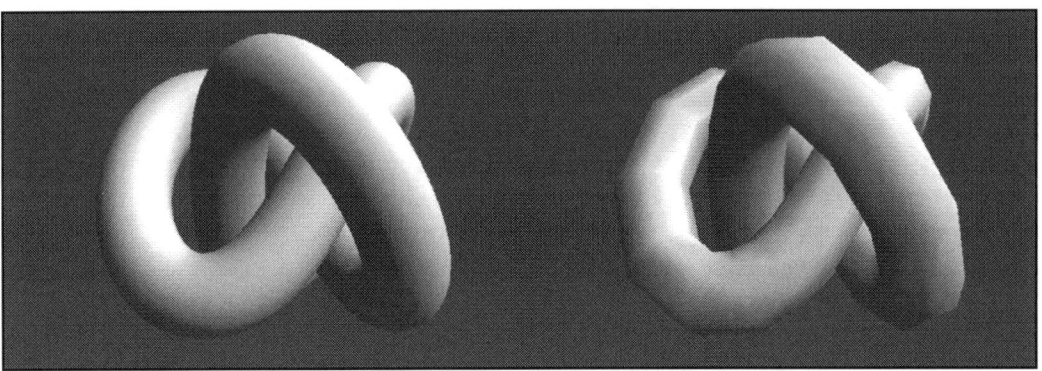

See also

- In Chapter 2, *Image Presentation*, see the following recipes:
    - *Creating a Vulkan Instance with WSI extensions enabled*
    - *Creating a logical device with WSI extensions enabled*
    - *Creating a swapchain with R8G8B8A8 format and a MAILBOX present mode*
- In Chapter 3, *Command Buffers and Synchronization*, the recipe *Beginning a command buffer recording operation*
- In Chapter 8, *Graphics and Compute Pipelines*, the recipe *Creating graphics pipelines*
- In Chapter 9, *Command Recording and Drawing*, the recipe *increasing the performance by increasing the number of separately rendered frames*
- In Chapter 10, *Helper Recipes*, the recipe *Loading a 3D model from an OBJ file*
- The following recipes in this chapter:
    - *Rendering a geometry with a fragment specular lighting*
    - *Rendering a normal mapped geometry*

Rendering a geometry with a fragment specular lighting

Specular lighting allows us to add bright highlights or reflections on the surface of a model. This way rendered geometry looks shinier and more glossy.

Lighting

An example of an image generated with this recipe looks like the following:

Getting ready

The most commonly used algorithm describing the way surfaces are lit is a **Blinn-Phong** model. It is an empirical model, which isn't physically correct but gives results that are more plausible in situations where rendered geometry is simplified. So it is well suited for 3D real-time graphics.

The **Blinn-Phong** model describes light leaving a given surface as a sum of four components:

- **Emissive**: The amount of light emitted by the surface
- : The amount of reflected light that is scattered around the whole scene and doesn't have any visible source (used to brighten up the geometry)

Ambient: The amount of reflected light that is scattered around the whole scene and doesn't have any visible source (used to brighten up the geometry) Diffuse: Describes the light reflected by rough surfaces (based on the Lambert lighting equation)

- **Specular**: Describes the light reflected by shiny, slick surfaces

Each of the above components may have a different color, which describes the surface material (diffuse color is usually taken from a texture). Each light source may also be represented with a separate color for each component (except the emissive). We can interpret it as how much given light source influences the ambient light available in the scene, how much diffuse lighting is emitted by the light source, and so on. We can, of course, modify the preceding algorithm to adjust it to our needs. This way we can achieve various results that are easy to calculate.

In this recipe, we will focus on the diffuse lighting and specular reflections. The former are described in the *Rendering a geometry with a vertex diffuse lighting* recipe. The latter are calculated with a dot product of a surface normal vector and a half vector. A half vector is a vector that is halfway between a view vector (from the lit point to the viewer) and the light vector (from the lit point to the light source):

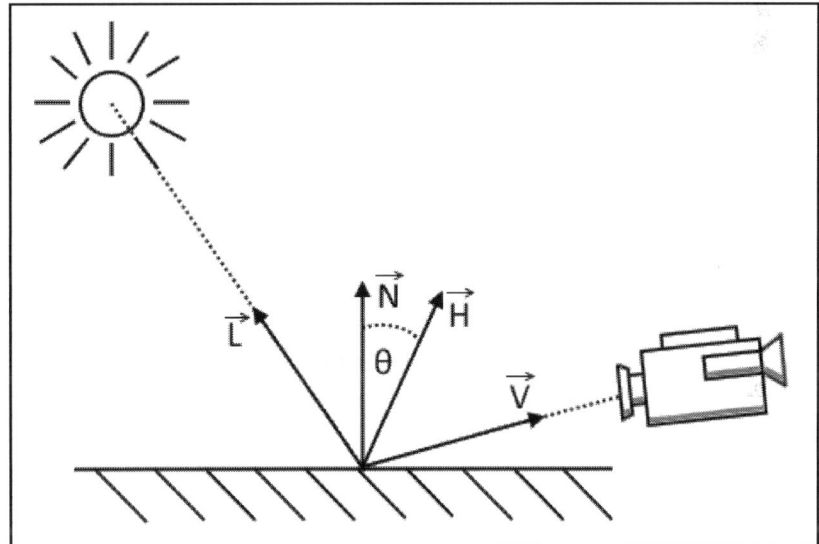

The calculated dot product value is responsible for creating shinny light reflections on slick surfaces. As the area lit this way may be too big, the calculated value is then raised to the power. The higher the power value, the smaller and more concentrated are light reflexes on an object's surface. In the shader, these are calculated like this:

```
pow( dot( half_vector, normal_vector ), shinniness );
```

Lighting

Normal vector is usually loaded along the geometry and provided by the application. The half vector is calculated as follows:

```
vec3 view_vector = normalize( eye_position.xyz - vert_position.xyz );
vec3 light_vector = normalize( light_position.xyz - vert_position.xyz );
vec3 half_vector = normalize( view_vector + light_vector );
```

To achieve correct results, all vectors must be normalized. Of course, specular highlights are not visible when the surface is not lit (or doesn't face the light source). So they should be calculated only when the diffuse component is greater than 0.

How to do it...

1. Prepare Vulkan resources as described in the *Rendering a geometry with a vertex diffuse lighting* recipe.
2. Create a pipeline layout using the prepared descriptor set layout with only a uniform buffer and also with a single push constant range accessed by a fragment shader stage, beginning at a 0th offset and of a 4 * sizeof(float) size (refer to the *Creating a pipeline layout* recipe from Chapter 8, *Graphics and Compute Pipelines*).
3. Create a shader module for a vertex shader stage using a SPIR-V assembly generated from the following GLSL code (refer to the *Converting GLSL shaders to SPIR-V assemblies* recipe from Chapter 7, *Shaders* and to *Creating a shader module* recipe from Chapter 8, *Graphics and Compute Pipelines*):

```
#version 450
layout( location = 0 ) in vec4 app_position;
layout( location = 1 ) in vec3 app_normal;
layout( set = 0, binding = 0 ) uniform UniformBuffer {
  mat4 ModelViewMatrix;
  mat4 ProjectionMatrix;
};
layout( location = 0 ) out vec3 vert_position;
layout( location = 1 ) out vec3 vert_normal;
void main() {
  vec4 position = ModelViewMatrix * app_position;

  vert_position = position.xyz;
  vert_normal = mat3( ModelViewMatrix ) * app_normal;
  gl_Position = ProjectionMatrix * position;
}
```

4. Create a shader module for a fragment shader stage using a SPIR-V assembly generated from the following GLSL code:

```
#version 450
layout( location = 0 ) in vec3 vert_position;
layout( location = 1 ) in vec3 vert_normal;
layout( push_constant ) uniform LightParameters {
  vec4 Position;
} Light;
layout( location = 0 ) out vec4 frag_color;
void main() {
  vec3 normal_vector = normalize( vert_normal );
  vec3 light_vector = normalize( Light.Position.xyz - vert_position );
  float diffuse_term = max( 0.0, dot( normal_vector, light_vector ) );

  frag_color = vec4( diffuse_term + 0.1 );
  if( diffuse_term > 0.0 ) {
    vec3 view_vector = normalize( vec3( 0.0, 0.0, 0.0 ) - vert_position.xyz );
    vec3 half_vector = normalize( view_vector + light_vector );
    float shinniness = 60.0;
    float specular_term = pow( dot( half_vector, normal_vector ), shinniness );
    frag_color += vec4( specular_term );
  }
}
```

5. Specify the pipeline shader stages with vertex and fragment shaders, both using a main function from the respective shader modules (refer to the *Specifying pipeline shader stages* recipe from Chapter 8, *Graphics and Compute Pipelines*).

6. Create a graphics pipeline using the pipeline layout and shader stages presented previously. The rest of pipeline parameters remain identical to those presented in the *Rendering a geometry with a vertex diffuse lighting* recipe.

7. Prepare a command buffer recording (or a rendering) function executed each frame. To do this, we need to begin a command buffer recording, copy data from the staging buffer to the uniform buffer (if needed), set an image memory barrier to transfer queue ownership for an image acquired from the swapchain, begin the render pass, set the viewport and scissor test states dynamically, bind the vertex buffers, descriptor sets and the graphics pipeline (refer to the *Rendering a geometry with a vertex diffuse lighting* recipe).

Lighting

8. Prepare a position of a light source and provide it to the shaders through push constants. For this operation, provide the pipeline layout, a `VK_SHADER_STAGE_FRAGMENT_BIT` shader stage, 0 offset and a size of `sizeof( float ) * 4`, and a pointer to the data, in which the light source's position is stored (refer to the *Providing data to shaders through push constants* recipe from `Chapter 9`, *Command Recording and Drawing*).
9. Finalize the command buffer by recording the model drawing operation, ending the render pass, setting another image memory barrier for the swapchain image and ending the command buffer.
10. Submit the command buffer to the graphics queue and present an image (refer to the *Preparing a single frame of animation* and *Increasing the performance through increasing the number of separately rendered frames* recipes from `Chapter 9`, *Command Recording and Drawing*).

How it works...

The whole source code is almost identical to the one presented in the *Rendering a geometry with a vertex diffuse lighting* recipe. The most important difference is in the vertex and fragment shaders, which perform lighting calculations based on data provided from the application. This time a light vector is not hardcoded in the shader. Instead, it is calculated using the data provided from the application. Positions and normal vectors are automatically read as vertex attributes. The position of a light source is read using a push constant, so we need to include a push constant range, when we create a pipeline layout:

```
std::vector<VkPushConstantRange> push_constant_ranges = {
  {
    VK_SHADER_STAGE_FRAGMENT_BIT,    // VkShaderStageFlags    stageFlags
    0,                                // uint32_t              offset
    sizeof( float ) * 4               // uint32_t              size
  }
};
InitVkDestroyer( LogicalDevice, PipelineLayout );
if( !CreatePipelineLayout( *LogicalDevice, { *DescriptorSetLayout },
push_constant_ranges, *PipelineLayout ) ) {
  return false;
}
```

Data to a push constant is provided during the command buffer recording operation:

```
BindVertexBuffers( command_buffer, 0, { { *VertexBuffer, 0 } } );
BindDescriptorSets( command_buffer, VK_PIPELINE_BIND_POINT_GRAPHICS,
*PipelineLayout, 0, DescriptorSets, {} );
BindPipelineObject( command_buffer, VK_PIPELINE_BIND_POINT_GRAPHICS,
```

```
*Pipeline );
std::array<float, 4> light_position = { 5.0f, 5.0f, 0.0f, 0.0f };
ProvideDataToShadersThroughPushConstants( command_buffer, *PipelineLayout,
VK_SHADER_STAGE_FRAGMENT_BIT, 0, sizeof( float ) * 4, &light_position[0] );
```

Through the push constant, we provide a position of a light source. This way our shaders becomes more universal, as we can calculate light vector directly in a shader and use it for lighting calculations.

In the following image, we can see the results of rendering a geometry lit with a diffuse and specular lighting calculated inside a fragment shader. The results of lighting calculations performed in the fragment shader are much better than if the same calculations were performed in the vertex shader. The lighting looks good even if the geometry is quite simple. But, of course, this comes with reduced performance.

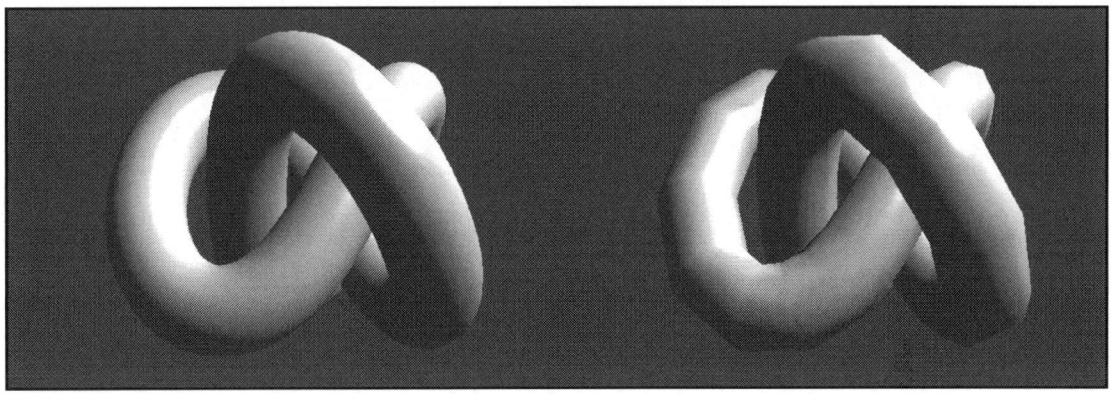

See also

- In Chapter 7, *Shaders*, the recipe *Converting GLSL shaders to SPIR-V assemblies*
- In Chapter 8, *Graphics and Compute Pipelines*, see the following recipes:
    - *Creating a shader module*
    - *Specifying pipeline shader stages*
    - *Creating a pipeline layout*
- In Chapter 9, *Command Recording and Drawing*, see the following recipes::
    - *Providing data to shaders through push constants*
- The following recipe in this chapter:
    - *Rendering a geometry with a vertex diffuse lighting*

Lighting

Rendering a normal mapped geometry

Normal mapping is a technique that allows us to increase the details of a model's surface without increasing its geometrical complexity. Using this technique, normal vectors associated with vertices are not used during lighting calculations. They are replaced with normal vectors read from an image (a texture). This way, the shape of a model is unchanged, so we don't need additional processing power to transform vertices. However, the lighting quality is much better and depends only on the quality of a normal map image instead of the complexity of the model.

An example of an image generated with this recipe looks like the following:

Getting ready

Normal map is an image, in which normal vectors acquired from a highly detailed geometry are stored. It is used to simulate the high amount of surface details on a simple (low-polygon) geometry.

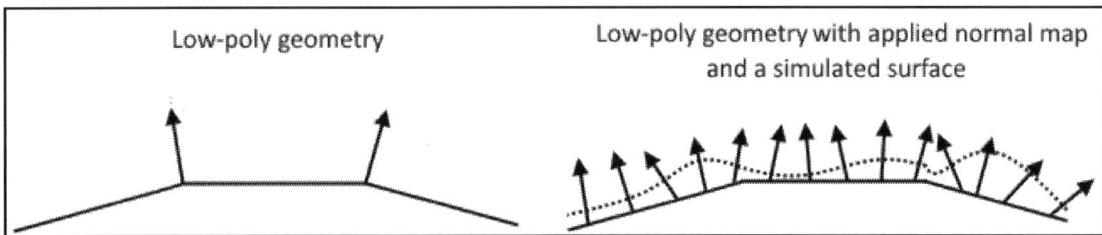

For simple lighting calculations, we just need to load positions and normal vectors, but normal mapping requires us to load (or generate) much more data for a given 3D model. Apart from the above attributes, we also need texture coordinates, so we can sample a normal map inside fragment shaders, and two additional vectors: tangent and bitangent. The normal vector is perpendicular to the surface at a given point and points in a direction that is away from the surface. Tangent and bitangent vectors are tangential to the surface. Tangent vector points in the direction on object's surface, in which texture image advances *horizontally*, from left to right (s component of texture coordinates is increasing). Bitangent points in the direction on object's surface, in which the texture image advances *vertically*, from top to bottom (t component of texture coordinates is decreasing). Additionally, all three vectors - a normal, tangent and bitangent - should be perpendicular to each other (small deviations are acceptable) and have a length equal to 1.0.

Normal, tangent and bitangent vectors are not used directly for lighting calculations. Instead, they form a rotation matrix, which can be used to convert a vector from texture (or tangent) space to a local model space or vice versa. This way we don't need to create a texture with normal vectors that can only be applied to a dedicated model, but we can prepare a general normal map and use it with an arbitrary geometry. Using the so called TBN matrix, we can load a normal vector from the texture and use it for lighting calculations performed in a coordinate system that is more convenient for us.

Lighting

How to do it...

1. Prepare Vulkan resources as described in the *Rendering a geometry with a vertex diffuse lighting* recipe.
2. Load texture data from a file with a normal map (refer to the *Loading texture data from a file* recipe from `Chapter 10`, *Helper Recipes*).
3. Create a two-dimensional combined image sampler that has a color aspect and format (in example `VK_FORMAT_R8G8B8A8_UNORM`) and supports `VK_IMAGE_USAGE_SAMPLED_BIT` and `VK_IMAGE_USAGE_TRANSFER_DST_BIT` usages (refer to the *Creating a combined image sampler* recipe from `Chapter 5`, *Descriptor Sets*).
4. Copy data loaded from a normal map into the created image using a staging buffer (refer to the *Using staging buffer to update an image with a device-local memory bound* recipe from `Chapter 4`, *Resources and Memory*).
5. Load a 3D model from a file. Apart from the vertex positions and normal vectors, load also texture coordinates and load or generate tangent and bitangent vectors. Create a (vertex) buffer and copy loaded model data to the buffer's memory using a staging buffer (refer to the *Loading a 3D model from an OBJ file* from `Chapter 10`, *Helper Recipes*).
6. Create a descriptor set layout with one uniform buffer accessed by a vertex shader at 0th binding and with one combined image sampler accessed by a fragment shader at 1st binding (refer to the *Creating a descriptor set layout* recipe from `Chapter 5`, *Descriptor Sets*).
7. Create a descriptor pool from which one uniform buffer descriptor and one combined image sampler descriptor can be allocated (refer to the *Creating a descriptor pool* recipe from `Chapter 5`, *Descriptor Sets*).
8. Allocate one descriptor set from the created pool using a descriptor set layout with one uniform buffer and one combined image sampler (refer to *Allocating descriptor sets* recipe from `Chapter 5`, *Descriptor Sets*).
9. Update the descriptor set with the uniform buffer accessed at the 0th binding and with the created combined image sampler with normal map data accessed at the 1st binding. Provide a `VK_IMAGE_LAYOUT_SHADER_READ_ONLY_OPTIMAL` value as the image's layout (refer to the *Updating descriptor sets* recipe from `Chapter 5`, *Descriptor Sets*).

10. Create a pipeline layout using the prepared descriptor set layout that also specifies a single push constant range accessed by a fragment shader stage, beginning at a 0th offset and of a 4 * sizeof(float) size (refer to the *Creating a pipeline layout* recipe from Chapter 8, *Graphics and Compute Pipelines*).

11. Create a shader module for a vertex shader stage using a SPIR-V assembly generated from the following GLSL code (refer to the *Converting GLSL shaders to SPIR-V assemblies* recipe from Chapter 7, *Shaders and to Creating a shader module* recipe from Chapter 8, *Graphics and Compute Pipelines*):

```
#version 450
layout( location = 0 ) in vec4 app_position;
layout( location = 1 ) in vec3 app_normal;
layout( location = 2 ) in vec2 app_texcoord;
layout( location = 3 ) in vec3 app_tangent;
layout( location = 4 ) in vec3 app_bitangent;
layout( set = 0, binding = 0 ) uniform UniformBuffer {
  mat4 ModelViewMatrix;
  mat4 ProjectionMatrix;
};
layout( location = 0 ) out vec3 vert_position;
layout( location = 1 ) out vec2 vert_texcoord;
layout( location = 2 ) out vec3 vert_normal;
layout( location = 3 ) out vec3 vert_tanget;
layout( location = 4 ) out vec3 vert_bitanget;
void main() {
  vec4 position = ModelViewMatrix * app_position;
  gl_Position = ProjectionMatrix * position;

  vert_position = position.xyz;
  vert_texcoord = app_texcoord;
  vert_normal = mat3( ModelViewMatrix ) * app_normal;
  vert_tanget = mat3( ModelViewMatrix ) * app_tangent;
  vert_bitanget = mat3( ModelViewMatrix ) * app_bitangent;
}
```

12. Create a shader module for a fragment shader stage using a SPIR-V assembly generated from the following GLSL code:

```
#version 450
layout( location = 0 ) in vec3 vert_position;
layout( location = 1 ) in vec2 vert_texcoord;
layout( location = 2 ) in vec3 vert_normal;
layout( location = 3 ) in vec3 vert_tanget;
layout( location = 4 ) in vec3 vert_bitanget;
layout( set = 0, binding = 1 ) uniform sampler2D ImageSampler;
```

Lighting

```glsl
layout( push_constant ) uniform LightParameters {
  vec4 Position;
} Light;
layout( location = 0 ) out vec4 frag_color;
void main() {
  vec3 normal = 2 * texture( ImageSampler, vert_texcoord ).rgb - 1.0;
  vec3 normal_vector = normalize( mat3( vert_tanget, vert_bitanget, vert_normal) * normal );
  vec3 light_vector = normalize( Light.Position.xyz - vert_position );
  float diffuse_term = max( 0.0, dot( normal_vector, light_vector ) ) * max( 0.0, dot( vert_normal, light_vector ) );
  frag_color = vec4( diffuse_term + 0.1 );
  if( diffuse_term > 0.0 ) {
    vec3 half_vector = normalize(normalize( -vert_position.xyz ) + light_vector);
    float specular_term = pow( dot( half_vector, normal_vector ), 60.0 );
    frag_color += vec4( specular_term );
  }
}
```

13. Specify pipeline shader stages with vertex and fragment shaders, both using a `main` function from respective shader modules (refer to the *Specifying pipeline shader stages* recipe from Chapter 8, *Graphics and Compute Pipelines*).

14. Specify a pipeline vertex input state with five attributes that are read from the same 0th binding. The binding should be created with data read per vertex and a stride equal to `14 * sizeof( float )` (refer to the *Specifying pipeline vertex input state* recipe from Chapter 8, *Graphics and Compute Pipelines*). The first attribute should have the following parameters:
    - 0 value for `location`
    - 0 value for `binding`
    - VK_FORMAT_R32G32B32_SFLOAT value for `format`
    - 0 value for `offset`

15. The second attribute should be defined as follows:
    - 1 value for `location`
    - 0 value for `binding`
    - VK_FORMAT_R32G32B32_SFLOAT value for `format`
    - `3 * sizeof( float )` value for `offset`

16. The third attribute should have the following definition:
    - 2 value for `location`
    - 0 value for `binding`
    - `VK_FORMAT_R32G32_SFLOAT` value for `format`
    - `6 * sizeof( float )` value for `offset`

17. The fourth attribute should be specified as follows:
    - 3 value for `location`
    - 0 value for `binding`
    - `VK_FORMAT_R32G32B32_SFLOAT` value for `format`
    - `8 * sizeof( float )` value for `offset`

18. The fifth attribute should use these values:
    - 4 value for `location`
    - 0 value for `binding`
    - `VK_FORMAT_R32G32B32_SFLOAT` value for `format`
    - `11 * sizeof( float )` value for `offset`

19. In each frame of animation, record a command buffer, inside which copy data from the staging buffer to the uniform buffer, begin the render pass, set the viewport and scissor test state dynamically, bind the vertex buffer, the descriptor set and the graphics pipeline (refer to the *Rendering a geometry with a vertex diffuse lighting recipe*).

20. Prepare the position of a light source and provide it to shaders through push constants. For this operation, provide the pipeline layout, a `VK_SHADER_STAGE_FRAGMENT_BIT` shader stage, 0 offset and a size of `sizeof( float ) * 4`, and a pointer to the data, in which light source's position is stored (refer to the *Providing data to shaders through push constants* recipe from `Chapter 9, Command Recording and Drawing`).

21. Draw the model, record the rest of the required operations into the command buffer, submit the command buffer to the graphics queue, and present an image (refer to the *Preparing a single frame of animation and Increasing the performance through increasing the number of separately rendered frames* recipes from `Chapter 9, Command Recording and Drawing`).

Lighting

How it works...

To use normal mapping in our application, we need to prepare an image, in which normal vectors are stored. We must load the image's contents, create an image, and copy the data to the image's memory. We also need to create a sampler that, along with the image, will form a combined image sampler:

```
int width = 1;
int height = 1;
std::vector<unsigned char> image_data;
if( !LoadTextureDataFromFile( "Data/Textures/normal_map.png", 4,
image_data, &width, &height ) ) {
  return false;
}
InitVkDestroyer( LogicalDevice, Sampler );
InitVkDestroyer( LogicalDevice, Image );
InitVkDestroyer( LogicalDevice, ImageMemory );
InitVkDestroyer( LogicalDevice, ImageView );
if( !CreateCombinedImageSampler( PhysicalDevice, *LogicalDevice,
VK_IMAGE_TYPE_2D, VK_FORMAT_R8G8B8A8_UNORM, { (uint32_t)width,
(uint32_t)height, 1 },
  1, 1, VK_IMAGE_USAGE_SAMPLED_BIT | VK_IMAGE_USAGE_TRANSFER_DST_BIT,
VK_IMAGE_VIEW_TYPE_2D, VK_IMAGE_ASPECT_COLOR_BIT, VK_FILTER_LINEAR,
   VK_FILTER_LINEAR, VK_SAMPLER_MIPMAP_MODE_NEAREST,
VK_SAMPLER_ADDRESS_MODE_REPEAT, VK_SAMPLER_ADDRESS_MODE_REPEAT,
   VK_SAMPLER_ADDRESS_MODE_REPEAT, 0.0f, false, 1.0f, false,
VK_COMPARE_OP_ALWAYS, 0.0f, 1.0f, VK_BORDER_COLOR_FLOAT_OPAQUE_BLACK,
   false, *Sampler, *Image, *ImageMemory, *ImageView ) ) {
  return false;
}
VkImageSubresourceLayers image_subresource_layer = {
  VK_IMAGE_ASPECT_COLOR_BIT,     // VkImageAspectFlags    aspectMask
  0,                              // uint32_t              mipLevel
  0,                              // uint32_t              baseArrayLayer
  1                               // uint32_t              layerCount
};
if( !UseStagingBufferToUpdateImageWithDeviceLocalMemoryBound(
PhysicalDevice, *LogicalDevice,
static_cast<VkDeviceSize>(image_data.size()),
  &image_data[0], *Image, image_subresource_layer, { 0, 0, 0 }, {
(uint32_t)width, (uint32_t)height, 1 }, VK_IMAGE_LAYOUT_UNDEFINED,
  VK_IMAGE_LAYOUT_SHADER_READ_ONLY_OPTIMAL, 0, VK_ACCESS_SHADER_READ_BIT,
VK_IMAGE_ASPECT_COLOR_BIT, VK_PIPELINE_STAGE_TOP_OF_PIPE_BIT,
  VK_PIPELINE_STAGE_FRAGMENT_SHADER_BIT, GraphicsQueue.Handle,
FrameResources.front().CommandBuffer, {} ) ) {
  return false;
}
```

After that, we need to load a 3D model. We need to load positions, normal vectors, and texture coordinates. Tangent and bitangent vectors must also be loaded, but as the .obj format cannot store so many different attributes, we must generate them (this is performed inside the Load3DModelFromObjFile()):

```
uint32_t vertex_stride = 0;
if( !Load3DModelFromObjFile( "Data/Models/ice.obj", true, true, true, true,
Model, &vertex_stride ) ) {
  return false;
}
```

Now we need to modify the descriptor set described in the *Rendering a geometry with a vertex diffuse lighting* recipe. First, we start by creating a proper layout:

```
std::vector<VkDescriptorSetLayoutBinding> descriptor_set_layout_bindings =
{
  {
    0,
    VK_DESCRIPTOR_TYPE_UNIFORM_BUFFER,
    1,
    VK_SHADER_STAGE_VERTEX_BIT,
    nullptr
  },
  {
    1,
    VK_DESCRIPTOR_TYPE_COMBINED_IMAGE_SAMPLER,
    1,
    VK_SHADER_STAGE_FRAGMENT_BIT,
    nullptr
  }
};
InitVkDestroyer( LogicalDevice, DescriptorSetLayout );
if( !CreateDescriptorSetLayout( *LogicalDevice,
descriptor_set_layout_bindings, *DescriptorSetLayout ) ) {
  return false;
}
```

Next, a descriptor pool is required. From it a descriptor set is allocated:

```
std::vector<VkDescriptorPoolSize> descriptor_pool_sizes = {
  {
    VK_DESCRIPTOR_TYPE_UNIFORM_BUFFER,
    1
  },
  {
    VK_DESCRIPTOR_TYPE_COMBINED_IMAGE_SAMPLER,
    1
  }
```

Lighting

```
};
InitVkDestroyer( LogicalDevice, DescriptorPool );
if( !CreateDescriptorPool( *LogicalDevice, false, 1, descriptor_pool_sizes,
*DescriptorPool ) ) {
  return false;
}
if( !AllocateDescriptorSets( *LogicalDevice, *DescriptorPool, {
*DescriptorSetLayout }, DescriptorSets ) ) {
  return false;
}
```

When the descriptor set is allocated, we can update it with handles of the uniform buffer and the combined image sampler:

```
BufferDescriptorInfo buffer_descriptor_update = {
  DescriptorSets[0],
  0,
  0,
  VK_DESCRIPTOR_TYPE_UNIFORM_BUFFER,
  {
    {
      *UniformBuffer,
      0,
      VK_WHOLE_SIZE
    }
  }
};
ImageDescriptorInfo image_descriptor_update = {
  DescriptorSets[0],
  1,
  0,
  VK_DESCRIPTOR_TYPE_COMBINED_IMAGE_SAMPLER,
  {
    {
      *Sampler,
      *ImageView,
      VK_IMAGE_LAYOUT_SHADER_READ_ONLY_OPTIMAL
    }
  }
};
UpdateDescriptorSets( *LogicalDevice, { image_descriptor_update }, {
buffer_descriptor_update }, {}, {} );
```

This time we have not two but five vertex attributes, so we also need to modify the vertex input state:

```
std::vector<VkVertexInputBindingDescription>
vertex_input_binding_descriptions = {
  {
    0,
    vertex_stride,
    VK_VERTEX_INPUT_RATE_VERTEX
  }
};
std::vector<VkVertexInputAttributeDescription>
vertex_attribute_descriptions = {
  {
    0,
    0,
    VK_FORMAT_R32G32B32_SFLOAT,
    0
  },
  {
    1,
    0,
    VK_FORMAT_R32G32B32_SFLOAT,
    3 * sizeof( float )
  },
  {
    2,
    0,
    VK_FORMAT_R32G32_SFLOAT,
    6 * sizeof( float )
  },
  {
    3,
    0,
    VK_FORMAT_R32G32B32_SFLOAT,
    8 * sizeof( float )
  },
  {
    4,
    0,
    VK_FORMAT_R32G32B32_SFLOAT,
    11 * sizeof( float )
  }
};
VkPipelineVertexInputStateCreateInfo vertex_input_state_create_info;
SpecifyPipelineVertexInputState( vertex_input_binding_descriptions,
vertex_attribute_descriptions, vertex_input_state_create_info );
```

Lighting

The preceding attributes are read in the vertex shader, which transforms the vertex position to a clip space using the model-view and projection matrices. Additionally, the view-space position and unmodified texture coordinates are passed to the fragment shader. Normal, tangent and bitangent vectors are also passed to the fragment shader, but they are first transformed to a view space with the model-view matrix:

```
vec4 position = ModelViewMatrix * app_position;
gl_Position = ProjectionMatrix * position;

vert_position = position.xyz;
vert_texcoord = app_texcoord;
vert_normal = mat3( ModelViewMatrix ) * app_normal;
vert_tangent = mat3( ModelViewMatrix ) * app_tangent;
vert_bitangent = mat3( ModelViewMatrix ) * app_bitangent;
```

The most important part, from the normal mapping perspective, takes place in the fragment shader. It first reads the normal vector from the texture. Usually, textures store values that are in the 0.0-1.0 range inclusive (unless we use signed-normalized texture formats: SNORM). However, all the components of normal vectors may have values in the -1.0-1.0 range, so we need to expand the loaded normal vector like this:

```
vec3 normal = 2 * texture( ImageSampler, vert_texcoord ).rgb - 1.0;
```

The fragment shader calculates diffuse and specular lighting in the same way as described in the *Rendering a geometry with a fragment specular lighting* recipe. It just takes the normal vector loaded from the texture instead of the one provided from the vertex shader. There is just one additional thing it needs to perform: all the vectors (light and view) are in the view space, but the normal vector stored in the normal map is in the tangent space, so it also needs to be converted to the same view space. This is done with a TBN matrix formed from the normal, tangent and bitangent vectors. They are provided from the vertex shader. Because the vertex shader transforms them from the model space into a view space (by multiplying them by the model-view matrix), the created TBN matrix converts the normal vector from the tangent space directly into the view space:

```
vec3 normal_vector = normalize( mat3( vert_tanget, vert_bitanget,
vert_normal) * normal );
```

mat3() is a constructor for creating a 3x3 matrix from three-component vectors. Using such a matrix, we can perform rotations and scaling, but no translation. Since we want to transform directions (unit-length vectors), this is exactly what we need in this situation.

Normal mapping can give us impressive lighting even on very simple (low-poly) geometry. In the image below, on the left we can see normal mapped geometry with many polygons; while on the right, similar geometry is presented but with fewer vertices.

See also

- In Chapter 4, *Resources and Memory*, the recipe *Using staging buffer to update an image with a device local memory bound*
- In Chapter 5, *Descriptor Sets*, the recipe *Creating a combined image sampler*
- In Chapter 10, *Helper Recipes*, see the following recipes:
    - *Loading texture data from a file*
    - *Loading a 3D model from an OBJ file*
- Also, look at the following recipes in the same chapter:
    - *Rendering a geometry with a vertex diffuse lighting*
    - *Rendering a geometry with a fragment specular lighting*

Lighting

Drawing a reflective and refractive geometry using cubemaps

In real-life, transparent objects both transmit light rays, and also reflect them. If an object's surface is viewed from high angles, we see more light being reflected. Looking at an object's surface more directly, we see more light being transmitted through the object. Simulating such an effect may generate very plausible results. In this recipe, we will see how to render a geometry that is both refractive and reflective.

An example of an image generated with this recipe looks like:

Getting ready

Cubemaps are textures with images covering six sides of a cube. They usually store the view of a scene from a given position. The most common use for cubemaps are skyboxes. They are also handy when we want to map reflections on a surface of a given model. Another example of common use is to simulate transparent objects (that is made of glass), which refract light rays. Very low resolution cubemaps (in example 4x4 pixels) can even be used directly for ambient lighting.

Chapter 11

Cubemaps contain six two-dimensional images. All of them are square and have the same size. In Vulkan, cubemaps are created using 2D images with six array layers, for which a cubemap image view is created. Through it, the six array layers are interpreted as cubemap faces in the following order: +X, -X, +Y, -Y, +Z, -Z.

Images courtesy of Emil Persson (http://www.humus.name)

Six sides of a cubemap correspond to six directions, as if we stayed in one position, turned around, and took photos of the world around us. Using such a texture, we can simulate the world being reflected from the surface of the object or being transmitted through the object. However, when an object moves too far from the place the texture was created for, the illusion is broken until we apply a new texture that is valid for the new position.

How to do it...

1. Prepare Vulkan resources as described in the *Rendering a geometry with a vertex diffuse lighting* recipe.
2. Load a 3D model data from file with vertex positions and normal vectors. This model will be displayed as the one reflecting and transmitting the environment (refer to the *Loading a 3D model from an OBJ file* recipe from `Chapter 10`, *Helper Recipes*).
3. Create a (vertex) buffer with a memory object and use it store the vertex data for our model (refer to the *Creating a buffer, Allocating and binding memory object to a buffer* and *Using staging buffer to update buffer with a device-local memory bound* recipes from `Chapter 4`, *Resources and Memory*).
4. Load a 3D model containing vertex positions of a cube. This model will be used to display the environment being reflected (refer to the *Drawing a skybox* recipe from `Chapter 12`, *Advanced Rendering Techniques*).
5. Create a buffer, along with a memory object bound it, to hold the vertex data of the environment (skybox).
6. Create a two-dimensional combined image sampler with six array layers and a cube image view. It must support `VK_IMAGE_USAGE_SAMPLED_BIT` and `VK_IMAGE_USAGE_TRANSFER_DST_BIT` uses. A `VK_SAMPLER_ADDRESS_MODE_CLAMP_TO_EDGE` sampler address mode must be used for all addressing dimensions (refer to the *Creating a combined image sampler* recipe from `Chapter 5`, *Descriptor Sets*).
7. Load texture data for all six sides of a cubemap from files (refer to the *Loading texture data from a file* recipe from `Chapter 10`, *Helper Recipes*).
8. Upload each loaded texture to a separate array layer of a created combined image sampler. Textures should be uploaded in the following order: positive and negative X, positive and negative Y, positive and negative Z (refer to the *Using staging buffer to update an image with a device-local memory bound* from `Chapter 4`, *Resources and Memory*).
9. Create a descriptor set layout with two descriptor resources: a uniform buffer accessed in a vertex shader at 0th binding and with a combined image sampler accessed in a fragment shader at 1st binding (refer to the *Creating a descriptor set layout* recipe from `Chapter 5`, *Descriptor Sets*).
10. Create a descriptor pool, from which one uniform buffer descriptor and one combined image sampler descriptor can be allocated (refer to the *Creating a descriptor pool* recipe from `Chapter 5`, *Descriptor Sets*).

11. Allocate a descriptor set from the created pool using the descriptor set layout with a uniform buffer and a combined image sampler resources (refer to the *Allocating descriptor sets* recipe from Chapter 5, *Descriptor Sets*).
12. Update (populate) the descriptor set with the uniform buffer accessed at the 0th binding and with the created combined image sampler (cubemap) accessed at the 1st binding. Provide a VK_IMAGE_LAYOUT_SHADER_READ_ONLY_OPTIMAL value as the cubemap's layout (refer to the *Updating descriptor sets* recipe from Chapter 5, *Descriptor Sets*).
13. Create a pipeline layout using the prepared descriptor set layout that also specifies a single push constant range accessed by a fragment shader stage, beginning at a 0th offset and of a 4 * sizeof(float) size (refer to the *Creating a pipeline layout* recipe from Chapter 8, *Graphics and Compute Pipelines*).
14. Create a graphics pipeline used for drawing a reflective and refractive model. Start by creating a shader module for a vertex shader stage using a SPIR-V assembly generated from the following GLSL code (refer to the *Converting GLSL shaders to SPIR-V assemblies* recipe from Chapter 7, *Shaders* and to Creating a shader module recipe from Chapter 8, *Graphics and Compute Pipelines*):

```
#version 450
layout( location = 0 ) in vec4 app_position;
layout( location = 1 ) in vec3 app_normal;
layout( set = 0, binding = 0 ) uniform UniformBuffer {
  mat4 ModelViewMatrix;
  mat4 ProjectionMatrix;
};
layout( location = 0 ) out vec3 vert_position;
layout( location = 1 ) out vec3 vert_normal;
void main() {
  vert_position = app_position.xyz;
  vert_normal = app_normal;

  gl_Position = ProjectionMatrix * ModelViewMatrix *
app_position;
}
```

15. Create a shader module for a fragment shader stage using a SPIR-V assembly generated from the following GLSL code:

```
#version 450
layout( location = 0 ) in vec3 vert_position;
layout( location = 1 ) in vec3 vert_normal;
layout( set = 0, binding = 1 ) uniform samplerCube Cubemap;
layout( push_constant ) uniform LightParameters {
```

```glsl
    vec4 Position;
} Camera;
layout( location = 0 ) out vec4 frag_color;
void main() {
  vec3 view_vector = vert_position - Camera.Position.xyz;

  float angle = smoothstep( 0.3, 0.7, dot( normalize( -
view_vector ), vert_normal ) );

  vec3 reflect_vector = reflect( view_vector, vert_normal );
  vec4 reflect_color = texture( Cubemap, reflect_vector );

  vec3 refrac_vector = refract( view_vector, vert_normal, 0.3 );
  vec4 refract_color = texture( Cubemap, refrac_vector );

  frag_color = mix( reflect_color, refract_color, angle );
}
```

16. Specify pipeline shader stages with vertex and fragment shaders, both using a `main` function from the respective shader modules (refer to the *Specifying pipeline shader stages* recipe from `Chapter 8`, *Graphics and Compute Pipelines*).
17. Create a graphics pipeline for drawing a model using the preceding pipeline shader stages definition, with the rest of the pipeline's parameters defined in the same way as in the *Rendering a geometry with a vertex diffuse lighting* recipe.
18. Create a graphics pipeline for drawing an environment being reflected--a skybox (refer to the *Drawing a skybox* recipe from `Chapter 12`, *Advanced Rendering Techniques*).
19. To render a frame, record a command buffer in each iteration of a rendering loop. In the command buffer, copy data from the staging buffer to the uniform buffer, begin the render pass, set the viewport and scissor test states dynamically and bind the descriptor set (refer to the *Rendering a geometry with a vertex diffuse lighting* recipe).
20. Bind the graphics pipeline and the vertex buffer created for the reflective/refractive model.
21. Prepare the position of a camera, from which the scene is observed and provide it to shaders through push constants. For this operation, provide the pipeline layout, a `VK_SHADER_STAGE_FRAGMENT_BIT` shader stage, 0 offset and a size of `sizeof( float ) * 4`, and a pointer to the data, in which the camera's position is stored (refer to the *Providing data to shaders through push constants* recipe from `Chapter 9`, *Command Recording and Drawing*).
22. Draw the model (refer to the *Drawing a geometry* recipe from `Chapter 9`, *Command Recording and Drawing*).

23. Bind the graphics pipeline and the vertex buffer created for the skybox and draw it.
24. Record the rest of the required operations into the command buffer, submit the command buffer to the graphics queue, and present an image (refer to the *Preparing a single frame of animation and Increasing the performance through increasing the number of separately rendered frames* recipes from `Chapter 9`, *Command Recording and Drawing*).

How it works...

We start this recipe by loading and preparing buffers for two models: the first being the one simulating our main scene (reflective/refractive model); and second being used to draw the environment itself (a skybox). We need to copy vertex data using staging buffers to both vertex buffers.

Next, we need to create a cubemap. We do this by creating a combined image sampler. The image must be of a 2D type, must have six array layers, and must support `VK_IMAGE_USAGE_SAMPLED_BIT` and `VK_IMAGE_USAGE_TRANSFER_DST_BIT` usages. The format of the image depends on the case, but usually a `VK_FORMAT_R8G8B8A8_UNORM` would be a good choice. The created sampler must use a `VK_SAMPLER_ADDRESS_MODE_CLAMP_TO_EDGE` addressing mode for all sampling dimensions (u, v, and w), otherwise we might see the edges of all cubemap faces:

```
if( !CreateCombinedImageSampler( PhysicalDevice, *LogicalDevice,
  VK_IMAGE_TYPE_2D, VK_FORMAT_R8G8B8A8_UNORM, { 1024, 1024, 1 }, 1, 6,
    VK_IMAGE_USAGE_SAMPLED_BIT | VK_IMAGE_USAGE_TRANSFER_DST_BIT,
  VK_IMAGE_VIEW_TYPE_CUBE, VK_IMAGE_ASPECT_COLOR_BIT, VK_FILTER_LINEAR,
    VK_FILTER_LINEAR, VK_SAMPLER_MIPMAP_MODE_NEAREST,
  VK_SAMPLER_ADDRESS_MODE_CLAMP_TO_EDGE,
  VK_SAMPLER_ADDRESS_MODE_CLAMP_TO_EDGE,
    VK_SAMPLER_ADDRESS_MODE_CLAMP_TO_EDGE, 0.0f, false, 1.0f, false,
  VK_COMPARE_OP_ALWAYS, 0.0f, 1.0f, VK_BORDER_COLOR_FLOAT_OPAQUE_BLACK,
    false, *CubemapSampler, *CubemapImage, *CubemapImageMemory,
  *CubemapImageView ) ) {
    return false;
}
```

Lighting

Next, we need to upload data to the cubemap image. In this sample we load data from six separate files and copy it to six layers of an image like this:

```
std::vector<std::string> cubemap_images = {
  "Data/Textures/Skansen/posx.jpg",
  "Data/Textures/Skansen/negx.jpg",
  "Data/Textures/Skansen/posy.jpg",
  "Data/Textures/Skansen/negy.jpg",
  "Data/Textures/Skansen/posz.jpg",
  "Data/Textures/Skansen/negz.jpg"
};
for( size_t i = 0; i < cubemap_images.size(); ++i ) {
  std::vector<unsigned char> cubemap_image_data;
  int image_data_size;
  if( !LoadTextureDataFromFile( cubemap_images[i].c_str(), 4,
cubemap_image_data, nullptr, nullptr, nullptr, &image_data_size ) ) {
    return false;
  }
  VkImageSubresourceLayers image_subresource = {
    VK_IMAGE_ASPECT_COLOR_BIT,
    0,
    static_cast<uint32_t>(i),
    1
  };
  UseStagingBufferToUpdateImageWithDeviceLocalMemoryBound( PhysicalDevice,
*LogicalDevice, image_data_size, &cubemap_image_data[0],
    *CubemapImage, image_subresource, { 0, 0, 0 }, { 1024, 1024, 1 },
VK_IMAGE_LAYOUT_UNDEFINED, VK_IMAGE_LAYOUT_SHADER_READ_ONLY_OPTIMAL,
    0, VK_ACCESS_SHADER_READ_BIT, VK_IMAGE_ASPECT_COLOR_BIT,
VK_PIPELINE_STAGE_TOP_OF_PIPE_BIT, VK_PIPELINE_STAGE_FRAGMENT_SHADER_BIT,
    GraphicsQueue.Handle, FrameResources.front().CommandBuffer, {} );
}
```

We also need a descriptor set through which a fragment shader will be able to access the cubemap. To allocate a descriptor set its layout is required:

```
std::vector<VkDescriptorSetLayoutBinding> descriptor_set_layout_bindings =
{
  {
    0,
    VK_DESCRIPTOR_TYPE_UNIFORM_BUFFER,
    1,
    VK_SHADER_STAGE_VERTEX_BIT,
    nullptr
  },
  {
    1,
    VK_DESCRIPTOR_TYPE_COMBINED_IMAGE_SAMPLER,
```

```
      1,
      VK_SHADER_STAGE_FRAGMENT_BIT,
      nullptr
    }
};
InitVkDestroyer( LogicalDevice, DescriptorSetLayout );
if( !CreateDescriptorSetLayout( *LogicalDevice,
descriptor_set_layout_bindings, *DescriptorSetLayout ) ) {
    return false;
}
```

Descriptor sets are allocated from pools. So now we create one and allocate the descriptor set itself:

```
std::vector<VkDescriptorPoolSize> descriptor_pool_sizes = {
    {
      VK_DESCRIPTOR_TYPE_UNIFORM_BUFFER,
      1
    },
    {
      VK_DESCRIPTOR_TYPE_COMBINED_IMAGE_SAMPLER,
      1
    }
};
InitVkDestroyer( LogicalDevice, DescriptorPool );
if( !CreateDescriptorPool( *LogicalDevice, false, 1, descriptor_pool_sizes,
*DescriptorPool ) ) {
    return false;
}
if( !AllocateDescriptorSets( *LogicalDevice, *DescriptorPool, {
*DescriptorSetLayout }, DescriptorSets ) ) {
    return false;
}
```

One last step connected with descriptor resources is to update the created set with handles of resources that should be accessed in shaders:

```
BufferDescriptorInfo buffer_descriptor_update = {
    DescriptorSets[0],
    0,
    0,
    VK_DESCRIPTOR_TYPE_UNIFORM_BUFFER,
    {
      {
        *UniformBuffer,
        0,
        VK_WHOLE_SIZE
      }
```

Lighting

```
    }
};
ImageDescriptorInfo image_descriptor_update = {
    DescriptorSets[0],
    1,
    0,
    VK_DESCRIPTOR_TYPE_COMBINED_IMAGE_SAMPLER,
    {
        {
            *CubemapSampler,
            *CubemapImageView,
            VK_IMAGE_LAYOUT_SHADER_READ_ONLY_OPTIMAL
        }
    }
};
UpdateDescriptorSets( *LogicalDevice, { image_descriptor_update }, {
buffer_descriptor_update }, {}, {} );
```

After descriptor sets, it's time to create a render pass and a graphics pipeline, or rather two pipelines: one for drawing the model, and one for drawing the environment (a skybox). A graphics pipeline used for the model is very similar to the one created in the *Rendering a geometry with a vertex diffuse lighting* recipe, except it uses different shader programs and a push constant range, so we need to include it during pipeline layout creation:

```
std::vector<VkPushConstantRange> push_constant_ranges = {
    {
        VK_SHADER_STAGE_FRAGMENT_BIT,
        0,
        sizeof( float ) * 4
    }
};
InitVkDestroyer( LogicalDevice, PipelineLayout );
if( !CreatePipelineLayout( *LogicalDevice, { *DescriptorSetLayout },
push_constant_ranges, *PipelineLayout ) ) {
    return false;
}
```

The vertex shader, as usual, calculates the clip space position of a vertex and passes the unmodified position and normal vector to the fragment shader:

```
vert_position = app_position.xyz;
vert_normal = app_normal;

gl_Position = ProjectionMatrix * ModelViewMatrix * app_position;
```

Calculating reflections or refractions is most easily done in the world space and we should transform both vectors to this coordinate system. However, to simplify the recipe, the above vertex shader makes an assumption that the model is already provided in the world space, that's why unmodified vectors (position and normal) are passed to the fragment shader. It then takes these vectors and uses them to calculate both reflected and refracted vectors with built-in `reflect()` and `refract()` functions. Calculated vectors are used to read values from the cubemap. They are then mixed together based on the viewing angle:

```
vec3 view_vector = vert_position - Camera.Position.xyz;

float angle = smoothstep( 0.3, 0.7, dot( normalize( -view_vector ),
vert_normal ) );

vec3 reflect_vector = reflect( view_vector, vert_normal );
vec4 reflect_color = texture( Cubemap, reflect_vector );

vec3 refrac_vector = refract( view_vector, vert_normal, 0.3 );
vec4 refract_color = texture( Cubemap, refrac_vector );

frag_color = mix( reflect_color, refract_color, angle );
```

As for the creation of a graphics pipeline used for the skybox rendering, there is a dedicated *Drawing a skybox* recipe in `Chapter 12`, *Advanced Rendering Techniques*.

One last thing we should focus on is a command buffer recording. Here we render two objects, not one, so first we need to set an appropriate state required to properly draw the model:

```
BindDescriptorSets( command_buffer, VK_PIPELINE_BIND_POINT_GRAPHICS,
*PipelineLayout, 0, DescriptorSets, {} );
BindPipelineObject( command_buffer, VK_PIPELINE_BIND_POINT_GRAPHICS,
*ModelPipeline );
BindVertexBuffers( command_buffer, 0, { { *ModelVertexBuffer, 0 } } );
ProvideDataToShadersThroughPushConstants( command_buffer, *PipelineLayout,
VK_SHADER_STAGE_FRAGMENT_BIT, 0, sizeof( float ) * 4,
&Camera.GetPosition()[0] );
for( size_t i = 0; i < Model.Parts.size(); ++i ) {
   DrawGeometry( command_buffer, Model.Parts[i].VertexCount, 1,
Model.Parts[i].VertexOffset, 0 );
}
```

Lighting

Immediately after the preceding code, we render the skybox:

```
BindPipelineObject( command_buffer, VK_PIPELINE_BIND_POINT_GRAPHICS,
*SkyboxPipeline );
BindVertexBuffers( command_buffer, 0, { { *SkyboxVertexBuffer, 0 } } );
for( size_t i = 0; i < Skybox.Parts.size(); ++i ) {
  DrawGeometry( command_buffer, Skybox.Parts[i].VertexCount, 1,
Skybox.Parts[i].VertexOffset, 0 );
}
```

Of course, we don't need to render the environment--the reflections (and refractions) are stored in the texture. However, usually we also want to see the environment being reflected, not only the reflections.

All the knowledge in this recipe combined with the *Rendering a geometry with a vertex diffuse lighting* recipe, should generate the results seen in the following image:

See also

- In Chapter 5, *Descriptor Sets*, the recipe *Creating a combined image sampler*
- In Chapter 9, *Command Recording and Drawing*, the recipe *Providing data to shaders through push constants*
- In Chapter 10, *Helper Recipes*, see the following recipes:
    - *Loading texture data from a file*
    - *Loading a 3D model from an OBJ file*
- The recipe *Rendering a geometry with a vertex diffuse lighting*, in this chapter

Adding shadows to the scene

Lighting is one of the most important operations performed by 3D applications. Unfortunately, due to the specifics of graphics libraries and the graphics hardware itself, lighting calculations have one major drawback--they don't have information about positions of all drawn objects. That's why generating shadows requires a special approach and advanced rendering algorithms.

There are several popular techniques targeted at efficient generation of natural looking shadows. Now we will learn about a technique called shadow mapping.

An example of an image generated with this recipe looks like:

Getting ready

The shadow mapping technique requires us to render a scene twice. Firstly, we render objects that cast shadows. They are rendered from the light's point of view. This way we store depth values in a depth attachment (color values are not required).

Then, in the second step, we render the scene as we normally do, from the camera's point of view. Inside shaders we use the shadow map generated in the first step. The vertex position is projected onto the shadow map and its distance from the light position is compared with the value read from the shadow map. If it is greater, it means a given point is covered in shadow, otherwise it is normally lit.

How to do it...

1. Prepare the Vulkan resources as described in the *Rendering a geometry with a vertex diffuse lighting* recipe.
2. Load the 3D models with vertex positions and normal vectors. Store loaded data in a (vertex) buffer.
3. Create a uniform buffer with `VK_BUFFER_USAGE_TRANSFER_DST_BIT` and `VK_BUFFER_USAGE_UNIFORM_BUFFER_BIT` usages that are big enough to hold data for three 16-element matrices of floating-point values (refer to the *Creating a uniform buffer* recipe from `Chapter 5, Descriptor Sets`).
4. Create a staging buffer supporting a `VK_BUFFER_USAGE_TRANSFER_SRC_BIT` usage, which is able to hold data for three matrices each with 16 floating-point elements. The buffer's memory object should be allocated on a memory that is host-visible (refer to the *Creating a buffer* and *Allocating and binding memory object to a buffer* recipes from `Chapter 4, Resources and Memory`).
5. Create a combined image sampler that should act as a shadow map. The image should be two-dimensional with one of the supported depth formats (`VK_FORMAT_D16_UNORM` must always be supported), and should support `VK_IMAGE_USAGE_SAMPLED_BIT` and `VK_IMAGE_USAGE_DEPTH_STENCIL_ATTACHMENT_BIT` usages (refer to the *Creating a combined image sampler* recipe from `Chapter 5, Descriptor Sets`).
6. Create a descriptor set layout with two descriptor resources: a uniform buffer accessed in a vertex shader at 0th binding and with a combined image sampler accessed in a fragment shader at 1st binding (refer to the *Creating a descriptor set layout* recipe from `Chapter 5, Descriptor Sets`).
7. Create a descriptor pool, from which one uniform buffer descriptor and one combined image sampler descriptor can be allocated (refer to the *Creating a descriptor pool* recipe from `Chapter 5, Descriptor Sets`).
8. A descriptor set from the created pool using the descriptor set layout with a uniform buffer and a combined image sampler resources (refer to the *Allocating descriptor sets* recipe from `Chapter 5, Descriptor Sets`).
9. Update (populate) the descriptor set with the uniform buffer accessed at the 0th binding and with the created combined image sampler (shadow map) accessed at the 1st binding. Provide a `VK_IMAGE_LAYOUT_DEPTH_STENCIL_READ_ONLY_OPTIMAL` value as the image's layout (refer to the *Updating descriptor sets* recipe from `Chapter 5, Descriptor Sets`).

10. Prepare data for a render pass used for drawing the whole scene into the shadow map. This render pass should have only one attachment, which has the same format as the combined image sampler's format. The image should be cleared on load, its initial layout may be undefined. The image contents should be stored at the end of the render pass and the final layout should be set to a VK_IMAGE_LAYOUT_DEPTH_STENCIL_READ_ONLY_OPTIMAL (refer to the *Specifying attachments descriptions* recipe from Chapter 6, *Render Passes and Framebuffers*).
11. The render pass used for shadow map generation should have just one subpass with only a depth attachment, for which framebuffer's 0th attachment with a VK_IMAGE_LAYOUT_DEPTH_STENCIL_ATTACHMENT_OPTIMAL layout should be used (refer to the *Specifying subpass descriptions* recipe from Chapter 6, *Render Passes and Framebuffers*).
12. Specify two subpass dependencies for the render pass (refer to the *Specifying dependencies between subpasses* recipe from Chapter 6, *Render Passes and Framebuffers*). Use the following values for the first dependency:
    - VK_SUBPASS_EXTERNAL value for srcSubpass
    - 0 value for dstSubpass
    - VK_PIPELINE_STAGE_FRAGMENT_SHADER_BIT value for srcStageMask
    - VK_PIPELINE_STAGE_EARLY_FRAGMENT_TESTS_BIT value for dstStageMask
    - VK_ACCESS_SHADER_READ_BIT value for srcAccessMask
    - VK_ACCESS_DEPTH_STENCIL_ATTACHMENT_WRITE_BIT value for dstAccessMask
    - VK_DEPENDENCY_BY_REGION_BIT value for dependencyFlags
13. Use the following values for the second render pass dependency:
    - 0 value for srcSubpass
    - VK_SUBPASS_EXTERNAL value for dstSubpass
    - VK_PIPELINE_STAGE_LATE_FRAGMENT_TESTS_BIT value for srcStageMask
    - VK_PIPELINE_STAGE_FRAGMENT_SHADER_BIT value for dstStageMask
    - VK_ACCESS_DEPTH_STENCIL_ATTACHMENT_WRITE_BIT value for srcAccessMask
    - VK_ACCESS_SHADER_READ_BIT value for dstAccessMask
    - VK_DEPENDENCY_BY_REGION_BIT value for dependencyFlags

Lighting

14. Create a render pass using the above parameters (refer to the *Creating a render pass* recipe from `Chapter 6`, *Render Passes and Framebuffers*).
15. Create a framebuffer compatible with the created render pass. The Framebuffer should have one attachment, for which the image view created along with the shadow map's combined image sampler should be used. Framebuffer should also have the same dimensions as the shadow map image (refer to the *Creating a framebuffer* recipe from `Chapter 6`, *Render Passes and Framebuffers*).
16. Create a second render pass used for drawing the scene normally into a swapchain (refer to the *Rendering a geometry with a vertex diffuse lighting* recipe).
17. Create a pipeline layout using the prepared descriptor set layout. Also, specify a single push constant range accessed by a vertex shader stage, beginning at a 0th offset and of a `4 * sizeof( float )` size (refer to the *Creating a pipeline layout* recipe from `Chapter 8`, *Graphics and Compute Pipelines*).
18. Create a graphics pipeline used for drawing a scene into the shadow map. Start by creating a shader module for a vertex shader stage using a SPIR-V assembly generated from the following GLSL code (refer to the *Converting GLSL shaders to SPIR-V assemblies* recipe from `Chapter 7`, *Shaders* and to *Creating a shader module* recipe from `Chapter 8`, *Graphics and Compute Pipelines*):

```
#version 450
layout( location = 0 ) in vec4 app_position;
layout( set = 0, binding = 0 ) uniform UniformBuffer {
  mat4 ShadowModelViewMatrix;
  mat4 SceneModelViewMatrix;
  mat4 ProjectionMatrix;
};
void main() {
  gl_Position = ProjectionMatrix * ShadowModelViewMatrix * app_position;
}
```

19. Specify pipeline shader stages with a vertex shader only, which uses a `main` function from the prepared shader module (refer to the *Specifying pipeline shader stages* recipe from `Chapter 8`, *Graphics and Compute Pipelines*).

20. Specify a pipeline vertex input state with one attribute that is read from the 0th binding. The binding should be created with data read per vertex and a stride equal to 6 * sizeof(float) (refer to the *Specifying pipeline vertex input state* recipe from Chapter 8, *Graphics and Compute Pipelines*). The attribute should have the following parameters:
    - 0 value for location
    - 0 value for binding
    - VK_FORMAT_R32G32B32_SFLOAT value for format
    - 0 value for offset
21. Specify the viewport and scissor test parameters with one viewport, whose dimensions match the size of the shadow map image (refer to the *Specifying pipeline viewport and scissor test state* recipe from Chapter 8, *Graphics and Compute Pipelines*).
22. Create a graphics pipeline using the previously specified parameters. Skip the blending state, because the render pass used for the shadow map generation doesn't have any color attachments (rasterization must be enabled though, because otherwise no fragments will be generated and their depth won't be stored in the shadow map). Also, don't use dynamic states, because the size of the shadow map doesn't change (refer to the *Creating graphics pipelines* recipe from Chapter 8, *Graphics and Compute Pipelines*).
23. Create another graphics pipeline used for rendering a shadowed scene. This time, create a shader module for a vertex shader stage using a SPIR-V assembly generated from the following GLSL code:

```
#version 450

layout( location = 0 ) in vec4 app_position;
layout( location = 1 ) in vec3 app_normal;

layout( set = 0, binding = 0 ) uniform UniformBuffer {
  mat4 ShadowModelViewMatrix;
  mat4 SceneModelViewMatrix;
  mat4 ProjectionMatrix;
};

layout( push_constant ) uniform LightParameters {
  vec4 Position;
} Light;

layout( location = 0 ) out vec3 vert_normal;
layout( location = 1 ) out vec4 vert_texcoords;
layout( location = 2 ) out vec3 vert_light;
```

Lighting

```
        const mat4 bias = mat4(
          0.5, 0.0, 0.0, 0.0,
          0.0, 0.5, 0.0, 0.0,
          0.0, 0.0, 1.0, 0.0,
          0.5, 0.5, 0.0, 1.0 );

        void main() {
          gl_Position = ProjectionMatrix * SceneModelViewMatrix *
        app_position;

          vert_normal = mat3( SceneModelViewMatrix ) * app_normal;
          vert_texcoords = bias * ProjectionMatrix *
        ShadowModelViewMatrix * app_position;
          vert_light = (SceneModelViewMatrix * vec4( Light.Position.xyz,
        0.0 ) ).xyz;
        }
```

24. Create a shader module for a fragment shader stage using a SPIR-V assembly generated from the following GLSL code:

```
#version 450

layout( location = 0 ) in vec3 vert_normal;
layout( location = 1 ) in vec4 vert_texcoords;
layout( location = 2 ) in vec3 vert_light;

layout( set = 0, binding = 1 ) uniform sampler2D ShadowMap;

layout( location = 0 ) out vec4 frag_color;

void main() {
  float shadow = 1.0;
  vec4 shadow_coords = vert_texcoords / vert_texcoords.w;

  if( texture( ShadowMap, shadow_coords.xy ).r < shadow_coords.z - 0.005 )
{
    shadow = 0.5;
  }

  vec3 normal_vector = normalize( vert_normal );
  vec3 light_vector = normalize( vert_light );
  float diffuse_term = max( 0.0, dot( normal_vector, light_vector ) );

  frag_color = shadow * vec4( diffuse_term ) + 0.1;
}
```

25. Specify pipeline shader stages with vertex and fragment shaders, both using a `main` function from a respective shader modules.
26. Specify a pipeline vertex input state with two attributes that are read from the same 0th binding. The binding should be created with data read per vertex and a stride equal to `6 * sizeof( float )`. The first attribute should have the following parameters:
    - 0 value for `location`
    - 0 value for `binding`
    - `VK_FORMAT_R32G32B32_SFLOAT` value for `format`
    - 0 value for `offset`
27. The second attribute should have the following definition:
    - 1 value for `location`
    - 0 value for `binding`
    - `VK_FORMAT_R32G32B32_SFLOAT` value for `format`
    - `3 * sizeof( float )` value for `offset`
28. Create a graphics pipeline for rendering the shadowed scene using the above shader stages and two attributes, with the rest of the parameters similar to those defined in the *Rendering a geometry with a vertex diffuse lighting* recipe.
29. Prepare a view matrix, which can be a multiplication of rotation, scaling and translation matrices used to draw the scene from the light's perspective (refer to the *Preparing a translation matrix, Preparing a rotation matrix* and *Preparing a scaling matrix* recipes from `Chapter 10`, *Helper Recipes*). Copy the contents of the concatenated matrix to the staging buffer at a 0 offset (refer to the *Mapping, updating and unmapping host-visible memory* recipe from `Chapter 4`, *Resources and Memory*).
30. Prepare a view matrix used to draw the scene normally, from the camera's perspective. Copy the contents of this matrix to the staging buffer at a `16 * sizeof( float )` offset.
31. Prepare a perspective projection matrix based on the aspect ratio of the swapchain's dimensions (refer to the *Preparing a perspective projection matrix* recipe from `Chapter 10`, *Helper Recipes*). Copy the contents of the matrix to the staging buffer at a `32 * sizeof( float )`. Remember to recreate the projection matrix and copy it to the staging buffer each time the application's window is resized (refer to the *Mapping, updating and unmapping host-visible memory* recipe from `Chapter 4`, *Resources and Memory*).

Lighting

32. In each frame of animation, record a command buffer. Start by checking whether any of the view or projection matrices were modified: if they were, copy the contents of the staging buffer to the uniform buffer, guarded by the proper pipeline barriers (refer to the *Copying data between buffers* recipe from `Chapter 4, Resources and Memory`).
33. Begin a render pass used for drawing the scene from the light's perspective into the shadow map. Bind the vertex buffer, descriptor set, and the pipeline used to fill the shadow map. Draw the geometry and end the render pass.
34. Transfer ownership of the acquired swapchain image if necessary. Set the viewport and scissor test states dynamically, bind the graphics pipeline created for rendering the shadowed scene, and draw the geometry once again. End the command buffer recording, submit the command buffer to the queue, and present an image.

How it works...

We start by creating a combined image sampler, in which depth information from the light's perspective will be stored:

```
if( !CreateCombinedImageSampler( PhysicalDevice, *LogicalDevice,
VK_IMAGE_TYPE_2D, DepthFormat, { 512, 512, 1 }, 1, 1,
   VK_IMAGE_USAGE_DEPTH_STENCIL_ATTACHMENT_BIT | VK_IMAGE_USAGE_SAMPLED_BIT,
VK_IMAGE_VIEW_TYPE_2D, VK_IMAGE_ASPECT_DEPTH_BIT, VK_FILTER_LINEAR,
   VK_FILTER_LINEAR, VK_SAMPLER_MIPMAP_MODE_NEAREST,
VK_SAMPLER_ADDRESS_MODE_CLAMP_TO_EDGE,
VK_SAMPLER_ADDRESS_MODE_CLAMP_TO_EDGE,
   VK_SAMPLER_ADDRESS_MODE_CLAMP_TO_EDGE, 0.0f, false, 1.0f, false,
VK_COMPARE_OP_ALWAYS, 0.0f, 1.0f, VK_BORDER_COLOR_FLOAT_OPAQUE_BLACK,
   false, *ShadowMapSampler, *ShadowMap.Image, *ShadowMap.Memory,
*ShadowMap.View ) ) {
   return false;
}
```

The combined image sampler, along with uniform buffer, will be accessed in shaders, so we need a descriptor set through which shaders will have access to both. Despite the fact that we render the scene twice using two different pipelines, we can use one descriptor set to avoid unnecessary state switching:

```
std::vector<VkDescriptorSetLayoutBinding> descriptor_set_layout_bindings =
{
  {
    0,
    VK_DESCRIPTOR_TYPE_UNIFORM_BUFFER,
```

```
      1,
      VK_SHADER_STAGE_VERTEX_BIT,
      nullptr
    },
    {
      1,
      VK_DESCRIPTOR_TYPE_COMBINED_IMAGE_SAMPLER,
      1,
      VK_SHADER_STAGE_FRAGMENT_BIT,
      nullptr
    }
  };
  InitVkDestroyer( LogicalDevice, DescriptorSetLayout );
  if( !CreateDescriptorSetLayout( *LogicalDevice,
  descriptor_set_layout_bindings, *DescriptorSetLayout ) ) {
    return false;
  }

  std::vector<VkDescriptorPoolSize> descriptor_pool_sizes = {
    {
      VK_DESCRIPTOR_TYPE_UNIFORM_BUFFER,
      1
    },
    {
      VK_DESCRIPTOR_TYPE_COMBINED_IMAGE_SAMPLER,
      1
    }
  };
  InitVkDestroyer( LogicalDevice, DescriptorPool );
  if( !CreateDescriptorPool( *LogicalDevice, false, 1, descriptor_pool_sizes,
  *DescriptorPool ) ) {
    return false;
  }
  if( !AllocateDescriptorSets( *LogicalDevice, *DescriptorPool, {
  *DescriptorSetLayout }, DescriptorSets ) ) {
    return false;
  }
```

We also need to populate the descriptor set with the handles of a uniform buffer and the combined image sampler:

```
  BufferDescriptorInfo buffer_descriptor_update = {
    DescriptorSets[0],
    0,
    0,
    VK_DESCRIPTOR_TYPE_UNIFORM_BUFFER,
    {
      {
```

Lighting

```
      *UniformBuffer,
      0,
      VK_WHOLE_SIZE
    }
  }
};

ImageDescriptorInfo image_descriptor_update = {
  DescriptorSets[0],
  1,
  0,
  VK_DESCRIPTOR_TYPE_COMBINED_IMAGE_SAMPLER,
  {
    {
      *ShadowMapSampler,
      *ShadowMap.View,
      VK_IMAGE_LAYOUT_DEPTH_STENCIL_READ_ONLY_OPTIMAL
    }
  }
};
UpdateDescriptorSets( *LogicalDevice, { image_descriptor_update }, {
buffer_descriptor_update }, {}, {} );
```

The next step is to create a dedicated render pass for storing the depth information in the shadow map. It doesn't use any color attachments, because we only need depth data. We also create a framebuffer. It can have fixed dimensions as we don't change the size of the shadow map:

```
std::vector<VkAttachmentDescription> shadow_map_attachment_descriptions = {
  {
    0
    DepthFormat,
    VK_SAMPLE_COUNT_1_BIT,
    VK_ATTACHMENT_LOAD_OP_CLEAR,
    VK_ATTACHMENT_STORE_OP_STORE,
    VK_ATTACHMENT_LOAD_OP_DONT_CARE,
    VK_ATTACHMENT_STORE_OP_DONT_CARE,
    VK_IMAGE_LAYOUT_UNDEFINED,
    VK_IMAGE_LAYOUT_DEPTH_STENCIL_READ_ONLY_OPTIMAL
  }
};
VkAttachmentReference shadow_map_depth_attachment = {
  0,
  VK_IMAGE_LAYOUT_DEPTH_STENCIL_ATTACHMENT_OPTIMAL
};
std::vector<SubpassParameters> shadow_map_subpass_parameters = {
  {
    VK_PIPELINE_BIND_POINT_GRAPHICS,
```

```
          {},
          {},
          {},
          &shadow_map_depth_attachment,
          {}
      }
  };
  std::vector<VkSubpassDependency> shadow_map_subpass_dependencies = {
      {
          VK_SUBPASS_EXTERNAL,
          0,
          VK_PIPELINE_STAGE_FRAGMENT_SHADER_BIT,
          VK_PIPELINE_STAGE_EARLY_FRAGMENT_TESTS_BIT,
          VK_ACCESS_SHADER_READ_BIT,
          VK_ACCESS_DEPTH_STENCIL_ATTACHMENT_WRITE_BIT,
          VK_DEPENDENCY_BY_REGION_BIT
      },
      {
          0,
          VK_SUBPASS_EXTERNAL,
          VK_PIPELINE_STAGE_LATE_FRAGMENT_TESTS_BIT,
          VK_PIPELINE_STAGE_FRAGMENT_SHADER_BIT,
          VK_ACCESS_DEPTH_STENCIL_ATTACHMENT_WRITE_BIT,
          VK_ACCESS_SHADER_READ_BIT,
          VK_DEPENDENCY_BY_REGION_BIT
      }
  };
  InitVkDestroyer( LogicalDevice, ShadowMapRenderPass );
  if( !CreateRenderPass( *LogicalDevice, shadow_map_attachment_descriptions,
  shadow_map_subpass_parameters, shadow_map_subpass_dependencies,
    *ShadowMapRenderPass ) ) {
    return false;
  }
  InitVkDestroyer( LogicalDevice, ShadowMap.Framebuffer );
  if( !CreateFramebuffer( *LogicalDevice, *ShadowMapRenderPass, {
  *ShadowMap.View }, 512, 512, 1, *ShadowMap.Framebuffer ) ) {
    return false;
  }
```

Next, we create two graphics pipelines. They both use the same push constant range to lower the number of variables (though only the second pipeline uses it in shaders):

```
  std::vector<VkPushConstantRange> push_constant_ranges = {
      {
          VK_SHADER_STAGE_VERTEX_BIT,
          0,
          sizeof( float ) * 4
      }
```

```
};
InitVkDestroyer( LogicalDevice, PipelineLayout );
if( !CreatePipelineLayout( *LogicalDevice, { *DescriptorSetLayout },
push_constant_ranges, *PipelineLayout ) ) {
  return false;
}
```

The first pipeline is for the shadow map generation. It uses very simple shaders that read only vertex positions and render the scene from the light's point of view.

The second pipeline renders the scene normally into the swapchain image. Its shaders are more complicated. A vertex shader calculates the position normally, but also converts the normal vector and the light vector into the view space for correct lighting calculations:

```
vert_normal = mat3( SceneModelViewMatrix ) * app_normal;
vert_light = (SceneModelViewMatrix * vec4( Light.Position.xyz, 0.0 ) ).xyz;
```

The most important thing that the vertex shader does is to calculate the vertex's position in the light source's view space. To do this, we multiply it by the light's model-view and projection matrices (perspective division is done in the fragment shader). The acquired result is used to fetch data from the shadow map. However, the calculated position values (after perspective division) are in the -1.0 - 1.0 range and reading data from textures using normalized texture coordinates requires providing the values in the 0.0 - 1.0 range. That's why we need to bias the result:

```
vert_texcoords = bias * ProjectionMatrix * ShadowModelViewMatrix *
app_position;
```

This way the fragment shader can project the interpolated position onto the shadow map and read the value from a proper coordinate:

```
float shadow = 1.0;
vec4 shadow_coords = vert_texcoords / vert_texcoords.w;
if( texture( ShadowMap, shadow_coords.xy ).r < shadow_coords.z - 0.005 ) {
  shadow = 0.5;
}
```

The value read from the shadow map is compared with the point's distance from the light's position (offset by a small value). If the distance is greater than the value stored in the shadow map, the point is lying in a shadow and shouldn't be lit. We need to add the small offset, so the surface of an object doesn't cast shadows on itself (only on parts that are further away). We also don't fully discard the lighting to avoid the shadows being too dark, hence the value 0.5 assigned to the shadow variable.

The above calculations can be performed using a textureProj() and a sampler2DShadow. This way perspective division, offsetting the distance and comparing it to a reference value is performed automatically.

The rest of the resources created in this recipe are similar to those presented in the *Rendering a geometry with a vertex diffuse lighting* recipe. Rendering/recording a command buffer requires us, apart from the usual stuff, to render the scene twice. Firstly, we fill the shadow map by drawing all objects from the light's perspective. The shadow map is then used during the rendering of all the objects normally from the camera's perspective:

```
BeginRenderPass( command_buffer, *ShadowMapRenderPass,
*ShadowMap.Framebuffer, { { 0, 0, }, { 512, 512 } }, { { 1.0f, 0 } },
VK_SUBPASS_CONTENTS_INLINE );
BindVertexBuffers( command_buffer, 0, { { *VertexBuffer, 0 } } );
BindDescriptorSets( command_buffer, VK_PIPELINE_BIND_POINT_GRAPHICS,
*PipelineLayout, 0, DescriptorSets, {} );
BindPipelineObject( command_buffer, VK_PIPELINE_BIND_POINT_GRAPHICS,
*ShadowMapPipeline );
DrawGeometry( command_buffer, Scene[0].Parts[0].VertexCount +
Scene[1].Parts[0].VertexCount, 1, 0, 0 );
EndRenderPass( command_buffer );
if( PresentQueue.FamilyIndex != GraphicsQueue.FamilyIndex ) {
  ImageTransition image_transition_before_drawing = {
    Swapchain.Images[swapchain_image_index],
    VK_ACCESS_MEMORY_READ_BIT,
    VK_ACCESS_MEMORY_READ_BIT,
    VK_IMAGE_LAYOUT_UNDEFINED,
    VK_IMAGE_LAYOUT_COLOR_ATTACHMENT_OPTIMAL,
    PresentQueue.FamilyIndex,
    GraphicsQueue.FamilyIndex,
    VK_IMAGE_ASPECT_COLOR_BIT
  };
  SetImageMemoryBarrier( command_buffer,
VK_PIPELINE_STAGE_COLOR_ATTACHMENT_OUTPUT_BIT,
VK_PIPELINE_STAGE_COLOR_ATTACHMENT_OUTPUT_BIT, {
image_transition_before_drawing } );
}
BeginRenderPass( command_buffer, *SceneRenderPass, framebuffer, { { 0, 0 },
Swapchain.Size }, { { 0.1f, 0.2f, 0.3f, 1.0f }, { 1.0f, 0 } },
VK_SUBPASS_CONTENTS_INLINE );

VkViewport viewport = {
  0.0f,
  0.0f,
  static_cast<float>(Swapchain.Size.width),
  static_cast<float>(Swapchain.Size.height),
  0.0f,
```

Lighting

```
    1.0f,
};
SetViewportStateDynamically( command_buffer, 0, { viewport } );

VkRect2D scissor = {
  {
    0,
    0
  },
  {
    Swapchain.Size.width,
    Swapchain.Size.height
  }
};
SetScissorsStateDynamically( command_buffer, 0, { scissor } );
BindPipelineObject( command_buffer, VK_PIPELINE_BIND_POINT_GRAPHICS,
*ScenePipeline );
ProvideDataToShadersThroughPushConstants( command_buffer, *PipelineLayout,
VK_SHADER_STAGE_VERTEX_BIT, 0, sizeof( float ) * 4,
&LightSource.GetPosition()[0] );
DrawGeometry( command_buffer, Scene[0].Parts[0].VertexCount +
Scene[1].Parts[0].VertexCount, 1, 0, 0 );
EndRenderPass( command_buffer );
```

The following image shows different models casting shadows on a flat plane:

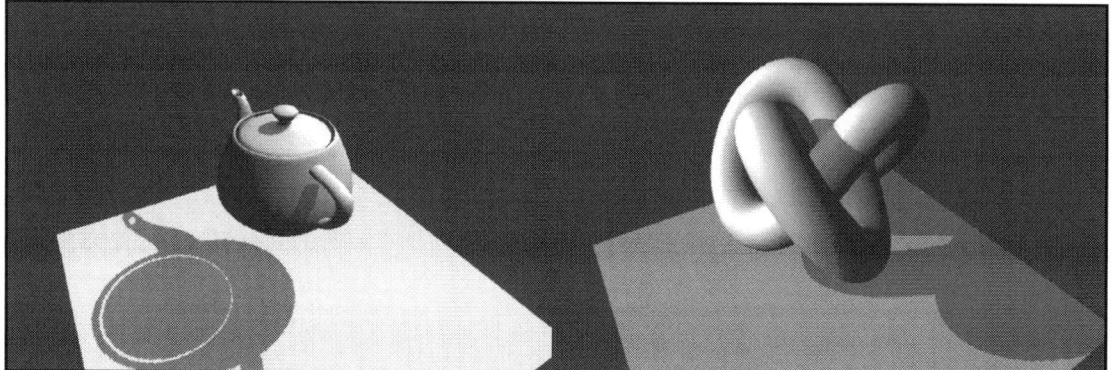

See also

- In Chapter 5, *Descriptor Sets*, see the recipe:
    - *Creating a combined image sampler*
- In Chapter 6, *Render Passes and Framebuffers*, see the following recipes:
    - *Creating a render pass*
    - *Creating a framebuffer*
- The recipe *Rendering a geometry with a vertex diffuse lighting,* in this chapter

12
Advanced Rendering Techniques

In this chapter, we will cover the following recipes:

- Drawing a skybox
- Drawing billboards using geometry shaders
- Drawing particles using compute and graphics pipelines
- Rendering a tessellated terrain
- Rendering a full-screen quad for post-processing
- Using input attachments for a color correction post-process effect

Introduction

Creating 3D applications, such as games, benchmarks or CAD tools, usually requires, from a rendering perspective, the preparation of various resources, including meshes or textures, drawing multiple objects on the scene, and implementing algorithms for object transformations, lighting calculations, and image processing. They all can be developed in any way we want, in a way that is most suitable for our purpose. But there are also many useful techniques that are commonly used in the 3D graphics industry. Descriptions for these can be found in books and tutorials with examples implemented using various 3D graphics APIs.

Advanced Rendering Techniques

Vulkan is still a relatively new graphics API, so there aren't too many resources that present common rendering algorithms implemented with the Vulkan API. In this chapter, we will learn how to use Vulkan to prepare various graphics techniques. We will learn about important concepts from a collection of popular, advanced rendering algorithms found in games and benchmarks and how they match with the Vulkan resources.

In this chapter, we will focus only on the code parts that are important from the perspective of a given recipe. Resources that are not described (for example, command pool or render pass creation) are created as usual (refer to the *Rendering a geometry with a vertex diffuse lighting* recipe from `Chapter 11`, *Lighting*).

Drawing a skybox

Rendering 3D scenes, especially open world ones with vast viewing distances, requires many objects to be drawn. However, the processing power of current graphics hardware is still too limited to render as many objects as we see around us every day. So, to lower the number of drawn objects and to draw the background for our scene, we usually prepare an image (or a photo) of distant objects and draw just the image instead.

In games where players can freely move and look around, we can't draw a single image. We must draw images in all directions. Such images form a cube, and an object on which background images are placed is called a skybox. We render it in such a way that it is always in the background, at the furthest depth value available.

Getting ready

Drawing a skybox requires the preparation of a cubemap. It contains six square images containing a view in all world directions (right, left, up, down, backward, forward), as in the following image:

Chapter 12

Images courtesy of Emil Persson (http://www.humus.name)

In Vulkan, cubemaps are special image views created for images with six array layers (or a multiple of six). Layers must contain images in the +X, -X, +Y, -Y, +Z, -Z order.

Cubemaps can be used not only for drawing skyboxes. We can use them to draw reflections or transparent objects. They can be used for lighting calculations as well (refer to the *Drawing a reflective and refractive geometry using cubemaps* recipe in Chapter 11, *Lighting*).

How to do it...

1. Load a 3D model of a cube from a file and store vertex data in a vertex buffer. Only vertex positions are required (refer to the *Loading a 3D model from an OBJ file* recipe in `Chapter 10`, *Helper Recipes*).

2. Create a combined image sampler with a square `VK_IMAGE_TYPE_2D` image that has six array layers (or a multiple of six), a sampler that uses a `VK_SAMPLER_ADDRESS_MODE_CLAMP_TO_EDGE` addressing mode for all coordinates and a `VK_IMAGE_VIEW_TYPE_CUBE` image view (refer to the *Creating a combined image sampler* recipe in `Chapter 5`, *Descriptor Sets*).
3. Load image data for all six sides of a cube and upload it to the image's memory using a staging buffer. Image data must be uploaded to six array layers in the following order: +X, -X, +Y, -Y, +Z, -Z (refer to the *Loading texture data from a file* recipe in `Chapter 10`, *Helper Recipes*, and to the *Using a staging buffer to update an image with a device-local memory bound* recipe in `Chapter 4`, *Resources and Memory*).
4. Create a uniform buffer in which transformation matrices will be stored (refer to the *Creating a uniform buffer* recipe in `Chapter 5`, *Descriptor Sets*).
5. Create a descriptor set layout with the uniform buffer accessed by a vertex stage and a combined image sampler accessed by a fragment stage. Allocate a descriptor set using the preceding layout. Update the descriptor set with the uniform buffer and the cubemap/combined image sampler (refer to the *Creating a descriptor set layout*, *Allocating descriptor sets* and *Updating descriptor sets* recipes in `Chapter 5`, *Descriptor Sets*).
6. Create a shader module with a vertex shader created from the following GLSL code (refer to the *Creating a shader module recipe* in `Chapter 8`, *Graphics and Compute Pipelines*):

```
#version 450
layout( location = 0 ) in vec4 app_position;
layout( set = 0, binding = 0 ) uniform UniformBuffer {
  mat4 ModelViewMatrix;
  mat4 ProjectionMatrix;
};

layout( location = 0 ) out vec3 vert_texcoord;

void main() {
  vec3 position = mat3(ModelViewMatrix) * app_position.xyz;
  gl_Position = (ProjectionMatrix * vec4( position, 0.0 )).xyzz;
  vert_texcoord = app_position.xyz;
}
```

7. Create a shader module with a fragment shader created from the following GLSL code:

   ```
   #version 450
   layout( location = 0 ) in vec3 vert_texcoord;
   layout( set = 0, binding = 1 ) uniform samplerCube Cubemap;
   layout( location = 0 ) out vec4 frag_color;

   void main() {
     frag_color = texture( Cubemap, vert_texcoord );
   }
   ```

8. Create a graphics pipeline from the preceding modules with vertex and fragment shaders. The pipeline should use one vertex attribute with three components (vertex positions) and a VK_CULL_MODE_FRONT_BIT value for the rasterization state's culling mode. Blending should be disabled. The pipeline's layout should allow access to the uniform buffer and the cubemap/combined image sampler (refer to the *Specifying pipeline shader stages, Specifying pipeline vertex input state, Specifying pipeline rasterization state, Specifying pipeline blend state, Creating a pipeline layout, Specifying graphics pipeline creation parameters* and *Creating a graphics pipeline* recipes from Chapter 8, *Graphics and Compute Pipelines*).

9. Draw the cube with the rest of a rendered geometry (refer to the *Binding descriptor sets* recipe from Chapter 5, *Descriptor Sets*, to the *Binding a pipeline object* recipe from Chapter 8, *Graphics and Compute Pipelines* and to the *Binding vertex buffers* and *Drawing a geometry* recipes from Chapter 9, *Command Recording and Drawing*).

10. Update a model view matrix in the uniform buffer each time a user (a camera) moves in the scene. Update a projection matrix in the uniform buffer each time the application window is resized.

How it works...

To render a skybox we need to load or prepare a geometry forming a cube. Only positions are required as they can also be used for texture coordinates.

Next, we load six cubemap images and create a combined image sampler with a cube image view:

```
InitVkDestroyer( LogicalDevice, CubemapImage );
InitVkDestroyer( LogicalDevice, CubemapImageMemory );
InitVkDestroyer( LogicalDevice, CubemapImageView );
InitVkDestroyer( LogicalDevice, CubemapSampler );
if( !CreateCombinedImageSampler( PhysicalDevice, *LogicalDevice,
VK_IMAGE_TYPE_2D, VK_FORMAT_R8G8B8A8_UNORM, { 1024, 1024, 1 }, 1, 6,
  VK_IMAGE_USAGE_SAMPLED_BIT | VK_IMAGE_USAGE_TRANSFER_DST_BIT,
VK_IMAGE_VIEW_TYPE_CUBE, VK_IMAGE_ASPECT_COLOR_BIT, VK_FILTER_LINEAR,
  VK_FILTER_LINEAR, VK_SAMPLER_MIPMAP_MODE_NEAREST,
VK_SAMPLER_ADDRESS_MODE_CLAMP_TO_EDGE,
VK_SAMPLER_ADDRESS_MODE_CLAMP_TO_EDGE,
  VK_SAMPLER_ADDRESS_MODE_CLAMP_TO_EDGE, 0.0f, false, 1.0f, false,
VK_COMPARE_OP_ALWAYS, 0.0f, 1.0f, VK_BORDER_COLOR_FLOAT_OPAQUE_BLACK,
  false, *CubemapSampler, *CubemapImage, *CubemapImageMemory,
*CubemapImageView ) ) {
  return false;
}
std::vector<std::string> cubemap_images = {
  "Data/Textures/Skansen/posx.jpg",
  "Data/Textures/Skansen/negx.jpg",
  "Data/Textures/Skansen/posy.jpg",
  "Data/Textures/Skansen/negy.jpg",
  "Data/Textures/Skansen/posz.jpg",
  "Data/Textures/Skansen/negz.jpg"
};
for( size_t i = 0; i < cubemap_images.size(); ++i ) {
  std::vector<unsigned char> cubemap_image_data;
  int image_data_size;
  if( !LoadTextureDataFromFile( cubemap_images[i].c_str(), 4,
cubemap_image_data, nullptr, nullptr, nullptr, &image_data_size ) ) {
    return false;
  }
  VkImageSubresourceLayers image_subresource = {
    VK_IMAGE_ASPECT_COLOR_BIT,
    0,
    static_cast<uint32_t>(i),
    1
  };
  UseStagingBufferToUpdateImageWithDeviceLocalMemoryBound( PhysicalDevice,
```

```
  *LogicalDevice, image_data_size, &cubemap_image_data[0],
    *CubemapImage, image_subresource, { 0, 0, 0 }, { 1024, 1024, 1 },
VK_IMAGE_LAYOUT_UNDEFINED, VK_IMAGE_LAYOUT_SHADER_READ_ONLY_OPTIMAL,
    0, VK_ACCESS_SHADER_READ_BIT, VK_IMAGE_ASPECT_COLOR_BIT,
VK_PIPELINE_STAGE_TOP_OF_PIPE_BIT, VK_PIPELINE_STAGE_FRAGMENT_SHADER_BIT,
    GraphicsQueue.Handle, FrameResources.front().CommandBuffer, {} );
}
```

The created cube image view, along with a sampler, is then provided to the shaders through a descriptor set. We also need a uniform buffer in which transformation matrices will be stored and accessed in the shaders:

```
std::vector<VkDescriptorSetLayoutBinding> descriptor_set_layout_bindings =
{
  {
    0,
    VK_DESCRIPTOR_TYPE_UNIFORM_BUFFER,
    1,
    VK_SHADER_STAGE_VERTEX_BIT,
    nullptr
  },
  {
    1,
    VK_DESCRIPTOR_TYPE_COMBINED_IMAGE_SAMPLER,
    1,
    VK_SHADER_STAGE_FRAGMENT_BIT,
    nullptr
  }
};
InitVkDestroyer( LogicalDevice, DescriptorSetLayout );
if( !CreateDescriptorSetLayout( *LogicalDevice,
descriptor_set_layout_bindings, *DescriptorSetLayout ) ) {
  return false;
}

std::vector<VkDescriptorPoolSize> descriptor_pool_sizes = {
  {
    VK_DESCRIPTOR_TYPE_UNIFORM_BUFFER,
    1
  },
  {
    VK_DESCRIPTOR_TYPE_COMBINED_IMAGE_SAMPLER,
    1
  }
};
InitVkDestroyer( LogicalDevice, DescriptorPool );
if( !CreateDescriptorPool( *LogicalDevice, false, 1, descriptor_pool_sizes,
*DescriptorPool ) ) {
```

Advanced Rendering Techniques

```
    return false;
}

if( !AllocateDescriptorSets( *LogicalDevice, *DescriptorPool, {
*DescriptorSetLayout }, DescriptorSets ) ) {
    return false;
}

BufferDescriptorInfo buffer_descriptor_update = {
    DescriptorSets[0],
    0,
    0,
    VK_DESCRIPTOR_TYPE_UNIFORM_BUFFER,
    {
        {
            *UniformBuffer,
            0,
            VK_WHOLE_SIZE
        }
    }
};

ImageDescriptorInfo image_descriptor_update = {
    DescriptorSets[0],
    1,
    0,
    VK_DESCRIPTOR_TYPE_COMBINED_IMAGE_SAMPLER,
    {
        {
            *CubemapSampler,
            *CubemapImageView,
            VK_IMAGE_LAYOUT_SHADER_READ_ONLY_OPTIMAL
        }
    }
};

UpdateDescriptorSets( *LogicalDevice, { image_descriptor_update }, {
buffer_descriptor_update }, {}, {} );
```

To draw a skybox we don't need a separate, dedicated *render pass*, as we can render it along the normal geometry. What's more, to save processing power (image fill rate), we usually draw a skybox after the (opaque) geometry and before the transparent objects. It is rendered in such a way so that its vertices are always at the far clipping plane. This way it doesn't cover geometry that had been already drawn and doesn't get clipped away either. This effect is achieved with a special vertex shader. Its most important part is the following code:

```
vec3 position = mat3(ModelViewMatrix) * app_position.xyz;
gl_Position = (ProjectionMatrix * vec4( position, 0.0 )).xyzz;
```

First, we multiply the position by a modelview matrix. We take only the rotation part of the matrix. A player should always be in the center of the skybox, or the illusion will be broken. That's why we don't want to move the skybox, we need only to rotate it as a response to the player looking around.

Next, we multiply the viewspace position of a vertex by a projection matrix. The result is stored in a 4-element vector, with the last two components being the same and equal to the z component of the result. In modern graphics hardware, a perspective projection is performed by dividing the position vector by its w component. After that, all vertices, whose x and y components fit into the <-1, 1> range (inclusive) and z component fits into the <0, 1> range (inclusive), are inside the clipping volume and are visible (unless they are obscured by something else). So, calculating the vertex position in a way that makes its last two components equal, guarantees that the vertex will lie on the far clipping plane.

Apart from the vertex shader and a cube image view, skybox needs only one additional special treatment. We need to remember polygon facingness. Usually, we draw geometry with backface culling, as we want to see its external surface. For the skybox, we want to render its internal surface, because we look at it from the inside. That's why, if we don't have a mesh prepared especially for the skybox, we probably want to cull front faces during skybox rendering. We can prepare the pipeline rasterization info like this:

```
VkPipelineRasterizationStateCreateInfo rasterization_state_create_info;
SpecifyPipelineRasterizationState( false, false, VK_POLYGON_MODE_FILL,
VK_CULL_MODE_FRONT_BIT, VK_FRONT_FACE_COUNTER_CLOCKWISE, false, 0.0f, 1.0f,
0.0f, 1.0f, rasterization_state_create_info );
```

Apart from that, the graphics pipeline is created in the usual way. To use it for drawing, we need to bind the descriptor set, the vertex buffer, and the pipeline itself:

```
BindVertexBuffers( command_buffer, 0, { { *VertexBuffer, 0 } } );

BindDescriptorSets( command_buffer, VK_PIPELINE_BIND_POINT_GRAPHICS,
*PipelineLayout, 0, DescriptorSets, {} );

BindPipelineObject( command_buffer, VK_PIPELINE_BIND_POINT_GRAPHICS,
*Pipeline );

for( size_t i = 0; i < Skybox.Parts.size(); ++i ) {
  DrawGeometry( command_buffer, Skybox.Parts[i].VertexCount, 1,
Skybox.Parts[i].VertexOffset, 0 );
}
```

The following images have been generated using this recipe:

See also

- In Chapter 5, *Descriptor Sets*, see the following recipes:
    - *Creating a combined image sampler*
    - *Creating a descriptor set layout*
    - *Allocating descriptor sets*
    - *Updating descriptor sets*
    - *Binding descriptor sets*

- In Chapter 8, *Graphics and Compute Pipelines*, see the following recipes:
    - *Creating a shader module*
    - *Specifying pipeline shader stages*
    - *Creating a graphics pipeline*
    - *Binding a pipeline object*
- In Chapter 9, *Command Recording and Drawing*, see the following recipes:
    - *Binding vertex buffers*
    - *Drawing a geometry*
- In Chapter 10, *Helper Recipes*, see the following recipes:
    - *Loading texture data from a file*
    - *Loading a 3D model from an OBJ file*
- In Chapter 11, *Lighting*, see the following recipe:
    - *Drawing a reflective and refractive geometry using cubemaps*

Drawing billboards using geometry shaders

Simplifying geometry drawn in a distance is a common technique for lowering the processing power needed to render the whole scene. The simplest geometry that can be drawn is a flat quad (or a triangle) with an image depicting the look of an object. For the effect to be convincing, the quad must always be facing camera:

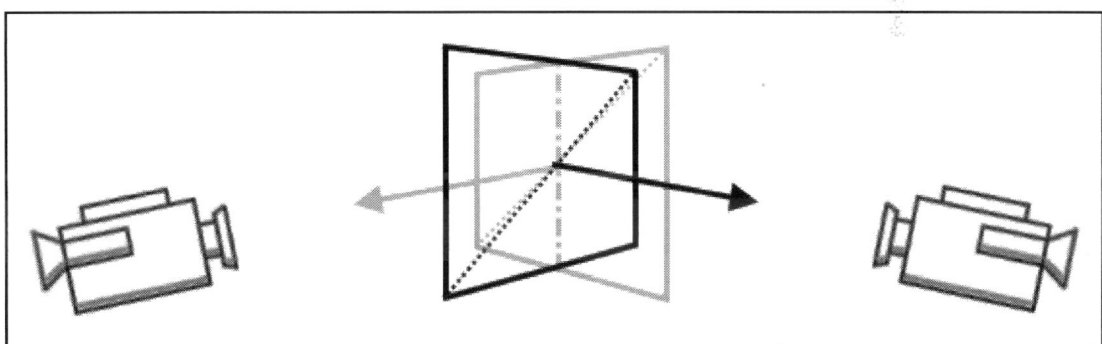

Flat objects that are always facing camera are called billboards. They are used not only for distant objects as the lowest level of detail of a geometry, but also for particle effects.

One straightforward technique for drawing billboards is to use geometry shaders.

How to do it...

1. Create a logical device with the `geometryShader` feature enabled (refer to the *Getting features and properties of a physical device* and *Creating a logical device* recipes from `Chapter 1`, *Instance and Devices*).
2. Prepare positions for all billboards with one vertex per single billboard. Store them in a vertex buffer (refer to the *Creating a buffer* recipe from `Chapter 4`, *Resources and Memory*).
3. Create a uniform buffer for at least two 4x4 transformation matrices (refer to the *Creating a uniform buffer* recipe from `Chapter 5`, *Descriptor Sets*).
4. If billboards should use a texture, create a combined image sampler and upload the texture data loaded from a file to the image's memory (refer to the *Creating a combined image sampler* recipe from `Chapter 5`, *Descriptor Sets* and to the *Loading texture data from a file* recipe from `Chapter 10`, *Helper Recipes*).
5. Prepare a descriptor set layout for a uniform buffer accessed by vertex and geometry stages and, if billboards need a texture, a combined image sampler accessed by a fragment shader stage. Create a descriptor set and update it with the created uniform buffer and the combined image sampler (refer to the *Creating a descriptor set layout, Allocating descriptor sets,* and *Updating descriptor sets* recipes from `Chapter 5`, *Descriptor Sets*).
6. Create a shader module with a vertex shader created from the following GLSL code (refer to the *Creating a shader module* recipe from `Chapter 8`, *Graphics and Compute Pipelines*):

```
#version 450
layout( location = 0 ) in vec4 app_position;
layout( set = 0, binding = 0 ) uniform UniformBuffer {
  mat4 ModelViewMatrix;
  mat4 ProjectionMatrix;
};

layout( push_constant ) uniform TimeState {
  float Time;
} PushConstant;

void main() {
  gl_Position = ModelViewMatrix * app_position;
}
```

7. Create a shader module containing a geometry shader created from the following GLSL code:

```glsl
#version 450
layout( points ) in;
layout( set = 0, binding = 0 ) uniform UniformBuffer {
  mat4 ModelViewMatrix;
  mat4 ProjectionMatrix;
};

layout( triangle_strip, max_vertices = 4 ) out;
layout( location = 0 ) out vec2 geom_texcoord;

const float SIZE = 0.1;

void main() {
  vec4 position = gl_in[0].gl_Position;

  gl_Position = ProjectionMatrix * (gl_in[0].gl_Position + vec4(
  -SIZE, SIZE, 0.0, 0.0 ));
  geom_texcoord = vec2( -1.0, 1.0 );
  EmitVertex();

  gl_Position = ProjectionMatrix * (gl_in[0].gl_Position + vec4(
  -SIZE, -SIZE, 0.0, 0.0 ));
  geom_texcoord = vec2( -1.0, -1.0 );
  EmitVertex();

  gl_Position = ProjectionMatrix * (gl_in[0].gl_Position + vec4(
  SIZE, SIZE, 0.0, 0.0 ));
  geom_texcoord = vec2( 1.0, 1.0 );
  EmitVertex();

  gl_Position = ProjectionMatrix * (gl_in[0].gl_Position + vec4(
  SIZE, -SIZE, 0.0, 0.0 ));
  geom_texcoord = vec2( 1.0, -1.0 );
  EmitVertex();

  EndPrimitive();
}
```

8. Create a shader module with a fragment shader that uses a SPIR-V assembly generated from the following GLSL code:

```
#version 450
layout( location = 0 ) in vec2 geom_texcoord;
layout( location = 0 ) out vec4 frag_color;

void main() {
  float alpha = 1.0 - dot( geom_texcoord, geom_texcoord );
  if( 0.2 > alpha ) {
    discard;
  }
  frag_color = vec4( alpha );
}
```

9. Create a graphics pipeline. It must use shader modules with the preceding vertex, geometry and fragment shaders. Only one vertex attribute (a position) is needed. It will be used to draw geometry using a VK_PRIMITIVE_TOPOLOGY_POINT_LIST primitive. The pipeline should have access to the uniform buffer with transformation matrices and (if needed) a combined image texture (refer to the *Specifying pipeline shader stages, Specifying pipeline vertex input state, Specifying pipeline input assembly state, Creating a pipeline layout, Specifying graphics pipeline creation parameters*, and *Creating a graphics pipeline* recipes from Chapter 8, *Graphics and Compute Pipelines*).

10. Draw the geometry inside a render pass (refer to the *Binding descriptor sets* recipe from Chapter 5, *Descriptor Sets*, to the *Binding a pipeline object* recipe from Chapter 8, *Graphics and Compute Pipelines*, and to the *Binding vertex buffers* and *Drawing a geometry* recipes from Chapter 9, *Command Recording and Drawing*).

11. Update a modelview matrix in the uniform buffer each time the user (a camera) moves in the scene. Update a projection matrix in the uniform buffer each time the application window is resized.

How it works...

First, we start by preparing the positions for billboards. Billboards are drawn as point primitives, so one vertex corresponds to a one billboard. How we prepare the geometry is up to us and we don't need other attributes. A geometry shader converts a single vertex into a camera-facing quad and calculates texture coordinates.

In this example we don't use a texture, but we will use texture coordinates to draw circles. All we need to access are transformation matrices stored in a uniform buffer generated like this:

```
std::vector<VkDescriptorSetLayoutBinding> descriptor_set_layout_bindings =
{
  {
    0,
    VK_DESCRIPTOR_TYPE_UNIFORM_BUFFER,
    1,
    VK_SHADER_STAGE_VERTEX_BIT | VK_SHADER_STAGE_GEOMETRY_BIT,
    nullptr
  }
};
InitVkDestroyer( LogicalDevice, DescriptorSetLayout );
if( !CreateDescriptorSetLayout( *LogicalDevice,
descriptor_set_layout_bindings, *DescriptorSetLayout ) ) {
  return false;
}

std::vector<VkDescriptorPoolSize> descriptor_pool_sizes = {
  {
    VK_DESCRIPTOR_TYPE_UNIFORM_BUFFER,
    1
  }
};
InitVkDestroyer( LogicalDevice, DescriptorPool );
if( !CreateDescriptorPool( *LogicalDevice, false, 1, descriptor_pool_sizes,
*DescriptorPool ) ) {
  return false;
}

if( !AllocateDescriptorSets( *LogicalDevice, *DescriptorPool, {
*DescriptorSetLayout }, DescriptorSets ) ) {
  return false;
}

BufferDescriptorInfo buffer_descriptor_update = {
  DescriptorSets[0],
  0,
  0,
  VK_DESCRIPTOR_TYPE_UNIFORM_BUFFER,
  {
    {
      *UniformBuffer,
      0,
      VK_WHOLE_SIZE
    }
```

Advanced Rendering Techniques

```
    }
};

UpdateDescriptorSets( *LogicalDevice, {}, { buffer_descriptor_update }, {},
{} );
```

The next step is to create a graphics pipeline. It uses a single vertex attribute (a position) defined in the following way:

```
std::vector<VkVertexInputBindingDescription>
vertex_input_binding_descriptions = {
    {
        0,
        3 * sizeof( float ),
        VK_VERTEX_INPUT_RATE_VERTEX
    }
};

std::vector<VkVertexInputAttributeDescription>
vertex_attribute_descriptions = {
    {
        0,
        0,
        VK_FORMAT_R32G32B32_SFLOAT,
        0
    }
};

VkPipelineVertexInputStateCreateInfo vertex_input_state_create_info;
SpecifyPipelineVertexInputState( vertex_input_binding_descriptions,
vertex_attribute_descriptions, vertex_input_state_create_info );
```

We draw vertices as points, so we need to specify an appropriate primitive type during the pipeline creation:

```
VkPipelineInputAssemblyStateCreateInfo input_assembly_state_create_info;
SpecifyPipelineInputAssemblyState( VK_PRIMITIVE_TOPOLOGY_POINT_LIST, false,
input_assembly_state_create_info );
```

The rest of the pipeline parameters are fairly typical. The most important parts are the shaders.

A vertex shader transforms the vertex from the local space to the view space. Billboards must always face the camera, so it is easier to perform calculations directly in the view space.

A geometry shader does almost all the work. It takes one vertex (a point) and emits a triangle strip with four vertices (a quad). Each new vertex is offset a bit to the left/right and up/down to form a quad:

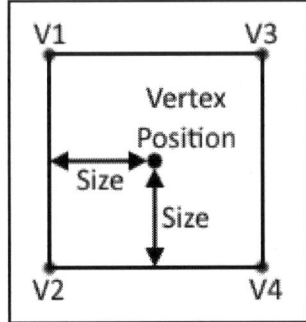

Additionally, a texture coordinate is assigned to the generated vertex based on the direction/offset. In our example, the first vertex is prepared like this:

```
vec4 position = gl_in[0].gl_Position;

gl_Position = ProjectionMatrix * (gl_in[0].gl_Position + vec4( -SIZE, SIZE,
0.0, 0.0 ));
geom_texcoord = vec2( -1.0, 1.0 );
EmitVertex();
```

The remaining vertices are emitted in a similar way. As we transformed vertices to the view space in the vertex shader, the generated quad is always facing the screen plane. All we need to do is to multiply generated vertices by a projection matrix to transform them to the clip space.

A fragment shader is used to discard some fragments to form a circle from the quad:

```
float alpha = 1.0 - dot( geom_texcoord, geom_texcoord );
if( 0.2 > alpha ) {
  discard;
}
```

In the following example, we can see billboards rendered in the positions of a mesh's vertices. The circles seen in the image are flat; they are not spheres:

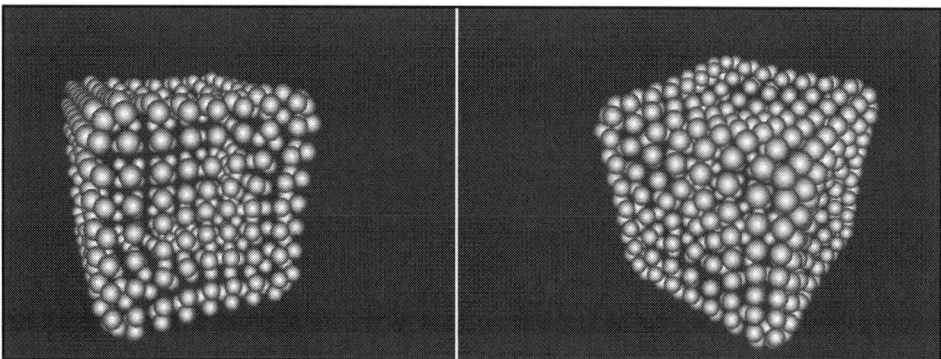

See also

- In Chapter 1, *Instances and Devices*, see the following recipes:
    - *Getting features and properties of a physical device*
    - *Creating a logical device*
- In Chapter 5, *Descriptor Sets*, see the following recipes:
    - *Creating a uniform buffer*
    - *Creating a descriptor set layout*
    - *Allocating descriptor sets*
    - *Updating descriptor sets*
    - *Binding descriptor sets*
- In Chapter 7, *Shaders*, see the *Writing geometry shaders* recipe
- In Chapter 8, *Graphics and Compute Pipelines*, see the following recipes:
    - *Creating a shader module*
    - *Specifying pipeline shader stages*
    - *Specifying a pipeline vertex binding description, attribute description, and input state*
    - *Specifying a pipeline input assembly state*
    - *Creating a pipeline layout*
    - *Specifying graphics pipeline creation parameters*
    - *Creating a graphics pipeline*
    - *Binding a pipeline object*

- In Chapter 9, *Command Recording and Drawing*, see the following recipes:
    - *Binding vertex buffers*
    - *Drawing geometry recipes*

Drawing particles using compute and graphics pipelines

Due to the nature of graphics hardware and the way objects are processed by the graphics pipeline, it is quite hard to display phenomena such as clouds, smoke, sparks, fire, falling rain, and snow. Such effects are usually simulated with particle systems, which are a large number of small sprites that behave according to the algorithms implemented for the system.

Because of the very large number of independent entities, it is convenient to implement the behavior and mutual interactions of particles using compute shaders. Sprites mimicking the look of each particle are usually displayed as billboards with geometry shaders.

In the following example, we can see an image generated with this recipe:

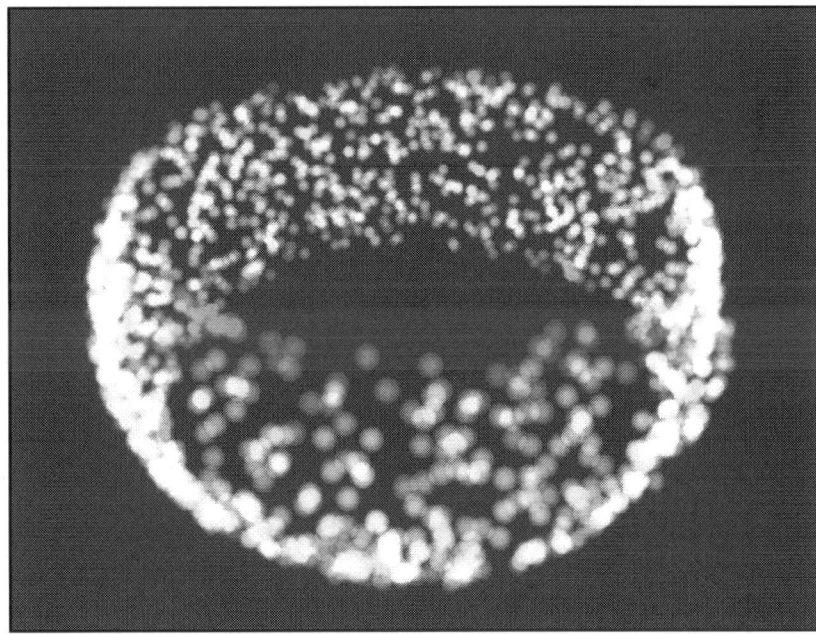

Advanced Rendering Techniques

How to do it...

1. Create a logical device with the `geometryShader` feature enabled. Request a queue that supports graphics operations and a queue that supports compute operations (refer to the *Getting features and properties of a physical device* and *Creating a logical device* recipes from `Chapter 1`, *Instance and Devices*).
2. Generate the initial data (attributes) for a particle system.
3. Create a buffer that will serve both as a vertex buffer and a storage texel buffer. Copy the generated particle data to the buffer (refer to the *Creating a storage texel buffer* recipe from `Chapter 5`, *Descriptor Sets*, and to the *Using staging buffer to update buffer with a device-local memory bound* recipe from `Chapter 4`, *Resources and Memory*).
4. Create a uniform buffer for two transformation matrices. Update it each time the camera is moved or the window is resized (refer to the *Creating a uniform buffer* recipe from `Chapter 5`, *Descriptor Sets*).
5. Create two descriptor set layouts: one with a uniform buffer accessed by vertex and geometry stages; and the second with a storage texel buffer accessed by a compute stage. Create a descriptor pool and allocate two descriptor sets using the above layouts. Update them with the uniform buffer and the storage texel buffer (refer to the *Creating a descriptor set layout, Creating a descriptor pool, Allocating descriptor sets* and *Updating descriptor sets*, recipes from `Chapter 5`, *Descriptor Sets*).
6. Create a shader module with a compute shader created from the following GLSL code (refer to the *Creating a shader module* recipe from `Chapter 8`, *Graphics and Compute Pipelines*):

```
#version 450
layout( local_size_x = 32, local_size_y = 32 ) in;
layout( set = 0, binding = 0, rgba32f ) uniform imageBuffer
StorageTexelBuffer;

layout( push_constant ) uniform TimeState {
  float DeltaTime;
} PushConstant;

const uint PARTICLES_COUNT = 2000;

void main() {
  if( gl_GlobalInvocationID.x < PARTICLES_COUNT ) {
    vec4 position = imageLoad( StorageTexelBuffer,
      int(gl_GlobalInvocationID.x * 2) );
    vec4 color = imageLoad( StorageTexelBuffer,
      int(gl_GlobalInvocationID.x * 2 + 1) );
```

```
            vec3 speed = normalize( cross( vec3( 0.0, 1.0, 0.0 ),
            position.xyz ) ) * color.w;

            position.xyz += speed * PushConstant.DeltaTime;

            imageStore( StorageTexelBuffer, int(gl_GlobalInvocationID.x
            *
            2), position );
        }
    }
```

7. Create a compute pipeline that uses the shader module with the compute shader and has access to the storage texel buffer and a push constant range with one floating point value (refer to the *Specifying pipeline shader stages, Creating a pipeline layout recipe,* and *Creating a compute pipeline* recipes from Chapter 8, *Graphics and Compute Pipelines*).
8. Create a graphics pipeline with vertex, geometry, and fragment shaders as described in the *Drawing billboards using geometry shaders* recipe. The graphics pipeline must fetch two vertex attributes, draw vertices as VK_PRIMITIVE_TOPOLOGY_POINT_LIST primitives and must have blending enabled (refer to the *Specifying pipeline vertex input state, Specifying pipeline input assembly state, Specifying pipeline blend state,* and *Creating a graphics pipeline* recipes from Chapter 8, *Graphics and Compute Pipelines*).
9. To render a frame, record a command buffer that dispatches compute work and submit it to a queue that supports compute operations. Provide a semaphore to be signaled when the queue finishes processing the submitted command buffer (refer to the *Providing data to shaders through push constants* and *Dispatching a compute work recipes* from Chapter 9, *Command Recording*, and the *Submitting command buffers to the queue* recipe from Chapter 3, *Command Buffers and Synchronization*).
10. Also, in each frame record a command buffer that draws billboards as described in the *Drawing billboards using geometry shaders* recipe. Submit it to the queue that supports graphics operations. During submission, provide a semaphore, which is signaled by the compute queue. Provide it as a wait semaphore (refer to the *Synchronizing two command buffers* recipe from Chapter 3, *Command Buffers and Synchronization*).

How it works...

Drawing particle systems can be divided in two steps:

- We calculate and update positions of all particles with compute shaders
- We draw particles in updated positions using graphics pipeline with vertex, geometry, and fragment shaders

To prepare a particle system, we need to think about the data needed to calculate positions and draw all particles. In this example we will use three parameters: position, speed and color. Each set of these parameters will be accessed by a vertex shader through a vertex buffer, and the same data will be read in a compute shader. A simple and convenient way to access a very large number of entries in stages other than the vertex shader is to use a texel buffer. As we want to both read and store data, we will need a storage texel buffer. It allows us to fetch data from a buffer treated as a 1-dimensional image (refer to the *Creating a storage texel buffer* recipe from `Chapter 5, Descriptor Sets`).

First, we need to generate initial data for our particle system. For the data available in a storage texel buffer to be properly read, it must be stored according to a selected format. Storage texel buffers have a limited set of formats that are mandatory, so we need to pack the parameters of our particles to one of them. Positions and colors require at least three values each. In our example, particles will move around the center of the whole system, so the velocity can be easily calculated based on the particle's current position. We just need to differentiate the speed of particles. For this purpose one value for scaling our velocity vector is enough.

So we end up with seven values. We will pack them into two RGBA vectors of floating-point values. First we have three X, Y, Z components of a position attribute. The next value is unused in our particle system, but for the data to be correctly read, it needs to be included. We will store a `1.0f` value as a fourth component of the position attribute. After that there are R, G, B values for a color, and a value scaling the speed vector of a particle. We randomly generate all values and store them in a vector:

```
std::vector<float> particles;

for( uint32_t i = 0; i < PARTICLES_COUNT; ++i ) {
  Vector3 position = /* generate position */;
  Vector3 color = /* generate color */;
  float speed = /* generate speed scale */;
  particles.insert( particles.end(), position.begin(), position.end() );
  particles.push_back( 1.0f );
  particles.insert( particles.end(), color.begin(), color.end() );
  particles.push_back( speed );
}
```

The generated data is copied to the buffer. We create a buffer that will serve both as a vertex buffer during rendering and as a storage texel buffer during position calculations:

```
InitVkDestroyer( LogicalDevice, VertexBuffer );
InitVkDestroyer( LogicalDevice, VertexBufferMemory );
InitVkDestroyer( LogicalDevice, VertexBufferView );
if( !CreateStorageTexelBuffer( PhysicalDevice, *LogicalDevice,
VK_FORMAT_R32G32B32A32_SFLOAT, sizeof( particles[0] ) * particles.size(),
  VK_BUFFER_USAGE_TRANSFER_DST_BIT | VK_BUFFER_USAGE_VERTEX_BUFFER_BIT |
VK_BUFFER_USAGE_STORAGE_TEXEL_BUFFER_BIT, false,
  *VertexBuffer, *VertexBufferMemory, *VertexBufferView ) ) {
  return false;
}

if( !UseStagingBufferToUpdateBufferWithDeviceLocalMemoryBound(
PhysicalDevice, *LogicalDevice, sizeof( particles[0] ) * particles.size(),
  &particles[0], *VertexBuffer, 0, 0, VK_ACCESS_TRANSFER_WRITE_BIT,
VK_PIPELINE_STAGE_TOP_OF_PIPE_BIT, VK_PIPELINE_STAGE_VERTEX_INPUT_BIT,
  GraphicsQueue.Handle, FrameResources.front().CommandBuffer, {} ) ) {
  return false;
}
```

Additionally, we need a uniform buffer, through which we will provide transformation matrices. A uniform buffer along the storage texel buffer will be provided to shaders through descriptor sets. Here we will have two separate sets. In the first set, we will have only a uniform buffer accessed by vertex and geometry shaders. The second descriptor set is used in a compute shader to access storage texel buffer. For this purpose we need two separate descriptor set layouts:

```
std::vector<VkDescriptorSetLayoutBinding> descriptor_set_layout_bindings =
{
  {
    0,
    VK_DESCRIPTOR_TYPE_UNIFORM_BUFFER,
    1,
    VK_SHADER_STAGE_VERTEX_BIT | VK_SHADER_STAGE_GEOMETRY_BIT,
    nullptr
  },
  {
    0,
    VK_DESCRIPTOR_TYPE_STORAGE_TEXEL_BUFFER,
    1,
    VK_SHADER_STAGE_COMPUTE_BIT,
    nullptr
  }
};
```

Advanced Rendering Techniques

```
DescriptorSetLayout.resize( 2 );
InitVkDestroyer( LogicalDevice, DescriptorSetLayout[0] );
InitVkDestroyer( LogicalDevice, DescriptorSetLayout[1] );
if( !CreateDescriptorSetLayout( *LogicalDevice, {
descriptor_set_layout_bindings[0] }, *DescriptorSetLayout[0] ) ) {
  return false;
}
if( !CreateDescriptorSetLayout( *LogicalDevice, {
descriptor_set_layout_bindings[1] }, *DescriptorSetLayout[1] ) ) {
  return false;
}
```

Next, we need a pool from which we can allocate two descriptor sets:

```
std::vector<VkDescriptorPoolSize> descriptor_pool_sizes = {
    {
      VK_DESCRIPTOR_TYPE_UNIFORM_BUFFER,
      1
    },
    {
      VK_DESCRIPTOR_TYPE_STORAGE_TEXEL_BUFFER,
      1
    }
};
InitVkDestroyer( LogicalDevice, DescriptorPool );
if( !CreateDescriptorPool( *LogicalDevice, false, 2, descriptor_pool_sizes,
*DescriptorPool ) ) {
  return false;
}
```

After that, we can allocate two descriptors sets and update them with the created buffer and buffer view:

```
if( !AllocateDescriptorSets( *LogicalDevice, *DescriptorPool, {
*DescriptorSetLayout[0], *DescriptorSetLayout[1] }, DescriptorSets ) ) {
  return false;
}

BufferDescriptorInfo buffer_descriptor_update = {
  DescriptorSets[0],
  0,
  0,
  VK_DESCRIPTOR_TYPE_UNIFORM_BUFFER,
  {
    {
      *UniformBuffer,
      0,
      VK_WHOLE_SIZE
```

```
      }
    }
  };

  TexelBufferDescriptorInfo storage_texel_buffer_descriptor_update = {
    DescriptorSets[1],
    0,
    0,
    VK_DESCRIPTOR_TYPE_STORAGE_TEXEL_BUFFER,
    {
      {
        *VertexBufferView
      }
    }
  };

  UpdateDescriptorSets( *LogicalDevice, {}, { buffer_descriptor_update }, {
  storage_texel_buffer_descriptor_update }, {} );
```

The next important step is the creation of graphics and compute pipelines. When a movement is involved, calculations must be performed based on real-time values, as we usually cannot rely on fixed time intervals. So the compute shader must have access to a value of time that has elapsed since the last frame. Such a value may be provided through a push constant range. We can see the code required to create the compute pipeline here:

```
  std::vector<unsigned char> compute_shader_spirv;
  if( !GetBinaryFileContents( "Data/Shaders/Recipes/12 Advanced Rendering
  Techniques/03 Drawing particles using compute and graphics
  pipelines/shader.comp.spv", compute_shader_spirv ) ) {
    return false;
  }

  VkDestroyer<VkShaderModule> compute_shader_module( LogicalDevice );
  if( !CreateShaderModule( *LogicalDevice, compute_shader_spirv,
  *compute_shader_module ) ) {
    return false;
  }
  std::vector<ShaderStageParameters> compute_shader_stage_params = {
    {
      VK_SHADER_STAGE_COMPUTE_BIT,
      *compute_shader_module,
      "main",
      nullptr
    }
  };
  std::vector<VkPipelineShaderStageCreateInfo>
  compute_shader_stage_create_infos;
  SpecifyPipelineShaderStages( compute_shader_stage_params,
```

[621]

Advanced Rendering Techniques

```
  compute_shader_stage_create_infos );
VkPushConstantRange push_constant_range = {
  VK_SHADER_STAGE_COMPUTE_BIT,
  0,
  sizeof( float )
};

InitVkDestroyer( LogicalDevice, ComputePipelineLayout );
if( !CreatePipelineLayout( *LogicalDevice, { *DescriptorSetLayout[1] }, {
push_constant_range }, *ComputePipelineLayout ) ) {
  return false;
}

InitVkDestroyer( LogicalDevice, ComputePipeline );
if( !CreateComputePipeline( *LogicalDevice, 0,
compute_shader_stage_create_infos[0], *ComputePipelineLayout,
VK_NULL_HANDLE, VK_NULL_HANDLE, *ComputePipeline ) ) {
  return false;
}
```

Compute shaders read data from the storage texel buffer defined as follows:

```
layout( set = 0, binding = 0, rgba32f ) uniform imageBuffer
StorageTexelBuffer;
```

Data from the storage texel buffer is read using the `imageLoad()` function:

```
vec4 position = imageLoad( StorageTexelBuffer, int(gl_GlobalInvocationID.x
* 2) );
vec4 color = imageLoad( StorageTexelBuffer, int(gl_GlobalInvocationID.x * 2
+ 1) );
```

We read two values so we need two `imageLoad()` calls, because each such operation returns one element of a format defined for the buffer (in this case, a 4-component vector of floats). We access the buffer based on a unique value of a current compute shader instance.

Next, we perform calculations and update the positions of the vertices. Calculations are performed so the particles move around the center of the scene based on the position and an up vector. A new vector (speed) is calculated using the `cross()` function:

Chapter 12

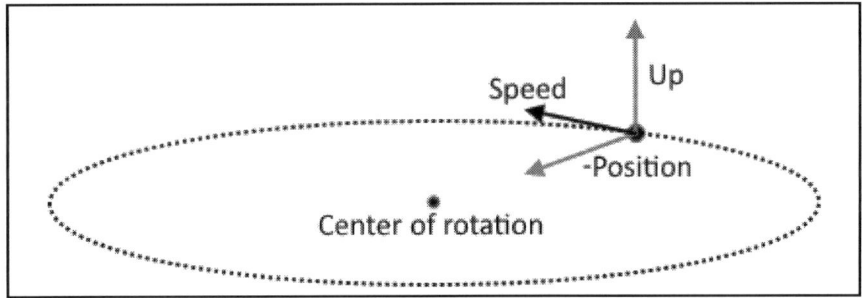

This calculated speed vector is added to the fetched position and the result is stored in the same buffer using the `imageStore()` function:

```
imageStore( StorageTexelBuffer, int(gl_GlobalInvocationID.x * 2), position
);
```

We don't update a color or speed, so we store only one value.

Because we access the data of only one particle, we can read values from and store values in the same buffer. In more complicated scenarios, such as when there are interactions between particles, we can't use the same buffer. The order in which compute shader invocations are executed is unknown, so we would end up with some invocations accessing unmodified values, but others would read data that has already been updated. This would impact the accuracy of performed calculations and probably result in an unpredictable system.

Graphics pipeline creation is very similar to the one presented in the *Drawing billboards using geometry shaders* recipe. The difference is that it fetches two attributes instead of one:

```
std::vector<VkVertexInputBindingDescription>
vertex_input_binding_descriptions = {
  {
    0,      VK_VERTEX_INPUT_RATE_VERTEX
  }
};

std::vector<VkVertexInputAttributeDescription>
vertex_attribute_descriptions = {
  {
    0,
    0,
    VK_FORMAT_R32G32B32A32_SFLOAT,
    0
  },
  {
```

```
        1,
        0,
        VK_FORMAT_R32G32B32A32_SFLOAT,
        4 * sizeof( float )
    }
};

VkPipelineVertexInputStateCreateInfo vertex_input_state_create_info;
SpecifyPipelineVertexInputState( vertex_input_binding_descriptions,
vertex_attribute_descriptions, vertex_input_state_create_info );
```

We also render vertices as point primitives:

```
VkPipelineInputAssemblyStateCreateInfo input_assembly_state_create_info;
SpecifyPipelineInputAssemblyState( VK_PRIMITIVE_TOPOLOGY_POINT_LIST, false,
input_assembly_state_create_info );
```

One last difference is that here we enable additive blending, so the particles look like they are glowing:

```
std::vector<VkPipelineColorBlendAttachmentState> attachment_blend_states =
{
    {
        true,
        VK_BLEND_FACTOR_SRC_ALPHA,
        VK_BLEND_FACTOR_ONE,
        VK_BLEND_OP_ADD,
        VK_BLEND_FACTOR_ONE,
        VK_BLEND_FACTOR_ONE,
        VK_BLEND_OP_ADD,
        VK_COLOR_COMPONENT_R_BIT |
        VK_COLOR_COMPONENT_G_BIT |
        VK_COLOR_COMPONENT_B_BIT |
        VK_COLOR_COMPONENT_A_BIT
    }
};
VkPipelineColorBlendStateCreateInfo blend_state_create_info;
SpecifyPipelineBlendState( false, VK_LOGIC_OP_COPY,
attachment_blend_states, { 1.0f, 1.0f, 1.0f, 1.0f },
blend_state_create_info );
```

The drawing process is also divided into two steps. First, we record a command buffer that dispatches compute work. Some hardware platforms may have a queue family that is dedicated to math calculations, so it may be preferable to submit command buffers with compute shaders to that queue:

```
if( !BeginCommandBufferRecordingOperation( ComputeCommandBuffer,
VK_COMMAND_BUFFER_USAGE_ONE_TIME_SUBMIT_BIT, nullptr ) ) {
  return false;
}

BindDescriptorSets( ComputeCommandBuffer, VK_PIPELINE_BIND_POINT_COMPUTE,
*ComputePipelineLayout, 0, { DescriptorSets[1] }, {} );

BindPipelineObject( ComputeCommandBuffer, VK_PIPELINE_BIND_POINT_COMPUTE,
*ComputePipeline );

float time = TimerState.GetDeltaTime();
ProvideDataToShadersThroughPushConstants( ComputeCommandBuffer,
*ComputePipelineLayout, VK_SHADER_STAGE_COMPUTE_BIT, 0, sizeof( float ),
&time );

DispatchComputeWork( ComputeCommandBuffer, PARTICLES_COUNT / 32 + 1, 1, 1
);

if( !EndCommandBufferRecordingOperation( ComputeCommandBuffer ) ) {
  return false;
}

if( !SubmitCommandBuffersToQueue( ComputeQueue.Handle, {}, {
ComputeCommandBuffer }, { *ComputeSemaphore }, *ComputeFence ) ) {
  return false;
}
```

Drawing is performed in the normal way. We just need to synchronize the graphics queue with a compute queue. We do this by providing an additional wait semaphore when we submit a command buffer to the graphics queue. This semaphore must be signaled by a compute queue when it finishes processing the submitted command buffer in which the compute shaders are dispatched.

Advanced Rendering Techniques

The following sample images show the same particle system rendered with different numbers of particles:

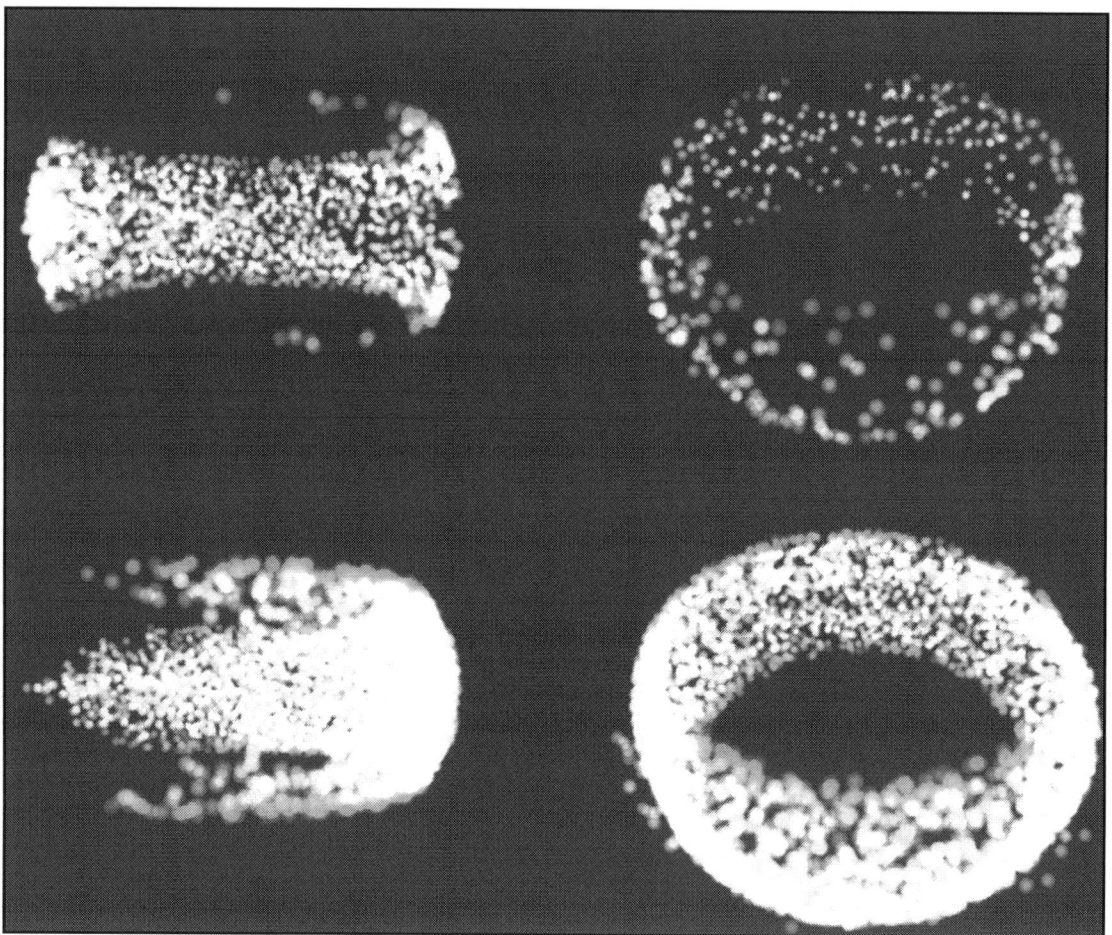

See also

- In Chapter 1, *Instances and Devices*, see the Getting features and properties of a physical device recipe
- In Chapter 5, *Descriptor Sets*, see the following recipes:
    - *Creating a storage texel buffer*
    - *Creating a descriptor set layout*
    - *Creating a descriptor pool*
    - *Allocating descriptor sets*
    - *Updating descriptor sets*
- In Chapter 7, *Shaders*, see the Writing compute shaders recipe
- In Chapter 8, *Graphics and Compute Pipelines*, see the following recipes:
    - *Creating a shader module*
    - *Creating a compute pipeline*
    - *Creating a graphics pipeline*
- In Chapter 9, *Command Recording and Drawing*, see the following recipes:
    - *Providing data to shaders through push constants*
    - *Drawing a geometry*
    - *Dispatching a compute work*

Rendering a tessellated terrain

3D scenes with open worlds and long rendering distances usually also contain vast terrains. Drawing ground is a very complex topic and can be performed in many different ways. Terrain in a distance cannot be too complex, as it will take up too much memory and processing power to display it. On the other hand, the area near the player must be detailed enough to look convincing and natural. That's why we need a way to lower the number of details with increasing distance or to increase the terrain's fidelity near the camera.

Advanced Rendering Techniques

This is an example of how the tessellation shaders can be used to achieve high quality rendered images. For a terrain, we can use a flat plane with low number of vertices. Using tessellation shaders, we can increase the number of primitives of the ground near the camera. We can then offset generated vertices by the desired amount to increase or decrease the height of a terrain.

The following screenshot is an example of an image generated using this recipe:

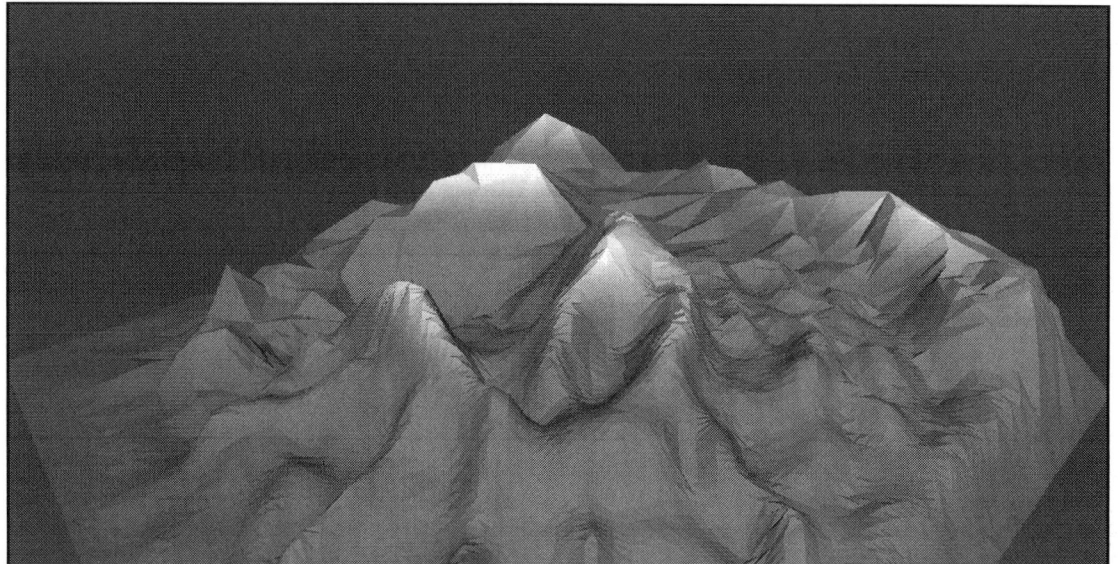

Getting ready

Drawing a terrain usually requires the preparation of height data. This can be generated on the fly, procedurally, according to some desired formulae. However, it can also be prepared earlier in the form of a texture called a height map. It contains information about the terrain's height above (or below) a specified altitude, in which a lighter color indicates a greater height and a darker color indicates a lower height. An example of such a height map can be seen in the following image:

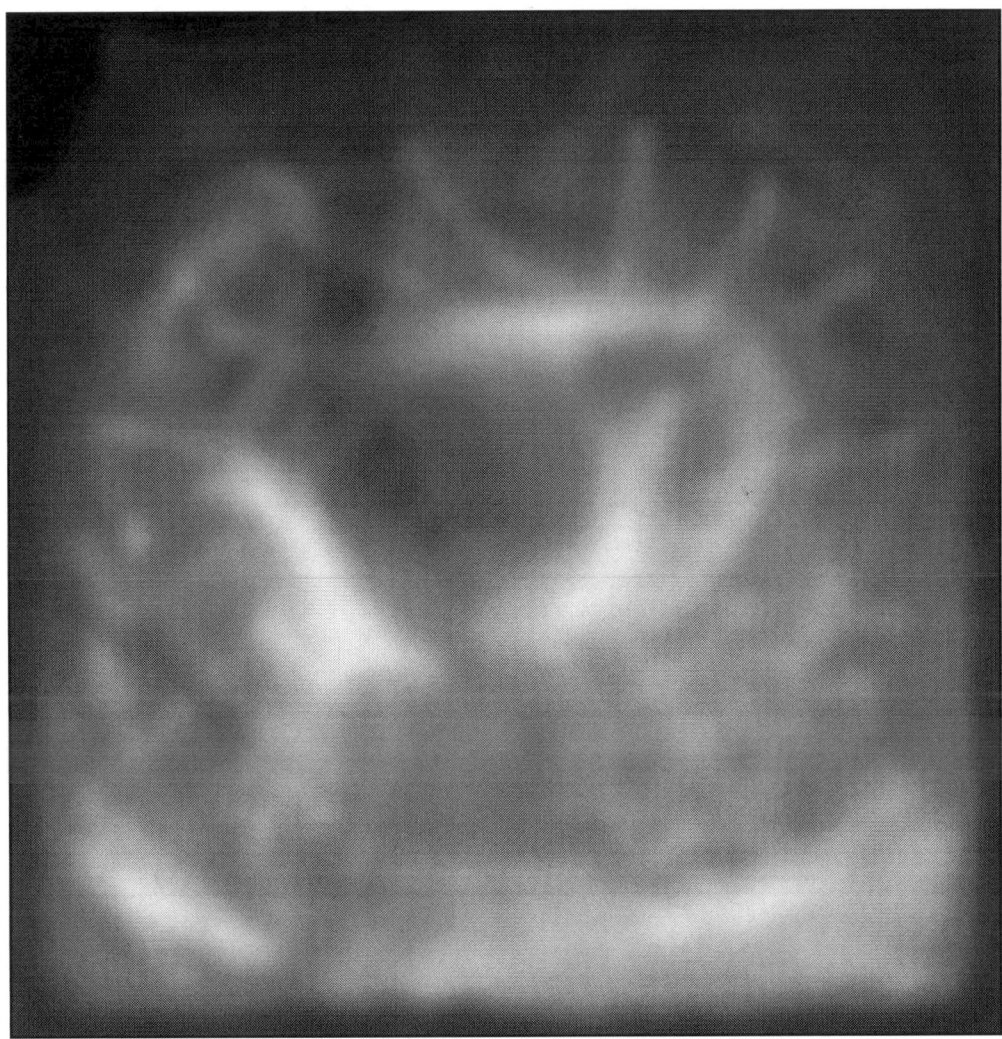

Advanced Rendering Techniques

How to do it...

1. Load or generate a model of a flat, horizontally-aligned plane. Two attributes--position and texture coordinate--will be needed. Upload the vertex data to a vertex buffer (refer to the *Loading a 3D model from an OBJ file* recipe from `Chapter 10`, *Helper Recipes* and to the *Creating a buffer* and *Using staging buffer to update buffer with a device-local memory bound* recipes from `Chapter 4`, *Resources and Memory*).
2. Create a uniform buffer for two transformation matrices (refer to the *Creating a uniform buffer* recipe from `Chapter 5`, *Descriptor Sets*).
3. Load height information from an image file (refer to the *Loading texture data from a file* recipe from `Chapter 10`, *Helper Recipes*). Create a combined image sampler and copy the loaded height data to image's memory (refer to the *Creating a combined image sampler* recipe from `Chapter 5`, *Descriptor Sets* and to the *Using the staging buffer to update an image with a device-local memory bound* recipe from `Chapter 4`, *Resources and Memory*).
4. Create a descriptor set layout with one uniform buffer accessed by tessellation control and geometry stages and one combined image sampler accessed by tessellation control and evaluation stages (refer to the *Creating a descriptor set layout* recipe from `Chapter 5`, *Descriptor Sets*). Allocate a descriptor set using the prepared layout. Update it with the created uniform buffer and sampler and image view handles (refer to the *Allocating descriptor sets* and *Updating descriptor sets* recipes from `Chapter 5`, *Descriptor Sets*).
5. Create a shader module with a SPIR-V assembly for a vertex shader created from the following GLSL code (refer to the *Creating a shader module* recipe from `Chapter 8`, *Graphics and Compute Pipelines*):

```
#version 450
layout( location = 0 ) in vec4 app_position;
layout( location = 1 ) in vec2 app_texcoord;
layout( location = 0 ) out vec2 vert_texcoord;

void main() {
  gl_Position = app_position;
  vert_texcoord = app_texcoord;
}
```

[630]

6. Create a shader module for a tessellation control stage. Use the following GLSL code to generate a SPIR-V assembly from:

```
#version 450
layout( location = 0 ) in vec2 vert_texcoord[];
layout( set = 0, binding = 0 ) uniform UniformBuffer {
 mat4 ModelViewMatrix;
 mat4 ProjectionMatrix;
};

layout( set = 0, binding = 1 ) uniform sampler2D ImageSampler;
layout( vertices = 3 ) out;
layout( location = 0 ) out vec2 tesc_texcoord[];

void main() {
  if( 0 == gl_InvocationID ) {
    float distances[3];
    float factors[3];

    for( int i = 0; i < 3; ++i ) {
      float height = texture( ImageSampler, vert_texcoord[i]
      ).x;
      vec4 position = ModelViewMatrix * (gl_in[i].gl_Position +
      vec4( 0.0, height, 0.0, 0.0 ));
      distances[i] = dot( position, position );
    }
    factors[0] = min( distances[1], distances[2] );
    factors[1] = min( distances[2], distances[0] );
    factors[2] = min( distances[0], distances[1] );

    gl_TessLevelInner[0] = max( 1.0, 20.0 - factors[0] );
    gl_TessLevelOuter[0] = max( 1.0, 20.0 - factors[0] );
    gl_TessLevelOuter[1] = max( 1.0, 20.0 - factors[1] );
    gl_TessLevelOuter[2] = max( 1.0, 20.0 - factors[2] );
  }
  gl_out[gl_InvocationID].gl_Position =
  gl_in[gl_InvocationID].gl_Position;
  tesc_texcoord[gl_InvocationID] =
  vert_texcoord[gl_InvocationID];
}
```

7. Create a shader module for a tessellation evaluation shader created from the following GLSL code:

```glsl
#version 450
layout( triangles, fractional_even_spacing, cw ) in;
layout( location = 0 ) in vec2 tesc_texcoord[];
layout( set = 0, binding = 1 ) uniform sampler2D HeightMap;
layout( location = 0 ) out float tese_height;
void main() {
  vec4 position = gl_in[0].gl_Position * gl_TessCoord.x +
                  gl_in[1].gl_Position * gl_TessCoord.y +
                  gl_in[2].gl_Position * gl_TessCoord.z;
  vec2 texcoord = tesc_texcoord[0] * gl_TessCoord.x +
                  tesc_texcoord[1] * gl_TessCoord.y +
                  tesc_texcoord[2] * gl_TessCoord.z;
  float height = texture( HeightMap, texcoord ).x;
  position.y += height;
  gl_Position = position;
  tese_height = height;
}
```

8. Create a shader module for a geometry shader and use the following GLSL code:

```glsl
#version 450

layout( triangles ) in;
layout( location = 0 ) in float tese_height[];

layout( set = 0, binding = 0 ) uniform UniformBuffer {
  mat4 ModelViewMatrix;
  mat4 ProjectionMatrix;
};
layout( triangle_strip, max_vertices = 3 ) out;
layout( location = 0 ) out vec3  geom_normal;
layout( location = 1 ) out float geom_height;

void main() {
  vec3 v0v1 = gl_in[1].gl_Position.xyz -
  gl_in[0].gl_Position.xyz;
  vec3 v0v2 = gl_in[2].gl_Position.xyz -
  gl_in[0].gl_Position.xyz;
  vec3 normal = normalize( cross( v0v1, v0v2 ) );

  for( int vertex = 0; vertex < 3; ++vertex ) {
    gl_Position = ProjectionMatrix * ModelViewMatrix *
    gl_in[vertex].gl_Position;
    geom_height = tese_height[vertex];
    geom_normal = normal;
```

```
        EmitVertex();
    }

    EndPrimitive();
}
```

9. Create a shader module that contains a source code of a fragment shader. Generate a SPIR-V assembly from the following GLSL code:

```
#version 450
layout( location = 0 ) in vec3  geom_normal;
layout( location = 1 ) in float geom_height;
layout( location = 0 ) out vec4 frag_color;

void main() {
    const vec4 green = vec4( 0.2, 0.5, 0.1, 1.0 );
    const vec4 brown = vec4( 0.6, 0.5, 0.3, 1.0 );
    const vec4 white = vec4( 1.0 );
    vec4 color = mix( green, brown, smoothstep( 0.0, 0.4,
    geom_height ) );
    color = mix( color, white, smoothstep( 0.6, 0.9, geom_height )
    );

    float diffuse_light = max( 0.0, dot( geom_normal, vec3( 0.58,
    0.58, 0.58 ) ) );
    frag_color = vec4( 0.05, 0.05, 0.0, 0.0 ) + diffuse_light *
    color;
}
```

10. Create a graphics pipeline using the above five shader modules. The pipeline should fetch two vertex attributes: a 3-component position and a 2-component texture coordinate. It must use VK_PRIMITIVE_TOPOLOGY_PATCH_LIST primitives. A patch should consist of three control points (refer to the *Specifying pipeline input assembly state, Specifying pipeline tessellation state, Specifying graphics pipeline creation parameters,* and *Creating a graphics pipeline* recipes from Chapter 8, *Graphics and Compute Pipelines*).

11. Create the remaining resources and draw the geometry (refer to the *Rendering a geometry with a vertex diffuse lighting* recipe from Chapter 11, *Lighting*).

How it works...

We start the process of drawing a terrain by loading a model of a flat plane. It may be a simple quad with a little bit more than four vertices. Generating too many vertices in a tessellation stage may be too expensive performance-wise, so we need to find a balance between the complexity of a base geometry and the tessellation factors. We can see a plane used as a base for the tessellated terrain in the following image:

In this example, we will load height information from a texture. We do this in the same way as we load data from files. Then we create a combined image sampler and upload loaded data to its memory:

```
int width = 1;
int height = 1;
std::vector<unsigned char> image_data;
if( !LoadTextureDataFromFile( "Data/Textures/heightmap.png", 4, image_data,
&width, &height ) ) {
  return false;
}

InitVkDestroyer( LogicalDevice, HeightSampler );
InitVkDestroyer( LogicalDevice, HeightMap );
InitVkDestroyer( LogicalDevice, HeightMapMemory );
InitVkDestroyer( LogicalDevice, HeightMapView );
if( !CreateCombinedImageSampler( PhysicalDevice, *LogicalDevice,
VK_IMAGE_TYPE_2D, VK_FORMAT_R8G8B8A8_UNORM, { (uint32_t)width,
(uint32_t)height, 1 },
  1, 1, VK_IMAGE_USAGE_SAMPLED_BIT | VK_IMAGE_USAGE_TRANSFER_DST_BIT,
VK_IMAGE_VIEW_TYPE_2D, VK_IMAGE_ASPECT_COLOR_BIT, VK_FILTER_LINEAR,
  VK_FILTER_LINEAR, VK_SAMPLER_MIPMAP_MODE_NEAREST,
VK_SAMPLER_ADDRESS_MODE_CLAMP_TO_EDGE,
VK_SAMPLER_ADDRESS_MODE_CLAMP_TO_EDGE,
  VK_SAMPLER_ADDRESS_MODE_CLAMP_TO_EDGE, 0.0f, false, 1.0f, false,
VK_COMPARE_OP_ALWAYS, 0.0f, 1.0f, VK_BORDER_COLOR_FLOAT_OPAQUE_BLACK,
  false, *HeightSampler, *HeightMap, *HeightMapMemory, *HeightMapView ) ) {
  return false;
}

VkImageSubresourceLayers image_subresource_layer = {
  VK_IMAGE_ASPECT_COLOR_BIT,
  0,
  0,
  1
};
if( !UseStagingBufferToUpdateImageWithDeviceLocalMemoryBound(
PhysicalDevice, *LogicalDevice,
static_cast<VkDeviceSize>(image_data.size()),
&image_data[0], *HeightMap, image_subresource_layer, { 0, 0, 0 }, {
(uint32_t)width, (uint32_t)height, 1 }, VK_IMAGE_LAYOUT_UNDEFINED,
VK_IMAGE_LAYOUT_SHADER_READ_ONLY_OPTIMAL, 0, VK_ACCESS_SHADER_READ_BIT,
VK_IMAGE_ASPECT_COLOR_BIT, VK_PIPELINE_STAGE_TOP_OF_PIPE_BIT,
VK_PIPELINE_STAGE_FRAGMENT_SHADER_BIT, GraphicsQueue.Handle,
FrameResources.front().CommandBuffer, {} ) ) {
return false;
}
```

Advanced Rendering Techniques

A uniform buffer with transformation matrices is also required, so the vertices can be transformed from local space to a view space and to the clip space:

```
InitVkDestroyer( LogicalDevice, UniformBuffer );
InitVkDestroyer( LogicalDevice, UniformBufferMemory );
if( !CreateUniformBuffer( PhysicalDevice, *LogicalDevice, 2 * 16 * sizeof(
float ), VK_BUFFER_USAGE_TRANSFER_DST_BIT |
VK_BUFFER_USAGE_UNIFORM_BUFFER_BIT,
  *UniformBuffer, *UniformBufferMemory ) ) {
  return false;
}

if( !UpdateStagingBuffer( true ) ) {
  return false;
}
```

The next step is to create a descriptor set for the uniform buffer and the combined image sampler. A uniform buffer is accessed in the tessellation control and geometry stages. Height information is read in the tessellation control and evaluation stages:

```
std::vector<VkDescriptorSetLayoutBinding> descriptor_set_layout_bindings =
{
  {
    0,
    VK_DESCRIPTOR_TYPE_UNIFORM_BUFFER,
    1,
    VK_SHADER_STAGE_TESSELLATION_CONTROL_BIT |
VK_SHADER_STAGE_GEOMETRY_BIT,
    nullptr
  },
  {
    1,
    VK_DESCRIPTOR_TYPE_COMBINED_IMAGE_SAMPLER,
    1,
    VK_SHADER_STAGE_TESSELLATION_CONTROL_BIT |
VK_SHADER_STAGE_TESSELLATION_EVALUATION_BIT,
    nullptr
  }
};
InitVkDestroyer( LogicalDevice, DescriptorSetLayout );
if( !CreateDescriptorSetLayout( *LogicalDevice,
descriptor_set_layout_bindings, *DescriptorSetLayout ) ) {
  return false;
}

std::vector<VkDescriptorPoolSize> descriptor_pool_sizes = {
  {
    VK_DESCRIPTOR_TYPE_UNIFORM_BUFFER,
```

```
          1
        },
        {
          VK_DESCRIPTOR_TYPE_COMBINED_IMAGE_SAMPLER,
          2
        }
      };
      InitVkDestroyer( LogicalDevice, DescriptorPool );
      if( !CreateDescriptorPool( *LogicalDevice, false, 1, descriptor_pool_sizes,
      *DescriptorPool ) ) {
        return false;
      }

      if( !AllocateDescriptorSets( *LogicalDevice, *DescriptorPool, {
      *DescriptorSetLayout }, DescriptorSets ) ) {
        return false;
      }
```

Next, we can update the descriptor set with the uniform buffer handle and with sampler and image view handles as they don't change during the lifetime of our application (that is, we don't need to recreate them when the window size is modified).

```
      BufferDescriptorInfo buffer_descriptor_update = {
        DescriptorSets[0],
        0,
        0,
        VK_DESCRIPTOR_TYPE_UNIFORM_BUFFER,
        {
          {
            *UniformBuffer,
            0,
            VK_WHOLE_SIZE
          }
        }
      };

      std::vector<ImageDescriptorInfo> image_descriptor_updates = {
        {
          DescriptorSets[0],
          1,
          0,
          VK_DESCRIPTOR_TYPE_COMBINED_IMAGE_SAMPLER,
          {
            {
              *HeightSampler,
              *HeightMapView,
              VK_IMAGE_LAYOUT_SHADER_READ_ONLY_OPTIMAL
            }
```

```
    }
  }
};

UpdateDescriptorSets( *LogicalDevice, image_descriptor_updates, {
buffer_descriptor_update }, {}, {} );
```

The next step is to create a graphics pipeline. This time we have a very complex pipeline with all five programmable graphics stages enabled:

```
std::vector<ShaderStageParameters> shader_stage_params = {
  {
    VK_SHADER_STAGE_VERTEX_BIT,
    *vertex_shader_module,
    "main",
    nullptr
  },
  {
    VK_SHADER_STAGE_TESSELLATION_CONTROL_BIT,
    *tessellation_control_shader_module,
    "main",
    nullptr
  },
  {
    VK_SHADER_STAGE_TESSELLATION_EVALUATION_BIT,
    *tessellation_evaluation_shader_module,
    "main",
    nullptr
  },
  {
    VK_SHADER_STAGE_GEOMETRY_BIT,
    *geometry_shader_module,
    "main",
    nullptr
  },
  {
    VK_SHADER_STAGE_FRAGMENT_BIT,
    *fragment_shader_module,
    "main",
    nullptr
  }
};

std::vector<VkPipelineShaderStageCreateInfo> shader_stage_create_infos;
SpecifyPipelineShaderStages( shader_stage_params, shader_stage_create_infos
);
```

Why do we need all five stages? A vertex shader is always required. This time it only reads two input attributes (position and texcoord) and passes it further down the pipeline.

When tessellation is enabled, we need both the control and evaluation shader stages. The tessellation control shader, as the name suggests, controls the tessellation level of processed patches (the amount of generated vertices). In this recipe, we generate vertices based on the distance from the camera: the closer the vertices of a patch are to the camera, the more vertices are generated by the tessellator. This way, the terrain in the distance is simple and doesn't take much processing power to be rendered; but, the closer to the camera, the more complex the terrain becomes.

We can't choose one tessellation level for the whole patch (in this case a triangle). When two neighboring triangles are tessellated with different factors, different number of vertices will be generated on their common edge. Vertices from each triangle will be placed in different locations and they will be offset by different values. This will create holes in our ground:

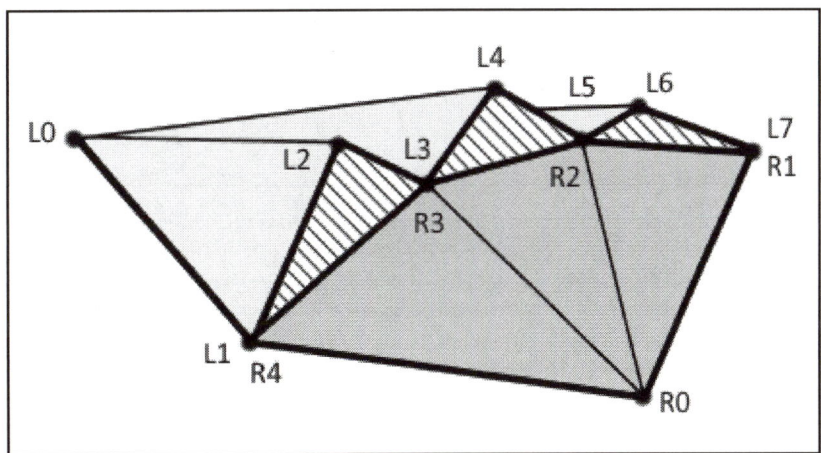

In the preceding image we see two triangles: the left formed from vertices L0-L1-L7, and right formed from vertices R0-R1-R4. The other vertices are generated by the tessellator. Triangles share an edge: L1-L7 or R1-R4 (points L1 and R4 indicate the same vertex; similarly points L7 and R1 indicate the same vertex); but the edge is tessellated with different factors. This causes discontinuities (indicated by stripes) in the surface formed by the two triangles.

Advanced Rendering Techniques

To avoid this problem, we need to calculate a tessellation factor for each triangle edge in such a way that it is fixed across triangles that share the same edge. In this example, we will calculate tessellation factors based on the distance of a vertex from the camera. We will do this for all vertices in a triangle. Then, for a given triangle edge, we will choose a greater tessellation factor that was calculated from one of the edge's vertices:

```
float distances[3];
float factors[3];

for( int i = 0; i < 3; ++i ) {
  float height = texture( ImageSampler, vert_texcoord[i] ).x;
  vec4 position = ModelViewMatrix * (gl_in[i].gl_Position + vec4( 0.0,
  height, 0.0, 0.0 ));
  distances[i] = dot( position, position );
}
factors[0] = min( distances[1], distances[2] );
factors[1] = min( distances[2], distances[0] );
factors[2] = min( distances[0], distances[1] );

gl_TessLevelInner[0] = max( 1.0, 20.0 - factors[0] );
gl_TessLevelOuter[0] = max( 1.0, 20.0 - factors[0] );
gl_TessLevelOuter[1] = max( 1.0, 20.0 - factors[1] );
gl_TessLevelOuter[2] = max( 1.0, 20.0 - factors[2] );
```

In the preceding tessellation control shader code, we calculate a distance (squared) from all vertices to the camera. We need to offset positions by the amount read from the height map, so the whole patch is in the correct place and the distance is properly calculated.

Next, for all triangle edges, we take the smaller distance of edge's two vertices. As we want a tessellation factor to increase with decreasing distance, we need to invert the calculated factor. Here we take a hardcoded value of 20 and subtract a chosen distance value. As we don't want the tessellation factor to be smaller than 1.0, we perform additional clamping.

The tessellation factor calculated like this exaggerates the effect of decreasing the number of generated vertices with increasing distance. This is done on purpose so that we can see how triangles are tessellated and how the number of details increases near the camera. However, in real-life examples we should prepare such a formula so that the effect is barely visible.

Next, a tessellation evaluation shader takes the weights of generated vertices to calculate a valid position of the new vertices. We do the same for texture coordinates, as we need to load height information from the height map:

```
vec4 position = gl_in[0].gl_Position * gl_TessCoord.x +
                gl_in[1].gl_Position * gl_TessCoord.y +
                gl_in[2].gl_Position * gl_TessCoord.z;

vec2 texcoord = tesc_texcoord[0] * gl_TessCoord.x +
                tesc_texcoord[1] * gl_TessCoord.y +
                tesc_texcoord[2] * gl_TessCoord.z;
```

After the position of a new vertex is calculated, we need to offset it, so the vertex is placed at an appropriate height:

```
float height = texture( HeightMap, texcoord ).x;
position.y += height;
gl_Position = position;
```

The tessellation evaluation shader stage is followed by the geometry shader stage. We can omit it but here we use it to calculate the normal vector of the generated triangle. We take one normal vector for all the triangle's vertices, so we will perform a flat shading in this sample.

The normal vector is calculated with the `cross()` function, which takes two vectors and returns a vector that is perpendicular to those provided. We provide vectors forming two edges of a triangle:

```
vec3 v0v1 = gl_in[1].gl_Position.xyz - gl_in[0].gl_Position.xyz;
vec3 v0v2 = gl_in[2].gl_Position.xyz - gl_in[0].gl_Position.xyz;
vec3 normal = normalize( cross( v0v1, v0v2 ) );
```

Finally, the geometry shader calculates the clip space positions of all vertices and emits them:

```
for( int vertex = 0; vertex < 3; ++vertex ) {
  gl_Position = ProjectionMatrix * ModelViewMatrix *
gl_in[vertex].gl_Position;
  geom_height = tese_height[vertex];
  geom_normal = normal;
  EmitVertex();
}

EndPrimitive();
```

Advanced Rendering Techniques

To simplify the recipe, a fragment shader is also simple. It mixes three colors based on the height above ground: green for grass in the lower parts, grey/brown for rocks in the middle, and white for snow in mountain tops. It also performs simple lighting calculations using the diffuse/Lambert light model.

The preceding shaders form a graphics pipeline used to draw a tessellated terrain. During pipeline creation we must remember to think about primitive topology. Because of the enabled tessellation stages, we need to use a VK_PRIMITIVE_TOPOLOGY_PATCH_LIST topology. We also need to provide a tessellation state during pipeline creation. As we want to operate on triangles, we specify that a patch contains three control points:

```
VkPipelineInputAssemblyStateCreateInfo input_assembly_state_create_info;
SpecifyPipelineInputAssemblyState( VK_PRIMITIVE_TOPOLOGY_PATCH_LIST, false,
input_assembly_state_create_info );
VkPipelineTessellationStateCreateInfo tessellation_state_create_info;
SpecifyPipelineTessellationState( 3, tessellation_state_create_info );
```

The remaining parameters used for pipeline creation are defined in the usual way. We also don't need to do anything special during rendering. We just draw a plane with the preceding graphics pipeline bound, and we should see a geometry resembling a terrain. We can see examples of results generated with this recipe in the following images:

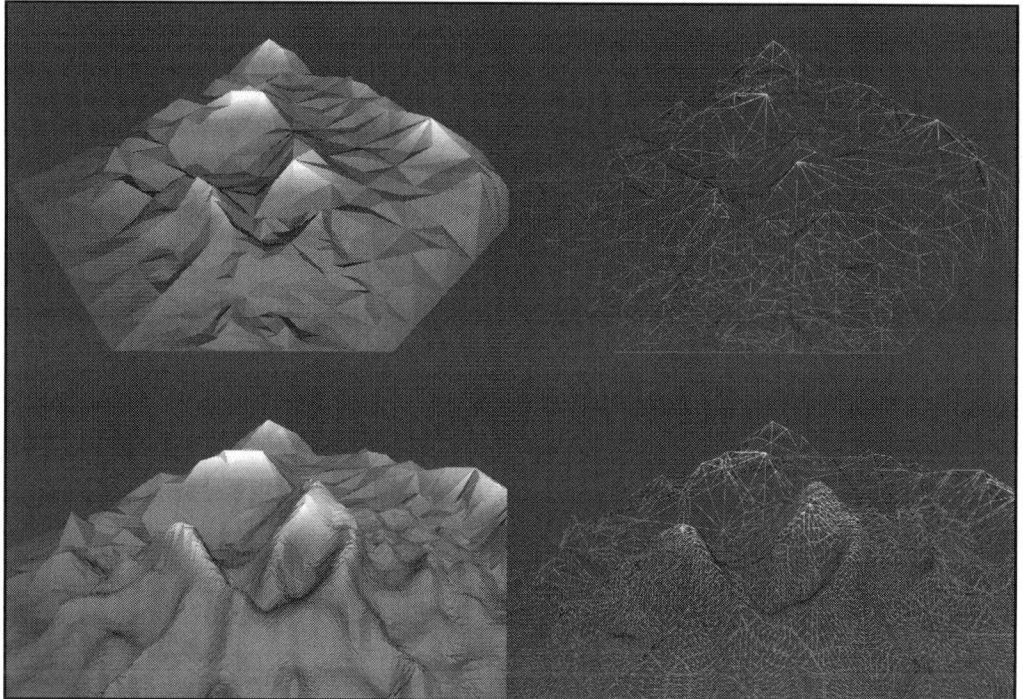

See also

- In `Chapter` 4, *Resources and Memory*, see the *Creating a buffer* recipe
- In `Chapter` 5, *Descriptor Sets*, see the following recipes:
    - *Creating a combined image sampler*
    - *Creating a uniform buffer*
    - *Creating a descriptor set layout*
    - *Allocating descriptor sets*
    - *Updating descriptor sets*
- In `Chapter` 7, *Shaders*, see the following recipes:
    - *Writing tessellation control shaders*
    - *Writing tessellation evaluation shaders*
    - *Writing geometry shaders*
- In `Chapter` 8, *Graphics and Compute Pipelines*, see the following recipes:
    - *Creating a shader module*
    - *Specifying the pipeline input assembly state*
    - *Specifying the pipeline tessellation state*
    - *Creating a graphics pipeline*
- In `Chapter` 10, *Helper Recipes*, see the following recipes:
    - *Loading texture data from a file*
    - *Loading a 3D model from an OBJ file*
- In `Chapter` 11, *Lighting*, see the *Rendering a geometry with a vertex diffuse lighting* recipe

Rendering a full-screen quad for post-processing

Image processing is another class of techniques commonly used in 3D graphics. Human eyes perceive the world around us in a way that is almost impossible to simulate directly. There are many effects which cannot be displayed by just drawing a geometry. For example, bright areas seem larger than dark areas (this is usually referred to as bloom); objects seen at our focus point are sharp, but the further from the focus distance, these objects become more fuzzy or blurred (we call this effect a depth of field); color can be perceived differently during the day and at night, when with very little lighting, everything seems more blueish.

Advanced Rendering Techniques

These phenomena are easily implemented as post-processing effects. We render the scene normally into an image. After that, we perform another rendering, this time taking the data stored in an image and processing it according to a chosen algorithm. To render an image, we need to place it on a quad that covers the whole scene. Such a geometry is usually called a fullscreen quad.

How to do it...

1. Prepare vertex data for the quad's geometry. Use the following values for four vertices (add texture coordinates if needed):
   - `{ -1.0f, -1.0f, 0.0f }` for top left vertex
   - `{ -1.0f, 1.0f, 0.0f }` for bottom left vertex
   - `{ 1.0f, -1.0f, 0.0f }` for top right vertex
   - `{ 1.0f, 1.0f, 0.0f }` for bottom right vertex
2. Create a buffer that will serve as a vertex buffer. Allocate a memory object and bind it to the buffer. Upload vertex data to the buffer using a staging resource (refer to the *Creating a buffer, Allocating and binding memory object to a buffer,* and *Using staging buffer to update buffer with a device-local memory bound* recipes from `Chapter 4`, *Resources and Memory*).
3. Create a combined image sampler. Remember to provide valid uses that depend on the way the image will be accessed during rendering and post-processing: rendering a scene into an image requires a `VK_IMAGE_USAGE_COLOR_ATTACHMENT_BIT`; sampling an image (reading data using a sampler) requires a `VK_IMAGE_USAGE_SAMPLED_BIT`; for image load/stores we must provide a `VK_IMAGE_USAGE_STORAGE_BIT`; other uses may also be necessary (refer to the *Creating a combined image sampler* recipe from `Chapter 5`, *Descriptor Sets*).
4. Create a descriptor set layout with one combined image sampler. Create a descriptor pool and allocate a descriptor set from it using the created layout. Update the descriptor set with the image view's and sampler handles. Do it each time an application window is resized and an image is recreated (refer to the *Creating a descriptor set layout, Creating a descriptor pool, Allocating descriptor sets,* and *Updating descriptor sets* recipes from `Chapter 5`, *Descriptor Sets*).

5. If we want to access many different image coordinates, create a separate, dedicated render pass with one color attachment and at least one subpass (refer to the *Specifying attachments descriptions*, *Specifying subpass descriptions*, *Specifying dependencies between subpasses*, and *Creating a render pass* recipes from Chapter 6, *Render Passes and Framebuffers*).

6. Create a shader module with a SPIR-V assembly for a vertex shader created from the following GLSL code (refer to the *Creating a shader module* recipe from Chapter 8, *Graphics and Compute Pipelines*):

```
#version 450
layout( location = 0 ) in vec4 app_position;
void main() {
  gl_Position = app_position;
}
```

7. Create a shader module for a fragment shader created from the following GLSL code:

```
#version 450
layout( set = 0, binding = 0 ) uniform sampler2D Image;
layout( location = 0 ) out vec4 frag_color;
void main() {
  vec4 color = vec4( 0.5 );
  color -= texture( Image, gl_FragCoord.xy + vec2( -1.0, 0.0 ) );
  color += texture( Image, gl_FragCoord.xy + vec2(  1.0, 0.0 ) );

  color -= texture( Image, gl_FragCoord.xy + vec2(  0.0, -1.0 ) );
  color += texture( Image, gl_FragCoord.xy + vec2(  0.0,  1.0 ) );

  frag_color = abs( 0.5 - color );
}
```

8. Create a graphics pipeline using the preceding shader modules. It must read one vertex attribute with vertex positions (and potentially a second attribute with texture coordinates). Use a `VK_PRIMITIVE_TOPOLOGY_TRIANGLE_STRIP` topology and disable face culling (refer to the *Specifying pipeline vertex input state*, *Specifying pipeline input assembly state*, *Specifying pipeline rasterization state*, and *Creating a graphics pipeline* recipes from `Chapter 8`, *Graphics and Compute Pipelines*).
9. Render a scene into the created image. Next, start another render pass and draw the full-screen quad using the prepared graphics pipeline (refer to the Beginning a render pass and Ending a render pass recipes from `Chapter 6`, *Render Passes and Framebuffers*, to the *Binding descriptor sets* recipe from `Chapter 5`, *Descriptor Sets*, and to the *Binding vertex buffers* and *Drawing a geometry* recipes from `Chapter 9`, *Command Recording and Drawing*).

How it works...

Image post-processing can be performed using compute shaders. However, when we want to display an image on screen, we must use a swapchain. Storing data in an image from within shaders requires images to be created with the storage image use. Unfortunately, such usage may not be supported on swapchain images, so it would require the creation of additional, intermediate resources, which further increase the complexity of a code.

Using a graphics pipeline allows us to process image data inside fragment shaders and store the results in color attachments. Such usage is mandatory for swapchain images, so this way feels more natural for image processing implemented with the Vulkan API. On the other hand, the graphics pipeline requires us to draw a geometry, so we need not only vertex data, and vertex and fragment shaders, but also a render pass and a framebuffer as well. That's why using compute shaders may be more efficient. So, everything depends on the features supported by the graphics hardware (available swapchain image usages) and the given situation.

In this recipe, we will present the method to draw a full-screen quad during an image postprocessing phase. First, we need the vertex data itself. It can be prepared directly in the clip space. This way we can create a much simpler vertex shader and avoid multiplying the vertex position by a projection matrix. After the perspective division, for the vertices to fit into a view, values stored in x and y components of their positions must fit into a <-1, 1> range (inclusive) and a value in a z component must be inside a <0, 1> range. So, if we want to cover the whole screen, we need the following set of vertices:

```
std::vector<float> vertices = {
  -1.0f, -1.0f, 0.0f,
  -1.0f,  1.0f, 0.0f,
   1.0f, -1.0f, 0.0f,
   1.0f,  1.0f, 0.0f,
};
```

We can add normalized texture coordinates if needed or we can rely on the built-in gl_FragCoord value (when writing GLSL shaders), which contain screen coordinates of a currently processed shader. When we use input attachments, we even don't need texture coordinates, as we can access only the sample associated with the currently processed fragment.

Vertex data needs to be stored in a buffer serving as a vertex buffer. So we need to create it, allocate a memory object and bind it to the buffer and upload vertex data to the buffer:

```
InitVkDestroyer( LogicalDevice, VertexBuffer );
if( !CreateBuffer( *LogicalDevice, sizeof( vertices[0] ) * vertices.size(),
VK_BUFFER_USAGE_TRANSFER_DST_BIT | VK_BUFFER_USAGE_VERTEX_BUFFER_BIT,
*VertexBuffer ) ) {
  return false;
}

InitVkDestroyer( LogicalDevice, BufferMemory );
if( !AllocateAndBindMemoryObjectToBuffer( PhysicalDevice, *LogicalDevice,
*VertexBuffer, VK_MEMORY_PROPERTY_DEVICE_LOCAL_BIT, *BufferMemory ) ) {
  return false;
}

if( !UseStagingBufferToUpdateBufferWithDeviceLocalMemoryBound(
PhysicalDevice, *LogicalDevice, sizeof( vertices[0] ) * vertices.size(),
&vertices[0], *VertexBuffer, 0, 0,
  VK_ACCESS_VERTEX_ATTRIBUTE_READ_BIT, VK_PIPELINE_STAGE_TOP_OF_PIPE_BIT,
VK_PIPELINE_STAGE_VERTEX_INPUT_BIT, GraphicsQueue.Handle,
FrameResources.front().CommandBuffer, {} ) ) {
  return false;
```

Advanced Rendering Techniques

Next, we need a way to access texel data inside the fragment shader. We can use an input attachment if we want to access data stored in a color attachment from any of the previous subpasses in the same render pass. We can use a storage image, separate the sampler and the sampled image or a combined image sampler. The latter is used in this recipe. To simplify this recipe and the code, we read texture data from a file. But usually we will have an image into which the scene will be rendered:

```
int width = 1;
int height = 1;
std::vector<unsigned char> image_data;
if( !LoadTextureDataFromFile( "Data/Textures/sunset.jpg", 4, image_data,
&width, &height ) ) {
  return false;
}

InitVkDestroyer( LogicalDevice, Sampler );
InitVkDestroyer( LogicalDevice, Image );
InitVkDestroyer( LogicalDevice, ImageMemory );
InitVkDestroyer( LogicalDevice, ImageView );
if( !CreateCombinedImageSampler( PhysicalDevice, *LogicalDevice,
VK_IMAGE_TYPE_2D, VK_FORMAT_R8G8B8A8_UNORM, { (uint32_t)width,
(uint32_t)height, 1 },
  1, 1, VK_IMAGE_USAGE_SAMPLED_BIT | VK_IMAGE_USAGE_TRANSFER_DST_BIT,
VK_IMAGE_VIEW_TYPE_2D, VK_IMAGE_ASPECT_COLOR_BIT, VK_FILTER_NEAREST,
  VK_FILTER_NEAREST, VK_SAMPLER_MIPMAP_MODE_NEAREST,
VK_SAMPLER_ADDRESS_MODE_CLAMP_TO_EDGE,
VK_SAMPLER_ADDRESS_MODE_CLAMP_TO_EDGE,
  VK_SAMPLER_ADDRESS_MODE_CLAMP_TO_EDGE, 0.0f, false, 1.0f, false,
VK_COMPARE_OP_ALWAYS, 0.0f, 1.0f, VK_BORDER_COLOR_FLOAT_OPAQUE_BLACK, true,
  *Sampler, *Image, *ImageMemory, *ImageView ) ) {
  return false;
}

VkImageSubresourceLayers image_subresource_layer = {
  VK_IMAGE_ASPECT_COLOR_BIT,
  0,
  0,
  1
};
if( !UseStagingBufferToUpdateImageWithDeviceLocalMemoryBound(
PhysicalDevice, *LogicalDevice,
static_cast<VkDeviceSize>(image_data.size()),
  &image_data[0], *Image, image_subresource_layer, { 0, 0, 0 }, {
(uint32_t)width, (uint32_t)height, 1 }, VK_IMAGE_LAYOUT_UNDEFINED,
  VK_IMAGE_LAYOUT_SHADER_READ_ONLY_OPTIMAL, 0, VK_ACCESS_SHADER_READ_BIT,
VK_IMAGE_ASPECT_COLOR_BIT, VK_PIPELINE_STAGE_TOP_OF_PIPE_BIT,
  VK_PIPELINE_STAGE_FRAGMENT_SHADER_BIT, GraphicsQueue.Handle,
```

```
    FrameResources.front().CommandBuffer, {} ) ) {
      return false;
    }
```

In the preceding code, we create a combined image sampler and specify that we will access it with unnormalized texture coordinates. Usually we provide coordinates in the <0.0, 1.0> range (inclusive). This way we don't need to worry about the image's size. On the other hand, for post-processing we usually want to address the texture image using screen space coordinates, and that's when unnormalized texture coordinates are used--they correspond to the image's dimensions.

To access an image, we also need a descriptor set. We don't need a uniform buffer as we don't transform the geometry-drawn vertices are already in the correct space (the clip space). Before we can allocate a descriptor set, we create a layout with one combined image sampler accessed in a fragment shader stage. After that, a pool is created and one descriptor set is allocated from the pool:

```
    VkDescriptorSetLayoutBinding descriptor_set_layout_binding = {
      0,
      VK_DESCRIPTOR_TYPE_COMBINED_IMAGE_SAMPLER,
      1,
      VK_SHADER_STAGE_FRAGMENT_BIT,
      nullptr
    };
    InitVkDestroyer( LogicalDevice, DescriptorSetLayout );
    if( !CreateDescriptorSetLayout( *LogicalDevice, {
    descriptor_set_layout_binding }, *DescriptorSetLayout ) ) {
      return false;
    }

    VkDescriptorPoolSize descriptor_pool_size = {
      VK_DESCRIPTOR_TYPE_COMBINED_IMAGE_SAMPLER,
      1
    };
    InitVkDestroyer( LogicalDevice, DescriptorPool );
    if( !CreateDescriptorPool( *LogicalDevice, false, 1, { descriptor_pool_size
    }, *DescriptorPool ) ) {
      return false;
    }

    if( !AllocateDescriptorSets( *LogicalDevice, *DescriptorPool, {
    *DescriptorSetLayout }, DescriptorSets ) ) {
      return false;
    }

    ImageDescriptorInfo image_descriptor_update = {
      DescriptorSets[0],
```

```
    0,
    0,
    VK_DESCRIPTOR_TYPE_COMBINED_IMAGE_SAMPLER,
    {
      {
        *Sampler,
        *ImageView,
        VK_IMAGE_LAYOUT_SHADER_READ_ONLY_OPTIMAL
      }
    }
  };

  UpdateDescriptorSets( *LogicalDevice, { image_descriptor_update }, {}, {},
  {} );
```

In the preceding code we also update the descriptor set with the handles of created sampler and image view. Unfortunately, the image into which we render a scene will usually fit into a screen. This means that we must recreate it when the size of an application's window is changed and, to do that, we must destroy the old image and create a new one with new dimensions. After such an operation we must update the descriptor set again with the handle of the new image (the sampler doesn't need to be recreated). So we must remember to update the descriptor set each time the application window size is changed.

One last thing is the creation of a graphics pipeline. It uses only two shader stages: vertex and fragment. The number of attributes fetched by the vertex shader depend on whether we need texture coordinates (and other dedicated attributes) or not. The full-screen quad's geometry should be drawn using a `VK_PRIMITIVE_TOPOLOGY_TRIANGLE_STRIP` topology. We also don't need any blending.

The most important part of the post-processing is performed inside the fragment shader. The work to be done depends on the technique we want to implement. In this recipe, we present an edge detection algorithm:

```
vec4 color = vec4( 0.5 );

color -= texture( Image, gl_FragCoord.xy + vec2( -1.0,  0.0 ) );
color += texture( Image, gl_FragCoord.xy + vec2(  1.0,  0.0 ) );

color -= texture( Image, gl_FragCoord.xy + vec2(  0.0, -1.0 ) );
color += texture( Image, gl_FragCoord.xy + vec2(  0.0,  1.0 ) );

frag_color = abs( 0.5 - color );
```

In the preceding fragment shader code, we sample four values around the fragment being processed. We take a negated value from one sample to the left and add a value read from one sample to the right. This way we know the difference between samples in a horizontal direction. When the difference is big, we know there is an edge.

We do the same operation for a vertical direction to detect horizontal lines too (the vertical difference, or a gradient, is used to detect horizontal edges; the horizontal gradient allows us to detect vertical edges). After that we store a value in the output variable. We additionally take the `abs()` value, but this is done only for visualization purposes.

In the preceding fragment shader, we access multiple texture coordinates. This can be done on combined image samplers (input attachments allow us to access only a single coordinate associated with a fragment being processed). However, to bind an image to a descriptor set as a resource other than an input attachment, we must end the current render pass and start another one. In a given render pass, images cannot be used for attachments and for any other non-attachment purpose at the same time.

Using the preceding setup, we should see the following result (on the right) with the original image seen on the left:

See also

- In Chapter 4, *Resources and Memory*, see the following recipes:
    - *Creating a buffer*
    - *Allocating and binding a memory object to a buffer*
    - *Using the staging buffer to update a buffer with a device-local memory bound*

Advanced Rendering Techniques

- In Chapter 5, *Descriptor Sets*, see the following recipes:
    - *Creating a combined image sampler*
    - *Creating a descriptor set layout*
    - *Allocating descriptor sets*
    - *Binding descriptor sets*
    - *Updating descriptor sets*
- In Chapter 6, *Render Passes and Framebuffers*, see the following recipes:
    - *Beginning a render pass*
    - *Ending a render pass*
- In Chapter 8, *Graphics and Compute Pipelines*, see the following recipes:
    - *Creating a shader module*
    - *Specifying the pipeline vertex input state*
    - *Specifying the pipeline input assembly state*
    - *Specifying the pipeline rasterization state*
    - *Creating a graphics pipeline*
- In Chapter 9, *Command Recording and Drawing*, see the following recipes:
    - *Binding vertex buffers*
    - *Drawing a geometry*

Using input attachments for a color correction post-process effect

There are many various post-process techniques used in 3D applications. Color correction is one of them. This is relatively simple, but it can give impressive results and greatly improve the look and feel of a rendered scene. Color correction can change the mood of the scene and induce the desired feelings for the users.

Usually, a color correction effect requires us to read data of a single, currently processed sample. Thanks to this property, we can implement this effect using input attachments. This allows us to perform post-processing inside the same render pass in which the whole scene is rendered, thus improving the performance of our application.

The following is an example of an image generated with this recipe:

How to do it...

1. Create a fullscreen quad with additional resources required during postprocessing phase (refer to the *Rendering a full-screen quad for post processing* recipe).
2. Create a descriptor set layout with one input attachment accessed in a fragment shader stage. Allocate a descriptor set using the prepared layout (refer to the *Creating a descriptor set layout* and *Allocating descriptor sets* recipes from `Chapter 5, Descriptor Sets`).
3. Create a 2D image (along with a memory object and an image view) into which the scene will be drawn. Specify not only a `VK_IMAGE_USAGE_COLOR_ATTACHMENT_BIT` usage, but also a `VK_IMAGE_USAGE_INPUT_ATTACHMENT_BIT` usage during image creation. Recreate the image each time the application's window is resized (refer to the *Creating an input attachment* recipe from `Chapter 5, Descriptor Sets`).

Advanced Rendering Techniques

4. Update the descriptor set with input attachment using the handle of the created image. Do it each time an application window is resized and an image is recreated (refer to the *Updating descriptor sets* recipe from Chapter 5, *Descriptor Sets*).
5. Prepare all the resource required to normally render the scene. When creating a render pass used for rendering the scene, add one additional subpass at the end of the render pass. Specify the attachment used in previous subpasses as a color attachment to be an input attachment in the additional subpass. A swapchain image should be used as a color attachment in the additional subpass (refer to the *Specifying subpass descriptions* and *Creating a render pass* recipes from Chapter 6, *Render Passes and Framebuffers*).
6. Create a shader module with a vertex shader created from the following GLSL code (refer to the *Creating a shader module* recipe from Chapter 8, *Graphics and Compute Pipelines*):

```
#version 450
layout( location = 0 ) in vec4 app_position;
void main() {
  gl_Position = app_position;
}
```

7. Create a shader module with a fragment shader created from the following GLSL code:

```
#version 450
layout( input_attachment_index = 0, set = 0, binding = 0 )
uniform subpassInput InputAttachment;
layout( location = 0 ) out vec4 frag_color;

void main() {
  vec4 color = subpassLoad( InputAttachment );
  float grey = dot( color.rgb, vec3( 0.2, 0.7, 0.1 ) );
  frag_color = grey * vec4( 1.5, 1.0, 0.5, 1.0 );
}
```

8. Create a graphics pipeline used for drawing a post-process phase. Use the preceding vertex and fragment shader modules. Prepare the rest of the pipeline parameters according to the *Rendering a fullscreen quad for postprocessing* recipe.
9. In each frame of animation, draw the scene normally into a created image, then progress to the next subpass (refer to the *Progressing to the next subpass* recipe from `Chapter 6`, *Render Passes and Framebuffers*). Bind the created graphics pipeline used for post-processing, bind the descriptor set with the input attachment, bind the vertex buffer with full-screen quad data, and draw the full-screen quad (refer to the *Binding descriptor sets* recipe from `Chapter 5`, *Descriptor Sets*, to the *Binding a pipeline object* recipe from `Chapter 8`, *Graphics and Compute Pipelines*, and to the *Binding vertex buffers* and *Drawing a geometry* recipes from `Chapter 9`, *Command Recording and Drawing*).

How it works...

Creating a postprocessing effect that is rendered inside the same render pass as the scene is performed in two steps.

In the first step, we need to prepare resources for the base scene: its geometry, textures, descriptor sets, and pipeline objects, among others. In the second step, we do the same for the full-screen quad, as described in the *Rendering a fullscreen quad for postprocessing* recipe.

The two most important resources prepared solely for the post-processing phase are an image and a graphics pipeline. The image will serve as a color attachment when we are rendering the scene in a normal way. We just render the scene into the image instead of rendering it into a swapchain image. The image must serve both as a color attachment during scene rendering, but also as an input attachment during post-processing. We must also remember to recreate it when the size of the application's window is changed:

```
InitVkDestroyer( LogicalDevice, SceneImage );
InitVkDestroyer( LogicalDevice, SceneImageMemory );
InitVkDestroyer( LogicalDevice, SceneImageView );
if( !CreateInputAttachment( PhysicalDevice, *LogicalDevice,
VK_IMAGE_TYPE_2D, Swapchain.Format, { Swapchain.Size.width,
Swapchain.Size.height, 1 }, VK_IMAGE_USAGE_COLOR_ATTACHMENT_BIT |
VK_IMAGE_USAGE_INPUT_ATTACHMENT_BIT, VK_IMAGE_VIEW_TYPE_2D,
VK_IMAGE_ASPECT_COLOR_BIT, *SceneImage, *SceneImageMemory, *SceneImageView
) ) {
return false;
}
```

Advanced Rendering Techniques

Accessing an image as an input attachment requires us to use a descriptor set. It must contain at least our input attachment, so we need to create a proper layout. Input attachments can be accessed only inside fragment shaders, so the creation of a descriptor set layout, a descriptor pool, and an allocation of a descriptor set may look like this:

```
std::vector<VkDescriptorSetLayoutBinding>
scene_descriptor_set_layout_bindings = {
  {
    0,
    VK_DESCRIPTOR_TYPE_INPUT_ATTACHMENT,
    1,
    VK_SHADER_STAGE_FRAGMENT_BIT,
    nullptr
  }
};
InitVkDestroyer( LogicalDevice, PostprocessDescriptorSetLayout );
if( !CreateDescriptorSetLayout( *LogicalDevice,
scene_descriptor_set_layout_bindings, *PostprocessDescriptorSetLayout ) ) {
  return false;
}

std::vector<VkDescriptorPoolSize> scene_descriptor_pool_sizes = {
  {
    VK_DESCRIPTOR_TYPE_INPUT_ATTACHMENT,
    1
  }
};
InitVkDestroyer( LogicalDevice, PostprocessDescriptorPool );
if( !CreateDescriptorPool( *LogicalDevice, false, 1,
scene_descriptor_pool_sizes, *PostprocessDescriptorPool ) ) {
  return false;
}

if( !AllocateDescriptorSets( *LogicalDevice, *PostprocessDescriptorPool, {
*PostprocessDescriptorSetLayout }, PostprocessDescriptorSets ) ) {
  return false;
}
```

We must also update the descriptor set with the handle of our color attachment/input attachment image. As the image gets recreated when the size of the application's window is changed, we must update the descriptor too:

```
ImageDescriptorInfo scene_image_descriptor_update = {
  PostprocessDescriptorSets[0],
  0,
  0,
  VK_DESCRIPTOR_TYPE_INPUT_ATTACHMENT,
```

```
    {
      {
        VK_NULL_HANDLE,
        *SceneImageView,
        VK_IMAGE_LAYOUT_SHADER_READ_ONLY_OPTIMAL
      }
    }
};

UpdateDescriptorSets( *LogicalDevice, { scene_image_descriptor_update },
{}, {}, {} );
```

The next thing we need to describe is the preparation of a render pass. In this recipe the render pass is common for both the scene rendering and the post-processing phase. The scene is rendered in its own, dedicated subpass (or subpasses). The post-processing phase adds an additional subpass for rendering a full-screen quad.

Usually, we define two render pass attachments: a color attachment (a swapchain image) and a depth attachment (an image with a depth format). This time we need three attachments: the first one is a color attachment for which the created image will be used; the depth attachment is the same as usual; and the third attachment is also a color attachment, for which a swapchain image will be used. This way, the scene is rendered normally into two (color and depth attachments). Then, the first attachment is used as an input attachment during post-processing; and the full-screen quad is rendered into the second color attachment (a swapchain image) so the final image appears on screen.

The following code sets up the render pass attachment:

```
std::vector<VkAttachmentDescription> attachment_descriptions = {
  {
    0,
    Swapchain.Format,
    VK_SAMPLE_COUNT_1_BIT,
    VK_ATTACHMENT_LOAD_OP_CLEAR,
    VK_ATTACHMENT_STORE_OP_DONT_CARE,
    VK_ATTACHMENT_LOAD_OP_DONT_CARE,
    VK_ATTACHMENT_STORE_OP_DONT_CARE,
    VK_IMAGE_LAYOUT_UNDEFINED,
    VK_IMAGE_LAYOUT_SHADER_READ_ONLY_OPTIMAL
  },
  {
    0,
    DepthFormat,
    VK_SAMPLE_COUNT_1_BIT,
    VK_ATTACHMENT_LOAD_OP_CLEAR,
    VK_ATTACHMENT_STORE_OP_DONT_CARE,
    VK_ATTACHMENT_LOAD_OP_DONT_CARE,
```

Advanced Rendering Techniques

```
    VK_ATTACHMENT_STORE_OP_DONT_CARE,
    VK_IMAGE_LAYOUT_UNDEFINED,
    VK_IMAGE_LAYOUT_DEPTH_STENCIL_ATTACHMENT_OPTIMAL
  },
  {
    0,
    Swapchain.Format,
    VK_SAMPLE_COUNT_1_BIT,
    VK_ATTACHMENT_LOAD_OP_DONT_CARE,
    VK_ATTACHMENT_STORE_OP_STORE,
    VK_ATTACHMENT_LOAD_OP_DONT_CARE,
    VK_ATTACHMENT_STORE_OP_DONT_CARE,
    VK_IMAGE_LAYOUT_UNDEFINED,
    VK_IMAGE_LAYOUT_PRESENT_SRC_KHR
  }
};
```

The render pass has two subpasses defined as follows:

```
VkAttachmentReference depth_attachment = {
  1,
  VK_IMAGE_LAYOUT_DEPTH_STENCIL_ATTACHMENT_OPTIMAL
};

std::vector<SubpassParameters> subpass_parameters = {
  {
    VK_PIPELINE_BIND_POINT_GRAPHICS,
    {},
    {
      {
        0,
        VK_IMAGE_LAYOUT_COLOR_ATTACHMENT_OPTIMAL,
      }
    },
    {},
    &depth_attachment,
    {}
  },
  {
    VK_PIPELINE_BIND_POINT_GRAPHICS,
    {
      {
        0,
        VK_IMAGE_LAYOUT_SHADER_READ_ONLY_OPTIMAL,
      }
    },
    {
      {
```

```
                2,
                VK_IMAGE_LAYOUT_COLOR_ATTACHMENT_OPTIMAL,
            }
        },
        {},
        nullptr,
        {}
    }
};
```

We also can't forget about the render pass subpass dependencies. They are very important here as they synchronize the two subpasses. We can't read data from a texture until the data is written into it, so we need dependencies between the 0 and the 1 subpass (for the image serving as color and input attachment. Similarly, dependencies are needed for a swapchain image:

```
std::vector<VkSubpassDependency> subpass_dependencies = {
    {
        0,
        1,
        VK_PIPELINE_STAGE_COLOR_ATTACHMENT_OUTPUT_BIT,
        VK_PIPELINE_STAGE_FRAGMENT_SHADER_BIT,
        VK_ACCESS_COLOR_ATTACHMENT_WRITE_BIT,
        VK_ACCESS_INPUT_ATTACHMENT_READ_BIT,
        VK_DEPENDENCY_BY_REGION_BIT
    },
    {
        VK_SUBPASS_EXTERNAL,
        1,
        VK_PIPELINE_STAGE_TOP_OF_PIPE_BIT,
        VK_PIPELINE_STAGE_COLOR_ATTACHMENT_OUTPUT_BIT,
        VK_ACCESS_MEMORY_READ_BIT,
        VK_ACCESS_COLOR_ATTACHMENT_WRITE_BIT,
        VK_DEPENDENCY_BY_REGION_BIT
    },
    {
        1,
        VK_SUBPASS_EXTERNAL,
        VK_PIPELINE_STAGE_COLOR_ATTACHMENT_OUTPUT_BIT,
        VK_PIPELINE_STAGE_TOP_OF_PIPE_BIT,
        VK_ACCESS_COLOR_ATTACHMENT_WRITE_BIT,
        VK_ACCESS_MEMORY_READ_BIT,
        VK_DEPENDENCY_BY_REGION_BIT
    }
};
```

The graphics pipeline used during post-processing phase is a standard one. Only two things are different: the graphics pipeline is used inside the subpass with index 1 (not 0 as in other recipes--the scene is rendered in the subpass 0); and the fragment shader loads color data, not from the combined image sampler, but from the input attachment. The input attachment inside the fragment shader is defined as follows:

```
layout( input_attachment_index = 0, set = 0, binding = 0 ) uniform
subpassInput InputAttachment;
```

We read data from it using the `subpassLoad()` function. It takes only the uniform variable. Texture coordinates are unnecessary, because through an input attachment we can read data only from the coordinate associated with the fragment being processed.

```
vec4 color = subpassLoad( InputAttachment );
```

The fragment shader then takes the loaded color, calculates a sepia color from it, and stores it in an output variable (a color attachment). All this combined should lead us to create the following results. On the left we see the scene rendered normally. On the right we see a post-processing effect applied:

See also

- In Chapter 5, *Descriptor Sets*, see the following recipes:
    - *Creating an input attachment*
    - *Creating a descriptor set layout*
    - *Allocating descriptor sets*
    - *Updating descriptor sets*
    - *Binding descriptor sets*
- In Chapter 6, *Render Passes and Framebuffers*, see the following recipes:
    - *Specifying subpass descriptions*
    - *Creating a render pass*
    - *Progressing to the next subpass*
- In Chapter 8, *Graphics and Compute Pipelines*, see the following recipes:
    - *Creating a shader module*
    - *Binding a pipeline object*
- In Chapter 9, *Command Recording and Drawing*, see the following recipes:
    - *Binding vertex buffers*
    - *Drawing a geometry*
- The recipe *Rendering a full-screen quad for post-processing*, in this chapter

Index

2

2D image
  creating 199, 201
2D view
  creating 199, 201

3

3D model
  loading, from OBJ file 526, 527

A

application
  waiting, for all submitted commands to finish 156, 157
  waiting, until commands submitted to queue are finished 155
attachments 259
attachments descriptions
  specifying 292
available device extensions
  checking 40
available Instance extensions
  checking 27
available physical devices
  enumerating 37, 38
available queue families
  checking 44, 45, 47
available queue properties
  checking 44, 45, 47

B

biding 234
billboards
  drawing, geometry shaders used 607, 608, 609, 610, 611, 613, 614
blend constants 406

blend constants states
  setting, dynamically 468
Blinn-Phong model
  about 552
  ambient 552
  diffuse 552
  emissive 552
  specular 552
buffer memory barrier
  setting 172, 173, 174, 175
buffer view
  creating 178, 179
  destroying 228, 229
buffers
  about 164
  creating 165, 166, 167
  data, copying between 207, 208, 209
  destroying 231
  memory object, allocating to 168, 169, 170, 171
  memory object, binding to 168, 169, 170, 171
  VK_BUFFER_USAGE_INDEX_BUFFER_BIT 166
  VK_BUFFER_USAGE_INDIRECT_BUFFER_BIT 166
  VK_BUFFER_USAGE_STORAGE_BUFFER_BIT 166
  VK_BUFFER_USAGE_STORAGE_TEXEL_BUFFER_BIT 166
  VK_BUFFER_USAGE_TRANSFER_DST_BIT 166
  VK_BUFFER_USAGE_TRANSFER_SRC_BIT 166
  VK_BUFFER_USAGE_UNIFORM_BUFFER_BIT 166
  VK_BUFFER_USAGE_UNIFORM_TEXEL_BUFFER_BIT 166
  VK_BUFFER_USAGE_VERTEX_BUFFER_BIT 166

C

color correction post-process effect
  input attachments, using for 652, 653, 654, 655, 656, 660
color image
  creating 450, 451, 452
combined image sampler
  creating 241, 242, 243
command buffer recording operation
  beginning 131, 132, 133, 134
  ending 135, 136
command buffers
  about 126
  allocating 129, 130, 131
  freeing 160, 161
  primary command buffers 130
  processing, checking 153
  recording 478, 479, 481, 482, 483, 484, 486
  recording, on multiple threads 487, 488, 490, 491
  resetting 136, 137
  secondary command buffers 130
  submitting, to queue 147, 148, 149, 150
  synchronizing 151
command pool
  creating 126, 127, 128
  destroying 161, 162
  resetting 137, 138
compute pipeline
  creating 427, 428, 429
  used, for drawing particles 615, 616, 625, 626
compute queues
  logical devices, creating with 63, 64, 65
compute shaders
  writing 351, 352, 353
compute work
  dispatching 475, 476
Computer Aided Design (CAD) 521
concurrent access 167
cosine law 535
CUBEMAP view
  layered 2D image, creating with 202, 203
cubemaps
  about 599
  used, for drawing reflective/refractive geometry 570, 571, 572, 574, 575, 577, 579, 580

D

data
  copying, between buffers 207, 208, 209
  copying, from buffer to image 209, 210, 211, 212
  copying, from image to buffer 213, 214, 216
dependencies
  specifying, between subpasses 300, 301
depth bias 405
depth bias states
  setting, dynamically 467
depth bounds 405
depth-stencil image
  clearing 452, 454
descriptor pool
  creating 266
  destroying 288
  resetting 286, 287
descriptor set layout
  creating 264, 265
  destroying 289
descriptor sets
  allocating 268, 270
  binding 277, 278, 279
  freeing 285, 286
  updating 272, 273, 274, 275, 277
descriptors
  about 234
  creating, with texture 279, 280, 281, 282
  creating, with uniform buffer 279, 280, 281, 282
device queue
  obtaining 61, 62, 63
device-level functions
  about 25
  loading 56, 57, 59, 60
device-local memory 201, 204
diffuse lighting 535

E

exclusive sharing mode 167, 173

F

fence
  creating 141, 142, 143
  destroying 157, 158
  resetting 145, 146
  waiting for 143, 144, 145
file
  texture data, loading from 522, 524, 525
first-person perspective (FPP) 502
format of swapchain images
  selecting 101, 102, 103, 104
fragment shaders
  writing 348, 350, 358, 359
fragment specular lighting
  geometry, rendering with 551, 552, 553, 554, 555, 556
framebuffer
  creating 307, 308, 309
  destroying 328
  preparing, with color and depth attachments 317, 318, 319, 320
full-screen quad
  rendering, for post-processing 644, 646, 647, 648, 651
functions
  loading, exported from Vulkan Loader library 22, 23

G

geometry shaders
  logical devices, creating with 63, 64, 65
  polygon normals, displaying with 362, 363, 364, 365, 366, 367
  used, for drawing billboards 607, 608, 609, 610, 611, 613, 614
  writing 344, 345, 346, 347
geometry
  about 55
  drawing 470, 471
  rendering, with fragment specular lighting 551, 552, 553, 554, 555, 556
  rendering, with vertex diffuse lighting 534, 535, 536, 538, 539, 540, 541, 542, 543, 545, 547
global-level functions
  loading 24, 25, 26
GLSL shaders
  converting, to SPIR-V assemblies 332, 333
glslangValidator 332
graphics pipeline creation parameters
  specifying 411, 412, 413, 414, 415, 416
graphics pipeline
  blend constants 406
  creating 424, 426, 434, 435, 436
  depth bias 405
  depth bounds 405
  line width 405
  scissor 405
  stencil compare mask 405
  stencil reference value 406
  stencil write mask 405
  used, for drawing particles 615, 616, 625, 626
  viewports 405
graphics
  logical devices, creating with 63, 64, 65

H

handles of swapchain images
  obtaining 109, 110
host-visible 171
host-visible memory
  mapping 204, 205, 206, 207
  unmapping 204, 205, 206, 207
  updating 204, 205, 206, 207

I

image acquisition 115
image memory barrier
  setting 189, 190, 191, 192, 194, 196
image processing 643
image view
  creating 196
  destroying 227
images
  about 164
  creating 180, 181, 182, 183, 184
  destroying 228
  memory object, allocating to 185, 186
  memory object, binding to 185, 186
  presenting 119, 120

index buffer
  binding 458
index of queue family
  selecting, with desired capabilities 47, 48, 49
indexed geometry
  drawing 473
input attachments
  creating 259, 260, 261, 262
  using, for color correction post-process effect 652, 653, 654, 655, 656, 660
instance-level functions
  about 25
  loading 33, 34, 36, 37

L

layered 2D image
  creating, with CUBEMAP view 202, 203
lighting 533
line width 405
line width states
  setting, dynamically 466
linear tiling 183
logical device
  about 50
  creating 51, 52, 53, 55, 56
  creating, with compute queues 63, 64, 65
  creating, with geometry shaders 63, 64, 65
  creating, with graphics 63, 64, 65
  creating, with WSI extensions enabled 84, 85
  destroying 67, 68

M

mailbox presentation mode
  setting 111, 112, 113
memory access types
  VK_ACCESS_HOST_READ_BIT 175
  VK_ACCESS_HOST_WRITE_BIT 175
  VK_ACCESS_INDEX_READ_BIT 175
  VK_ACCESS_INDIRECT_COMMAND_READ_BIT 175
  VK_ACCESS_MEMORY_READ_BIT 175
  VK_ACCESS_MEMORY_WRITE_BIT 175
  VK_ACCESS_SHADER_READ_BIT 175
  VK_ACCESS_SHADER_WRITE_BIT 175
  VK_ACCESS_TRANSFER_WRITE_BIT 175

VK_ACCESS_UNIFORM_READ_BIT 175
VK_ACCESS_VERTEX_ATTRIBUTE_READ_BIT 175
memory object
  allocating, to buffer 168, 169, 170, 171
  allocating, to images 185, 186
  binding, to buffer 168, 169, 170, 171
  binding, to images 185, 186
  freeing 229, 230
multiple graphics pipelines
  creating, on multiple threads 440, 441, 442
multiple pipeline cache objects
  merging 421, 422, 423
multiple threads
  command buffers, recording on 487, 488, 489, 490, 491
multisampling 392

N

normal mapped geometry
  rendering 558, 559, 560, 563, 565, 566, 568, 569
normal mapping 558
number of swapchain images
  selecting 94, 95

O

OBJ file
  3D model, loading from 526
orthographic projection matrix
  preparing 519, 520, 521

P

particles
  drawing, compute pipeline used 615, 616, 625, 626
  drawing, graphics pipeline used 615, 616, 625, 626
patch 384
performance
  increasing, through increased number of separately rendered frames 498, 499, 500, 503, 504
perspective projection matrix
  preparing 515, 516, 517, 518

physical device
  features, obtaining 42, 43
  properties, obtaining 42, 43
pipeline blend state
  specifying 398, 399, 400, 402
pipeline cache object
  creating 417, 418
pipeline cache
  data, retrieving from 419, 420, 421
  destroying 445
pipeline depth
  specifying 394, 396, 397
pipeline dynamic states
  specifying 403, 404, 405
pipeline input assembly state
  specifying 381, 383
pipeline layout
  creating 407, 408, 410, 431, 432
  destroying 446
pipeline multisample state
  specifying 392, 394
pipeline object
  binding 429, 430
pipeline rasterization state
  specifying 389, 390, 392
pipeline shader stages
  specifying 373, 374, 375
pipeline tessellation state
  specifying 383
pipeline vertex binding description
  specifying 377, 378, 380
pipeline viewport
  specifying 385, 386, 389
pipeline
  destroying 443, 444
polygon normals
  displaying, with geometry shaders 362, 363, 364, 365, 366, 367
post-processing
  full-screen quad, rendering for 644, 646, 647, 648, 651
presentation mode
  selecting 86, 87, 88, 89, 90
presentation surface
  capabilities, obtaining of 92, 93

  creating 76, 77, 79, 80
  destroying 123
primary command buffers 130
push constants
  about 255
  used, for providing data to shaders 460
  using, in shaders 356, 357, 358

Q

queue family
  selecting, that supports presentation to surface 81, 82, 83
queue
  about 44
  command buffers, submitting to 147, 148, 149, 150
  operation types 46

R

R8G8B8A8 format
  swapchain, creating with 111, 112, 113
reflective geometry
  drawing, cubemaps used 570, 571, 572, 573, 575, 576, 579, 580
refractive geometry
  drawing, cubemaps used 570, 571, 572, 574, 575, 576, 579, 580
render pass attachments
  clearing 454
render pass
  about 291
  beginning 322, 323, 324
  creating 303, 304, 305, 306
  destroying 329
  ending 326, 327
  preparing, for geometry rendering 310, 312, 313, 315, 316
  preparing, for postprocess subpasses 310, 312, 313, 316
  preparing, with color and depth attachments 317, 318, 319, 320
role-playing game (RPG) 502
rotation matrix
  preparing 509, 510, 512

[667]

S

sampled image
  creating 237, 238, 239, 241
sampler
  creating 234, 235, 236, 237
  destroying 290
scaling matrix
  preparing 513, 514, 515
scene
  shadows, adding to 581, 582, 583, 584, 585, 587, 592, 594
scissor 405
scissor states
  setting, dynamically 464, 465
scissor test state
  specifying 385, 386, 389
secondary command buffer
  executing, inside primary command buffer 477, 478
secondary command buffers 130
semaphore
  creating 139, 140, 141
  destroying 158
shader module
  creating 371, 372
  destroying 447, 448
shaders
  push constants, using in 356, 357, 358
shadows
  adding, to scene 581, 582, 583, 584, 585, 587, 588, 593
single frame of animation
  preparing 492, 493, 494, 495, 496, 497
size of swapchain images
  selecting 96, 97
skybox
  drawing 598, 600, 601, 602, 605, 606
SPIR-V assemblies
  GLSL shaders, converting to 332, 333
stages 331
staging buffer
  used, for updating buffer with device-local memory bound 216, 217, 218, 219, 220, 221
  used, for updating image with device-local memory bound 222, 223, 224

staging resources 164
stencil compare mask 405
stencil reference value 406
stencil state
  specifying 394, 395, 397
stencil write mask 405
storage buffer
  creating 257
storage image
  creating 243, 244, 245, 246
storage texel buffer
  creating 250, 251, 252, 254
subpass descriptions
  specifying 295, 296, 297, 299
subpass
  progressing to 325, 326
swapchain images
  acquiring 115, 118
  desired usage scenarios, selecting of 98, 99
swapchain
  creating 105, 106, 107
  creating, with R8G8B8A8 format 111, 112, 113
  destroying 122

T

tessellated terrain
  rendering 627, 628, 629, 630, 631, 632, 634, 635, 636, 640, 641, 642
tessellation 337
tessellation control shaders
  writing 337, 338, 339, 340
tessellation evaluation shaders
  writing 341, 342, 343
tessellation shaders 55
texture data
  loading, from file 522, 524, 525
texture
  descriptors, creating with 279, 280, 281, 282
texturing 358, 522
texturing vertex
  writing 359
tinyobjloader
  reference 526
transformation of swapchain images
  selecting 100, 101

[668]

translation matrix
  preparing 506, 508

U

uniform buffer
  creating 254, 255, 256
  descriptors, creating with 279, 280, 281, 282
uniform texel buffer
  creating 247, 248

V

validation layers
  enabling 13, 14, 15
vertex buffers
  binding 456
vertex diffuse lighting
  geometry, rendering with 534, 535, 538, 539, 540, 541, 542, 543, 545, 547
vertex processing 334
vertex shaders
  writing 334, 337
  writing, that multiples vertex position by projection matrix 354, 355

viewport states
  setting, dynamically 462, 463
viewports 405
VkPhysicalDeviceFeatures structure
  features 43
Vulkan 10, 72
Vulkan API functions
  preparing, for loading 18, 20, 21
Vulkan Instance
  creating 29, 30, 32
  creating, with WSI extensions enabled 72, 73, 74, 75
  destroying 68, 69
Vulkan Loader library
  connecting with 16, 17
  functions, loading exported from 22, 23
  releasing 69, 70
Vulkan's SDK
  downloading 10, 11, 12
  reference 10

W

Wavefront OBJ 526

Made in the USA
San Bernardino, CA
27 March 2018